SIGNALS & SYSTEMS

SIGNALS & SYSTEMS

The Analog and Digital Domains

RAJIV KAPADIA

JAICO PUBLISHING HOUSE

Ahmedabad Bangalore Bhopal Bhubaneswar Chennai
Delhi Hyderabad Kolkata Lucknow Mumbai

Published by Jaico Publishing House
A-2 Jash Chambers, 7-A Sir Phirozshah Mehta Road
Fort, Mumbai - 400 001
jaicopub@jaicobooks.com
www.jaicobooks.com

SIGNALS & SYSTEMS
ISBN 978-81-7992-989-6

First Jaico Impression: 2009
Third Jaico Impression: 2012

Printed by
Pashupati Printers (P) Ltd.
1/429/16, Gali No.1, Friends Colony, Industrial Area
G.T. Road, Shahdara, Delhi - 110 095

Dedication

I dedicate this book to my parents

Jayraj & Veena,

and to my two children

Ajay & Tara

Contents

Preface

The primary objective of this book is

1. To show the students how both the analog and the discrete signals are used;
2. To help the reader to easily analyze the analog and the digital systems;
3. To expose to the practitioners of analog and digital systems the difficulties that they might face in analyzing these systems, and how to overcome these difficulties.

All or portions of this book are usable by the following groups of people:

– Upper-division engineering and engineering technology students. (Third year and Fourth year.)
– Applied Engineering students.
– Practicing engineers, technology professionals and engineering managers.

Engineers and/or engineering technology students who have had a course in circuit analysis using frequency response analysis methods and a course in integral and differential calculus will easily be able to benefit by reading this book. Throughout the book I have tried to use a simple conversational tone and have demonstrated all the important derivations using calculus where appropriate. When the results are to be used I have tried to show that many times the result can be used by a minimum use of calculus.

All the chapters in the book progress in a logical manner. First the concept of the signal is introduced which naturally leads the student to what the signal can do and hence the concept of the system. Now that the students are introduced to what a system is, their natural curiosity will lead them to the study of how the system is analyzed and controlled. This is taught by the transform theory.

The book also contains numerous solved examples to emphasize the important points of the subject covered in the chapter. In addition to the solved examples there are end of the chapter homework problems. These homework problems are coordinated with the solved examples and the subject covered in the chapter. If you have difficulty with the homework problems then a review of the solved examples will point you in the right direction. The solved examples and the homework problems make this book an ideal reference text for students as well as technical professionals.

The primary emphasis throughout the book has been on developing a thorough understanding of the analysis of all types of systems in the world. So instead of treating a particular system here and a different system there, we have shown that all systems, whether they are thermal, or electrical, or mechanical or any other type can be represented by differential equations. Once you have the system represented as a differential equation then it does not matter what the fundamental system is. The analysis of the system proceeds in the same manner for all systems having similar differential equations.

The book tried to draw 'Pictures' for the students. The discussion in the chapter draws a word picture; the equations in the chapter draw a mathematical picture and the simulation done by the use of freeware software throughout the book draw a visual picture so the student can get the complete grasp of the discussion in the book. The use of simulation software to verify and to demonstrate the analysis that you have done is a major tool in engineering analysis. The book emphasizes first the understanding of the subject matter by use of equations and analysis and then confirms the analysis by the use of the simulation software, so the students get the best of both the worlds.

The entire book is divided into two halves. The first half deals with the analog system while the second half deals with the discrete representation of the systems. Since the analog and the discrete systems are kept separate it is much easier to refer to and understand one type of system or the other type. Also as the two domains are kept separate but the book is written along parallel lines it is much easier to relate the two domains as you study the discrete domain after studying the analog domain.

I have successfully, throughout the book, linked the concepts in the analog and the discrete domains together. The two domains are very similar and the concepts track each other in parallel. In this book the student will see that the two domains are indeed related to each other and how one domain points to what can be expected in the other domain.

The engineering profession is changing and this change is heading towards proof of concept. The proof of concept today is provided by software simulations. In this book I have used the state of the art and freely available software to first demonstrate the concept to the students and next to show to the students how they can employ the software to explore new ideas and use it to satisfy the proof of concept requirement.

At the end of each chapter there are several worked examples for the students to refer to. These worked examples guide the students through the interpretation of the important concepts. They provide the same function that a good tutor provides.

The book can be used in several different ways. For a one semester class the book can either be used sequentially from chapter 1 through to the end of the book. In this use you will first study the continuous time system and then the discrete time system. Another way to use the book is cover both the analog and the discrete systems together. When using the book in this way the sequence of chapters would be as follows:

Chapters 1→2→3→7→4→8→5→9→6→10

Either way you choose to use the book I am certain that you and your students will gain the most by covering all the chapters and at the same time completing all the chapter problems assigned to the students to attempt.

Rajiv Kapadia

CHAPTER 1

Signals and their Representations

1.1 DEFINITION OF A SIGNAL

A signal is a communication of information from the source of information to the destination of information. Signals come in various different forms and shapes. Take for example a square wave; this signal can convey information by the frequency of the wave. A square wave with a higher frequency could be understood to convey a higher value of the physical quantity that it is supposed to represent. Similarly a lower frequency wave could be understood to convey a lower value of the same physical quantity. A different way to convey information using a square wave would be by using its duty cycle. This is demonstrated in Figure 1.1. A larger duty cycle could be made to represent a higher value of a physical parameter and a lower duty cycle can be made to represent a lower value of the same physical quantity. The middle or the 50% duty cycle can be used to represent the idle state of the signal. In the idle state the signal does not carry any information.

The idea then is that the signal carries information in one of its parameters. So with every parameter that the signal has you can associate some information or message. In the above example we have seen two different parameters. Both the parameters can carry information simultaneously. So with our square wave, if we choose to, we can transmit two different items of information simultaneously. One piece of information is transmitted in the frequency of the square wave and the other information is transmitted in the duty cycle of the square wave.

In the above example the meaning of the signal was the same every time. So when you received the signal with a 30% duty cycle it meant exactly the same thing every time. The meaning of a signal, or the information that it carries does not have to be so rigid. We can decide to assign a different meaning to a signal by what has occurred before the signal that is received, or what other signal is being received simultaneously. Consider once again the signal with a 30% duty cycle, this

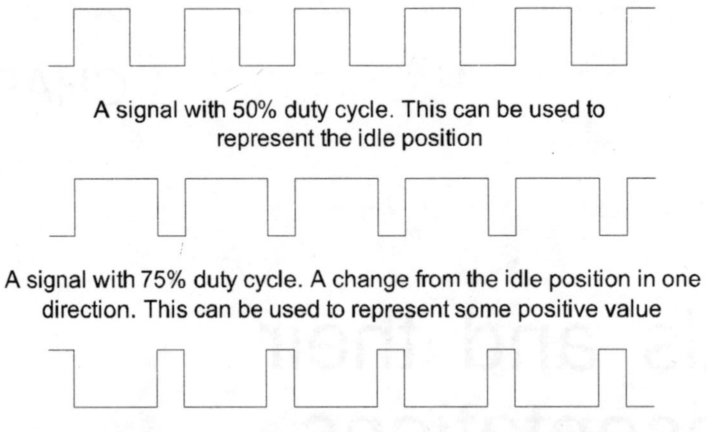

A signal with 50% duty cycle. This can be used to represent the idle position

A signal with 75% duty cycle. A change from the idle position in one direction. This can be used to represent some positive value

A signal with 25% duty cycle. A change from the idle position in the opposite direction. This can be used to represent some negative value

Figure 1.1: A signal demonstrating how a change in its parameter, the duty cycle, can be used to carry information

time we will monitor the frequency of the signal as well. We can now assign one meaning to the 30% duty cycle signal if the frequency of the signal is low and we can assign a different meaning to the same 30% duty cycle signal if the frequency is high. The idea we want to convey to you is that signals carry information. The information is coded in the signal by the sender and the information is interpreted by the receiver according to some rule that they have agreed upon earlier. The rule does not have to be rigid; it can be as flexible as the sender and the receiver want to make it.

One excellent example of this is the touch-tone dialing system. The touch-tone dialing system for the telephones uses two frequencies to identify the digit that is being dialed. One group of tones represent the row of the dialing matrix while the other tone represents the column of the dialing matrix. This is shown in Figure 1.2. Once the touch tone selects the row any of the digits on that row could be represented. To find out which digit is specifically dialed this time the column has to be determined from the column frequency. The digit located at the intersection of the row and the column is then the dialed digit for the telephone.

As we have seen in the previous examples, a signal has parameters that can carry information. The parameters of a signal are shape, size, duration etc. A signal can have a very broad range of shapes, amplitudes, frequencies, and other physical properties. Thus a signal can be a periodic waveform or it can be a one time event. The signal can take the shape of a table, a graph or a waveform on a CRT. Irrespective of the form of the signal, in this chapter we will examine the mathematical representation of the signal, their applications, how they are able to convey the information that they carry and other properties of the signal.

Example 1.1

List all the parameters in a signal that you can use to carry information.

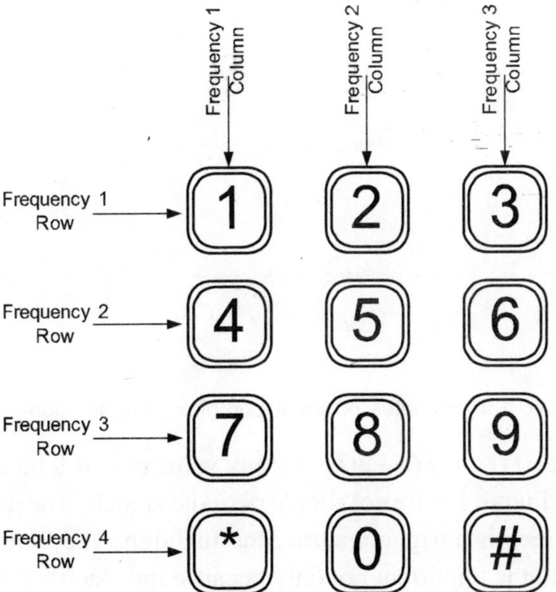

Figure 1.2: Decoding the Touch Telephone matrix

Solution 1.1

The parameters that can be used in a signal are: Amplitude; Frequency (or period); Phase. If the signal is a pulse signal then two additional parameters are also available. They are Duty Cycle and Pulse Position.

1.2 PERIODIC SIGNALS

1.2.1 Continuous Time Periodic Signals

A signal or a wave that repeats itself after some time is known as a periodic wave. The wave repeats itself over and over again forever. The repletion rate of a periodic wave is exactly same every time. There are many different periodic signals. Figure 1.3 shows some not so common but different periodic signals. The period of these signals is the time after which the signal repeats itself. In Figure 1.3 the period is identified as T seconds. The period is related to the frequency of the signal. The frequency of the signal is the number of times the signal repeats itself in one second. So the frequency of the signal, **f**, is the reciprocal of the period of the signal or **f = 1/T**. The frequency is identified as "Cycles per second" or as "radians per second". The two different ways of relating frequency are related to each other and the relation is 2π radians/second equals 1 cycle per second. The symbol used to represent the frequency in radians per second is ω, so $2\pi f = \omega$ or $\omega = 2\pi/T$.

A simple fact of periodic signals is that the signal repeats itself. When the signal repeats it takes on the same value that the signal had exactly one period ago or the same value the signal will have one period later. This holds true not just for one period but for any number of periods. We identify this

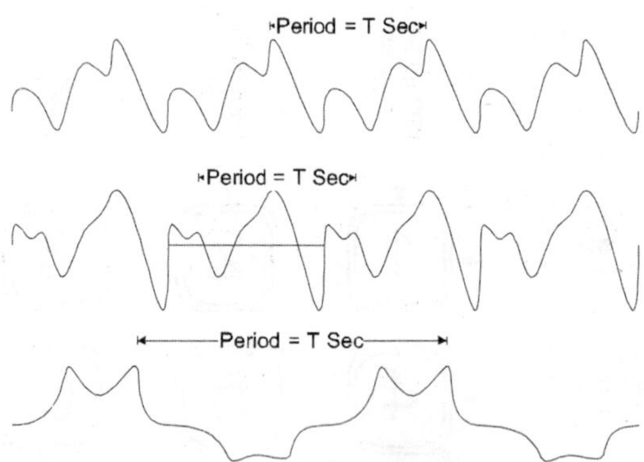

Figure 1.3: Samples of some complex periodic signals

in a simple equation form as $f(t) = f(t + nT)$ for any value of n as long as n is an integer.

The periodic signals in Figure 1.3 are not simple periodic signals. The most elementary periodic signal that you may have seen is a trigonometric Sine function. The Sine waveform is shown in Figure 1.4. The sine function is important not only because the electric power that is delivered to our homes and businesses is delivered by a Sine wave signal but also because most if not all the complex as well as the simple periodic waves like the ones shown in Figure 1.1 and in Figure 1.3 can be represented and reproduced by selectively adding an infinite number of sine and cosine functions of different amplitudes together. Figure 1.4 shows a typical sine wave along with some important parameters of the sine wave.

$$f(t) = 2Sin(\omega t + \theta) = F_m\, Sin(\omega t + \theta)$$

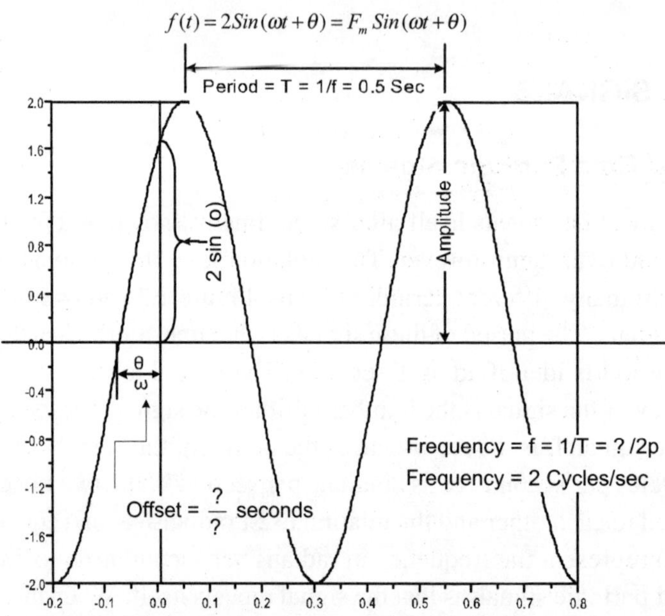

Figure 1.4: The Sine function. Demonstrating the relations between the different parameters. Two complete cycles are drawn.

The Amplitude of the wave is the peak to peak value divided by two. In Figure 1.4 the first peak has a value of +2 and the next peak has a value of -2 so the peak to peak difference is 4 and 4/2=2 so the amplitude of the wave is 2.

If the wave is not centered and symmetrical on the X-axis then the wave has a DC offset. The DC offset is the value of the highest peak minus the amplitude of the wave. In Figure since the wave is symmetrical about the X-axis the DC offset is zero.

The Phase offset occurs when a Sine wave does not pass through the origin when it is rising and it has no DC offset. The wave in Figure 1.4 has a phase offset since it does not pass through the origin when it is rising. The Phase offset is determined by solving the equation $A\text{Sin}(\theta) = Y$ axis intercept. In our example this is $2\text{Sin}(\theta) = 1.6$. Solving this we get $\theta = 53.13°$.

Example 1.2

Identify the appropriate parameters for Figure Example 1.2.

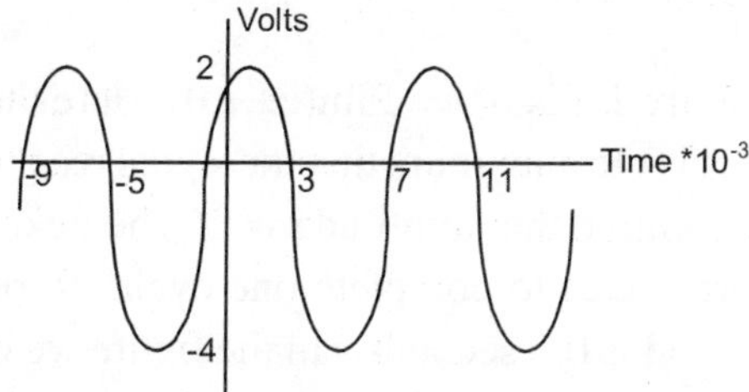

Figure Example 1.2: A periodic waveform

Solution 1.2

The Amplitude?	3 Volts
The Period?	$8*10^{-3}$ Seconds
The Frequency?	125 Hz
DC Offset?	-1 Volt
Phase Offset?	65 degrees

Example 1.3

Identify the appropriate parameters in the signal of Figure Example 1.3a and 1.3b

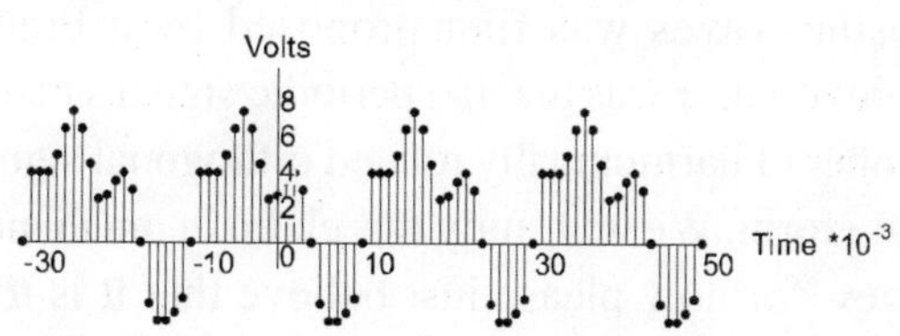

Figure Example 1.3a: A periodic sampled signal

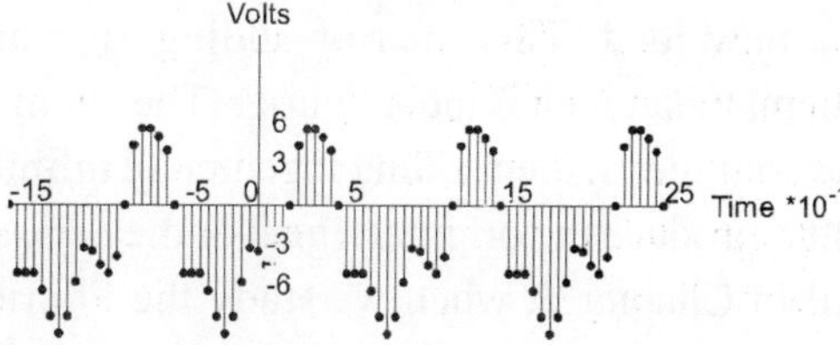

Fig. Example 1.3b: A periodic sampled signal

Solution 1.3

For the two figures the required parameters are:

Solution 1.3a

Magnitude of the 10th sample?	Zero
Period of the signal in samples?	20 Samples
Sampling period/interval?	0.001 seconds
Period of the signal in time?	0.02 seconds

Solution 1.3.b

Magnitude of the 10th sample?	Zero
Period of the signal in samples?	20 Samples
Sampling period/interval?	0.0005 seconds
Period of the signal in time?	0.01 seconds

The waveform drawn in Figure 1.4 is $f(t) = 2\text{Sin}(\omega t + \theta)$. Here the first parameter we see is the amplitude of the waveform. This is the maximum that the signal reaches above zero or the minimum it reaches below zero. In our example the amplitude is 2. The next parameter is the Period. The Period is the time the waveform takes to complete one cycle. In our example the period of the waveform is 0.5 units so the period is 0.5 seconds. (In the figure we have assumed that the units of time is seconds.) The frequency of a waveform is represented in one of two different ways. Frequency can be represented as either cycles-per-second or as radians-per-second. Since there are 2π radians in every cycle the two representations are related to each other by $\omega = 2\pi f$. The Frequency of the waveform is the reciprocal of the period. The frequency of the wave in the figure then is 2Hz or 4π radians. The third parameter in the expression for the signal is the Offset θ. A Sine wave with no (zero) offset would pass through the origin and would be rising as it passed through the origin. If the sine wave does not pass through the origin then the wave has an offset.

Figure 1.5a and 1.5b show how one particular complex waveform is built. To build this waveform we have used only the first eight terms. To build a complex waveform in general we will typically add an infinite number of sine and cosine terms with harmonically related frequencies and varying amplitudes. The idea of adding sine and cosine waves together to build a complex periodic wave is not a new idea. This idea of adding sine and cosine waves was first proposed by a French mathematician Jean Baptist Fourier. The claim made by Fourier was that if a periodic signal satisfies some conditions, then adding together an infinite number of harmonically related orthogonal signals could reproduce the original signal or the periodic waveform. We will study this claim in much more detail in Chapter 3, when we study the Fourier series, for now please just believe that it is true. Orthogonal signals that we need have some special properties which also we will study in Chapter 3. The simplest family of orthogonal signals is the set of sine and the cosine waves. So we will concentrate on using these signals to build a complex periodic signal. This, as the figures suggest, we will be doing by adding together sine and cosine waves that have different frequencies and

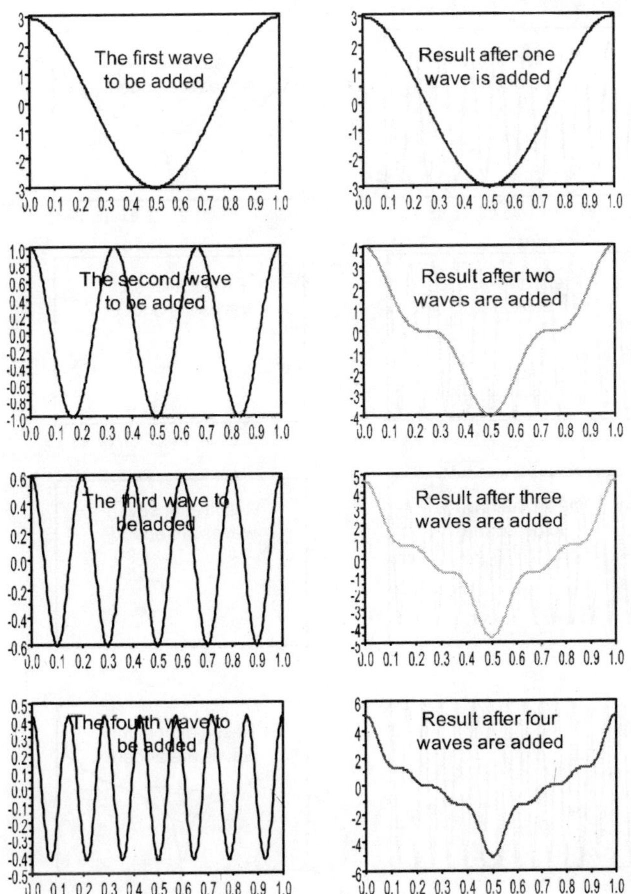

Figure 1.5a: To build the complex waveform shown on the right we add successive cosine terms. The terms to be added are shown on the left. After each addition we get the diagram on the right. Notice that both the amplitude and the frequency of the waveform to be added are changing.

different amplitudes, in the example shown the phase is zero for all the signals to be added, but in general the phase can also be different for the various waves to be added together.

The sine and the cosine waves are continuous periodic signals. The period of a function is the time it takes the signal to complete one repetition of the function. The period of the function is usually written as **T**. A function that is periodic with a period T satisfies Equation(1.1).

$$f(t \pm nT) = f(t) \tag{1.1}$$

Equation (1.1) says that the value of the function at any time t is the same as the value of the function at time $t \pm T$ or at time $t \pm 2T$ or at time $t \pm 3T$ or at time $t \pm nT$ for any value of n. The parameter T is known as the period of the function. The period is the time it takes the function to complete one cycle. The periodic function also has a frequency. The frequency of the periodic function is the number of cycles the function completes in one second. The frequency and the period

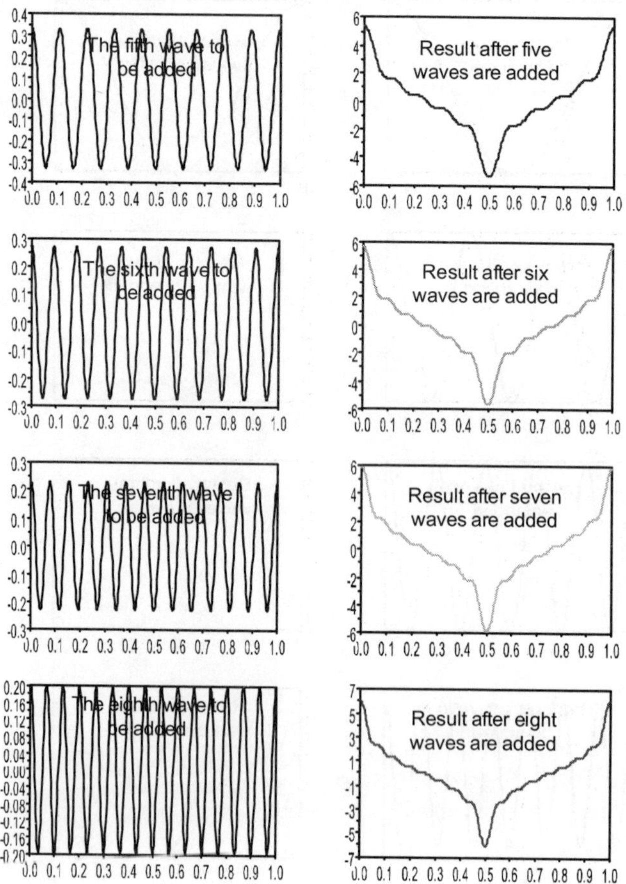

Figure 1.5b: When we continue adding more terms the complex wave starts to take a definite shape. Notice that both the frequency and the amplitude are adjusted for each successive function that is added.

are related to each other, so if you know one you also know the other. The reciprocal of the period is the frequency of the function. The frequency can be represented in one of two different ways. The frequency can be represented as number of cycles completed per second which is the unit of Hertz abbreviated as Hz or as number of radians completed per second. Since there are 2π radians in every revolution (cycle) the two representations of the frequency are also related to each other and the relation is shown in Equation(1.2).

$$f = \frac{1}{T} = 2\pi\omega \tag{1.2}$$

Example 1.4

A continuous time periodic signal has a frequency of 38 Hz. How many cycles does this signal complete in 0.85 seconds? What is the frequency of the signal in radians per second? How many radians does this signal travel in 0.6 seconds?

Solution 1.4

The frequency of the signal is 38 cycles per second.

Solution 1.4a

So in 0.85 seconds the signal will complete 38*0.85 = 32.3 cycles.

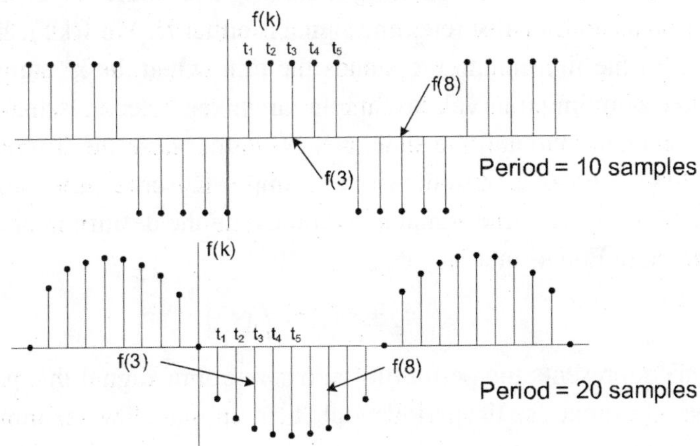

Figure 1.6: Typical discrete time periodic signals. Samples f(3) and f(8) for both the signals are identified.

Solution 1.4b

Since there are 2*π radians in each cycle the signal frequency in radians per second is 2*38*π = 238.761 radians per second.

Solution 1.4c

The signal will travel 238.761*0.6 = 143.2566 radians in 0.6 seconds.

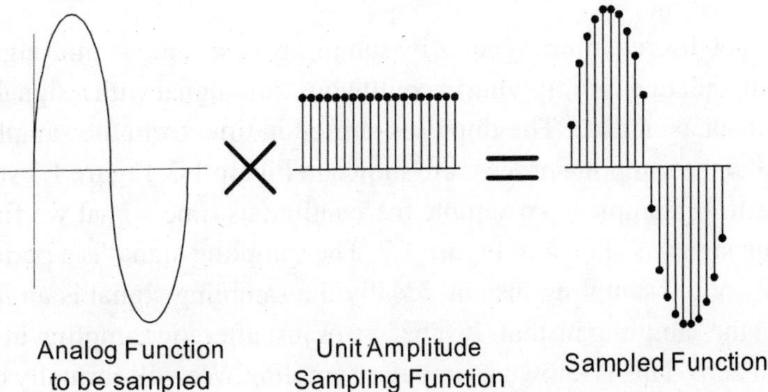

Figure 1.7: The sampling of an analog function is accomplished by modulating the analog function by a sampling function of amplitude 1. The sampling function is assumed to be made up of impulses shifted by sampling interval.

1.2.2 Discrete Time Periodic Signals

Periodic signals can exist as continuous time signals or as discrete time signals. A discrete time signal is a signal that is defined at discrete instants in time. The instances where the discrete time signal is defined are known as sampling instances or sampling times. Generally the sampling instances are equi-distance from each other or the sampling is done by a periodic waveform (this is shown in Figure 1.7.) The notation used for a discrete time signal is either $f(t_k)$ or f(kT). They both represent the same information. In the first notation t_k stands the time when the kth sample is taken. In the second notation T is the sampling interval. So samples are taken T seconds apart. So kT is the time of the kth sample. Once again one and the same as t_k. In either case the discrete time function is generally written as f(k). Here k represents the kth sample. Discrete time signals can be either periodic or aperiodic. If a discrete time signal is periodic then the definition of a periodic signal in discrete time is as shown in Equation(1.3).

$$f\left(t_k \pm nT\right) = f\left(t_k\right) \tag{1.3}$$

In Equation 1.3 nT represents the period of the discrete time signal this period is sometimes represented in number of samples so the period would be n samples. Two examples of discrete time periodic signals are shown in Figure 1.6.

1.3 SAMPLING A CONTINUOUS TIME SIGNAL

How do we get sampled signals is often a question that is asked. Sampled signals or discrete time signals are obtained in a variety of ways. First, the signal itself may be of a discrete nature so it exists only at discrete instants in time. A signal of this type is the result of a coin toss experiment that is recorded. Each successive result of the coin toss represents the next entry of the discrete time sequence. The coin tosses do not have to occur at equal time intervals. Since there is no value between two successive coin tosses, the result of a coin toss is defined only at the sampling instants or at discrete instants in time.

Another way to get discrete time signal is by sampling a continuous time signal. The sampling process consists of modulating (multiplying) a continuous time signal with a signal that is an impulse located at discrete instants in time. The impulses shifted in time form the sampling function. The sampling function and the sampling process are shown in Figure 1.7. Figure 1.7 shows a continuous time signal that has to be sampled. To sample the continuous time signal we first get a sampling signal. The sampling signal is shown in Figure 1.7. The sampling signal is a periodic impulse train that has a value only at the sampling instant. Ideally the sampling signal is an impulse so it has a value of 1 exactly at the sampling instant. Just before or just after the sampling instant the sampling signal has a value of zero. This is known as impulse sampling. We will formally define the impulse function and hence the impulse train in Section 1.4.3. For now the sampling function is as shown in Figure 1.7.

When we multiply the analog function and the impulse train sampling function at every instant in time we get the sampled signal that is shown in Figure 1.7. Since the sampling function has magnitude of one at the sampling instants only, the result of the product is equal the value of the analog function at the sampling instants. Since the sampling function has magnitude zero between the sampling instants, the result of sampling is zero between the sampling instants. Hence we get the sampled signal as shown in Figure 1.7. The sampled signal is defined only at the sampling instants and not between the sampling instants. Not defined does not mean zero. It is just not defined; we do not know what it is.

Note about discrete time signals. Even when a periodic analog signal is sampled with a periodic sampling signal the result may be a non periodic signal. We will see the specific reasons and examples of this in the second half of this book when we study the discrete time systems.

1.4 NON PERIODIC SIGNALS

There are many special functions that are not periodic. These functions have special properties and are useful to describe other functions which may be periodic or may be non periodic.

1.4.1 The Step Function

This function is generally written as U(t). The function is a continuous function of time with a single discontinuity at the point of activation. The point of activation of the function is when the argument of the function is zero. The argument of the function is that part of the function within the parenthesis. Before the function is activated the function equals zero, after the function is activated the function is one. So the definition of the unit step function is as shown in Figure 1.8a and in Equation (1.4).

From Equation (1.4) we see that when the argument of the function is positive the value of the function is 1; when the argument of the function is negative the value of the function is zero. At exactly the point of application of the function the function has a discontinuity and hence at the point of application the function is not defined. To get a function that has a step other then unity the unit step function is multiplied by the size of the step required. Thus the function 5U(t) will have a magnitude 5 step activated at $t = 0$. The step function $U(t_0 - t)$ is active for the negative time and it is active till $t = t_0$ and for $t > t_0$ the function is turned off and it is inactive or it has a value of zero. This would be a mirror image of the second function shown in Figure 1.8. When the function U(t) is multiplied by -1 then the function has a step in the negative direction.

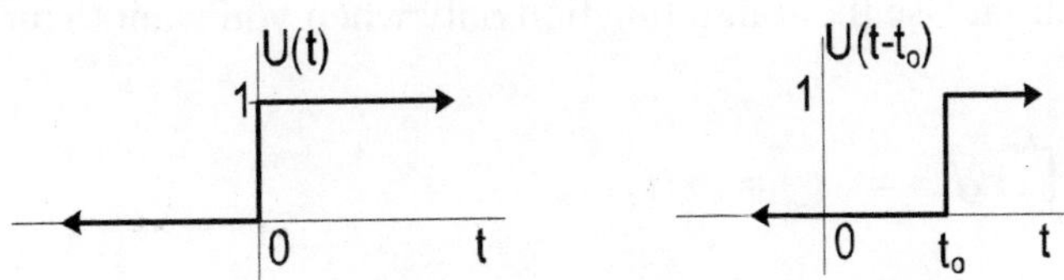

Figure 1.8a: The Unit Step Function

$$U(t)=\begin{cases}1 & t>0\\ 0 & t<0\end{cases} \quad \text{or} \quad U(t-t_0)=\begin{cases}1 & t>t_0\\ 0 & t<t_0\end{cases} \tag{1.4}$$

This function is very useful as a switch function. Since the Step function is zero till it is activated, it can be used to represent a switch that turns some other function on. After activation the Step function has a value 1 so that can be thought as the switch making contact. So a function of the type Sin(5πt)U(t) represents a sine function only after t = 0. Before t = 0 the function has a value zero. Here U(t), the step function, can be thought of as a switch function that turns the sine function on.

$$r(at)=ar(t)\ \begin{cases}at & t\geq 0\\ 0 & t<0\end{cases} \tag{1.5}$$

1.4.2 The Ramp Function

This function is generally written as r(t). This function is a continuous function. The ramp function is shown in Figure 1.8b. Similar to the step function the ramp function is also activated when its argument is zero. The function is zero when the argument of the function is negative, the function is non zero and has a slope equal to 'a' when the argument is positive. Equation 1.5 shows the definition of the ramp function. The ramp function is very important in generating the sweep signal of a CRT, the scan lines on the television.

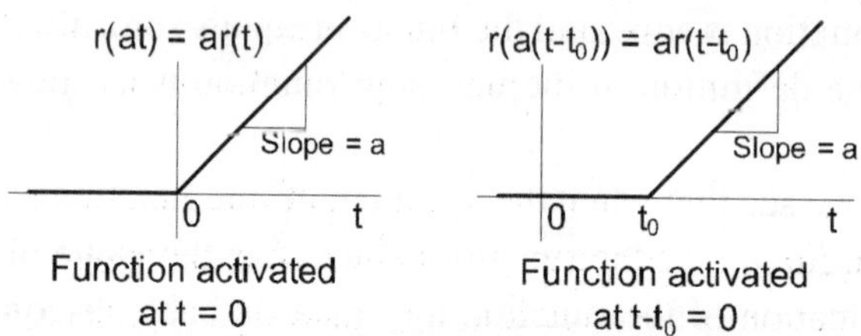

Figure 1.8b: The Ramp Function

The slope of the ramp function normally is unity. The slope can be changed by multiplying the ramp function by a constant. If the constant is negative then the ramp has a negative slope. Since the definition of the ramp function activates the ramp function when the argument is zero the ramp function also can be thought of as a switch function. This switch is however different from the simple switch represented by the Step function. So use only the Step function when you want to represent the switching action. Use the Ramp function only when you want to turn on a Ramp at a specific instant in time.

$$\int_{-\infty}^{\infty} U(t)\,dt \;=\; \int_{0}^{\infty} 1\,dt \;=\; t \;=\; r(t) \tag{1.6}$$

There is a distinct relation between the step function and the ramp function. The two functions are related to each other by the derivative (integral) relation. The derivative of the ramp function is the step function and the integral of the step function is the ramp function. This relation is shown in Equation (1.6).

1.4.3 The Impulse Function

This function is generally written as δ(t). This function is defined in a very special way. The function is defined as an integral. Being defined as an integral the function represents the area under the curve. When the area under any curve stays constant as the base of support of the function reduces to zero in the limit, then that function is an impulse function. So one definition of the impulse function is shown in Figure 1.9. Notice that as the base gets smaller and smaller the height of the function keeps on getting higher. In the limit then as the base approaches zero the height will tend to increase towards infinity. While this is happening the area under the curve stays constant at one. This is exactly what the definition of the function says. In our example the area is unity so this is the unit impulse.

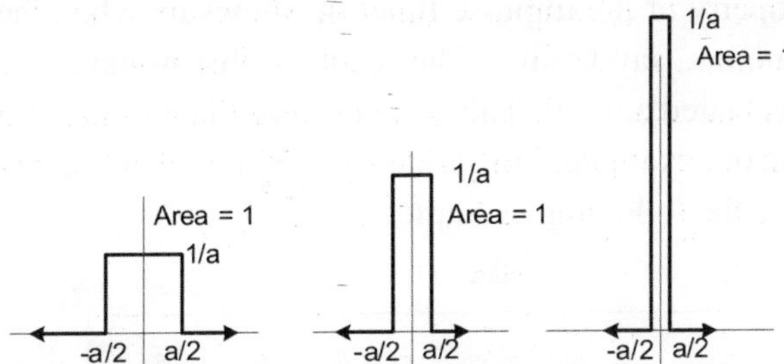

Figure 1.9: The definition of the Impulse Function. The area under the function is constant while the base of the function reduces to zero in a limit.

Another point that is very important to consider is as follows, we said that the area under the function has to be constant. This does not say anything about the shape of the function. In the example of Figure 1.9 we have chosen to use the square function. Say we have a triangular function with base equal to 2a and the height equal to 1/a then the area under the curve is still unity. Consider what happens to the area and the height of this function as the parameter **'a'** tends to zero. Now the base tends to zero while the height tends to infinity all the time maintaining the area under the curve equal to unity. This shows us that the shape of the impulse function is not unique, what is unique is that the area under the curve has to stay constant as the base of the function goes to zero. With this understanding we can write the definition of the impulse function as given in Equation (1.7).

$$\delta(t) = \underset{t \to 0}{Limit} \int_{-t}^{t} f(t)\, dt = \int_{0^-}^{0^+} f(t)\, dt = 1 \tag{1.7}$$

Equation(1.7) is rather special. If you remember from your calculus class the integral of a function at one point is zero. In Equation(1.7) the middle integral is an integral at one point, this one point being at t = 0. This integral, even though it is an integral at one point is not zero because the area under the curve – which is what the integral measures – is not zero even though the base of the function is zero. So the impulse function is defined as an integral at a point which is finite and not zero.

Just like the step and the ramp function, the impulse function is active when its argument is zero. So to have an impulse function active at say $t = t_o$ we would write it as $\delta(t-t_o)$. The sampling function shown in Figure 1.7 is an infinite sum of shifted unit impulses. This function can be written as $\sum_{n=-\infty}^{\infty}\delta(t-nT)$. In this function the sampling interval is T so the successive impulses are T seconds apart and located at t = nT. When all the infinite pulses are added together we get the impulse train which is then the sampling function that we have used in Figure 1.7. Just as with the Step and the Ramp functions we can change the strength (not the amplitude) of the impulse by multiplying it with a constant. When the unit impulse is multiplied by a constant then the area under the curve is increased to that value. So a function $5\delta(t)$ is an impulse of strength 5 and the area under the curve that makes up the impulse is 5 units.

One very important property of the impulse function shows up when the impulse function is multiplied with another function, say $f(t)\delta(t)$. The result of this product is a constant value f(0) which is the value of f(t) evaluated at t = 0. This is so because the impulse function has strength 1 and it is active only at t = 0 in our example. This property is exploited in sampling a continuous time signal, and is demonstrated in the following example.

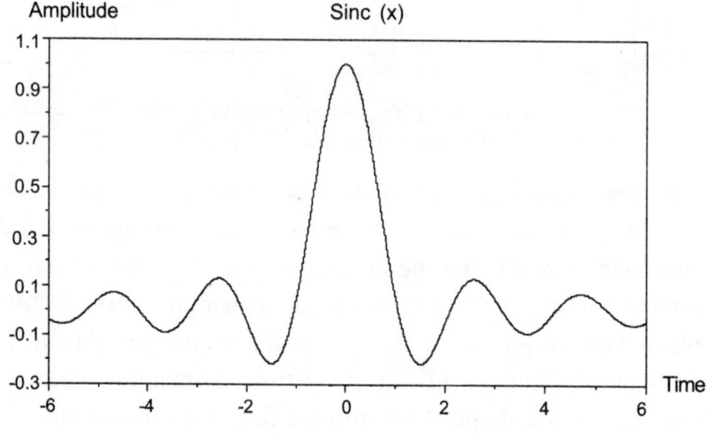

Figure 1.10: The Sinc function

Example 1.5

Evaluate the following integrals:

a $\int_{-5}^{5} 5Sin(38t)e^{-4t}\delta(t-.5)\,dt$

b $\int_{-\infty}^{\infty} 45Cos(45t)e^{0.05t}Sin^{-1}(0.45)\delta(t)\,dt$

Solution 1.5

Since both the integrals involve the impulse function the integral will have a value only where the impulse function is active.

Solution 1.5a

In this integral the impulse function is active at t = 0.5 seconds. So the integral will evaluate to: $5Sin(38*0.5)e^{-4*0.5} = 0.101418373$

Solution 1.5b

In this integral the impulse function is active at t=0 seconds. So the integral will evaluate to: $45Cos(45*(0))e^{0.05*(0)}Sin^{-1}(0.45) = 21.0044026$

1.4.4 The Sinc Function

The ***Sinc*** function is defined as shown in Equation 1.8 and is represented as shown in Figure 1.10. This function is extremely useful in the reconstruction of sampled signals. Just like the other functions that we have seen so far the Sinc function also can be located at different points on the time axis by shifting the function. The function is activated (located) where the argument is zero. The function is defined in Equation (1.8).

$$\text{sinc(x)} = \frac{\sin(\text{x})}{\text{x}} \qquad -\infty < x < \infty \tag{1.8}$$

With the Step, Ramp and the Impulse function we activated the function where the argument was equal to zero. This point was the first time where the function had a non zero value. With the Sinc function however the point where the argument is zero is not the first time the function has a non zero value. This point is not the starting point of the function. The function is only located (centered) where the argument is zero. The point where the argument is zero is the point where the function has unit value. The function has a non zero value from $-\infty$ to $+\infty$. Notice that where the argument of the function is zero both the numerator and the denominator values are zero. Thus the function assumes an indeterminate value where the argument is zero. To determine the value of the function at the point where the argument is zero you have to use L'Hospital's rule. To locate the Sinc function at some point other than at the origin (replace x by ($x-x_0$) to shift the function to x_0).

This function is also special in a different way. It passes through the X-axis every π radians. Since the numerator is a sine function and the sine function is zero every π radians the Sinc function also goes through zero every π radians.

1.4.5 The Signum Function

This function represents the sign of the argument. When the argument of the function is positive the value of this function is +1. When the argument of the function is negative the value of this function is -1 and when the argument of the function is zero the value of the function is zero. This is shown in Equation(1.9).

$$Signum \overset{\Delta}{=} \operatorname{sgn}(t) = \begin{cases} 1 & t > 0 \\ 0 & t = 0 \\ -1 & t < 0 \end{cases} \tag{1.9}$$

Figure 1.11: The sgn(t) function and the sgn(t-to) function.

Figure 1.11 shows the function sgn(t) function. Just as with all the other functions this function can also be located at some non zero point, the shifted version of the function is written as sgn(t-t_o) and is located at t = t_0. An alternate way of expressing this function is by the use of the unit step function that we have defined earlier. The definition with the unit step function is sgn(t) = -1 + 2U(t).

Now that we have seen some of the functions we can combine them together to form some interesting functions. Look at the functions given in Example 1.6. Each one of the functions represents one pulse of some function. They all look as if they are very complicated functions. When we resolve them into some of the fundamental functions you will see that they are indeed some very simple functions.

Example 1.6

For each of the pulse shown write the function as a sum of the simple functions that we have just seen.

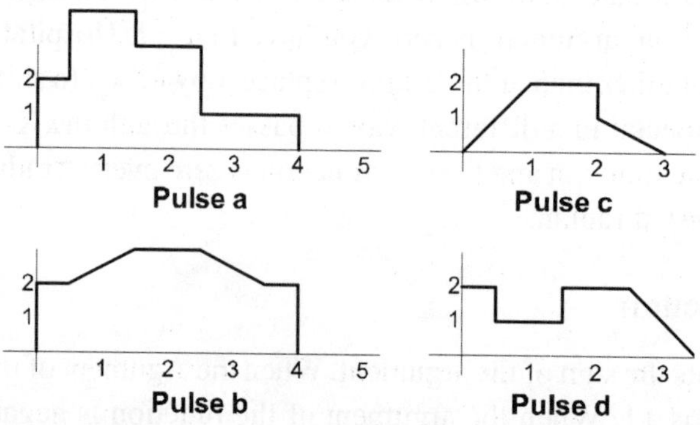

Figure Example 1.6: Represent these pulses as sum of simple step and ramp functions.

Solution 1.6

To write the various different pulses we will try to visualize how the pulse can be built using the pulse, ramp and the impulse functions which are located at different points in time.

Solution 1.6a

We can visualize this pulse as several different step functions added together. We begin with a step function active at time t = 0 and amplitude 2. So the first function is 2U(t). This function will be active from t= 0 to t = ∞.

Next we add another step function starting at t = 0.5 and amplitude 2. Thus the sum of the two step functions will be 4 which is what we want from t = 0.5 to t = 1.5.

At t = 1.5 we need a negative step of amplitude 1 which is –U(t-1.5). So adding the three together we will have the step height of 3 till t = 2.5.

At t = 2.5 we need a negative step of amplitude 2 which is –2U(t-2.5). So adding the four together we will have the step height of 1 till t = 4.

At t = 4 we need a negative step of amplitude 1 which is –U(t-4). So adding the five together we will have the step height of 0 which can continue till t = ∞.

Putting all the steps together we get the signal for pulse a as:

Pulse a = 2U(t) + 2U(t-0.5) – U(t-1.5) – 2U(t-2.5) –U(t-4).

Solution 1.6b

Pulse b has a ramp in it. We will have to remember to turn the ramp off when the signal is no longer increasing or decreasing. With this in mind we can write the signal for pulse b as:

Pulse b = 2U(t) + r(t-0.5) – r(t-1.5) –r(t-2.5) + r(t-3.5) -2U(t-4)

Solution 1.6c

Pulse c = 2r(t) -2r(t-1) –U(t-2) –r(t-2) + r(t-3)

Solution 1.6d

Pulse d = 2U(t) –U(t-0.5) + U(t-1.5) – 2r(t-2.5) + 2r(t-3.5)

Example 1.7

A pulse of a signal X(t) is shown in Figure Example 1.7. Sketch each of the following signals derived from the sketched pulse.

Solution 1.7

All the shown pulses are similar to the original pulses except the different pulses are either shifted and or stretched. This can be accounted for by adjusting the time variable in various ways as shown in the solution. In the following solution we will assume that the given pulse is x(t).

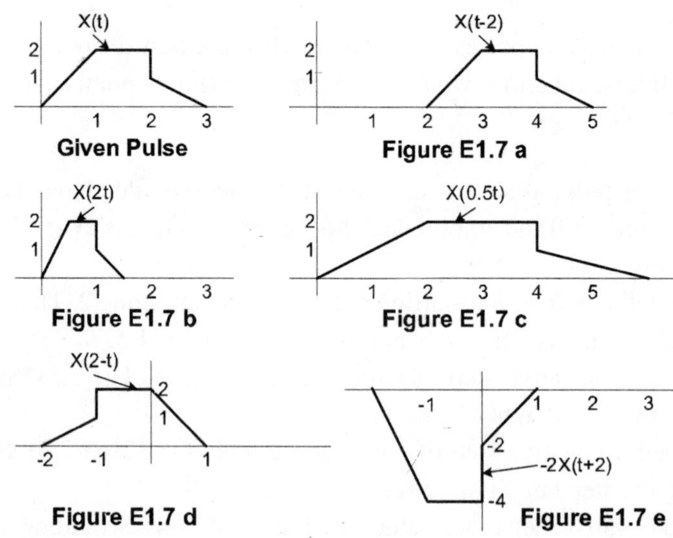

Figure Example 1.7: Various different representations for the signal pulse

Solution 1.7a

Pulse a is the same exact shape and size as the given pulse but shifted by 2 units of time, so pulse a = x(t-2).

Solution 1.7b

Pulse b is the same pulse as the given pulse except it has been compressed in time. To compress the pulse in time we multiply the time variable in the given pulse by the compression factor in this case 2 so pulse b = x(2t).

Solution 1.7c

Pulse c is the same pulse as the given pulse except it has been stretched in time. To stretch the pulse in time we multiply the time variable in the given pulse by the stretching factor in this case 0.5 so pulse c = x(0.5t).

Solution 1.7d

Pulse d is the same as the given pulse except it is first flipped along the y-axis and then it is shifted one unit to the right. Flipping the function is done by reversing the sign of the time variable. So pulse d = x(1-t).

Solution 1.7e

Pulse e is the same as the given pulse except it is scaled in amplitude by a factor of 2 and then it is flipped along the X-axis, finally the function is also shifted by 2 time units. Flipping the function along the X-axis is done by multiplying the function by -1 or by reversing the sign of the function. So pulse e = -2x(t+2).

1.5 REPRESENTING SIGNALS BY ORTHOGONAL FUNCTIONS

We have used signals and the definitions of various different types of signals earlier in this chapter and we will use them in the remainder of this book. Often there is a question, what are these signals? Where do they come from? Is there a difference in the signals if they are represented in a tabular format or the signal is collected as data from a sensor or if the signal is a mathematical expression? Is it possible to represent a complex waveform in terms of regular and simple functions? All these and other questions about signals are answered by representing the signal in its components.

This process of representing the signal in its components is similar to the process of resolving a vector in three dimension space into its x, y, and z components. The three components of the three dimension space have some special properties. Each component in the three dimension space resolves the original vector in only one of the three directions. Resolving the component in this way we are able to look at and examine the effect of the vector in any one direction. The X component tells us the effect of the vector in the X direction; similarly the Y component tells us the effect in the Y direction. We will use similar special properties to resolve a signal in its components. We do this in detail in Chapter 3. In Chapter 3 we will use the trigonometric functions, the Sine and the Cosine functions.

Here we examine the orthogonal functions in general and we first identify the properties of these functions and then list several different functions that possess these properties and can be used to represent a signal. Referring back again to the three vectors in three dimension space they are orthonormal to each other. Signals or vectors that are orthonormal to each other satisfy the following property:

Property 1: $\phi(i) \cdot \phi(j) = 0 \;\; i \neq j$; and $\phi(i) \cdot \phi(j) = 1 \;\; i = j$

We can interpret the first equation of property 1 graphically as the projection of the vector $\phi(j)$ in the direction of the vector $\phi(i)$ is zero, or that the two vectors are perpendicular to each other. This is shown in Figure 1.12. Figure 1.12 shows the three orthonormal vectors of the Cartesian co-ordinate system. Notice that the projection of any of the three vectors in the direction of any other vector will be zero. Hence we get the first equation in Property 1. The second equation in Property 1 says that the projection of the vector in its own direction is the vector it self. Since the self projection is 1 we call these vectors orthonormal. If the self projection is not equal to unity then the vectors are known as orthogonal.

Figure 1.12 also shows how the projection of a vector in the three dimensional space can be resolved into its three orthonormal components. The three orthonormal components completely define the vector R in the co-ordinate system. This is shown in Equation (1.10). When we examine the signals in Chapter 3 we want to accomplish something very similar to this for the various periodic functions. The periodic function may have (will have) more then three components but the concept is the same. We wish to resolve the periodic function along its various orthonormal components.

$$\vec{R} = R_1\vec{i} + R_2\vec{j} + R_3\vec{k} \;\; = \;\; \sum_{n=1}^{3} R_n \Phi_n \tag{1.10}$$

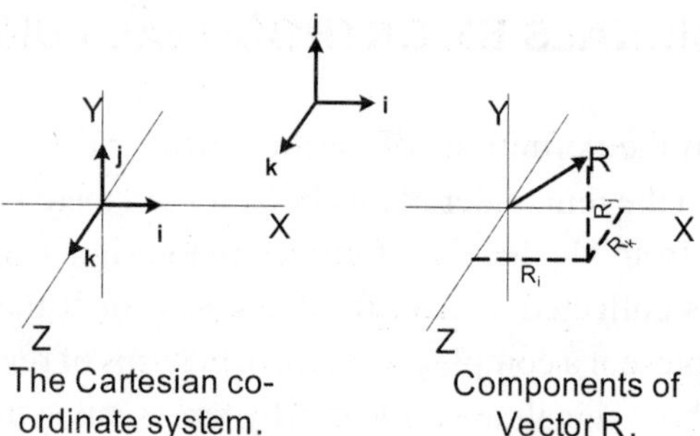

Figure 1.12: Three Orthonormal vectors in the Cartesian co-ordinate system. Components of Vector R.

To take the step that will resolve the periodic function along its orthonormal components we first write the periodic function in the same form as the vector R in Equation (1.10). Doing this will give us the equation $f(t) = \sum_{i=1}^{n} r_i \Phi_i$. In this equation the r_i components are the projections of the function *f(t)* in the direction of the orthonormal functions ϕ_i. The orthonormal functions have the same property that is described in Property 1 above.

One set of these functions, as we will see in Chapter 3, is the set of Sine or the Cosine functions. The cosine functions cos(1t); cos(2t) ... cos(nt) are all orthogonal to each other. They are not orthonormal. To show that the cos functions are orthogonal to each other we use property 1.

So $$\int_0^{2\pi} \cos(nt)\cos(mt)\,dt = \begin{cases} 0 & n \neq m \\ \pi & n = m \end{cases}$$

To make this set of functions orthonormal we need to multiply each of the functions by $\sqrt{1/\pi}$. We will be using this concept in great detail when we talk about Fourier series and Fourier transforms in Chapter 3. Similarly all the Sine functions are also orthogonal. They are not orthonormal. To show that the sine functions are orthogonal we use property 1 again.

So $$\int_0^{2\pi} \sin(nt)\sin(mt)\,dt = \begin{cases} 0 & n \neq m \\ \pi & n = m \end{cases}$$

1.6 ORTHOGONAL FUNCTIONS AND POLYNOMIALS

Orthogonal functions and polynomials play a very important part in signal estimation and signal detection. Earlier we have mentioned and have shown that all of the sine functions and the cosine functions are orthogonal. Here in this section we will list some of the other functions that are also orthogonal. We will not be going into detail of these orthogonal functions.

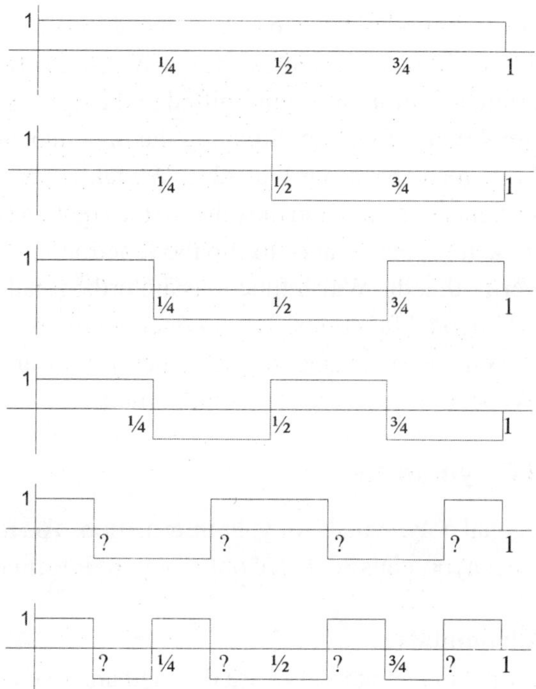

Figure 1.13: Several different Walsh functions

1.6.1 The Walsh Functions

Walsh functions form a complete set of orthogonal functions in the interval [0,1]. Walsh functions are used in the expansions of complex signals such as the EKG biomedical signal, the seismic data from earth quake recorders and speech signals. The Walsh functions have a special advantage compared to other orthogonal functions. Refer to Figure 1.13. Notice the values assumed by the Walsh functions, they are ± 1 so multiplication with any Walsh function is only a matter of checking the sign of the other function. Also since the Walsh functions are binary (assume only 2 values) they can easily be generated by logic circuits. The Ordered Walsh functions are written as $\Phi_w = \{Wal_w(I,t)$ $I = 0, 1, 2, \ldots N-1\}$. In this representation I is the index and it represents the Ith member of the set. The index also gives us information about the number of zero crossings in the interval [0,1]

$$Wal_w(2I + p, t) \overset{\Delta}{=} Wal_w(I, 2(t + 0.25)) + (-1)^{(I+p)} Wal_w(I, 2(t - 0.25)) \tag{1.11}$$

The crossing of the zero axis are analogous to the frequency of an analog function. In the Walsh function this is known as **Sequency**. When I=0 the sequency of the function is zero. When I is odd then the sequency of the function is (I + 1)/2. When I is even then the sequency of the function is (I)/2. The Walsh functions are defined by using a recursive relation. The relation is given by Equation (1.11)

In Equation (1.11) p = 0 or 1. The index of the Walsh function is I. The term $Wal_w(I,2(t+0.25))$

represents the Walsh function with index I as a block, reduced by a factor of 2 (shrunk to half its size) and shifted to the left. $Wal_w(I,2(t-0.25))$ represents the Walsh function with index I as a block, reduced by a factor of 2 (shrunk to half its size) and shifted to the right. So a new Walsh function is made up by one of its previous Walsh function. Studying the diagrams in Figure 1.13 will make it clear. For example $Wal_w(4,t)$ is made by using $Wal_w(2,t)$. We take two copies of $Wal_w(2,t)$ Shrink them to half their length, shift one to the left and the other to the right and check the sign for the one shifted to the right. In this case it is + so no need to flip the function.

You can very quickly verify that the Walsh functions are orthogonal as they satisfy property 1 that we have listed for the orthogonal functions. The product of any two Walsh functions is zero if the Walsh functions are not identical (not same) to each other, if they are identical (are same) then the product is one. So the Walsh functions are also orthonormal.

1.6.2 Other Orthogonal Polynomials

Here we list other orthogonal polynomials for your information. You may easily skip this section if you choose to do so. These polynomials are listed only for your information.

1.6.2.1 The Legender Polynomials

These functions are orthonormal in the interval -1 d≤t d≤1 and are given by the Equation (1.12).

$$\Theta_n(t) = \sqrt{n+\tfrac{1}{2}}\, P_n(t) \qquad -1 \le t \le 1$$

$$\text{Where } P_n(t) = \frac{1}{2^n}\frac{1}{n!}\frac{d^n\left(t^2-1\right)^n}{dt^n} \qquad n = 0, 1, 2, 3 \ldots$$

P_n are the Legender polynomials which possess the property;

$$\int_{-1}^{1} P_n^2(t)\,dt = \frac{1}{n+\tfrac{1}{2}} \tag{1.12}$$

And they are recursive with the Recursive relation

$$(n+1)P_{n+1}(t) = (2n+1)tP_n(t) - nP_{n-1}(t)$$

$$P_n(-t) = (-1)^n P_n(t)$$

The definition of the Legender polynomials is given in the second equation in Equation 1.13 and the recursive relations are given in the last two equations in Equation 1.13. Evaluation of the Legender polynomials is done by the recursive relation after the first polynomial has been evaluated. So we can evaluate the Legender polynomial $P_1(t)$ using the relation given in the second equation in Equation (1.12). This will evaluate to $P_1(t) = t$. Next we evaluate $P_2(t)$ using the recursive relation as

$$(1+1)P_2(t) = (2*1+1)tP_1(t) - 1P_0(t) = 3t^2 - 1 \text{ or } P_2(t) = 0.5(3t^2-1)$$

1.6.2.2 The Hermite Functions

These functions are orthonormal in the interval $-\infty < t < \infty$ and are given by Equation(1.13)

$$\Theta_n(t) = (2^n n! \sqrt{n})^{\frac{1}{2}} e^{-t^2/2} H_n(t) \tag{1.13}$$

$$H_n(t) = (-1)^n e^{t^2} \frac{d^n(e^{-t^2})}{dt^n} \qquad n = 0,1,2,\ldots$$

These functions are orthonormal in the interval -1 ≤t d≤1 the recursive properties of these functions are given in Equation (1.14).

$$H_n(t) = (-1)^n H_n(-t)$$
$$H_{n+1}(t) = 2tH_n(t) - 2nH_{n-1}(t) \tag{1.14}$$

1.6.2.3 The Chebyshev Functions

These functions are orthonormal in the interval -1 d≤t d≤1 and are given by the Equation (1.15)

$$\Theta_0(t) = \frac{1}{\sqrt{\pi}} \frac{1}{(1-t^2)^{1/4}} C_0(t) \qquad n = 0 \tag{1.15}$$

$$\Theta_n(t) = \frac{2}{\sqrt{\pi}} \frac{1}{(1-t^2)^{1/4}} C_n(t) \qquad n \geq 1$$

$$C_n(t) = \frac{(-2)^n n!}{(2n)!} \sqrt{(1-t^2)} \frac{d^n (1-t^2)^{n-1/2}}{dt^n}$$

The recursive properties of these functions are given in Equation (1.16).

$$C_1(t) - 2tC_n(t) = 0$$
$$C_{n+1}(t) - 2tC_n(t) + C_{n-1}(t) = 0 \qquad n \geq 1 \tag{1.16}$$

1.6.3 How do we use the Orthogonal Polynomials

These Orthogonal Polynomials are used to represent other complex functions as their individual components just as we did for the vector in three dimensional space earlier in Equation (1.10).

In order to approximate a function using say the Legender polynomials we would use the first equation in Equation(1.12). In Equation(1.12) we are trying to approximate the function $\Theta(t)$ and in approximating the function we need to determine the coefficients c_n for each of the various Legender polynomials.

This is done by the equation $c_n = 2\sqrt{n + \frac{1}{2}} \int_0^1 \Theta(t) P_n(t) dt$ and the evaluated coefficients are then attached to the various Legender polynomials. As we will see later when we study the Fourier series in detail the coefficient { $2\sqrt{n+\frac{1}{2}}$ } multiplying the integral is there to make the Legender polynomials orthonormal. More about representing the functions when we study the Fourier series.

1.7 POWER AND ENERGY SIGNALS

Signals can be classified as Power signals or as Energy signals or as neither. A power signal is one that has an average value (less than ∞) when the square of the signal is integrated over a time from minus infinity to infinity. An energy signal is one that has zero power but a finite value when the area under the square of the signal curve is evaluated from minus infinity to infinity. So the energy of a signal is calculated as shown in Equation (1.17). The signal f(t) in Equation (1.17) will be an energy signal if the integral is finite (less than infinity.)

$$E = \int_{-\infty}^{\infty} f^2(t)\, dt \tag{1.17}$$

The power of the signal is computed as shown in Equation (1.18). This signal will be a power signal if the average value of the integral is greater than zero but less than infinite. That is the Limit must be finite and not equal to zero. If this Limit is zero then the signal is most probably an energy signal. If the signal f(t) is a complex valued signal then the integral evaluated in both cases (Power and Energy) is that of the magnitude of the signal squared or $|f(t)|^2$ instead of $f^2(t)$.

$$P = \underset{T \to \infty}{Limit} \left[\frac{1}{2T} \int_{-T}^{T} f^2(t)\, dt \right] \tag{1.18}$$

If f(t) is a periodic signal then the power in each period is the same and it repeats itself every cycle. So for periodic signal we can replace, in Equation (1.18), T by its period. So instead of having T→ to ∞T is equal to the period of the signal.

The Energy and Power of a finite time signal are always finite as long as the amplitude of the signal is not infinite. A finite time signal is one that starts at a given time and then stops at a different time later.

$$E_k = \sum_{k=-\infty}^{\infty} f^2(k) \qquad \text{and} \qquad P_k = \underset{K \to \infty}{Limit} \frac{1}{2K+1} \sum_{-K}^{K} f^2(t_k) \tag{1.19}$$

When we have a discrete signal then we replace the integral with a summation. So when the signal is a discrete signal then the Power and the Energy in the signal are calculated by using Equation (1.19). In either the analog or the discrete case if the signal is a complex valued signal then $f^2(t)$ is replaced by the magnitude square of the signal which is $|f^2(t)|$. In Chapter 3 when we learn about Parsevals relation we will see that we can calculate the power in the signal either in the Time domain or in the Frequency domain.

Example 1.8

Calculate the Power and the Energy in each of the signals given.

a. $X_1(t) = 5e^{-0.5t}U(t)$

b. $X_2(t) = 4Cos(10\pi t + 30^0)$

Solution 1.8

We first calculate the Power and Energy in the first signal given in X1 and then we calculate the Power and Energy in the other signal given in X2.

Solution 1.8a

Using Equation (1.17) the energy in signal $X_1(t)$ can be determined as

$$E_{X_1} = \int_{-\infty}^{\infty}\left[5e^{-0.5t}U(t)\right]^2 dt = \int_0^{\infty} 25e^{-1.0t}\, dt = \frac{25}{-1}e^{-1t}\Big|_0^{\infty} = 25J$$

Similarly we can determine the power in the signal using Equation (1.18). This time the Power in the signal is $P_{X_1} = \underset{T\to\infty}{\text{Limit}}\frac{1}{2T}\int_{-T}^{T}\left[5e^{-0.5t}U(t)\right]^2 dt = 0$. Since this signal has finite energy it will have zero power. This is an Energy signal.

Solution 1.8b

The signal X_2 is a periodic signal. So we can use the periodic signal formula to compute the power. First the energy of the signal.

$$E_{X_2} = \int_{-\infty}^{\infty}\left[4Cos(10\pi t + 30^\circ)\right]^2 dt = \int_{-\infty}^{\infty}\left[8 + 8Cos\left(20\pi t + 60^\circ\right)\right] dt = \infty.$$

So the energy in this signal is infinite. Similarly we can determine the Power in the signal as

$$P_{X_2} = \underset{T\to\infty}{\text{Limit}}\frac{1}{2T}\int_{-T}^{T}\left[4Cos(10\pi t + 30^\circ)\right]^2 dt = \underset{T\to\infty}{\text{Limit}}\frac{1}{2T}\int_{-T}^{T}\left[8 + 8Cos\left(20\pi t + 60^\circ\right)\right] dt$$

$$P_{X_2} = \frac{8}{2} = 4W$$

Thus we see that signal X_1 has 25 Joules of energy and signal X_2 has 4 Watts of power.

1.8 INTERPOLATING SIGNALS BY POLYNOMIALS

A continuous function with continuous derivatives can be expanded in the form of its Taylor series if its value and the value of all its derivatives are also known at the point where the Taylor series is written. This is a very well known fact from Calculus. So we must know the function and its derivatives at the instant in time where we want to expand the function. Very often we do not know the value of the function at a specific instant in time. In cases like these we would like to estimate the value of the function at that instant in time. This will occur especially when we have a discrete function. In this case we will approximate the value of the function at a specific instant in time.

A discrete function is often an analog function that we have sampled as shown in Figure 1.7 earlier. When the analog function is sampled we know the exact value of the function only at the sampling instants. In between the sampling instants the function is not defined. It is not zero, it is just not defined. In cases such as these we need to estimate the value of the function at some time in between two sampling instants.

To estimate the function at these intermediate points, we make an assumption about the function. The assumption that we make about the function is that the function is going to be following the same path as the nth order polynomial that we choose to approximate the function by. This same assumption can be stated in an alternate way as follows: *The nth derivative of the function is constant.*

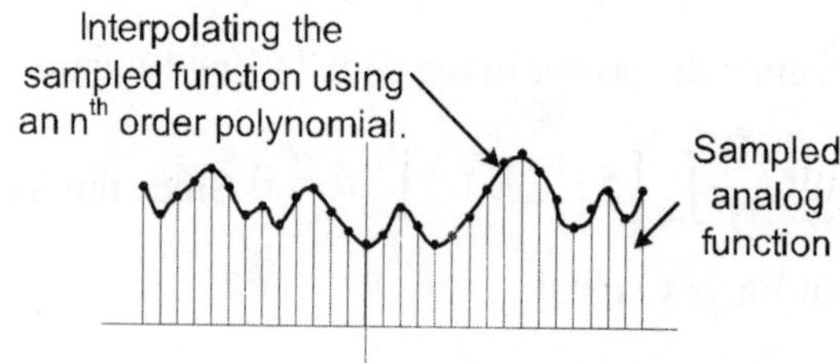

Figure 1.14: Interpolating the values of a sampled function between sample points by using an nth order polynomial.

What would happen if we chose to represent the function by an nth order function but the nth derivative of the function was not constant? If the nth derivative is not constant then we will be wrong in our estimation. However if the nth derivative is changing very, very slowly then our estimation will be quite reasonable. After all remember we are trying to approximate the sampled values. We are not claiming that they are exact. Here we will see how we can represent a sampled function by an nth order polynomial. Once we have represented the sampled function by an nth order polynomial then the values in between the various sampling instants can be approximated.

To determine the nth order polynomial we assume that the value of the function that we have at the sampling points is exactly correct and that the nth order polynomial passes through all the points. Then by using the polynomial and the time when the intermediate value is to be determined we can get the intermediate value. The simplest case is that of linear interpolation. For linear interpolation we determine the equation of a straight line passing through two adjacent sampling points. Then by using the equation of the straight line we can determine the value of the function at any point between these two sample points.

$$f(t_m) = \sum_{i=0}^{n} \alpha_i t_m^i \tag{1.20}$$

When we use linear interpolation we are making an assumption that the polynomial that we are using is a straight line between two points. This is because the first derivative of a straight line (a straight line equation is a first order polynomial) is constant. Similarly when we use the quadratic interpolation we know that the second derivative is a constant. In the same way if we know that the nth derivative of a function is constant then we will use the nth order polynomial to interpolate the values between the sampling instants.

$$\begin{aligned}
&\alpha_0 t_0^0 + \alpha_1 t_0^1 + \alpha_2 t_0^2 + \alpha_3 t_0^3 \cdots + \alpha_n t_0^{n-1} = f(t_0) \\
&\alpha_0 t_1^0 + \alpha_1 t_1^1 + \alpha_2 t_1^2 + \alpha_3 t_1^3 \cdots + \alpha_n t_1^{n-1} = f(t_1) \\
&\alpha_0 t_2^0 + \alpha_1 t_2^1 + \alpha_2 t_2^2 + \alpha_3 t_2^3 \cdots + \alpha_n t_2^{n-1} = f(t_2) \\
&\;\vdots \qquad \vdots \qquad \vdots \qquad \vdots \quad \cdots \quad \vdots \;=\; \vdots \\
&\alpha_0 t_n^0 + \alpha_1 t_n^1 + \alpha_2 t_n^2 + \alpha_3 t_n^3 \cdots + \alpha_n t_n^{n-1} = f(t_n)
\end{aligned} \tag{1.21}$$

Getting the first order polynomial was easy; all we had to do was to get the equation of the straight line from the two known sample points that are on either side of the instant where we wish to estimate the value. But how do we get the expression say for a fifth or a seventh order polynomial? To get a nth order polynomial we make use of n+1 known sample values. We always take one more sample value then the order of the polynomial with which we want to complete the interpolation. These n +1 sample values will be at n + 1 different instant in time. So with these n +1 sample values and the n +1 different time instants we can write out n + 1 simultaneous equation as shown in Equation (1.21). To get Equation (1.21) we expanded Equation (1.20).

Once all the coefficients α have been determined the value of the function between the sampling instants can be determined by using one of the n equations in Equation (1.21) for a particular instant in time. Equation (1.21) is a matrix equation of the type $\boldsymbol{\alpha}$ **T** = **f** which can be solved by either SCILAB or MATLAB. Once we get the n+1 constants α then the nth order polynomial will be known and the required value is estimated by substituting the value of time where the function is to be interpolated. An example of using the approximation is given in the solved problem section.

Students often are confused when the same point in a discrete sequence is interpolated by say the second order polynomial as well as the first order polynomial. So we are trying to approximate the value of say a function at $t = 0.85$ using the first (linear) order function and the same point of the same function at $t = 0.85$ using the second (quadratic) order approximation. Which one is right? It is possible that neither one of them is correct. That is the point of estimation. You are estimating; you are not predicting an exact value. So which method should you use? The way we choose the method to be used for interpolation is as follows.

The interpolation polynomial that you will use depends on:

1. The amount of computation you want to perform or have the time to do. Higher the order of the polynomial greater the amount of computation required.

2. The underlying or the governing curve from which the samples are obtained. If the samples are taken from say a 5th order curve then a 5th order curve will interpolate the function correctly.

In actual practice you will find that if the samples are taken close to each other then the linear or the first order approximation is good enough most of the time.

Example 1.9

For the function shown in Figure 1.15 interpolate the value of the function at the time required (t = 0.25) using the first order, second order and third order polynomial.

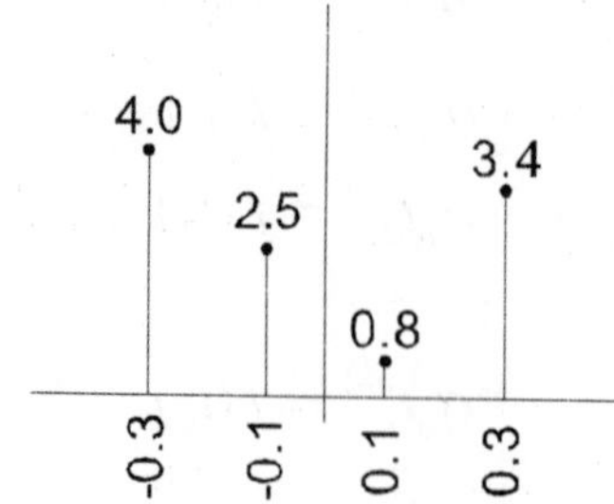

Figure 1.15: Determine the value of the function at t = 0.25

Solution 1.9

Using the values shown in Figure 1.15 to approximate the value of the function at t = 0.25.

Solution 1.9a

First Order approximation. For this we get two equations from which we will determine the coefficients α as shown in Equation (1.22).

$$\begin{aligned} \alpha_0 + 0.1\alpha_1 &= 0.8 \\ \alpha_0 + 0.3\alpha_1 &= 3.4 \end{aligned} \tag{1.22}$$

Solving the two Equations in Equation (1.22) we get $\alpha_0 = -0.5$ and $\alpha_1 = 13$. Substituting these values and the time at which we wish to approximate the function we get Equation (1.23).

$$-0.5 + 13(0.25) = f(0.25) = 2.75 \tag{1.23}$$

Solution 1.9b

Second Order approximation. For this we get three equations from which we will determine the coefficients α as shown in Equation (1.24).

$$\begin{aligned} \alpha_0 + (-0.1)\alpha_1 + (-0.1)^2\alpha_2 &= 2.5 \\ \alpha_0 + (0.1)\alpha_1 + (0.1)^2\alpha_2 &= 0.8 \\ \alpha_0 + (0.3)\alpha_1 + (0.3)^2\alpha_2 &= 3.4 \end{aligned} \tag{1.24}$$

Solving the three Equations in Equation (1.24) we get $\alpha_0 = 0.53875$, $\alpha_1 = -0.85$ and $\alpha_2 = 34.625$. Substituting these values and the time at which we wish to approximate the function we get Equation(1.25)

$$0.53875 - 0.85(0.25) + 34.625(0.25)^2 = f(0.25) = 2.4903125 \tag{1.25}$$

Solution 1.9c

Third Order approximation. For this we get four equations from which we will determine the coefficients α as shown in Equation(1.26)

$$\begin{aligned}
\alpha_0 + (-0.3)\alpha_1 + (-0.3)^2\alpha_2 + (-0.3)^3\alpha_3 &= 4.0 \\
\alpha_0 + (-0.1)\alpha_1 + (-0.1)^2\alpha_2 + (-0.1)^3\alpha_3 &= 2.5 \\
\alpha_0 + (0.1)\alpha_1 + (0.1)^2\alpha_2 + (0.1)^3\alpha_3 &= 0.8 \\
\alpha_0 + (0.3)\alpha_1 + (0.3)^2\alpha_2 + (0.3)^3\alpha_3 &= 3.4
\end{aligned} \tag{1.26}$$

Solving the four Equations in Equation (1.26) we get $\alpha_0 = 1.39375$, $\alpha_1 = -9.4375$ $\alpha_2 = 25.625$ and $\alpha_3 = 93.75$. Substituting these values and the time at which we wish to approximate the function we get Equation (1.27).

$$\begin{aligned}
&1.39375 - 9.4375(0.25) + 25.625(0.25)^2 + 93.75(0.25)^3 \\
&\qquad = \mathrm{f}(0.25) = 2.1007812
\end{aligned} \tag{1.27}$$

As you can see the approximation using the three different polynomials are relatively close but not exact but that is what approximation is all about. All you can get is an approximation and there is no guarantee that different approximation methods will give you the same approximate values.

1.9 CHAPTER SUMMARY

A signal is a means of transferring information from the source to the destination. The information is placed in the signal by modulating one of the parameters of the signal by the information that we wish to transfer. Any parameter of the signal can be modulated, some of these parameters are the amplitude, the frequency, the phase, the duty cycle or the pulse position. Sometimes it is possible to vary two or more parameters to place two or more information streams in the same signal.

The simplest continuous time periodic signal is the sine signal. The signal is defined by three parameters – the Amplitude, the Phase and the Frequency. The period of a periodic signal is the reciprocal of the frequency in cycles per second. The frequency of a periodic signal is defined in either cycles per second or in radians. One cycle per second equals to 2π radians.

A discrete time signal is defined at discrete instants in time. Being defined at discrete instants in time does not mean that the signal is zero between the discrete instants in time. It just means that we do not know what the signal is at that time. Discrete time signals can also be periodic or non-periodic. Often a discrete time signal is obtained by sampling a continuous time signal. The sampling process is similar to multiplying a continuous time signal by a periodic unit amplitude sampling function. This sampling function is made up of impulses which are equally spaced. The sampling function does not have to have the same frequency as the function being sampled. Most often the sampling function has a higher frequency then the function being sampled.

Some of the common non periodic signals are the Step function, the Ramp function, the Impulse function, the Sinc function and the Signum function. All these functions have an activation time. The function activates when the argument of the function is zero. Thus by changing the argument of the function we can activate the function at any time that we want it to be activated. This just shifts the function left or right depending on the argument.

Jean Baptist Fourier, a French scientist and mathematician was among the early pioneers to study the periodic signals. He found that any periodic signal can be resolved into its components by using orthonormal components. The orthonormal components that we will use in our study in Chapter 3 are the Sine and the Cosine signals. In this chapter we have identified several different functions that are also orthogonal.

When we have a sampled signal we know what the value of the signal is only at the sampling instants. If we need to know the value of the sampled function in-between the sampling instants then we need to use interpolation to determine (estimate) the values between the sampling instants. Interpolation is done by an nth order polynomial. Most of the times when we interpolate we will be using either the first order or the second order polynomials for interpolation.

1.10 HOMEWORK PROBLEMS

Definition of a Signal

Problem 1.10.1

a. List all the different parameters that can be used to transmit information on a Square wave.

Problem 1.10.2

For the Touch Tone telephone dialing system we have a key matrix that is arranged as a 4 x 3 matrix. To decode a key in this matrix we need 7 different frequencies

1. If the matrix were arranged as a 6 x 2 matrix how many different frequencies would be required?

2. If you had a different matrix arranged as a 5 x 4 matrix how many different frequencies would be required?

3. If there were say 24 buttons on some key pad then this key pad can be arranged as any of the following matrices. Which matrix would you recommend? Why?

24 x 1; 12 x 2; 8 x 3; 6 x 4.

Periodic Signals

Problem 1.10.3

Identify the periodic signals from the following. For the periodic signals identify their fundamental period.

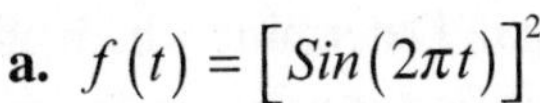

a. $f(t) = \left[Sin(2\pi t)\right]^2$

b. $f(t) = \sum_{r=-10}^{10} x(t+2r)$

c. $f(t) = \sum_{r=-\infty}^{\infty} x(t-3r)$

d. $f(n) = (-1)^n$

e. $f(n) = (-1)^{n^2}$

f. Signal shown in Figure Problem 1.3f

g. Signal shown in Figure Problem 1.3g

h. f(n) = Cos(2n)

i. f(n) = Cos(2πn)

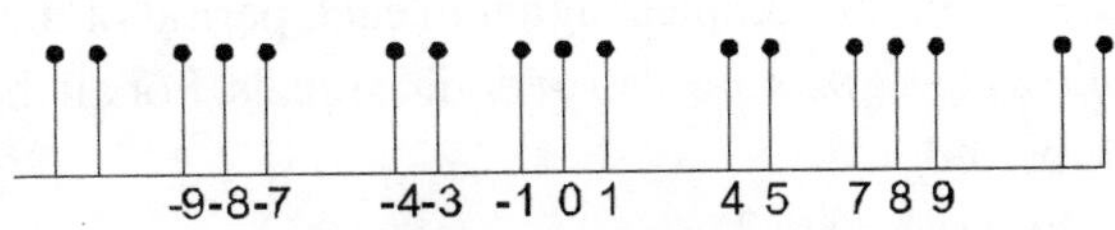

Figure Problem 1.3f

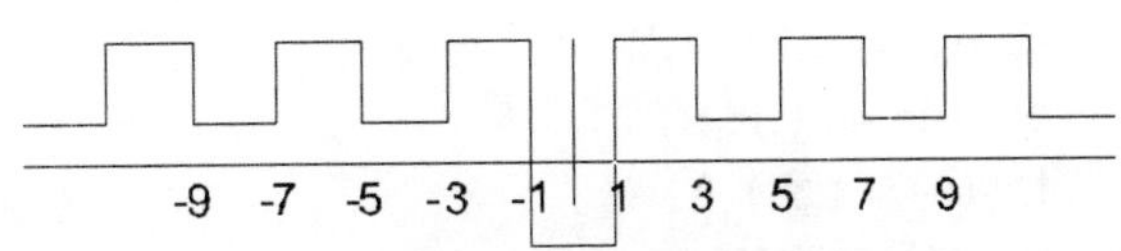

Figure Problem 1.3g

Problem 1.10.4

For the waves shown in Figure Problem 1.4 determine the period of the periodic signals. What is the frequency in Hz and in radians/sec for the waves shown in Figure Problem 1.4?

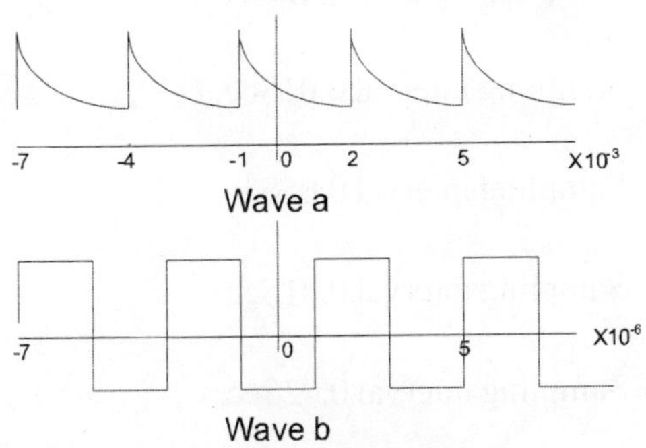

Figure Problem 1.4

Problem 1.10.5

Draw a Cosine Wave that has amplitude of 0.5 volts, a period of 30×10^{-6} seconds, an offset of 42° and a DC bias of 0.3 volts.

Problem 1.10.6

Identify the Power signals and the Energy signals among all the signals shown in Problem 1.10.3.

Sampling a Continuous time signal

Problem 1.10.7

Assume that x(t) is a periodic signal with period T. Also assume that x(n) is a signal that is the sampled version of x(t) with sampling rate of T/10 where T is the period of x(t). So there are 10 samples of the sampled signal in each period of the continuous time signal. Determine which of the following signals are also periodic signals. For all the signals that you identified as periodic determine the period.

a. y(n) = x(t-2)
b. y(n) = x(2-t)
c. y(n) = x((2-2t)
d. y(n) = x(0.5t+2)
e. y(n) = x(t)U(t)
f. y(n) = x(2t)
g. y(n) = x(t/4)
h. y(n) = $x(t^2)$

Problem 1.10.8

We wish to sample the following continuous time signals at the sampling intervals shown. Write out the first 10 samples of each signal.

a. 5Sin(6πt)U(t) Sampling interval 0.05Sec.

b. 5Sin(6πt +30°)U(t) Sampling interval 0.05Sec.

c. e^{-5t}Sin(4πt)U(t) Sampling interval 0.01Sec.

d. $e^{-(5+j6\pi)t}$Sin(8πt)U(t) Sampling interval 0.05Sec.

e. $5e^{-(5+j6\pi)t}$U(t) Sampling interval 0.01Sec.

f. $6e^{j6\pi t}$U(t) Sampling interval 0.02Sec.

Problem 1.10.9

Assume that x(t) is a periodic continuous time signal with period T. Also let x(n) be derived by sampling x(t) by a sampling function of equally spaced samples of x(t), that is x(n) = $x(nT_s)$ where T_s is the sampling interval. Under what condition is x(n) a periodic signal? Show that x(n) is periodic if and only if T/T_s is a rational number.

Non-Periodic Signals

Problem 1.10.10

Sketch the following signals:

a. Step function of step 3 activated at time t = 4 sec. 3U(t-4)

b. A sum of two step functions both of step 1.5. The first function is activated at t = 3 sec and the second function is activated at t = 8 sec.

c. $X_1(t) = 4U(t) - 2U(t-3)$

d. $X_2(t) = 3U(t) - 4U(t-5) + r(t-6) - r(t-8)$

e. $X_3(t) = 3U(t-5) * U(5-t)$

Problems 1.10.11

We have seen that the impulse function is independent of the shape of the function as long as the area under the curve stays constant. It is desired to build an impulse function with the shapes shown in Figure Problem 1.11. Determine the various parameters in each figure so the impulse function is a unit impulse.

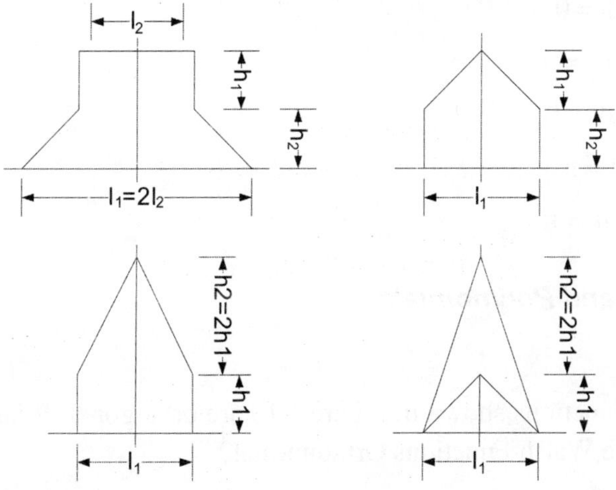

Figure Problem 1.11: Various possible shapes for an impulse function

Problem 1.10.12

Evaluate the value of each of the following integrals:

a. $\int \text{Sin}(16\pi t + 30^{o})\delta(t-4)\, dt$

b. $\int e^{-4t}\delta(t-0.04)\, dt$

c. $\int e^{-4t}U(t)\delta(t-0.04)\, dt$

d. $\int e^{-4t}U(t)\delta(t+0.04)\, dt$

Problem 1.10.13

From the sketch of the signals in Figure Problem 1.13 write the expression for the signal.

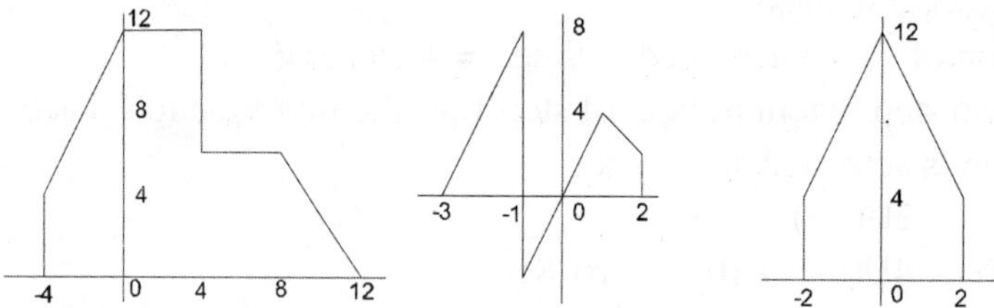

Figure Problem 1.13: From the sketch of the signals drawn write the expression to represent each signal.

Representing signals by Orthogonal Functions

Problem 1.10.14

Evaluate the following integrals over one period and prove the indicated result:

a. $\int \text{Sin}(16\pi t)\text{Sin}(8\pi t)\, dt = 0$

b. $\int \text{Cos}(16\pi t)\text{Sin}(8\pi t)\, dt = 0$

c. $\int \text{Sin}(16\pi t)\text{Cos}(8\pi t)\, dt = 0$

d. $\int \text{Sin}(8\pi t)\text{Sin}(8\pi t)\, dt = \pi$

e. $\int \text{Cos}(8\pi t)\text{Cos}(8\pi t)\, dt = \pi$

Orthogonal Functions and Polynomials

Problem 1.10.15

Show that the Walsh Functions shown in Figure 1.13 are orthogonal. What is the multiplying constant needed to make the Walsh Functions Orthonormal?

Problem 1.10.16

In Figure 1.13 you have the first 6 Walsh functions drawn. Draw the next two Walsh functions that follow.

Problem 1.10.17

Determine the relation between the sequency parameter I and the number of zero axis crossings for the Walsh functions.

Power and Energy Signals

Problem 1.10.18

For each of the following signals determine which signals are the energy signals and which signals are the power signals. Then proceed to determine the energy in the energy signals and the power in the power signals.

a. $x(t)=\begin{cases} t & 0\le t\le 1 \\ 2-t & 1\le t\le 2 \\ 0 & Otherwise \end{cases}$

b. $x(n)=\begin{cases} n & 0\le n\le 5 \\ 10-n & 5\le t\le 10 \\ 0 & Otherwise \end{cases}$

c. x(t) = Sin(4πt) + 2Cos(3πt)

d. $x(t)=\begin{matrix} 4Cos(\pi t) & -\pi\le t\le \pi \\ 0 & Otherwise \end{matrix}$

e. $x(n)=\begin{matrix} 4Cos(\pi n) & -4\le n\le 4 \\ 0 & Otherwise \end{matrix}$

Problem 1.10.19

Consider the signal 5Sin(4πt) after it undergoes the following operations.

a. The signal is passed through a square law device so $y(t) = x^2(t)$ or $y(t) = 25Sin^2(4\pi t)$. (Hint: Use the double angle trigonometric identity)

b. Passed through a half wave rectifier.

c. Passed through a full wave rectifier.

d. Passed through a symmetric clipper with clipping levels set at ±3volts.

For each of the above operations determine if the resulting signal is

i. Periodic: What is the resulting period if the signal is periodic?

ii. Energy Signal: What is the energy of the resulting signal?

iii. Power Signal: What is the power of the resulting signal?

Problem 1.10.20

For each of the signals listed below fill out the appropriate box in the corresponding matrix.

Signal	Periodic/ Aperiodic	Continuou/ Discrete	Energy/ Power	Deterministic/ Probabilistic	Band/Time Limited
U(t)					
U(t)-U(t-9)					
Cos(20t)+Cos(40t)					
Exp(-10t)					
Exp(-10t)U(t)					
tU(t)-(t-1)U(t-1)					
δ(t)					
tU(t)-(t-1)U(t-1)-(t-2)U(t-2)-(t-3)U(t-3)					

Problem 1.10.21

A pulse of a signal is shown in Figure Problem 1.21. Sketch each of the following signals derived from the sketched pulse.

a. X(2t)	b. X(2(t-4))
c. X(0.5t)	d. 4X(2(3-t))
e. X(t-5)	f. 3X(t) +4X(t-2)
g. X(t+5)	h. -2X(t) + 4X(t+2)
i. X(2-t)	j. 3X(2t) + 4X(2-t)

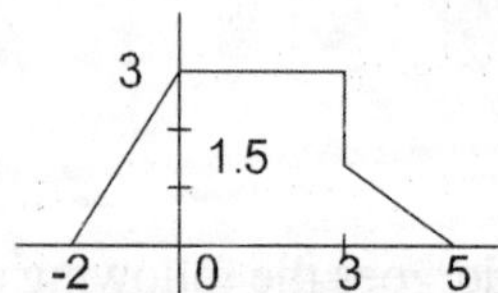

Figure Problem 1.21

Problem 1.10.22

Sketch the waveform of the following signals.

a. X(t) = U(t) – U(t-2)

b. X(t) = 0.5U(t+2) + U(t) – 2U(t-3) + ½U(t-5)

c. X(t) = -3U(t+3) + r(t) – r(t-5) -2U(t-7)

d. X(t) = U(-t) – U(t-5)

e. First write the expression for the pulse that will be a mirror image (on the X-axis) of the pulse given in Problem 1.10.22(b). Then sketch the pulse.

f. First write the expression for the pulse that will be a mirror image (on the Y-axis) of the pulse given in Problem 1.10.22(b). Then sketch the pulse.

g. Mirror image (on the X-axis) of the pulse given in Problem 1.10.22(c).

Problem 1.10.23

You are given a certain time limited signal x(n) in Figure Problem 1.23. Sketch and label each of the following signals. Where appropriate use linear interpolations.

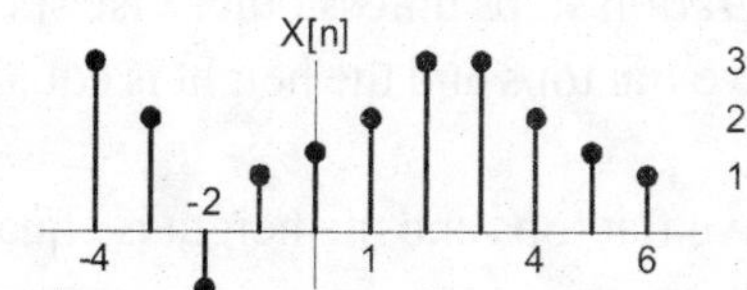

Figure Problem 1.23: Sampled signal X[n]

a. Y[n] = X[n-2]

b. Y[n] = X[1-n/2]

c. Y[n] = X[2+2n]

d. Y[n] = X[n]U[N-n] N= {-4,-2,0,2,4}

e. Y[n] = X[2-n]

f. Y[n] = X[2n+3]

g. Y[n] = X[n] – X[n-1]

Problem 1.10.24

Approximate the value at t = 0.06 using the sampled signals and the sample values given in Figure 1.15.

Problem 1.10.25 SCILAB Assignment:

a. Write the SCILAB script to draw a square wave of amplitude 5 volts, fundamental frequency 20 Hz., and 60% duty cycle.

b. Write the SCILAB script to draw a Sine wave of amplitude 3 volts, fundamental frequency 150 Hz., and an offset of 55°.

c. Write the SCILAB script to first add the first three odd harmonics of a Sine wave of amplitude 3/n volts where n equals the number of the harmonic, the fundamental frequency is 150 Hz., and an offset of each wave is 55*n°.

Problem 1.10.26

Use SCILAB to plot the solution to a differential equation that is given by:

a. $Y(t) = 10e^{-5t} + 3e^{-2t}Sin(5\pi t)$. Draw the plot from t = 0 to t = 1.25 seconds.

b. $Y(t) = 10e^{-5t} - 3e^{-2t}Sin(5\pi t)$. Draw the plot from t = 0 to t = 1.25 seconds.

Problem 1.10.27

Using SCILAB write the script to do numerical integration of a simple ramp function with slope 0.5 and the ramp activated from t = 0 to t = 2 as follows. For each case a, b, c and d use $\Delta t = 0.01$ the length of the time interval for integration steps unless otherwise specified.

a. Assume that all the strips have flat tops and the height is equal to height of the first edge of the strip.

b. Assume that all the strips have flat tops and the height is equal to height of the second edge of the strip.

c. Assume that all the strips have sloping tops and the top goes from the top of the first edge to the top of the second edge of the strip.

d. Compare the results of the above three integration methods with the result of actual integration that you can do using paper and pencil.

e. Repeat steps a, b, c and d with $\Delta t = 0.005$ the length of the time interval for integration steps.

f. Repeat steps a, b, c and d with $\Delta t = 0.001$ the length of the time interval for integration steps.

Problem 1.10.28

Use SCILAB to draw the following three plots:

a. $$x(t) = \sum_{i=1}^{20} \frac{1}{(2i-1)!} Sin((2i-1)\pi t)$$

b.

$$x(t) = \sum_{i=1}^{20} \frac{1}{(2i-1)!} Sin((2i-1)\pi t - 30^\circ)$$

c. $$x(t) = \sum_{i=1}^{20} \frac{1}{(2i-1)!} Sin((2i-1)\pi t \; - \; (2i-1)30^\circ)$$

After you have sketched all the three plots label them individually. Comment on the effect of the phase shift of each harmonic on the composite periodic wave. How would you shift a periodic wave?

CHAPTER 2

Continuous Time Systems

INTRODUCTION

Imagine that a sensor takes a measurement which is presented to an actuator that turns on a heater or opens a door or performs some action based upon the measurement taken by the sensor. What you have just imagined is a system. A system is then a collection of interconnected objects that accepts an input, modifies it to suit some predefined purpose and returns an output or performs an action. To study systems we need to somehow describe the collection of interconnected objects in their mathematical form. Once we have described all the components in their mathematical form, stripped of their individual characteristics, we will see that all systems behave in a very similar manner. So it does not matter that the system described is an electrical system, or a mechanical system, or a thermal system, or a hydraulic system or some other type of system. The mathematical equations describing all the systems are similar and hence all types of systems can be analyzed using the same tools for all types of systems. When we are able to solve the mathematical equations that describe the system, no matter what type of system we have, we are able to calculate a response from all types of systems. For this reason we will introduce different types of systems to get you to see and appreciate that there is indeed no difference in how we analyze the systems once we have reduced the systems to their mathematical representation. The only difference that exists is in the components that make up the system and the laws that the components must obey.

2.1 PROPERTIES OF CONTINUOUS TIME SYSTEMS

Systems, whether they are mechanical, electrical, thermal, economic or any other form can all be divided into several different categories. Here we will look at some of these divisions and what effect they have on the method of analysis before we actually start to analyze the systems.

Lumped Parameters or Distributed Parameter Systems

A lumped parameter system is a system that is comprised of a finite number of physical elements that are discrete and are to be interconnected. The lumped parameters may represent a capacitor in an electrical system or it may represent a point mass; as shown in Figure 2.1 in a mechanical system or it may represent a point source in a heating system. The lumped parameters such as the capacitor or the mass are energy storage elements. Parameters such as the heat source or the battery are the energy sources or elements such as the resistor or friction are energy dissipation elements. All these types of elements whether they are the energy sources, energy storage elements or the energy dissipation elements can all be described by differential equations. So we will be using differential equations to describe the lumped parameter systems.

If we do not represent the system components as a lumped capacitor or as a point mass, but rather we represent the components as spread out all along the system then we have a distributed parameter system. One common example of a distributed parameter system is the uniform

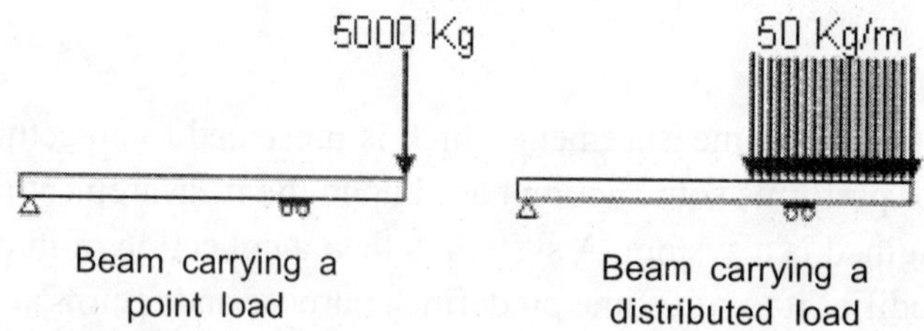

Figure 2.1: A lumped parameter system and a distributed parameter system

distributed load on a beam as shown in Figure 2.1. Another example is the inductance or the capacitance of a long transmission line. In this book we are going to concentrate only on lumped parameter systems. Very often it is possible to convert a distributed parameter system to a lumped parameter system. The conversion method will depend on the system.

Example 2.1

Is the overhead electric transmission line a lumped parameter or a distributed parameter system?

Solution 2.1

The over head electric line is generally modeled as a distributed parameter system. The resistance of the wire is specified as, for example, 0.1W/meter. In the same way the inductance and the capacitance of the wires are also specified on a per meter basis. Since they are specified on a per meter basis instead of as one fixed amount the system is a distributed parameter system.

Stochastic or Deterministic Systems

When some aspect of the system is of a statistical nature, then we have a stochastic system. If everything is known about the system (all the statistics of the system are known) then the system is a deterministic system. All the systems that we will be dealing with in this book are deterministic in nature. Some people will argue that all systems in nature are stochastic since there is always some random effect present in the system. They are of course correct but we will treat these small random effects as known and treat them as deterministic. In the appendix at the end of the book some statistical implications to systems are discussed. For those who are interested this will represent a very nice advanced topic as well as a continuation of what is covered in this book.

Example 2.2

Is the RADAR pulse that you receive back from an object a determinist or a stochastic system?

Solution 2.2

When you transmit the RADAR pulse everything about the pulse is completely known. However when you are receiving the signal back it is scattered by the target and it is corrupted by noise. Both these phenomena are stochastic so the complete system is a stochastic system. Whenever a stochastic element is introduced in the system anywhere the system becomes stochastic.

Linear and Non-linear

Systems that exhibit a linear relation between cause and effect can be classified as linear systems. This means that if the input doubles then the output will also double. Linear systems require components that are linear. Linear components are components whose value or size does not depend on the forces acting on them or the voltage across them. The size is the same whether the component is in the circuit or out of the circuit. As an example the mass of a car is independent of the speed of the car; the resistance of the resistor is independent of the current flowing through it.

There are many other definitions of linear systems and we will come across them as we continue our study, but there is one definition that we have to mention here. ***A linear system is one that obeys the principle of superposition.***

The principle of superposition tells us that if we have two different inputs; $x_1(t)$ and $x_2(t)$; to a system and know the outputs for these two inputs as; $y_1(t)$ and $y_2(t)$; then the system will be a linear system if and only if the following relation holds: A new input $x_3(t) = x_1(t) + x_2(t)$ has a new output $y_3(t)$. If $y_3(t)$ is equal to $y_1(t) + y_2(t)$ then the system is linear.

There are systems that may be conditionally linear, such a system will be linear in a certain range of input and output values. If either the input or the output range is exceeded then the system becomes non linear. It can not follow the principle of superposition in this extended range. An example of such a system is the operational amplifier. If we try to get an output voltage that exceeds the $\pm V_{cc}$ supply voltage then the output saturates and cannot follow a change in the input. So the operational amplifier is linear in the $\pm V_{cc}$ range only. Outside this range the Operational Amplifier is a non linear device. All the systems that we will analyze in this book will be linear systems; to show you an example or two we will point out some non-linear systems but we will not be doing a lot of work with non-linear systems.

Some systems can be identified as piece wise linear. When a system is piece wise linear it is linear in small increments, within each small range the system is linear. When you go from one piece wise linear segment to another piece wise linear segment the transition does not obey the laws of a linear system, the law of superposition. The system however is linear as long as you stay within one range. We will not be considering this type of system in this book; to show you an example or two we will point out some piece wise linear systems but we will not be doing a lot of work with piece wise linear systems.

Example 2.3

Is a system defined by the equation $y(t) = 4x(t) + 2$ a linear system?

Solution 2.3

To verify if the system is a linear system or not we first determine the output from the system when say $x(t)$ = some constant value 'a'.

In this case the output $y(t) = 4a+2$.

Next we determine the output when $x(t)$ is a different constant value say 'b'. In this case the output $y(t) = 4b+2$.

Finally we determine the output if $x(t)$ was equal to the sum of the two inputs say $x(t) = a+b$. In this case the output $y(t) = 4(a+b)+2$.

Now if the sum of the first two outputs is equal to the third output then the system is linear. In our case $\{4a+2\} + \{4b+2\}$ is not equal to $4(a+b)+2$ so the system is a non linear system.

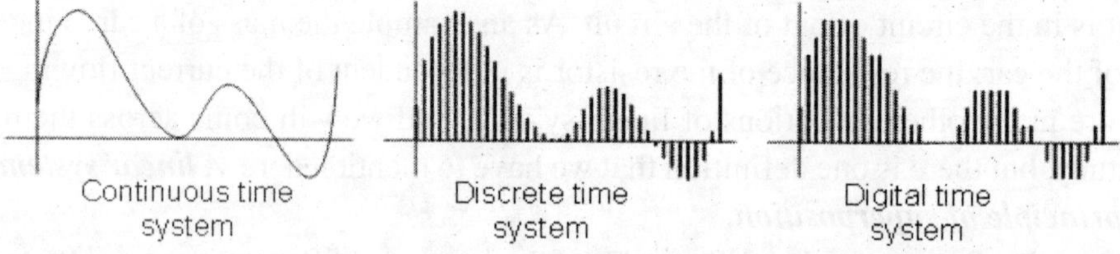

Figure 2.2: Difference between Continuous time, Discrete time and Digital systems. In the three graphs the same waveform is represented in the three different systems

Continuous, Discrete and Digital Systems

A continuous system is a system that is defined for all instants in time, from the time when the system starts up till the time when the system is shut down. In addition to the system being defined for all time the system can also take on any value on its output from its min to its max. So the system has a defined output that is anywhere between the max and the min and there is an output for every instant of time that the system is on. Some people also call this type of a system as an analog system.

A discrete time system is the sampled version of a continuous time system. So a discrete system can have an output that can take on any value from its maximum to its minimum but the output is defined only at the sampling instants. The system does not have a defined output in between the sampling instants. We can say that a discrete time system is continuous in its output but it is sampled in time. In between the sampling instants the system output is not zero. It is undefined we just do not know what it is because we are not observing it.

When we quantize the output of a discrete time system we get a digital system. Quantizing the output means that we use only a few (not infinite) levels to represent the output. The number of levels depends on the number of bits that we use to represent each quantized level. If the analog value of the continuous time or the discrete time system falls between two quantizing levels then the quantizing level closest to the analog value is chosen to represent the value at that instant in time. Quantizing thus introduces some error. So a digital system is defined only at discrete instants in time and its output can take on only discrete levels.

In this book we will consider all three types of systems. While we will consider all the three types of systems we will concentrate on the continuous systems in the first half of the book and in the second half of the book we will concentrate on the digital systems. While studying the systems pay close attention to the methods used to analyze the Continuous Time Systems and the Digital Systems. You will find that the methods of analysis for both these types of systems are very similar to each other.

Example 2.4

Is the system that records the temperature of your city at noon every day for the entire year without missing a day a Continuous time, a Discrete time or a Digital system?

Solution 2.4

The system that records the temperature of your city every day at noon will be a Discrete time system. The city has some temperature between the recording instants only we are not recording it. This system is not a Digital system since any temperature is possible.

Example 2.5

If the recorded temperature in Example 2.4 was recorded only in increments of 0.2°C then what kind of a system would we have?

Solution 2.5

This time since only a few values are permitted and the samples are taken at some selected instants of time the system is a digital system. The Temperature values are quantized so that they are reported in increments of 0.2°C.

Time varying and Time Invariant Systems

If the parameters of the components in a system change with time or are time dependent then we have a time varying system. Alternately if the parameters do not vary with time then we have time invariant systems. Another way of looking at a time invariant system is as follows.

Suppose you apply an input to a system at time t_o. This input will give you some output, say Y_o. Next, you apply the same input to the same system but not at time t_o but at a later time $t_o + t_1$. This delayed application of the input will also give you an output. If the output that you get from applying the delayed input at time $t_o + t_1$ has the same shape as the output you got by applying the input at time t_o, but it is delayed by time t_1 so it starts at time $t_o + t_1$ then the system that you have is a time invariant system. This is shown for you in Figure 2.3.

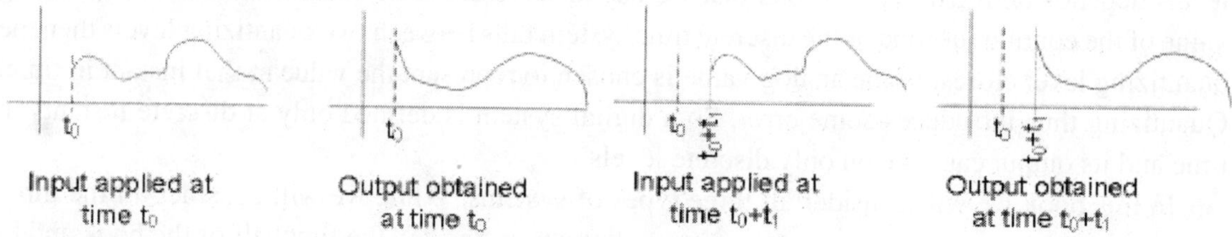

Figure 2.3: For a system to be time invariant the output due to a shifted input should be a shifted copy of the output due to an un-shifted input.

I am sure that you are aware that all components get worn out as we use the system. For example when we drive our car the piston in the cylinder starts to wear down due to friction, or when you use your MP3 player the dielectric in the capacitor starts to breakdown with age. Does this mean that the system with these components is time varying? (As the piston wears out the response from the car engine will not be the same.) Going strictly by the definition we have listed above the answer would be a definite yes. However the change in the parameters is so gradual and slow that for most practical purpose we consider that the parameters are not changing. If the change was not very gradual and extremely slow we would consider these systems as time varying and not time invariant. So when we say that the system is a time invariant system it is only approximately true but for most of the systems this assumption applies for a long period often for the life time of the system.

Example 2.6

An A/D converter requires 55mSec to complete a conversion. In the lab the students are required to measure a pre-set DC output of the power supply which is pre-set to 5.25 volts and then convert it to a digital representation by the A/D converter. One pair of diligent students measure the output on the power supply at time 12:05 while the other pair of students measure the output of the A/D converter at 12:15. Will both the pair of students measure the same output from the A/D converter? Is the system Time invariant?

Solution 2.6

In this example both the pairs of students will have the same output even though they started the measuring process 10 minutes apart. Since they get the same outputs in this example the system is a time invariant system. Both the pairs of students will measure the same output.

Causal and Anti-Causal Systems

Systems that anticipate inputs and produce an output before the input arrives are anti-causal (non-causal) systems. These systems begin to produce an output even before an input is applied. Thus the present output from the system depends not only on the past and the present inputs but on the future inputs also. On the other hand if the present output of the system depends only on the past and the present inputs then the system is a causal system. We will be considering only causal systems in this book. Science fiction writers who developed the TV series 'Star Trek' had a lot of fun with anti causal (non-causal) systems.

Example 2.7

Discrete time systems are described by difference equations. One such system is y[n] = 3x[n]+4x[n+1]-2x[n-1]. Is this a causal system or an anti causal system?

Solution 2.7

In the description of the system the sample instant n is assumed to be the present sample. So y[n] is the present output. Similarly x[n] is the present input, x[n-1] is the input just previous and x[n+1] is the next input. Since the present output depends on the next output the system is an anti causal system.

Example 2.8

Continuous time systems are described by differential equations. One such system is $y(t) = 3x(t)+4dx(t)/dt-2d^2x(t)/dt^2$. Is this a causal system or an anti causal system.

Solution 2.8

In this system since the output at time t is dependent only on the input at time t and its first two derivatives, which are also obtained at time t the system is a causal system.

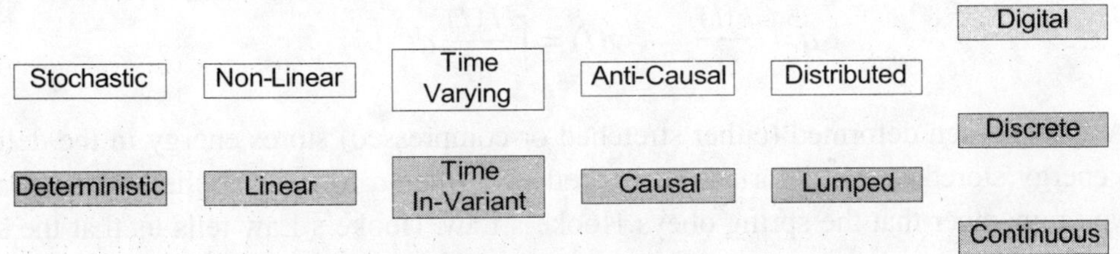

Figure 2.4: Different possible types of systems

Figure 2.4 shows the different possible combinations that make up a system. Every system is one type or another from each row in Figure 2.4. In this book all the systems that we analyze will be Deterministic; Linear; Time Invariant; Causal; Lumped Parameter and either Continuous or Discrete or Digital. The systems that we will be studying are shown shaded in Figure 2.4.

2.2 MODELING SYSTEMS

Systems that we are going to study are made up of several different components. In order to model the entire system we must know how to model the individual components. Once we have the models for the individual components then we can connect the models together as the system is connected and we will have the model for the system which we can then analyze. While building the model of the individual components we will pay particular attention to the physical laws that the component has to obey. Keeping this in mind we will build the models for the individual components. Spending extra time to build and understand the models of the individual components will then be well worth our time.

2.2.1 Mechanical Translation Elements

Here we will first make the models of the mechanical translation elements. We have three fundamental elements here. They are the mass, the spring and the viscous damper.

Mass: Any time you have bulk matter in a system that is part of that system you have mass present in the system. The model for mass is formed by Newton's laws of motion. The Newton's Laws of motion tell us that when a force acts on a mass, the mass acquires acceleration. We can write this as:

$$f(t) = Ma = M\frac{dv(t)}{dt} = M\frac{d^2x(t)}{dt^2} \tag{2.1}$$

In Equation(2.1) we have written the equation where the applied force is related to the Mass and the acceleration that the mass acquires. This equation can be inverted and written as shown in Equation(2.2). The Mass is an energy storage element; it stores energy either as potential energy or as kinetic energy.

$$a = \frac{f(t)}{M} \qquad v(t) = \int \frac{f(t)}{M}\,dt \tag{2.2}$$

Spring: A spring when deformed (either stretched or compressed) stores energy in the deformation. The energy stored or the deformation is produced when a force is applied to the spring. I am sure you remember that the spring obeys Hooke's Law. Hooke's Law tells us that the spring deformation is proportional to the applied force, or the applied force is equal to the spring constant multiplied by the spring deformation. So the model for the spring is given in Equation (2.3).

A larger force produces a larger deformation. The relation between the force and the deformation is a straight line relation. The spring is an energy storage element; it stores energy as elastic energy in the deformation.

$$f(t) = Kx(t) \tag{2.3}$$

Damper: When the applied force is proportional to the velocity we get a component that is a damper. There are many different types of dampers and each is modeled in its own way. We are using a simple model for the damper. The damper that we model is directly proportional to the velocity. The damper is an energy dissipation element as it consumes the energy stored in the other elements.

$$f(t) = Dv(t) = D\frac{dx(t)}{dt} \tag{2.4}$$

We can invert this equation also just as we inverted the equation for the mass. The inverted equation is shown in Equation 2.5.

$$v(t) = \frac{f(t)}{D} \quad x(t) = \int \frac{f(t)}{D}\,dt \tag{2.5}$$

2.2.2 Electrical Elements

Just like the mechanical translational elements that we modeled, we can also model the three basic electrical elements. The three electrical elements are the Capacitor, the Inductor, and the Resistor.

Capacitor: The Capacitor is an energy storage element. The energy stored in a capacitor is proportional to the voltage across the Capacitor. The voltage across the capacitor is built up by the current flowing into the Capacitor or the charge that is present on the plates of the Capacitor. To build the model for the electrical element capacitor we refer to the Kirchhoff's Laws. The Capacitor model is shown in Equation (2.6). The capacitor is an energy storage element; it stores energy in the electric field.

$$i(t) = C\frac{dv(t)}{dt} \qquad or \qquad v(t) = \frac{1}{C}\int i(t)\,dt \tag{2.6}$$

Inductor: The Inductor is an energy storage element. The energy stored in an Inductor is proportional to the current flowing through the inductor. The current flowing through the inductor is built up by having a voltage present across the two ends of the inductor. To build the model for the electrical element Inductor we refer to the Kirchhoff's Laws. The Inductor model is shown in Equation (2.7). The inductor is an energy storage element; it stores energy in the magnetic field.

$$v(t) = L\frac{di(t)}{dt} \qquad or \qquad i(t) = \frac{1}{L}\int v(t)\,dt \tag{2.7}$$

Resistor: The third electrical element is the resistor. The resistor is not an energy storage element. The resistor is an energy dissipation element. The model of the resistor is a straight line model that is given by the Ohm's Law. In the resistor the current and the voltage are directly proportional to each other and the constant of proportionality is the resistance of the resistor. The resistor model is given in Equation(2.8). The resistor is an energy dissipation element it consumes the energy stored in the other elements.

$$v(t) = Ri(t) \tag{2.8}$$

We have seen three electrical components and three mechanical components. Both these sets of components are described with very similar relations. Take for example the resistor and the damper, both of them dissipate energy and both have similar equations which are V=RI and f(t)=DV(t). So once we have replaced the component by its model we do not need to know if the actual component was a resistor or a damper. Similarly the spring and the capacitor have very similar relations, the spring relates the force to the displacement while the capacitor relates the voltage to charge. (Here we have replaced the integral of the current by charge). There exists a similar relation between the inductor and the mass. Can you determine the relation between these two circuit elements?

2.2.3 First Order Systems

Now that we have seen how to model some of the elementary components, our next step is to put these component models in some simple systems and get the models for the systems. Towards this end consider the electrical system in Figure 2.5. To model the system we use Kirchoff's voltage laws to write the equation for the current, and then we will use Ohm's law to get the equation for the output voltage. Completing these two steps we get the two equations as shown in Equation(2.9).

$$V(t) = L\frac{dI(t)}{dt} + RI(t) \quad and \quad V_o(t) = RI(t)$$

$$V(t) = \frac{L}{R}\frac{dV_o(t)}{dt} + V_o(t) \tag{2.9}$$

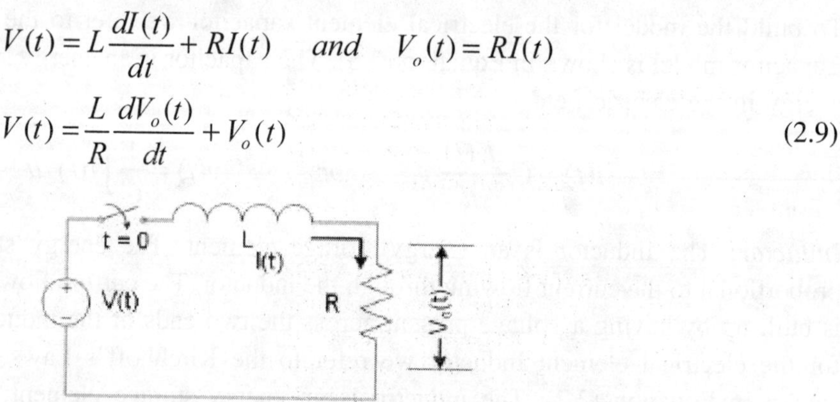

Figure 2.5: Example of a first order electrical system

Equation(2.9) is a first order, constant coefficient, linear differential equation. The systems that we described in this book can all be described by such differential equations. The only difference between Equation 2.9 and the equation describing a different system will be the order of the system, hence the order of the equation, and the coefficients of the equation. However since all the systems are described by linear constant coefficient differential equations the method of analyzing all these systems stays the same. So if you know how to solve the differential equation then you are able to analyze any system since all systems are described by differential equations. Here we will demonstrate how we solve a first order, constant coefficient, linear differential equation. Differential equations of the second order and higher will be solved in a later section. The solution process is a simple three step process:

Step 1.

Separate the variables in the differential equation. Get the time variable on one side of the equation and the other variable on the other side of the equation. When we do this for Equation 2.9 we get:

$$\frac{dV_o(t)}{V_o(t) - V(t)} = \frac{-R}{L} dt$$

Step 2.

With the variables separated we can integrate the equation from starting time to the ending time. Integrating the equation in Step 1 above we get:

$$\ln\left[V_o(t) - V(t)\right]\Big|_0^t = \frac{-R}{L} t\Big|_0^t$$

Step 3.

On substituting the limits and inverting the natural log function we get the solution of the differential equation in the form that we need it to be. For the Equation in Step 2 above we get:

$$V_o(t) = V(t) + \left(V_o(0) - V(t)\right)e^{\frac{-R}{L}t}$$

In step 3 the term $V_o(0)$ is the initial value of the variable of interest. This must be known to complete the solution. In the example chosen if there is no current flowing through the inductor at time t=0 then the voltage drop across the resistor will be zero just when the switch closes so $V_o(0) = 0$. For the system shown in Figure 2.5 the response for V(t) = 25; L = 0.5H and R = 50Ω is computed using SCILAB and it is shown in Figure 2.6. This response is computed using a SCILAB script. This SCILAB script is shown below.

```
R = 50;L = 0.5;V = 25;
F = -R/L;G = -F*V;
deff('ydot = Fig2_6(t,y)','ydot = F*y+G');
y0 = 0;t0 = 0;T = 0:0.001:0.06;
Y = ode(y0,t0,T,Fig2_6);
plot2d(T,Y)
xtitle('First Order Response Circuit of Figure 2.5','Time','Volts')
```

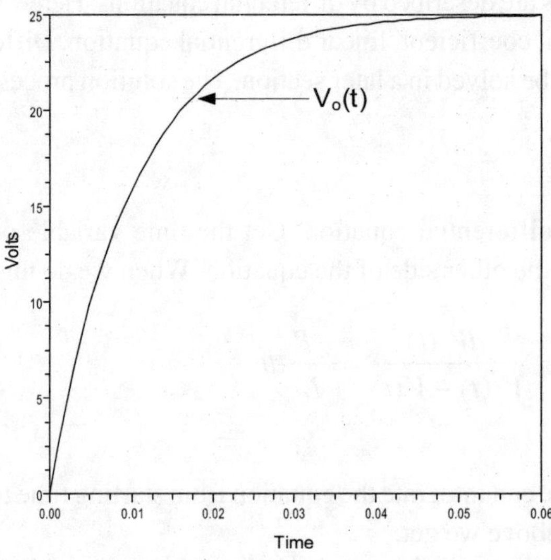

Figure 2.6: Response of a first order simple R-L circuit

Example 2.9

In the circuit of Figure 2.5 we will first replace the inductor by a capacitor and now if R=25Ω, C = 0.075F and V=-12.5 volts determine the voltage across the resistor for t>0.

Solution 2.9

We first write the Differential Equation describing the circuit. This equation is

$$V(t) = \frac{1}{C}\int_0^t i(t)\,dt + Ri(t)$$

Next we will differentiate this equation to get the differential equation we are interested in. So

$$0 = \frac{i(t)}{C} + R\frac{di(t)}{dt}$$

We will now separate the variables in this equation to get

$$-\left[\frac{1}{RC}\right]dt = \frac{di(t)}{i(t)} \quad \text{(step 1)}$$

Next we will integrate this equation from 0 to t to get

$$-\frac{t}{RC} = \ln\left[i(t)\right]_0^t \quad \text{(step 2)}$$

When we invert this equation we get

$$i(t) = i(0^+)e^{-\frac{t}{RC}} \quad \text{(step 3)}$$

This gives us the current flowing through the circuit. When we multiply the current by the resistance we get the voltage across the resistor.

2.2.4 Response of some simple systems

Now that we know how to solve the first order system let us look at some specific examples to see how we get the solution for systems from various different fields. Systems that can be described by a first order differential equation appear in many different fields such as physics, chemistry, economics, and of course engineering. As our first example we will consider an example from biology specifically how the population of fish in a pond will grow or shrink depending on the availability of food or the presence of predators or the birth of babies or the death of the old ones.

Fish in a pond are continuously being born and other fish as they become old die. The rate of birth and death of fish in a pond will depend on the number of fish that we have alive at any given time. More fish in the pond implies more fish are born during that generation as well as more fish die during that generation. So suppose P(t) is the number of fish in the pond at any given time. Then we can model the births of the fish as $B(t) = b_0 + \beta P(t)$. Here b_0 is the number of new fish introduced no matter what the population is and β is thc proportional number of fish that are introduced in the pond during this generation. Similarly we can model the deaths of the fish as $D(t) = d_0 + \delta P(t)$. Here d_0 is the number of old fish that die no matter what the population is and δ is the proportional number of fish that die in the pond uuring this generation.

Here we have decided to keep the model simple by using a straight line model for both the birth and the death rates. In this model b_0 and d_0 represent a constant number no matter how many fish we have in the pond. This could happen if the fish are stocked in the pond periodically by the game warden and a fixed number of fishing licenses given for people to catch fish in the pond during each generation.

Now the rate of change in the fish population at any time can be modeled as shown in the first equation in Equation(2.10). The first equation in Equation(2.10) tells us that the rate of change of the fish population equals the births minus the deaths of the fish. Substituting for the births and the deaths of the fish we get the second equation in Equation(2.10) and re-arranging that equation we get the final equation.

$$\begin{aligned}\frac{dP(t)}{dt} &= D(t) - B(t)\\ \frac{dP(t)}{dt} &= d_0 + \delta P(t) - b_0 - \beta P(t)\\ \frac{dP(t)}{dt} &+ (\beta - \delta)P(t) = b_0 - d_0\end{aligned} \tag{2.10}$$

To solve this fish population problem let us decide that the birth rate is $\beta = 0.25$ and the death rate $\delta = 0.175$. Also, independent of the population size, 225 fish are born (or somehow added to the pond) and 90 fish die (or somehow are removed from the pond) every generation so $b_0 = 225$ and

$d_o = 90$. We will also assume that the fish population in the pond begins with 1250 fish at the time when we start the exercise. So P(0) = 1250. This will be the initial condition that we need to complete the solution of the differential equation. With these numbers Equation(2.10) becomes

$$\frac{dP(t)}{dt} + 0.075P(t) = 135$$

The form of this equation is exactly similar to Equation(2.9) that we had for the electric circuit with one resistor and one inductor. To solve this equation we will follow the same three step procedure that we have established. The plot of the fish population is given in Figure 2.7 and the SCILAB script is also given.

Step 1.

Separate the variables in the differential equation. For the fish population problem we get:

$$\frac{dP(t)}{135 - 0.075P(t)} = dt$$

Step 2.

With the variables separated we can integrate the equation from starting time to the ending time.

For the fish population problem we get: $\ln\left(1800 - P(t)\right)\Big|_0^t = -0.075t$

Step 3.

Substituting the limits and inverting the equation we get after substituting the initial value:

$$P(t) = (1800 - 1250)e^{-0.075t} + 1800$$

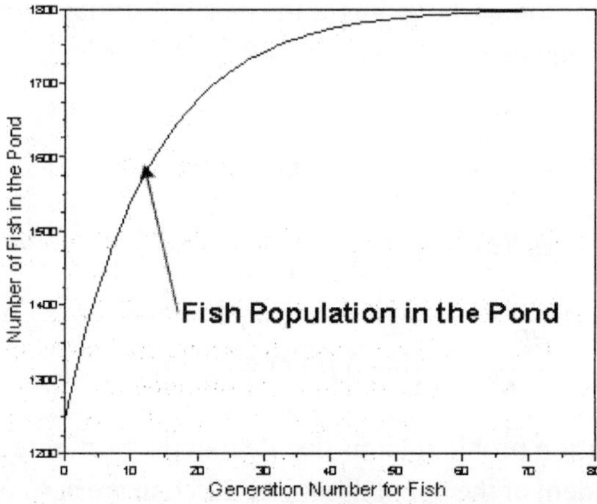

Figure 2.6a: Solution to the Fish in the Pond Problem

So in this example the fish population starts out with a population of 1250 but after a long time (about 75 generations) the population of fish will increase and rise up to a value of 1800. Thereafter it will stay steady at that population. The plot of this response is given in Figure 2.6a and the SCILAB script is also given.

```
b0 = 225;d0 = 90;b = 0.25;d = 0.175;
F = b0-d0;G = (b-d);
deff('pdot = Fig2_6a(t,p)','pdot = F-p*G');
P0 = 1250;t0 = 0;T = 0:1:70;
P = ode(P0,t0,T,Fig2_6a);
plot2d(T,P)
xtitle(' ','Generation Number for Fish','Number of Fish in the Pond')
xtitle('First Order Response to Fish Population Problem')
```

With a different birth and death rate the population will settle to a different value. Try it for yourself with different birth rates, death rates and initial populations. Try to solve for yourself with $b_o = 225$; $d_o = 90$; b = 0.5; d = 0.425 and P(0) = 6000. You should get the fish population reaching a steady state of 1805.

As a different example from a different field let us look at an example from the field of economics where we would try to estimate the price of a commodity based upon the supply and the demand of the commodity. The price of a commodity such as rice or wheat is proportional to the supply and the demand of the commodity in the market place at any time t. Here also we will assume that the supply and the demand curves are linear and that the supply S(t) = 0.5*P(t) – 27.5 and the demand for the commodity is D(t) = 50 – 0.65*P(t). Also assume that the initial price of the commodity is 48 Units.

$$\frac{dP(t)}{dt} = 0.2\left[D(t) - S(t)\right]$$

$$\frac{dP(t)}{dt} = 0.2\left[50 - 0.65P(t) - 0.5P(t) + 27.5\right]$$

$$\frac{dP(t)}{dt} + 0.23P(t) = 15.5 \tag{2.11}$$

The controlling equation for the price fluctuations are given in Equation (2.11). As you can see this equation is a simple first order, constant coefficient, linear differential equation and can be solved by the three step process that we have established. On solving the equation we get the following result.

$$P(t) = \left(P(0) - 67.39\right)e^{-t} + 67.39$$

When we substitute the initial value of the price in the equation we get

$$P(t) = 67.39 - 19.39\,e^{-t}$$

In this example the price starts out at 48 per unit and will increase to 67.39 per unit as time goes by. This example shows us another system, this time from economics, which has exactly similar dynamics and can be modeled as either the fish population or the electric circuit. What we gather from these examples is that once we model the system it does not matter where the system came from, the method of solution stays the same.

2.2.5 Higher Order Systems

In the previous section we saw how to solve the first order differential equation. Here we will develop a general method that is applicable to higher order differential equations that are linear with constant coefficients. Before we start talking about the solution procedure let us define some of the terms that we will need to know.

Order of the Equation: This is the highest order of derivative in the differential equation. So a third order differential equation will have the third order derivative present. It will not have any higher order derivatives. It may or may not have any lower order derivatives. This is a 3rd order Equation:

$$\frac{d^3 y(t)}{dt^3} + \alpha \frac{d^2 y(t)}{dt^2} - \beta\, y(t) = \gamma x(t)$$

Constant Coefficients: The coefficients of the derivatives are constants. They are not functions of time. In the 3rd order equation above if a; b; and g are constants then this is a constant coefficient equation.

Homogeneous Equation: A differential equation is a homogeneous equation if its driving function is zero. So a homogeneous equation will have all the derivatives on one side of the equation and the driving function of the equation will be zero. In the above equation if we set the driving function x(t) = 0 then we get a Homogeneous Equation.

Characteristic Equation: When you replace all the different order derivatives in the Homogeneous equation by the variable l raised to the appropriate power you get the characteristic equation. So you will replace the second order derivative with l^2 and the 5th order derivative with l^5. In the above equation the Homogeneous equation will be $l^3 + al^2 + b = 0$.

Complete Solution: The differential equation has a general solution and a particular solution. When the two solutions are combined together we get the complete solution. Sometimes the solution is also separated as the natural solution and the forced solution. Either way the complete solution is the General and the Particular solution together or the Natural and the Forced solution together.

Homogeneous Solution: This is the solution to the Homogeneous equation. This solution is obtained by using the characteristic equation. The homogeneous solution to the differential equation does not depend on the driving function.

Particular Solution: This is the solution of the differential equation that depends on the driving function.

Now that we know the various terms that we will come across we can turn our attention to the method that we plan to use to get the complete solution to a constant coefficient differential equation. Let us quickly review here what we need to do to get the solution of a higher order differential equation:

1. **We need to determine two solutions. The Homogeneous solution and the Particular solution.**
2. **The Homogenous equation is an equation that has its driving function set to zero. The Homogenous equation will have a solution of the type e^{lt} where l is the root of the characteristic equation obtained from the differential equation.**
3. **The particular solution is the solution that depends on the forcing function. In general it will contain all the derivatives of the forcing function as part of the solution.**

One of the solutions that we need to get is the Homogeneous solution. The Homogeneous solution is obtained by first solving the characteristic equation to determine the roots of the characteristic equation. Next the homogenous solution is assumed to be the type $\alpha e^{\lambda t}$ where the constant λ is the root of the characteristic equation. The characteristic equation will have as many roots as the order of the characteristic equation. So a fourth order equation will have four roots of the characteristic equation. Each of these roots will lead to a different solution of the type $\alpha e^{\lambda t}$.

There are some conditions that will modify the solutions of the characteristic equation and the solution is not of the type $\alpha e^{\lambda t}$. There are two conditions which are (1) when two or more roots of the characteristic equation are equal and (2) when two or more roots of the characteristic equation are complex conjugates of each other.

First we will examine the condition when we have two or more solutions of the homogeneous equation identical to each other. When this occurs we choose the solution of the type $t^n e^{\lambda t}$ for all the roots that are identical to each other instead of the solution $e^{\lambda t}$. In the solution $t^n e^{\lambda t}$ the power of the variable t will start with 1 when there are two roots that are identical and keep on increasing by 1 for each additional root that is identical. So if we have four roots that are identical then the homogeneous solution will be of the type $t^3 e^{\lambda t}$, $t^2 e^{\lambda t}$, $t^1 e^{\lambda t}$ and $t^0 e^{\lambda t}$.

The second condition when we modify the Homogeneous solution is when we have complex conjugate roots. When the roots of the characteristic equation are complex conjugates of each other then one root will be the complex conjugate of the other root. So we will have two roots λ and λ^*. When λ is complex then $e^{\lambda t}$ can be expanded by using Euler's identity. Euler's identity says that $e^{(a+jb)t} = e^{at}\{\mathrm{Cos}(bt) + j\mathrm{Sin}(bt)\}$.

So when we know the type of roots that are present in the characteristic equation the solution of the Homogeneous equation can be obtained. It is possible for the characteristic equation to contain real and distinct roots, real and repeated roots and complex conjugate roots simultaneously. Since all types of roots can occur simultaneously the solution may contain all three forms of solutions simultaneously.

Example 2.10

Determine the Homogeneous solution to the differential equation

$$3\ddot{y}(t)+7\dot{y}(t)+4y(t)=4tU(t)$$

Solution 2.10

We first write the Homogeneous Equation replacing the derivatives with λ and setting the driving function to zero.

This time we get $3\lambda^2 + 7\lambda + 4 = 0$. Solving this equation we get λ_1 and λ_2 = -1 and -1.333.

This time we have two distinct roots so the Homogeneous solution for this differential equation is $\alpha_1 e^{-1t} + \alpha_2 e^{-1.333t}$. When we solve the constants α_1 and α_2 (which we will do later) we will know the complete Homogeneous solution.

Example 2.11

Determine the Homogeneous solution to the differential equation

$$2\ddot{y}(t)+4\dot{y}(t)+2y(t)=4e^{-5t}U(t)$$

Solution 2.11

We first write the Homogeneous Equation replacing the derivatives with λ and setting the driving function to zero.

This time we get $2\lambda^2 + 4\lambda + 2 = 0$. Solving this equation we get λ_1 and $\lambda_2 = -1$.

This time we have two repeated roots so the Homogeneous solution for this differential equation is $\alpha_1 e^{-1t} + \alpha_2 t e^{-1t}$. Notice that the second function is modified to account for the repeated root.

When we solve the constants α_1 and α_2 (which we will do later) we will know the complete Homogeneous solution.

Now that we have the Homogeneous solution we can turn our attention to the other solution that we need to get the complete solution, this is the particular solution. When we look at the differential equation we first of all notice that it is an equation. Being an equation the left hand side has to equal the right hand side. On the left hand side we see all the derivatives and on the right hand side we see the forcing function. That means, when we choose a solution that is going to represent the Particular Solution of our differential equation, and substitute the assumed solution in the differential equation, the left hand side must still equal the right hand side. We will actually do this to determine some of the constants that we need to get.

So what type of solution should we assume as a particular solution. Knowing that we have derivatives on the LHS the solution that we will assume will have to have derivatives that satisfy the differential equation. These functions must be such that the derivative of the function is similar to the function itself. Only when we choose functions of this type will we be able to gather the solution together and equate the left hand side to the right hand side. Remember that we have an equation and the left hand side has to equal the right hand side. On the left hand side we have derivatives, so the derivative of the solution will have to have the same form as the solution itself. There are only a few functions that have this property. The functions that have these properties are listed in Table 2.1 below.

Table 2.1: Functions that can be used as particular solutions for linear differential equations

1	$\mathbf{t^{\beta}}$	β is a positive constant
2	$\mathbf{e^{\theta t}}$	θ is a constant
3	**Cos(γt)**	γ is a positive constant
4	**Sin(γt)**	γ is a positive constant
5	Any finite linear combination of 1 to 4 above.	

We have chosen these functions because all these functions have the special property that we are looking for. This special property is as follows: A derivative of the forcing functions in our differential equations will be a linear combination of the functions listed in Table 2.1 above. For example if the forcing function is $f(t) = t^2e^{-2t}$ then the derivatives of this forcing function will be some linear combination of t^2e^{-2t}, te^{-2t}, e^{-2t}. That is each function is a linear combination of other functions listed in Table 2.1 including the zeroth derivative. Verify this for yourself using the function $t^3\text{Sin}(5t)$ as the forcing function of a differential equation.

This simple fact tells us the procedure to follow to write out the particular solution for our differential equation. The procedure that we will follow to get the particular solution is listed below for you:

1. **List all the derivatives of the function f(t) including the function itself (zeroth derivative) as possible solutions.**
2. **Multiply each term in the solution by an unknown constant.**
3. **Substitute the solution and its derivatives in the differential equation as required.**
4. **Solve for the unknown constants by noting that the coefficient of each term on the right hand side has to equal the coefficient of a similar term on the left hand side.**

An example will make all this clear for you: Determine the particular solution for the differential equation shown in Equation(2.12)

$$\frac{d^2x}{dt^2} + 2\frac{dx}{dt} - 3 = 2t^2 + 5$$
$$x(0) = -3; \text{ and } \dot{x}(0) = 2 \tag{2.12}$$

The particular solution: This time the driving function is $2t^2 + 5$. The particular solution must include the derivatives of the driving function so the solution that we will choose will be of the form $\alpha t^2 + \beta t + \gamma$. The solution that we have chosen includes all the derivatives of the forcing function. This completes step 1 & 2 in the list above (we have multiplied the three terms by three different constants which are α, β and γ). Next, we have to determine the constants α, β, γ to complete the solution. To determine these constants substitute the solution in Equation(2.12) and evaluate the individual derivatives. On substituting the solution in the differential equation and resolving the derivatives we get Equation(2.13). This completes step 3 in the list above.

$$2\alpha + 2(\alpha t + \beta) - 3(\alpha t^2 + \beta t + \gamma) = 2t^2 + 5 \tag{2.13}$$

In Equation(2.13) there are actually three different equations buried. The three equations are obtained by noting that all the coefficients of the t^2 term on the left hand side must equal all the coefficients of the t^2 term on the right hand side. This condition gives us Equation(2.14)

$$2\alpha - 3\beta = 0 \tag{2.14}$$

Similarly when we equate the coefficient of the terms t^1 on the two sides of the equation we get Equation(2.15)

$$-3\alpha = 2 \tag{2.15}$$

Finally when we equate the coefficients that are constants (coefficients of t^0 power) we get Equation(2.16)

$$2\alpha + 2\beta - 3\gamma = 5 \tag{2.16}$$

On solving these three equations we get a = -2/3; b = -4/9 and g = -65/27. When we substitute the known values of the constants we get the particular solution that we are looking for. So the particular solution of our differential equation is shown in Equation(2.17). This completes step 4 in the list above.

$$\text{Particular Solution} = -\frac{2}{3}t^2 - \frac{4}{9}t - \frac{65}{27} \tag{2.17}$$

Now that we have the particular solution let us turn our attention to the other half of the solution so that we will have the complete solution of the differential equation. Remember that the complete solution is the sum of the homogeneous solution and the particular solution. Let us see how we go about getting the homogeneous solution to a differential equation. For this we will use the same differential equation that we used to obtain the particular solution. That differential equation is

$$\frac{d^2x}{dt^2} + 2\frac{dx}{dt} - 3 = 2t^2 + 5$$

To begin the homogeneous solution we first write the characteristic equation for this differential equation. The characteristic equation is ($\lambda^2 + 2\lambda - 3 = 0$). The solution of the characteristic equation is $\lambda = 3$ and $\lambda = -1$. With these roots we get the homogeneous solution as ($c_1e^{3t} + c_2e^{-t}$). Here c_1 and c_2 are the unknown constants that we will determine shortly.

To the homogeneous solution we must add the particular solution. The particular solution is the solution that we had just determined and is shown in Equation(2.17).

Using this particular solution we are in a position to write the complete solution to the differential equation. Remember that the complete solution is the homogenous solution and the particular solution all taken together. This then becomes Equation(2.18)

$$\text{Complete Solution} = c_1e^{3t} + c_2e^{-t} - \frac{2}{3}t^2 - \frac{4}{9}t - \frac{65}{27} \tag{2.18}$$

In this solution we still have to determine the constants c_1 and c_2. To determine these constants we will use the given initial conditions. (The initial conditions are given in Equation 2.12.) Using the given initial condition for x(0) we get Equation(2.19)

$$\begin{aligned} x(0) &= c_1e^{3(0)} + c_2e^{-(0)} - \frac{2}{3}(0) - \frac{4}{9}(0) - \frac{65}{27} = -3 \\ so\ c_1 + c_2 &= -3 + \frac{65}{27} = -0.5926 \end{aligned} \tag{2.19}$$

And using the given initial condition for the derivative of x(t) we get Equation(2.20)

$$\begin{aligned} \frac{dx(0)}{dt} &= 2 = 3c_1 - c_2 - \frac{4}{3}(0) - \frac{4}{9} - 0 \\ so\ 3c_1 - c_2 &= 2 + \frac{4}{9} = 2.4444 \end{aligned} \tag{2.20}$$

In Equation(2.19) and Equation(2.20) we get two simultaneous equations in c_1 and c_2. When we solve the two simultaneous equations we will get the values for the constants c_1 and c_2. Solving the two simultaneous equations we get $c_1 = 0.4629$, and then $c_2 = -1.0555$. With all the constants determined the complete solution of the differential equation is shown in Equation(2.21).

$$0.4629e^{3t} - 1.0555e^{-t} - \frac{2}{3}t^2 - \frac{4}{9}t - \frac{65}{27} \tag{2.21}$$

So let us review the method to get the complete solution for a differential equation.

Table 2.2: Solution Method for Higher order Differential Equations

1	Write the **Characteristic Equation** for the given differential equation.
2	Determine the **Roots** of the characteristic equation.
3	Using the roots of the characteristic equation write the homogeneous solution to the differential equation. Remember that the **Homogeneous Solution** will have some constants which we will determine later.
4	Determine the **Form of the Particular Solution** that you need by looking at the forcing function. The particular solution will include all the derivatives of the forcing function. Each term of the particular solution is also multiplied by an undetermined constant. We will determine these constants in the next step.
5	To determine the **Constants of the Particular Solution** substitute only the particular solution in the differential equation and evaluate the differentials. This will give you several simultaneous equations. Solve these simultaneous equations to determine the constants for the particular solution.
6	Combine the Homogeneous solution and the particular solution and use the given **Initial Conditions** in the complete solution to determine the constants that we added to the homogeneous solution in step 3 above. Each initial condition will give you a different equation. Solve them simultaneously for all the constants.

Another example will make this method clear. Determine the complete solution for the differential equation given in Equation(2.22)

$$\begin{aligned}&\frac{d^2y}{dt^2}+5\frac{dy}{dt}+6y=3t^2+4e^{-2t}\\&y(0)=-3;\quad \text{and}\quad \dot{y}(0)=2.25\end{aligned}\tag{2.22}$$

We will follow the steps that we have laid out in Table 2.2 above to get the complete solution for this differential equation.

Step 1.

Write the characteristic equation: The characteristic equation for this differential equation is $(\lambda^2 + 5\lambda + 6 = 0)$

Step 2.

Determine the roots of the characteristic equation: The roots of this characteristic equation are $\lambda = -2$ and $\lambda = -3$.

Step 3.

Write the homogeneous solution: The homogeneous solution to the differential equation is $c_1e^{-2t} + c_2e^{-3t}$. Here c_1 and c_2 are constants that have to be determined. We will use the given initial conditions in step 6 to determine these constants.

Step 4.

Determine the particular solution: This time the forcing function has a term t^2. The particular solution for the term t^2 will include t^2; t^1 and t^0 as part of the solution. The forcing function also includes another term e^{-2t} so the particular solution will include te^{-2t} as part of the particular solution. When we multiply these terms with the unknown constants we get the particular solution. This time the particular solution with the unknown constants is

$$\alpha t^2 + \beta t + \gamma + \delta te^{-2t}$$

Step 5.

Determine the constants of the particular solution: To determine the constants of the particular solution we will substitute the particular solution in the differential equation. Doing this will give us several simultaneous equations. They are listed in Equation(2.23).

$$\begin{aligned}
&2\alpha + 5\beta + 6\gamma = 0 && \textit{Coefficient of } t^0 \\
&10\alpha + 6\beta = 0 && \textit{Coefficient of } t^1 \\
&6\alpha = 6 && \textit{Coefficient of } t^2 \\
&4\delta - 10\delta + 6\delta = 0 && \textit{Coefficient of } te^{-2t} \\
&-4\delta + 5\delta + 6\delta = 4 && \textit{Coefficient of } e^{-2t}
\end{aligned} \tag{2.23}$$

Solving these equations we get the four constants as given in Equation(2.24)

$$\alpha = 1; \beta = -\frac{5}{3}; \gamma = \frac{19}{18}; \delta = \frac{4}{7} \tag{2.24}$$

Step 6.

Use initial conditions to determine the remaining constants: We know that y(0) = -3 so using this initial condition in the solution we get Equation(2.25). Equation(2.25) gives us one equation in c_1 and c_2.

$$\left. c_1e^{-2t} + c_2e^{-3t} + 1t^2 - \frac{5}{3}t + \frac{19}{18} + \frac{4}{7}te^{-2t} \right|_{t=0} = -3$$

$$c_1 + c_2 + \frac{19}{18} = -3 \tag{2.25}$$

Using the second initial condition for the derivative of y(t) we get another equation in c_1 and c_2. This is given in Equation(2.26).

$$-2c_1e^{-2t} - 3c_2e^{-3t} + 2t - \frac{5}{3} + 0 + \frac{4}{7}e^{-2t} - \frac{8}{7}te^{-2t}\bigg|_{t=0} = 2.25$$

$$-2c_1 - 3c_2 = 3.345 \tag{2.26}$$

Solving the two equations simultaneously we get $c_1 = -8.82166$ and $c_2 = 4.76611$. Now that we know all the constants we can write the complete solution as shown in Equation(2.27).

$$\underbrace{\underbrace{t^2 - \frac{5}{3}t + \frac{19}{18} + \frac{4}{7}te^{-2t}}_{\textit{Particular Solution}} \underbrace{-8.82166e^{-2t} + 4.76611e^{-3t}}_{\textit{Homogeneous Solution}}}_{\textit{Complete Solution}} \tag{2.27}$$

Example 2.12

Determine the Particular Solution to the differential equation

$$3\ddot{y}(t) + 7\dot{y}(t) + 4y(t) = 4tU(t)$$

Solution 2.12

In Example 2.10 we determined the Homogeneous solution for this differential equation as $\alpha_1 e^{-1t} + \alpha_2 e^{-1.333t}$. We will continue the solution here and determine the constants and the particular solution for this differential equation.

First we will choose the form of the particular solution. Since the driving function is tU(t) the form of the particular solution that we will choose is $c_1t + c_2$. Here we have to determine the two constants c_1 and c_2.

In order to determine the constants c_1 and c_2 we substitute the assumed particular solution in the difference equation and obtain two algebraic equations in c_1 and c_2 which we will solve to get the two constants. Substituting the assumed solution in the differential equation gives us $3(0) + 7c_1 + 4(c_1t + c_2) = 4t$.

From this we get that $c_1 = 1$ and $c_2 = -7$, so the particular solution is 4t-7.

Example 2.13

Determine the Particular Solution to the differential equation

$$2\ddot{y}(t) + 4\dot{y}(t) + 2y(t) = 4e^{-5t}U(t)$$

Solution 2.13

In Example 2.10 we determined the Homogeneous solution for this differential equation as $\alpha_1 e^{-1t} + \alpha_2 e^{-1.333t}$. We will continue the solution here and determine the constants and the particular solution for this differential equation.

Next we will choose the form of the particular solution. Since the driving function is e^{-5t} U(t) the form of the particular solution that we will choose is $c_1e^{-5t} + c_2$. Here we have to determine the two constants c_1 and c_2.

In order to determine the constants c_1 and c_2 we substitute the assumed particular solution in the difference equation and obtain two algebraic equations in c_1 and c_2 which we will solve to get the two constants. Substituting the assumed solution in the differential equation gives us

$$2(5^2)c_1e^{-5t} + 4(-5)c_1e^{-5t} + 2c_1e^{-5t} + 2c_2 = e^{-5t}.$$

From this we get the two constants as particular solution as $c_2 = 0$ and $c_1 = 0.03125$. So the particular solution is $0.03125e^{-5t}$.

2.2.6 Special case for Second Order Systems

Many of the systems that we come across in our study will be second order systems. Since we will come across many second order systems let us examine them in a little more detail and see what we can expect in terms of the various different solutions of the second order systems. Before we go into detail here please remember that a second order differential equation can be treated as a higher order differential equation and the solution as described in the 6 step procedure in Table 2.2 can be followed. Here we list some of the short cuts that you can take when the system or the differential equation that you have is a second order differential equation.

We begin by first looking at the homogeneous solution. The homogeneous solutions for second order systems will be of the type $e^{\lambda t}$ where λ is the root of the characteristic equation. The characteristic equation of the second order system is of the type $\alpha\lambda^2 + \beta\lambda + \gamma = 0$. The solution of this equation will be one of the following three cases:

- The roots of the characteristic equation are **Real and Distinct** so $\lambda_1 \neq \lambda_2$. In this case the homogeneous solution $y_h(t) = c_1e^{\lambda 1t} + c_2e^{\lambda 2t}$. Here c_1 and c_2 are constants that have to be determined.
- The roots of the characteristic equation are **Real and Identical** so $\lambda_1 = \lambda_2$. In this case the homogeneous solution $y_h(t) = c_1e^{\lambda 1t} + c_2te^{\lambda 1t}$. Here c_1 and c_2 are constants that have to be determined.
- The roots of the characteristic equation are **Complex Conjugates** so $\lambda_1 = \alpha + j\beta$ and $\lambda_2 = \alpha - j\beta$. Now the homogeneous solution $y_h(t) = c_1e^{\alpha t}\mathrm{Cos}(\beta t) + c_2e^{\alpha t}\mathrm{Sin}(\beta t)$. Here c_1 and c_2 are constants that have to be determined.

2.2.6.1 System with Real and Distinct Roots

Let us look at an example of a second order system such as an RLC circuit shown in Figure 2.7. Here we wish to determine the current i(t) for time $t > 0$. To solve this system we begin with writing the differential equation for the given system using Kirchoff's laws. The circuit equation after the switch closes is given in Equation(2.28).

$$L\frac{di(t)}{dt} + \frac{1}{C}\int i(t)dt + Ri(t) = V(t) \tag{2.28}$$

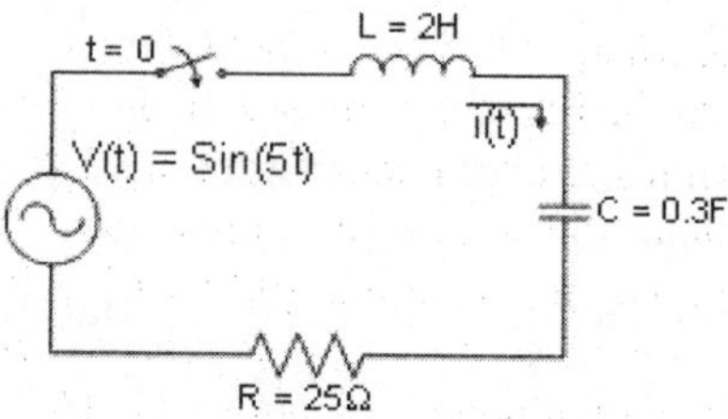

Figure 2.7: A second order RLC system. The roots of the Characteristic Equation are real and distinct

Equation(2.28) can be differentiated once and then written as Equation(2.29):

$$L\frac{d^2i(t)}{dt^2} + R\frac{di(t)}{dt} + \frac{i(t)}{C} = \frac{dV(t)}{dt} \tag{2.29}$$

This is a second order differential equation with constant coefficients so we can use our method of solution that we have outlined in Table 2.2 or we can use the short cut listed above. To solve this equation we also need to know the initial conditions. We will assume that the initial conditions which are the current in the inductor at time t = 0 is zero and the rate of change of current through the inductor at time t = 0 is 100 Amps/second. With this information we can begin the 6 step solution method.

Step 1.

Write the characteristic equation: The characteristic equation for this differential equation, using the given values for the components given in Figure 2.7 is $(2\lambda^2 + 25\lambda + 3.33 = 0)$

Step 2.

Determine the roots of the characteristic equation: The roots of this characteristic equation are real and distinct and are given in Equation(2.30)

$$\lambda_{1,2} = \frac{-25 \pm \sqrt{25^2 - 4*2*3.33}}{2*2} = -0.13465 \; or \; -12.365 \tag{2.30}$$

Step 3.

Write the homogeneous solution: Since the roots are real and distinct; from the above three cases we recognize the first case so, the homogeneous solution to the differential equation is $c_1e^{-0.134t} + c_2e^{-12.365t}$. Here c_1 and c_2 are constants that have to be determined. We will use the given initial conditions in step 6 to determine these constants.

Step 4.

Determine the particular solution: This time the forcing function has a term Sin(5t). The particular solution for this term include Sin(5t) and Cos(5t) as part of the solution. When we multiply these terms with the unknown constants we get the particular solution. This time the particular solution with the unknown constants is $\alpha Sin(5t) + \beta Cos(5t)$. The two constants have to be determined from the differential equation. This is done for you in Equations(2.31); (2.32); (2.33) and (2.34).

$$-2[25\alpha Sin(5t) + 25\beta Cos(5t)] + 25[5\alpha Cos(5t) - 5\beta Sin(5t)] + 3.33[\alpha Sin(5t) + \beta Cos(5t)] = 5Cos(5t) \quad (2.31)$$

Equating the coefficients of the Sin terms we get:

$$-50\alpha - 125\beta + 3.33\alpha = 0 \quad (2.32)$$

Equating the coefficients of the Cos terms we get:

$$-50\beta - 125\alpha + 3.33\beta = 5 \quad (2.33)$$

Solving these two equations we get

$$\alpha = -0.04647 \text{ and } \beta = 0.01735 \quad (2.34)$$

Step 5.

Determine the constants of the particular solution: To determine the constants of the particular solution we will substitute the particular solution in the differential equation. Doing this will give us two simultaneous equations. They are also listed in Equation (2.32) and in Equation(2.33). Solving these two equations determines the constants for the particular solution so now we know the entire Particular solution. The constants are given in Equation(2.34).

Step 6.

Use initial conditions to determine the remaining constants: We know that i(0) = 0 so using this initial condition in the complete solution we get one equation listed in Equation(2.35)

$$c_1 e^{-0.134(0)} + c_2 e^{-12.365(0)} - 0.04647 Sin(5*0) + 0.01735 Cos(5*0) = 0 \quad (2.35)$$

This simplifies to $c_1 + c_2 + 0.01735 = 0$

Using the other initial condition in the solution we get Equation(2.36)

$$-0.134 c_1 e^{-0.134(0)} - 12.365 c_1 e^{-12.365(0)} - 5(-0.04647) Cos(5*0) - 5(0.01735) Sin(5*0) = 100 \quad (2.36)$$

This simplifies to $-0.134c_1 - 12.365c_1 + 0.23235 = 100$

Solving Equation(2.35) and Equation(2.36) simultaneously we get the constants c_1 and c_2 as shown in Equation(2.37). Now that we know both the particular solution and the homogeneous solution we can get the complete solution. The complete solution is also shown in Equation(2.37)

$$c_1 = 8.1394 \text{ and } c_2 = 8.15676$$

$$8.1394e^{-0.134t} + 8.15676e^{-12.356t} - 0.04647\text{Sin}(5t) + 0.01735\text{Cos}(5t) \tag{2.37}$$

2.2.6.2 System with Real and Identical Roots

In the system shown in Figure 2.7 if we change the capacitor so that the new capacitor value is 0.0128F then we get the system shown in Figure 2.8. In this system the characteristic equation has identical roots. For this system the differential equation will be

$$L\frac{di(t)}{dt} + \frac{1}{C}\int i(t)dt + Ri(t) = V(t)$$

To get the complete solution we will follow a similar procedure to the one that we followed for the problem with two real and distinct roots. The procedure consists of the six steps for solving the differential equation. To begin we will first differentiate the circuit equation to get

$$L\frac{d^2i(t)}{dt^2} + R\frac{di(t)}{dt} + \frac{i(t)}{C} = \frac{dv(t)}{dt}$$

This is a second order differential equation with constant coefficients so we can use our method of solution that we have outlined in Table 2.2. We will also take advantage of the short cut for the second order systems. To solve this equation we also need to know the initial conditions. We will use the same initial conditions that we used in the previous section, which are the current in the inductor at time t = 0 is zero and the rate of change of current through the inductor at time t = 0 is 100 Amps/second. With this information we can begin the 6 step solution method.

Step 1.

Write the characteristic equation: The characteristic equation for this differential equation, using the given values for the components given in Figure 2.8 is ($2\lambda^2 + 25\lambda + 78.125 = 0$)

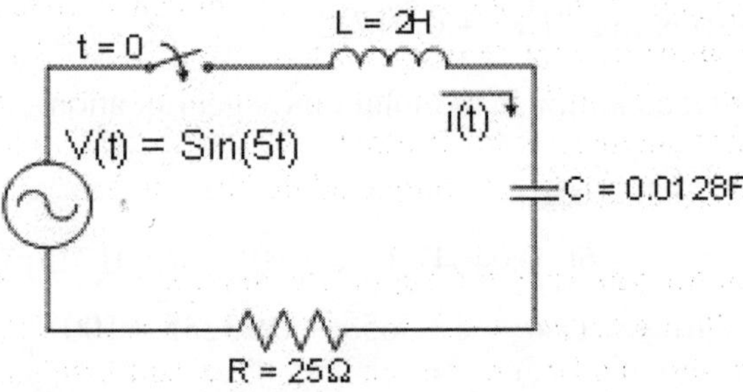

Figure 2.8: A Second order RLC system. The roots of the Characteristic Equation are identical to each other

Step 2.

Determine the roots of the characteristic equation: The roots of this characteristic equation are real and identical and are given in Equation(2.38)

$$\lambda_{1,2} = \frac{-25 \pm \sqrt{25^2 - 4*2*78.125}}{2*2} = -6.25 \text{ and } -6.25 \tag{2.38}$$

Step 3.

Write the homogeneous solution: Since the roots are real and identical the homogeneous solution to the differential equation is $c_1e^{-6.25t} + c_2te^{-6.25t}$. Here c_1 and c_2 are constants that have to be determined. Notice that the second term in the solution is multiplied with the time variable t so that it will be different from the first term. We will use the given initial conditions in step 6 to determine these constants.

Step 4.

Determine the particular solution: This time the forcing function has a term Sin(5t). The particular solution for this term will include Sin(5t) and Cos(5t) as part of the solution. When we multiply these terms with the unknown constants we get the particular solution. This time the particular solution with the unknown constants is $\alpha Sin(5t) + \beta Cos(5t)$. The two constants have to be determined from the differential equation.

$$-2[25\alpha Sin(5t) + 25\beta Cos(5t)] + 25[5\alpha Cos(5t) - 5\beta Sin(5t)]$$
$$+ 78.125[\alpha Sin(5t) + \beta Cos(5t)] = 5Cos(5t) \tag{2.39}$$

Equating the coefficients of the Sin terms in Equation(2.39) we get

$$-50\alpha - 125\beta + 78.125\alpha = 0 \tag{2.40}$$

Equating the coefficients of the Cos terms in Equation(2.39) we get

$$-50\beta - 125\alpha + 78.125\beta = 5 \tag{2.41}$$

Step 5.

Determine the constants of the particular solution: To determine the constants of the particular solution we will substitute the particular solution in the differential equation. Doing this will give us two simultaneous equations. This done for you in Equation(2.39), (2.40) and (2.41). This determines the constants for the particular solution so now we know the entire Particular solution.

Solving Equation(2.40) and Equation(2.41) we get

$$\alpha = -0.04213 \text{ and } \beta = -0.00948$$

Step 6.

Use initial conditions to determine the remaining constants: We know that i(0) = 0 so using this initial condition in the solution we get Equation(2.42)

$$c_1 e^{-6.25(0)} + c_2 (0) e^{-6.25(0)} - 0.04213 Sin(5*0) - 0.00948 Cos(5*0) = 0$$

This simplifies to $c_1 \quad -0.01735 = 0$ (2.42)

Next using the other initial condition in the solution will give us another equation in the two constants c_1 and c_2. This Equation is given in Equation(2.43)

$$-6.25 c_1 e^{-6.25(0)} + c_2 e^{-6.25(0)} - 6.25 c_2 (0) e^{-6.25(0)}$$
$$- 5*0.04213 Cos(5*(0)) + \ 5*0.00948 Sin(5*(0)) = 100$$

This Equation simplifies to $-6.25 c_1 + c_2 - 0.21 = 100$ (2.43)

Solving Equation(2.42) and Equation(2.43) simultaneously we get the constants c_1 and c_2 as shown in Equation(2.44). Now that we know both the particular solution and the homogeneous solution we can get the complete solution. The complete solution is also shown in Equation(2.44).

$$c_1 = 0.01735 \ and \ c_2 = 100.101$$
$$0.01735 e^{-6.25t} + 100.101 t e^{-6.25t} - 0.04213 Sin(5t) - 0.00948 Cos(5*t) \quad (2.44)$$

The above two examples show us that the method of solution of a second order system does not change as the roots of the characteristic equation change from real and distinct to real and identical. The only change that we have to make is in the assumption of the solution for the homogeneous equation. When we look at the next example where the roots are complex conjugates of each other we will see the same effect. The method of solution stays the same; we only adjust the type of solution that we choose for the homogeneous equation.

2.2.6.3 System with Complex Conjugate Roots

In the system shown in Figure 2.8 if we change the capacitor to a different capacitor with a value of 0.005F then we get the system shown in Figure 2.9. In this system the characteristic equation has Complex Conjugate roots. For this system the differential equation will be

$$L\frac{di(t)}{dt} + \frac{1}{C}\int i(t)dt + Ri(t) = V(t).$$

We will follow a similar procedure to the one that we followed for the problem with two real and distinct roots and also for two real and identical roots. The procedure consists of the six steps for solving the differential equation. To begin we will first differentiate the circuit equation as we have done twice before to get

$$L\frac{d^2i(t)}{dt^2} + R\frac{di(t)}{dt} + \frac{i(t)}{C} = \frac{dv(t)}{dt}$$

This is a second order differential equation with constant coefficients so we can use our method of solution that we have outlined in Table 2.2. To solve this equation we also need to know the initial conditions. We will use the same initial conditions that we used in the previous two sections, which are the current in the inductor at time t = 0 is zero and the rate of change of current through the inductor at time t = 0 is 100 Amps/second. With this information we can begin the 6 step solution method.

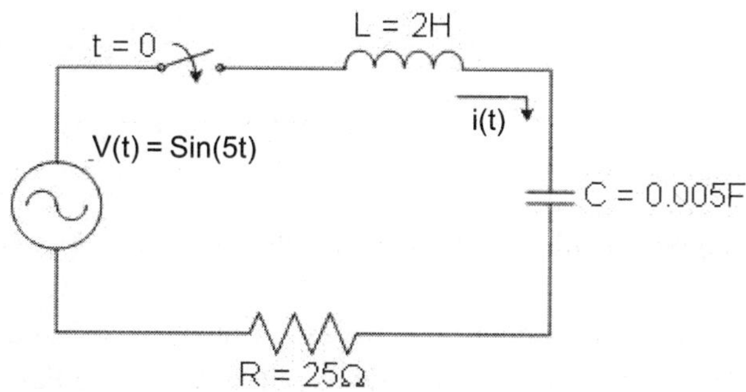

Figure 2.9: A Second order RLC system.
The roots of the Characteristic Equation are Complex Conjugates of each other

Step 1.

Write the characteristic equation: The characteristic equation for this differential equation, using the given values for the components in Figure 2.9 is ($2\lambda^2 + 25\lambda + 200 = 0$)

Step 2.

Determine the roots of the characteristic equation: The roots of this characteristic equation are complex conjugates and are given in Equation(2.45)

$$\lambda_{1,2} = \frac{-25 \pm \sqrt{25^2 - 4*2*200}}{2*2} = -6.25 \pm 31.225j \tag{2.45}$$

Step 3.

Write the homogeneous solution: Since the roots are complex conjugates of each other the homogeneous solution to the differential equation is $c_1e^{-6.25t}Sin(31.225t) + c_2e^{-6.25t}Cos(31.225t)$. Here c_1 and c_2 are constants that have to be determined. Notice that we have used Euler's Identity to choose the solution for the Homogeneous solution. We will use the given initial conditions in step 6 to determine these constants.

Step 4.

Determine the particular solution: This time the forcing function has a term Sin(5t). The particular solution for this term include Sin(5t) and Cos(5t) as part of the solution. When we multiply these terms with the unknown constants we get the particular solution. This time the particular solution with the unknown constants is $\alpha Sin(5t) + \beta Cos(5t)$. The two constants have to be determined from the differential equation. This is done in Equation (2.46)

$$-2[25\alpha Sin(5t) + 25\beta Cos(5t)] + 25[5\alpha Cos(5t) - 5\beta Sin(5t)] + 200[\alpha Sin(5t) + \beta Cos(5t)] = 5Cos(5t) \quad (2.46)$$

Equating the coefficients of the Sine terms we get Equation (2.47)

$$-50\alpha - 125\beta + 200\alpha = 0 \quad (2.47)$$

Equating the coefficients of the Cosine terms we get Equation(2.48)

$$-50\beta - 125\alpha + 200\beta = 5 \quad (2.48)$$

Step 5.

Determine the constants of the particular solution: To determine the constants of the particular solution we will substitute the particular solution in the differential equation. Solving Equation(2.47) and Equation(2.48) we get the two coefficients α=0.091 and β=0.109. This determines the constants for the particular solution so now we know the entire Particular solution.

Step 6.

Use initial conditions to determine the remaining constants: We know that i(0) = 0 so using this initial condition in the solution we get Equation (2.49).

$$c_1e^{-6.25(0)}Sin(31.225*0) + c_2e^{-6.25(0)}Cos(31.225*0) + 0.091Sin(5*0) + 0.109Cos(5*0) = 0 \quad (2.49)$$

This simplifies to $c_2 + 0.109 = 0$

Using the other initial condition in the solution will give us another equation in the two constants c_1 and c_2. This Equation is given in Equation (2.50).

$$-6.25c_1e^{-6.25(0)}Sin(31.225*(0)) + 31.225c_1e^{-6.25(0)}Cos(31.225*(0)) - 6.25c_2e^{-6.25(0)}Cos(31.225*(0)) - 31.225c_2e^{-6.25(0)}Sin(31.225*(0)) + 5*0.091Cos(5*(0)) - 5*0.109Sin(5*(0)) = 100 \quad (2.50)$$

Equation(2.50) simplifies to $31.225c_1 - 6.25c_2 + 0.445 = 100$

Solving the two Equations in the constants c_1 and c_2 we get c_1 = 3.166 and c_2 = 3.166. Now that we know both the Particular Solution and the Homogeneous solution we can get the complete solution. The complete solution is also shown in Equation(2.51)

$$3.166e^{-6.25t}Sin(31.225t) - 0.109e^{-6.25t}Cos(31.225t) - 0.091Sin(5t) - 0.109Cos(5*t) \quad (2.51)$$

The above three examples show us that the method of solution of a second order system does not change as the roots of the characteristic equation change from real and distinct to real and identical and finally to complex conjugates. The only change that we have to make is in the assumption of the solution for the homogeneous equation. The method of solution stays the same; we only adjust the type of solution that we choose for the homogeneous equation. This is summarized in Table 2.3.

Table 2.3: Types of roots of Characteristic Equations and the solution to be chosen.

Type of roots of the Characteristic Equation	Roots of the Characteristic Equation	Solution to be chosen
Real and distinct	λ_1 and λ_2	$C_1e^{\lambda 1t} + C_2e^{\lambda 2t}$
Real and identical	λ	$C_1e^{\lambda t} + C_2te^{\lambda t}$
Complex Conjugates	$\alpha + j\beta$; and $\alpha - j\beta$	$C_1e^{\alpha t}\text{Sin}(\beta t) + C_2e^{\alpha t}\text{ Cos}(\beta t)$

Solving second order differential equations are not any different than solving higher order differential equations. It is for that reason that we have not included many solved examples of solving second order systems. We have chosen particularly to include the solution of this differential equation because it has complex conjugate roots. It has been our experience that most students have most difficulty with this type of a system.

Example 2.14

Determine the Particular Solution to the differential equation

$$2\ddot{y}(t) + 4\dot{y}(t) + 10y(t) = 5U(t)$$

Solution 2.14

The Homogeneous equation for this system is $2\lambda^2 + 4\lambda + 10 = 0$. The roots of this equation are $\lambda_{1,2} = -1 \pm 2j$.

When the roots of the characteristic equation are complex the Homogeneous solution will be of the type $e^{-t}\{\alpha\text{Cos}(2t) + \beta\text{ Sin}(2t)\}$. The two constants α and β will be determined from the initial conditions.

Next we will choose the form of the particular solution. Since the driving function is a constant the particular solution will also be a constant so we will choose c_1 as the particular solution.

When we substitute the particular solution in the differential equation we get $c_1 = 0.5$. So the complete solution for this differential equation is obtained by combining the two solutions together $0.5 + e^{-t}\{\alpha\text{ Cos}(2t) + \beta\text{ Sin}(2t)\}$.

2.3 CHARACTERISTICS OF CONTINUOUS TIME SYSTEMS

In this section we will examine the various characteristics of continuous time systems. It will be useful to know and be able to identify the following properties during subsequent analysis of these systems. We listed some of these as properties of systems in Section 2.1.

2.3.1 Linear Systems

A system is characterized as a *Linear System* if it satisfies the relation in Equation(2.52)

$$H\{a_1f_1(t) \pm a_2f_2(t)\} = a_1H\{f_1(t)\} \pm a_2H\{f_2(t)\} = a_1Y_1(t) \pm a_2Y_2(t) \tag{2.52}$$

In Equation(2.52) H is the system operator, Y_1 is the response when only f_1 is the input, Y_2 is the response when only f_2 is the input, a_1 and a_2 are constants. If the entire relation, all three relations, in Equation(2.52) do not hold then the system is said to be non-linear.

What the above relation in Equation(2.52) tells us is that if to a system you apply input one only you will get output one. Similarly if you apply input two only you will get output two. Next if you combine the two inputs together and apply them simultaneously then you will get an output for the combined input. If this combined output that you obtained by applying the two inputs simultaneously is the same as the sum of the two outputs that you obtained when you applied the inputs individually, then the system is linear.

We are applying the combined input to the system in the first term in Equation(2.52); we are next applying the inputs individually to the system and then combining them in the second term of Equation(2.52); if now we find that the result for the two different applications are the same as shown in the third term in Equation(2.52) then the system that we have is a linear system if they are not then the system that we have is a non-linear system.

2.3.2 Time Invariant Systems

A system is characterized as a time invariant system if the output does not vary (does not change) when the time of application of the input is changed. This can be written as shown in Equation(2.53) and in Figure 2.10.

$$H\{f(t)\} = Y(t) \quad then \quad H\{f(t \pm \tau)\} = Y(t \pm \tau) \tag{2.53}$$

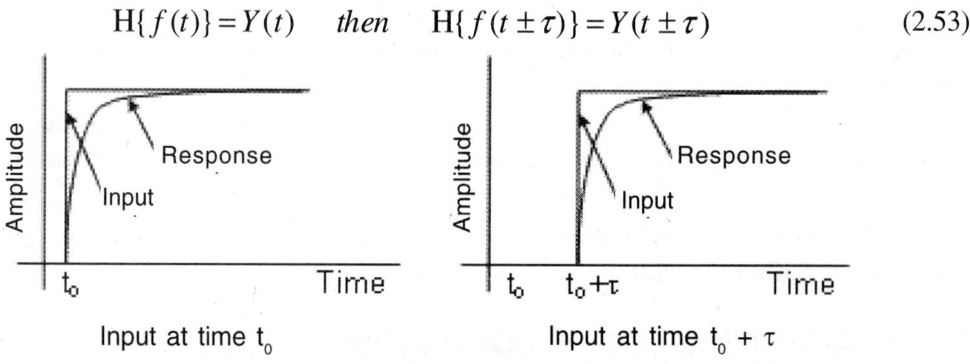

Figure 2.10: For an invariant system the response is identical but delayed when the input is delayed

If a system does not satisfy these conditions then the system is a time variant system. If the system is a spatial system instead of a time system then we call the system a shift invariant system if it satisfies Equation(2.53). When a system is both Linear and Invariant then it will satisfy Equation(2.54). In an LTI system we will have Equation(2.54) satisfied where τ_1 and τ_2 are both constants.

$$\begin{aligned} H\{a_1 f_1(t-\tau_1) \pm a_2 f_2(t-\tau_2)\} &= a_1 H\{f_1(t-\tau_1)\} \pm a_2 H\{f_2(t-\tau_2)\} \\ &= a_1 Y_1(t-\tau_1) \pm a_2 Y_2(t-\tau_2) \end{aligned} \tag{2.54}$$

An example of an LTI system is the system that we saw earlier in Figure 2.5. In Figure 2.5 we saw a system where the switch closed at time t = 0. The response to the system was shown in Figure 2.6. If instead of closing the switch at t = 0 seconds we were to close the switch at t = 1.5 seconds say. Then the response will start at time t = 1.5 seconds but the shape of the response would be the same. Note that the response is identical to Figure 2.6 except it starts at time 1.5 seconds instead of at time t = 0 seconds. Hence the system is time invariant.

2.3.3 Memory or Memory less

A system is said to have memory if the present output of the system depends on one or more of its past inputs. If the present output depends only on the present input then the system is memory less. A resistor has no memory. The present voltage across the resistor depends only on the present current that is flowing through the resistor. It makes no difference how much current was flowing through the resistor previously. A capacitor on the other hand has memory. The present voltage across the capacitor is the accumulation of charge that was flowing in and out of the capacitor from the time the capacitor was connected in the circuit. Any energy storage element will have memory. So systems that have energy storage elements will be systems that have memory.

2.3.4 Stability of the System

There are many different and varied definitions for stability. The most common and the most often used definition is the Bounded Input Bounded Output (BIBO). A system is said to be BIBO stable if the output is finite as long as the input is finite. It does not matter how large the input is, as long as it is finite the output will stay finite, it will not grow without limit. For a system to be BIBO stable the impulse response of the system must be absolutely integrable. This is shown in Equation(2.55). More on the impulse response and a detailed discussion of Equation(2.55) later.

$$|Y(t)| = \left| \int_{-\infty}^{\infty} h(\tau) f(t-\tau) d\tau \right| \le M \left| \int_{-\infty}^{\infty} h(\tau) d\tau \right| \le M \int_{-\infty}^{\infty} |h(\tau)| d\tau \le \infty \tag{2.55}$$

In Equation(2.55) the first and second terms just define how we get the response of the system. The absolute value bars make the response always positive. The third term removes the effect of the input. In the third term we make the input large and constant, as large as we want but still keep it finite. This is the largest the input will ever be. Now that the input is constant, it can be taken out of the integral, since it is a constant (a large constant) equal to some value M. Since this input is large and is always large the response due to the large input will be larger than an actual input which is not always so large. So the third term will always be greater than the second term. The fourth term moves the absolute value bars inside the integral. The absolute value bars are placed around the system function. This term is the impulse response of the system. The fourth term tells us that the output of the system has an upper bound given by some large constant M multiplied by the impulse response of the system. So if the impulse response of the system is finite then the system will be stable in the BIBO sense. If the impulse response of the system does not stay finite then the system will eventually become unstable. This tells us that for the system to be BIBO stable the impulse response of the system must be finite.

2.3.5 Causality

When a system is Causal it means that the system will not anticipate its input. Any signal that arrives at the input of the system at time t_0 will produce an output only at time t_0 or after time t_0 but never before time t_0. Because of this property for most systems when an input is applied at time $t = 0$ the integral that defines the system response can be modified as shown in Equation(2.56)

$$Y(t) = \int_{-\infty}^{t} f(\tau)h(t-\tau)d\tau = \int_{0}^{t} f(\tau)h(t-\tau)d\tau \qquad (2.56)$$

The third term in Equation(2.56) has its lower limit in the integral raised to zero from minus infinity because the input is applied at time $t = 0$ and the system is a causal system. In a causal system there is an implicit assumption that the input is zero for $t < 0$.

2.4 CONVOLUTION

Given two continuous time signals f(t) and h(t), the convolution of f(t) and h(t), written as f(t)*h(t) is defined as shown in Equation(2.57). The convolution integral is a very important integral for LTI systems. In the convolution integral, if f(t) is the input to the system, h(t) is the impulse response of the system then the evaluation of the convolution integral will give us the response of the system for the applied input. For the first integral we say f(t) convolved with h(t), and for the next integral we say h(t) convolved with f(t). Since they are both the same result we do not care which function is first. Each of the two integrals in Equation(2.57) is known as the convolution integral. The evaluation of the convolution integral is shown graphically in Figure 2.11.

$$\left(f(t) * h(t)\right) = \int_{-\infty}^{\infty} h(\tau)f(t-\tau)d\tau = \int_{-\infty}^{\infty} h(t-\tau)f(\tau)d\tau = \left(h(t) * f(t)\right) \qquad (2.57)$$

When you examine the convolution integral carefully there are three different steps that you have to perform to evaluate the convolution integral. You begin with the two functions to be convolved with each other. They are drawn on the top in Figure 2.11. The second step is to flip one of the two functions about the Y-axis; any one of the two functions can be flipped. Equation(2.57) also shows that you can flip any one of the two functions. In this example we have flipped the function f(t). The third step involves gradually shifting the flipped function all the way from $+\infty$ to $-\infty$ and performing the integral of the product of the two functions. The shift amount is recorded by the time variable t while the variable of integration is the variable τ. For each value of the time t the integral of the product of the two functions is evaluated. This is the area that is the overlap area for the two functions shown shaded in Figure 2.11. This is shown in Figure 2.12 in more detail.

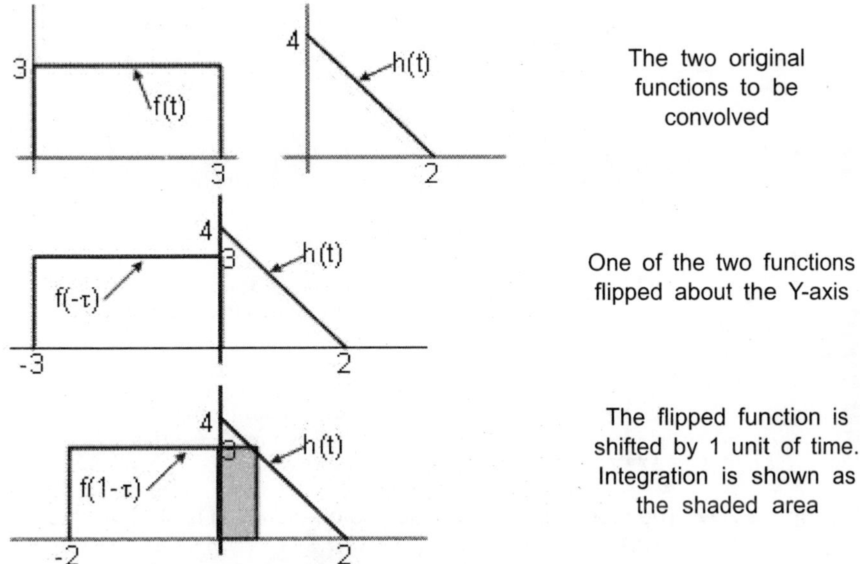

Figure 2.11: Pictorial start of convolution

2.4.1 Convolution by Pictures

Figure 2.12 shows how the convolution is to be completed. The diagram shows us two functions h(t) and f(t) that are to be convolved together. In a series of seven diagrams we complete the convolution. The second diagram in Figure 2.12 shows that one of the functions is flipped and we are ready to start the convolution. In the third diagram we begin the convolution; the flipped function is shifted by one unit of time. The overlap region is shown shaded. This is the result of convolution at time t = 1 seconds. We have to evaluate the convolution for all time t so for every instant of time t we need to determine the overlap area. We will do this mathematically in the next section. The next three diagrams (diagram 4, 5, and 6) evaluate the convolution for time t = 2, t = 3 and t = 4 seconds. The last diagram shows that there is no more overlap for the two functions so from t = 5 onwards the result of the convolution will always be zero.

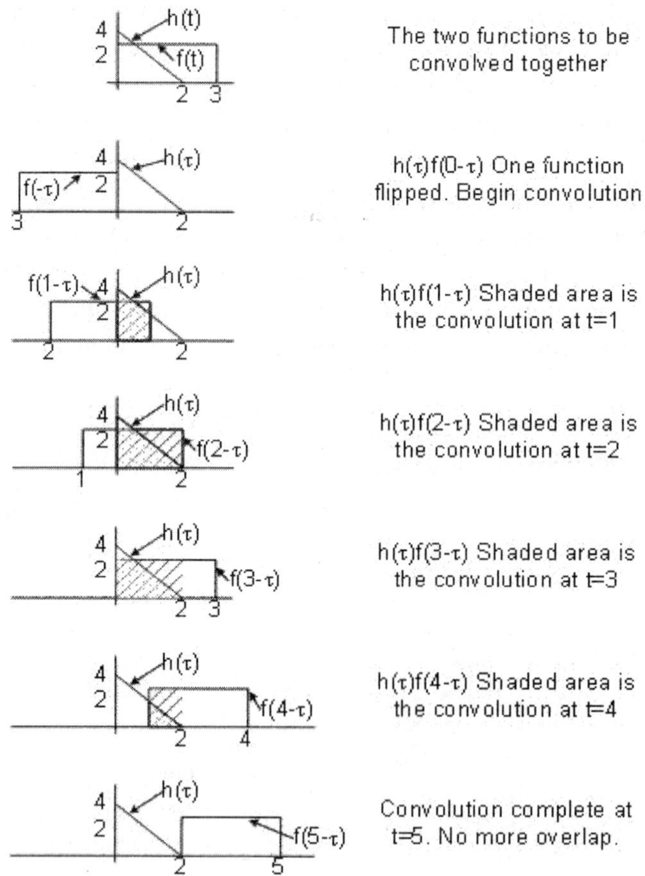

Figure 2.12: The progress of convolution as one function is slid over the other

Now let us do the same convolution using the convolution integral and obtain a closed form solution. We first note that as we slide the function f(t) there will be five different time intervals where the integral will have to be evaluated. The five time intervals are $t < 0$, (second diagram in Figure 2.12) $0 < t < 2$, (diagrams three and four in Figure 2.12) $2 < t < 3$, (fifth diagram in Figure 2.12) $3 < t < 5$, (sixth diagram in Figure 2.12) and $5 < t$ (last diagram in Figure 2.12). We will evaluate the convolution integral in each of these time intervals. We have chosen these five time intervals since the overlap function changes at the boundary of each of these five time intervals.

Interval t<0:

In this interval there is no overlap of the two functions so the convolution in this region is zero.

Interval 0<t<2:

In this region the rectangular function f(t) is starting to overlap the triangular function, the overlap is not yet complete. This result is shown in Equation(2.58)

$$\int_{-\infty}^{\infty}(4-2\tau)1d\tau=\int_{0}^{t}(4-2\tau)1d\tau=4\tau-\frac{2\tau^2}{2}\Big|_0^t$$
$$=(4t-t^2)\quad 0<t<2 \tag{2.58}$$

Interval 2<t<3:

In this region the rectangular function f(t) is completely overlapping the triangular function, the overlap has not yet started to decrease as the rectangular function crosses the triangular function. This result is shown in Equation(2.59).

$$\int_{-\infty}^{\infty}(4-2\tau)1d\tau=\int_{0}^{2}(4-2\tau)1d\tau=4\tau-\frac{2\tau^2}{2}\Big|_0^2$$
$$=(8-4)=4\qquad 2<t<3 \tag{2.59}$$

Interval 3<t<5:

In this region the rectangular function f(t) is starting out to slide away over the triangular function. So the overlap region is gradually decreasing. This result is shown in Equation(2.60). When $t>5$ the two functions have no overlap region so the result of convolution for $t>5=0$.

$$\int_{-\infty}^{\infty}(4-2\tau)1d\tau=\int_{t-3}^{2}(4-2\tau)1d\tau=4\tau-\frac{2\tau^2}{2}\Big|_{t-3}^2 \tag{2.60}$$
$$=(25-10t-t^2)\quad 3<t<5$$

The result of this convolution is drawn in Figure 2.13. The SCILAB script that can be used to calculate the convolution of two functions is also given.

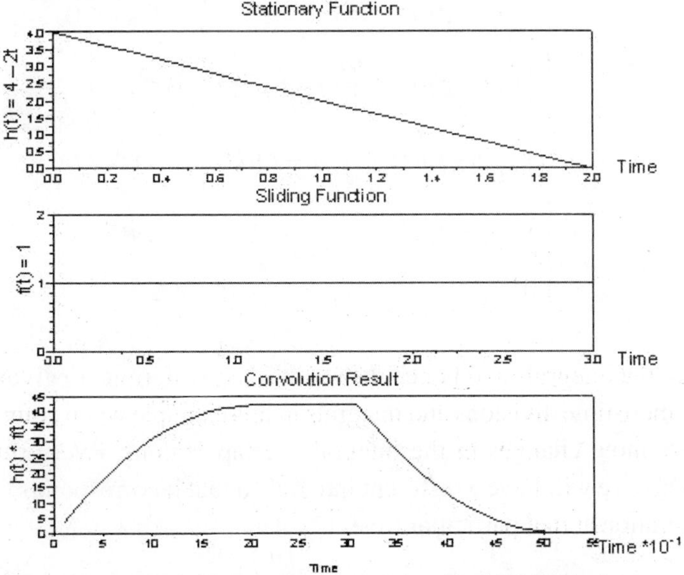

Figure 2.13: Result of convolution with SCILAB script

```
th=0:0.1:2;h=4-2*th;
tf=0:0.1:3;f=ones(1,length (tf));
[y]=convol(h,f);
subplot(3,1,1),plot2d(th,h)
xtitle(['Stationary function'],'Time',' h(t)=4-2t');
subplot(3,1,2),plot2d(tf,f)
xtitle(['Sliding function'],'Time',' f(t)=(1)');
subplot(3,1,3),plot2d(y);
xtitle(['Convolution Result'],'Time',' h(t)*f(t)');
```

2.4.2 Evaluating the Convolution Integral

Here is a different pair of functions to calculate the convolution. The two signals that we want to convolve are shown in Equation(2.61).

$$h(t)=\begin{cases}\dfrac{t}{2} & 0\le t\le 2\\ 0 & \text{otherwise}\end{cases}\qquad f(t)=\begin{cases}1 & -1\le t\le 0\\ -1 & 0\le t\le 1\\ 0 & \text{otherwise}\end{cases}\tag{2.61}$$

The required integrals and the limits of integration are given in Equation(2.62). Since the function f(t) is either +1 or -1 it only shows up as a sign change for the other function when the two functions are multiplied.

$$y(t)=\begin{cases}0 & t\le -1\\ \int_{-1}^{t}(t-\tau)d\tau & -1\le t\le 0\\ \int_{-1}^{0}(t-\tau)d\tau-\int_{0}^{t}(t-\tau)d\tau & 0\le t\le 1\\ \int_{t-2}^{0}(t-\tau)d\tau-\int_{0}^{1}(t-\tau)d\tau & 1\le t\le 2\\ \int_{t-2}^{1}(t-\tau)d\tau & 2\le t\le 3\\ 0 & t\le 3\end{cases}\tag{2.62}$$

The results of all the integrals and hence the result of convolution are given in Equation(2.63). Notice that we have more time divisions and integrals in this example when compared to the previous example as there are more changes in the integral overlap regions. Every time the shape of the overlap region changes we will have a different integral so that it corresponds to the overlap region that is under consideration at that particular time.

$$y(t)=\begin{cases}0 & t\le -1\\ \frac{1}{2}(t+1)^2 & -1\le t<0\\ \frac{1}{2}(-t^2+2t+1) & 0\le t<1\\ \frac{1}{2}(-t^2-2t+1)+2 & 1\le t<2\\ \frac{1}{2}(t^2-2t+1)-2 & 2\le t<3\\ 0 & 3<t\end{cases} \tag{2.63}$$

Example 2.15

Determine the result of convolution when x(t) = δ(t) an impulse function is convolved with h(t) = u(t)-u(t-2).

Solution 2.15

The convolution of any function with an impulse function is the first function again. So in this example the result of convolution is h(t) = u(t) – u(t-2).

Example 2.16

Determine the result of convolution when
x(t) = 2u(t) - 2u(t-2) is convolved with h(t) = u(t)-u(t-2).

Solution 2.16

Here we have two pulses that are being convolved together so the convolution integral is $\int_{-\infty}^{\infty} x(\tau)h(\tau-t)d\tau$. As we did in the previous example we will divide this integral into several different regions. Then perform the integral in each region to get the result of the convolution.

The first region is from $-\infty$ to 0. In this region since there is no overlap of the two functions the result of convolution in this region is zero.

The second region is from 0 to 2. In this region the functions begin to overlap and the region of overlap reaches its maximum value at t = 2. The integration is performed from 0 to t. So the integral is . $\int_0^t (2)(1)d\tau = 2t$. The third region is from 2 to 4. In this region the functions begin to decrease the overlap region from its maximum value at t = 2 to no overlap region when t = 4. When the time reaches 4 the two functions have no overlap region. The integration is performed from 2 to t. So the integral is $\int_2^t (2)(1)d\tau = 2t-4$.

The last region is from t = 4 to t = ∞. In this entire region there is no overlap region so the result of integration is zero.

Example 2.17

Evaluate the convolution of the following two functions $5e^{-3t}U(t)$ and {U(t-2)-U(t-5)}. The functions are shown in Figure Example 2.17.

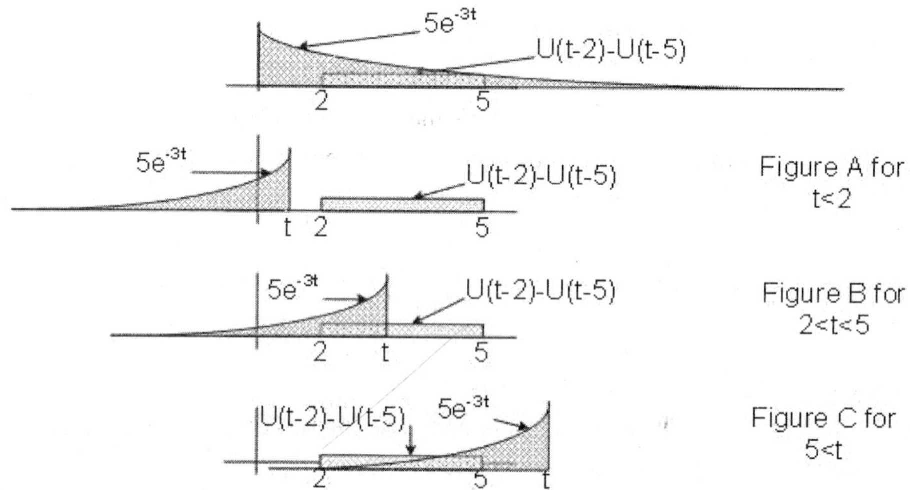

Figure Example 2.17: Convolution of an exponential function with a rectangular function

Solution 2.17

To evaluate this convolution we will assume that the rectangular pulse function is the stationary function and the exponential function is flipped first and then made to slide. With this refer to Figure Example 2.17.

For the time interval t < 2 the two functions do not overlap anywhere so the integral of the function is zero. This is shown in Figure Example 2.17; Figure A.

For the time interval 2 < t < 5 the two functions overlap but the overlap is not complete. This is shown in Figure Example 2.17; Figure B. The convolution integral in this region will be as shown in Equation (2.64)

$$\int_{2}^{t} 5e^{-3(t-\tau)} * 1d\tau = \frac{5}{3}e^{-3t}\, e^{3\tau}\Big|_{2}^{t} = \frac{5}{3}\left[1-e^{(6-3t)}\right] \tag{2.64}$$

For the time interval 5 < t the two functions completely overlap but the overlap region is only from t = 2 to t = 5. This is shown in Figure Example 2.17; Figure C. The convolution integral in this region will be as shown in Equation(2.65)

$$\int_{2}^{5} 5e^{-3(t-\tau)} d\tau = \frac{5}{3}e^{3(\tau-t)}\Big|_{2}^{5} = \frac{5}{3}\left[e^{(15-3t)} - e^{(6-3t)}\right] \tag{2.65}$$

Example 2.18

Evaluate the convolution of the following two functions $2e^{-2t}U(t)$ and $Sin(3\pi t)U(t)$.

Solution 2.18

To evaluate this convolution we will assume that the Sin function is the stationary function and the exponential function is flipped first and then made to slide. With this refer to Figure Example 2.18.

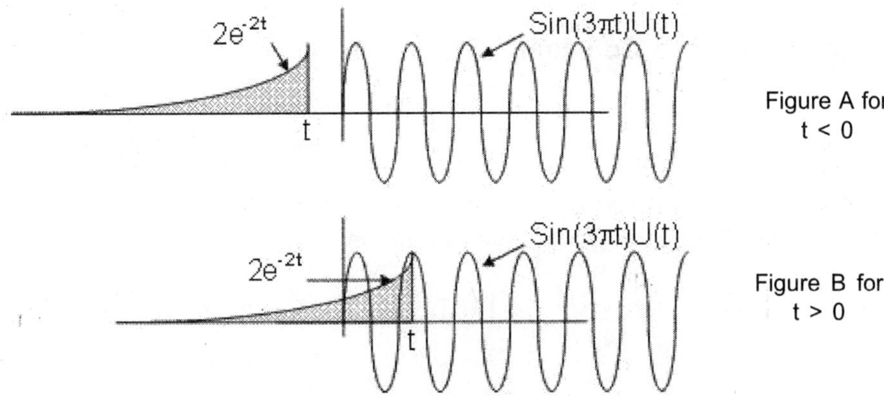

Figure Example 2.18: Convolution of the exponential function with a switched on Sine function

For the time interval t < 0 the two functions do not overlap anywhere so the integral of the function is zero. This is shown in Figure Example 2.18 – Figure A.

For the time interval t > 0 the two functions overlap completely. This is shown in Figure Example 2.18 – Figure B. The convolution integral in this region will be as shown in Equation(2.66)

$$\int_0^t 5e^{-3(t-\tau)} * Sin(3\pi\tau)d\tau = \frac{5}{3(1+\pi)} e^{-3(t-\tau)}[Cos(3\pi\tau) + Sin(3\pi\tau)]\Big|_0^t \qquad (2.66)$$

$$= \frac{5}{3(1+\pi)}\left\{e^0[Cos(3\pi t) + Sin(3\pi t)] - e^{-3t}[1+0]\right\}$$

2.4.3 Properties of Convolution

The convolution integral obeys several simple properties. Knowing these properties will enable us to use the convolution integral more intelligently.

2.4.3.1 Commutative

h(t)*f(t) = f(t)*h(t). This property tells us it does not matter which function is the first function and which is the second function, or which function is the fixed function and which function is the sliding function. This also means that it does not matter which one of the two functions is flipped and slid over the other function. This can be shown as in Equation(2.67). The second integral is obtained from the first by making a simple substitution of $(t - \tau) = \lambda$.

$$\int_{-\infty}^{\infty} h(\tau)f(t-\tau)d\tau = \int_{-\infty}^{\infty} f(\lambda)h(t-\lambda)d\lambda \tag{2.67}$$

Notice that there is no difference between the two integrals and they will evaluate to the same value.

2.4.3.2 Multiplication by a Constant

$$h(t)*[af(t)] = a[h(t)*f(t)].$$

Multiplying any one function in the convolution by a constant multiplies the entire result of convolution by a constant. This can be shown as in Equation(2.68). Since a is a constant it can be taken out of the integral without altering the result of the integration.

$$\int_{-\infty}^{\infty} ah(\tau)f(t-\tau)d\tau = a\int_{-\infty}^{\infty} h(\tau)f(t-\tau)d\tau = a[h(t)*f(t)] \tag{2.68}$$

2.4.3.3 Distributive

$$h(t)*[f_1(t) + f_2(t)] = h(t)*f_1(t) + h(t)*f_2(t).$$

Convolution of a sum of two signals with a third signal is the same as the convolution of the third signal with each of the other two signals individually and then adding the result of the two convolutions. This can be shown as in Equation(2.69). This holds true as the integral of a sum is the same as the sum of an integral.

$$\begin{aligned}\int_{-\infty}^{\infty} h(\tau)[f_1(t-\tau)+f_2(t-\tau)]d\tau &= \int_{-\infty}^{\infty} h(\tau)f_1(t-\tau)d\tau + \int_{-\infty}^{\infty} h(\tau)f_2(t-\tau)d\tau \\ &= h(t)*f_1(t)+h(t)*f_2(t)\end{aligned} \tag{2.69}$$

2.4.3.4 Associative

$$h(t) * [f(t) * g(t)] = [h(t) * f(t)] * g(t)$$

When three functions are convolved together it does not matter which two functions are convolved together first, then the result is convolved with the third. The result is the same. This can be shown as in Equation(2.70). In Equation(2.70) we have first written the two convolutions, then we have interchanged the order of the two integrals, next we substituted μ for $\lambda - \tau$, and finally we have substituted ν for $t-\tau$ to get the final result. Observe carefully that the first integral is in the same form as the fourth integral and hence convolution is associative.

$$\int_{-\infty}^{\infty}\left[\int_{-\infty}^{\infty} h(\tau)f(\lambda-\tau)d\tau\right]g(t-\lambda)d\lambda$$

$$= \int_{-\infty}^{\infty} h(\tau)\left[\int_{-\infty}^{\infty} f(\lambda-\tau)g(t-\lambda)d\lambda\right]d\tau$$

$$= \int_{-\infty}^{\infty} h(\tau)\left[\int_{-\infty}^{\infty} f(\mu)g(t-\mu-\tau)d\mu\right]d\tau \quad (2.70)$$

$$= \int_{-\infty}^{\infty} h(t-\upsilon)\left[\int_{-\infty}^{\infty} f(\mu)g(\upsilon-\mu)d\mu\right]d\upsilon$$

2.4.3.5 Limits of Convolution

If h(t) is time limited to (a,b) and f(t) is time limited to (c,d) then h(t)*f(t) is time limited to (a+c,b+d). It is easiest to reason this out. Assume that we are going to flip the function f(t). So the function f(-t) is now time limited to (-d,-c). The convolution will have a non zero value only when the two functions start to overlap. The overlap will begin when the function f(t) has been made to slide from –c time limit to zero and then it has to be slid further from zero to a, so the total time the function is made to slide is c+a before there is any overlap. So the function f(t) has to slide by a+c time before any overlap takes place. So the lower limit is the sum of the two lower limits. Similarly we can argue that the convolution will end when the function f(t) has been made to slide past the h(t) function. Since its limit is b time units and the flipped function f(t) has its time limit at –d time units the convolution result will have a zero result from time b+d time units onwards. So the upper limit is the sum of the two upper limits or it is b+d time units.

Looking at Figure 2.13 will make this clear. The limits for one function are 0 to 2 and for the limits for the other function are from 0 to 3 so the limits for the result of Convolution are from 0 to 5. Verify this result for all the convolutions that we have performed in this chapter.

2.4.4 Correlation

There are often occasions when it is necessary to compare one reference signal with one or more signals to determine which of these signals is most similar to the reference signal. Such a situation occurs in your cell phone. This is done by correlating the reference signal with all the other signals. For example in digital communication the transmitter uses an alphabet of a few signals. To determine which one of the few signals has been just received by the receiver; the receiver will use correlation of the received signal with all the signals in the transmitter's alphabet. The transmitter will have transmitted one of the signals from its alphabet.

$$R_{fh}(\tau) \overset{\Delta}{=} \int_{-\infty}^{\infty} f(t)h(t-\tau)dt \quad (2.71)$$

The measure of similarity between a pair of finite energy signals is given by their cross correlation. The cross-correlation of two functions is defined by Equation(2.71). In the definition given in Equation(2.71) the parameter τ is known as the lag parameter. The time function f(t) is the stationary function while the function h(t) is the shifted function. The function h(t) is shifted to the right for positive τ and it is shifted left for negative τ. The order of subscripts in $R_{fh}(\tau)$ tells us which is the stationary function and which is the shifted function. If we make a substitution in Equation(2.71) of $t - \tau = t'$ then we will get $R_{hf}(-\tau)$ which shows that now the shifted function is the function f(t) and it is shifted to the left. This is shown in Equation (2.72). In correlation the variable τ represents the amount of shift. As the amount of shift is changed the result of correlation also changes.

$$R_{fh}(\tau) = \int_{-\infty}^{\infty} f(t'+\tau)\,h(t')\,dt' = R_{hf}(-\tau) \tag{2.72}$$

Note that the integral is almost the same as the equation of convolution except the function, when correlation is to be performed, is not flipped. For this reason the second function in the integral is $(t-\tau)$ for correlation instead of $(\tau - t)$ as it appears in convolution.

When the two functions h(t) and f(t) in the correlation equation are the same then the correlation is known as auto-correlation. When the functions are different then the correlation is known as cross-correlation. It is interesting to see the auto correlation of a function w(t) that is formed by the addition of two functions say $w(t) = \{af(t) - h(t - \tau)\}$.

$$\begin{aligned} R_{ww}(0) &= \int_{-\infty}^{\infty} \{af(t) - h(t-\tau)\}^2\, dt \\ &= \int_{-\infty}^{\infty} \left[a^2 f^2(t) - 2af(t)h(t-\tau) + h^2(t-\tau)\right] dt \\ &= a^2 R_{ff}(0) - 2aR_{fh}(\tau) + R_{hh}(0) \end{aligned} \tag{2.73}$$

The auto correlation with no shift shown in Equation(2.73) of the function w will always be a positive quantity since it is a squared function. We can write the auto correlation result of Equation(2.73) as a matrix equation as shown in Equation(2.74).

$$[a \;\; 0]\begin{bmatrix} R_{ff}(0) & R_{fh}(\tau) \\ R_{fh}(\tau) & R_{hh}(0) \end{bmatrix}\begin{bmatrix} a \\ 0 \end{bmatrix} \geq 0 \tag{2.74}$$

From Equation(2.74) we get the relation that $R_{ff}(0)R_{hh}(0) \geq R_{fh}^2(\tau)$. This fact is of great importance, and it is routinely used in signal detection. Finally if we make h(t) = f(t) in Equation(2.74) we get a very special relation given in Equation(2.75)

$$R_{ff}^2(0) \geq R_{ff}^2(\tau) \tag{2.75}$$

which shows us that $R_{ff}(0)$ is always greater than $R_{ff}(\tau)$. The auto correlation is always greatest when there is no shift involved or the auto-correlation of a function is a maximum when the amount of shift is zero.

The RADAR uses correlation to determine the distance from the target. The radar sends out a pulse and starts a timer. Then it keeps on computing the correlation of the received or the reflected pulse with the pulse that it transmitted. When the computed correlation reaches its maximum value, the assumption is that the received pulse and the transmitted pulses have been lined up and the amount of shift is zero. The radar converts the time it takes for the correlation to reach maximum into the distance of the object from the radar. Since the received pulse is a replica of the transmitted pulse the radar computes the auto-correlation to determine the distance of the object.

Example 2.19

The Auto correlation of a complex sequence is defined as

$$R_x(n) = \sum_{k=-\infty}^{\infty} x^*[k]x[n+k].$$

Show that a. With a proper choice of the signal g[n] we can compute $R_x[n] = x[n]*g[n]$

b. Identify the signal g[n]

Solution 2.19

On comparing the integrals for the convolution and the correlation we find there is similarity:

$$Convolution = \int_{-\infty}^{\infty} x(\tau)g(t-\tau)\,d\tau$$

$$\text{and the } Correlation = \int_{-\infty}^{\infty} x(\tau)g(\tau-t)\,d\tau.$$

On comparing the two integrals we find the function g(t) is flipped in the convolution integral while it is not flipped for the correlation function. Using the same rational for the discrete time convolution and the discrete time correlation we can say that the auto correlation can be computed by performing the convolution if we first flip the function that is shifted and then perform the convolution. Performing the convolution will flip the function a second time which will right side the function so the result will be auto correlation. So the signal g[n] will have to be x[-n] to perform the auto correlation by performing the convolution.

A matched filter is a signal detection device in your cell phone, it functions by calculating the correlation between the received signal and the ideal template of the expected signal that is stored in the matched filter. A matched filter has several different expected signals. Then to decide which signal is received by the matched filter the correlation is computed. This correlation is computed with the received signal and a template of all the possible signals that could be received. The largest correlation identifies the received signal since that will represent the auto-correlation while all the others will represent cross-correlation. Radar systems also detect items by using correlation between the transmitted pulse and the reflected pulse.

$$\rho_{fh}(\tau)=\frac{R_{fh}(\tau)}{\sqrt{R_{ff}(0)R_{hh}(0)}} \tag{2.76}$$

Correlation as we have been computing is dependent on the amplitude of the two signals. Two signals with large amplitudes will have a larger coefficient than two signals with smaller amplitudes. To examine correlation without the effect of amplitudes the correlation coefficient is computed instead of the correlation only. The correlation coefficient is defined as shown in Equation(2.76) and uses the fact that the auto correlation is largest when the signals have zero lag. The range of the correlation coefficient is between -1 and +1. So when $\rho_{fh}(\tau) = -1$ then the two signals are negatively correlated and when $\rho_{fh}(\tau) = +1$ then the two signals are completely (or positively) correlated and when $\rho_{fh}(\tau) = 0$ then the two signals are un-correlated. Negative correlation means when one signal is increasing the other is decreasing, completely correlated means that when one signal is increasing the other signal is also increasing, un-correlated means that there is no relation between the two signals. They may both increase or decrease at the same time or they may increase or decrease at different times. We cannot tell one way or the other.

2.5 THE IMPULSE RESPONSE OF A CONTINUOUS TIME LTI SYSTEM

In Section 2.4 we have shown the convolution integral and hinted that the convolution integral is used to determine the response of a system. In this section we will determine the impulse response of a system using the convolution integral and then using the property of a LTI (linear time invariant) system actually show that the response of a system can be obtained by the convolution integral.

We define the impulse response of a system as *the response of the system to a unit impulse applied to the input of the system at time t=0.* The impulse response, denoted as h(t), also assumes that the system is at rest before the application of the impulse. Being at rest means that there is no energy stored in the system when the impulse arrives.

Before we work with a general signal x(t) as input we will find it extremely beneficial to first represent the general signal as a sum of shifted impulse pulses. To do this we once again write the impulse function as a sum of two step functions shifted in time as shown in Equation(2.77).

$$\hat{\delta}(t)=\frac{1}{\Delta}\left[U(t)-U(t-\Delta)\right] \tag{2.77}$$

Now consider an approximation of a continuous time function x(t) by adding together shifted and weighted impulse functions. The weight assigned to the impulse function is equal to the value of the function x(t) at the location of the impulse as in Equation(2.78).

$$x(t)=\sum_{k=-\infty}^{\infty}x(k\Delta)\hat{\delta}(t-k\Delta)\Delta \tag{2.78}$$

Equation(2.78) is only an approximation of the function x(t) but the approximation gets better and better as Δ gets to be smaller and smaller till Δ→0. In the limit as Δ→0 the approximation is exact. The approximation of the function by rectangular impulses is shown in Figure 2.14. In Equation (2.79) we show the same by a limit equation as Δ→0. In the limit the summation becomes an integral and the function defined in Equation(2.77) becomes an impulse δ(t).

$$x(t)=\underset{\Delta\to 0}{Limit}\sum_{k=-\infty}^{\infty}x(k\Delta)\hat{\delta}(t-k\Delta)\Delta=\int_{-\infty}^{\infty}x(\tau)\delta(t-\tau)\,d\tau \tag{2.79}$$

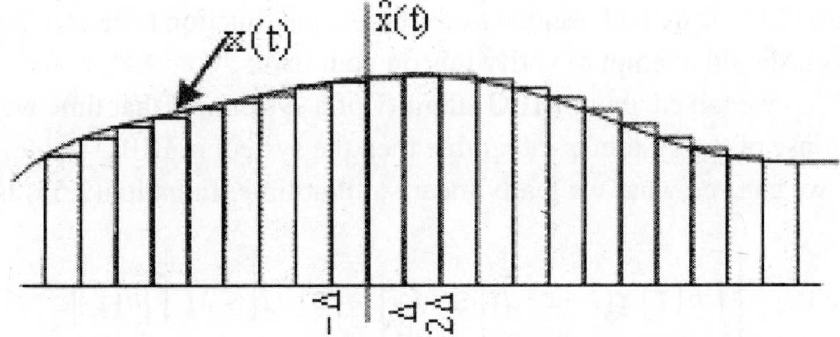

Figure 2.14: Approximation of a continuous time function as described in Equation 2.79

The integral in this equation represents the shifting property of the impulse. That is why we said earlier that a continuous time function can be represented as shifted weighted impulses. Suppose now that the system has a transfer function h(t), the output of the system y(t) will be the convolution of the input with the system function. Further suppose that the input to the system is an impulse function, then we get Equation(2.80).

$$y(t)=\int_{-\infty}^{\infty}h(\tau)\delta(t-\tau)\,d\tau=h(t) \tag{2.80}$$

This equation tells us that the system function h(t) is the response to the system when the input to the system is an impulse. Hence h(t) is known as the impulse response of the system. This is usually written as $h(t)=H\{\delta(t)\}$. Now when we have a general input x(t) to a system then the response from the system will be as shown in Equation(2.81)

$$y(t)=\int_{-\infty}^{\infty}h(\tau)x(t-\tau)\,d\tau \tag{2.81}$$

Example 2.20

Consider a system with an impulse response $h(t) = e^{-0.2t}u(t)$. Let the input to this system be a step input x(t) = u(t). Determine the response y(t) from this system.

Solution 2.20

Since we know the input and the impulse response from the system we can directly apply Equation (2.81) to determine the response from the system. This is done in Equation(2.82)

$$\begin{aligned} y(t) &= \int_0^t x(\tau)h(t-\tau)\,d\tau \\ &= \int_0^t 4e^{-0.2(t-\tau)}\,d\tau = 4e^{-0.2t}e^{0.2\tau}\Big|_0^t \\ &= 4e^{-0.2t}\left(e^{0.2t}-1\right) = \left[4-4e^{-0.2t}\right]u(t) \end{aligned} \tag{2.82}$$

Notice that since the convolution integral does not differentiate between which function is the stationary function and which function is the shifted function the result would be the same as that shown in Equation(2.82) if we had decided to shift the input function instead of the system function. As an exercise you should attempt to verify this on your own.

In Section 2.3.4 we talked about BIBO stability of a system. At that time we mentioned that if the impulse response of the system is integrable then the system in BIBO stable. Referring back to Equation (2.55) we can see what we really meant at that time. Equation(2.55) is repeated for you here.

$$|Y(t)| = \left|\int_{-\infty}^{\infty} h(\tau)x(t-\tau)\,d\tau\right| \le M\left|\int_{-\infty}^{\infty} h(\tau)\,d\tau\right| \le M\int_{-\infty}^{\infty}|h(\tau)|\,d\tau \le \infty \tag{2.55}$$

In this equation h(t) is the impulse response of the system and x(t) is the input to the system. When we make the input as large as possible but not infinite *(Bounded input)* we can get it out of the integral since it is now a constant. The integral now is the integral of the impulse response of the system. If the integral of the impulse response of the system is bounded then the output will also be bounded. Thus BIBO stability condition says that if the integral of the absolute impulse response is bounded then the system is stable.

2.6 CHAPTER SUMMARY

2.6.1 Properties of Continuous time systems

Systems are classified in many different ways. In this book we will be considering only the Deterministic; Linear; Time Invariant; Causal; Lumped parameter systems.

A **Deterministic** system is a system in which the input is known. The input is not a stochastic input.

A **Linear** system is a system that obeys the principle of superposition. Often a system will be linear within a small and a specific range. In this case we will consider the system acting only in this range. Some times we call such a system as piece wise linear.

A **Time Invariant** system is a system whose output will be a delayed by the exact same amount as the input but the shape of the output will be maintained.

A **Causal** system is a system that does not anticipate its input. In a causal system the output to a particular input will arrive only after the input has been received by the system. So for a causal system we can also say that the output is dependent only on the present and the past inputs.

A **Lumped Parameter** system is a system that assumes that its parameters that make up the system are assumed to be acting at a point. The parameters even though they occupy finite space are thought of as if they act as if they are effectively present at only one point.

2.6.2 System Modeling

The modeling of systems is done by differential equations. Once the system is modeled by its differential equations then the system that is one type (say mechanical) is not any different from a system that is a different type (say electrical or hydraulic or some other.)

The Mechanical translation elements that make up a mechanical system are the Mass Spring and the Damper. The mass obeys Newton's law of motion; the Force acting on the mass will give the mass an acceleration. The relation between the force and the mass is $F = M\alpha$. The Spring obeys Hooke's Law. In a spring the force is proportional to the deformation. This is written as $F = kx$. In a damper the force is proportional to the velocity. The damper is an energy consumption element. It dissipates energy stored in the mass and the spring.

The Electrical elements are similar to the mechanical elements. The element Inductor tries to maintain a constant current flowing through it. We have shown that the inductor is similar to the mass of the mechanical system. The element Capacitor tries to maintain a constant voltage across its terminal. We have shown that the Capacitor is similar to the spring of the mechanical system. The element Resistor obeys the Ohms Law. It is the proportionality constant between the current and the voltage. The resistor is similar to the damper. Both the damper and the resistor consume energy.

2.6.3 System Descriptions

Systems are described by differential equations. The types of systems that we will come across are described by linear constant coefficient differential equations. We first learnt how to solve the first order differential equation. The procedure was a simple three step process. First separate the variables, then integrate and finally invert to get the solution in the standard form. This gave us the complete solution.

With higher order (second order and higher) differential equations the method is a six step process. The six steps gave us both the required solutions, the homogeneous solution as well as the particular solution. The six steps that we listed in detail in Table 2.2 are outlined below for you once again:

- Write the **Characteristic** Equation. The characteristic equation is formed by setting the driving function to zero.
- Determine the **Roots** of the Characteristic Equation.
- Choose an appropriate **Homogeneous** solution. Attach undetermined constants to the Homogeneous solution.

- Choose the form of the **Particular** solution to be used this time by examining the driving function. Include all the derivatives of the solution also.
- Solve for the **Constants** of the particular solution by substituting the solution in the equation.
- Use the **Initial Conditions** to determine the constants of the Homogeneous solution.

With Second order systems we are able to use a slightly different method of solution. (Although we can use the above method any way as the second order equation can be thought of as a higher order equation.) We use this alternate method because second order equations have only three different types of roots. The roots of the second order system can be real and distinct; real and identical or complex conjugates. That is it. So the homogeneous solution is chosen according to the type of roots you expect. The different types of roots that you may get and the conditions for the roots are listed in detail in Table 2.3, the solutions for the three types of roots are given below.

- Real and distinct roots: Homogeneous solution is two exponentials (decaying exponentials for real systems) with different decay rates.
- Real and identical roots: Homogeneous solution is two exponentials (decaying exponentials for real systems) with identical (decay rates for real systems) rates, with one exponential multiplied with t the time variable and the other not to keep them different.
- Complex conjugate roots: Homogeneous solution is either a pure Sine or a pure Cosine function if the roots are purely imaginary. Homogeneous solution consists of decaying Sine or a Cosine function if the roots are complex conjugates (the functions will be decaying for real systems).

2.6.4 Characteristics of Continuous Time Systems

Continuous time systems that we will study are **Linear** which means that these systems obey the principle of superposition. These systems are **Time Invariant** which means that if the input is delayed the output will also be appropriately delayed. These systems either have **Memory** or are **without Memory**. If a system has memory then its present output depends on its present input and also on its past inputs. If a system has no memory then the present output is dependent only on the present input. These systems are **BIBO Stable** which means that if the input to the system is not infinite then the output of the system will also be finite. These systems are **Causal** which means that the present output of the system depends only on the past and the present inputs. It does not depend on the future inputs. The system does not anticipate its input.

2.6.5 Convolution

This is an operation that is performed whenever a signal goes through a system. The transfer function of the system is convolved with the input to get the response of the system. To perform convolution we take one function - any one of the two will do - and we flip it. Then we slide the flipped function, starting at $-\infty$ all across the function that is not flipped, all the way to $+\infty$. While the sliding is in progress we integrate the product of the two functions. The result of the integration is the result of convolution. Convolution is described pictorially in Figure 2.12 in the text.

Properties of Convolution are:

- Convolution is **Commutative**.
- **Multiplication** of one function **by a constant** multiplies the result of convolution by the same constant.
- Convolution is **Distributive**.
- Convolution is **Associative**.
- The limits of convolution. The lower limit is the **sum of the lower limits** of the two functions and the upper limit is the **sum of the upper limits** of the two functions.

Correlation

Correlation is very similar to Convolution. In correlation we slide one function without flipping it. Correlation is a measure of the similarity of the two functions. Correlation is usually reported as the correlation coefficient. The range of the correlation coefficient is -1 to +1. +1 showing perfect correlation, -1 showing perfect anti correlation and a zero showing that the two functions are uncorrelated to each other.

When the two functions in the correlation are the same then we get auto correlation. Auto correlation is maximum when the lag (the amount of relative shift) is zero.

2.7 HOMEWORK PROBLEMS

Properties of Continuous Time Systems

Problem 2.7.1

For each of the impulse responses listed below, determine whether the corresponding system is Linear, Causal, Time Invariant, with memory and stable.

a) $h(t) = e^2|t|$
b) $h(t) = e^2tU(t-1)$
c) $h(t) = U(t+1) - U(t-1)$
d) $h(t) = 3\delta(t-2)$
e) $h(t) = Cos(2\pi t)U(t)$
f) $h(t) = 5te^{-0.3t}U(t)$
g) $h(t) = e^{2t}U(t-1) + 2$
h) $h(t) = (0.5)^tU(t)$
i) $h(t) = 3\delta(t) + 2\delta(t-2)$
j) $h(t) = e^{-0.5t}Cos(2\pi t) - e^{-0.4t}Sin(5\pi t)$

Problem 2.7.2

Determine the forced response for the systems described by the following differential equation with the supplied inputs.

$$(a)\ \dot{y}(t)+8y(t)=x(t); \quad x(t)=U(t); \quad y(0)=1.25$$

$$(b)\ \ddot{y}(t)+4\dot{y}(t)+7y(t)=x(t); \quad x(t)=e^{-2t}U(t); \quad y(0)=1;\ \dot{y}(0)=0.5$$

$$(c)\ \ddot{y}(t)+4\dot{y}(t)+4y(t)=x(t); \quad x(t)=Sin(2\pi t)U(t); \quad y(0)=-2;\ \dot{y}(0)=1$$

$$(d)\ \ddot{y}(t)+4\dot{y}(t)+2y(t)=x(t); \quad x(t)=t^3U(t); \quad y(0)=2;\ \dot{y}(0)=0.4$$

Problem 2.7.3

A system consists of a general time domain signal x(t) and a modulating signal Sin(200πt). The output of the system is the product of the signal x(t) and the modulating signal. So the output of the system y(t) = x(t)Sin(200πt). Is this system Linear? Is this system time varying? Is this system Causal? Does this system have Memory? Does the input signal x(t) make any difference?

Problem 2.7.4

Given a system that is defined as follows. The output from the system is the input multiplied by a pure cosine function. So y(t) = x(t)Cos(20πt). Determine if this system is

a. Linear or non linear?
b. Time invariant or time varying?
c. Causal or anti causal?
d. Instantaneous or does the system have memory?

Problem 2.7.5

A system has the relationship as follows: $y(t) = 8h(t) + 3.5h^{0.5}(t)$.

a. An input to this system is $x_a(t) = u(t)$. What is the output from the system?
b. Second input to this system is $x_b(t) = Sin(4\pi t)$. What is the output now?
c. Third input to the system is $x(t) = x_a(t) + x_b(t)$. Show that this system is a non linear system.
d. Through some special circuits it is possible to square the second term only of the system response. Now determine the answers to parts a; b and c above.

Problem 2.7.6

You are given a differential equation that describes a system. This system is driven by various different input functions. For each of the input functions determine the complete solution assuming zero initial conditions.

$$7\dddot{y}(t)+5\ddot{y}(t)-2\dot{y}(t)+6=2x(t)$$

$$(a)\ x(t)=2U(t-2)$$

$$(b)\ x(t)=3e^{-3t}U(t)$$

$$(c)\ x(t)=[t^3+e^{-2t}]U(t)$$

$$(d)\ x(t)=Sin(3\pi t)U(t)$$

System Modeling

Problem 2.7.7

Write the differential equation describing the relation between the input voltage and the output current in each of the electric circuits shown in Figure 2.7.5. Solve the differential equation using time domain methods.

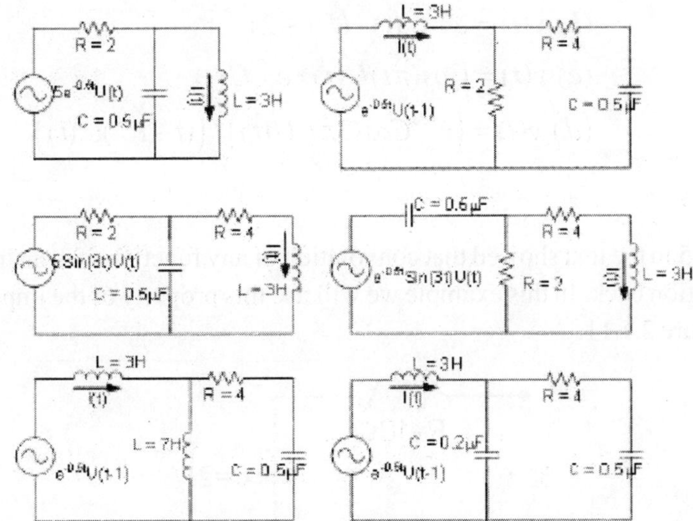

Figure 2.7.7: First determine the differential equation that relates the source voltage and the 3H inductor. Then solve the differential equation and plot the current through the 3H inductor. Assume that all the initial conditions are zero.

Problem 2.7.8

Solve the differential equations obtained in Problem 2.7.6 using the SCILAB ODE command.

Problem 2.7.9

Write the differential equation that relates the output voltage to the input voltage for the circuit shown in Figure 2.7.9. Solve the differential equation assuming the initial conditions given.

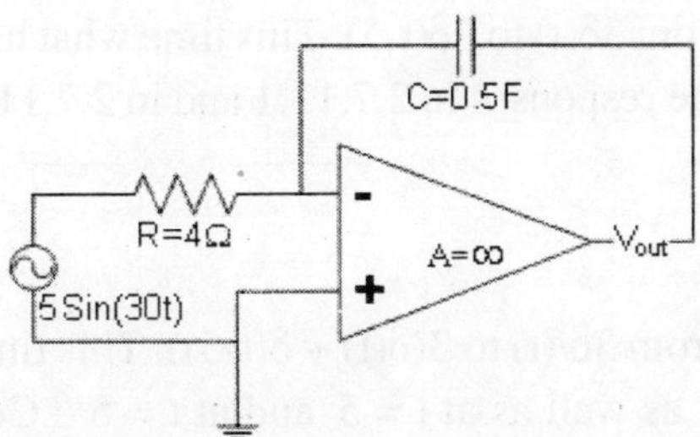

Figure 2.7.9: Write the Equation relating the input voltage to the output voltage. Solve assuming that the capacitor voltage is 0.5 volts at time t = 0

Convolution

Problem 2.7.10

Evaluate the continuous time convolution of the four pairs of signals given below:

$$(a)\ y(t) = U(t+1) * U(t-1)$$

$$(b)\ y(t) = e^{-2t}U(t) * U(t+2)$$

$$(c)\ y(t) = Cos(\pi t)U(t) * e^{-2t}U(t)$$

$$(d)\ y(t) = \left(e^{-2t}Cos(3\pi t)U(t)\right) * \left((t - t^{-2})U(t)\right)$$

Problem 2.7.11

Example 2.15 in the text showed that convolution of any function with an impulse function gives us the same function back. In this example we will use this property of the impulse function to study the circuit in Figure 2.7.11.

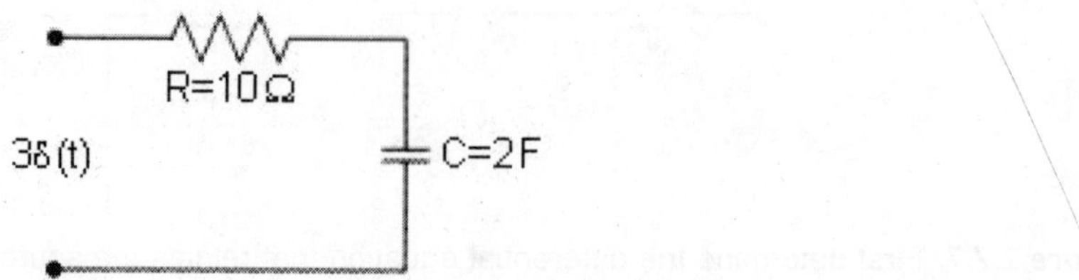

Figure 2.7.11: Determine the voltage across the capacitor assuming zero initial conditions

2.7.11.1

The impulse is applied at time t = 0⁺. What is the voltage across the capacitor at t=0⁻. What is the voltage across the capacitor at t = 0⁺. Earlier you learnt that the voltage across the capacitor cannot change instantaneously. Does this example violate this principle? How do you explain the change in the capacitor voltage?

2.7.11.2

This time change the input from 3δ(t) to 3δ(t-5). This time what happens to the capacitor voltage at t = 5⁻ and at t = 5⁺? Compare the responses in 2.7.11.1 and in 2.7.11.2. Does the comparison show that the system is time invariant?

2.7.11.3

This time change the input from 3δ/(t) to 3(δ(t) + δ(t-5)). This time what happens to the capacitor voltage at t = 0⁻ and at t = 0⁺ as well as at t = 5⁻ and at t = 5⁺? Compare this response with the responses in 2.7.11.1 and in 2.7.11.2. Is the present response equal to the sum of the two earlier responses? This shows that the present system is a linear system also.

Problem 2.7.12

When we discussed convolution we mentioned that it does not matter which function we flip and shift. Show that this is indeed true at least for the following two functions. Perform the convolution first by flipping function (a) and then by flipping function (b). Show that the results of both the convolutions are the same. The two functions are shown in Figure 2.7.12.

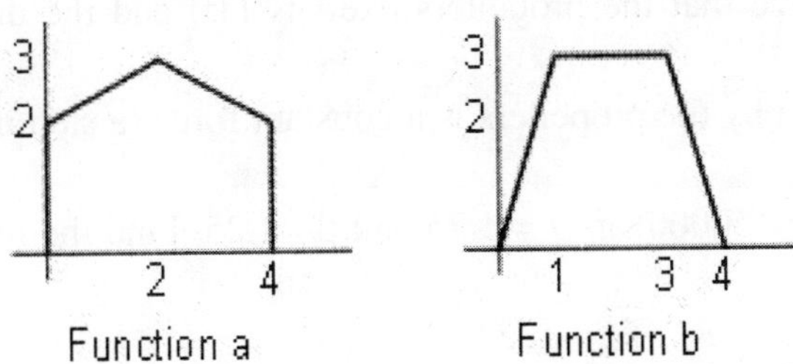

Fig. 2.7.12: Convolve the two functions shown

Problem 2.7.13

To show that convolution is time invariant repeat the convolution of the two functions shown in Figure 2.7.12 but this time shift the functions as shown.

Problem 2.7.13.1

Shift function (a) by 2 time units to the right (delay).

Problem 2.7.13.2

Shift function (b) by 3 time units to the left (early).

When you draw the result of convolving the two shifted functions as required in Problem 2.7.13.1 and 2.7.13.2 you should find that the result of shifted convolution has the same shape as the convolution of Problem 2.7.13 but the result is either delayed or advanced as the case may be for the shifted functions.

Problem 2.7.14

In the chapter we mentioned that when the parameters of a system change with time then we have a time varying system. As an example of a simple time varying system consider the following.

a. Consider an airplane carrying flame retardant chemical that it will drop on a fire. As the plane drops the chemical the mass of the plane will change. As this change is not gradual we will have to treat the mass of the plane as a time varying function. Say the mass of the plane changes according to the rule $M(t) = M_0 - \mu t$. Here M_0 is the base mass of the plane and μ is the rate at which the mass is decreasing from the plane. With this the equation of motion becomes

$$\frac{d\left[M(t)v(t)\right]}{dt}+\alpha v(t)=F(t)$$

$$\left(M_0-v(t)\right)\frac{dv(t)}{dt}+(\alpha-\mu)v(t)=F(t)$$

In these equations the force that the propellers exert is F(t) and the drag force that has to be overcome is $\alpha v(t)$.

b. If the force exerted by the propellers is a constant force (a step input) determine the step response for the airplane.

c. Assuming that M_0=150000Kg, α = 1.75 and μ =1.25. Find the response to the step input applied at time t=0.

2.8 FURTHER READING

2.8.1

A summary and many worked examples for everything that we will cover in this text are found in:

1. Hsu, H. P., *Signals and Systems*, Schaum's Outline Series. (McGraw Hill, 1995)

2.8.2

A general treatment of Differential Equations can be found in:

1. Boyce W.E., and DiPrima, R.C., *Elementary Differential Equations*, Sixth Edition. (Wiley, 1997)

2. Kreyszig, E., *Advanced Engineering Mathematics*, 7th edition (John Wiley & Sons New York)

2.8.3

The role of Differential Equations and Block diagrams descriptions in Feedback control systems are found in:

1. Dorf, R.C. and Bishop, R.H., *Modern Control System*, Seventh Edition. (Addison-Wesley, 1995)

2. Strang, G., *Linear Algebra and its applications*, 3rd edition (Harcourt Bruce Javanovich, New York)

3. Aseltine, J. A., *Transform Methods in Linear System Analysis*, (McGraw Hill, New York)

CHAPTER 3

Spectrum of Periodic Signals

INTRODUCTION

Have you ever wondered if there is any relation between a periodic signal and a sinusoid of the same frequency? Between a periodic signal and a sinusoid of a frequency that is harmonically related to the frequency of the periodic signal? Many great scientists and mathematicians have wondered about this and have conjectured with different results. For example Bernoulli in the middle of the 18th century experimented with the vibrations of plucked strings. He conjectured that the vibration modes can be resolved into various sinusoids. Lagrange on the other hand conjectured that abrupt changes (finite jumps or discontinuities) in the magnitude of a signal can not be represented by the smooth variations of the sinusoids. It was towards the end of the 18th century that a French mathematician by the name of Jean Batiste Joseph Fourier showed without a doubt that it is possible to represent any periodic wave by an infinite sum of harmonically related sine and cosine waves provided the periodic wave satisfied some simple conditions. We will see these conditions in the next section.

Representing a periodic wave by its Fourier series has many advantages. First it permits us to observe the frequency content of the signal. By knowing the frequency content of the signal we are able to identify the frequency domain parameters, such as the bandwidth, energy concentration, etc of the signal. It was this study of the frequency content of the human voice signals that enabled the telephone company to band limit the telephone signal to less than 3000 Hz and yet deliver very good fidelity at the other end of the telephone line. This is possible because most of the energy of the signal is contained in the band of frequencies between 300 Hz and 3000 Hz. Another advantage that we will get by representing the signal in its frequency domain is that the differential equations become algebraic equations. We will look at this effect in more detail after we have studied the Fourier Transform and the Laplace Transform.

3.1 THE FOURIER SERIES

Recall Figure 1.3a and Figure 1.3b. In both these figures we added various sine waves of different frequency and different amplitude to get a complex pulse of a triangular looking periodic wave. So by selectively choosing the proper frequency and the amplitude of the sine wave we are able to build a different complex periodic wave. In this section we will first see the conditions that the complex periodic wave must satisfy so that it can be represented by the sine waves. Then we will go forward and determine the equations that enable us to determine the frequency and the amplitude of the various sine waves that are necessary. Before continuing with the analysis of a complex periodic wave let us look at two examples.

$$x(t) = Sin(\omega t) + \tfrac{1}{3}Sin(3\omega t) + \tfrac{1}{5}Sin(5\omega t) + \tfrac{1}{7}Sin(7\omega t) + \tfrac{1}{9}Sin(9\omega t)\,..... \quad (3.1)$$

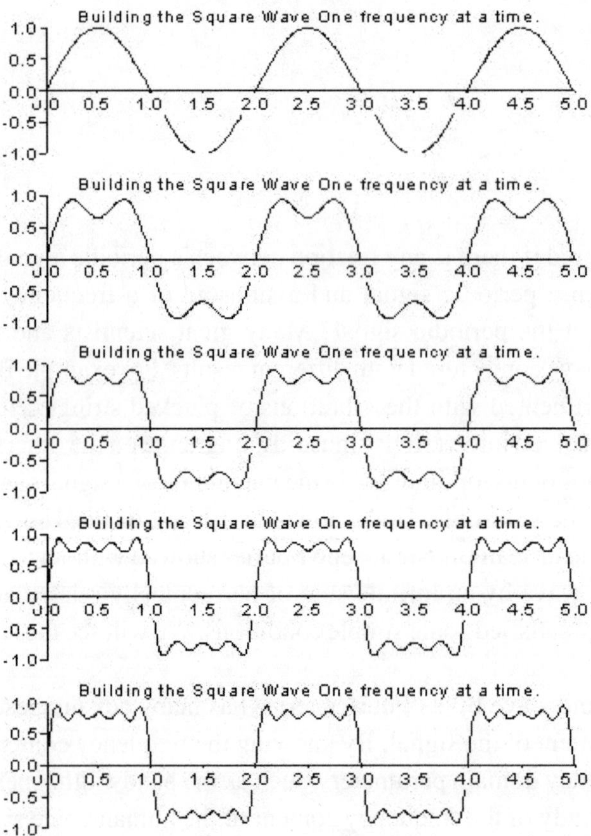

Figure 3.1: In this figure we build a square wave by adding the odd order harmonics one at a time. With only the first five terms we see the shape of the square wave

First consider the function defined in Equation 3.1. Several partial sums of the wave in Equation 3.1 are plotted in Figure 3.1 using a SCILAB script also included following the Figure 3.1. The first figure represents the Sine wave at the fundamental frequency. The second plot represents the sum of the sine wave of the fundamental frequency and the third harmonic (the first two terms in Equation(3.1). The amplitude of the third harmonic is 1/3 of the amplitude of the fundamental. The third plot is the sum of the fundamental, the third harmonic and the fifth harmonic (the first three terms in Equation(3.1). The amplitude of the third harmonic is 1/3 that of the fundamental and the amplitude of the fifth harmonic is 1/5 that of the fundamental. The fourth and the fifth plots are drawn with similar progression. From the Figure 3.1 you can easily visualize that if we continue in this manner we will end up with a square wave.

```
*********************************
SCILAB script to add together successive Sin Waves of differing amplitudes and frequencies
each diagram is drawn by adding the next odd harmonic.
*********************************
t=0:0.01:5;
s=zeros(t);
for i=1:2:9
  s=s+1/i*sin(i*%pi*t);
  subplot(5,1,(i+1)/2);
  plot2d(t,s,axesflag=5)
  xtitle(['Building the Square Wave One frequency at a time.'])
end
*********************************
```

As a second example consider the function described in Equation(3.2). The plot of this wave along with the SCILAB script is shown in Figure 3.2. This plot is drawn in the same manner as we drew the square wave plot in Figure 3.1. Each succeeding plot adds one more term to build the function. The reader will easily be able to imagine that the plot is that of a saw tooth wave.

$$x(t) = Sin(\omega t) - \tfrac{1}{2}Sin(2\omega t) + \tfrac{1}{3}Sin(3\omega t) - \tfrac{1}{4}Sin(4\omega t) + \tfrac{1}{5}Sin(5\omega t) ..... \tag{3.2}$$

```
*********************************
SCILAB script to build the Saw-Tooth wave.
*********************************
t=0:0.01:5;
s=zeros(t);
for i=1:1:5
  s=s+(-1)^(i+1)*1/i*sin(i*%pi*t);
  subplot(5,1,i);
  plot2d(t,s,axesflag=5)
  xtitle(['Building the Sawtooth Wave One frequency at a time.'])
end
*********************************
```

These two examples show us without a doubt that it is possible to build various different periodic functions using only simple harmonically related trigonometric functions. Next we turn our attention to the conditions that the functions that can be represented by harmonically related trigonometric functions must satisfy.

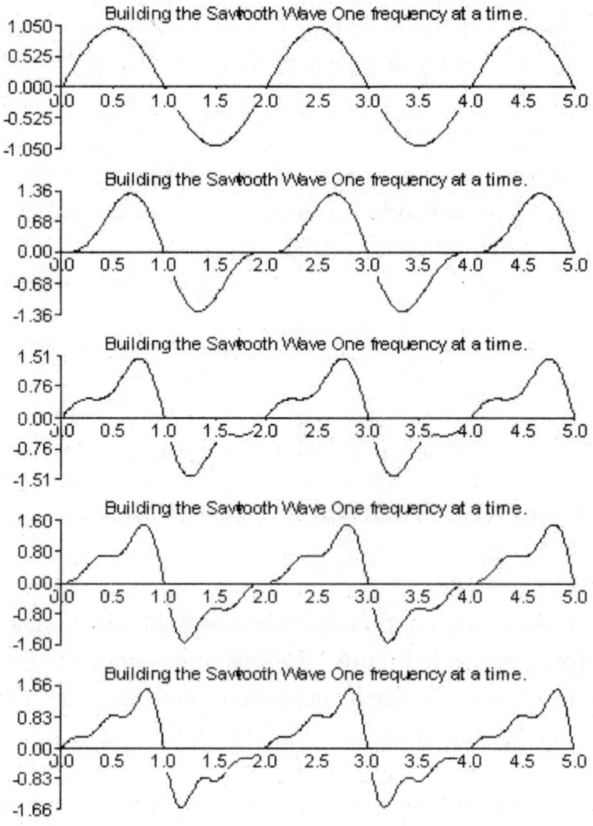

Figure 3.2: In this figure we build a Sawtooth wave by alternately adding and subtracting the first five harmonics one at a time. Shape of the wave is seen.

3.1.1 The Dirichlet Conditions

We have just seen that it is definitely possible to represent some periodic function by adding together harmonically related trigonometric functions. Here we examine the conditions, which if present in a function, do permit the function to be represented by harmonically related trigonometric functions. There are three conditions and together they are known as the **Dirichlet Conditions.**

- **The discontinuities that may be present in a function must be finite.** In other words the function must be absolutely integrable or that the function must be bounded. A function such as tan(nπt) or cotan(nπt) has an unbounded value and hence it cannot be represented by harmonically related trigonometric functions.

• **The number of discontinuities in a function must be finite.** In other words if there are any jumps in the value of the function then there are only a finite number of such jumps in the function. A function that has an infinite number of discontinuities no matter how small cannot be represented by the Fourier series.

• **The number of maximums and the number of minimums that can be present in the function must be finite.** In other words the number of times the function reaches its maximum value or its minimum value is finite. Consider the function of Figure 3.1, in each cycle it reaches its maximum value only a few times. Such a function can be represented by harmonically related trigonometric functions. On the other hand a function such as Cos(nπ/t), this function would have an infinite number of maximums or minimums in the range $0<t<1$. This function cannot be represented by harmonically related trigonometric functions.

Any function that satisfies all the three Dirichlet conditions can be represented by harmonically related trigonometric functions. These conditions are sufficient but all the conditions are not necessary. What this means is that any function that meets these conditions can definitely be represented by the Fourier series. But there are functions that do not satisfy all the conditions and yet can be represented by the Fourier series. The necessary conditions (the conditions that each and every function must satisfy to be represented by harmonically related trigonometric functions) to represent a function by its Fourier series are not yet known.

3.1.1.1 Some important integrals that we will need:

When we integrate either Sin(nw_0t) or Cos(nw_0t) over one complete cycle we know that the result is zero. There are some special integral relations when the two functions are multiplied together. These relations are integral relations shown in Equation(3.3); Equation(3.4) and Equation(3.5):

$$I_1 = \int_T Sin(m\omega_0 t)Sin(n\omega_0 t)dt = \begin{cases} 0 & m \neq n \\ T/2 & m = n \end{cases} \tag{3.3}$$

$$I_2 = \int_T Cos(m\omega_0 t)Cos(n\omega_0 t)dt = \begin{cases} 0 & m \neq n \\ T/2 & m = n \end{cases} \tag{3.4}$$

$$I_3 = \int_T Sin(m\omega_0 t)Cos(n\omega_0 t)dt = 0 \ for \ \forall \ n, m \tag{3.5}$$

You remember from Chapter 1 the conditions that functions must satisfy to be orthogonal and/or orthonormal. Since the integrals evaluate as shown the functions Sin($n\omega_0t$) and Cos($n\omega_0t$) are orthogonal functions. To make the functions orthonormal the integral should evaluate to 1 when n = m in integrals I_1 and I_2. The integrals in Equation(3.3) and Equation(3.4) will evaluate to 1 if we multiply each integral by the factor 2/T. So the factor that makes the functions orthonormal is 2/T.

3.1.2 The Trigonometric Fourier series

What Fourier suggested is that a function that satisfies all the given conditions (the Dirichlet conditions) can be represented in the integral square sense (refer to the Generalized Fourier Series in Section 3.4 for a more detail view of the integral square sense) by a sum of infinite harmonically related trigonometric functions. Harmonically related means that the period of the fundamental function in the infinite series is an integral multiple of the period of any of the other functions. So if the period of the fundamental is T then the period of the nth harmonic is T/n. We can also make a similar statement about the frequency relation. If the frequency of the fundamental is f_o then the frequency of the nth harmonic is nf_o. We can say this in another way thus: in one period of the fundamental we have n periods of the nth harmonic. What Fourier showed us is that any function can be represented as shown in Equation(3.6).

$$f(t) = a_0 + \sum_{n=1}^{\infty} a_n Cos(n\omega_0 t) + \sum_{n=1}^{\infty} b_n Sin(n\omega_0 t) \tag{3.6}$$

In Equation(3.6) when we are able to evaluate the constant a_0 and the two infinite sequence of constants a_n and b_n then we will have all the information that we need to represent the signal f(t) in its Fourier representation. The procedure of evaluating these infinite coefficients is very straight forward and does not involve any new techniques. All you need to know is to integrate by parts some simple functions. The necessary equations to evaluate the Fourier coefficients are shown in Equation(3.7); Equation(3.8) and Equation(3.9). Each one of the three equations evaluates one of the three sets of coefficients. In all the three equations, T is the period of the function f(t), it is also the period of the fundamental Sin or Cosine wave used to evaluate the constants a_n and b_n. All the three integrals that we evaluate are over one period of the periodic function which is also the period of the fundamental. When we evaluate these three integrals and obtain the constants a_0, a_n and b_n we will have determined the **Trigonometric Fourier Series** for the function f(t).

$$a_0 = \frac{1}{T} \int_{t_0}^{t_0+T} f(t)dt \tag{3.7}$$

$$a_n = \frac{2}{T} \int_{t_0}^{t_0+T} f(t) Cos(n\omega_0 t)dt \tag{3.8}$$

$$b_n = \frac{2}{T} \int_{t_0}^{t_0+T} f(t) Sin(n\omega_0 t)dt \tag{3.9}$$

It is easy to see how we get these three equations. First if we integrate the Fourier series definition in Equation(3.6) over one period of the fundamental we get Equation(3.10). Completing this integration will give us Equation(3.7). All the integrations in Equation(3.10) are over an integral number of cycles for every value of n. Since the integrals are over a complete cycle it does not matter where in time we begin the integration. Also since a_n and b_n are both constants the 2nd and the 3rd integrals in Equation(3.10) on the right hand side are both zero for every value of n. This is because the integral of either the Sine or the Cosine over any complete cycle is zero. Hence we get the result for a_0 in Equation(3.7). Remember that a_0 is also a constant.

$$\int_{t_0}^{t_0+T} f(t)dt = \int_{t_0}^{t_0+T} a_0 dt + \int_{t_0}^{t_0+T} \sum_{n=1}^{\infty} a_n Cos(n\omega_0 t)dt + \int_{t_0}^{t_0+T} \sum_{n=1}^{\infty} b_n Sin(n\omega_0 t)dt \tag{3.10}$$

Next we multiply the definition in Equation(3.6) by $Cos(m\omega_0 t)$ and then integrate this over one period of the fundamental. This will give us Equation(3.11). All the integrations in Equation(3.11) is over an integral number of cycles for every value of n and any specific value of m. Also since a_0, a_n and b_n are all constants the 1st and the 3rd integrals on the right hand side are both zero for any value of m and n. In the second integral on the right hand side, when n ? m the result of integration will be equal to zero, when n = m then and only then the integral will have a non zero value.

$$\begin{aligned} \int_{t_0}^{t_0+T} f(t)Cos(m\omega_0 t)dt &= \int_{t_0}^{t_0+T} a_0 Cos(m\omega_0 t)dt \\ &+ \int_{t_0}^{t_0+T} \sum_{n=1}^{\infty} a_n Cos(m\omega_0 t)Cos(n\omega_0 t)dt \\ &+ \int_{t_0}^{t_0+T} \sum_{n=1}^{\infty} b_n Cos(m\omega_0 t)Sin(n\omega_0 t)dt \end{aligned} \tag{3.11}$$

So by choosing a specific value for m we are able to evaluate a specific constant a_n where n = m. This way by choosing different values of m we get the result for all the a_n terms in Equation(3.8)

Finally we multiply the definition in Equation(3.6) by $Sin(m\omega_0 t)$ and then integrate the function over one period of the fundamental. This will give us Equation 3.7. The integration in Equation(3.12) is over an integral number of cycles for every value of n and any specific value of m. Also since a_0, a_n and b_n are all constants the 1st and the 2nd integrals on the right hand side are both zero for any value of m and n. In the third integral on the right hand side, when $n \neq m$ the result of integration will be equal to zero, when n = m then and only then the integral will have a non zero value. So by choosing a specific value for m we are able to evaluate a specific constant b_n where n = m. This way by choosing different values of m we get the result for all the b_n terms in Equation(3.9).

$$\int_{t_0}^{t_0+T} f(t)Sin(m\omega_0 t)dt = \int_{t_0}^{t_0+T} a_0 Sin(m\omega_0 t)dt$$

$$+ \int_{t_0}^{t_0+T} \sum_{n=1}^{\infty} a_n Sin(m\omega_0 t)Cos(n\omega_0 t)dt$$

$$+ \int_{t_0}^{t_0+T} \sum_{n=1}^{\infty} b_n Sin(m\omega_0 t)Sin(n\omega_0 t)dt \tag{3.12}$$

One example will show us right away how to use the results that we have just obtained. Here we will develop the trigonometric Fourier series for the function shown in Figure 3.3. We begin by determining the value for the coefficient a_o. For this we will evaluate the equation in Equation(3.7). This is shown in Equation(3.13). We integrate from t=-1 to t=3 as this covers one complete cycle. On your own you should integrate from t=0 to t=4 as this also covers one complete cycle. When you are done with the integration you should come up with the same answer for the constant a_0. This shows that you can select any/most convenient complete cycle to complete your integration.

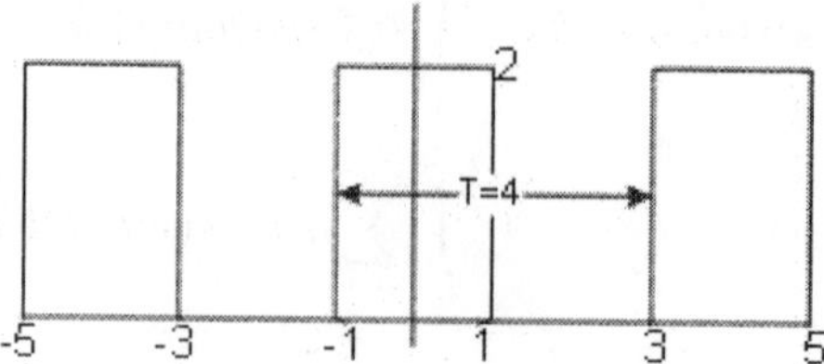

Figure 3.3: A square periodic function whose Trigonometric Fourier series is determined in the Example

$$a_o = \frac{1}{4}\int_{-1}^{3} f(t)dt = \frac{1}{4}\int_{-1}^{1} 2dt = \frac{4}{4} = 1 \tag{3.13}$$

Next we will evaluate the constants a_n. For this we will first multiply the function f(t) by $\cos(m\omega_o t)$ and then integrate. This is shown in Equation(3.14). In Equation(3.14) we have made use of the fact that $Sin(-m\omega_o t) = -Sin(m\omega_o t)$. Here also you should determine the coefficients a_n by completing the integral from t=0 to t=4 as you did before when you determined the constant a_0.

$$a_n = \frac{2}{4}\int_{-1}^{3} f(t)Cos(m\omega_0 t)dt = \frac{2}{4}\int_{-1}^{1} 2Cos(m\omega_0 t)dt$$

$$= \frac{4}{4\, m\omega_0}\left[Sin(m\omega_0) - Sin(-m\omega_0)\right] \tag{3.14}$$

$$= \begin{cases} \dfrac{2Sin(m\omega_0)}{m\omega_0} & \text{when m is Odd} \\ 0 & \text{when m is Even} \end{cases}$$

Finally we will evaluate the constants b_n. For this we will first multiply the function f(t) by sin($m\omega_0 t$) and then integrate. This is shown in Equation(3.15). In Equation(3.15) we have made use of the fact that Cos($-m\omega_0 t$) = Cos($m\omega_0 t$). Here also you should determine the coefficients b_n by completing the integral from t = 0 to t = 4 as you did before when you determined the constant a_0 and the constants a_n.

$$b_n = \frac{2}{4}\int_{-1}^{3} f(t)\,Sin(m\omega_0 t)\,dt \tag{3.15}$$

$$= \frac{2}{4}\int_{-1}^{1} 2Sin(m\omega_0 t)\,dt$$

$$= \frac{4}{4m\omega_0}\left[Cos(m\omega_0) - Cos(-m\omega_0)\right] = 0$$

The plot of this Fourier series is shown using SCILAB in Figure 3.4. The SCILAB script is given below. We have drawn only the first five terms of the infinite number of terms which make up the complete Fourier series.

$$f(t) = \frac{8}{\pi^2}\left[\begin{array}{l} Sin((t-\tau)) - \frac{1}{3^2}Sin(3(t-\tau)) \\ \qquad + \frac{1}{5^2}Sin(5(t-\tau)) \\ \qquad - \frac{1}{7^2}Sin(7(t-\tau)) + \cdots \end{array}\right] \tag{3.16}$$

```
******************************
SCILAB script the plot the wave obtained using Equations(3.13); (3.14) and (3.15)
******************************
t=-5:0.001:5;y=ones(t);
for i = 1:2:9
  y=y+ 2*sin(i*%pi/2)/(i*%pi/2)*cos(i*%pi/2*t);
  subplot(5,1,(i+1)/2)
   plot2d(t,y)
  xtitle(['Building function in Figure 3.3 One frequency at a time.'])
end
******************************
```

From the plot of Figure 3.4 you may have noticed a few things that are rather odd. First we see ripples in the graph. We do not have these ripples in the plot of Figure 3.3. So what is going on? According to the Fourier series that we have developed, the number of terms that have to be added

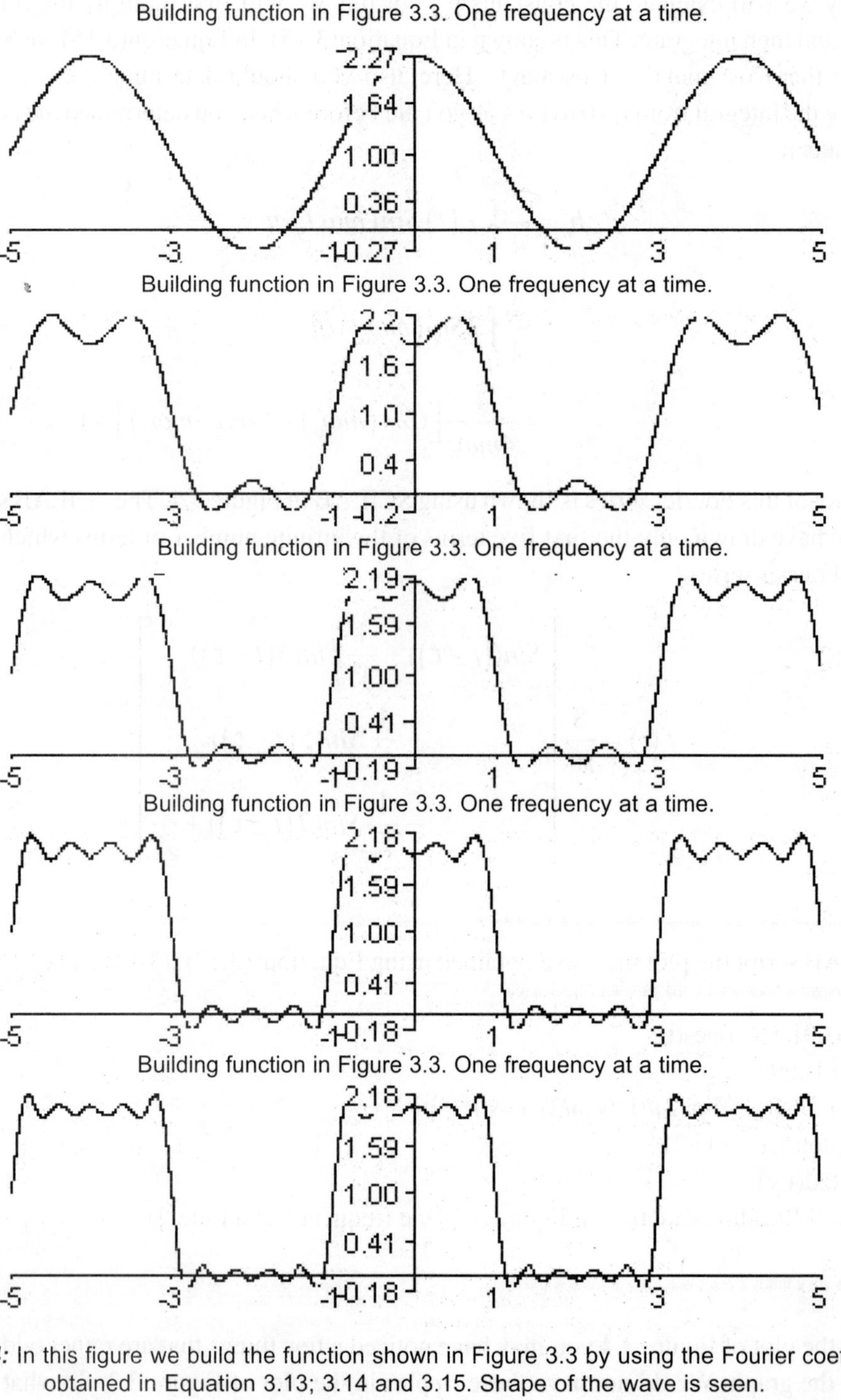

Building function in Figure 3.3. One frequency at a time.

Building function in Figure 3.3. One frequency at a time.

Building function in Figure 3.3. One frequency at a time.

Building function in Figure 3.3. One frequency at a time.

Building function in Figure 3.3. One frequency at a time.

Figure 3.4: In this figure we build the function shown in Figure 3.3 by using the Fourier coefficients obtained in Equation 3.13; 3.14 and 3.15. Shape of the wave is seen.

to duplicate the plot of Figure 3.3 is infinite. Here we have added only the first five terms and hence we see the ripples. As we add more and more terms the ripples will get closer and closer. This is evident from the first few terms that we have drawn. With infinite terms added the ripples will become a straight line.

Another thing that we notice is the sharp overshoots and undershoots at the discontinuities in the Figure of 3.4. The overshoot and undershoot appears to be more pronounced then just appearing from the ripples. These overshoots and undershoots are known as Gibbs phenomenon. We will talk about this in Section 3.1.4.

Example 3.1

Determine the Trigonometric Fourier series of the function shown in Figure Example 3.1.

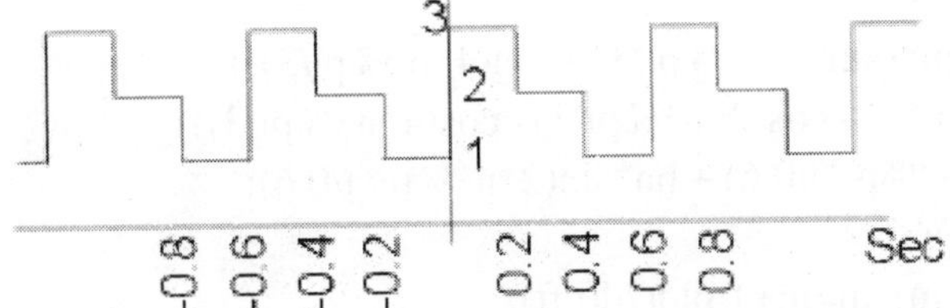

Figure Example 3.1: Compute the Trigonometric Fourier series of the function shown

Solution 3.1

Since we have to compute the Trigonometric Fourier series we will begin by computing the constant a_0.

The average value is computed as

$$a_0 = \frac{1}{0.6}\left[\int_0^{0.2} 3\,dt + \int_{0.2}^{0.4} 2\,dt + \int_{0.4}^{0.6} 1\,dt\right]$$

When we complete the evaluation of the three integrals we will get $a_0 = 2$

The coefficients a_n are computed by evaluating these three integrals.

$$a_n = \frac{2}{T_o}\left[\int_0^{0.2} 3\,Cos\left(\frac{2n\pi t}{T_o}\right)dt + \int_{0.2}^{0.4} 2\,Cos\left(\frac{2n\pi t}{T_o}\right)dt + \int_{0.4}^{0.6} Cos\left(\frac{2n\pi t}{T_o}\right)dt\right]$$

When we evaluate the three integrals we get the coefficient a_n to be

$$a_n = \frac{1}{n\pi}\left[Sin\left(\frac{2n\pi}{3}\right) + Sin\left(\frac{4n\pi}{3}\right)\right]$$

Similarly the coefficients b_n are computed by evaluating these three integrals.

$$b_n = \frac{2}{T_o}\left[\int_0^{0.2} 3\,Sin\left(\frac{2n\pi t}{T_o}\right)dt + \int_{0.2}^{0.4} 2\,Sin\left(\frac{2n\pi t}{T_o}\right)dt + \int_{0.4}^{0.6} Sin\left(\frac{2n\pi t}{T_o}\right)dt\right]$$

When we evaluate the three integrals we get the coefficient b_n to be

$$b_n = \frac{1}{n\pi}\left[2 - Cos\left(\frac{2n\pi}{3}\right) - Cos\left(\frac{4n\pi}{3}\right)\right]$$

The result of building the function is shown in Figure Solution 3.1 and the SCILAB script is given below.

```
****************************************
//Solution 3.1
****************************************
t=0:0.001:1.2;a0=2;
ft=a0*ones((t));m=1;
for n=1:1:100
  an=clean(1/n/%pi*(sin(2*n*%pi/3) + sin(4*n*%pi/3)));
  bn=clean(1/n/%pi*(2 - cos(2*n*%pi/3) - cos(4*n*%pi/3)));
  ft=ft+an*cos(2*n*%pi*t/0.6) + bn*sin(2*n*%pi*t/0.6);
  if (m==n/20) then
  subplot(100/20,1,m); m=m+1;plot2d(t,ft);
  end
end
```

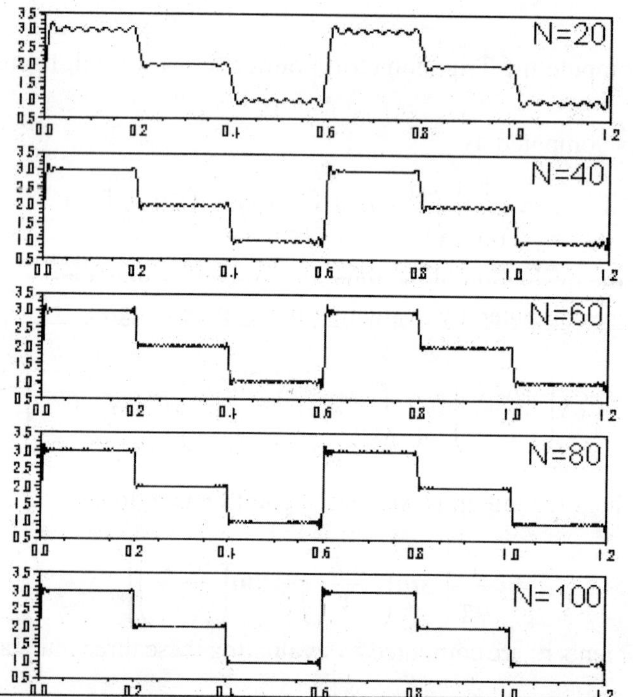

Figure Solution 3.1: The function of Example 3.1 is built up in increments of 20 terms added. Notice that the Gibbs phenomenon persists and the oscillations have the same amplitude at the discontinuities.

Example 3.2

How would you modify the Fourier series that you computed in Example 3.1 to determine the Fourier series of function shown in Figure Example 3.2?

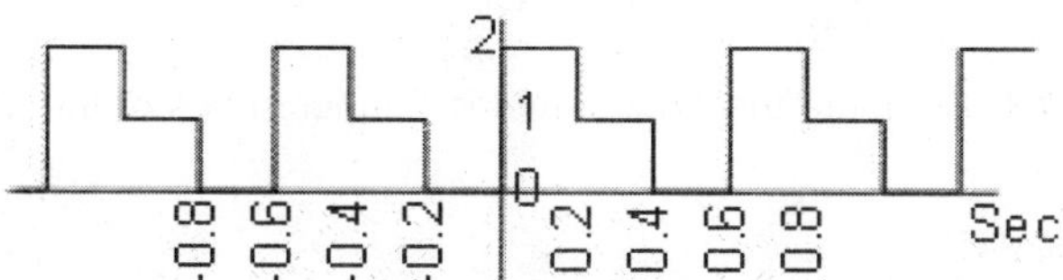

Figure Example 3.2: Compute the Trigonometric Fourier series of the function shown

Solution 3.2

When you compare the figures of Example 3.1 and Example 3.2 the only difference we see is that the function of Example 3.2 has a constant one volt of DC bias reduced when compared to the Figure for Example 3.1. The DC bias is reflected in the constant a_o so decreasing a_o by one, from 2 to 1 will give us the Fourier series for Example 3.2. The constants a_n and b_n stay the same. The constant a_o only affects the DC level present in the signal.

Example 3.3

How would you modify the Fourier series that you computed in Example 3.1 to determine the Fourier series of function shown in Figure Example 3.3?

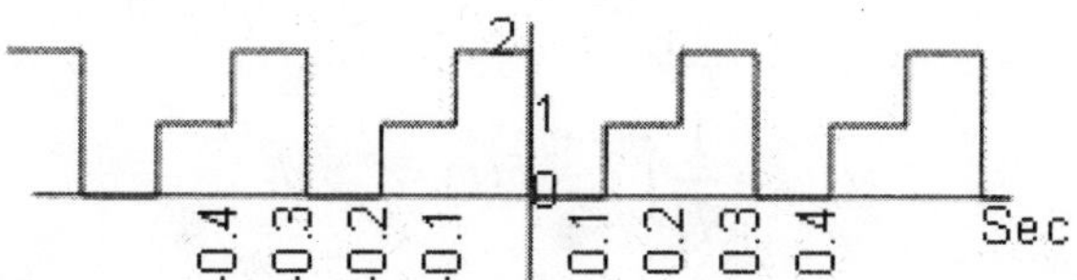

Figure Example 3.3: Compute the Trigonometric Fourier series of the function shown

Solution 3.3

When we compare the figures of Example 3.2 and that of Example 3.3 we see that they are mirror images of each other. A mirror image function of f(t) is formed by replacing t = -t so the Fourier series of Example 3.2 can be modified by changing t = -t to get the Fourier series of Example 3.3.

Example 3.4

How would you modify the Fourier series that you computed in Example 3.1 to determine the Fourier series of function shown in Figure Example 3.4?

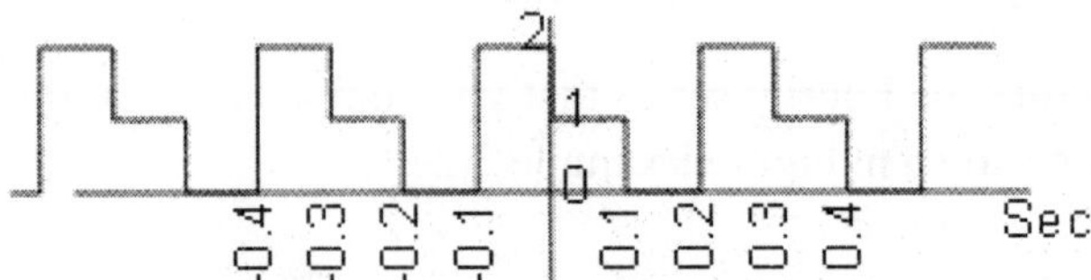

Figure Example 3.4: Compute the Trigonometric Fourier series of the function shown

Solution 3.4

Once again we see that there is a very direct relation between the Figure of Example 3.2 and that of Example 3.4. This time the relation is the advance of the figure by 2π/3 radians. So by advancing each harmonic by 2nπ/3 we get the Fourier series of the figure shown in Example 3.4. Notice that to shift each harmonic the proper amount we had to shift the harmonic by not just 2π/3 radians but by 2nπ/3 radians where n is the harmonic number.

The Fourier series in Complex Exponential Form. We have just seen the Fourier series in the trigonometric representation. The same series can also be represented in an alternate form. This is the exponential form. The two forms are related to each other and one can be derived from the other. So the two forms are just two different ways of representing the same information. The Fourier series in its exponential form is written as shown in Equation(3.17).

$$f(t) = \sum_{n=-\infty}^{\infty} \alpha_n e^{jn\omega_0 t} \tag{3.17}$$

$$\alpha_n = \frac{1}{T}\int_{t_0}^{t_0+T} f(t)e^{-jn\omega_0 t}\,dt \tag{3.18}$$

For the Fourier series in this representation we have to determine all the constants α_n. The constants are determined as shown in Equation(3.18). All the α_n constants are complex valued constants. They serve the same function as the a_0; a_n and b_n constants in the trigonometric Fourier series. They define the amplitude and the phase of each of the harmonic waves that make up the periodic waveform. The advantage of using the exponential Fourier series is that you need to evaluate only one integral and all the coefficients are known.

$$e^{\pm jx} = Cos(x) \pm jSin(x)$$
$$Sin(x) = \frac{e^{jx} - e^{-jx}}{2j} \qquad Cos(x) = \frac{e^{jx} + e^{-jx}}{2} \tag{3.19}$$

The exponential form of the Fourier series is related to the trigonometric form of the Fourier series because both the sine and the cosine functions can be expressed in terms of the exponential function. The basis of this relation is the Euler's Identity. This identity can be written as shown in

Equation(3.19). When we use the relations in Equation(3.19), the coefficient $2\alpha_n$ in Equation(3.18) equals a_n+jb_n in Equation(3.6) and $2\alpha_{-n}$ in Equation(3.18) equals $a_n - jb_n$ in Equation(3.6). Notice that with this relation the coefficients α_n and the coefficients α_{-n} are complex conjugates of each other so we get $\alpha_n = \alpha^*_{-n}$. That is the coefficients are complex conjugates of each other. This often helps in determining the α_n coefficients.

Example 3.5

Determine the exponential Fourier series for the square wave of Figure 3.3

Solution 3.5

The result is shown in Equation(3.20) below. We begin by determining the α_n coefficients. The α_n coefficients are determined in Equation(3.20)

$$\alpha_n = \frac{1}{4}\int_{-1}^{3} f(t)e^{-jn\left(\pi/2\right)t}dt = \frac{1}{4}\int_{-1}^{1} 2e^{-jn\left(\pi/2\right)t}dt$$

$$\alpha_n = \frac{2}{4}\left[\left.\frac{-e^{-jn\left(\pi/2\right)t}}{jn\left(\pi/2\right)}\right|_{-1}^{1}\right] = \frac{2}{4}\left[\frac{e^{\frac{jn\pi}{2}} - e^{-\frac{jn\pi}{2}}}{jn\left(\pi/2\right)}\right] \tag{3.20}$$

Recognizing that $e^{-jn(\pi/2)} = (-j)^n$ and $e^{jn(\pi/2)} = (j)^n$ allows us to re-write the expression in a simpler form. When n is even the α_n coefficients are zero and when n is odd the α_n coefficients alternate in sign. So

$$\alpha_n = \begin{cases} \dfrac{1}{n\pi}, n = 1, 5, 9, \cdots \\ \dfrac{-1}{n\pi}, n = 3, 7, 11, \cdots \end{cases} \quad and\ \alpha_0 = \frac{1}{4}\int_{-1}^{1} 2dt = 1 \tag{3.21}$$

In Equation(3.21) we have used the fact that

$$e^{-jn\left(\frac{\pi}{2}\right)} = \left(e^{-j\left(\frac{\pi}{2}\right)}\right)^n = \left(Cos\left(\frac{\pi}{2}\right) - jSin\left(\frac{\pi}{2}\right)\right)^n = (-j)^n \tag{3.22}$$

Now that we know α_n we can write the exponential Fourier series as

$$f(t) = \frac{1}{0.6}\sum_{n=-\infty}^{\infty} \alpha_n e^{\frac{-j2n\pi}{0.6}}$$

With the use of the exponential representation of the Fourier series we can visualize the Fourier coefficients as amplitude and phase. To do this we can write the α_n coefficients as $\alpha_n = |\alpha_n| e^{j\Phi_n}$. In this relation the magnitude of the α_n coefficient equals $|\alpha_n| = \sqrt{a_n^2 + b_n^2}$ and the phase

$\Phi_n = \tan^{-1}\left(\frac{\text{Im}(\alpha_n)}{\text{Re}(\alpha_n)}\right)$. The important significance of this can be understood by drawing the magnitude and the phase spectrum separately. The magnitude spectrum tells us the amplitude of each of the sine and the cosine waves that we must have. And the phase spectrum tells us by how much the particular sine wave is shifted in phase in relation to the fundamental.

Both the Fourier series; the trigonometric and the exponential Fourier series; are equal to each other as they should be. The work involved in using the exponential Fourier series is much less and the result is the same. I will recommend that you practice developing the exponential Fourier series as it requires less work. Since the exponential Fourier series uses complex numbers and complex algebra many students find it confusing. But a little bit of practice and you will have no difficulty in mastering this concept and you will also appreciate the ease of developing the exponential Fourier series.

Very often you might wonder how you can determine the frequency content that can be obtained from say a musical instrument. For example you might have a great interest in playing the sitar. This is a stringed instrument and you might wonder does it make any difference how much I pluck the string or if I pluck the string far from the center does the frequency output from the string change? Now you can just determine the Fourier series of the plucked string to determine the harmonic content. An astute student will naturally ask: the plucked string is not a periodic signal, so how do I determine its Fourier series? This is easily answered as shown in Example 3.6.

Example 3.6

If you had a non periodic signal and wanted to determine its Fourier coefficients then one common method used is to assume that the signal that you have is one period of an imaginary periodic signal. This concept is shown in Figure Example 3.6. Assume that a Sitar string is plucked and has the initial shape as shown in Figure Example 3.6. Determine the Fourier coefficients of the sitar note.

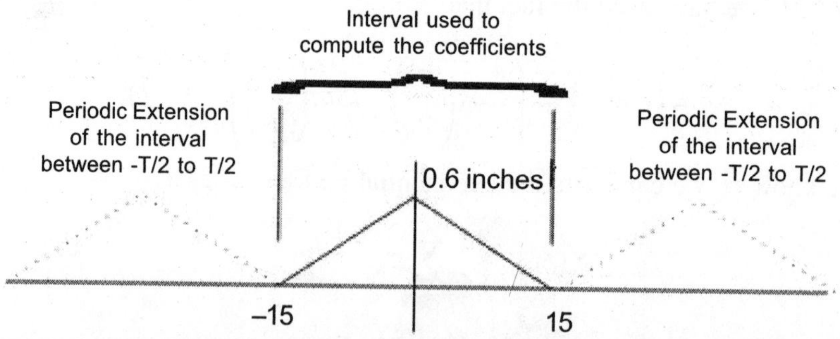

Figure Example 3.6: Extending the non periodic signal to obtain its Fourier coefficients. A plucked Sitar String

Solution 3.6

To evaluate the Fourier coefficients we integrate the function over one period which is from -T/2 to T/2 as shown below. We first evaluate the DC term a_0 as shown in Equation(3.23).

$$a_0 = \int_{-X/2}^{X/2} f(x)\,dx = \int_{-15}^{0}(0.04x+0.6)\,dx + \int_{0}^{15}(-0.04x+0.6)\,dx$$
$$= \left[\frac{0.04x^2}{2} + 0.6x\right]_{-15}^{0} + \left[\frac{-0.04x^2}{2} + 0.6x\right]_{0}^{15} \tag{3.23}$$
$$a_0 = (0+0-(4.5-9)) + (-4.5+9-0-0) = 9$$

Next to evaluate the coefficients a_n we multiply the function by $Cos(n\omega_0 x)$ and then integrate.

$$a_n = \int_{-X/2}^{X/2} f(x)\,Cos(n\omega_0 x)\,dx$$
$$= \int_{-15}^{0}(0.04x+0.6)\,Cos(n\omega_0 x)\,dx \int_{0}^{15}(-0.04x+0.6)\,Cos(n\omega_0 x)\,dx \tag{3.24}$$
$$= \frac{0.04xSin(n\omega_0 x)}{n\omega_0} + \frac{0.6Sin(n\omega_0 x)}{n\omega_0} + \frac{0.04Cos(n\omega_0 x)}{n^2\omega_0^2}\Bigg|_{-15}^{0}$$
$$+ \frac{(-0.04)xSin(n\omega_0 x)}{n\omega_0} + \frac{0.6Sin(n\omega_0 x)}{n\omega_0} + \frac{(-0.04)Cos(n\omega_0 x)}{n^2\omega_0^2}\Bigg|_{0}^{15}$$

When we substitute the limits and note that $\omega_0 = \frac{\pi}{15}$ we get all the a_n coefficients.

$$a_n = \frac{9}{n^2\pi^2}\left[1 - Cos(n\pi)\right] \qquad a_n = \begin{cases} 0 & \textit{when n is even} \\ \dfrac{18}{n^2\pi^2} & \textit{when n is odd} \end{cases}$$

Finally we determine the coefficients b_n. Following an exercise similar to Equation(3.24) except using Sin $(n\omega_0 x)$ we will find that all the b_n coefficients evaluate to zero. (Do not take my word for this. Prove it for yourself by evaluating the required integrals.) Now that we have all the coefficients available we are able to determine the spectrum of a sitar string so the Fourier series for the plucked sitar string will be as shown in Equation(3.25)

$$f(x) = 9 + \frac{18}{\pi^2}Cos\left(\frac{\pi x}{15}\right) + \frac{18}{9\pi^2}Cos\left(\frac{3\pi x}{15}\right) + \frac{18}{25\pi^2}Cos\left(\frac{5\pi x}{15}\right) + \frac{18}{49\pi^2}Cos\left(\frac{7\pi x}{15}\right) + \cdots \tag{3.25}$$

3.1.3 Gibbs Phenomenon:

The individual terms and the partial sum approximations for a square wave is shown in Figure 3.4. The behavior of the partial sum in the vicinity of the discontinuities at ±1, ±3 and ±5 is of particular interest to us here. We note that each partial sum approximation passes through the average value (mid point) of the discontinuity. This is a feature of the Fourier series convergence requirement. On both the sides of the discontinuity the approximation exhibits a ripple. (Overshoot or undershoot.) The sizes of this overshoot or undershoot remains constant. As the number of terms used to arrive at the approximation increases the maximum height of the ripple does not seem to change. In fact it has been shown that if only a finite number of terms are used to approximate the function at a discontinuity the ripple stays at 9%. This is shown in Figure 3.5.

This ripple in the partial sum of a Fourier series is known as the Gibbs Phenomenon in honor of the mathematical physicist J. Willard Gibbs. He was the first to explain this phenomenon in 1899. The square wave satisfies the Dirichlet conditions and so we know that the Fourier series approximation ultimately converges to the square wave for all the values of t except at the discontinuities. From Figure 3.5 we see that for any given number of terms in the Fourier series the accuracy of the partial sum approximation increases and the approximation is best at times that are distant from the discontinuity. When examining the approximation near the discontinuity the approximation is worst. Examine Figure 3.5 to see the effect of Gibbs Phenomenon on the Fourier series of a square wave drawn with various numbers of terms used. Each successive plot in Figure 3.5 uses 9 additional terms but the amount of overshoot or the amount of undershoot at the discontinuity does not change from the first plot to the last plot.

3.1.4 Least Squares Approximation property of Fourier Series:

Very often students wonder why or how can an infinite sum of smooth functions approximate a discontinuous function as we have seen in all the figures so far. Another fact that the students wonder is if the Gibbs phenomenon always persists, as we showed in the previous section, then at what stage will the Fourier series represent the function? The answer to these and many other questions are tied together and the answer lies in the Least Squares approximation property of the Fourier series. It can be explained as follows: How would you measure the error between the function f(t) and its Fourier series approximation. In order to measure this error we will approximate the function f(t) by a finite number of its harmonics instead of the infinite harmonics that the Fourier series requires. Then we will measure the error between the finite approximation and the infinite representation. For this reason define the approximation of the function limited to terms from -N to N as shown in Equation(3.26):

$$f_N(t) = \sum_{n=-N}^{N} \beta_n e^{jn\omega_o t} \tag{3.26}$$

In this approximation we want to select the coefficients β_n in such a way that the mean square error resulting from the approximation is minimized. The error function ε is defined as $\varepsilon(t) = f(t) - f_N(t)$. This equation can be written as

$$\varepsilon(t) = \sum_{n=-\infty}^{\infty} \alpha_n e^{jn\omega_o t} - \sum_{n=-N}^{N} \beta_n e^{jn\omega_o t} = \sum_{n=-\infty}^{\infty} \sigma_n e^{jn\omega_o t} \tag{3.27}$$

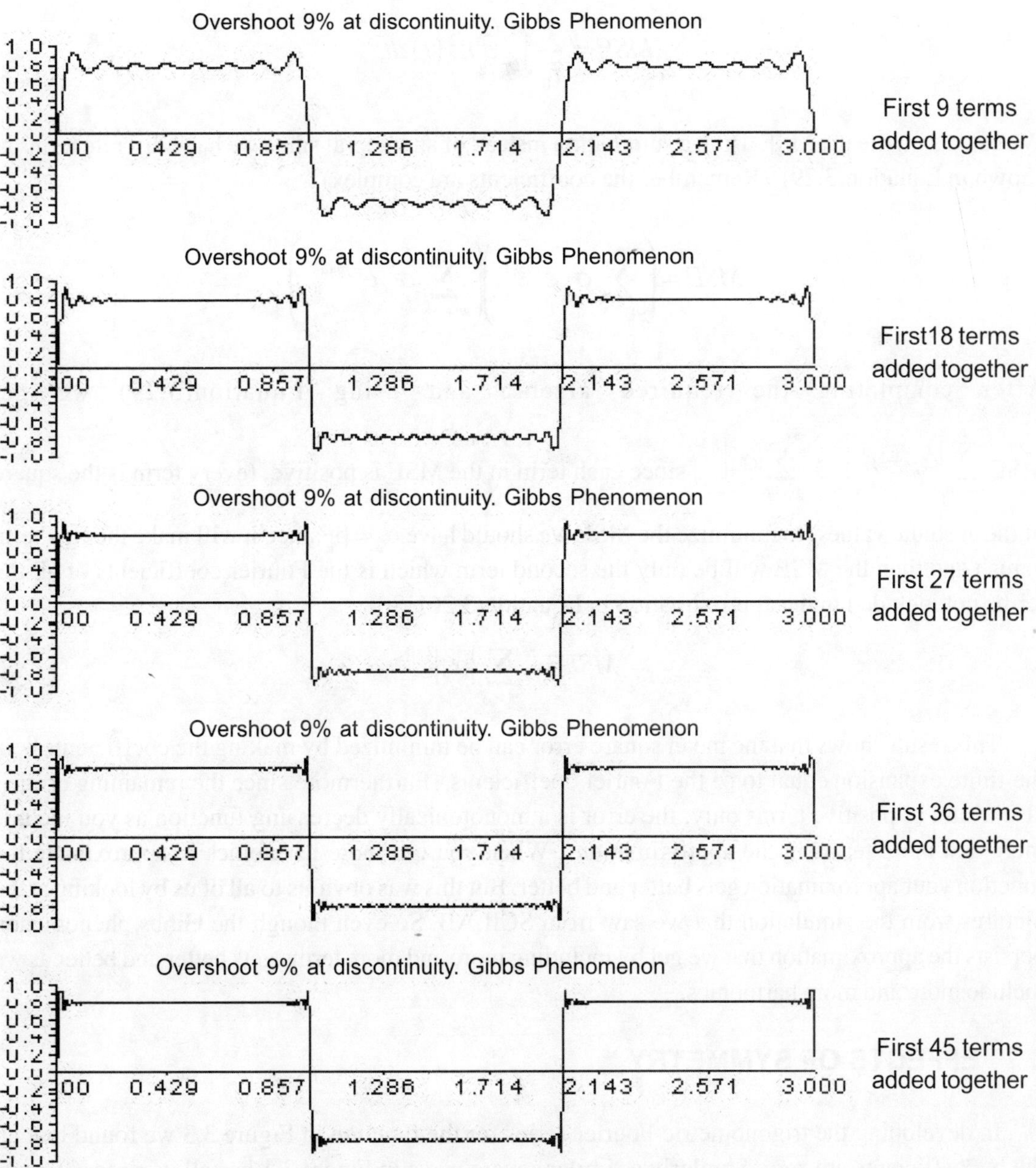

Figure 3.5: Plot of Square wave being built. Presence of Gibbs Phenomenon is very obvious from the various plots

In Equation(3.27) $\sigma_n = \alpha_n - \beta_n$ for $\{-N \le n \le N\}$ and $\sigma_n = \alpha_n$ for $N < |n|$. Now that we have the error function defined we want to see what it will be in one period of the original function, so we define the Mean Square Error as shown in Equation(3.28)

$$MSE = \frac{1}{T_0}\int_{-T_0/2}^{T_0/2} \varepsilon^2(t)\,dt \tag{3.28}$$

We can also write the MSE using a summation instead of an integral since we have discrete terms as shown in Equation(3.29). (Remember the coefficients are complex).

$$MSE = \left(\sum_{n=-\infty}^{\infty} \sigma_n e^{jn\omega_0 t}\right)\left(\sum_{m=-\infty}^{\infty} \sigma_m^* e^{-jm\omega_0 t}\right) \tag{3.29}$$

After completing the required algebra and using Equation(3.29) we get MSE $\sum_{n=-N}^{N}|\alpha_n - \beta_n|^2 + \sum_{|n|>N}|\alpha_n|^2$, since each term in the MSE is positive, (every term is the square of the absolute values) to minimize the MSE we should have $\alpha_n = \beta_n$ since it will make the first term vanish and then the MSE will be only the second term which is the Fourier coefficients of all the terms not included in the approximation in Equation(3.26). So

$$MSE = \sum_{|n|>N} |\alpha_n|^2 \tag{3.30}$$

This result shows that the mean square error can be minimized by making the coefficients β_i in the finite expansion equal to αi the Fourier coefficients. Furthermore since the remaining error is also a sum of positive terms only; the error is a monotonically decreasing function as you include more and more terms in the approximations. When you use more harmonics to approximate the function your approximation gets better and better. But this was obvious to all of us by looking at the pictures from the simulation that we saw from SCILAB. So even though the Gibbs phenomenon persists the approximation that we get by including more and more terms gets better and better as we include more and more harmonics.

3.2 EFFECTS OF SYMMETRY

In developing the trigonometric Fourier series for the function in Figure 3.3 we found that all the b_n coefficients are zero. Similarly a similar square wave in Figure 3.1 has all its a_n coefficients equal to zero. An astute student will ask "Is there a pattern that we can recognize which permits us to say when either the a_n or the b_n sequence of coefficients will be zero?" The answer to this question is obviously yes and it can be found in the symmetry of the function f(t). There are two main types of symmetry that will simplify our task in evaluating the coefficients. There are other subtypes of symmetry also. They also reduce the work involved somewhat but the effort spent in trying to identify the symmetry is almost the same as the effort spent in evaluating the Fourier series without resorting to the symmetry conditions. So we will concentrate only on the Odd symmetry and the Even symmetry. We will not concern ourselves with the half-wave and the quarter-wave symmetry.

3.2.1 Even Function

A function is said to have even symmetry when f(t) = f(-t). Functions that satisfy this property are said to be even functions. The term Even is used because polynomial functions with only even exponents possess this property. For even periodic functions the Fourier coefficients b_n are all zero. This is because the b_n coefficients are the coefficients of the odd functions (Sin). So when you want to determine the Fourier series of an even function you need to only determine the a_0 and the a_n coefficients for functions that possess even symmetry. An even function can be recognized from the plot of the function by placing an imaginary mirror vertically on the Y-axes. If the reflection that you see in the mirror is the same as the function on the other side of the mirror (the reflection and the function on the other side overlap) then the function you have is the even function. When you have an even function you can integrate over only half the period of the waveform instead of the entire period of the waveform. When the integration is done you double the value of each of the coefficients. Sometimes this saves you an additional integration. This is the only advantage we gain. The figure of an even function is shown in Figure 3.6 along with the equations that evaluate the a_0 and the a_n coefficients. Notice that to determine the Fourier series of the function we have integrated only from t = 0 to t = 5 instead of from t = 0 to t = 10 or from t = -5 to t = 5 which is the entire period. This is done in Example 3.7.

Example 3.7

Determine the Fourier series of the even symmetric function shown in Figure 3.6.

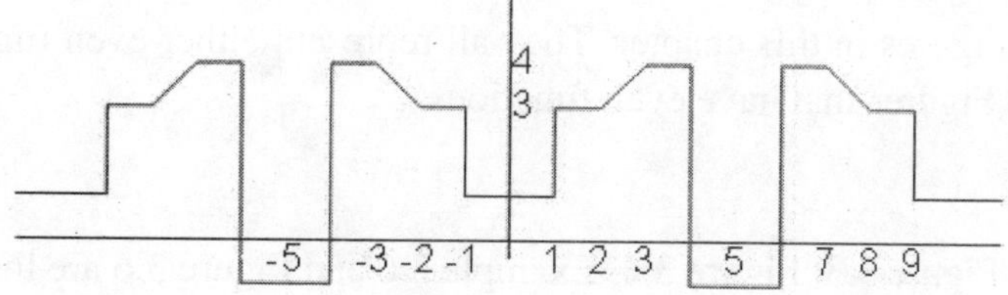

Figure 3.6: Diagram of an even function whose Fourier series is to be determined

Solution 3.7

We first determine the constant a_0 as shown in Equation(3.31). Notice that since the function is even and symmetric we have integrated it over only half the period and doubled the result. This is because the function is symmetric and even.

$$a_0 = \frac{2}{10}\left[\int_0^1 1\,dt + \int_1^2 3\,dt + \int_2^3 (t+1)\,dt + \int_3^4 4\,dt + \int_4^5 -1\,dt\right]$$

$$a_0 = \frac{2}{10}\left[1+3+\left(\frac{t^2}{2}+t\right)_2^3 +4-1\right] = 2.1 \tag{3.31}$$

Similarly we can determine the a_n coefficients as shown in Equation(3.32). Notice here also we have doubled the result and determined the integrals only for half the period.

$$a_n = \frac{4}{10}\left[\begin{array}{l}\int_0^1 1Cos(n\omega_0 t)\,dt + \int_1^2 3Cos(n\omega_0 t)\,dt + \int_2^3 (t+1)\,Cos(n\omega_0 t)\,dt \\ \qquad + \int_3^4 4Cos(n\omega_0 t)\,dt + \int_4^5 -1Cos(n\omega_0 t)\,dt\end{array}\right]$$

$$a_n = \frac{4}{10}\left[\begin{array}{l}Sin(n\omega_0) + 3Sin(2n\omega_0) - 3Sin(n\omega_0) \\ \quad +4Sin(3n\omega_0) - 4Sin(2n\omega_0) + \frac{1}{n\omega_0}Cos(3n\omega_0) \\ \quad -\frac{1}{n\omega_0}Cos(2n\omega_0) + 4Sin(4n\omega_0) \\ \quad -4Sin(3n\omega_0) - Sin(5n\omega_0) + Sin(4n\omega_0)\end{array}\right] \tag{3..32}$$

And finally because of even symmetry all the b_n coefficients will be zero. So we do not have to attempt to determine them. On your own you should verify that integrating the function over the entire period (and not doubling the result) will give you the same result as the one obtained in Equation(3.31) and Equation(3.32)

Example 3.8

Examine all the Figures in this chapter. They all represent either even functions or odd functions. Identify all the Figures that have even functions.

Solution 3.8

The functions in Figure 3.3, Figure 3.4, Example 3.6 and Figure 3.6 are the even functions.

3.2.2 Odd Function

A function is said to have odd symmetry when f(t) = -f(-t). Functions that satisfy this property are said to be odd functions. The term Odd is used because polynomial functions with only odd exponents possess this property. For odd periodic functions the Fourier coefficients a_n are all zero (this does not necessarily apply to a_0). This is because the a_n coefficients are the coefficients of the even functions (Cosin). Since the term a_0 represents the average value, it is neither even nor odd, so it may be present or it may be absent in an even function or an odd function. When you have an odd function you need to only determine the a_0 and the b_n coefficients for functions that possess odd symmetry. You need to determine a_0 as it represents the dc or the average or the offset value. The coefficient a_0 will be zero if the waveform is symmetric about the x-axes. An odd function can be recognized from the plot of the function by placing two imaginary mirrors vertically on the Y-axes and the X-axes. If the reflection that you see in the corner at the origin is the same as the function on the other side of the corner in the mirror (the reflection and the function on the other side overlap) then the function you have is an odd function. When you have an odd function you can integrate only over half the period of the waveform instead of the entire period of the waveform, then you have to double the value of each of the b_n coefficients. The figure of an odd function is shown in Figure 3.7 along with the equations that evaluate the a_0 and the b_n coefficients. Notice also that we have integrated only for half the period which is from t = -2 to t = 1 instead of from t = -2 to t = 4 which is the entire period.

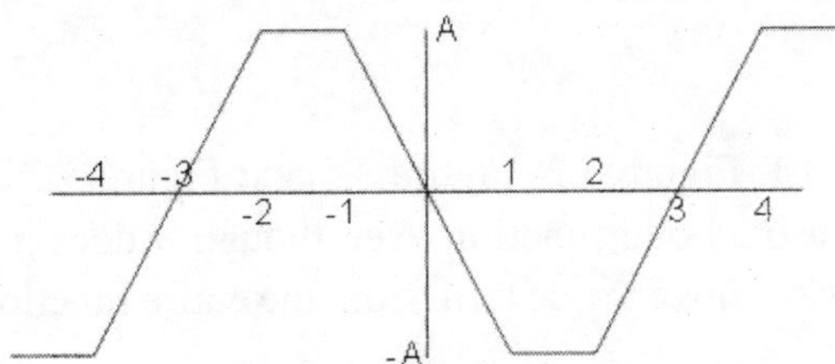

Figure 3.7: Diagram and the Fourier series of an odd function

Example 3.9

Determine the Fourier series of the odd symmetric function shown in Figure 3.7.

Solution 3.9

We first determine the constant a_0 as shown in Equation(3.33). Notice that it is also zero in this example since the function is symmetric about the X-axis. The average value being zero has nothing to do with the function itself being odd or even. To determine the constant for the even function integrate over the entire period not just half the period.

$$a_0 = \int_{-2}^{-1} A\,dt + \int_{-1}^{1} -At\,dt + \int_{1}^{2} (-A)\,dt + \int_{2}^{4} A(t-3)\,dt$$

$$a_0 = At\Big|_{-2}^{-1} - A\frac{t^2}{2}\Big|_{-1}^{1} - At\Big|_{1}^{2} + A\left(\frac{t^2}{2} - 3t\right)\Big|_{2}^{4} = 0 \qquad (3.33)$$

Next since we know that this is an odd function we do not need to determine all the a_n coefficients since they are all zero. Finally we will determine the b_n coefficients as shown in Equation(3.34).

Here we will integrate over only half the period and then double the coefficient to get the exact value of the b_n coefficients.

$$b_n = \frac{4}{T}\left[\int_{-2}^{-1} ASin(n\omega_0 t)\,dt + \int_{-1}^{1}(-At)\,Sin(n\omega_0 t)\,dt\right]$$

$$b_n = \frac{4}{T}\left[\left(\frac{-A}{n\omega_0}Cos(n\omega_0 t)\Big|_{-2}^{-1}\right) + \left(\frac{-At}{n\omega_0}Cos(n\omega_0 t)\Big|_{-1}^{1}\right) - \left(\frac{A}{n^2\omega_0^2}Sin(n\omega_0 t)\Big|_{-1}^{1}\right)\right] \tag{3.34}$$

$$b_n = \frac{4A}{2n\pi}\left[Cos\left(\frac{n\pi}{3}\right) + Cos\left(\frac{2n\pi}{3}\right) - \frac{6}{n\pi}Sin\left(\frac{n\pi}{3}\right)\right]$$

Example 3.10

Examine all the figures in this chapter. They all represent either even functions or odd functions. Identify all the figures that have odd functions.

Solution 3.10

The functions in Figure 3.1, Figure 3.2, Figure 3.5 and Figure 3.7 are the odd functions. The function in Example 3.1 is also an odd function even though it does not look like it satisfies the condition f(t) = -f(-t), but if we remove the dc term from the entire function we find that the function is an odd function.

3.3 PARSEVAL'S THEOREM

The information that this theorem gives us is that the energy or the power in a signal may be measured either in the frequency domain or in the time domain and that this measurement is the same in either domain. The Parseval's relation for Fourier series is given in Equation(3.35)

$$\text{E} = Energy\ in\ f(t) = \int_{t_0}^{t_0+T} |f(t)|^2\,dt = \sum_{-\infty}^{\infty} |\alpha_n|^2 \tag{3.35}$$

In Equation(3.35) the integral is in the time domain. The integral represents the energy in the function as we have seen earlier in Chapter 1 section 1.7. The summation in Equation(3.35) is the summation of the square of the Fourier coefficients of the function. So this relation tells us that we can determine the energy in the function either in the time domain or in the frequency domain. The Parseval's relation also enables us to identify the energy in a sub-band of frequencies or in a frequency range of interest. To determine the result for the Fourier series representation we will use the exponential representation of the Fourier series. The energy in one period of a continuous time signal in the time domain is given by:

$$E_f = \int_{t_0}^{t_0+T} |f(t)|^2 \, dt \tag{3.36}$$

In this expression if we replace the function f(t) by its Fourier representation as given in Equation(3.17) and repeated here $f(t) = \sum_{-\infty}^{\infty} \alpha_n j^{-jn\omega_0 t}$ we get Equation(3.36). If we substitute this in the equation for Energy we get Equation(3.37)

$$E_f = \int_{t_0}^{t_0+T} f(t) f^*(t) dt = \int_{t_0}^{t_0+T} f(t) \left[\sum_{-\infty}^{\infty} \alpha_n^* e^{jn\omega_0 t} \right] dt \tag{3.37}$$

In Equation(3.37) we have assumed a complex valued function as this is the most general type of a function, further since we are replacing for the function f*(t) we have used the complex conjugate of the Fourier series. Since Equation(3.37) is a well behaved equation we can interchange the order of the summation and the integration. Doing this we get Equation(3.38)

$$E_f = \sum_{-\infty}^{\infty} \alpha_n^* \underbrace{\int_{t_0}^{t_0+T} f(t) e^{jn\omega_0 t} \, dt}_{\text{Defination of } a_n} = \sum_{-\infty}^{\infty} \alpha_n^* \alpha_n = \sum_{-\infty}^{\infty} |\alpha_n|^2 \tag{3.38}$$

Equation(3.38) shows that the energy in the time domain function f(t) can be obtained from its Fourier coefficients. The quantity $|\alpha_n|^2$ is referred to as the Energy Spectrum. From the Energy Spectrum if we choose only a few coefficients in a narrow band of frequencies then we would get the energy in that narrow band of frequencies. Say coefficients n for n = ±10 then we will get the energy in the frequency range of the first ten harmonics. Thus Parseval's relation gives us a means of determining energy in a band of frequencies. It was by this relation that the telephone company was able to determine that most of the energy of the voice signal lies in the frequency range of 300 Hz to 3000 Hz and hence limit the telephone transmission to that frequency range instead of using the entire frequency spectrum.

Example 3.11

Determine the power in the fundamental and the first 10 harmonics in the function of Figure Example 3.1.

Solution 3.11

The Fourier series for the function of Example 3.1 is repeated here.

$$a_n = \frac{1}{n\pi}\left[Sin\left(\frac{2n\pi}{3}\right) + Sin\left(\frac{4n\pi}{3}\right)\right] \text{ and } b_n = \frac{1}{n\pi}\left[2 - Cos\left(\frac{2n\pi}{3}\right) - Cos\left(\frac{4n\pi}{3}\right)\right].$$

If we examine all the a_n terms closely we find that they are all zero. So we only need the b_n coefficients to determine the power in the signals. The power in the first 10 harmonics is given in the table below.

Harmonic Number	Power in this harmonic	Power in the signal so far.
One	1.43	1.43
Two	0.72	2.15
Three	0.48	2.63
Four	0.36	2.99
Five	0.29	3.28
Six	0.28	3.56
Seven	0.20	3.76
Eight	0.18	3.94
Nine	0.16	4.10
Ten	0.14	4.24

We can clearly see that the increase in power in each succeeding harmonic is decreasing. It is for this reason that after the first few harmonics we begin to see the correct shape of the function. Most of the power of the function is already contained in the first few harmonics. The total power in the periodic signal is 4.666 so we are approaching the total power very quickly.

3.4 THE GENERALIZED FOURIER SERIES

The Fourier series that we have just studied and the Fourier Transform that we will study in the next chapter are tools for resolving power and energy signals in terms of individual fundamental components. When we want to represent the energy or the power in the Fourier series we are able to identify the energy or the power in say the nth harmonic. We are able to do this because the nth harmonic does not interfere with any other harmonic. A rather neat way of saying this is that all the harmonics are mutually perpendicular to each other. The projection of any one harmonic on any other harmonic is identically equal to zero. This is known as the property of Orthogonality. We saw this in Chapter 1 and here we see how it is used to develop the Fourier series.

Another way to look at the property of Orthogonality is to look at a vector in three dimension space. The vector in three dimension space is made up of the x-component, the y-component and the z-component. The projection of the x-component on either the y-component or the z-component is zero. So the x-component is orthogonal to the y-component and the z-component. This is shown in Figure 3.8.

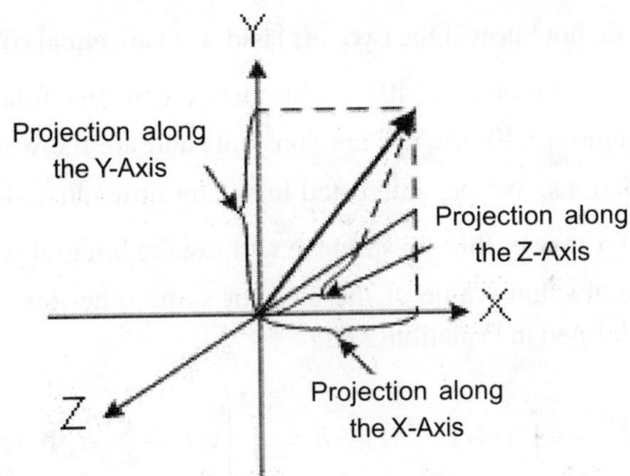

Figure 3.8: Three Orthogonal projections of a vector in three dimensional space.

Just as in Figure 3.8 the X-component of the vector has no effect on the Y-component of the vector and the Z-component of the vector. In the same way any one harmonic of a periodic wave has no effect on any other harmonic of the periodic wave since all the harmonics are orthogonal to each other.

$$\int_{t_0}^{t_0+T} \Phi_n(t)\Phi^*_m(t)dt = \begin{cases} 0 & n \neq m \\ finite & n = m \end{cases} \tag{3.39}$$

Two functions are orthogonal to each other if they satisfy Equation(3.39). Equation(3.39) says: Take two similar functions (functions from the same class of functions) and integrate the product of one function and the complex conjugate of the other function. If the result of the integration satisfies the conditions shown in Equation(3.39) then the two functions are orthogonal. When the two functions are orthogonal to each other then the integral shown in Equation(3.39) is zero. When the functions are not orthogonal then the integral is not zero. If in Equation(3.39), the integral of the functions $\Phi_n(t)$ and its conjugate are normalized then the finite result of the integration when n=m is equal to 1 and the functions are said to be orthonormal.

To develop a generalized Fourier series we will try to represent the function y(t) in terms of the fundamental orthonormal functions as shown in Equation(3.40). Equation(3.40) says that we have the function y(t) and we want to represent it in its components. To do this we will try to represent this function as a sum of different amplitude orthogonal functions as

$$y(t) = \sum_{n=1}^{N} d_n \Phi(t).$$

Equation(3.40) suggests us a way to see if this representation is indeed true. So

$$y(t) \overset{?}{=} \hat{y}(t) = \sum_{n=1}^{N} d_n \Phi_n(t) \tag{3.40}$$

Since right now we do not know if the two $y(t)$ and $\hat{y}(t)$ are equal so we have placed a question mark over the equal sign. So Equation(3.40) is a question, are the two functions $y(t)$ and $\hat{y}(t)$ equal to one another? In Equation(3.40) the d_n's are constants and are the weights assigned to the individual orthonormal functions. We are interested in seeing how close the two functions $y(t)$ and $\hat{y}(t)$ are to each other. To answer this question we will use the integral square error. This is a much better measure than the absolute value of the error or some other similar measure of error. The integral square error is defined in Equation(3.41)

$$error = \mathcal{E}_n = \int_{t_0}^{t_0+T} \left|y(t) - \hat{y}(t)\right|^2 dt = \int_{t_0}^{t_0+T} \left|y(t) - \sum_{n-1}^{N} d_n \Phi_n(t)\right|^2 dt \tag{3.41}$$

Expanding the square in the last integral in Equation(3.41) and noting that in general y(t), d_n and Φ_n can all be complex quantities we get Equation(3.42) where the * next to any quantity denotes that this is the complex conjugate of that quantity. Multiplying out the two square brackets in Equation(3.42) we get Equation(3.43)

$$\mathcal{E}_n = \int_{t_0}^{t_0+T} \left[y(t) - \sum_{n=1}^{N} d_n \Phi_n(t)\right]\left[y^*(t) - \sum_{n=1}^{N} d_n^* \Phi_n^*(t)\right] dt \tag{3.42}$$

Equation(3.43) makes use of the fact that the Φ_n's are orthonormal to each other. So when the product $\Phi_n(t)\Phi_n^*(t)$ is integrated we get a '1' also the result when $\Phi_n(t)\Phi_m^*(t)$ are integrated is a zero. These results are obtained since Φ_n's are orthonormal functions.

$$\mathcal{E} = \int_{t_0}^{t_0+T} |y(t)|^2 dt - \sum_{n=1}^{N}\left[d_n^* \int_{t_0}^{t_0+T} y(t)\Phi_n^*(t)dt + d_n \int_{t_0}^{t_0+T} y(t)^* \Phi_n(t)dt \right] + \sum_{n=1}^{N} |d_n|^2 \tag{3.43}$$

Next we want to complete the square in Equation(3.43). To do this we will add and subtract the quantity $\sum_{n=1}^{N}\left|\int_{t_0}^{t_0+T} y(t)\Phi^*(t)dt\right|^2$. After adding and subtracting the factor and completing the required algebra (it is much easier if you work backward from Equation (3.44) to (3.43)) we get Equation(3.44).

$$\mathcal{E} = \int_{t_0}^{t_0+T} |y(t)|^2 dt - \sum_{n=1}^{N}\left|\int_{t_0}^{t_0+T} y(t)\Phi_n^*(t)dt\right|^2 + \sum_{n=1}^{N}\left|d_n - \int_{t_0}^{t_0+T} y(t)\Phi_n^*(t)dt\right|^2 \tag{3.44}$$

When we examine Equation(3.44) we see that it consists of three absolute value squared terms, we will examine the last term first. This term is always positive as it is a squared term. Since this term is always positive it will always increase the error by whatever value it has. The smallest that this term can be is zero. So to minimize the error (without considering the first two terms for now) we must make this last term go to zero. No matter what the first two terms are the last term must be made to go to zero to have the error as small as possible. To make the last term go to zero we must choose the d_n coefficients as shown in Equation(3.45)

$$d_n = \int_{t_0}^{t_0+T} y(t)\Phi_n^*(t)dt \qquad n = 1,2,3\ldots N \tag{3.45}$$

This choice of the d_n coefficients minimizes the error function. The d_n coefficients are known as the generalized Fourier Coefficients. With this choice of the d_n coefficients the error is given in Equation(3.46). In Equation(3.46) we have substituted the d_n terms in place of the integral since they are equal to each other.

$$\mathcal{E} = \int_{t_0}^{t_0+T} |y(t)|^2\, dt - \sum_{n=1}^{N} |d_n|^2 \tag{3.46}$$

We often wish the error to be zero. Can this error ever go to zero? Yes this error can and does go to zero for a special choice of functions Φ_n's. This set of Φ_n's is referred to as a complete set. The trigonometric functions that we have used earlier in this chapter (the Sin and the Cos terms as well as the exponential terms) are one example of the complete set of functions. When the functions Φ_n's are a complete set the error can go to zero so we get Equation(3.47)

$$\underset{N\to\infty}{\text{Limit}}\ \mathcal{E}_{n,\min} = 0 \ \text{ Gives us}$$

$$\int_{t_0}^{t_0+T} |y(t)|^2\, dt = \sum_{n=1}^{N\to\infty} |d_n|^2 \tag{3.47}$$

Equation(3.47) I am sure you will recognize as the Generalized Parseval's Theorem and Equation(3.47) as the Generalized Fourier Series. This is interesting stuff. These equations tell us that we can choose any set of orthogonal functions and represent any periodic signal in terms of the orthogonal functions that we have chosen. Go back to the end of Chapter 1 and refer to the various different orthogonal functions that we have listed. Since these functions are orthogonal it is possible to expand any function in terms of these orthogonal functions also. So we are not limited to the Sin and the Cos functions

3.5 CHAPTER SUMMARY

Fourier Series:

The Fourier series permits us to represent a periodic signal by an infinite sum of sine and cosine functions. Each of the sine and the cosine functions are harmonically related to the fundamental. The period of the fundamental is the same as the period of the periodic signal.

The Dirichlet Conditions:

A function that satisfies the Dirichlet conditions can be represented by a Fourier series. The Dirichlet conditions are sufficient conditions. The necessary conditions for a function to be represented by its Fourier series are not yet known.

The Dirichlet conditions can be stated in layman terms as: The function will have a finite number of maximums (and/or minimums) in one period; the function will have a finite number of discontinuities (jumps) in one period and each of these discontinuities is finite.

The Fourier series is not unique for a function. You can easily define two functions that have identical Fourier series. As an example define one function with a discontinuity. At the discontinuity define the function to be equal to the low value of the discontinuity. For a function that is different but having the same Fourier series change the definition of the function at the discontinuity to some other value. Any other value will do. Now the two functions have identical Fourier series but the two functions are different.

The Trigonometric Fourier series:

The definition of the trigonometric Fourier series is given in Equation(3.6). In the definition the coefficient a_0 represents the average value of the function. This parameter either lifts of drops the entire function. The coefficients a_n's represent the coefficients of the Cosine harmonic waves. These coefficients are the coefficients of the even functions. The coefficients b_n's represent the coefficients of the Sine harmonic waves. These coefficients are the coefficients of the odd functions.

When a phase shift is added to each of the harmonic terms the entire function is shifted to the right or the left. The phase shift that is added to each harmonic is proportional to the harmonic number so the phase shift added to the fundamental is θ then the phase added to the nth harmonic will be nθ. If the phase is not added in this way the function that you will get is different from the original function.

The Exponential Fourier series:

This is just another way of representing the Fourier series. The Trigonometric and the Exponential Fourier series are related to each other. The magnitude $|\alpha_n| = \sqrt{a_n^2 + b_n^2}$ and the phase $\Phi_n = \tan^{-1}\left(\dfrac{\text{Im}(\alpha_n)}{\text{Re}(\alpha_n)}\right)$. The Exponential Fourier series permits us to plot the magnitude and the phase spectrum of the periodic signal.

Gibbs Phenomenon:

When we replace a function by its Fourier series we need an infinite number of terms. When we are approximating the function by a reduced number of terms in the Fourier series, we see that where ever there is a discontinuity there are overshoots and undershoots present. The overshoot and undershoot are about 9% and they stay the same when we use only finite terms from the Fourier series. Only when we use infinite terms will the Gibbs phenomenon vanish. The Gibbs phenomenon shows up only when we truncate the Fourier series to a finite number of terms.

The Effects of Symmetry:

Symmetry of the waveform permits us to determine the Fourier series by integrating only over half the period of the waveform. The other half is symmetrical so it is identical to the first half. Hence, in a symmetrical wave we determine the coefficient over half the period and just double the appropriate coefficient to get the proper value of the coefficient.

We have explored two kinds of symmetry: Even symmetry exists when the function exhibits $f(t) = f(-t)$. In the text we identified this kind of symmetry by placing a mirror vertically on the Y-axis and looking at the reflection. Odd symmetry exists when the function exhibits $f(t) = -f(-t)$. In the text we identified this kind of symmetry by placing a mirror vertically on the Y-axis and on the X-axis and looking at the reflection in the corner thus formed. When we have an even symmetric waveform then the b_n coefficients are all zero and only the a_n coefficients need to be determined. When we have an odd symmetric waveform then the a_n coefficients are all zero and only the b_n coefficients need to be determined.

Parseval's Theorem:

This theorem relates the energy or the power in a signal in the time domain to the Fourier coefficients. Now we have means of determining the energy or the power in a signal in either the time domain or in the frequency domain. This relation also permits us to determine energy or the power of a signal in a sub-band of frequencies. To determine the power in a sub-band of frequencies we use the Fourier coefficients only on these frequencies.

The Generalized Fourier series:

The general theory tells us that we do not have to use the sine or the cosine functions only. To represent a function in the form of a series we first need to find a complete set of orthonormal functions. Sine and cosine are only one example. Other functions that can be used are the Bessel functions, Walsh functions and many other functions.

The Generalized Fourier series also shows us that the Fourier series is derived by minimizing the integral square error. So if we do not use the entire infinite sequence of the orthonormal functions there will be some error. This is obvious when we compare Figure 3.3 with Figure 3.4. In Figure 3.4 we have used only five terms and hence we have error. But we see that Figure 3.4 shows what the function will look like very quickly.

3.6 HOMEWORK PROBLEMS

Orthogonal and Orthonormal Functions.

Problem 3.6.1

Prove the Cos($2n\omega_0 t$) is orthogonal to Cos($m\omega_0 t$). That is show that when $m = 2n$ the integral is non zero, and when $m \neq 2n$ the integral is zero. What is the scaling factor that would make it an orthonormal function?

Problem 3.6.2

Prove the Sin($n\omega_0 t$) is orthogonal to Sin($5m\omega_0 t$). That is show that when $m = 5n$ the integral is non zero, and when $m \neq 5n$ the integral is zero. What is the scaling factor that would make it an orthonormal function?

Problem 3.6.3

Prove the Sin($3n\omega_0 t$) is orthogonal to Cos($2m\omega_0 t$) for all values of n and m. That is show that when $2m = 3n$ the integral is zero, and that the integral is zero also when $2m \neq 3n$.

Trigonometric Fourier Series

Problem 3.6.4

Determine the trigonometric Fourier series for the three square waves shown in Figure P3.6.4. Is it possible to deduce the Fourier series of the second function from the Fourier series of the first? Is it possible to deduce the Fourier series of the third from the Fourier series of the first and also from the second? In general is it possible to obtain the Fourier series of any one from the Fourier series of any other? Explain how? (Hint: Each waveform is obtained by shifting the previous waveform by 90^0. For more help refer to the Fourier series in Examples 1, 2, 3, 4 in this chapter).

Problem 3.6.5

Determine the Exponential Fourier series for the three Triangle waves shown in Figure P3.6.5. Is it possible to deduce the Fourier series of the second function from the Fourier series of the first? Is it possible to deduce the Fourier series of the third from the Fourier series of the first and also from the second? In general is it possible to obtain the Fourier series of any one from the Fourier series of any other? Explain how? (Hint: Each waveform is obtained by shifting the previous waveform by 90^0. For more help refer to the Fourier series in Examples 1, 2, 3, 4 in this chapter).

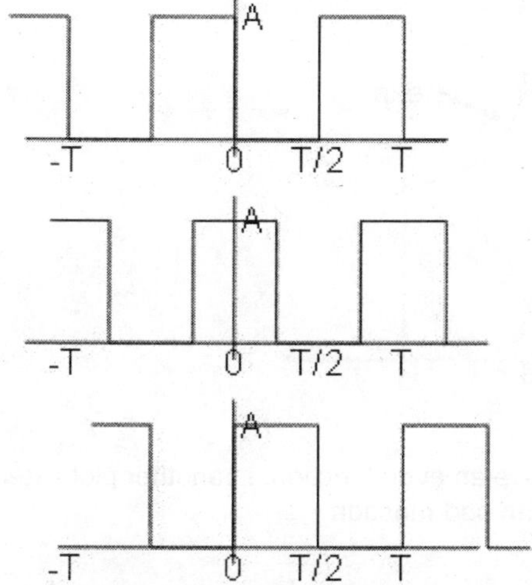

Figure P3.6.4: Three similar square waves. Related by 90° phase shift.

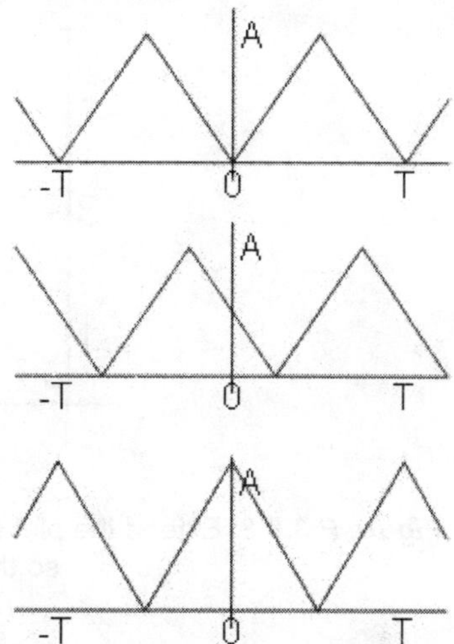

Figure P 3.6.5: Three similar Triangle waves. Related by 90° phase shift.

Problem 3.6.6

Identify which plot in Figure P3.6.4 is an even function and which plot is an odd function. Use the concept of even function and odd function to determine the trigonometric Fourier series for all three plots in Figure P3.6.4. Are the functions related by the shift relation? Show that the functions are related by a phase shift relation.

Problem 3.6.7

Identify which plot in Figure P3.6.5 is an even function and which plot is an odd function. Use the concept of even function and odd function to determine the trigonometric Fourier series for all three plots in Figure P3.6.5. Are the functions related by the shift relation? Show that the functions are related by a phase shift relation.

Even and Odd Functions

Problem 3.6.8

Only a part of a waveform is drawn in Figure P3.6.8. Complete the periodic waveform using the plot drawn as a starting point and knowing that the plot is supposed to be (a) an even function (b) an odd function.

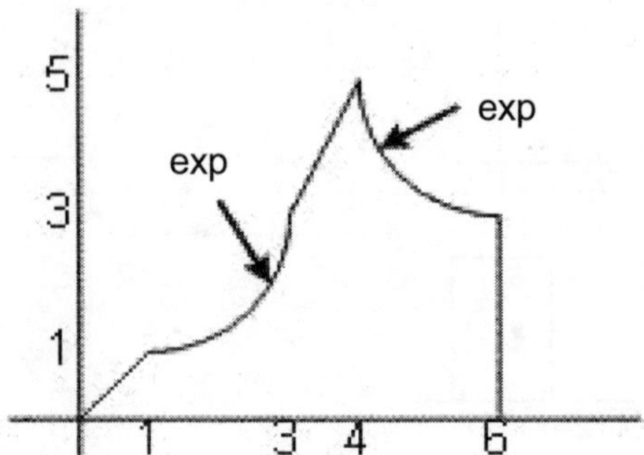

Figure P 3.6.8: Extend the plot so that you have an even function. In another plot extend so that you have an odd function

Properties of the Fourier Series.

Problem 3.6.9

In Problem 3.6.4 you determined the relation between Fourier coefficients of waves that were shifted in Phase. For this example assume that all the waveform of Problem 3.6.4 is scaled so that the period is now 2T. (The period of all the waveforms in problem 3.6.4 is T) What is the Fourier series of the scaled function? What will be the Fourier series if the period was ½T. Is it possible to write the Fourier series of the scaled function directly from the Fourier series of the original function? (Write the Fourier series without actually computing the Fourier Series).

Problem 3.6.10

In Problem 3.6.5 you determined the relation between Fourier coefficients of waves that were shifted in Phase. For this example assume that all the waveform of Problem 3.6.5 is scaled so that the period is now 2T. What is the Fourier series of the scaled function? What will be the Fourier series if the period was ½T. Is it possible to write the Fourier series of the scaled function directly from the Fourier series of the original function? (Write the Fourier series without actually computing the Fourier Series).

Problem 3.6.11

Determine the Fourier series of the three functions shown in Figure 3.6.11.

Problem 3.6.12

Functions 'A' and 'B' in Figure 3.6.11 are added together to form function 'C' in Figure P 3.6.11. Show that the Fourier series of function 'C' is the sum of the Fourier series of functions 'A' and 'B'.

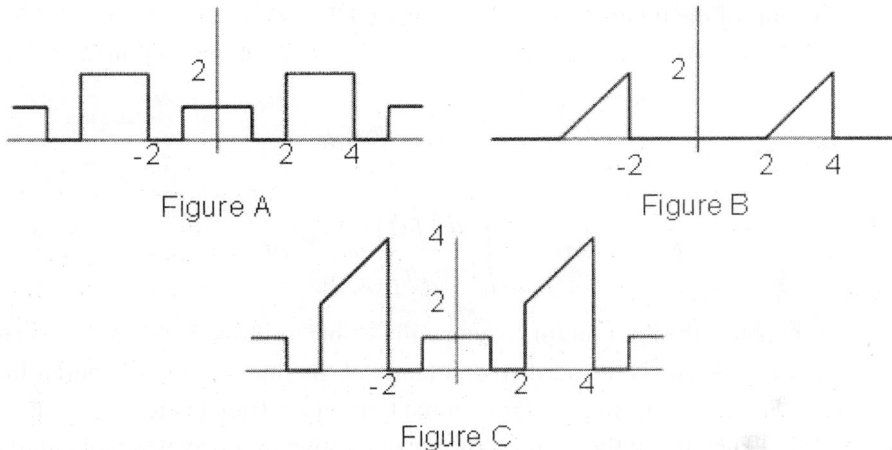

Figure P 3.6.11: Determine the Fourier series of Figures A; B; and C. Show that the sum of the Fourier series of Figures A and B equals the Fourier series of Figure C.

Problem 3.6.13

Some other properties of symmetry for Fourier series are specific to the form of the Fourier series. Prove the following properties for the Exponential Fourier series.

- C_n is real and an even function of n if f(t) is real and even itself.
- C_n is imaginary and an odd function of n if f(t) is real and odd itself.

Problem 3.6.14

Using SCILAB build a function that is defined as $f(t) = 3S\,\text{in}(5\omega t) + 1Sin(35\omega t)$. What is the Fourier series of this function?

Problem 3.6.15

Determine the Fourier series of a function with a discontinuity such as the one shown in Figure 3.3. Determine the value of the Fourier series at the discontinuity. In Figure 3.3 determine the value of the Fourier series at t = 1, 3, 5, etc. In other words show that the Fourier converges to the average value at the discontinuity.

Problem 3.6.16

Fourier series has many interesting properties. One of the properties is that if a function has a derivative and the derivative is also a periodic function then the Fourier series of the derivative can easily be obtained from the Fourier series of the original function. Towards this end define α_n as the

Fourier coefficients of the function to be differentiated. Define α_n' as the Fourier coefficients of the differentiated function. Then the definition of α_n and α_n' is as shown in Equation(3.48).

$$\alpha_n = \int_{t_0}^{t_0+T} f(t)e^{-jn\omega_0 t}\,dt$$

$$\alpha_n' = \int_{t_0}^{t_0+T} \frac{d(f(t))}{dt} e^{-jn\omega_0 t}\,dt \tag{3.48}$$

When you evaluate the integral for α_n' you will be able to show that the relation between α_n and α_n' is $\alpha_n' = (jn\omega_0)\alpha_n$. Which is the derivative relation of the function in the Fourier integral.

Prove this relation by deriving the exponential Fourier coefficients for a triangle wave as shown in Figure P3.6.16. Then using the relation for the derivative of a waveform obtain the exponential Fourier coefficients for the square wave shown also in Figure P3.6.16.

The converse of the relation in Problem 3.6.16 is that there are two functions that are related by the integral relation. So define α_n as the Fourier coefficients of the function to be integrated. Define α_n' as the Fourier coefficients of the integrated function. Then the definition of α_n and α_n' is as shown in Equation(3.49). Evaluate the coefficients α_n' and determine the relation to the coefficients α_n.

$$\alpha_n = \int_{t_0}^{t_0+T} f(t)e^{-jn\omega_0 t}\,dt$$

$$\alpha_n' = \int_{t_0}^{t_0+T} \left[\int_{-\infty}^{\infty} f(t)dt\right] e^{-jn\omega_0 t}\,dt \tag{3.49}$$

Show that

$$\alpha_n = \begin{cases} \frac{4A}{(\pi n)^2} & \text{For all odd n} \\ 0 & \text{For all even n} \end{cases}$$

$$\alpha_n' = \begin{cases} \frac{2A}{|n|\pi} & n = \pm 1, \pm 5, \pm 9, \ldots \\ \frac{-2A}{|n|\pi} & n = \pm 3, \pm 7, \pm 11, \ldots \\ 0 & \text{n is even} \end{cases}$$

FigureP 3.6.16: Derive the Fourier Coefficients for the Square wave by using the relation in Equation (3.49)

Problem 3.6.17

Use SCILAB to plot the series

$f(t) = (2/\pi)[Cos(\omega_0 t)-1/3\ Cos(3\omega_0 t)+ 1/5\ Cos(5\omega_0 t)- 1/7\ Cos(7\omega_0 t)+ 1/9\ Cos(9\omega_0 t)]$

Comment on the similarity to the square wave drawn in Figure 3.1. Is f(t) an even function or an odd function? Can you comment on why this series is alternating while the series for the diagram 3.1 had all added terms?

Problem 3.6.18

Use SCILAB to plot the series given in Problem 3.6.17 but this time shift each frequency component by 45*n degrees where n represents the harmonic number of the frequency component. So the component $Cos(5\omega_0 t)$ becomes $Cos(5\omega_0 t+45*5^o)$. Comment on the resulting plot.

Problem 3.6.19

Use SCILAB to plot the series given in Problem 3.6.17 but this time replace the time t by -t. Comment on the resulting plot.

3.7 FURTHER READING

Fourier series is typically taught in the first or the second circuits class to Electrical Engineering students. At the time when Fourier series is taught the student is not quite ready to use this powerful tool. A typical student is able to use this tool only after he has a couple of system oriented classes under his belt. The topic of Fourier series can also be treated as a purely mathematical topic. So it is also covered in the Advanced Mathematics classes. Here I choose to cite reading material that is more mathematical in nature, the system relation and application of Fourier series is referred to in the reading material of the next chapter.

1. E Kreyszig. *Advanced Engineering Mathematics* 6th Edition J Wiley 1988
2. A Papoulis. *Signal Analysis* McGraw Hill 1977.

CHAPTER 4

Transform of Time Domain Signals

4.1 SPECTRUM OF PERIODIC SIGNALS

In this chapter we study several integral transforms. The chief among these is the Fourier Transform. Fourier transform plays a crucial role in any type of signal processing. Unlike the Fourier series which is essentially for periodic functions of time, the Fourier transform permits us to determine the frequency content of time limited signals. A time limited signal is present for a finite duration of time only. We know when it starts and when it ends. A periodic signal on the other hand is assumed to have been on since forever and is assumed to go on till forever. A periodic signal does not have a beginning or an end.

The Fourier integral may be viewed as the limiting form of the Fourier series. Consider what happens when you take one period of a periodic function, within this chosen period we leave the function as it is but outside this period we pad the function with zero values every all the way to infinity. Now you view this new function as a periodic function. What is the period of this function? Since one period of the function extends from $+\infty$ to $-\infty$ the period of this signal must be infinite! With this point of view the Fourier integral is useful for providing us with the spectral content of a pulse type of a signal or a time limited signal.

Just as we had to be careful to see what conditions are required for the Fourier series to converge we will also have to see what conditions the functions must satisfy for the Fourier integral converge. The Fourier integral converges only for a restricted class of signals, for this reason it does not find widespread use as it is but it forms a foundation for many, many other transforms. The Fourier integral however provides us an easy transition to more general transforms for system analysis. One of these general transforms is the Laplace transform. In this chapter we derive the Fourier transform and prove several of its properties and theorems we also develop several of the Fourier transform pairs. We will cover the Laplace Transform in the next chapter.

Both the Fourier series and the Fourier transform have similar properties and results and have a close resemblance to each other. I am sure that you expected this; we will deduce the Fourier transform from the Fourier series by stretching the period to infinity. There are many important applications where Fourier transforms can be used. Some applications that we will come across are analytically representing non periodic signals; solving differential equations; analyzing and processing signals for medical imaging; weather prediction; seismology; acoustic radar and sonar.

We finish this chapter with a related transform that is the Hilbert transform. The Hilbert Transform tries to tell us the relation between the real part and the imaginary part of the Fourier transform when you have a causal, stable, real signal. The relation is interesting in that it tells us that the real part and the imaginary part of the Fourier transform are related to each other when the time domain signal satisfies the causal, stable, real requirement.

4.2 THE FOURIER TRANSFORM

Recall from the Fourier series that the spectral components of a periodic signal were related by the harmonics of the fundamental. The various spectral lines of the periodic signal, in the frequency domain, are all separated by the frequency of the fundamental. As the period of the fundamental becomes larger, its frequency becomes smaller; hence the harmonics come closer to each other. This was apparent from the Fourier series of Figure 3.3 in the last chapter. To repeat this very important point let us calculate the Fourier series of Figure 4.1 then we will get a clear idea of the effect of the period on the Fourier series. The Fourier series for the pulse waveform in Figure 4.1 is given in the exponential format in Equation(4.1). The SCILAB script to draw this plot is also given below.

$$C_n = \frac{A\tau}{T}\frac{Sin(\frac{n\pi\tau}{T})}{\frac{n\pi\tau}{T}} = \frac{A\tau}{T}Sinc\left(\frac{n\pi\tau}{T}\right) \tag{4.1}$$

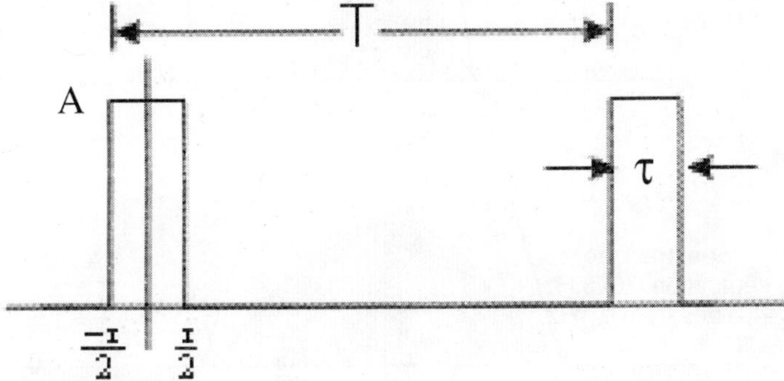

Figure 4.1: Pulse waveform to study the effect of increasing the period

```
***********************************
The SCILAB script to draw the Fourier series of
the pulse in Figure 4.1 with varying period.
***********************************
n=-80:1:80;
A=2;tau=1;T=10;
x1=(A*tau/T)*sinc(n*%pi*tau/T);
subplot(3,1,1)
plot2d3(n/T,x1,frameflag=6,axesflag=5)
x2=(A*tau/(2*T))*sinc(n*%pi*tau/(2*T));
subplot(3,1,2)
plot2d3(n/(2*T),x2,frameflag=6,axesflag=5)
x3=(A*tau/(4*T))*sinc(n*%pi*tau/(4*T));
subplot(3,1,3)
plot2d3(n/(4*T),x3,frameflag=6,axesflag=5)
```

Now let us draw the amplitude spectrum of Fourier series of the waveform of Figure 4.1. The spectrum is drawn in Figure 4.2. The three plots in Figure 4.2 are drawn as the period gets larger

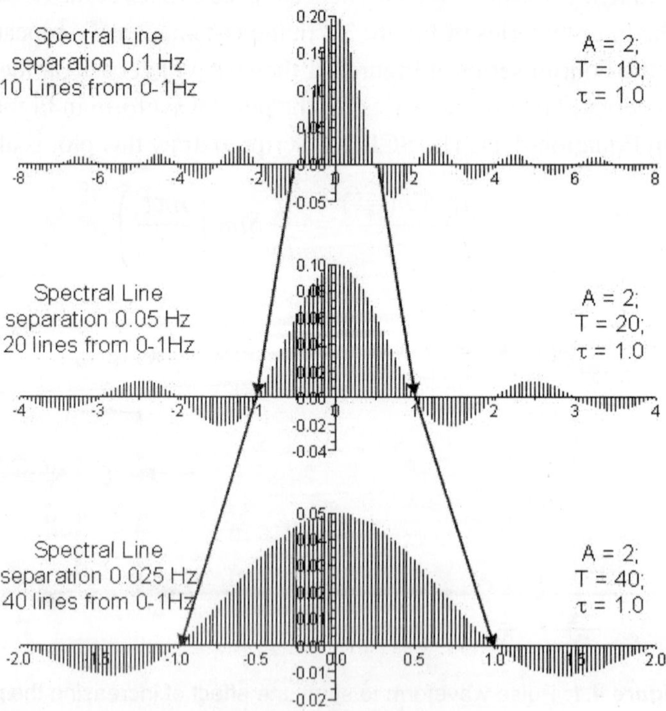

Figure 4.2: Fourier spectrum of a square pulse. The spectral lines get closer together as the period of the square pulse increases.

from T = 10.0 to T = 20.0 to T = 40.0. As T becomes larger the separations between the various harmonics becomes smaller and smaller. Thus the spectrum of the pulse train is getting tighter and tighter as the various harmonics get closer together with increasing T. We see this by counting the number of frequency pulses between 0Hz and 1Hz in all the three plots. We find that the number of harmonics that are present double since the period doubles. We could stretch the period of the pulse to infinity. If we stretch the period of the pulse T to infinity then the discrete harmonics become a continuous variation and the Fourier series becomes the Fourier Transform. This is shown mathematically in the following discussion.

The three diagrams in Figure 4.2 each show about 160 spectral lines. The frequency scale in each succeeding figure is expanded so the 160 spectral lines occupy a smaller and smaller frequency interval. Hence in each succeeding plot the spectral lines are getting closer together since the 160 spectrum lines occupy a smaller frequency interval; this happens because the period T of the time domain function is getting larger and larger.

Assume that we have a periodic signal that satisfies the Dirichlet conditions so it can be expanded in Fourier series. So we can write Equation 4.2.

Our goal here is to study the two equations given in Equation 4.2 as the period of the waveform becomes infinite. When the period starts to grow and becomes infinite the pulse train will become just one pulse at the origin. One pulse at the origin is a time limited signal as it begins at a specific time instant and it ends at a specific time instant.

$$x(t)=\sum_{n=-\infty}^{\infty} C_n e^{jn\omega_0 t}$$

$$C_n=\frac{1}{T_0}\int_{-\frac{T_0}{2}}^{\frac{T_0}{2}} x(t)e^{-jn\omega_0 t}\,dt \tag{4.2}$$

Let us examine how the infinite period alters the various different terms in Equation 4.2. First consider just the exponential function $e^{-jn\omega_0 t}$ in Equation(4.2). The quantity $n\omega_0$ changes by an amount ω_0 with every increment in the variable n. So as we change n by 1 we get $\Delta\omega_0 = (n+1)\omega_0 - n\omega_0 = \omega_0 = 2\pi/T_0$. This equation shows us that the incremental change in frequency becomes smaller and smaller as the period T_0 gets larger and larger. In the limit as $T_0 \to \infty$ the frequency differential $\Delta\omega$ becomes $d\omega$.

Next look at the quantity $n\omega_0$, as $T_0 \to \infty$ this quantity tends to $2\pi n/T_0 = nd\omega$. Since n is infinitely variable over all the integer values of n the factor $nd\omega$ becomes the continuous variable ω. We will make these replacements in Equation(4.2) which will transform Equation(4.2) to Equation(4.3). We have written Equation(4.3) after we multiply and divide Equation(4.2) by 2π to get it in the form that we need.

$$C_{n\infty} = \underset{T_0 \to \infty}{\text{Limit}} \frac{1}{2\pi} \frac{2\pi}{T_0} \int_{-\frac{T_0}{2}}^{\frac{T_0}{2}} x(t)\, e^{-jn\frac{2\pi}{T_0}t}\, dt$$

$$C_{n\infty} = \frac{1}{2\pi}\left[\int_{-\infty}^{\infty} x(t) e^{-j\omega t}\, dt\right] d\omega \tag{4.3}$$

In Equation(4.3) the function in the square brackets is the Fourier Transform of the function x(t) which is given in Equation(4.4)

$$F\{x(t)\} = X(\omega) = \int_{-\infty}^{\infty} x(t) e^{-j\omega t}\, dt \tag{4.4}$$

Using Equation(4.4) we can write the expression for $C_n = (1/2\pi)X(\omega)d\omega$. When we substitute this value for C_n into Equation(4.2) we can write the expression for the function x(t) as shown in Equation(4.5). The infinite summation becomes an integral as the variable ω is a continuous variable so we get Equation(4.5)

$$x(t) = \underset{T_0 \to \infty}{\text{Limit}} \sum_{-\infty}^{\infty} \frac{1}{2\pi} X(\omega) d\omega e^{jn\omega_0 t}$$

$$x(t) = \underset{T_0 \to \infty}{\text{Limit}} \frac{1}{2\pi} \sum_{-\infty}^{\infty} X(\omega) e^{jn\omega_0 t} d\omega = \frac{1}{2\pi}\int_{-\infty}^{\infty} X(\omega) e^{j\omega t} d\omega \tag{4.5}$$

These equations give us the Fourier transform relation. The relations are given in Equation(4.6). The relation identifies the frequency content in a time limited signal.

$$X(\omega) = \int_{-\infty}^{\infty} x(t) e^{-j\omega t}\, dt$$

$$x(t) = \frac{1}{2\pi}\int_{-\infty}^{\infty} X(\omega) e^{j\omega t}\, d\omega \tag{4.6}$$

To use the Fourier transform of a function we must first obtain the Fourier transform of that function. So let us examine how we compute the Fourier transform of some everyday signals that we are familiar with.

Example 4.1

Calculate the Fourier transform of the impulse δ(t).

Solution 4.1

The Fourier transform of an impulse is directly obtained by using the definition equation thus.

$$\mathbb{F}[\delta(t)] = \int_{-\infty}^{\infty} \delta(t) e^{-j\omega t}\, dt = e^{-j\omega 0} = 1$$

Example 4.2

Calculate the Fourier transform of a decaying exponential $e^{-\alpha t}U(t)$.

Solution 4.2

The Fourier transform of an exponential is also directly obtained by using the definition equation. Notice that the exponential begins at t = 0 (due to the presence of U(t)) hence we change the lower limit on the integral from $-\infty$ to 0 thus.

$$\mathbb{F}\left[e^{-\alpha t}U(t)\right]=\int_{-\infty}^{\infty} e^{-\alpha t}U(t)e^{-j\omega t}\,dt$$

$$=\int_{0}^{\infty} e^{-(\alpha+j\omega)t}\,dt=\left.\frac{e^{-(\alpha+j\omega)t}}{-(\alpha+j\omega)}\right|_{0}^{\infty}=\frac{1}{(\alpha+j\omega)}$$

Example 4.3

Determine the Fourier transform of a sinusoid $Cos(3\omega t)u(t)$

Solution 4.3

The Fourier transform of a sinusoid $Cos(3\omega t)u(t)$ is directly obtained by using the definition equation and the solution to the previous example thus.

$$\mathbb{F}\left[Cos(3t)\right]=\mathbb{F}\left[\frac{e^{j3t}+e^{-j3t}}{2}\right]$$

$$=\tfrac{1}{2}\int_{-\infty}^{\infty}\left[e^{-j(\omega-3)t}U(t)+e^{-j(\omega+3)t}U(-t)\right]dt$$

$$=\tfrac{1}{2}\delta(\omega-3)+\tfrac{1}{2}\delta(\omega+3)$$

4.2.1 Symmetry relations for the Fourier Transform

When the signal x(t) has some special properties then the Fourier transform of this signal also exhibits some similar special properties. One that we have just seen is that the transform of a time limited signal is a continuous function. In this section we will examine the relation between the time domain function and the Fourier transform of this function when the time domain function has some special properties.

Real and Imaginary part of the Transform:

In general the signal x(t) can be a complex quantity. When x(t) is complex we can determine the real part and the imaginary part of the transform as shown in Equation(4.7)

$$F\{x(t)\}=\int_{-\infty}^{\infty} x(t)e^{-j\omega t}\,dt=\int_{-\infty}^{\infty}\left[x_R(t)+jx_I(t)\right]\left[Cos(\omega t)-jSin(\omega t)\right]dt$$

$$F\{x(t)\} = \int_{-\infty}^{\infty} [x_R(t)Cos(\omega t) + x_I(t)Sin(\omega t)]dt \tag{4.7}$$

$$+ j\int_{-\infty}^{\infty} [x_I(t)Cos(\omega t) - x_R(t)Sin(\omega t)]dt$$

$$F\{x(t)\} = X_R(\omega) + jX_I(\omega)$$

Even and Odd part of the Transform:

In general the signal x(t) can be broken in its even part and its odd part as shown in Equation(4.8). When x(t) is written in its even and its odd parts the transform of the even part can be written as shown in Equation(4.9)

$$\begin{aligned} x(t) &= x_e(t) + x_o(t) \\ x_e(t) &= \tfrac{1}{2}\{x(t) + x(-t)\} \\ x_o(t) &= \tfrac{1}{2}\{x(t) - x(-t)\} \end{aligned} \tag{4.8}$$

$$\begin{aligned} F\{x(t)\} &= \int_{-\infty}^{\infty} [x_e(t) + x_o(t)]e^{-j\omega t}\,dt \\ F\{x_e(t)\} &= \frac{1}{2}\int_{-\infty}^{\infty} [x(t) + x(-t)]e^{-j\omega t}\,dt \\ &= \frac{1}{2}\int_{-\infty}^{\infty} x(t)e^{-j\omega t}\,dt + \frac{1}{2}\int_{-\infty}^{\infty} x(-t)e^{-j\omega t}\,dt \\ &= \frac{1}{2}X(\omega) - \frac{1}{2}X(-\omega) = \frac{1}{2}(X(\omega) - X(-\omega)) \end{aligned} \tag{4.9}$$

And the transform of the odd part can be written as shown in Equation(4.10)

$$\begin{aligned} F\{x(t)\} &= \int_{-\infty}^{\infty} [x_e(t) + x_o(t)]e^{-j\omega t}\,dt \\ F\{x_o(t)\} &= \frac{1}{2}\int_{-\infty}^{\infty} [x(t) - x(-t)]e^{-j\omega t}\,dt \\ &= \frac{1}{2}\int_{-\infty}^{\infty} x(t)e^{-j\omega t}\,dt + \frac{1}{2}\int_{-\infty}^{\infty} x(-t)e^{-j\omega t}\,dt \\ &= \frac{1}{2}X(\omega) + \frac{1}{2}X(-\omega) \end{aligned} \tag{4.10}$$

Transform of the complex conjugate signal:

The Fourier transform of the conjugate of the signal x(t) can be determined as shown in Equation(4.11)

$$\begin{aligned} F\{x^*(t)\} &= \int_{-\infty}^{\infty} x^*(t)e^{-j\omega t}\,dt = \left[\int_{-\infty}^{\infty} x(t)e^{j\omega t}\,dt\right]^* \\ F\{x^*(t)\} &= \left[\int_{-\infty}^{\infty} x(t)e^{-j(-\omega)t}\,dt\right]^* = X^*(-\omega) \end{aligned} \tag{4.11}$$

Conjugate Symmetric and Conjugate anti-symmetric part of the Transform:

In general the signal x(t) can be broken in its conjugate symmetric and its conjugate anti-symmetric part. A function is conjugate symmetric when it satisfies Equation(4.12)

$$\begin{aligned} x(t) &= x^*(-t) \\ x_R(t) + jx_I(t) &= x_R(-t) - jx_I(-t) \end{aligned} \tag{4.12}$$

So a conjugate symmetric function is even in its real part but it is odd in its imaginary part. A function is conjugate anti symmetric when it satisfies Equation(4.13)

$$\begin{aligned} x(t) &= -x^*(-t) \\ x_R(t) + jx_I(t) &= -x_R(-t) + jx_I(-t) \end{aligned} \tag{4.13}$$

So a conjugate anti symmetric function is odd in its real part but it is even in its imaginary part. What is the Fourier transform of a function x(t) that is conjugate symmetric? We use the result from Equation(4.11) to get the result that we want.

$$\begin{aligned} F\{x_{CS}(t)\} &= F\{\tfrac{1}{2}[x(t) + x^*(-t)]\} \\ &= \frac{1}{2}[X(\omega) + X^*(\omega)] \\ &= X_R(\omega) \end{aligned} \tag{4.14}$$

Similarly the Fourier transform of a conjugate anti symmetric function will be

$$F\{x_{CA}(t)\} = jX_{im}(\omega)$$

4.2.2 The Properties of Fourier Transform:

Here we will list and derive some of the properties of the Fourier Transforms. As we go through these properties you will find that most of the properties are very similar to the properties of the

Fourier series. For most of the properties the proof is a direct application of the Fourier transform just as in the Fourier series. Please pay close attention to these properties as almost the same properties will come up when we talk about the Laplace transforms in Chapter 5 and they are almost identical.

4.2.2.1 Linearity:

The Fourier transform is a linear transform, so if $x(t) \Leftrightarrow X(\omega)$[1] and $v(t) \Leftrightarrow V(\omega)$ are two Fourier transform pairs then for any scalars, we have Equation(4.15)

$$ax(t) + bv(t) \overset{F}{\Leftrightarrow} aX(\omega) + bV(\omega) \tag{4.15}$$

This property can be proved in various different ways. Here we will first use an example of the three time domain functions shown in Figure 4.3.

Example 4.4

Examine the three functions shown in Figure 4.3. When you add the function $x_1(t)$ to the function $x_2(t)$ you will get the function $x_3(t)$. Show that the Fourier transform of $x_3(t)$ is equal to the Fourier transform of $x_1(t) + x_2(t)$.

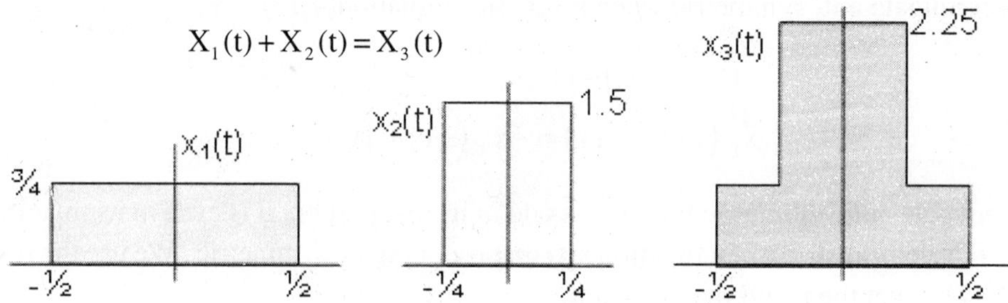

Figure 4.3: Displaying the Linearity property of the Fourier Transform

Solution 4.4

When we add the function $x_1(t)$ to the function $x_2(t)$ we get the function $x_3(t)$. Then the linearity property says that the Fourier transform of the function $x_3(t)$ equals the sum of the fourier transforms of $x_1(t)$ and $x_2(t)$. The following derivation makes this very clear. We first define the Fourier transforms of the signals $x_1(t)$ and $x_2(t)$. This is done in Equation(4.16)

$$\begin{aligned} X_1(\omega) &= \int_{-\infty}^{\infty} x_1(t)e^{-j\omega t}dt = \int_{-0.5}^{0.5} 0.75e^{-j\omega t}dt \\ X_2(\omega) &= \int_{-\infty}^{\infty} x_1(t)e^{-j\omega t}dt = = \int_{-0.25}^{0.25} 1.5e^{-j\omega t}dt \end{aligned} \tag{4.16}$$

[1] The notation $x(t) \Leftrightarrow X(\omega)$ implies that $X(\omega)$ is the Fourier Transform of $x(t)$.

Next we will define the Fourier transform of the signal $x_3(t)$. Then we will show that the Fourier transform of $x_3(t)$ is the same as the sum of the Fourier transform of the signals $x_1(t)$ and $x_2(t)$. This is shown in Equation(4.17).

$$\begin{aligned} X_3(\omega) &= \int_{-\infty}^{\infty} x_3(t) e^{-j\omega t} dt \\ &= \int_{-0.5}^{-0.25} 0.75(t) e^{-j\omega t} dt + \int_{-0.25}^{0.25} 2.25(t) e^{-j\omega t} dt + \int_{0.5}^{0.25} 0.75(t) e^{-j\omega t} dt \\ &= \int_{-0.5}^{-0.25} 0.75(t) e^{-j\omega t} dt + \int_{-0.25}^{0.25} (1.5+0.75)(t) e^{-j\omega t} dt + \int_{0.5}^{0.25} 0.75(t) e^{-j\omega t} dt \\ &= \int_{-0.5}^{0.5} 0.75(t) e^{-j\omega t} dt + \int_{-0.25}^{0.25} 1.5(t) e^{-j\omega t} dt \end{aligned} \tag{4.17}$$

Equation(4.17) begins with the calculation of the Fourier transform of $x_3(t)$ but we are able to arrange the integrals so that the Fourier transform of $x_3(t)$ as shown in Equation(4.17) equals the sum of the two integrals for the Fourier transforms of $x_1(t)$ and $x_2(t)$ which are shown in Equation(4.16). This then tells us that the linearity property is satisfied.

Figure 4.4 shows the result of Example 4.4 pictorially, the Fourier transform of $x_1(t)$ is plotted in the top left corner of Figure 4.4 and the Fourier transform of $x_2(t)$ is plotted in the top right corner of Figure 4.4. We next add these two Fourier transforms to get the figure in the center of Figure 4.4. This is the transform of the sum of the two Fourier transforms. The Fourier transform of $x_3(t)$ is now plotted independently in the bottom of Figure 4.4. When we compare the bottom plot and the middle plot we find that they are identical. This proves the linearity property for the Fourier transforms. This is shown in Figure 4.4. The SCILAB script follows.

****

The SCILAB script for the plot of Figure 4.4 is given below.

****

```
w=-30:1/2:30;
x1=0.75*2*sinc(w/2); // Fourier Transform of signal x1(t)
x2=1.5*4*sinc(w/4); // Fourier Transform of signal x2(t)
x3=0.75*2*sinc(w/2)+ 1.5*4*sinc(w/4); // Fourier Transform of signal x3(t)
//Plot the Fourier transform of the signal x1(t).
subplot(3,2,1);plot2d3(w,x1,frameflag=6,axesflag=4);
xtitle(['Fourier Transform of the signal X1']);
//Plot the Fourier transform of the signal x2(t).
subplot(3,2,2);plot2d3(w,x2,frameflag=6,axesflag=4);
```

```
xtitle(['Fourier Transform of the signal X2']);
//Plot the sum of the Fourier transforms of the signals x1(t)and x2(t).
subplot(3,1,2);plot2d3(w,x1+x2,frameflag=6,axesflag=4);
xtitle(['Sum of the Fourier transforms of signal X1 and X2']);
//Plot the Fourier transform of the signal x3(t).
subplot(3,1,3);plot2d3(w,x3,frameflag=6,axesflag=4);
xtitle(['Fourier Transform of the signal X3. Identical to the sum of X1 and X2']);
****************************
```

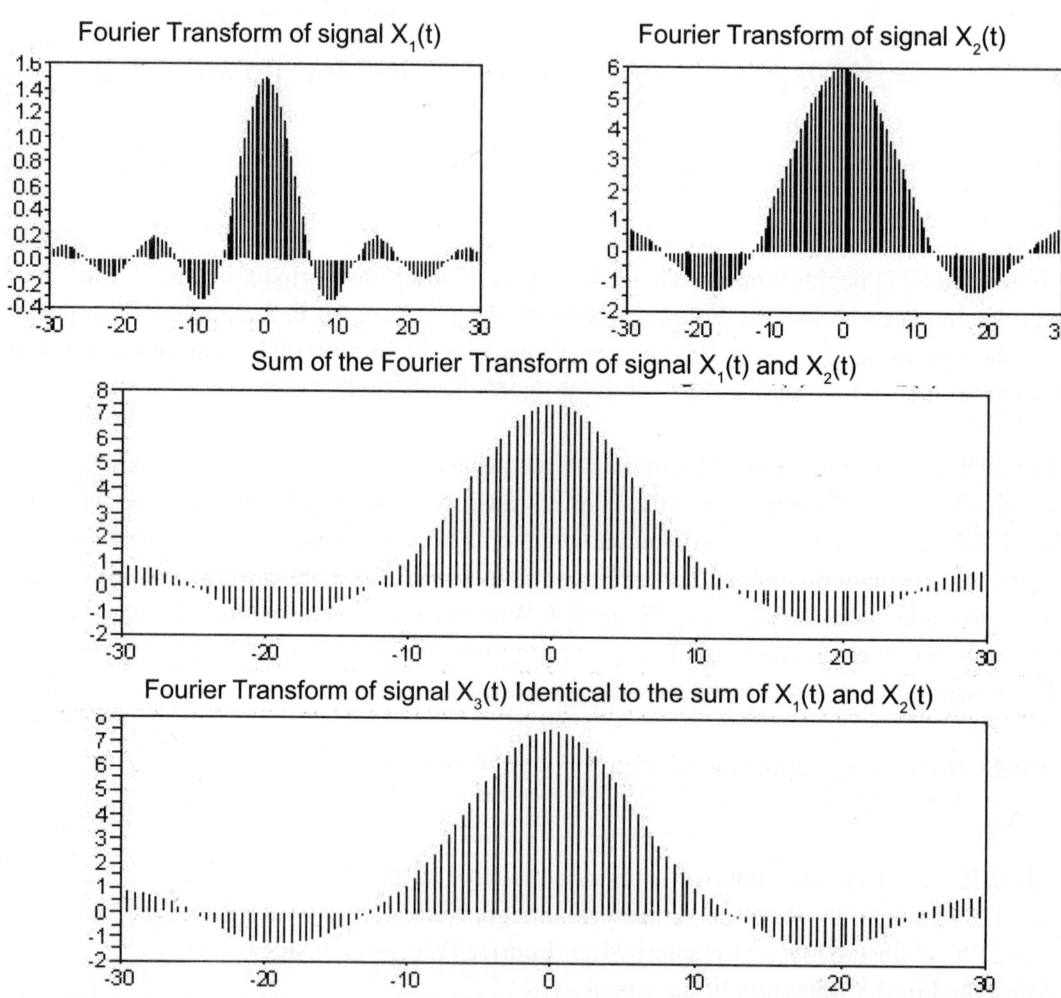

Figure 4.4: Demonstrating the Linearity Property. The two bottom figures are identical to each other.

Example 4.4 proves the Linearity property for a particular signal. Next in order to prove this property in general we would proceed in the exact same manner and arrive at the same conculsion. This is done for you in Equation(4.18)

$$\begin{aligned} &F(x_3(t)) = F(ax_1(t)) + F(bx_2(t)) \\ &F(ax_1(t) + bx_2(t)) = a\int_{-\infty}^{\infty} x_1(t)e^{-j\omega t}dt + b\int_{-\infty}^{\infty} x_2(t)e^{-j\omega t}dt \\ &\qquad = F_1(\omega) + F_2(\omega) = F_3(\omega) \end{aligned} \tag{4.18}$$

4.2.2.2 Shift in Time:

If the Fourier transform, of $x(t) \Leftrightarrow X(\omega)$ then the Fourier transform of a time shifted function $x(t-\tau)$ is given by Equation(4.19). To prove this property we begin with the Fourier transform definition. Then using a substitution of t' by $t-\tau$ we get the required Fourier transform property. This is shown in Equation(4.19). This property can be proved directly by substituting $t' = t-t_0$ in the integral.

$$F\{x(t \pm t_0)\} \overset{E}{\Leftrightarrow} e^{\pm j\omega t_0} X(\omega) \tag{4.19}$$

Example 4.5

In Example 4.1 we determined the Fourier transform of an impulse. Here we will determine the Fourier transform of an impulse at $t-t_0$.

Solution 4.5

Applying the time shift property we find that the Fourier transform of $\delta(t-t_0)$ is $e^{j\omega t_0}$.

4.2.2.3 Scale Change:

If the Fourier transform of $x(t) \Leftrightarrow X(\omega)$ then for any constant α the Fourier transform of $x(\alpha t)$ is given by Equation(4.20). Notice that Equation(4.20) tries to maintain the scale parameter α as a positive constant always. Keep this in mind when you are completing the proof of the property. The proof of this property is given in Equation(4.21). The effect of the scaling property is shown in Figure 4.5.

$$F\{x(\alpha t)\} \overset{F}{\Leftrightarrow} \frac{1}{|\alpha|} X\left(\frac{\omega}{\alpha}\right) \tag{4.20}$$

$$\begin{aligned} F\{x(\alpha t)\} &= \int_{-\infty}^{\infty} x(\alpha t)e^{-j\omega t}\,dt \qquad \text{let } t' = \alpha t \\ &= \int_{-\infty}^{\infty} x(t')e^{-j\left(\frac{\omega}{\alpha}\right)t'} \frac{dt'}{|\alpha|} \end{aligned} \tag{4.21}$$

$$= \frac{1}{|\alpha|} X\left(\frac{\omega}{\alpha}\right)$$

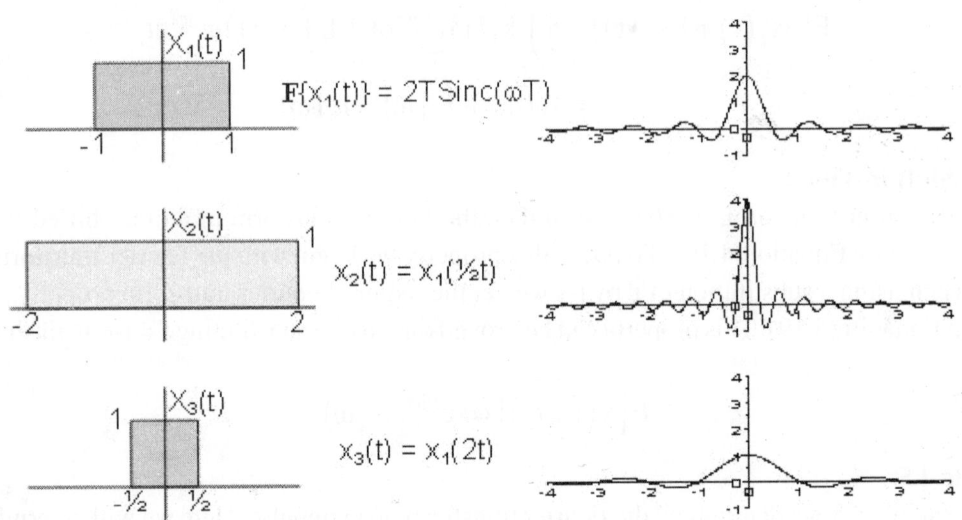

Figure 4.5: The scaling property of the Fourier Transform. Figure on the left shows the time domain function. Figure on the right shows the Fourier transform of the function. Examine the effect of the scale parameter.

The first row in Figure 4.5 gives us a time domain function and its Fourier transform. Next we scale the time domain function so that it is stretched out to twice its width. So the Fourier domain function is scaled in both magnitude and in width with a scaling factor of 0.5. In the bottom row we scale the function with a scale factor of 2 and again we see the effect of scaling in both magnitude and in width. Another effect of the time scale is that when we make the time domain function wider it requires a smaller frequency range to represent the function. The function acts as a low pass function. When we make the function narrower it requires many more frequencies to represent the function. A side effect and a consequence of this theorem shows up when $\alpha = -1$. In this case we get the Fourier transform property of a time reversal.

4.2.2.4 Duality in Fourier Transforms:

The time domain signal and its Fourier transform are duals of each other as the only difference between the Fourier transform and its inverse is the sign change in the exponent and the change in the variable of integration. So if a time domain function and its Fourier transform are known, then the Fourier transform of the Fourier transform has a shape that is similar to the original time domain function. This is shown pictorically in Figure 4.6. In Figure 4.6 the top two figures are a Fourier transform pair. In the bottom two figures the time domain function has the same shape as the Fourier transform of the square pulse in the top two figures. So the Fourier transform of the new time domain shape has the same shape as the original time domain function.

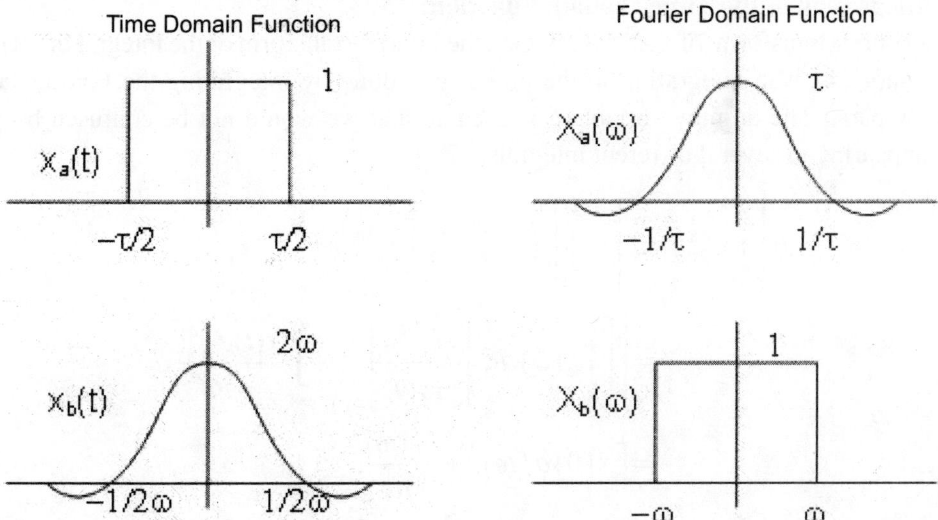

Figure 4.6: Showing the Duality of the Fourier Transform. Notice that the Fourier Transform of the Fourier Transform shape is the same shape as the original Time domain function.

4.2.2.5 Translation in the Frequency Domain:

This property is the dual of the 4.2.2.2 Shift in Time property. If the Fourier transform, of $x(t)\Leftrightarrow X(\omega)$ then the Fourier transform of $e^{j\omega_0 t}x(t)$ is given by Equation(4.22). Notice that Equation(4.22) shows that the Fourier transform of the new function has the same shape as the Fourier transform of the old function but is shifted in frequency by the amount ω_0.

$$F\left[e^{j\omega_0 t}x(t)\right] \overset{F}{\Leftrightarrow} X(\omega-\omega_o) \tag{4.22}$$

This property is proved in the same manner as the other properties. Equation(4.23) shows us how.

$$F\left[e^{j\omega_0 t}x(t)\right] = \int_{-\infty}^{\infty} x(t)e^{j\omega_0 t}e^{-j\omega t}dt = \int_{-\infty}^{\infty} x(t)e^{-j(\omega-\omega_0)t}dt = X(\omega-\omega_0) \tag{4.23}$$

Example 4.6

Determine the Fourier transform of a decaying sinusoid
$e^{-\alpha t}Cos(\omega t)U(t)$ using the translation in frequency theorem

Solution 4.6

We know that the Fourier transform of an sinusoid Cos(3ωt) is ½δ(ω-3) + ½δ(ω-3). We are going to translate this to frequency α. So the new Fourier transform will be a translation of the original transform hence:

$$\mathbb{F}\left[e^{-j\alpha t}Cos(3t)u(t)\right] = X(\omega-\alpha) = \tfrac{1}{2}\{\delta(\omega-3-\alpha)+\delta(\omega+3-\alpha)\}$$

4.2.2.6 Integration of the Time Domain Function:

If the Fourier transform, of $x(t) \Leftrightarrow X(\omega)$ then the Fourier transform of the integral of x(t) is given by Equation(4.24). The integration in the property is done by integrating the Fourier transform function by parts. The dummy variable ζ is used so that we would not be confused by the time variable appearing in several different integrals.

$$\begin{aligned} F\left[\int_0^t x(\xi)\,d\xi\right] &= \int_{-\infty}^{\infty}\left[\int_0^t x(\xi)\,d\xi\right]e^{-j\omega t}dt \\ &= \left[\left[\int_0^t x(\xi)\,d\xi\right]\frac{-e^{-j\omega t}}{-j\omega}\right]_{-\infty}^{\infty} - \int_{-\infty}^{\infty}\frac{x(t)e^{-j\omega t}}{-j\omega}dt \\ &= \left[x(0)\delta(\omega)\right] + \frac{X(\omega)}{j\omega} \end{aligned} \tag{4.24}$$

Example 4.7

Determine the Fourier transform of the unit step function using the Integration theorem.

Solution 4.7

We know that the integral of the unit impulse function is the unit step function

$$\int_{-\infty}^{t}\delta(\lambda)d\lambda = U(t).$$

So to determine the Fourier transform of the unit step function we will use the integral theorem and the Fourier transform of the impulse function:

$$\mathbb{F}\left[\int_{-\infty}^{t}\delta(\lambda)d\lambda\right] = \frac{X(\omega)}{j\omega} + x(0)\delta(\omega) = \frac{1}{j\omega} + \frac{\delta(\omega)}{2}$$

4.2.2.7 Differentiation of the Time Domain:

If the Fourier transform of $x(t) \Leftrightarrow X(\omega)$ then the Fourier transform of the derivative of x(t) is given by Equation(4.25).

$$F\left[\frac{dx(t)}{dt}\right] = j\omega X(\omega) \quad \text{and} \quad F\left[\frac{d^n x(t)}{dt^n}\right] = (j\omega)^n X(\omega) \tag{4.25}$$

This property is directly proved by using the definition of the Fourier transform and integrating it by parts with the derivative of x(t) as the first function and the exponential as the second function as shown in Equation(4.26)

$$F\left[\frac{dx(t)}{dt}\right]=\int_{-\infty}^{\infty}\frac{dx(t)}{dt}e^{-j\omega t}dt$$

$$F\left[\frac{dx(t)}{dt}\right]=\left[x(t)e^{-j\omega t}\Big|_{-\infty}^{\infty}+(j\omega)\int_{-\infty}^{\infty}x(t)e^{-j\omega t}dt\right] \tag{4.26}$$

$$F\left[\frac{dx(t)}{dt}\right]=\left[x(t)\bullet 0-0\bullet e^{i\omega\infty}+(j\omega)X(\omega)\right]=j\omega X(\omega)$$

This concept of the derivative of the function can be extended further to higher order derivatives. Extending the concept to higher order derivatives gives us the second expression in Equation(4.25).

Earlier in Example 4.1 we determined the Fourier transform of the impulse. We also know that the impulse is the derivative of a step function. Here we will use the derivative theorem to determine the Fourier transform of an impulse. This is shown in detail in Equation(4.27).

$$F\left[\frac{dU(t)}{dt}\right]=\int_{-\infty}^{\infty}\frac{dU(t)}{dt}e^{-j\omega t}\,dt$$

$$=e^{-j\omega t}U(t)\Big|_{-\infty}^{\infty}-(-j\omega)\int_{-\infty}^{\infty}U(t)e^{-j\omega t}\,dt \tag{4.27}$$

$$=0-0+(j\omega)\int_{0}^{\infty}e^{-j\omega t}\,dt=(j\omega)\left[\frac{-1}{j\omega}e^{-j\omega t}\Big|_{0}^{\infty}\right]=1$$

4.2.2.8 The Convolution Property:

Non periodic convolution. Consider the convolution of two non periodic continuous time signals x(t) and h(t). Define the result of convolution to be a signal y(t) so by definition we have

y(t) = x(t)*h(t). This can be written as an equation $y(t)=x(t)*h(t)=\int_{-\infty}^{\infty}h(\tau)x(t-\tau)d\tau$. To evaluate this transform we begin with the definition shown in Equation(4.28). We will substitute Equation(4.28) into the definition of convolution to get Equation(4.29)

$$x(t-\tau)\Leftrightarrow\frac{1}{2\pi}\int_{-\infty}^{\infty}X(j\omega)e^{j\omega(t-\tau)}d\omega \tag{4.28}$$

$$y(t)=\int_{-\infty}^{\infty}h(\tau)\left[\frac{1}{2\pi}\int_{-\infty}^{\infty}X(j\omega)e^{j\omega(t-\tau)}d\omega\right]d\tau \tag{4.29}$$

Completing the integral in Equation(4.29) we get Equation(4.30). Equation(4.30) shows us that the inverse transform of the product of two Fourier transform functions is the time domain function which is the result of convolving the two time domain functions. Or the Fourier transform of the convolution of two time domain functions is the product of the Fourier transforms of the two individual time domain functions.

$$\begin{aligned} y(t) &= \frac{1}{2\pi}\int_{-\infty}^{\infty} X(j\omega)\left[\int_{-\infty}^{\infty} h(\tau)e^{j\omega(t-\tau)}d\tau\right]d\omega \\ &= \frac{1}{2\pi}\int_{-\infty}^{\infty} X(j\omega)e^{j\omega t}\left[\int_{-\infty}^{\infty} h(\tau)e^{-j\omega\tau}d\tau\right]d\omega \\ &= \frac{1}{2\pi}\int_{-\infty}^{\infty} X(j\omega)H(j\omega)e^{j\omega t}d\omega = \frac{1}{2\pi}\int_{-\infty}^{\infty} Y(j\omega)e^{j\omega t}d\omega \end{aligned} \tag{4.30}$$

Equation(4.30) shows us that y(t) is the inverse Fourier transform of the product of two Fourier domain functions. Since y(t) is equal to the convolution of two time domain functions, we can conclude that the inverse Fourier transform of the product of two Fourier domain functions equals the convolution of two time domain functions. This is written as

$$y(t) = x(t)*h(t) \overset{FT}{\Leftrightarrow} Y(j\omega) = X(j\omega)\bullet H(j\omega)$$

The convolution occurs when a signal goes through a system or a filter. Say for example you have a rectangular pulse and you pass this pulse through a filter whose impulse response is also rectangular as shown in Figure 4.7. The response of the filter in the time domain then is the convolution of the input signal and the filter time response. This can be easily evaluated in the frequency domain by using the convolution theorem as shown below.

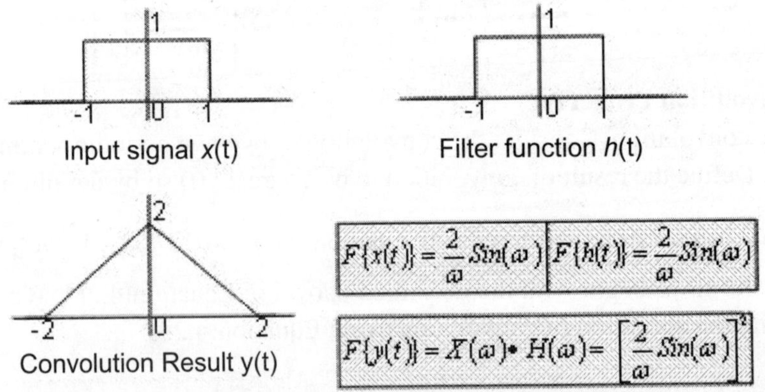

Figure 4.7: We want to know the Fourier representation of the result of Convolution. It is not so difficult to obtain the Fourier transform of the triangular function but since we know that this function is the result of Convolution of two time domain signals we can determine its Fourier representation by using the convolution Theorem. The result is shown in the boxes in the Figure.

4.2.2.9 Parseval's Relation:

Earlier in the Fourier series we have seen that the energy in the time domain representation of a signal is equal to the energy in the frequency domain representation. This is true also for the non-periodic signal and its Fourier transform representation. The energy in the time domain of a continuous time non-periodic signal is shown in Equation(4.31)

$$E_x = \int_{-\infty}^{\infty} |x(t)|^2 dt = \int_{-\infty}^{\infty} x(t)x^*(t)dt \tag{4.31}$$

Here we will assume that x(t) is the most general signal and hence we will assume that it is a complex signal. Being a complex signal the magnitude squared of the signal is the product of the signal and its complex conjugate. The Fourier transform of the conjugate of signal x(t) is given in Equation(4.31). We will replace the signal x*(t) in Equation(4.31) by its Fourier transform. The Fourier transform of the signal x*(t) is shown in Equation(4.32)

$$x^*(t) = \frac{1}{2\pi}\int_{-\infty}^{\infty} X^*(j\omega)e^{-i\omega t}d\omega \tag{4.32}$$

After the substitution we will interchange the order of integration and examine the resulting equation. This is done for you in Equation(4.33).

$$\begin{aligned}
E_x &= \int_{-\infty}^{\infty} x(t)\left[\frac{1}{2\pi}\int_{-\infty}^{\infty} X^*(j\omega)e^{-j\omega t}\, d\omega\right]dt \\
E_x &= \frac{1}{2\pi}\int_{-\infty}^{\infty} X^*(j\omega)\underbrace{\left[\int_{-\infty}^{\infty} x(t)e^{-j\omega t}\, dt\right]}_{\text{Fourier Transform of } x(t)}d\omega \\
E_x &= \frac{1}{2\pi}\int_{-\infty}^{\infty} X^*(j\omega)X(j\omega)d\omega = \frac{1}{2\pi}\int_{-\infty}^{\infty}|X(j\omega)|^2 d\omega
\end{aligned} \tag{4.33}$$

When we look at Equation(4.31) and Equation(4.33) we can conclude that the energy in a signal can be represented in either the time domain or in the frequency domain. This is the Parseval's relation for the Fourier transforms. As you can see that this is the same relation as the Parseval's relation for the Fourier series. We will see this over and over again as we study other transforms. This relation tells us that the signal energy stays the same no matter which domain we look at the representation of a signal. Another use of this relation is to determine the energy content of the signal in a specific band of frequencies. If we replace the limits of the integration from $\pm\infty$ to $\pm\omega_0$ then we will determine the energy in the signal from $\omega = 0$ to $\omega = \omega_0$.

Table 4.1: The Fourier Transform Pairs

	Time Domain	Frequency Domain
1	$f(t)=\begin{cases}1 & \|t\|\le a\\ 0 & Otherwise\end{cases}$	$F(\omega)=2\dfrac{Sin(a\omega)}{\omega}$
2	$f(t)=Ae^{-at}U(t)$	$F(\omega)=\dfrac{A}{a+j\omega}$
3	$f(t)=Ae^{-a\|t\|}$	$F(\omega)=\dfrac{2aA}{a^2+\omega^2}$
4	$f(t)=\begin{cases}A\left(1-\dfrac{\|t\|}{a}\right) & \|t\|<a\\ 0 & Otherwise\end{cases}$	$F(\omega)=aA\left[\dfrac{Sin(a\omega/2)}{a\omega/2}\right]^2$
5	$f(t)=Ae^{-a^2t^2}$	$F(\omega)=A\dfrac{\sqrt{\pi}}{a}e^{\left(\frac{\omega}{2a}\right)^2}$
6	$f(t)=\begin{cases}ACos(\omega_o t)e^{-at} & t\ge 0\\ 0 & t\le 0\end{cases}$	$F(\omega)=A\dfrac{a+j\omega}{(a+j\omega)^2+\omega_0^2}$
7	$f(t)=\begin{cases}ASin(\omega_o t)e^{-at} & t\ge 0\\ 0 & t\le 0\end{cases}$	$F(\omega)=A\dfrac{\omega_0}{(a+j\omega)^2+\omega_0^2}$
8	$f(t)=\begin{cases}ACos(\omega_o t) & \|t\|\ge a\\ 0 & Otherwise\end{cases}$	$F(\omega)=A\left[\dfrac{Sin(a(\omega-\omega_0))}{\omega-\omega_0}+\dfrac{Sin(a(\omega+\omega_0))}{\omega+\omega_0}\right]$
9	$f(t)=A\delta(t)$	$F(\omega)=A$
10	$f(t)=AU(t)$	$F(\omega)=A\left[\pi\delta(\omega)-j\dfrac{1}{\omega}\right]$
11	$f(t)=\begin{cases}A & t>0\\ 0 & t=0\\ -A & t<0\end{cases}$	$F(\omega)=-2jA\dfrac{1}{\omega}$
12	$f(t)=A$	$F(\omega)=2\pi A\,\delta(\omega)$
13	$f(t)=ACos(\omega_0 t)$	$F(\omega)=\pi A[\delta(\omega-\omega_0)+\delta(\omega+\omega_0)]$
14	$f(t)=ASin(\omega_0 t)$	$F(\omega)=j\pi A[\delta(\omega+\omega_0)-\delta(\omega-\omega_0)]$
15	$f(t)=\sum_{n=-\infty}^{\infty}\delta(t-nT)\overset{\Delta}{=}\mathrm{Comb_T(t)}$	$F(\omega)=\dfrac{2\pi A}{T}\sum_{n=-\infty}^{\infty}\delta\left(\omega-\dfrac{2\pi n}{T}\right)=\dfrac{2\pi A}{T}COMB_{2\pi/T}(\omega)$

Table 4.2: Fourier Transform Properties

	Property Name	Time Domain Function	Frequency Domain Function
1	Linearity	$Ax_1(t) \pm Bx_2(t)$	$AX_1(\omega) \pm BX_2(\omega)$
2	Shift in the Time Domain	$X(t \pm t_0)$	$e^{\pm jwto} X(\omega)$
3	Scale change	$x(at)$	$1/\lvert a\rvert \cdot X(\omega/a)$
4	Differentiation in the Time Domain	$\frac{d^n x(t)}{dt^n}$	$(j\omega)^n X(\omega)$
5	Integration in the Time Domain	$\left[\int_0^t x(\xi)d\xi\right]$	$\frac{X(\omega)}{j\omega}$
6	Convolution	$x(t)*h(t)$	$X(\omega)H(\omega)$
7	Parseval's Relation	$E_x = \int_{-\infty}^{\infty} \lvert x(t)\rvert^2 dt$	$E_x = \frac{1}{2\pi}\int_{-\infty}^{\infty} \lvert X(\omega)\rvert^2 d\omega$

Table 4.3: Fourier Transform Symmetry Relations

	Time Function	Fourier Transform
1	$x^*(t)$	$X^*(-\omega)$
2	$x_{CS}(t)$	$X_R(\omega)$
3	$x_{CA}(t)$	$jX_I(\omega)$
4	$x_R(t)$	$X_{CS}(\omega)=½\,[X(\omega)+X^*(-\omega)]$
5	$x_I(t)$	$X_{CA}(\omega)=½\,[X(\omega)-X^*(-\omega)]$

4.3 CHARACTERISTICS OF LINEAR SYSTEMS

4.3.1 Distortionless system

The Fourier transform that we have just completed discussing has many important uses in the study of systems and filters. In this section we use a filter as a system and study further the importance of the Fourier Transform. We know that the output of a system is a convolution of the system input and the system impulse response. So to get the output of a system we would normally have to evaluate the convolution integral. The convolution integral in the time domain becomes a simple algebraic product in the frequency domain. We have seen this earlier and is shown again in Equation(4.34)

$$\underbrace{y(t) = h(t) * x(t)}_{\text{Convolution in the time domain}} \qquad \underbrace{Y(\omega) = H(\omega) \bullet X(\omega)}_{\text{Product in the Frequency domain}} \tag{4.34}$$

Since an algebraic product is much simpler than convolution we will find it easier to study the system characteristics in the frequency domain. We will study different types of filters that will influence or alter the input signal so that the output signal is a signal that is required. When the input signal goes through the filter it will be altered in a specified manner by the filter.

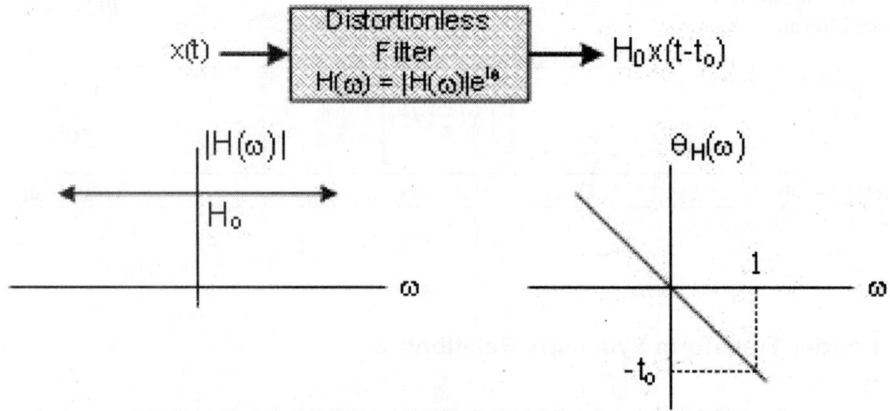

Figure 4.8: Transfer function of a distortionless filter. Constant magnitude across the entire spectrum and linear phase across the entire spectrum.

Filtering is often used to eliminate frequencies in a specific band of frequencies such as the very low or the very high frequencies in audio amplifiers, or to block off a band of frequencies to eliminate vibration in a device, or to enhance/amplify different frequency bands by specific amounts as in a graphics equalizer in your stereo. In this chapter we have already discussed that the output signal of a system y(t) is the convolution of the input signal x(t) with the impulse response of the system h(t). This is given by the relation in the time and the frequency domain as shown in Equation(4.34).

Since we know that in general the Fourier transform is a complex quantity so we can write Equation(4.34) to specifically show the effect of the system on the magnitude and the phase in Equation(4.36)

$$|Y(\omega)| = |H(\omega)||X(\omega)| \quad \text{and} \quad e^{j\theta_{Y(\omega)}} = e^{j\theta_{Y(\omega)} + j\theta_{X(\omega)}} \tag{4.35}$$

$$|Y(\omega)|e^{j\theta_{Y(\omega)}} = |H(\omega)|e^{j\theta_{H(\omega)}}\,|X(\omega)|e^{j\theta_{X(\omega)}} \tag{4.36}$$

Equation(4.36) shows that the output magnitude is the product of the magnitude of the input signal and the magnitude of the impulse response of the system. The phase of the output is the sum of the input phase and the phase of the impulse response of the system. Equation(4.36) shows that the output spectrum will be affected in both the magnitude and the phase by the system or the filter spectrum. That is the system will distort or alter the output spectrum.

Often we want to consider a **distortionless filter.** What is a distortionless filter anyway? In the general case a filter is considered distortionless when the output is identical to the input over the entire frequency spectrum except perhaps a change in the magnitude and a possible time lag. This is shown graphically in Figure 4.8. With a distortionless filter the output in the Frequency domain is $H_o e^{-j\omega t_o} X(\omega)$. When the magnitude response of the filter is constant as shown in Figure 4.8 then there is no amplitude distortion. If the magnitude of the filter is not constant across the frequency spectrum then the filter is said to have **amplitude distortion.** When the phase of the filter varies linearly across the frequency spectrum as shown in Figure 4.8 then there is no phase distortion. If the phase of the filter is not linear across the frequency spectrum then the filter is said to have **phase distortion.** In the next section we will examine some of the phase and the frequency characteristics of different filters.

4.3.2 Characteristics of linear filters

An Ideal Low Pass Filter:

The frequency domain characteristics of this filter are shown in Figure 4.9. The magnitude is constant only in the pass band which extends from $-\omega_o$ to ω_o and in this region the phase displays linear characteristics. In the pass band the filter permits the signal to pass through with ideal transmission characteristics and in the stop band the signal is completely blocked.

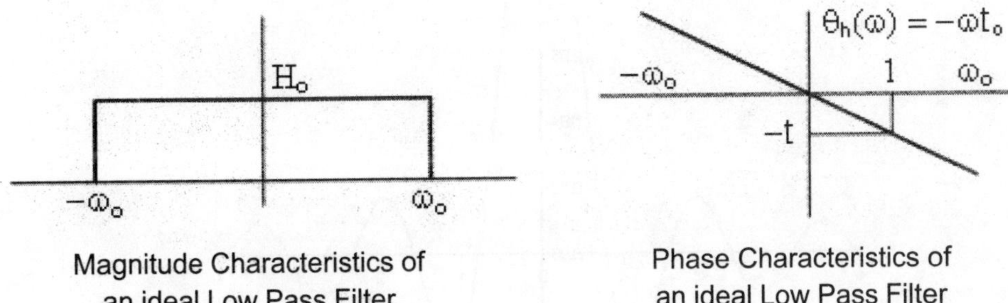

Figure 4.9: Frequency domain Characteristics of an ideal Low Pass Filter

$$h(t) = \frac{1}{2\pi}\int_{-\infty}^{\infty} H(\omega)e^{j\omega t}d\omega = \frac{1}{2\pi}\int_{-\omega_o}^{\omega_o} H_o e^{j\omega t}d\omega$$

$$h(t) = \frac{H_o}{2\pi}\int_{-\omega_o}^{\omega_o} e^{j\omega t}d\omega = \frac{\omega_o H_o}{\pi}\text{Sinc}(\omega_o t) \qquad (4.37)$$

The inverse Fourier transform of the filter will give us the impulse response of the filter and will show us the filter in the time domain. The impulse response is shown in Equation(4.37). The SCILAB script to plot the function of Equation(4.37) is given below.

```
****************************
SCILAB Script to draw the impulse response of an ideal Low Pass Filter.
****************************
w0=4; H0=2;t=linspace(-4,4,201);
lpf=(w0*H0/%pi)/sinc(w0*t);
plot2d3(t,lpf)
```

The time domain expression in Equation(4.37) and the plot in Figure 4.10 suggests that the time domain function is not zero for t<0. This is shown in the impulse response plot in Figure 4.10. So the ideal low pass filter anticipates that the input will come at t = 0 and starts producing an output long before t = 0. This of course is not possible in a practical system; a system that anticipates your input and produces an output is possible only in science fiction novels. In a laboratory such a system is not possible. This is proof that an ideal low pass filter is a non-realizable system. This means that you cannot build one in a laboratory with real components such as resistors, capacitors etc. You can come close to it but you cannot build it exactly.

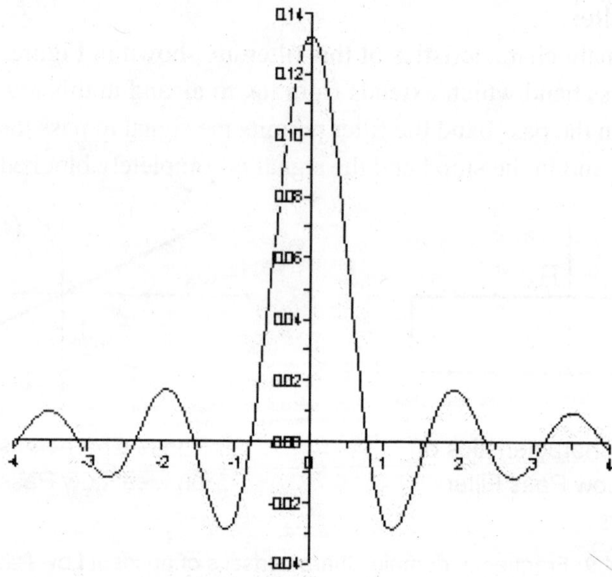

Figure 4.10: The impulse response of an ideal Low Pass Filter

An Ideal High Pass Filter:

The frequency domain characteristics of this filter are shown in Figure 4.11. The magnitude is constant only in the pass band which extends from $-\infty$ to $-\omega_0$ and then from ω_0 to ∞. In the region from $-\omega_0$ to ω_0 the filter has the stop band. In the pass band region the phase displays linear characteristics. In the pass band the filter permits the signal to pass through with ideal transmission characteristics and in the stop band the signal is completely blocked.

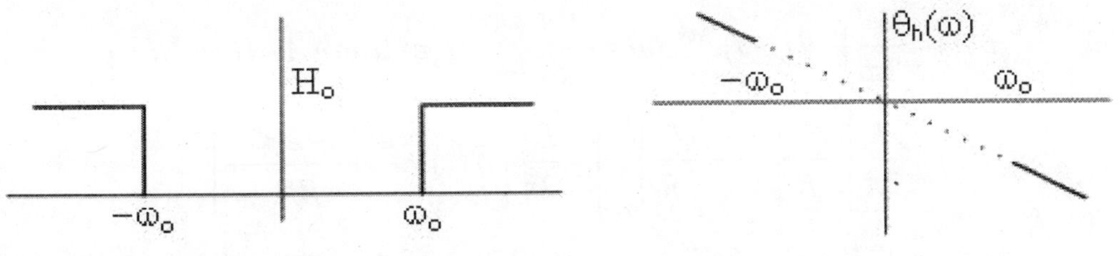

Magnitude Characteristics of an ideal High Pass Filter

Phase Characteristics of an ideal High Pass Filter

Figure 4.11: Frequency domain characteristics of an Ideal High Pass Filter

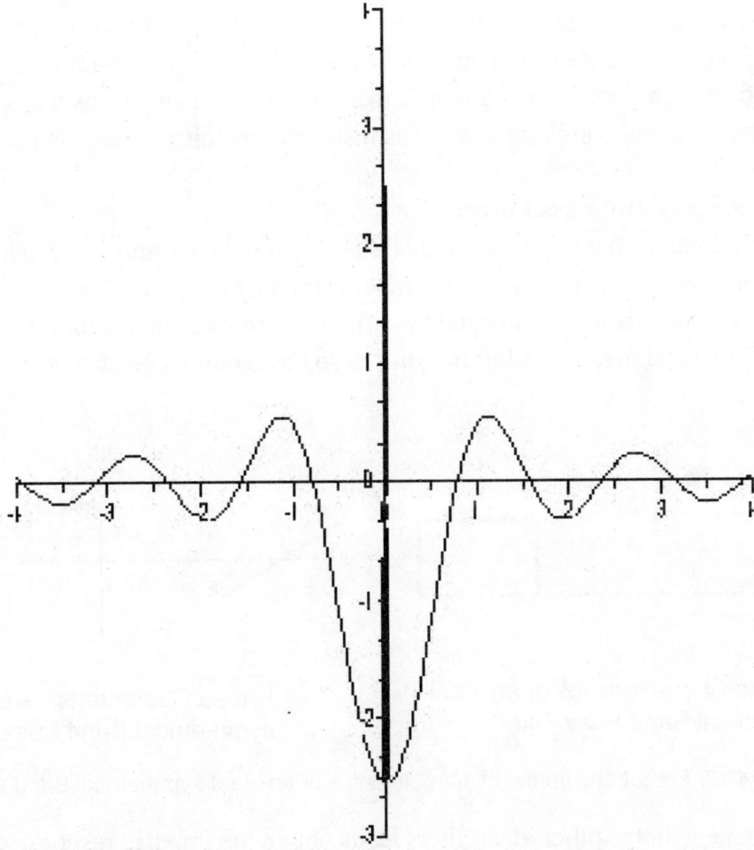

Figure 4.12: The impulse response of an ideal High Pass Filter. Notice the presence of the impulse.

The inverse Fourier transform of the filter will give us the impulse response of the filter and will show us the filter in the time domain. This is shown in Equation(4.38).

$$h(t)=\frac{1}{2\pi}\int_{-\infty}^{\infty}H(\omega)e^{j\omega t}d\omega=\frac{1}{2\pi}\left[\int_{-\infty}^{-\omega_o}H_oe^{j\omega t}d\omega+\int_{\omega_o}^{\infty}H_oe^{j\omega t}d\omega\right]$$

$$h(t)=\frac{H_o}{2\pi}\left[\frac{e^{j\omega t}}{jt}\Bigg|_{-\infty}^{-\omega_o}+\frac{e^{j\omega t}}{jt}\Bigg|_{\omega_o}^{\infty}\right]=\frac{H_o}{2\pi}\left[\delta(t)-\frac{e^{j\omega_o t}-e^{-j\omega_o t}}{jt}\right] \tag{4.38}$$

$$h(t)=H_o\left[\delta(t)-\frac{\omega_o}{\pi}Sinc(\omega_o t)\right]$$

The time domain expression in Equation(4.38) suggests that the time domain function is not zero for t<0. This is shown in the impulse response plot in Figure 4.12. So the ideal high pass filter anticipates that the input will come at t = 0 and starts producing an output long before t = 0. This of course is not possible in a practical system; a system that anticipates your input and produces an output is possible only in science fiction novels. In a laboratory such a system is not possible. This is proof that an ideal high pass filter is a non-realizable system. This means that you cannot build one in a laboratory with real components such as resistors, capacitors etc.

An Ideal Symmetrical Band Pass Filter:

The frequency domain characteristics of this filter are shown in Figure 4.13. The ideal filter has two pass bands, one centered at $\omega = \omega_c$ and the other centered at $\omega = -\omega_c$. When you carefully examine the pass band characteristics of the band pass filter the characteristics look very much like the characteristics of the ideal low pass filter but shifted so the center frequency is $\omega = \omega_c$ and $\omega = -\omega_c$ instead of zero.

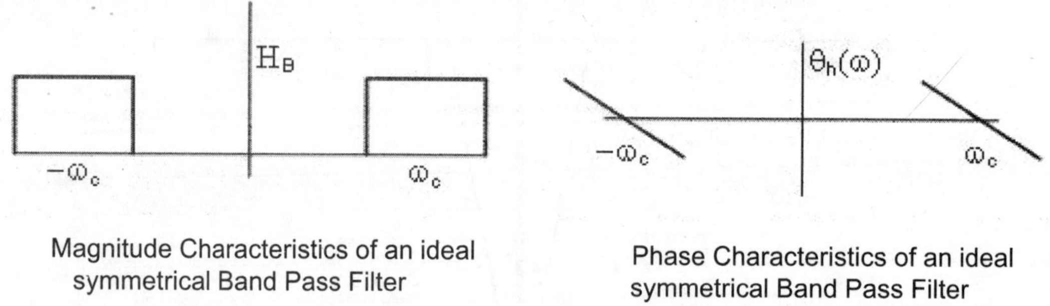

Magnitude Characteristics of an ideal symmetrical Band Pass Filter

Phase Characteristics of an ideal symmetrical Band Pass Filter

Figure 4.13: Frequency domain Characteristics of an ideal symmetrical Band Pass Filter

As we have done with the other ideal filters let us obtain the impulse response of this filter and see how it relates to the impulse response of the ideal low pass filter. But before we proceed with the mathematical analysis it will be informative to do this intuitively. Assuming that the band pass filter is the shifted version of the ideal low pass filter then the impulse response of the band pass filter should be the same as the impulse response of the low pass filter that is modulated by a carrier frequency of $\omega = \omega_c$ So intuitively we predict that the impulse response of the band pass filter will be the impulse response of the low pass filter but multiplied by a carrier with a frequency of $\omega = \omega_c$.

Let us obtain the impulse response of the ideal band pass filter as we have done for the other filters. This is done for you in Equation(4.39). Examining Equation(4.39) we see that our intuitive reasoning is indeed true. The impulse response of the band pass filter is the same as the impulse response of the low pass filter multiplied by the carrier signal Cos(ω_ct). The factor of 2 just represents gain and comes about because we have two replicas of the band pass filters while we had only one replica of the low pass filter.

$$
\begin{aligned}
h(t) &= \frac{1}{2\pi}\int_{-\infty}^{\infty} H(\omega)e^{j\omega t}d\omega = \frac{1}{2\pi}\left[\int_{-\omega_c-\omega_o}^{-\omega_c+\omega_{oo}} H_o e^{j\omega t}d\omega + \int_{\omega_c-\omega_o}^{\omega_c+\omega_{oo}} H_o e^{j\omega t}d\omega\right] \\
&= \frac{H_o}{2\pi}\left[\frac{e^{j\omega t}}{jt}\bigg|_{-\omega_c-\omega_o}^{-\omega_c+\omega_o} + \frac{e^{j\omega t}}{jt}\bigg|_{\omega_c-\omega_o}^{\omega_c+\omega_o}\right] \\
&= \frac{H_o}{2\pi}\left[Sin((\omega_c-\omega_o)t) - Sin((\omega_c+\omega_o)t)\right] \\
&= \frac{2H_o\omega_o}{\pi}\left[Sinc(\omega_o t)Cos(\omega_o t)\right] = 2h_{lpf}Cos(\omega_o t)
\end{aligned}
\tag{4.39}
$$

The expression in Equation(4.39) is the same expression as that of an amplitude modulated signal with Cos(ω_ct) being the carrier signal. Here the carrier frequency is the same as the center frequency of the band pass filter. So our intuitive reasoning was indeed correct and the band pass filter can be visualized as a modulated version of the low pass filter. As we have already noted earlier an ideal low pass filter is not a realizable filter so also the ideal band pass filter. This filter is also not realizable. The impulse response of the ideal band pass filter is shown in Figure 4.14. The SCILAB script for the plot is given below.

```
***************************
SCILAB script to draw the plot of Figure 4.14
***************************
w0=5.0; H0=2;t=linspace(-2,2,801);
lpf=(w0*H0/%pi)*sinc(w0*t);
subplot(2,1,1);
plot2d1(t,lpf,frameflag=6,axesflag=5)
x=cos(4*w0*t);
bpf=x.*lpf;
subplot(2,1,2);
plot2d1(t,bpf)
****************************
```

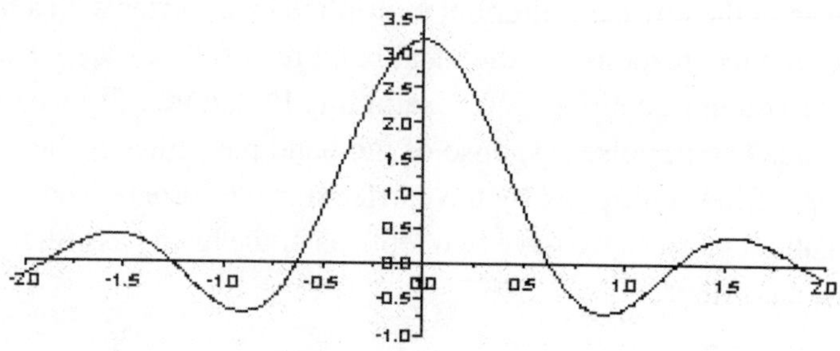

Impulse response of an Ideal Low Pass Filter

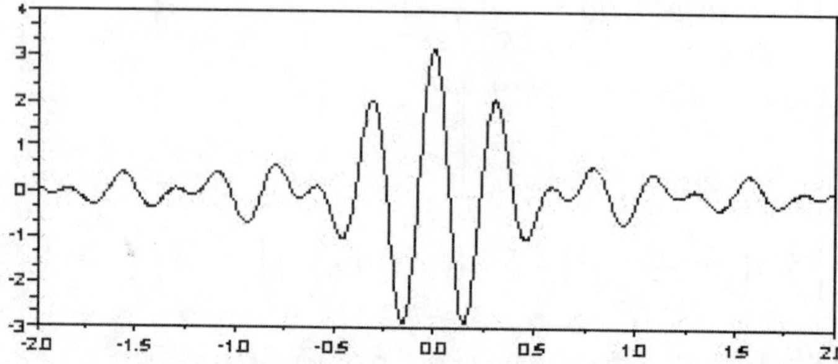

Figure 4.14: The impulse response of an Ideal Band Pass Filter. Notice the effect of amplitude modulation over a low pass filter.

4.4 DESIGNING ANALOG FILTERS

In the previous section we have seen the characteristics of ideal filters. We have also seen that the ideal filters are not realizable in a laboratory as they are all non-causal. In this section we will explore how practical analog filters are designed. Even though we have seen that there are four different types of filters the design of practical filters always begins with the design of low pass filters. Once the low pass filter is designed then the filter is transformed to the type of filter that is required. We do this towards the end of this section. Design of analog filters is a very straight forward procedure and if you follow the specified steps you will also come up with a very good design. Design of analog filters is an art that is as old as electrical engineering. So there are extensive tables available to design just about any filter. Since we can transform any type of a filter to any other type of filter we will begin our study by seeing how the low pass filter is designed.

A typical low pass filter has a magnitude response as shown in Figure 4.15. The magnitude characteristics in the pass band and the stop band are generally not constant as the ideal filter tried to portray, the magnitude characteristics oscillate between set limits. In a filter, the pass band extends from $0 \leq \Omega < \Omega_p$ and in this region the magnitude response is specified as shown in Equation(4.40)

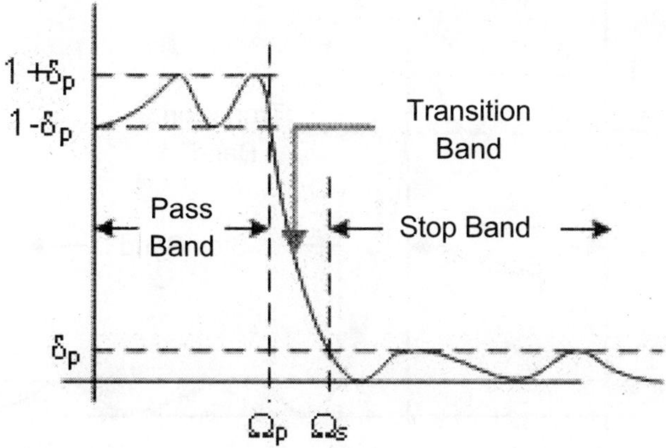

Figure 4.15: Filter specifications in standard format

$$1-\delta_p \le |H_{LP}(j\Omega)| \le 1+\delta_p \qquad \text{for } \Omega < \Omega_p \tag{4.40}$$

In a filter, the stop band extends from $\Omega \ge \Omega_s$ and in this region the magnitude response is specified as shown in Equation(4.41)

$$|H_{LP}(j\Omega)| \le \delta_s \qquad \text{for } \Omega \ge \Omega_s \tag{4.41}$$

In Figure 4.15 we have specified tolerances in both the pass band and the stop band, these fluctuations in both the bands are known as *Ripples*. The ripples are usually specified in dB as maximum pass band ripple of α_p and minimum stop band ripple of α_s. These ripples are computed as shown in Equation(4.42)

$$\alpha_p = -20\log_{10}(1-\delta_p)\,\text{dB}$$

$$\alpha_s = -20\log_{10}(\delta_s)\,\text{dB} \tag{4.42}$$

Sometimes the filter is specified in its normalized format. The normalized format of filter specifications is shown in Figure 4.16. In the normalized representation the maximum gain in the pass band is assumed to be unity and the ripple is specified as $1/\sqrt{(1+\varepsilon^2)}$. This represents the minimum gain in the pass band. In the stop band the ripple is specified as A^{-1}. So in the normalized specifications the maximum pass band gain is 0dB and the minimum attenuation in the stop band is $20\log_{10}(A)$.

The transition band extends from the end of the pass band which is at Ω_p to the beginning of the stop band which is at Ω_s. This band is generally specified as a ratio $\tau = \Omega_s/\Omega_p$ of the two edge frequencies. Notice that the transition ratio defined in this way will always be greater than one (remember these are the specification for a low pass filter).

Another parameter that is also defined in filter design is known as the discrimination parameter. This parameter is defined as shown in Equation(4.43)

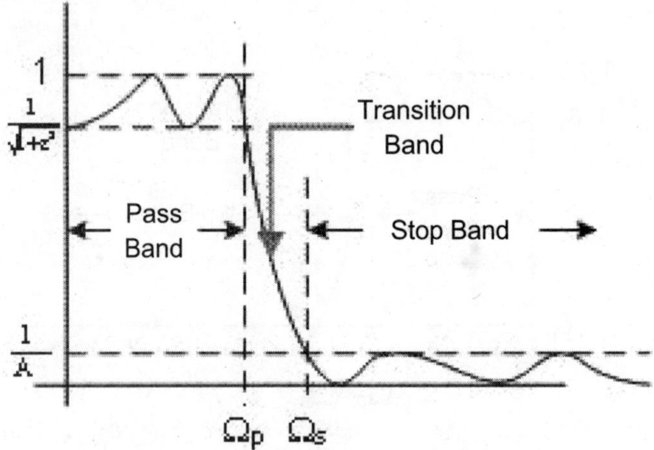

Fig.4.16: Filter specifications in normalized format

$$\tau_1 = \frac{\varepsilon}{\sqrt{A^2 - 1}} \tag{4.43}$$

When we are designing low pass filters we will first determine the two parameters τ and τ_1 as shown above. Once these parameters are determined the design of the low pass filter is a straight forward process.

4.4.1 Butterworth Approximation

The Butterworth response for a filter is a monotonically decreasing response. Since it is a monotonically decreasing response it is a smooth response, there are no ripples. The maximum gain in the pass band occurs at $\Omega = 0$ and from there on the magnitude is always decreasing. The minimum gain in the pass band occurs at Ω_p. The maximum gain in the stop band occurs at Ω_s. The magnitude squared response of the Butterworth approximation is given in Equation(4.44)

$$\left|H_{LP}(j\Omega)\right|^2 = \frac{1}{1 + \left(\frac{\Omega}{\Omega_c}\right)^{2N}} \tag{4.44}$$

In the magnitude response for the Butterworth approximation Ω_c is the 3dB cutoff frequency. To design a required Butterworth filter we need to determine the order of the filter N and the 3dB cutoff frequency Ω_c. They are determined by solving the two Equations(4.45)

$$\left|H_{LP}(j\Omega_p)\right|^2 = \frac{1}{1 + \left(\frac{\Omega_p}{\Omega_c}\right)^{2N}} = \frac{1}{1+\varepsilon^2}$$

$$\left|H_{LP}(j\Omega_s)\right|^2 = \frac{1}{1+\left(\dfrac{\Omega_s}{\Omega_c}\right)^{2N}} = \frac{1}{A^2} \tag{4.45}$$

The first equation in Equation(4.45) uses the known magnitude at the pass band edge while the second equation in Equation(4.45) uses the known magnitude at the stop band edge. When we solve the two equations simultaneously we will get the order of the required filter. The order of the filter is determined from Equation(4.46)

$$N = \frac{1}{2}\frac{\log_{10}\left(\dfrac{A^2-1}{\varepsilon^2}\right)}{\log_{10}\left(\dfrac{\Omega_s}{\Omega_p}\right)} = \frac{\log_{10}\left(\dfrac{1}{\tau_1}\right)}{\log_{10}(\tau)} \tag{4.46}$$

The order of the filter is always an integer value so we generally round N up to the next higher integer if it turns out that the result in Equation(4.46) is a fraction. When you substitute this value of N back in one of the two equations in Equation(4.45) you will get the value of the cutoff frequency for this filter. Once you know both these parameters the transfer function of the Butterworth filter can be written as shown in Equation(4.47)

$$H_{LP}(j\Omega) = \frac{\Omega_c^N}{\prod_{(i=0)}^{(N-1)}(s-p_i)} \qquad p_i = \Omega_c e^{j\pi\left[\frac{N+2i-1}{2N}\right]} \tag{4.47}$$

So we can list the steps to design the Butterworth filter.

- From the given specifications determine A and ε. Once these parameters are known we can compute the discrimination parameter τ_1.
- From the edge of the pass band and the stop band frequencies determine the transition ratio parameter τ.
- Substitute the two parameters in Equation(4.46) to get the order of the filter.
- Determine the poles of the filter using Equation(4.47) to get the transfer function of the filter.

Example 4.8

Determine the transfer function of a Butterworth low pass filter which has a pass band edge at 1KHz with an attenuation of 0.8dB, and has stop band edge at 5KHz with an attenuation of 35dB.

Solution 4.8

For this example we are given the gain at the pass band edge as -0.8dB. So using the first equation in Equation(4.45) we can determine ε.

$$-0.8 = 10\log_{10}\left(\frac{1}{1+\varepsilon^2}\right)$$

$$\varepsilon = 0.449738$$

We are also given the gain at the stop band edge as -35dB. So using the second equation in Equation(4.45) we can determine A.

$$-35 = 10\log_{10}\left(\frac{1}{A^2}\right)$$

$$A^2 = 3162.28$$

Now thatweknow ε and A we can determine the two parameters τ and τ_1

$$\tau = \frac{5000}{1000} = 5$$

$$\tau_1 = \frac{\varepsilon}{\sqrt{A^2-1}} = \frac{0.449738}{56.2252} = \frac{1}{125}$$

Now that we know these parameters we can determine the order of the filter

$$N = \frac{\log_{10}\left(\frac{1}{\tau_1}\right)}{\log_{10}(\tau)} = \frac{\log_{10}(125)}{\log_{10}(5)} = 3.000088 \approx 4$$

So we have determined that the order of the filter is 4. Next we determine the cutoff frequency by using this value of N in Equation(4.45)

$$|H_{LP}(j\Omega_p)|^2 = \frac{1}{1+\left(\frac{1000}{\Omega_c}\right)^8} = \frac{1}{1+(0.449738)^2}$$

$$\Omega_c = 1221.3694\text{Hz}$$

Now that we know the order and the cutoff frequency we can determine the pole locations using Equation(4.47)

$$p_0 = 1221.34e^{j\pi\left[\frac{4-0-1}{8}\right]} = 1221.34\left[\text{Cos}\left(\frac{3\pi}{8}\right) + j\text{Sin}\left(\frac{3\pi}{8}\right)\right]$$

$$p_1 = 1221.34e^{j\pi\left[\frac{4-2-1}{8}\right]} = 1221.34\left[\text{Cos}\left(\frac{\pi}{8}\right) + j\text{Sin}\left(\frac{\pi}{8}\right)\right]$$

$$p_2 = 1221.34e^{j\pi\left[\frac{4-4-1}{8}\right]} = 1221.34\left[\mathrm{Cos}\left(\frac{-1\pi}{8}\right) + j\mathrm{Sin}\left(\frac{-1\pi}{8}\right)\right]$$

$$p_3 = 1221.34e^{j\pi\left[\frac{4-6-1}{8}\right]} = 1221.34\left[\mathrm{Cos}\left(\frac{-3\pi}{8}\right) + j\mathrm{Sin}\left(\frac{-3\pi}{8}\right)\right]$$

Thus the required filter is designed.

4.4.2 Chebyshev Approximation

The Chebyshev response for a filter is known for its equiripple response in the pass band (Type 1) and smooth (or monotonic) response in the stop band or for its smooth response in the pass band (Type 2) and equiripple in the stop band. The two responses are shown in Figure 4.17.

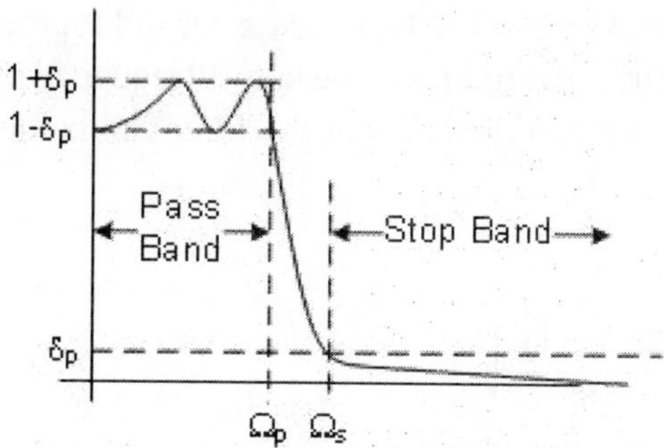

Chebyshev Type 1 response. Equiripple in the pass band and monotonic in the stop band.

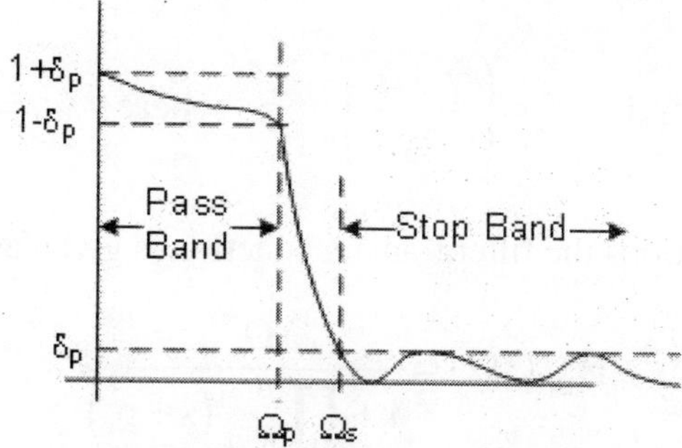

Chebyshev Type 2 response. Monotonic in the pass band and equiripple in the stop band.

Figure 4.17: Showing the two type of responses of the Chebyshev type of filters.

Chebyshev Type 1 Filter:

The magnitude squared response of the Chebyshev filter is given in Equation(4.48)

$$\left|H_{LP}(j\Omega)\right|^2 = \frac{1}{1+\varepsilon^2 T_N^2\left(\dfrac{\Omega}{\Omega_p}\right)} \tag{4.48}$$

In Equation(4.48) T_N is the Chebyshev polynomial of order N and the parameter for this polynomial is the ratio (Ω/Ω_p). This Nth order polynomial is defined by the relation shown in Equation(4.49)

$$T_N(\Omega) = \begin{cases} \mathrm{Cos}\left(N\mathrm{Cos}^{-1}(\Omega)\right) & |\Omega| < 1 \\ \mathrm{Cosh}\left(N\mathrm{Cosh}^{-1}(\Omega)\right) & |\Omega| > 1 \end{cases} \tag{4.49}$$

Notice that the magnitude response of the Chebyshev filter depends on the pass band frequency. In the normalized filter this is always chosen to be 1. Just as we did for the Butterworth filter, here also we have to determine the order of the filter and the cutoff frequency of the filter in order to design the filter. Once these two are known the poles of the filter can be determined from the relations given in Equation(4.50)

$$\begin{aligned} p_i &= \sigma_i + j\Omega_i \\ \sigma_i &= -\Omega_p \xi \mathrm{Sin}\left(\frac{\pi(2i-1)}{2N}\right) \\ \Omega_i &= \Omega_p \varsigma \mathrm{Cos}\left(\frac{\pi(2i-1)}{2N}\right) \end{aligned} \tag{4.50}$$

$$\varsigma = \left(\frac{\gamma^2+1}{2\gamma}\right) \quad \text{and} \quad \xi = \left(\frac{\gamma^2-1}{2\gamma}\right) \quad \text{where} \quad \gamma = \left(\frac{1+\sqrt{1+\varepsilon^2}}{\varepsilon}\right)^{\frac{1}{N}}$$

Once we know the pole locations the filter transfer function is given as shown in Equation(4.51)

$$H_{LP}(j\Omega) = \frac{\Omega_c^N}{1+\prod_{(i=0)}^{(N-1)}(s+p_i)} \tag{4.51}$$

The order of the filter is determined from the attenuation specification in the stop band as shown in Equation(4.52)

$$\left|H_{LP}(j\Omega_s)\right|^2 = \frac{1}{1+\varepsilon^2\left\{\mathrm{Cosh}\left(N\mathrm{Cosh}^{-1}(\Omega_s)\right)\right\}^2} = \frac{1}{A^2} \tag{4.52}$$

Solving Equation(4.52) for the order of the filter we get Equation (4.53).

$$N = \frac{\cosh^{-1}\left(\frac{\sqrt{A^2-1}}{\varepsilon}\right)}{\cosh^{-1}\left(\frac{\Omega_s}{\Omega_p}\right)} = \frac{\cosh^{-1}\left(\frac{1}{\tau_1}\right)}{\cosh^{-1}(\tau)} \tag{4.53}$$

So we can list the steps to design the Chebyshev filter.

- From the given specifications determine A and ε. Once these parameters are known we can compute the discrimination parameter τ_1.
- From the edge of the pass band and the stop band frequencies determine the transition ratio parameter τ.
- Substitute the two parameters in Equation(4.53) to get the order of the filter.
- Determine the poles of the filter using Equation(4.50) to get the transfer function of the filter.

Example 4.9

Repeat Example 4.8 for the Chebyshev type 1 filter. Determine the transfer function of a Chebyshev Type 1 low pass filter which has a pass band edge at 1KHz with an attenuation of 0.8dB, and has stop band edge at 5KHz with an attenuation of 35dB.

Solution 4.9

Once again since the edge frequencies and the respective gains are the same as in Example 4.8 the parameters will evaluate to the same values so we have

$$\varepsilon = 0.449738; \quad A^2 = 3162.28; \quad \tau = 5; \quad \tau_1 = \frac{1}{125}$$

Using these parameters we can solve for the order of the filter. In this example we get

$$N = \frac{\cosh^{-1}\left(\frac{\sqrt{A^2-1}}{\varepsilon}\right)}{\cosh^{-1}\left(\frac{\Omega_s}{\Omega_p}\right)} = \frac{\cosh^{-1}(125)}{\cosh^{-1}(5)} = 2.408554 \approx 3$$

Now that we know the order of the filter and the pass band edge frequency we can determine the pole locations for the filter using Equation(4.50).

Chebyshev Type 2 Filter:

The magnitude squared response of the Chebyshev type 2 filter is given in Equation(4.54)

$$\left|H_{LP}(j\Omega)\right|^2 = \frac{1}{1+\varepsilon^2\left[\dfrac{T\left(\frac{\Omega_s}{\Omega_p}\right)}{T\left(\frac{\Omega_s}{\Omega}\right)}\right]^2} \tag{4.54}$$

This response is smooth in the pass band and has ripples in the stop band. This filter is different from the Butterworth and the Chebyshev type 1 filter because this response has both zeros and poles while the other two responses are designed only with poles. Again to design the filter using the type 2 approximation we need to determine the order of the filter. The order of the type 2 filter is the same as the order of the type 1 filter. So the filter order is determined as shown in Equation(4.53). Once the order is determined we need to identify the poles and the zeros of the filter. The poles are located at locations which are computed as shown in Equation(4.55)

$$p_i = \rho_i + j\Theta_i$$

$$\rho_i = -\Omega_p \xi \text{Sin}\left(\frac{\pi(2i-1)}{2N}\right)$$

$$\Theta_i = \Omega_p \varsigma \text{Cos}\left(\frac{\pi(2i-1)}{2N}\right)$$

$$\varsigma = \left(\frac{\gamma^2+1}{2\gamma}\right) \quad \text{and} \quad \xi = \left(\frac{\gamma^2-1}{2\gamma}\right) \quad \text{where} \quad \gamma = \left(A+\sqrt{A^2-1}\right)^{\frac{1}{N}} \tag{4.55}$$

and the zeros are located at locations which are computed as shown in Equation(4.56)

$$z_i = j\frac{\Omega_s}{\text{Cos}\left[\dfrac{\pi(2i-1)}{2N}\right]} \tag{4.56}$$

So the only difference between the design of the type 1 and type 2 Chebyshev filter is the determination of the zeros for the filter.

4.4.3 Filter Transformation and Scaling

All the different types of designs that we have examined in this section dealt with the design of low pass filters. Once the low pass filter is designed then the filter can be scaled and transformed to any other type of filter that you need. In the transformations shown below S_{LP} is the Laplace[1] opera-

[1] We will talk about the Laplace operator in the next chapter. For now think of s as a variable. The importance of S will become clear after we cover the next chapter.

tor in the low pass filter transfer function. In the same way S_{HP} is the Laplace operator in the high pass filter transfer function; S_{BP} is the Laplace operator in the band pass filter transfer function and S_{BS} is the Laplace operator in the band stop filter transfer function. In the same way Ω_P represents the pass band frequency, Ω_{P1} and Ω_{P2} represent the two edge frequencies of the band pass and the band stop filters and $\Omega_o^2 = \Omega_{P_1} \bullet \Omega_{P_2}$. The transformation and the scaling are done by an invertible transformation as shown below.

4.4.3.1 Frequency Scaling

In the previous section we have discussed that the low pass filters are generally designed as normalized filters. Normalized filters, after they are designed have to be scaled so that they are operating at the frequency range of interest. Frequency scaling is done in a very straight forward manner by first determining the frequency scale factor, then multiplying the frequency variable with the scale factor. The scaling of the filters and the transformation of the filters can be done simultaneously. That is what we have done in the following three transformations.

4.4.3.2 Low Pass to High Pass:

To transform a Low pass filter to a high pass filter we first design the low pass filter using any method that you choose and determine the transfer function in the Laplace domain. Then we make the substitution shown in Equation(4.57)

$$S_{LP} = \frac{\Omega_{P_{(LP)}} \Omega_{P_{(HP)}}}{S_{HP}} \tag{4.57}$$

The required frequency transformation is done by Equation(4.58)

$$\Omega_{LP} = -\frac{\Omega_{P(LP)} \Omega_{P(HP)}}{\Omega_{HP}} \tag{4.58}$$

Equation(4.58) tells us that we can determine the corresponding frequencies in the low pass and the high pass filters by appropriately substituting in the correct values. So for example if the High Pass filter has a pass band frequency of 5KHz and the Low Pass filter has a pass band frequency or 750Hz then the frequency in the low pass filter that corresponds to the frequency of 8KHz in the high pass filter is $\frac{750*5000}{8000} = 468.75$. So the response at 468.75Hz in the low pass filter will be the same as the response at 8000Hz in the high pass filter.

4.4.3.3 Low Pass to Band Pass:

To transform a low pass filter to a band pass filter we first design the low pass filter using any method that you choose and determine the transfer function in the Laplace domain variable. Then we make the substitution shown in Equation(4.59). In this equation Ω_o is the center frequency of the band pass filter which is equal to $\Omega_o^2 = \Omega_{s1}\Omega_{s2}$ and the band width of the filter is Ω_{s2} - Ω_{s1}

$$s_{LP} = \frac{\Omega_{P_{(LP)}}\left(s_{BP}^2 + \Omega_{O_{(BP)}}^2\right)}{s_{BP}\left(\Omega_{P2_{(BP)}} - \Omega_{P1_{(BP)}}\right)} \tag{4.59}$$

The required frequency transformation is done by Equation(4.60)

$$\Omega_{LP} = \frac{\Omega_{P_{(LP)}}\left(\Omega_{BP}^2 - \Omega_{O_{(BP)}}^2\right)}{\Omega_{BP}\left(\Omega_{P2_{(BP)}} - \Omega_{P1_{(BP)}}\right)} \tag{4.60}$$

4.4.3.4 Low Pass to Band Stop:

To transform a low pass filter to a band stop filter we first design the low pass filter using any method that you choose and determine the transfer function in the Laplace domain. Then we make the substitution shown in Equation(4.61). In this equation Ω_o is the center frequency of the band stop filter which is equal to $\Omega_o^2 = \Omega_{s1}\Omega_{s2}$ and the band width of the filter is Ω_{s2} - Ω_{s1}

$$s_{LP} = \frac{\Omega_{S_{(LP)}} s_{BS}\left(\Omega_{S2_{(BS)}} - \Omega_{S1_{(BS)}}\right)}{\left(s_{BS}^2 + \Omega_{O_{(BS)}}^2\right)} \tag{4.61}$$

The required frequency transformation is done by Equation(4.62)

$$\Omega_{LP} = \frac{\Omega_{S_{(LP)}} \Omega_{BS}\left(\Omega_{S2_{(BS)}} - \Omega_{S1_{(BS)}}\right)}{\left(\Omega_{BS}^2 - \Omega_{O_{(BS)}}^2\right)} \tag{4.62}$$

Example 4.10

We need a filter to select a band of audio frequencies from with a center frequency of 10Krad. The filter has to be the Chebyshev type 1 filter with 1dB of ripple in the pass band. The band width of the filter is 1Krad. Maximum stop band gain allowed is -15dB and this occurs at 8Krad and at 12.5Krad.

Solution 4.10

This time we are given the specifications in the band pass filter so we first need to transform the specifications to the low pass filter. For this we will need to determine the pass band frequency of the low pass filter. Since we are designing a normalized low pass filter we will choose the pass band edge to be 1 radian. Then the stop band edge will be determined by the frequency translation equation given in Equation(4.60). Using this equation we get the stop band edge at

$$\Omega_{LP(stop)} = \frac{1\left(12500^2 - 10000^2\right)}{12500(1000)} = 4.5 .$$

Next we determine the filter parameters.
For our example we get $\tau = 4.5/1 = 4.5$.

Also from allowed ripple we get $-1 = 10\log_{10}(\varepsilon)$ so $\varepsilon = 0.794$

From the attenuation in the stop band we get $-15 = 10\log(1/A^2)$ so $A^2 = 31.6227$.

With A^2 and ε determined we can get $\tau_1 = 0.794/(31.6227-1)^{1/2} = 0.14348$.

Using these two parameters, τ and τ_1 we get the order of the filter using Equation(4.53). This time we get the order of the filter as 1.204 or 2.

A second order Chebyshev low pass filter is given by $H(s) = \dfrac{1}{s^2 + 1.0977s + 1}$

Finally to convert this filter to the band pass filter we substitute for s in this equation according to Equation(4.59) so we get $s_{LP} = \dfrac{1\left(s_{BP}^2 + 10000^2\right)}{s_{BP}(1000)}$ after substitution we get the required band pass filter as $H_{BP}(s) = \dfrac{10^8 s^2}{s^4 + 1097.7s^3 + 4*10^8 s^2 + 1.0977*10^{11} + 10^8}$

4.5 HILBERT TRANSFORMS

Have you ever wondered about the Amplitude Modulated (AM) signal? In the AM signal both the sidebands carry the same information. So when we transmit a signal using AM we use up twice as much band width as required. If somehow we could separate the upper sideband from the lower sideband then the bandwidth required to transmit the signal would be cut in half since we would be transmitting only one of the two side bands. Is such a scheme possible? To study this let us investigate the Fourier transform of a very special signal.

To begin we know that any signal in the time domain can be represented as a sum of its odd part and its even part as shown in Equation(4.63)

$$x(t) = x_e(t) + x_o(t)$$

$$x_e(t) = \tfrac{1}{2}\{x(t) + x(-t)\}$$
$$x_o(t) = \tfrac{1}{2}\{x(t) - x(-t)\} \quad (4.63)$$

Next suppose that the signal x(t) is a causal signal. Since x(t) is a causal signal the entire signal x(t) can be determined from only the even part of the signal as shown in Equation(4.64)

$$x(t) = 2x_e(t) - x(0)\delta(t) \quad (4.64)$$

Similarly since x(t) is a causal signal the entire signal - except the signal at x(0) can also be determined from the odd part of the signal as shown in Equation(4.65)

$$x(t) = 2x_o(t) + x(0)\delta(t) \quad (4.65)$$

Relations in Equations(4.64) and(4.65) hold because the signal x(t) is a causal signal and hence x(-t) = 0. Next let us consider what happens to the Fourier transform of x(t).

$$F[x(t)] = 2F[x_e(t)] = 2\int_{-\infty}^{\infty} x_e(t)Cos(\omega t)d\omega = 2X_e(\omega)$$
$$F[x(t)] = 2F[x_o(t)] = 2\int_{-\infty}^{\infty} x_o(t)Sin(\omega t)d\omega = 2X_o(\omega) \quad (4.66)$$

Question:

What would we get if we were to determine the inverse transform of either $X_e(\omega)$ *or* $X_o(\omega)$?

Another relation that is important and related to the topic at hand is written as $X(\omega) = X_R(\omega) + jX_I(\omega)$. Here $X_R(\omega)$ is the real part of the Fourier transform of $X(\omega)$ and $X_I(\omega)$ is the imaginary part of the transform of $X(\omega)$. Referring back to the symmetry properties of the Fourier transform we see that when x(t) is a real signal then $X_R(\omega)$ is the transform of $x_e(t)$ and that $X_I(\omega)$ is the transform of $x_o(t)$. So for a causal, real, stable signal x(t); $X_R(\omega)$ will completely determine x(t) or $X(\omega)$. This can be done as follows.

1. First determine $x_e(t)$ as the inverse transform of $X_R(t)$.
2. From $x_e(t)$ determine x(t) for t > 0 which is a causal signal.
3. From x(t) determine $X(\omega)$.

So for a causal, real, stable signal $x_e(t)$ or $X_R(\omega)$ is equivalent to knowing the complete signal x(t). This construction also suggests that for a real, causal, signal the real part and the imaginary part of the Fourier transform of the signal are related to each other. This relation can be described as shown in Equation(4.67)

$$X(\omega) = \frac{1}{\pi}\int_{-\pi}^{\pi} X_R(\theta)U(\omega-\theta)d\theta - x(0) \quad (4.67)$$

In Equation(4.67) $U(\omega)$ is the Fourier transform of the unit step function. The unit step function is used to ensure that the function x(t) is a causal function. (If it already is then multiplying it with 1 in the region t > 0 will not change the function in any way.) We determined the Fourier transform of the unit step function in Example 4.7 and the Fourier transform of the unit step function is shown in Equation(4.68)

$$U(\omega)=\frac{\delta(\omega)}{2}+\frac{1}{j\omega} \tag{4.68}$$

With this representation of the unit step function we can substitute Equation(4.68) in Equation(4.67) to get Equation(4.69). In Equation(4.69) we are only going to look at the principal value.

$$\begin{aligned} X(\omega)&=\tfrac{1}{\pi}\int_{-\pi}^{\pi}X_R(\theta)\left[\frac{\delta(\omega-\theta)}{2}+\frac{1}{j(\omega-\theta)}\right]d\theta \\ X(\omega)&=\tfrac{1}{\pi}\mathfrak{P}\int_{-\pi}^{\pi}\frac{X_R(\theta)}{(\omega-\theta)}d\theta \\ X(\omega)&=\tfrac{1}{\pi}\mathfrak{P}\int_{-\pi}^{\pi}\frac{X_I(\theta)}{(\omega-\theta)}d\theta \end{aligned}\Bigg\}\text{Principal Value} \tag{4.69}$$

Details of all this math are really beyond the scope of this book but the result is interesting and useful, besides it is not so difficult to employ. The useful part of the Hilbert transform can be explained by looking at the Cosine and the Sine functions of the Fourier transform of $e^{j\omega_o t}$. The Cosine wave has two spectral impulses located at $\pm\omega_o$. Each of these impulses in the frequency domain has a strength equal to ½ the amplitude of the Cosine wave. Similarly the Sin wave also has two spectral impulses located at $\pm\omega_o$. Each of these impulses in the frequency domain has a strength equal to ½ the amplitude of the Sine wave. The two Cosine components are real while the two Sine components are imaginary. If we draw these four spectral components on one plot in three dimensions then we get Figure 4.18.

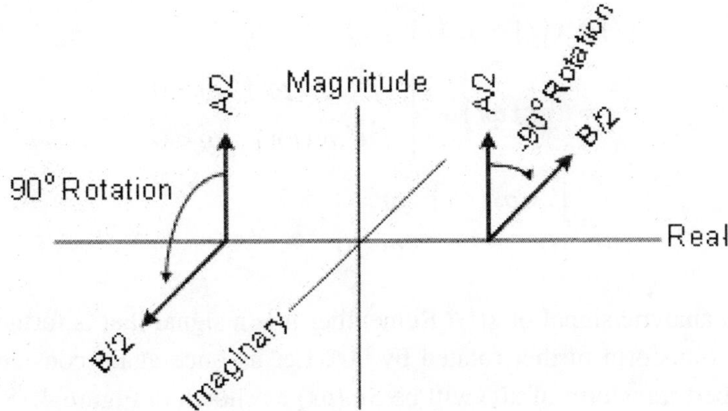

Figure 4.18: Special components of Cosine → A/2 and Sine → B/2. The Cosine components are both positive while one Sine component is positive and the other is negative.

In the Frequency domain to turn the Cosine wave into a Sine wave we can rotate the positive frequency impulse by -90° and the negative frequency impulse by +90°. This is what is shown in Figure 4.18 and this is what happens to any signal that we put through a Hilbert transformer. The Hilbert transformer will rotate the positive frequency components by -90° and the negative frequency impulse by +90°. So when we take a signal x(t) and whose Fourier transform is X(ω) and pass x(t) through a Hilbert transformer then the Fourier transform of the signal that is the Hilbert transform of x(t) will be as shown in Equation(4.70)

$$\widehat{X}(\omega) = \begin{cases} -jX(\omega) & \text{For } \omega > 0 \\ jX(\omega) & \text{For } \omega < 0 \end{cases} \tag{4.70}$$

This shows that the component that is in the positive frequency range is rotated by -90° which is the same as multiplying it by -j and the component that is in the negative frequency range is rotated by +90° which is the same as multiplying it by j. Now that we know what the Hilbert transform is and what it does let see how we are able to use the Hilbert transform. The Hilbert transform is used to create an 'Analytic signal'. An analytic signal is defined as $x_+(t) = x(t) + j\hat{x}(t)$. This equation shows that the analytic signal is formed by adding to the original signal its Hilbert transform further rotated by 90°. This is done for us in Equation(4.71)

$$\begin{aligned} x(t) &= Cos(\omega t) \\ \hat{x}(t) &= \begin{cases} -jCos(\omega t) & \omega > 0 \\ jCos(\omega t) & \omega < 0 \end{cases} = j(Sign(\omega))Cos(\omega t) \\ x_+(t) &= x(t) + j\hat{x}(t) \\ &= Cos(\omega t) + \begin{cases} -j^2 Cos(\omega t) & \omega > 0 \\ j^2 Cos(\omega t) & \omega < 0 \end{cases} \\ &= \begin{cases} 2Cos(\omega t) & \omega > 0 \\ 0 & \omega < 0 \end{cases} \end{aligned} \tag{4.71}$$

So what is an analytic signal of x(t)? Remember it is a signal that is formed by adding to the signal its Hilbert transform further rotated by 90°. Let us once again consider the signal x(t) = Cos(ωt). The Hilbert transform of x(t) will be Sin(ωt) as shown in Figure 4.18. Next we will proceed to form the analytic signal of x(t). For this we will need to further rotate the Hilbert transform of Cos(ωt), which is Sin(ωt) by another 90°. Refer to Figure 4.19. When we rotate the positive frequency component by 90° we get an impulse that is the same as the positive frequency impulse for the Cos(ωt); while when we rotate the negative frequency impulse we get an impulse that is negative of the impulse for the Cos(ωt). This is shown in Equation(4.71) and in Figure 4.19.

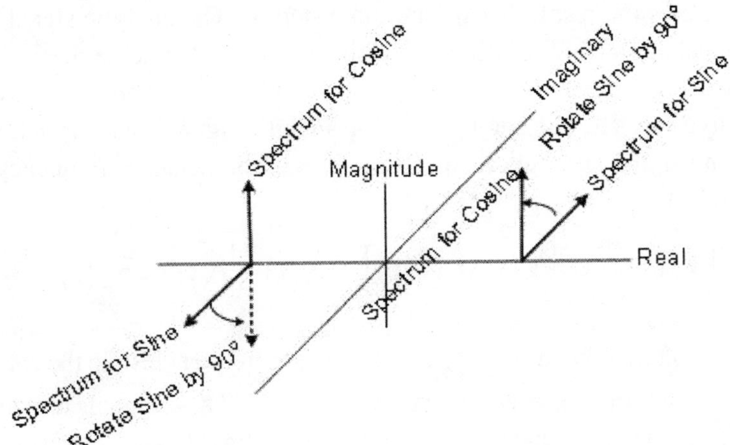

Figure 4.19: The phasor for Sine is multiplied by 'j' which is the same as rotating it by 90°. When the Sine phasor is rotated by 90° it adds to the Cosine phasor in the positive frequency range while it subtracts in the negative frequency range. So the resulting plot is the spectrum of full amplitude in the positive frequency region while in the negative frequency range the two spectrums cancel each other.

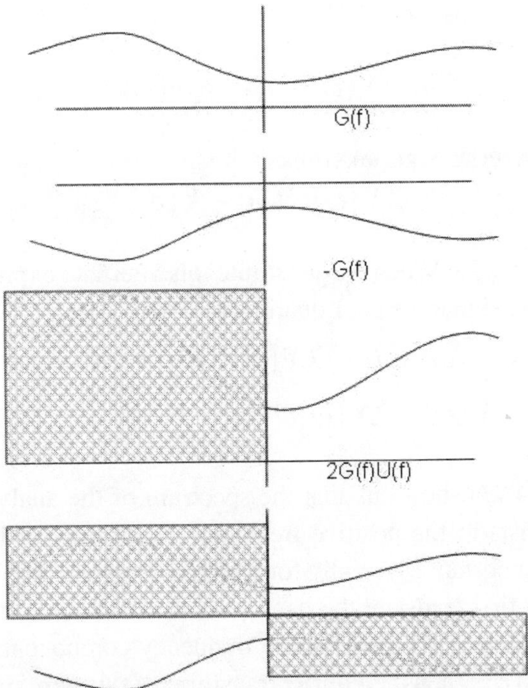

Figure 4.20: Signal Sign(f)G(f) = 2G(f)U(f)–G(f)

Equation(4.71) shows the result that we are interested in. The analytic signal is a single side band signal. This signal has a band only in the positive frequency range, in the negative frequency range there is no signal. This result is very interesting. Another related and interesting signal is the conjugate of the analytic signal. The conjugate of the analytic signal is also an analytic signal - i.e. it is a single side band signal and it has a spectrum only in the negative frequency range. This is shown in Equation(4.72)

$$\left[x_+(t)\right]^* = \left[x(t) + j\hat{x}(t)\right]^* = x(t) - j\hat{x}(t) = x_-(t) \tag{4.72}$$

This last signal $x_-(t)$ has a spectrum only in the negative frequencies. So the analytic signal and its complex conjugate form the complete spectrum of a signal. These signals are important as they permit us to separate out the upper and the lower side bands of modulated signals. A signal that has a spectrum in either only the positive frequency range or in only the negative frequency range is a signal that has only one side band. So at the time of transmission we can encode two different messages in the signal, one message in the upper side band and a different message in the lower side band.

This signal with two messages is then transmitted. At the receiver this process is repeated and the two side bands are separated from each other so that we get both the independent messages. What do we get if we continue to investigate this signal a little further? What will be the Fourier transform of the analytic signal?

$$X_+(\omega) = X(\omega) + j(-jSign(\omega)X(\omega))$$

In this equation we can write Sign(ω)X(ω)as

$$2X(\omega)U(\omega) - X(\omega)$$

This is shown in Figure 4.20. When we substitute this alternate expression for Sign(ω)X(ω) in the equation for the analytic signal we get Equation(4.73)

$$\begin{aligned} X_+(\omega) &= X(\omega) + j(-j2X(\omega)U(\omega) + jX(\omega)) \\ &= X(\omega) + 2X(\omega)U(\omega) - X(\omega) = 2X(\omega)U(\omega) \end{aligned} \tag{4.73}$$

Once again Equation(4.73) shows us that the spectrum of the analytic signal is a single side band spectrum; it only exists in the positive frequency range only or in the negative frequency range. This result is very important especially for band pass signals. We will see that the net effect of the analytic signal is to first translate the band pass signal down to the base band, double the magnitude of the spectrum, chop off the negative frequency component. Next if we multiply this single side band signal with $e^{j\omega_0 t}$ then the Fourier transform of this new signal will occupy the same one sided spectrum of the original signal but will be shifted in frequency to the frequency band at $\omega_0(t)$ as shown in Equation(4.74)

$$\breve{X}(\omega)=2X(\omega-\omega_o)U(\omega-\omega_o) \tag{4.74}$$

$$\breve{X}(\omega)=\begin{cases}2X(\omega-\omega_o) & \omega>\omega_o\\ X(0) & \omega=\omega_o\\ 0 & \omega<\omega_o\end{cases}$$

This signal has a one sided spectrum at the carrier frequency range. Also the carrier is suppressed and the spectrum is not symmetrical so we can look at either the upper or the lower side band. One example will make this clear. Consider a signal x(t) = 4Cos(4πt) - 6Sin(6πt) which is a base band signal, we will modulate this signal with a carrier signal that is Cos(400πt) so that it will be a band pass signal. The modulated signal then will be given in Equation(4.75)

$$\begin{aligned}x_m(t)=&2Cos\left(2\pi(200+2)t\right)+2Cos\left(2\pi(200-2)t\right)+\\&-3Sin\left(2\pi(200+3)t\right)-3Sin\left(2\pi(200-3)t\right)\end{aligned} \tag{4.75}$$

We next determine the Hilbert transform of the modulated signal. This is given in Equation(4.76)

$$\begin{aligned}\hat{x}_m(t)=&2Sin\left(2\pi(200+2)t\right)+2Sin\left(2\pi(200-2)t\right)+\\&-3Cos\left(2\pi(200+3)t\right)-3Cos\left(2\pi(200-3)t\right)\end{aligned} \tag{4.76}$$

Now that we have the signal and its Hilbert transform we can determine the analytic signal corresponding to the signal x(t). This is given in Equation(4.77).

This last equation, Equation(4.77), shows that the signal is the same as the original signal multiplied by a rotating phasor at the carrier frequency but it is a single side band signal. This is what the Hilbert transformer does for us.

$$\begin{aligned}x_{+m}(t)=&x_m(t)+j\hat{x}_m(t)\\ x_{+m}(t)=&2Cos\left(2\pi(200+2)t\right)+2Cos\left(2\pi(200-2)t\right)+\\&-3Sin\left(2\pi(200+3)t\right)-3Sin\left(2\pi(200-3)t\right)\\&+2Sin\left(2\pi(200+2)t\right)+2Sin\left(2\pi(200-2)t\right)+\\&-3Cos\left(2\pi(200+3)t\right)-3Cos\left(2\pi(200-3)t\right)\end{aligned} \tag{4.77}$$

Combining the terms together and doing some algebra we get

$$x_{+m}(t)=\left[4Cos(4\pi t)-6Sin(6\pi t)\right]e^{j400\pi t}$$

4.6 CHAPTER SUMMARY

Fourier Transforms:

In this chapter we have considered an alternate representation of signals. Now we are not limited to looking at and examining signals only in the time domain. With the Fourier Transform we can look at and study the signals in the Frequency domain. The following are the major points that we examined in this chapter.

The Fourier transform of a signal is a continuous function which gives us information about the frequency content of a time limited signal. We derived the Fourier transform by looking at one pulse of a periodic signal. We stretched out the period of this pulse by padding zeros to the pulse till the period of the pulse was infinite.

Symmetry Properties of Fourier Transforms:

The Fourier transforms display symmetry. If the signal in the time domain is real and an even function then the Fourier transform will be real and even function of frequency. In the same way if the Fourier transform of a real odd signal is an imaginary and an odd function of frequency.

Fourier Transforms of signals:

We have summarized several different Fourier transforms in Table 4.1, in Table 4.2 we have summarized several different properties of the Fourier transform and in Table 4.3 we have summarized the symmetry relations of the Fourier transform.

Ideal Filters:

We discussed three different types of ideal filters. When we discussed these ideal filters we were able to prove that ideal filters are not realizable since ideal filters are non causal filters. The three different types of ideal filters are the Low pass; the High pass and the Band pass filter. We also showed that the Band pass filter is a modulation of the low pass filter.

Design of Analog Filters:

Design of the analog filters is generally done by first designing a low pass filter. The low pass filter can be designed either as the Butterworth approximation or as the Chebychev approximation. To design the low pass filter as any one of these approximations requires that we determine the cutoff frequency of the low pass filter and the required order of the filter. Once these two parameters are determined the poles of the filter can be determined directly.

The Butterworth filter has a monotonic response which is greatest at zero frequency and from then on it is decreasing. The response has the most attenuation at the specified pass band edge so this is the frequency that is used to determine the order of the filter and the cutoff frequency. The response has the least attenuation at the specified stop band edge so this is the second frequency that is used to determine the order of the filter and the cutoff frequency. The two equations are solved simultaneously to determine the two required parameters.

The Chebychev filters come as either type1 or as type 2. In the type 1 filter the pass band has the ripples while the stop band has the smooth response and the filter is an all pole filter. In the type 2 filter the stop band has the ripples while the pass band has the smooth response and the filter needs both zeros and poles to build the filter. To determine the order of the filter we use the specified gain at the pass band edge. Once the order of the filter is known the cutoff frequency of the filter can be computed by noting that the gain at the cutoff frequency is -3dB.

The Hilbert Transform:

The Hilbert transform of a signal is essential to determine the analytic signal of a time domain signal. The analytic signal of a time domain signal is a single side band signal. The Hilbert transform further showed us that for a real part and the imaginary part of a real causal stable signal are not independent and are related to each other. The Hilbert transform of a signal is obtained by rotating the positive frequency components of a signal by -90^0 and rotating the negative frequency components by $+90^0$.

4.7 HOMEWORK PROBLEMS

Definition of Fourier Transform

Problem 4.7.1

Use the definition of the Fourier transform to determine the following {You are given $x(t) \Leftrightarrow X(\omega)$}:

4.6.1.1 $xa(t) = x(-t)$

4.6.1.2 $xb(t) = x^*(t)$

4.6.1.3 $xc(t) = x^*(-t)$

Problem 4.7.2

Show that the Magnitude function of the Fourier transform $|X(\omega)| = (X_R(\omega)^2 + X_I(\omega)^2)^{1/2}$ is an even function and the Phase function $\tan^{-1}(\theta) = [X_I(\omega)/X_R(\omega)]$ of the Fourier transform is an odd function.

Problem 4.7.3

Using the definition of Fourier Transform obtain the Fourier transform of the following signals:

4.6.3.1 $x_1(t) = ae^{-\alpha t}u(t) \quad \alpha>0$

4.6.3.2 $x_2(t) = ae^{\alpha t}u(-t) \quad \alpha>0$

4.6.3.3 $x_3(t) = ae^{-|\alpha|t}u(t) \quad \alpha>0$

4.6.3.4 $x_4(t) = x_2(t) - x_1(t) \quad \alpha>0$

Symmetry Relations

Problem 4.7.4

Prove the following:

4.7.4.1 When x(t) is an odd function (i.e., x(t) = -x(-t)) then show that

$$X(\omega) = 2j\int_0^{\infty} x(t)\sin(\omega t)dt$$

4.7.4.2 When x(t) is an even function (i.e., x(t) = x(-t)) then show that

$$X(\omega) = 2\int_0^{\infty} x(t)\cos(\omega t)dt$$

4.7.4.3 When x(t) is a conjugate anti symmetric function then show that its Fourier transform is purely imaginary. $\{x_{ca}(t) = \frac{1}{2}\{x(t) - x^*(-t)\}$

4.7.4.4 When x(t) is a conjugate symmetric function then show that its Fourier transform is purely real. $\{x_{cs}(t) = \frac{1}{2}\{x(t) + x^*(-t)\}$

4.7.4.5 When X(ω) is a conjugate anti symmetric function then show that its inverse Fourier transform is purely imaginary.

4.7.4.6 When X(ω) is a conjugate symmetric function then show that its inverse Fourier transform is purely real.

Properties of Fourier Transforms

Problem 4.7.5

Using the Fourier transform properties determine the Fourier transform of the following functions. Assume you know the Fourier transform of x(t)⇔X(w):

4.7.5.1 $\mathbb{F}\{tx(t)\}$

4.7.5.2 $\mathbb{F}\{e^{-j\alpha t}x(t)\} \quad \alpha > 0$

4.7.5.3 $\mathbb{F}\{e^{-j\alpha t}tx(t)\} \quad \alpha > 0$

Problem 4.7.6

Using the Fourier transform properties determine the Fourier transform of the following functions. Assume you know the Fourier transform of x(t)⇔X(w):

4.7.6.1 $\mathbb{F}\{x(\alpha t)\} \quad \alpha > 0$

4.7.6.2 $\mathbb{F}\{x(-\alpha t)\} \quad \alpha > 0$

4.7.6.3 Using the result from problem 4.7.6.2 determine the Fourier transform of the mirror image of a function when you know the Fourier transform of a function.

Problem 4.7.7

First show that the Fourier transform of a pulse shown in Figure 4.21 is given by AτSinc(ωτ). Then using various different theorems of the Fourier transform determine the Fourier transform of the other figures shown in Figure 4.21.

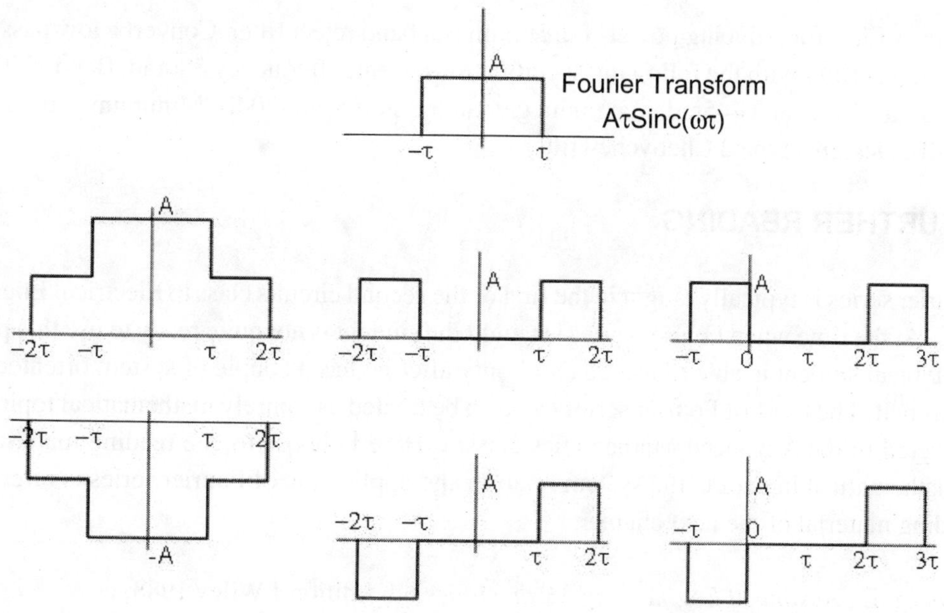

Figure 4.21: You are given the Fourier Transform of a rectangular pulse. Using Fourier transform Theorems determine the Fourier transforms of all the other functions shown. Verify your answer by directly calculating the Fourier transform of each.

Filters and Filter Design

Problem 4.7.8

An anti aliasing filter of the low pass type is to be designed to have a gain variation less than 1.5dB in the pass band that extends from 0rad to 20rad. The stop band for the filter has to begin at 25rad with a maximum gain not to exceed -20dB.

4.7.8.1 Determine the required Chebychev filter transfer function for this filter.
4.7.8.2 Determine the required Butterworth filter transfer function for this filter.

Problem 4.7.9

To reduce power source hum in signals a high pass filter is often used. Design a high pass filter by transforming a low pass filter. The required filter has to have pass band starting at 450rad with minimum gain in the pass band of -1.25dB. The stop band of the high pass filter extends up to 350rad with a maximum gain in the stop band being -20dB. Determine the transfer function for a Butterworth filter.

Problem 4.7.10

A better filter for reducing power source hum is a band reject filter. Convert a low pass filter to the band reject filter with the following specifications: Center frequency 380rad, Bandwidth 60rad, stop bands at 325rad and 445rad, maximum gain in the stop band -30dB. Minimum gain in the pass band -2dB. Design a type 2 Chebychev filter.

4.8 FURTHER READING

Fourier series is typically taught in the first or the second circuits class to Electrical Engineering students. At the time when Fourier series is taught the student is not quite ready to use this powerful tool. A typical student is able to use this tool only after he has a couple of system oriented classes under his belt. The topic of Fourier series can also be treated as a purely mathematical topic. So it is also covered in the Advanced Mathematics classes. Here I choose to cite reading material that is more mathematical in nature, the system relation and application of Fourier series is referred to in the reading material of the next chapter.

1. Kreyszig, E., *Advanced Engineering Mathematics* 6th Edition J Wiley 1988.

2. Papoulis, A., *Signal Analysis* McGraw Hill 1977.

CHAPTER 5

The Laplace Transform

INTRODUCTION

In this chapter we study a very useful transform which is similar to the Fourier transform but it is much more powerful than the Fourier transform. We will see that the power of the Laplace transform comes from the fact that the negative exponential used to transform the time domain signal has both the real part and an imaginary part. The negative exponential for the Fourier transform has only the imaginary part. The presence of the negative real part in the exponent forces the function to go to zero as $t \rightarrow \infty$. This makes it possible for many more functions to possess a Laplace transform even when they cannot have a Fourier transfer. Since the difference between the two transforms is so slight we will see that there are many similarities between the two transforms, due to the similarities of the two transforms we will find that the properties of two transforms are very similar to each other, there are however enough differences between the two transforms for us to study the two of them individually. In this chapter we will study what makes the Laplace transform so much more desirable then the Fourier transform.

In the previous chapter we saw that the Fourier transform has difficulty in applications when the input is a function that starts from say $t = 0$ onwards. This is because we have no way of introducing initial conditions with the Fourier transforms as the Fourier transform is always defined from $-\infty$ to $+\infty$, you must compute what is going on within the system from $-\infty$. You cannot say that the sum total of the effect at time $t = 0$ is such and such. That is what the initial conditions accomplish. In these cases the Fourier transform falls apart. There is no way of including initial conditions in the Fourier transform. These difficulties are overcome by the Laplace transform.

The evaluation of the Fourier transform and its inverse is along the imaginary axis as Fourier transform uses the exponential $e^{-j\omega t}$. The Laplace transform moves the evaluation from the imaginary axis to an axis located at some real value σ away from the imaginary axis by using the exponential $e^{(\sigma+j\omega)t}$. The addition of the factor $e^{-\sigma t}$ to the Laplace transform will make the transform more useful as it will permit the transform converge for many more functions. The value of σ can be either positive or negative or zero. When σ is zero the Fourier transform and the Laplace transform are identical to each other.

$$\begin{aligned} L\{x(t)\} &= X(s) = \int_{-\infty}^{\infty} x(t)e^{-st}dt \\ L^{-1}\{X(s)\} &= \frac{1}{2\pi j}\int_{\sigma-j\omega}^{\sigma+j\omega} X(s)e^{st}ds \end{aligned} \tag{5.1}$$

The Laplace Transform pair is shown in Equation(5.1). In this representation the term L{x(t)} is the short form notation for the integral that is on the right hand side. Similarly the term L-1{X(s)} is the short form notation for the integral appearing on the right hand side of that equation.

5.1 THE BILATERAL AND THE ONE-SIDED LAPLACE TRANSFORM

In order to better understand the difference between the Fourier and the Laplace transforms consider first the Fourier transform of a function x(t) that is Fourier transformable. So we have Equation(5.2)

$$\begin{aligned} F\{x(t)\} &= \dot{X}(j\omega) = \int_{-\infty}^{\infty} x(t)e^{-j\omega t}dt \\ F^{-1}\{X(j\omega)\} = x(t) &= \frac{1}{2\pi}\int_{-\infty}^{\infty} X(j\omega)e^{j\omega t}d\omega \end{aligned} \tag{5.2}$$

Next consider the definition of another function f(t) as $f(t) = x(t)e^{-\sigma t}$ where σ is a real number. The Fourier transform of f(t) and its inverse are given in Equation(5.3)

$$\begin{aligned} F\{f(t)\} &= \int_{-\infty}^{\infty} f(t)e^{-\omega t}dt = \int_{-\infty}^{\infty} x(t)e^{-\sigma t}e^{-j\omega t}dt = X(\sigma+j\omega) \\ F^{-1}\{X(\sigma+j\omega)\} &= f(t) = x(t)e^{-\sigma t} = \frac{1}{2\pi}\int_{-\infty}^{\infty} X(\sigma+j\omega)e^{j\omega t}d\omega \\ x(t) &= \frac{1}{2\pi}\int_{-\infty}^{\infty} X(\sigma+j\omega)e^{\sigma t}e^{j\omega t}d\omega \end{aligned} \tag{5.3}$$

In Equation(5.3) the quantity σ+jω is the complex frequency. This complex frequency shifts the axis of convergence of the Fourier transform from the imaginary axis to some positive value σ into the right half of the complex plane. This is the difference between the Laplace transform and the Fourier transform. When we use the Laplace transform we generally replace the complex frequency σ+jω by s. Replacing σ+jω by s in Equation(5.3) we get Equation(5.4).

$$X(s)=\int_{-\infty}^{\infty}x(t)e^{-st}dt$$

$$x(t)\ =\frac{1}{2\pi}\int_{\sigma-j\infty}^{\sigma+j\infty}X(s)e^{st}ds \tag{5.4}$$

Figure 5.1 shows graphically what we have been discussing in Equations(5.3) and (5.4). The advantage of using Laplace transform over the Fourier transform becomes clear from Figure 5.1. In Figure 5.1, we see a plot of a function x(t) that has a pole in the right half of the s-plane, (pole at c in the figure). This function will not converge when we try to determine its Fourier transform, and hence this function will not have a Fourier transform. The same function will have a Laplace transform if the poles of the function are at some value $c<\sigma$. The region of convergence of the Laplace transform is shown as the shaded region in Figure 5.1. The path of integration (for the inverse transform) is shown along the edge of the shaded region.

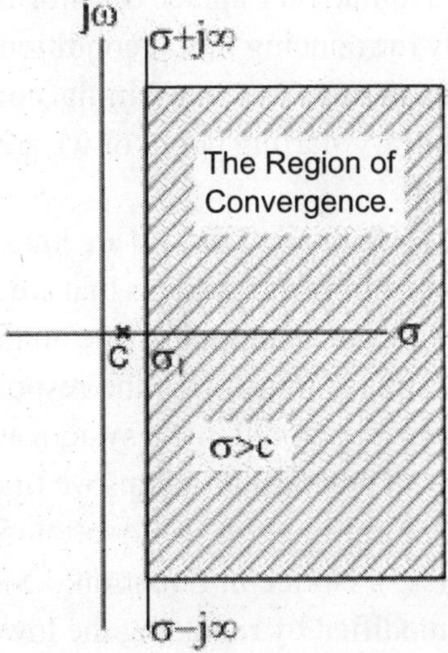

Figure 5.1: The region of convergence and the path of integration for the Laplace Transform

Equation(5.4) shows that the path of integration for the Laplace transform has been shifted from the imaginary axis (which was the path of integration for the Fourier transform) to a parallel axis. The new axis is at a point on the real axis where the real part is σ. The integration takes place on this axis at σ from $-j\infty$ to $+j\infty$. In this form, Equation(5.4), we have the definition of the bilateral or the two-sided Laplace transform pair.

Often we are faced with a question: if the Fourier transform of a function does not exist can the Laplace transform exist? To answer this we refer to Equation(5.2) first. In Equation(5.2) we assumed that the Fourier transform of the function x(t) existed. That is the integral of $x(t)e^{-j\omega t}$ converges. What if the integral of $x(t)e^{-j\omega t}$ does not converge? Then the Fourier transform will not exist. Now consider the effect of multiplying the function $x(t)e^{-j\omega t}$ by $e^{-\sigma t}$. Very often the integral of

$x(t)e^{-(\sigma+j\omega)t}$ will converge. This is because the multiplying function, $e^{-\sigma t}$, is a decaying function which may force the function $x(t)e^{-j\omega t}$ to converge. So even if the Fourier transform of x(t) does not exist the Fourier transform of $x(t)e^{-\sigma t}$ could exist if we make σ large enough. This will be so because the exponential, $e^{-\sigma t}$ is a monotonically decreasing function. The function $e^{-\sigma t}$ would make the transform integral converge. So the Fourier transform of $x(t)e^{-\sigma t}$ would exist, but that is the Laplace transform of x(t). So the Laplace transform of a function could exist even when the Fourier transform of the function may not exist. The presence of the convergence factor $e^{-\sigma t}$ in the integral of the Laplace transform permits us to evaluate the integral even for difficult functions for which the Fourier transform does not exist.

The Laplace transform in the form of Equation(5.1) is not very useful. A much more useful result is obtained by using the one sided transform. The bilateral Laplace transform begins at $t = -\infty$ and extends to $t = \infty$. In this form the transform is not a very useful transform since all the systems that we propose to use the Laplace transform in have a starting point. The systems have not been running from time immemorial. With a unilateral Laplace transform we are able to add this starting point other than $t = -\infty$. This is done by introducing initial conditions. We are able to add a starting point for the systems since the transform permits us to have initial conditions. With initial conditions we can analyze systems from some arbitrary starting point, or we are also able to consider functions that are zero or non existent for time $t<0$.

Functions and systems that start at $t = 0$, or are 0 for $t<0$ are known as causal functions or causal systems. We restrict considerations to functions and systems that are zero for $t<0$ because in physical systems we do not expect and nor do we have an output before an input is applied, usually we treat this time as $t = 0$. So with the use of Laplace transforms the response of physical systems can be determined from the knowledge of the energy stored in the system at $t = 0$ (the initial condition) and the response to the system for $t>0$. So in all practical problems we first assume that the input function is zero for $t<0$ and the two sided transform integral in Equation(5.4) is replaced by a one sided transform integral shown in Equation(5.5). Notice in Equation(5.5) the inverse transform does not change only the forward transform is modified by replacing the lower limit on the integral by zero.

$$X(s) = \int_0^{\infty} x(t)e^{-st}dt$$

$$x(t) = \frac{1}{2\pi}\int_{\sigma-j\infty}^{\sigma+j\infty} X(s)e^{st}ds \tag{5.5}$$

5.2 TABLE OF LAPLACE TRANSFORM PAIRS

Let us first see how we use the Laplace transform integral to calculate the Laplace transform of some simple functions that we will be using often.

Example 5.1

Calculate the Laplace transform of the impulse $\delta(t)$.

Solution 5.1

The Laplace transform of the impulse can be directly obtained from the definition equation of the Laplace transform $L[\delta(t)] = \int_0^\infty \delta(t)e^{-st}\,dt$. By using the property of the impulse function we get the L[δ(t)] = 1.

Example 5.2

Calculate the Laplace Transform of the unit step function U(t).

Solution 5.2

The Laplace transform of the unit step function can be directly obtained from the definition equation of the Laplace transform $L[u(t)] = \int_0^\infty u(t)e^{-st}\,dt = \left.\frac{e^{-st}}{-s}\right|_0^\infty = \left.\frac{e^{-(\sigma+j\omega)t}}{-s}\right|_0^\infty = \frac{1}{s}$.

Example 5.3

Calculate the Laplace Transform of a decaying exponential function $e^{-at}u(t)$.

Solution 5.3

The Laplace transform of a decaying exponential function can be directly obtained from the definition equation of the Laplace transform.

$$L\left[e^{-\alpha t}\right] = \int_0^\infty e^{-\alpha t}e^{-st}\,dt = \int_0^\infty e^{-(s+\alpha)t}\,dt = \left.\frac{e^{-(s+\alpha)t}}{(s+\alpha)}\right|_0^\infty = \frac{1}{(s+\alpha)}$$

Example 5.4

Calculate the Laplace Transform of a sinusoid function Cos(αωt).

Solution 5.4

The Laplace transform of a sinusoid function can be directly obtained from the definition equation of the Laplace transform

$$L[Cos(\alpha t)] = \int_0^\infty Cos(\alpha t)e^{-st}\,dt = \tfrac{1}{2}\int_0^\infty \left(e^{\alpha t} + e^{-\alpha t}\right)e^{-st}\,dt$$

$$= \tfrac{1}{2}\left[\left.\frac{e^{-(s+\alpha)t}}{-(s+\alpha)}\right|_0^\infty + \left.\frac{e^{-(s+\alpha)t}}{-(s+\alpha)}\right|_0^\infty\right] = \frac{s}{\left(s^2+\alpha^2\right)}$$

The other Laplace transform pairs can be derived in a similar manner.

Table 5.1: A few selected Laplace Transform pairs

$x(t)=\frac{1}{2\pi j}\int_{\sigma-j\infty}^{\sigma+j\infty} X(s)e^{st}ds$	$X(s)=\int_0^\infty x(t)e^{-st}dt$
e^{-at}	$\frac{1}{s+a}$
te^{-at}	$\frac{1}{(s+a)^2}$
$Sin(\omega t)$	$\frac{\omega}{s^2+\omega^2}$
$Cos(\omega t)$	$\frac{s}{s^2+\omega^2}$
$e^{-at}Sin(\omega t)$	$\frac{\omega}{(s+a)^2+\omega^2}$
$e^{-at}Cos(\omega t)$	$\frac{s+a}{(s+a)^2+\omega^2}$
$tSin(\omega t)$	$\frac{2\omega s}{(s^2+\omega^2)^2}$
$tCos(\omega t)$	$\frac{s^2-\omega^2}{(s^2+\omega^2)^2}$

5.3 PROPERTIES OF THE LAPLACE TRANSFORM

Just as we saw when we were studying the Fourier transform that the Fourier transform has some nice properties that help us in understanding the transform better and also to build more transform pairs. The Laplace transform also has some properties that will help us to understand the transform and to expand our collection of transform pairs. To prove the Laplace transform properties we will use the one sided Laplace transform as that is the transform that is most often used. All the properties are summarized in Table 5.2.

5.3.1 Linearity:

This property is listed in Equation(5.6).

$$\begin{aligned} L\{\alpha_1 x_1(t) \pm \alpha_2 x_2(t)\} &= L\{\alpha_1 x_1(t)\} \pm L\{\alpha_2 x_2(t)\} \\ &= \alpha_1 X_1(s) \pm \alpha_2 X_2(s) \end{aligned} \tag{5.6}$$

Table 5.2: Properties of the Laplace Transform

Linearity	$L\{\alpha_1 x_1(t)+\alpha_2 x_2(t)\}$	$\alpha_1 X_1(s)+\alpha_2 X_2(s)$
Time Derivative	$L\left(\dfrac{dx(t)}{dt}\right)$	$sX(s)-x(0^+)$
Time Integral	$L\left(\int_{-\infty}^{t} x(\xi)d\xi\right)$	$\dfrac{1}{s}X(s)+\dfrac{1}{s}x^{(-1)}(0^+)$
Shift in Time	$L\{x(t-\tau)U(t-\tau)\}$	$e^{-s\tau}X(s)$
Shift in Frequency	$L\{e^{-\alpha t}x(t)\}$	$X(s+\alpha)$
Multiplication by t	$L\{tx(t)\}$	$-\dfrac{dX(s)}{ds}$
Time Scaling	$L\{x(t/\alpha)\}$	$\alpha X(\alpha s)$
Initial Value	$\lim_{t\to 0} x(t)$	$\lim_{s\to\infty} sX(s)$
Final Value	$\lim_{t\to\infty} x(t)$	$\lim_{s\to 0} sX(s)$

To prove this property we will first assume that the two functions $x_1(t)$ and $x_1(t)$ are Laplace transformable and α_1 and α_2 are two constants. We begin by writing the definition of the Laplace transform as shown in Equation(5.7). Evaluating the Laplace transform we prove the Linearity property.

$$\begin{aligned} L\{\alpha_1 x_1(t)\pm\alpha_2 x_2(t)\} &= \int_0^\infty (\alpha_1 x_1(t)\pm\alpha_2 x_2(t))e^{-st}dt \\ &= \int_0^\infty (\alpha_1 x_1(t))e^{-st}dt \pm \int_0^\infty (\alpha_2 x_2(t))e^{-st}dt \qquad (5.7) \\ &= \alpha_1 X_1(s)\pm\alpha_2 X_2(s) \end{aligned}$$

Example 5.5

Calculate the Laplace Transform of a linear function $(e^{-5t}+e^{-3t})u(t)$

Solution 5.5

We know the Laplace transform of the two exponentials individually and then we can use the Linearity theorem to find the Laplace transform of the combination as:

$$L\left[\left(e^{-3t}+e^{-5t}\right)u(t)\right] = \int_0^\infty \left(e^{-3t}+e^{-5t}\right)e^{-st}dt$$

$$= \int_0^\infty e^{-3t}e^{-st}+e^{-5t}e^{-st}dt = \frac{1}{s+3}+\frac{1}{s+5}$$

5.3.2 Time Derivative:

The derivative of a function that is Laplace transformable has a special relation with the function itself. This relation is expressed in Equation(5.8)

$$L\left\{\frac{dx(t)}{dt}\right\} = sX(s) - x(0^+) \tag{5.8}$$

To prove the relation in Equation(5.8) we once again begin with the definition of the Laplace transform and integrate by parts to get:

$$\begin{aligned} L\left\{\frac{dx(t)}{dt}\right\} &= \int_0^\infty \frac{dx(t)}{dt} e^{-st} dt \\ &= x(t)e^{-st}\Big|_0^\infty + s\int_0^\infty x(t)e^{-st} dt \\ &= sX(s) - x(0^+) \end{aligned} \tag{5.9}$$

In arriving at Equation(5.9) we have made use of the fact that

$$\operatorname*{Limit}_{t\to\infty}\left(x(t)e^{-st}\right) = 0 \tag{5.10}$$

If this was not true then the Laplace transform does not exist. This limit will exist as long as x(t) does not increase faster than the negative exponential decreases. In the limit we have two functions, one is increasing towards ∞ while the other is decreasing towards zero, so whenever the function decreasing towards zero wins the Laplace transform will exist. This is the same as saying that x(t) does not have a pole to the right of σ in the Laplace transform.

$$\begin{aligned} L\{x(t-\tau)u(t-\tau)\} &= \int_0^\infty x(t-\tau)u(t-\tau)e^{-st} dt \\ &= \int_{-\tau}^\infty x(t')u(t')e^{-s(t'+\tau)} dt' \\ &= e^{-s\tau}\int_0^\infty x(t')e^{-st'} dt' = e^{-s\tau}X(s) \end{aligned}$$

We will find that this theorem plays a big part when we want to solve differential equations. We will see this in Section 5.5 in this chapter. Notice how the initial condition is introduced into the transform just when it is needed.

Example 5.6

Use the differentiation theorem to calculate the Laplace Transform of Sin(3t) given that the Laplace transform of Cos(3t) = $s/(s^2+3^2)$.

Solution 5.6

We know that the derivative of Cos(3t) = -1/3Sin(3t). So we can derive the Laplace transform of Sin(3t) by using the derivative theorem and the Linearity theorem. L[-1/3Cos(3t)] = L[sin(3t)]. So when we use these two theorems we get:

$$L\left[Sin(3t)\right] = L\left[\frac{d\left(-\frac{1}{3}Cos(3t)\right)}{dt}\right] = -\tfrac{1}{3}\left[sX(s) - x(0^-)\right]$$

$$= -\tfrac{1}{3}\left[\frac{s \bullet s}{s^2+3^2} - 1\right] \quad = -\tfrac{1}{3}\left[\frac{s^2 - s^2 - 3^2}{s^2+3^2}\right] = \frac{3}{s^2+3^2}$$

which is the Laplace transform of Sin(3t).

5.3.3 Time Integral:

The Laplace transform of the integral of a function that is Laplace transformable is shown in Equation(5.11). The notation used in Equation(5.11) and (5.12) is as follows. When a function is raised to a negative power this is written in (), this implies that the function is integrated once if the negative power is 1. The function is integrated n times if the negative power is n.

$$L\left\{\int_{-\infty}^{t} x(\xi)\,d\xi\right\} = \frac{1}{s}X(s) + \frac{1}{s}x^{(-1)}\left(0^+\right) \tag{5.11}$$

In Equation(5.11) the term $x^{(-1)}(0^+)$ is the initial value of the integral of x(t). The initial value corresponds to the evaluation of the integral from time - ∞ to the time when the Laplace transform begins which is time t = 0. The proof is given in Equation(5.12).

In Equation(5.12) the term $x^{(-1)}(0^+)$ represents the value of the integral at t = 0^+ which is also the initial condition.

$$L\left\{\int_{-\infty}^{t} x(\xi)\,d\xi\right\} = \int_{0}^{\infty}\left\{\int_{-\infty}^{t} x(\xi)\,d\xi\right\}e^{-st}dt$$

$$= \left[\frac{-e^{-st}}{s}\int_{-\infty}^{t} x(\xi)\,d\xi\right]_0^{\infty} + \frac{1}{s}\int_{0}^{\infty} x(t)e^{-st}dt \tag{5.12}$$

$$= \frac{1}{s}\int_{0}^{\infty} x(t)e^{-st}dt + \frac{1}{s}\int_{-\infty}^{0} x(\xi)\,d\xi = \frac{1}{s}X(s) + \frac{1}{s}x^{(-1)}\left(0^+\right)$$

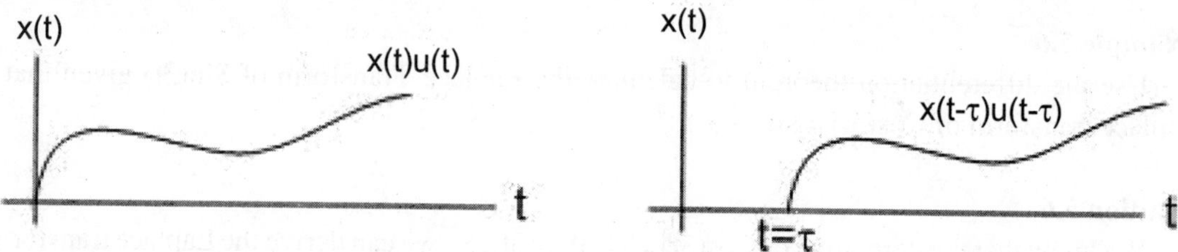

Figure 5.2: A function x(t) starting at t = 0 and a shifted copy of the same function starting at t = τ

5.3.4 Shift in the Time Domain:

When a time domain function is shifted in time the Laplace domain function undergoes a rotation as shown in Equation(5.13). The shift of the time domain function is shown in Figure 5.2. This property is proved in Equation(5.14)

$$L\{x(t-\tau)U(t-\tau)\} = e^{s\tau}X(s) \tag{5.13}$$

$$\begin{aligned} L\{x(t-\tau)U(t-\tau)\} &= \int_0^\infty x(t-\tau)U(t-\tau)e^{-st}\,dt \\ &= \int_0^\infty x(t')e^{-s(t'+\tau)}\,dt' = e^{-s\tau}\int_0^\infty x(t')e^{-st'}\,dt' \\ &= e^{-s\tau}X(s) \end{aligned} \tag{5.14}$$

5.3.5 Shift in the Frequency Domain:

When a time domain function is multiplied by e^{at} the Laplace domain function undergoes a shift as shown in Equation(5.15). The shift of the frequency domain function is shown in Figure 5.3.

$$L\{e^{-\alpha t}x(t)\} = X(s+\alpha) \tag{5.15}$$

In Figure 5.3 we assume that the time domain function has a Laplace transform as shown in

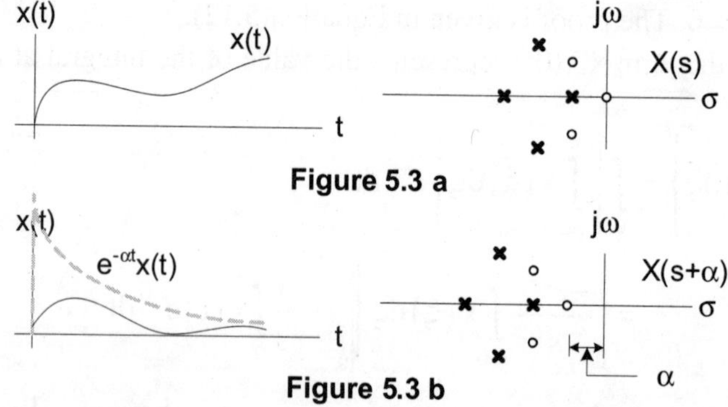

Figure 5.3: A function x(t) and its Laplace transform are shown in Figure 5.3a. The function e^{at} x(t) and its Laplace transform showing shift in the Laplace domain are shown in Figure 5.3b.

Figure 5.3a. When we multiply the time domain function by e^{at} and we determine the Laplace transform of this new function we find that the new Laplace transform has the same shape except it is shifted in the s-domain. This property is proved in Equation(5.16). The shape of the Laplace transform function is represented by its pole-zero plot in Figure 5.3. Notice that the shape of the Laplace transform remains the same except it is shifted by α units.

$$L\{e^{-\alpha t}x(t)\} = \int_0^\infty e^{-\alpha t}x(t)e^{-st}dt = \int_0^\infty x(t)e^{-(s+\alpha)t}dt$$

$$= \int_0^\infty x(t)e^{-(s')t}dt \tag{5.16}$$

$$= \int_0^\infty x(t)e^{-s't}dt' = X(s') = X(s+\alpha)$$

Example 5.7

Use the shift in the Frequency domain theorem to calculate the Laplace Transform of $e^{-4t}Sin(3t)$ given that the Laplace transform of $Sin(3t) = 3/(s^2+3^2)$

Solution 5.7

We are given the Laplace transform of Sin(3t) and we have to use the Frequency shift theorem. Applying the theorem we get the new transform directly by replacing s by (s+4)

thus: $L\left[e^{-4t}Sin(3t)\right] = \left[\dfrac{3}{(s+4)^2+3^2}\right]$

5.3.6 Multiplication by t:

When the time domain function is multiplied by the time variable then the Laplace transform of the new function is the negative derivative of the Laplace transform of the original function. This property is proved in Equation(5.17)

$$L\{tx(t)\} = -\frac{dX(s)}{ds}$$

$$= \int_0^\infty tx(t)e^{-st}dt = -\int_0^\infty \frac{d\{x(t)e^{-st}\}}{ds} \tag{5.17}$$

$$= \frac{-d\left[\int_0^\infty x(t)e^{-st}dt\right]}{ds} = -\frac{dX(s)}{ds}$$

Example 5.8

Use the multiplication by t theorem to calculate the Laplace Transform of tSin(3t) given that the

Laplace transform of Sin(3t) = $3/(s^2+3^2)$.

Solution 5.8

We are given the Laplace transform of Sin(3t) and we have to use the multiplication by t theorem. This theorem requires that we differentiate the Frequency domain function with respect to s and then change its sign. Applying the theorem we get the new transform as shown

$$L\left[tSin(3t)\right] = -\frac{dX(s)}{ds} = -\frac{d\left(\frac{3}{s^2+3^2}\right)}{ds}$$

$$=3\frac{2s}{\left(s^2+3^2\right)^2} = \frac{6s}{\left(s^2+3^2\right)^2}$$

5.3.7 Time Scaling:

When the function in the time domain is scaled by a positive constant α then the function in the Laplace domain is scaled by the reciprocal of the scaling factor or 1/α. This is shown in Equation(5.18) and proved in Equation(5.19).

$$L\left\{x\left(t/\alpha\right)\right\} = \alpha X(\alpha s) \qquad \alpha > 0 \tag{5.18}$$

The effect of time scale is to bring the poles and zeros either closer together if α>1 or to spread them apart if α<1.

$$L\left\{x\left(t/\alpha\right)\right\} = \int_0^\infty x\left(t/\alpha\right)e^{-st}dt$$

$$= \alpha\int_0^\infty x(t')e^{-s\alpha t'}dt' = \alpha\int_0^\infty x(t')e^{-s't'}dt' \tag{5.19}$$

$$= \alpha X(s') = \alpha X(\alpha s)$$

Example 5.9

Use the time scale theorem to calculate the Laplace Transform of e^{-6t} when it is written as $e^{-3(2t)}$. Here the beginning function is e^{-3t} which is scaled in time so t' = 2t.

Solution 5.9

We know the Laplace transform of e^{-3t} is 1/(s+3) and we are given the scale factor here as ½. When we apply the theorem we get

$$L\left[e^{-6t}\right] = L\left[e^{-3(2t)}\right] = \frac{\frac{1}{2}}{s/2+3} = \frac{1}{s+6}$$

just as we expected it to be. This example gives us an idea what happens to the poles and the zeros of the function in the Frequency domain when we scale the function in the time domain. In this example the pole moved from s = -3 to s = -6.

5.3.8 Initial and Final Value Theorem:

The initial value theorem relates the initial value of the time domain function to its value in the Laplace domain. This theorem is listed in Equation(5.20). The final value theorem relates the final value of the time domain function to its value in the Laplace domain. This theorem is listed in Equation(5.21).

$$\text{Initial value } \lim_{t\to 0^+} x(t) = \lim_{s\to\infty} sX(s) \text{ if the limit exists.} \tag{5.20}$$

$$\text{Final value } \lim_{t\to \infty} x(t) = \lim_{s\to 0} sX(s) \text{ if the limit exists.} \tag{5.21}$$

The final value will be determined provided sF(s) is analytic on the imaginary axis($\sigma = 0$) and on the right half ($\sigma > 0$) of the s-plane.

5.4 THE INVERSE LAPLACE TRANSFORM

The inverse Laplace transform can be obtained by using the inverse transform integral. Using the inverse transform integral requires that we perform the integral in the complex domain. Most people find it very difficult to evaluate a complex integral. Fortunately for us there is a much easier way to determine the inverse Laplace transform. The easiest way is to look up the Laplace transform pairs shown in Table 5.1. Or to use one of the Laplace transform theorems to obtain one transform from another. A sample of Laplace transform theorems are given in Table 5.2. The table lookup method uses the result of the inverse Laplace transform integral without evaluating the inverse transform integral. This is possible because the time domain function and its Laplace transform are unique to each other, they have a one-to-one correspondence. So as soon as you find a Laplace domain function in the table that is the same as the Laplace domain function that you have, its inverse is obtained by looking up the entry on the other side of the table.

For many cases the Laplace domain function will be a quotient of two polynomials in the s-domain. These functions generally will not appear in the table of the Laplace transform pairs. In these cases we will re-write the Laplace domain function into several partial fractions in such a way that each partial fraction appears in the table of Laplace transform pairs. Most of the time when we examine the ratio of two polynomials we will find that in the ratio the power of the numerator polynomial is less than the power of the denominator polynomial. This is what we want and this is what will be our starting point. Such a fraction is known as a proper fraction. Sometimes the power of the numerator polynomial could be higher than the power of the denominator polynomial. In this case we begin by dividing the numerator polynomial with the denominator polynomial. The result will be a polynomial in s and an extra term that is a proper fraction. This is shown in Equation(5.22).

$$F(s) = \alpha_0 + \alpha_1 s + \alpha_2 s^2 + ... + \frac{\beta_1}{(s - s_1)} +$$
$$\frac{\beta_2}{(s - s_2)} + ... + \frac{\beta_{p1}}{(s - s_p)} + \frac{\beta_{p2}}{(s - s_p)^2} + ... + \frac{\beta_{pk}}{(s - s_p)^k} \quad (5.22)$$

Equation(5.22) contains three types of terms. The first set of terms is a polynomial in s; $\alpha_0 + \alpha_1 s + \alpha_2 s^2 \cdots$, the next set of terms $\frac{\beta_1}{(s - s_1)} + \frac{\beta_2}{(s - s_2)}$ are the individual roots which may be real or occur as complex conjugate pairs, finally the last set of terms $\frac{\beta_{p1}}{(s - s_p)} + \frac{\beta_{p2}}{(s - s_p)^2} + ... + \frac{\beta_{pk}}{(s - s_p)^k}$ are the repeated roots. We have chosen to write the fractions in this way for a very special reason. Each individual term in equation(5.22) appears in the Laplace transform Table 5.1 and hence its inverse transform is known. The only things that we have to determine in Equation(5.22) are the coefficients β's (the coefficients α's are only present when the order of the numerator is greater than the order of the denominator. In this case we divide the numerator by the denominator and obtain the proper fraction. The coefficient α's are known when we complete the division.) These β coefficients are known as the residues at the poles. To determine the residues at each of the poles we first obtain an auxiliary function F'(s) which is a proper fraction from the original s-domain function F(s). This auxiliary function F'(s) is a proper fraction obtained by subtracting the first polynomial in s; this is shown in Equation (5.23)

$$F'(s) = F(s) - (\alpha_0 + \alpha_1 s + \alpha_2 s^2 + ...) \quad (5.23)$$

The auxiliary function F'(s) then will be as expanded and re-written as shown in Equation(5.24). The auxiliary function is a proper fraction. Once we have the proper fraction the inverse transform of the function F'(s) can be obtained.

$$F'(s) = \frac{\beta_1}{(s - s_1)} + \frac{\beta_2}{(s - s_2)} + ... \frac{\beta_{p1}}{(s - s_p)} + \frac{\beta_{p2}}{(s - s_p)^2} + ... + \frac{\beta_{pk}}{(s - s_p)^k} \quad (5.24)$$

In the next section we will see how to determine the values of the individual β's. From now on we will assume that the Laplace domain function is reduced to an auxiliary function when we attempt to find its inverse Laplace transform.

5.4.1 Finding the inverse at individual real roots:

In order to determine the value of β_1 we must make sure that every term except the one with β_1 on the right hand side in Equation(5.24) is zero. We can obtain this condition if we multiply the entire Equation(5.24) by the denominator of the term that has β_1 as the numerator coefficient, and then evaluate the resulting equation at the pole location $s = s_1$. This is shown in Equation(5.25).

$$\beta_1 = \underset{s \to s_1}{\text{Limit}}\left[(s - s_1)F'(s)\right] \tag{5.25}$$

Once the coefficient β_1 has been evaluated the inverse transform is found by looking up and using entry 2 in Table 5.1. This will give us the inverse Laplace transform for the single pole as $\beta_1 e^{-s_1 t}$. The coefficient β_1 is known as the residue at pole $s=s_1$. Repeating this procedure for every individual pole we can determine the numerator values for the partial fractions and hence the inverse transform by table lookup. Example 5.10 shows how this is done.

Example 5.10

Determine the inverse Laplace transform of the following function.

$$F(s) = \frac{38(s^2 + 3s + 6)}{s(s+3)(s+6)(s+8)}$$

Solution 5.10

We first examine the function F(s). We see that it is already a proper fraction so we do not need to form an auxiliary function. Next we begin by re-writing the function as partial fractions thus

$$F(s) = \frac{\beta_1}{s} + \frac{\beta_2}{s+3} + \frac{\beta_3}{s+6} + \frac{\beta_4}{s+8}$$

Now we have to determine the four residues. They are determined as shown here:

$$\beta_1 = \left[\frac{s\left(38\left(s^2 + 3s + 6\right)\right)}{s(s+3)(s+6)(s+8)}\right]_{s=0} = \frac{(38)(6)}{(3)(6)(8)} = 1.5833$$

$$\beta_2 = \left[\frac{(s+3)\left(38\left(s^2 + 3s + 6\right)\right)}{s(s+3)(s+6)(s+8)}\right]_{s=-3} = \frac{(38)(9 + (-9) + 6)}{(-3)(3)(5)} = -5.0666$$

$$\beta_3 = \left[\frac{(s+6)\left(38\left(s^2 + 3s + 6\right)\right)}{s(s+3)(s+6)(s+8)}\right]_{s=-6} = \frac{(38)(36 + (-18) + 6)}{(-6)(-3)(2)} = 25.3333$$

$$\beta_4 = \left[\frac{(s+8)\left(38\left(s^2 + 3s + 6\right)\right)}{s(s+3)(s+6)(s+8)}\right]_{s=-8} = \frac{(38)(64 + (-24) + 6)}{(-8)(-5)(-2)} = -21.85$$

Now that we have determined all the residues we can write the inverse Laplace transform by looking up the appropriate pair in Table 5.1. This time we get

$$f(t) = (1.5833 - 5.0666e^{-3t} + 25.3333e^{-6t} - 21.85e^{-8t})u(t)$$

5.4.2 Finding the inverse of complex conjugate roots:

If the single root s_k is complex then there will also be a root located at the conjugate of s_k. Both these complex conjugate roots are considered together to determine the inverse Laplace transform. Since the roots are complex conjugates of each other the residues β_k and $\beta_k{}^*$ will also be complex conjugates of each other. For these complex poles the coefficients are determined as shown in Equation(5.26).

$$\beta_k = \underset{s \to s_k}{\text{Limit}}\left[(s - s_k)F'(s)\right]$$

$$\beta_k^* = \underset{s \to s_k^*}{\text{Limit}}\left[(s - s_k^*)F'(s)\right] \quad (5.26)$$

Then by using entry 2 in Table 5.2 in Section 5.4 we find that the inverse Laplace transform for the complex conjugate poles as $\beta_k e^{-s_1 t} + \beta_k^* e^{-s_1^* t}$. It is possible to combine these two complex conjugate terms into a more useful form as shown in Equation(5.27) (remember that β_k and s_1 and their conjugate are complex). Using $\beta_k = a_k + jb_k$ and the Euler's Identity we get Equation(5.27)

$$\begin{aligned}\left(\beta_k e^{-s_1 t} + \beta_k^* e^{-s_1^* t}\right) &= (a_k + jb_k)e^{(\sigma_k + j\omega_k)t} + (a_k - jb_k)e^{(\sigma_k - j\omega_k)t} \\ &= e^{\sigma_k t}\left\{\begin{array}{l}(a_k + jb_k)(\cos(\omega_k t) + j\sin(\omega_k t)) \\ \quad + (a_k - jb_k)(\cos(\omega_k t) - j\sin(\omega_k t))\end{array}\right\} \\ &= 2e^{\sigma_k t}\{a_k(\cos(\omega_k t)) - b_k(\sin(\omega_k t))\}\end{aligned} \quad (5.27)$$

On carefully examining the table of inverse Laplace transform pairs we find that this transform corresponds to either transform pair 4, and/or the transform pair 5.

Example 5.11

Determine the inverse Laplace transform of the following function $F(s) = \dfrac{(s+5)}{s(s^2+4s+5)}$

Solution 5.11

We first examine the function F(s). We see that it is already a proper fraction so we do not need to form an auxiliary function. Next we begin by re-writing the function as partial fractions thus

$$F(s) = \frac{\beta_1}{s} + \frac{\beta_2}{s+2+1j} + \frac{\beta_2^*}{s+2-1j}$$

Now we have to determine the three residues. They are determined as shown here:

$$\beta_1 = \left.\frac{(s+6)}{(s^2+4s+5)}\right|_{s=0} = \frac{6}{5} = 1.2$$

and

$$\beta_2 = \left.\frac{(s+6)}{s(s+2-j)}\right|_{s=-2-j} = -0.6 - 0.7j$$

and the other residue is the complex conjugate of this one so $\beta_2^* = -0.6+0.7j$. Now that we have the residues we can write the inverse transform using the pairs from the Laplace transform tables. This gives

$$f(t) = (1.2 - 2e^{-2t}\{0.6\cos(t) - 0.7\mathrm{Sin}(t)\})u(t)$$

5.4.3 Finding the inverse when the roots are repeated:

When there are multiple roots then the coefficients in the partial fraction expansion β_{p1}, β_{p2}, β_{p3}, … β_{pk} must be each evaluated. This time however a simple application of Equation(5.25) will not give us the residue coefficients. The procedure must be modified slightly as follows.

Multiply both sides of Equation(5.24) by the highest power of the repeated root or $(s-s_p)^k$ so that you will get Equation(5.28).

$$(s-s_p)^k F'(s) = (s-s_p)^k\left[\frac{\beta_1}{(s-s_1)} + \ldots + \frac{\beta_1}{(s-s_r)}\right] + \beta_{p1}(s-s_p)^{k-1} + \ldots + \beta_{p(k-1)}(s-s_p) + \beta_{pk} \tag{5.28}$$

In Equation(5.28) when we take the limit as $s \to s_p$ all the terms on the right hand side vanish except the last which is β_{pk}. Now evaluating the expression at the pole location will permit us to determine the coefficient β_{pk}.

$$\beta_{pr} = \frac{1}{(k-r)}\left\{\frac{d^{k-r}}{ds^{k-r}}\left[F'(s)(s-s_p)^k\right]\right\}_{s=s_p} \tag{5.29}$$

Next suppose we differentiate the Equation(5.28) once with respect to the variable s and then take the limit as $s \to s_p$. Then all the terms except $\beta_{p(k-1)}$ will vanish. Now evaluating the expression at the pole location will permit us to determine the coefficient $\beta_{p(k-1)}$. If we differentiate equation(5.28) twice then all the coefficients except $\beta_{p(k-2)}$ will vanish. This way, repeatedly finding successive derivatives and then evaluating the limit as $s \to s_p$ will give us all the individual coefficients. This procedure is summarized in Equation(5.29). The several solved examples that follow will clear this concept further for you.

Example 5.12

Determine the inverse Laplace transform of the following function $F(s)=\frac{38(s+3))}{(s+6)^2(s+8)}$.

Solution 5.12

We first examine the function F(s). We see that it is already a proper fraction so we do not need to form an auxiliary function. Next we begin by re-writing the function as partial fractions thus

$$F(s)=\frac{\beta_1}{(s+6)^2}+\frac{\beta_2}{(s+6)}+\frac{\beta_3}{(s+8)}$$

In this we have to determine the coefficients β_i's. They are determined thus:

$$\beta_1=\left.\frac{38(s+3)}{(s+8)}\right|_{s=-6}=-57$$

$$\beta_2=\left.\frac{d\left[\frac{38(s+3)}{(s+8)}\right]}{ds}\right|_{s=-6}=\frac{38(s+8)-38(s+6)}{(s+8)^2}=47.5$$

$$\beta_3=\left.\frac{38(s+3)}{(s+6)^2}\right|_{s=-8}=-47.5$$

Now that we have the residues we can write the inverse transform using the pairs from the Laplace transform tables. This gives

$$f(t) = (57te^{-6t} + 47.5\,e^{-6t} - 47.5e^{-8t})u(t)$$

Example 5.13

Determine the inverse Laplace transform of the following function.

$$F(s)=\frac{38(s+3)}{(s+6)^2(s^2+5s+8.5)}$$

Solution 5.13

We first examine the function F(s). We see that it is already a proper fraction so we do not need to form an auxiliary function. Next we begin by re-writing the function as partial fractions thus

$$F(s)=\frac{\beta_1}{(s+6)^2}+\frac{\beta_2}{(s+6)}+\frac{\beta_3}{(s+2.5+j1.5)}+\frac{\beta_3^*}{(s+2.5-j1.5)}$$

Here we to determine the coefficients β_i's. They are determined thus:

$$\beta_1=\left.\frac{38(s+3)}{(s^2+5s+8.5)}\right|_{s=-6}=-7.862$$

$$\beta_2=\left.\frac{d\left[\frac{38(s+3)}{(s^2+5s+8.5)}\right]}{ds}\right|_{s=-6}=\left.\frac{38(s^2+5s+8.5)-38(s+3)(2s+5)}{ds}\right|_{s=-6}=-1.175$$

$$\beta_3=\left.\frac{38(s+3)}{(s+6)^2(s+2.5-1.5j)}\right|_{s=-2.5-1.5j}=0.5875+1.25j$$

$$\beta_3^*=0.5875-1.25j$$

Now that we have the residues we can write the inverse transform using the pairs from the Laplace transform tables. This gives

$$f(t) = (-7.862te^{-6t}\ -1.175e^{-6t}\ +2e^{-2.5t}\{0.5875Cos(1.5t)-1.25Sin(1.5t\})u(t)$$

5.5 USING LAPLACE TRANSFORM TO SOLVE DIFFERENTIAL EQUATIONS WITH INITIAL CONDITIONS

One of the primary applications of Laplace transforms is to solve differential equations with initial conditions. We first saw how to solve differential equations with initial conditions in Chapter 2 Section 2.2.5 and in Section 2.2.6. There we solved the differential equation in the time domain. Here we will be solving similar differential equations but we will be solving them in the Laplace domain. After we have seen how differential equations are solved in the Laplace domain we will be able to compare the two different methods. We begin our solution of differential equations by noting that the Laplace transform of the derivative of any time domain function is given by the differentiation theorem. This is the second entry in Table 5.1.

$$L\left[\frac{dx(t)}{dt}\right]=sX(s)-x(0^+) \tag{5.30}$$

It is repeated for your convenience in Equation(5.30). Notice that the Laplace transform of the derivative also contains a term that allows us to include the initial condition. This term is the $x(0^+)$. There are similar initial condition terms in all the other higher order derivatives also. Do you remember the Laplace transform of say the third derivative of x(t)? In the third order derivative of x(t) can identify the initial condition terms in all the derivatives. The answer is given at the bottom of this page.[1]

In Equation(5.30) the term $x(0^+)$ represents the value of x(t) just after time t = 0, hence we use the strange notation of 0^+. So the initial condition is included in the Laplace transform at time $t = 0^+$. We will demonstrate the Laplace transform method of solving a differential equation by first considering a simple example and then we will follow the same method to tackle more difficult examples.

Example 5.14

As our first example we will solve the differential equation with initial conditions given in Equation(5.31).

$$\frac{dy(t)}{dt} + 6y(t) = x(t); \qquad x(t) = 3e^{-5t}$$
$$\text{initial condition } y(0^+) = 4 \tag{5.31}$$

Solution 5.14

Equation(5.31) tells us that the initial value of y(t) at $t = 0^+$ is 4 and that the driving function is $3e^{-5t}$. The first step in using the Laplace transform to solve the differential equation is to find the Laplace transform of the differential equation. This is shown in Equation(5.32). Equation(5.32) also contains the solution for Y(s) in the Laplace domain.

$$sY(s) - y(0^+) + 6Y(s) = X(s)$$
$$\text{Solving for } Y(s) \text{ we get } Y(s) = \frac{1}{s+6}\left[y(0^+) + X(s)\right] \tag{5.32}$$

In Equation(5.32) we can substitute the initial condition and the Laplace transform of the driving function X(s). Doing this and expanding the Laplace domain function in order to get the inverse Laplace transform we get Equation(5.33).

$$Y(s) = \frac{1}{s+6}[4 + X(s)] = \frac{1}{s+6}\left[4 + \frac{3}{s+5}\right] = \frac{4}{s+6} + \frac{3}{s+5} - \frac{3}{s+6} \tag{5.33}$$

On obtaining the inverse Laplace transform of Equation(5.33) by looking up the Laplace transform pairs in Table 5.2 in Section 5.4 we get the solution to the differential equation in the time domain. This is shown for you in Equation(5.34).

---

1 $L\left[\frac{d^3x(t)}{dt^3}\right] = s^3X(s) - s^2x(0^+) - s\frac{dx(0^+)}{dt} - \frac{d^2x(0^+)}{dt^2}$

$$\begin{aligned} y(t) &= 4e^{-6t} + 3e^{-5t} - 3e^{-6t} \\ &= 1e^{-6t} + 3e^{-5t} \end{aligned} \tag{5.34}$$

Using Laplace transforms, gives us the complete solution to the differential equation with initial conditions very quickly and easily. This method is a lot simpler than the solution method that we learnt in Chapter 2. To recap the method the steps we followed are as follows:

Step 1.

Obtain the Laplace transform of the differential equation.

Step 2.

Solve the equation for the variable of interest in the Laplace domain. This solution will be an algebraic solution not a differential solution.

Step 3.

Substitute the initial condition values and the Laplace transform of the driving function. Separate in partial fractions. This is the solution of the differential equation in the Laplace domain.

Step 4.

Determine the inverse Laplace transform of the solution to get the solution in the time domain.

Example 5.15

As a second example let us consider a spring mass damper system as shown in Figure 5.4. The differential equation for the system and the initial conditions for the variables are given with the Figure 5.4.

Solution 5.15

To solve this differential equation we find the Laplace transform of the system equation first and re-arrange to get Equation(5.35).

$$Y(s) = \frac{X(s)}{4s^2 + 8s + 200} + \frac{(4s+8)y(0+) + 4\frac{dy(0^+)}{dt}}{4s^2 + 8s + 200}$$

$$Y(s) = \frac{3(1-e^{-2s})}{s(4s^2 + 8s + 200)} + \frac{20s + 28}{4s^2 + 8s + 200}$$

$$Y((s) = \frac{0.75(1-e^{-2s})}{s((s+1)^2 + 7^2)} + \frac{20(s+1)}{((s+1)^2 + 7^2)} + \frac{1.143(7)}{(s+1)^2 + 7^2} \tag{5.35}$$

When we factor the equation and get the inverse Laplace transform of Equation(5.35) we get Equation(5.36). This is the solution to the motion of the Mass in the system shown in Figure 5.4. In Equation 5.34 the term e^{-2s} represents a delay in the time domain. Notice how easy it is to use the Laplace transform method to solve the differential equations.

This example shows that the Laplace transform method is indeed very easy when it comes to solving differential equations. The four steps set out for us are very straight forward and simple to apply. The only difficult part is finding the inverse Laplace transform of the function that is the solution to the differential equation in the Laplace domain.

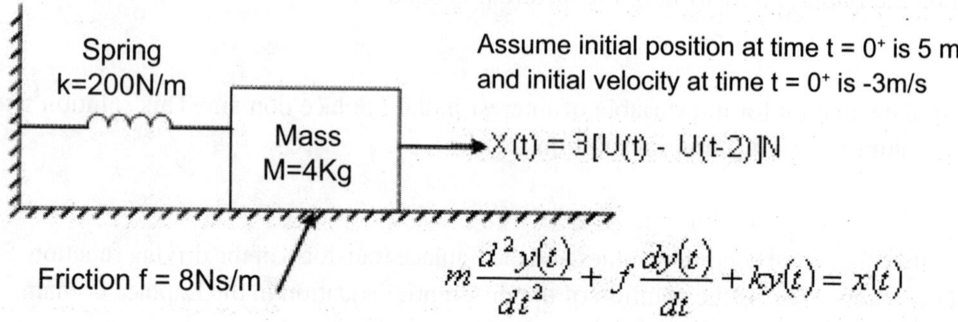

Figure 5.4: A Spring-Mass-Damper mechanical system

$$\begin{aligned}y(t)=&0.015\left[u(t)-u(t-2)\right]-0.015\left[e^{-t}\mathrm{Cos}(7t)\right]u(t)+0.00643\left[e^{-t}\mathrm{Sin}(7t)\right]u(t)\\&-0.015\left[e^{-t}\mathrm{Cos}(7t)\right]u(t-2)+0.00643\left[e^{-t}\mathrm{Sin}(7t)\right]u(t-2)\\&+20e^{-t}\mathrm{Cos}(7t)u(t)+1.143e^{-t}\mathrm{Sin}(7t)u(t)\end{aligned} \qquad (5.36)$$

Example 5.16

Determine the solution to the differential equation

$$\frac{d^4y(t)}{dt}+\frac{11d^3y(t)}{dt}+\frac{74.5d^2y(t)}{dt}+\frac{267dy(t)}{dt}+306y(t)=114\delta(t)+38\frac{d\delta(t)}{dt}$$

using the Laplace transform method assuming that all the initial conditions are zero.

Solution 5.16

We first determine the Laplace transform of the differential equation. This will be $(s^4 + 11s^3 + 74.5s^2 + 267s + 306)Y(s) = (38s+114)$. Next we write this as partial fraction. So

$$Y(s)=\frac{38(s+3)}{(s+6)^2(s^2+5s+8.5)}$$

This solves the differential equation in the Laplace domain. When we find the inverse Laplace transform of this equation we will have the solution in the time domain. Look back and you will find that we computed the inverse transform of this Laplace domain function in Example 5.13. So that is the solution of this differential equation.

Example 5.17

Determine the solution to the differential equation given using the Laplace transform method

$$\frac{d^2y(t)}{dt}+\frac{3dy(t)}{dt}+2y(t)=4u(t)$$

$$\frac{dy(0^+)}{dt}=2; \quad y(0^+)=-1$$

Solution 5.17

We first determine the Laplace transform of the differential equation. This will be

$$(s^2+3s+2)Y(s)\text{ -}y(0+)\text{ - }s\frac{dy(0+)}{dt}=\frac{4}{s}$$

Next we write this as partial fraction. So

$$Y(s)=\frac{4}{s(s^2+3s+2)}+\frac{-1}{(s^2+3s+2)}+\frac{2s}{(s^2+3s+2)}$$

This solves the differential equation in the Laplace domain and it also includes the initial conditions. When we complete the inverse Laplace transform of this equation we will have the solution in the time domain. The inverse Laplace transform can easily be obtained from Equation(5.37). Notice that Equation(5.37) clearly shows which part of the solution comes from which initial condition.

$$Y(s)=\underbrace{\frac{2}{s}+\frac{2}{(s+2)}+\frac{4}{(s+1)}}_{\text{Due to the Driving Function}}-\underbrace{\frac{-1}{(s+2)}+\frac{1}{(s+1)}}_{\text{Initial Condition at } y(0^+)}+\underbrace{\frac{4}{(s+2)}+\frac{2}{(s+1)}}_{\text{Initial Condition at } \frac{dy(0^+)}{dt}} \tag{5.37}$$

5.6 TRANSFER FUNCTIONS OF LTI SYSTEMS

5.6.1 Block Diagram Representation:

Earlier in Chapter 2 we have been describing systems in terms of their mathematical representation. A different type of representation for the system is in the form of the Block Diagram. To represent the system in its Block Diagram format we draw a rectangular block to represent a component or an action within the system. The blocks are connected by directed line segments (arrows) that represent the direction of signal flow. Each line segment is labeled to identify the signal that is flowing through that line segment. Within each block is the action that is performed by that block. The blocks may represent hardware or an algorithm or something else. It does not matter. As we have seen earlier in Chapter 2 that once we represent a system by its equations all systems look and act alike. In the same way each block in the block diagram tells us what action is performed on the input signal by the block to get the output signal. It does not matter how the block does its thing.

The principle that we follow when we use a block diagram is as follows. Refer to the blocks in Figure 5.5. If the block diagram is represented in the TIME domain then the output from the block is the convolution of the input and the impulse response of the block. If the block diagram is represented in the FREQUENCY domain then the output from the block is the product of the input with the frequency domain representation of the impulse response of the block (this is known as the Transfer Function of the block.)

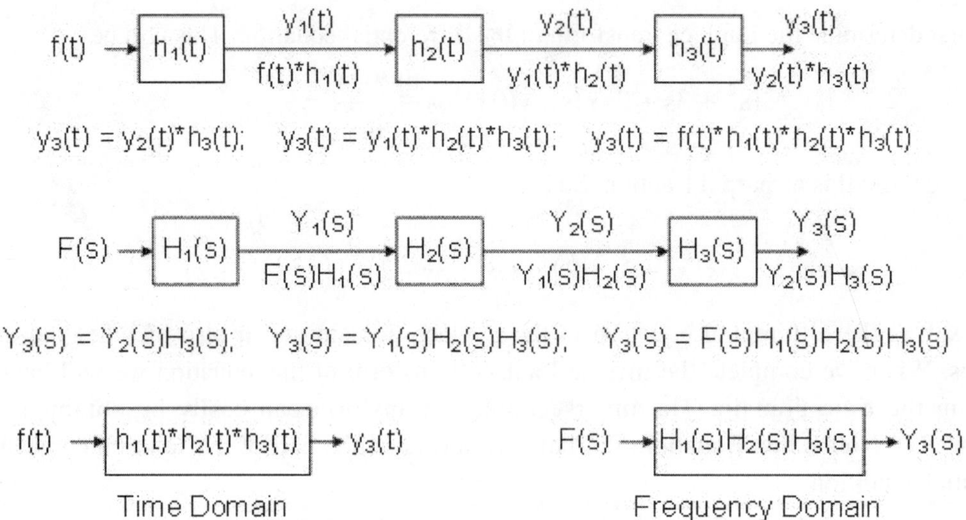

Figure 5.5: A cascade connection is similar to a single block. In the time domain this is equal to the convolution of all the blocks in the cascade chain. In the frequency domain this is equal to the product of all the blocks in the cascade chain.

On carefully looking at the block diagram we see that the input to a block is connected to the output of a previous block. Since each block represents one part of a system each block has some output impedance and input impedance. The presence of the output impedance and the input impedance in two connected blocks has the effect of loading the block that provides the output by the input impedance of the block that accepts the output as its input. The loading is present because the two impedances form a voltage divider. Proper attention must be paid to this loading effect for the system to function efficiently and properly. The loading effect does not in any way alter the function of the system or the block. Since most of the time when we are looking at the block diagram we are mostly interested with the functioning of the system we make an assumption that at the output of each block we have a unity gain buffer. The purpose of having the buffer is to simply eliminate the effect of loading. Now that we have eliminated the effect of loading we can concentrate on the functions of the various blocks.

5.6.1.1 The Cascade Connection:

The first connection that we will examine is known as the cascade connection. In this connection the output of one block is the input to the next block and the output of the second block is the input to the third block and so on. This connection is shown in Figure 5.5. In a series connection the overall block function is the product of all the blocks in the series. So as shown in Figure 5.5 the overall block is equivalent to $H_1(s)H_2(s)H_3(s)$

5.6.1.2 The Parallel Connection:

Another connection that we often come across is the parallel connection. In the parallel connection the same signal goes through several blocks and the output of several blocks are combined together at the output by a summing junction. The summing junction will add together the output of several blocks and combine them into one composite signal. This connection is shown in Figure 5.6. In a parallel connection the overall block function is the sum of all the blocks that are in parallel. This is as shown in Figure 5.6 the overall block is equivalent to $H_1(s)+H_2(S)+H_3(s)$.

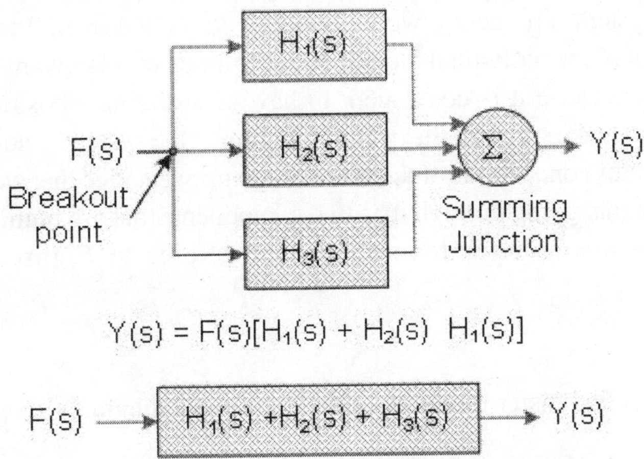

Figure 5.6: A parallel connection is similar to a single block with a transfer function equal to the sum of the transfer functions of all the blocks in the parallel stack

The Feedback Connection:

A third connection that we often come across is the feedback connection. In the feedback connection the signal from the output of one of the blocks is routed back to the input of an earlier block through which the signal has already traveled. Usually the feedback signal is subtracted but it can also be added sometimes. This connection is shown in Figure 5.7. In a feedback connection the overall block function is a combination of the blocks in the forward and the feedback path. So as shown in Figure 5.7 the overall block is equivalent to $\frac{H_1(s)F(s)}{1+H_1(s)H_2(s)}$. Using these three types of connections we can put together many different, varied and unique systems.

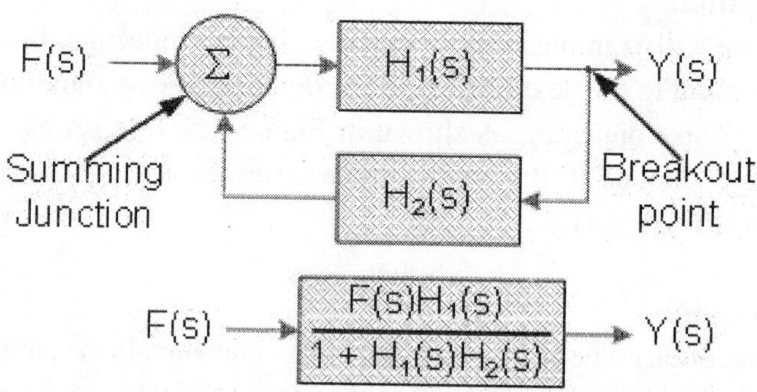

Figure 5.7: A feedback connection is similar to a single block with a transfer function that is a combination of the blocks in the forward and the feedback path.

Block Diagram Algebra:

The various connections that we have seen are all used in some combination to make up the block diagram of a system. Frequently we will want to know the overall transfer function of the system rather than that of the individual blocks. At other times we may want to move a block either forward or backward because it is convenient to have it in the new position. In doing all these movements we want to make sure that the overall function of the system is not altered in any way. In going through the various connections of the block diagrams we notice that we can treat the function of the block and the signal going through it as two components that are multiplied to get the output signal. A couple of examples will make it clear. Refer to Figure 5.8 along with the following discussion.

Example 5.18

Determine the overall transfer functions of the three block diagrams given in Figure 5.8 a, b, c.

Solution 5.18

Figure 5.8 a:

In this figure we see a cascade connection along with a parallel connection. To evaluate the cascade connection we combine the two blocks with functions $H_1(s)$ and $H_2(s)$ together. This gives us $H_1(s)H_2(s)$. The cascade connection is in parallel with another connection that has its function as $H_3(s)$. The two paths are combined together by a summing block so the overall function for the block is the sum of the functions of the two parallel paths.

This gives us $Y(s) = F(s)[\, H_1(s)H_2(s) + H_3(s)]$

Figure 5.8 b:

In this Figure 5.8 b we see a feedback connection, a feed forward connection along with a parallel connection. In Block Diagram Algebra whenever you see a feedback connection you will also see a summing junction. The signal after the summing junction is going to be the signal that will help us to evaluate the overall function in block diagrams with feedback. For this reason we will assign a name to the signal just after the summing junction. In this diagram we have assigned the name $E_1(s)$ to the signal just after the summing junction.

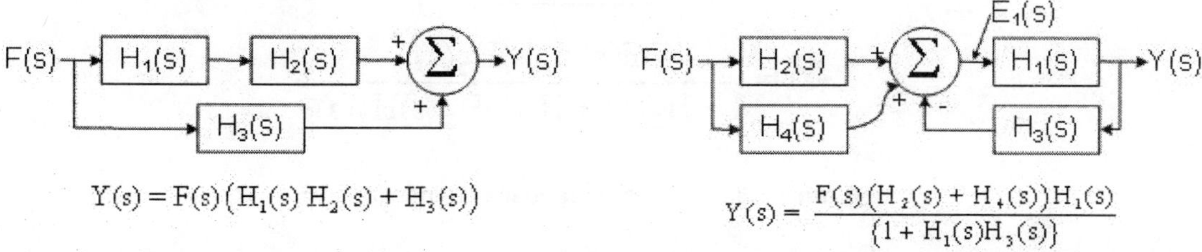

Figure 5.8a: Feed forward and a parallel connection ***Figure 5.8b:*** Feedback; feed forward and parallel connection

Next we pretend that we have broken the loop just after the summing junction. So the signal $E_1(s)$ will have two ends. One end is just after the summing junction and the other end is at the input of the block right after the summing junction which in this case is $H_1(s)$. We begin with the signal $E_1(s)$ at the input of the block $H_1(s)$ and go around the block diagram till we come back to the signal $E_1(s)$ just after the summing junction. When we equate the two $E_1(s)$ signals we will get the transfer function for the block diagram. Study the sequence of equations listed in Equation(5.38) to see how this is done.

$$\begin{aligned}
Y(s) &= E_1(s)H_1(s) \\
E_1(s) &= F(s)[H_2(s) + H_4(s)] - Y(s)H_3(s) \\
Y(s) &= \{F(s)[H_2(s) + H_4(s)] - Y(s)H_3(s)\}H_1(s) \\
Y(s)[1 + H_1(s)H_3(s)] &= F(s)[H_2(s) + H_4(s)]H_1(s) \\
Y(s) &= \frac{F(s)[H_2(s) + H_4(s)]H_1(s)}{1 + H_1(s)H_3(s)}
\end{aligned} \tag{5.38}$$

Figure 5.8 c:

In this Figure 5.8 c we see a double feedback connection. Because of the presence of the double feedback connection there are two summing junctions and we need to break the signal at two places. This time we have labeled the two signals as $E_1(s)$ and $E_2(s)$. We will write the equation from the input of block $H_1(s)$ to the point after the second summing junction where we have the signal $E_2(s)$ and then from the input of the block $H_2(s)$ to the starting point just after the first summing junction and the signal $E_1(s)$. Study the sequence of equations listed in Equation(5.39) to see how this is done.

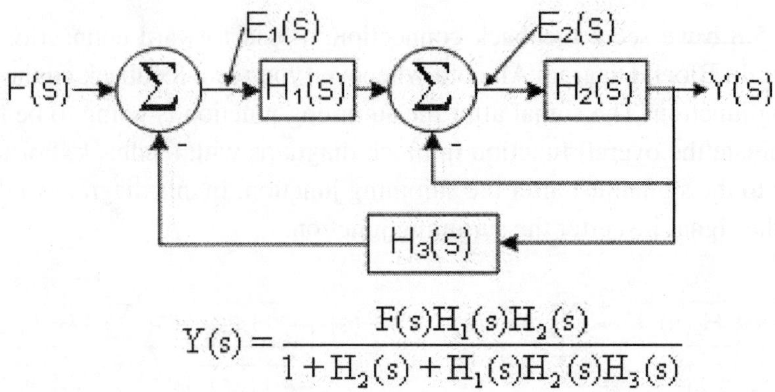

$$Y(s) = \frac{F(s)H_1(s)H_2(s)}{1 + H_2(s) + H_1(s)H_2(s)H_3(s)}$$

Figure 5.8c: A double feedback connection

Doing the algebra systematically and solving the equations from the output side of the summing junction to the input side of the summing junction gives you the entire transfer function of the block diagram.

$$\begin{aligned}
Y(s) &= E_2(s)H_2(s) \\
E_1(s) &= F(s) - Y(s)H_3(s) \\
E_2(s) &= E_1(s)H_1(s) - Y(s) \\
Y(s) &= \left[E_1(s)H_1(s) - Y(s)\right]H_2(s) \\
Y(s) &= \left[\left(F(s) - Y(s)H_3(s)\right)\right]H_1(s) - Y(s)H_3(s)]H_2(s) \\
Y(s) &= F(s)H_1(s)H_2(s) - Y(s)H_3(s)H_2(s)H_1(s) - Y(s)H_2(s) \\
Y(s) &= \frac{F(s)H_2(s)H_1(t)}{1 + H_2(s) + H_3(s)H_2(s)H_1(s)}
\end{aligned} \tag{5.39}$$

5.7 THE BODE PLOTS

5.7.1 The Logarithmic Plots:

The Laplace domain function that we have obtained for a system can be viewed as the transfer function of the system in the frequency domain. To see how the system will behave at various frequencies we can draw the frequency response plot of the transfer function. The frequency response plot can be drawn in many different formats. Each of these formats represents the magnitude of the transfer function and the phase of the transfer function at different frequency points. In my opinion the plot that is the easiest to draw and the one that is the easiest to interpret is the Bode plot. The other plots provide us with the same information but the information is packaged differently. Some of you may have heard of the Nyquist plot or the Nichols plot. If you want to draw either of these two plots by hand then it is much easier (many fewer calculations) if you draw the Bode plot first.

The Bode plot is actually two different plots. The first plot draws the log-magnitude of the function against the frequency while the second plot draws the phase of the function against the frequency. We use the log-magnitude plot as it gives us straight line approximations which are very close to the exact value. This makes it even easier to draw and interpret the Bode Plot. The ease comes from the fact that multiplications and divisions are converted to additions and subtractions when you use the log function. The Bode plot is drawn on a semi-log graph paper with the log-magnitude and the phase drawn on the linear scale while the frequency is represented on a logarithmic scale on the plot. Also the use of the logarithms expands the low frequency range and permits us to draw an approximate asymptotic plot very quickly. With a little practice you will be able to draw the asymptotic Bode plot by inspection - that means no calculations. Once the Bode plot is drawn we can obtain enough data to quickly draw one of the other frequency response plots in any frequency range of interest. So whenever I teach how to draw one or the other frequency plots (such as the Nyquist or the Nichols Plots) I always ask my students to first draw the Bode plot and get the data from the Bode plot to draw the other plots.

5.7.2 The Frequency Transfer Function:

A general Laplace transform function can be written as shown in Equation(5.40):

$$F(s)=\frac{K_m(s+T_1)(s+T_2)^r}{s^m(s+T_a)(s^2+\alpha T_b s+T_b^2)} \tag{5.40}$$

In Equation(5.40) K_m represents a gain constant, $(s+T_1)$ represents a single real zero; $(s+T_2)^r$ represents real zeros of order r; s^m represents m poles at the origin; $(s+T_a)$ represents a single real pole and $(s^2 + \alpha T_b s + T_b^2)$ represents a complex conjugate pole. We can of course have complex conjugate zeros and multiple order poles but you will get the idea of how to handle them when we discuss how the Bode plot is drawn for the ones that we have chosen. When we are trying to draw the bode plot we are interested in determining what happens at different frequencies to the magnitude and the phase. To convert Equation(5.40) to a frequency response equation we replace $s \rightarrow j\omega$ and re-write the equation in a slightly different format as shown in Equation(5.41). Notice that each factor in the equation has been adjusted so that it is written as 1 + some other factor. This will adjust the gain constant so we have a different gain constant.

$$F(s)\Big|_{s=j\omega}=F(j\omega)=\frac{K_m'(1+j\omega T_1)(1+j\omega T_2)^r}{(j\omega)^m(1+j\omega T_a)\left(1+\frac{2\xi}{\omega_n}j\omega+\left(\frac{j\omega}{\omega_n}\right)^2\right)} \tag{5.41}$$

The function in Equation(5.41) is a complex quantity. Since it is a complex quantity we can write it in its polar form as magnitude and phase. So separating the magnitude and the phase part of Equation(5.41) and taking the logarithm of the magnitude of Equation(5.41) gives us Equation(5.42) and Equation(5.43) gives us the phase.

$$\log_{10}\left[F(j\omega)\right] = \log_{10}\left(K_m^{'}\right) + \log_{10}\left|1+j\omega T_1\right| + r\log_{10}\left|1+j\omega T_2\right| \\ -m\log_{10}\left|j\omega\right| - \log_{10}\left|1+j\omega T_a\right| - \log_{10}\left|1+\frac{2\xi}{\omega_n}j\omega+\left(\frac{j\omega}{\omega_n}\right)^2\right| \tag{5.42}$$

$$\arg\left(F(j\omega)\right) = \arg\left(K_m^{'}\right) + \arg\left(1+j\omega T_1\right) + (r)\arg\left(1+j\omega T_2\right) \\ -(m)\arg\left(j\omega\right) - \arg\left(1+j\omega T_a\right) - \arg\left(1+\frac{2\xi}{\omega_n}j\omega+\left(\frac{j\omega}{\omega_n}\right)^2\right) \tag{5.43}$$

The magnitude equation is further modified slightly to give us the log-magnitude form and the phase equations is further modified slightly to give us the tangent form of the equation. The modified equations are shown in Equation(5.44) and in Equation(5.45). We will be using these equations to draw the Bode plot. The equation shown in Equation(5.44) is the log magnitude equation. The log-magnitude function is a simple modification of the log function. This is how the modification is done: $\mathrm{Lm}\left(F(\omega)\right) = 20\log_{10}\left|F(j\omega)\right|$. Completing the modification gives us the log-magnitude of the function F(s). The units of the log-magnitude function are decibels abbreviated as dB. With this change the two equations change to those shown in Equation(5.44) and Equation(5.45):

$$\mathrm{Lm}\left(\mathrm{F}(\omega)\right) = \mathrm{Lm}\left|K_m^{'}\right| + \mathrm{Lm}\left|1+\mathrm{j}\omega T_1\right| + (r)\mathrm{m}\left|1+\mathrm{j}\omega T_2\right| \\ -(m)\mathrm{Lm}\left|\mathrm{j}\omega\right| - \mathrm{Lm}\left|1+\mathrm{j}\omega T_a\right| - \mathrm{Lm}\left|1+\frac{2\xi}{\omega_n}\mathrm{j}\omega+\left(\frac{j\omega}{\omega_n}\right)^2\right| \tag{5.44}$$

$$\arg\left(F(j\omega)\right) = \arg\left(K_m^{'}\right) + \tan^{-1}\left(\omega T_1\right) + (r)\tan^{-1}\left(\omega T_2\right) \\ -(m)\left(90^\circ\right) - \tan^{-1}\left(\omega T_a\right) - \tan^{-1}\left(\frac{(2\xi\omega)/(\omega_n)}{1-(\omega/\omega_n)^2}\right) \tag{5.45}$$

Remember that both the log-magnitude and the phase equations are functions of frequency. We will plot them on semi-log graph paper with the frequency drawn on the log scale and the log-magnitude and the phase drawn on the linear scale. This way we will get two graphs. The two graphs that we get together are known as the Bode plots.

5.7.3 Drawing the Bode Plots:

The log-magnitude equation shown in Equation(5.44) has four different unique factors. Since the Log-magnitudes for these factors are all added together we can draw each factor individually and then add the individual plots together across the frequency axis to get a complete plot. Since each of the term except the gain constant K_m can appear either as a single or multiple order we will pay close attention to the order of the term also. Looking at Equation(5.44) we see that the magnitude plot for the poles and zeros are identical except for the sign. Poles are subtracted while zeros are added. So we will draw the graph and then either add or subtract the factor depending on whether it is a zero or a pole.

5.7.3.1 Drawing the Gain Constant:

Since the constant is independent of the frequency its plot will be a horizontal straight line at $Lm(|K'_m|) = 20\log_{10}(K'_m)$ at all frequency values. The effect of the constant is to either raise or lower the entire log-magnitude plot by the amount of $Lm(|K'_m|)$. When the gain constant is a fraction then the plot will be lowered. This plot is shown in Figure 5.9.

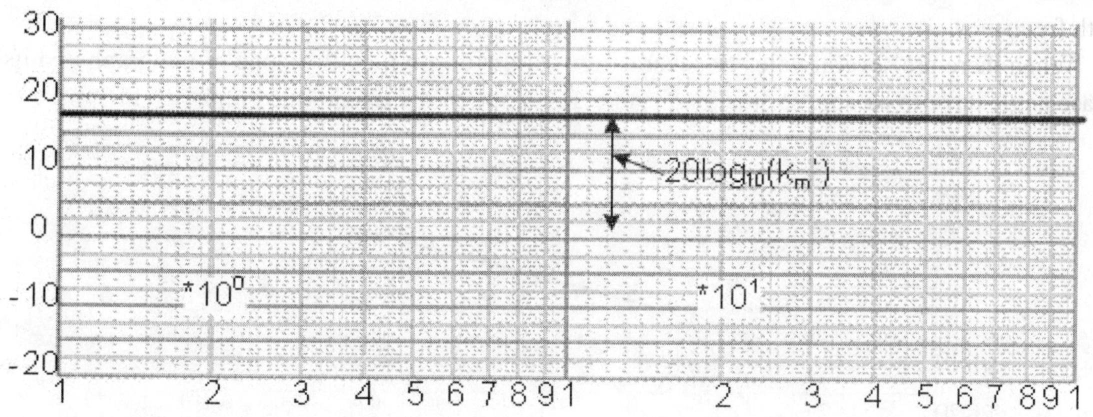

Figure 5.9: Plot of the gain constant. Stays constant over the entire frequency range.

5.7.3.2 Drawing Poles and Zeros at the origin:

The factor $j\omega$ usually appears in the denominator as poles at the origin, sometimes it may appear as a zero at the origin, it will however never appear as both the pole and a zero at the origin simultaneously. The log-magnitude for this factor is shown in Equation(5.44):

$$Lm(\omega) = 20\log_{10}|j\omega| = 20\log_{10}(\omega)$$

When the $j\omega$ factor is in the denominator as a pole then the quantity in Equation(5.44) will be negative, when the $j\omega$ factor is in the numerator as a zero then the quantity in Equation(5.44) will be positive. When we draw a plot of this function on a semi log graph paper we get a straight line graph with a slope of -20dB/decade for poles located at the origin or with a slope of 20dB/decade for zeros located at the origin. The graph for a pole or a zero at the origin is shown in Figure 5.10. Note that the plot of the pole or zero at the origin passes through the 0-dB axis at w=1.

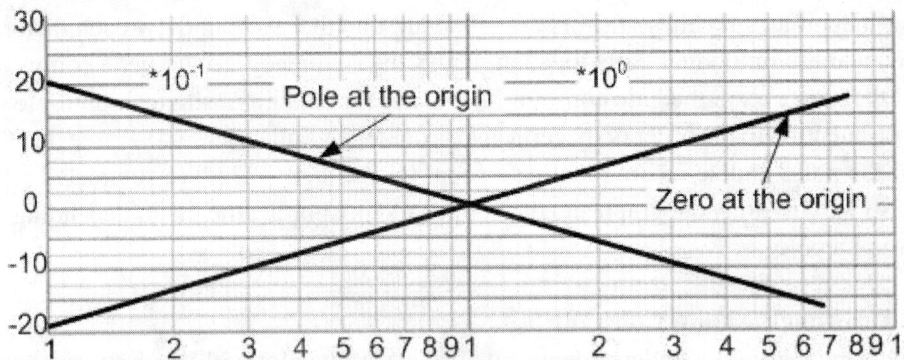

Figure 5.10: Plot of a pole or a zero at the origin

The phase for each pole present at the origin is a constant -90, the phase plot for each zero present at the origin is a constant +90. The phase of the poles or zeros at the origin does not change with frequency.

When there are several poles or several zeros at the origin then the slope of the graph and its phase angle have to be appropriately adjusted. The slope of the magnitude graph and the phase in

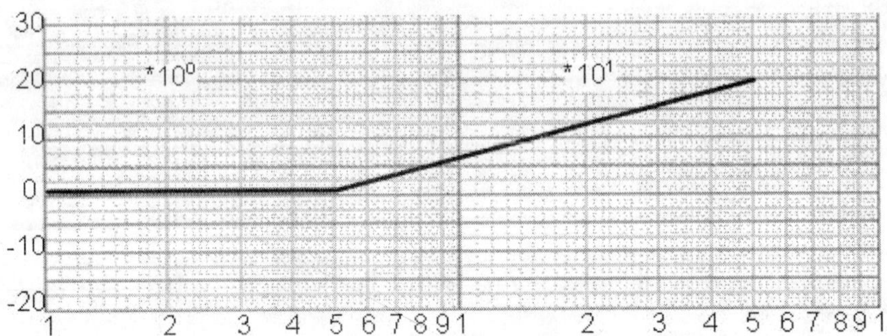

Figure 5.11a: Bode plot of a Zero with a corner frequency of 5

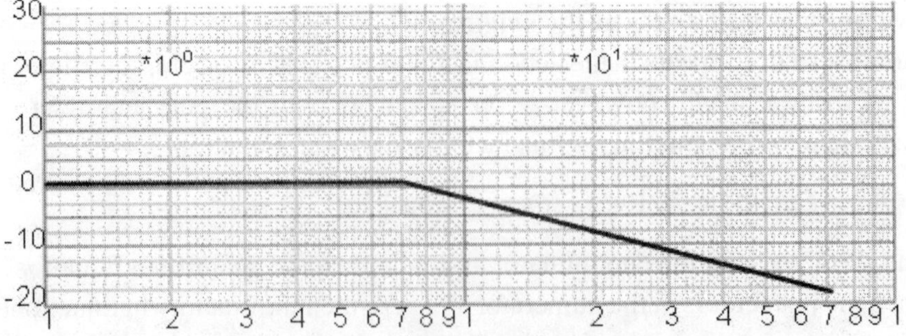

Figure 5.11b: Bode plot of a Pole with a corner frequency of 7

the phase graph are multiplied by the number of poles or zeros at the origin. So, if there are m poles at the origin then the slope of the graph will be -20m dB/decades. When there are m poles at the origin then the phase of these m poles at the origin will be -90m° degrees. Similarly, if there are m zeros at the origin then the slope of the graph will be 20m dB/decades. When there are m zeros at the origin then the phase of these m zeros at the origin will be 90m° degrees.

When we are drawing the magnitude graph for the poles or the zeros at the origin, we begin by noting that the graph always passes through the 0dB axis at $\omega = 1$. This is because the $\log_{10}(1) = 0$. So we draw a line at ± 20m dB/decade passing through the 0dB axis at $\omega = 1$. The graph of the poles and zeros at the origin are shown in Figure 5.10.

5.7.3.3 Drawing Real Poles and Zeros:

The factor $(1 + j\omega T)$ can appear in either the numerator or the denominator or in both the places simultaneously. It may appear either individually or as a multiple factor in either the numerator or the denominator or both. Log-magnitude for the $(1 + j\omega T)$ factor is shown in Equation(5.46):

$$Lm(1+\omega T) = 20\log_{10}|1 + j\omega T| = 20\log_{10}\left(1 + \omega^2 T^2\right)^{\frac{1}{2}} \tag{5.46}$$

When the $(1 + j\omega T)$ factor is in the denominator as a pole then the quantity on the right in Equation 5.43 will be negative, when it is in the numerator as a zero then the quantity on the right in Equation 5.43 will be positive. To draw either the pole or the zero we consider two ranges, one when $\omega T \gg 1$ and the other when $\omega T \ll 1$.

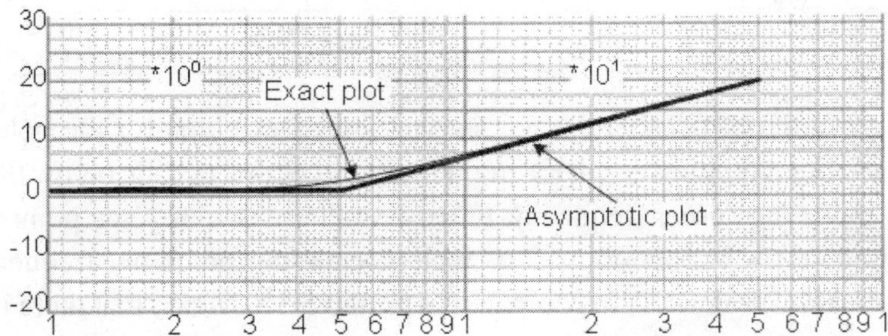

Figure 5.12a: Comparing an exact plot with an asymptotic plot for a zero with a corner frequency of 5

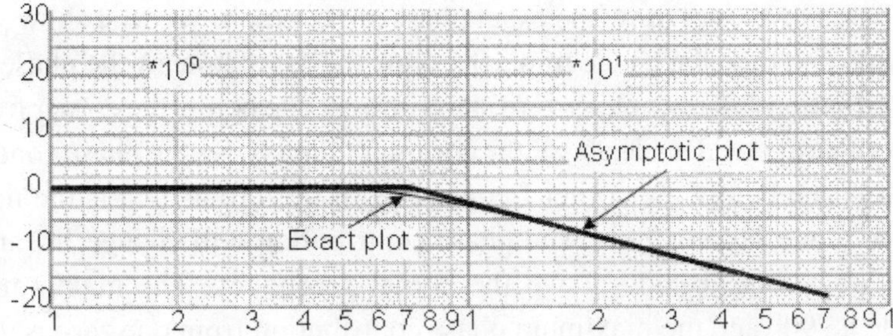

Figure 5.12b: Bode plot of a Pole with a corner frequency of 7

When $\omega T \ll 1$:

In this case $Lm(1 + j\omega T) \approx Lm(1) = 20\log_{10}(1) = 0$. So the plot of $Lm(1 + j\omega T)$ is on the 0dB axis whenever $\omega T \ll 1$. This is the asymptote of the plot when $\omega T \ll 1$. This asymptote has a slope of 0dB/decade.

When $\omega T \gg 1$:

In this case $Lm(1 + j\omega T) \approx Lm(j\omega T) = 20\log_{10}(\omega T)$. So the plot of $Lm(1 + j\omega T)$ is a straight line with a slope of 20dB/decade whenever $\omega T \gg 1$. This is the asymptote of the plot when $\omega T \gg 1$. This asymptote has a slope of -20dB/decade for poles and a slope of +20dB/decade for zeros.

So the asymptotes for the factor $(1+j\omega T)$ are two straight lines. If we were to extend these asymptotes then these two asymptotes intersect each other at $\omega T = 1$ or $\omega = 1/T$. The frequency, 1/T, at which the two asymptotes intersect each other, is known as the corner frequency of the pole/zero and it is denoted as ω_{cf}. So the asymptotic plot for the pole or the zero begins with a horizontal straight line on the 0dB axis from very low frequencies until the corner frequency. Then from the corner frequency the graph has a slope of either -20dB/decade for a pole or +20dB/decade for a zero. This asymptotic plot in the range $0.1\omega \ll \omega_{cf} \ll 10\omega$ is an approximation but this approximation is very good. Examine the error between the approximate and the exact values given in Table 5.3.

Table 5.3: Error in using an asymptote pole for real poles/zeros.

Frequency Ratio $\frac{\omega}{\omega_{cf}}$	0.1	0.25	0.5	0.75	1.0	1.31	2	4	10
Error in dB	0.04	0.26	0.97	2.0	3.01	2.0	0.97	0.26	0.04

On examining the error column in Table 5.3 we see that the exact graph for the poles or the zeros has the same value as the asymptotic graph for frequencies either one decade below the corner frequency or one decade above the corner frequency. In between these two extreme points there is some error but the maximum error is only about 3dB which occurs at the corner frequency. The exact and the asymptotic magnitude graphs are compared in Figure 5.12. Notice that there is almost no difference between the two graphs.

The phase angle graph can also be drawn as an asymptote. But an exact phase angle graph is easy to draw so most of the time we will draw the exact phase angle graph. We first show you how to draw the asymptote graph and then the exact graph. To draw the asymptote of the phase plot we assume that the phase contribution for any pole or zero starts one decade below the corner frequency and reaches its maximum value at one decade above the corner frequency. So the phase contribution for a pole or zero at one decade below the corner frequency will be zero as that is the minimum phase contribution from any one pole or zero. The phase contribution will change linearly till it reaches its maximum value at one decade above the corner frequency. The maximum phase contribution from one pole is -90° and the maximum phase contribution from one zero is 90°. This is shown in Figure 5.13. Drawing this straight line will give us an approximate phase plot.

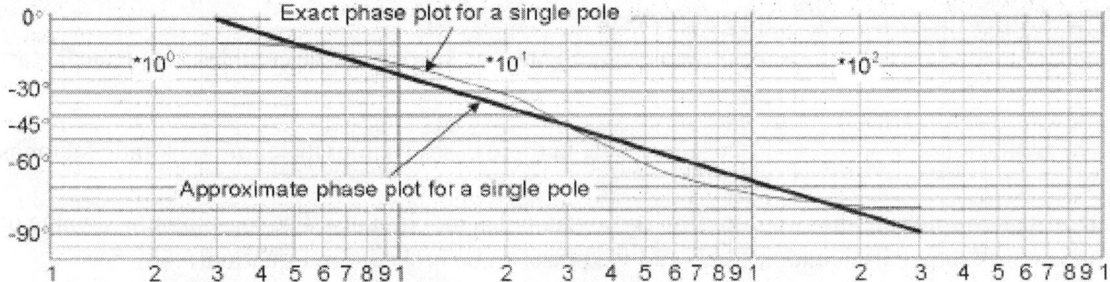

Figure 5.13: Comparison of approximate and exact phase plot for a pole with a corner frequency of 30

To draw the exact phase shift graph for a pole or a zero we again begin at one decade below the corner frequency for the pole or the zero. At this point we calculate the phase shift using $\tan^{-1}(\omega/\omega_{cf})$. Next we pick about 8-10 frequency points equally spaced between $0.1\omega_c \leq \omega \leq 10\omega_{cf}$ and for each of these frequency points we calculate the phase shift. A typical phase shift for a pole is calculated for you in Table 5.4. Using these values the plot of the calculated points is drawn by connecting the points with a smooth curve to get the phase shift graph. The exact phase plot is also shown in Figure 5.13 so you can compare the exact with the approximate plots.

Table 5.4 Phase shift for a typical real pole or zero

$\frac{\omega}{\omega_{cf}}$	0.1	0.25	0.5	0.8	1.0	1.25	2.0	4.0	10.0
phase	5.7	14.04	26.56	38.66	45	51.34	63.43	75.96	82.3

When there are several poles or zeros at the same corner frequency then the slope of the magnitude graph and its phase angle of the phase graph have to be appropriately adjusted. The slope of the magnitude graph is multiplied by the number of poles or zeros at that corner frequency. So, if there are m poles at a particular corner frequency then the slope of the magnitude graph will be -20m dB/decades. The phase of these m poles with the same corner frequency will be m times the phase of one pole at that corner frequency.

Drawing the graph for the pole or the zero is a very simple procedure. We begin the graph at very low frequencies, at least one decade less than the corner frequency. From there draw a horizontal straight line at 0dB up to the corner frequency. Now from the corner frequency we draw the second asymptote. This is at -20dB/decade if we are drawing the graph for a pole or at +20dB/decade if we are drawing the graph for a zero. This asymptote continues at the same slope up to the highest frequency that is represented on the graph. To this graph we then add the phase graph. The phase graph is drawn by plotting the 8-10 points that we calculated and then connecting them by a smooth curve.

5.7.3.4 Drawing Quadratic Poles and Zeros:

The quadratic factors appear as complex conjugate poles or zeros. The complex conjugate factors have the form $\left[1+\frac{j2\xi\omega}{\omega_{cf}}-\frac{\omega^2}{\omega_{cf}^2}\right]$ where ξ <1. In these cases we plot the entire quadratic factor as one instead of plotting the two complex conjugate poles individually. The log-magnitude value of this factor is shown in Equation(5.47) and the phase value is shown in Equation(5.48).

$$Lm\left[1+\frac{j2\xi\omega}{\omega_{cf}}-\frac{\omega^2}{\omega_{cf}^2}\right]=20\log_{10}\left[\left(1-\frac{\omega^2}{\omega_{cf}^2}\right)^2+\left(\frac{2\xi\omega}{\omega_{cf}}\right)^2\right]^{1/2} \tag{5.47}$$

$$\arg\left[\left(1-\frac{\omega^2}{\omega_{cf}^2}\right)+\left(\frac{j2\xi\omega}{\omega_{cf}}\right)\right]=\tan^{-1}\left(\frac{\frac{2\xi\omega}{\omega_{cf}}}{\left(1-\frac{\omega^2}{\omega_{cf}^2}\right)}\right) \tag{5.48}$$

When the quadratic factor is in the denominator as a pole then the quantity on the right in Equation(5.47) will be negative, when it is in the numerator as a zero then the quantity on the right in Equation(5.47) will be positive. To plot the quadratic factor we consider two ranges, as we did for the single poles, when we are trying to draw the magnitude plot, one range is when ωT» 1 and the other range is when ωT« 1.

When ωT« 1 the low frequency asymptote is represented by Lm[1] = 0 so the asymptote is drawn on the 0 dB axis. This range extends from very low frequencies until about one decade less than the corner frequency. So, in this range there is no difference between a single pole and a complex conjugate pole when the asymptote for the frequencies is less than the corner frequency. When ωT» 1 then the Log-magnitude value is approximately given by the second order term in Equation(5.47) or

$$20\log_{10}\left(\frac{\omega^2}{\omega_{cf}^2}\right)=40\log_{10}\left(\frac{\omega}{\omega_{cf}}\right).$$

This is an asymptote of 40dB/decade, which makes perfect sense since this is an asymptote for two poles. This range extends from about one decade above the corner frequency till infinite frequency. The two asymptotes for the complex conjugate poles cross at the corner frequency.

From Equation(5.47) we see that when the frequency of interest is at or near the corner frequency a resonant condition exists. Due to the resonant condition the Log-magnitude graph will significantly depart from its asymptotes. The amount of departure depends on the value of the damping coefficient ξ. As ξ approaches zero the resonant peak will be sharper and higher. Some typical values of the Log-magnitude and the phase plot for the quadratic factor are shown in Figure 5.14 and Table 5.5

lists the maximum overshoot for poles or the undershoot for zeros for various values of the damping factor. This amount of correction can be added to your asymptote graphs if you need an exact plot.

From Figure 5.14 you can see that there is no overshoot and the approximation using the

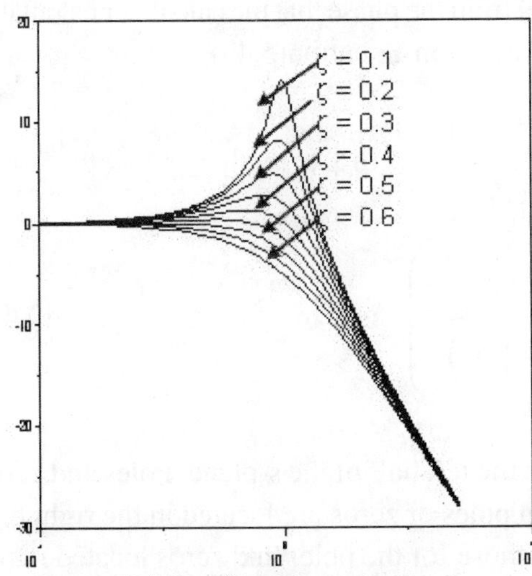

Figure 5.14 a Magnitude Plot notice the overshoot at the corner frequency for small values of the damping ratio ζ.

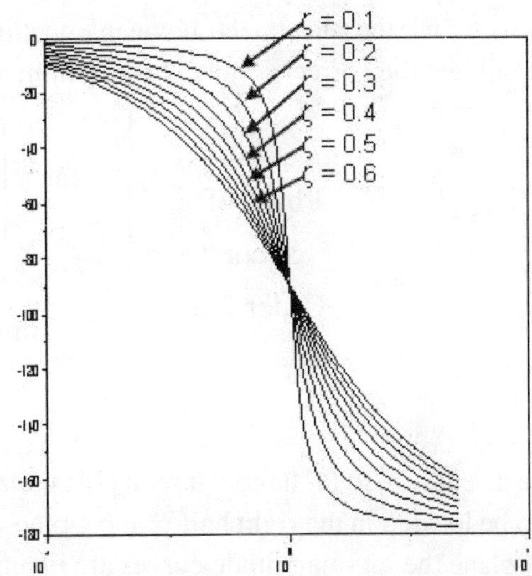

Figure 5.14 b Phase Plot notice that all the curves pass through 90° at the corner frequency. For small values of the damping ratio ζ the phase change is very abrupt at the corner frequency.

Figure 5.14: Bode plot of a complex conjugate pole pair for various values of the damping ratio

asymptotes holds for $\xi > 0.7$ for $\xi < 0.7$ there is a sharp peak at the corner frequency. To include the peak at the corner frequency we first draw the asymptote plot and then at the corner frequency we add the appropriate amount of overshoot for the poles or the undershoot for the zeros.

The phase plot is drawn in the same way as the phase plot for the single poles. We calculate the phase shift for different frequency values. The range of frequency values used is once again from one decade less than the corner frequency to one decade more than the corner frequency. Equation(5.48) is used for this calculation.

Table 5.5 Correction to include the effect of a low damping factor

Damping Ratio	0.1	0.2	0.3	0.4	0.5	0.6	0.7	0.8
Correction in dB	13.76	6.25	4.7	3.2	1.5	0.5	-2.0	-3.5

A note about using Equation(5.48): The denominator of the argument of the inverse tangent function is a difference between two terms. As long as ω/ω_{cf} is less than one (or the denominator is a positive quantity) the calculation using a standard scientific calculator will give the correct result. When ω/ω_{cf} is greater than 1 (or the denominator is a negative quantity) then the denominator of the argument becomes negative. The standard scientific calculator which gives us the result in the first or the fourth quadrant only will give an erroneous result in this case. To correct for the calculator peculiarity we use the adjustment shown in Equation(5.49) from the phase that the calculator calculates and we will get the correct result. This is summarized for you in Equation(5.49).

$$\text{Phase of a Second Order Pole} = \begin{cases} \tan^{-1}\left(\dfrac{\frac{2\xi\omega}{\omega_{cf}}}{1-\left(\frac{\omega}{\omega_{cf}}\right)^2}\right) & \omega \le \omega_{cf} \\ 180-\tan^{-1}\left(\dfrac{\frac{2\xi\omega}{\omega_{cf}}}{1-\left(\frac{\omega}{\omega_{cf}}\right)^2}\right) & \omega \ge \omega_{cf} \end{cases} \tag{5.49}$$

5.7.3.5

The discussion so far has dealt with poles or zeros in the left half of the s-plane. Poles and zeros can also be located in the right half of the s-plane. When poles or zeros are located in the right half of the s-plane the log-magnitude curves are identical as those for the poles and zeros located in the left half of the s-plane. The phase curves are not the same, they are different. For example the angle for the factor $(1-j\omega T)$ varies from 0 to -90° as ω varies from low frequencies to very large frequencies. So with poles or zeros in the right half of the s-plane we need no adjustment for the log magnitude graph and for the phase portion of the graph we need to change the sign of the phase due to the pole or the zero. So a right half pole will have positive phase shift while a right half zero will have a negative phase shift.

Example 5.19

As a simple example of drawing the Bode plot of an s-domain transfer function consider the function given in Equation(5.50). We will draw the Bode plot of this s-domain function.

$$F(s) = \frac{132(s+2)}{s(s+0.5)(s^2+0.4s+64)} \tag{5.50}$$

Solution 5.19

We will first re-write the s-domain transfer function in the standard form and replace s→jω. Doing this will give us the function shown in Equation(5.51).

$$F(j\omega) = \frac{8(1+\frac{j\omega}{2})}{j\omega(1+\frac{j\omega}{0.5})(1+\frac{j0.4\omega}{8}+(\frac{j\omega}{8})^2)} \tag{5.51}$$

Step 1.

Since this function includes both the pole at the origin and a gain >1 we will draw these first. We first draw the plot for the pole at the origin. This plot has a -20dB/decade slope and passes through the 0dB axis at $\omega = 1$. After we have drawn the plot for the pole at the origin we lift it up by the amount of the gain which is $20\log_{10}(8) = 18.06$dB. This is shown in Figure 5.15. The plot so far is up to point A from the extreme left edge of the plot.

Step 2.

Our next pole occurs at $\omega = 0.5$ radians/sec so we have to back up the plot drawn so far till this corner frequency. This is point B on the plot. At point B on the plot we have a pole. So the slope of the graph has to reflect the contributions of two poles. The slope of -20dB/decade from the pole at the origin and another -20dB/decade due to the pole at $\omega = 0.5$ so the total contribution is in the form of the slope of -40dB/decade. The graph is then drawn from here until the next break point which is at $\omega = 2$ radians/sec and shown as a graph from point B to point C on the plot.

Step 3.

At point C we have a zero in the transfer function. The zero introduces a slope of +20dB/ decade. So the new slope of the plot will be -20dB/decade to reflect the presence of two poles and one zero. This slope will continue till the next corner frequency which is located at 8 radians/sec and is shown on the graph by point D.

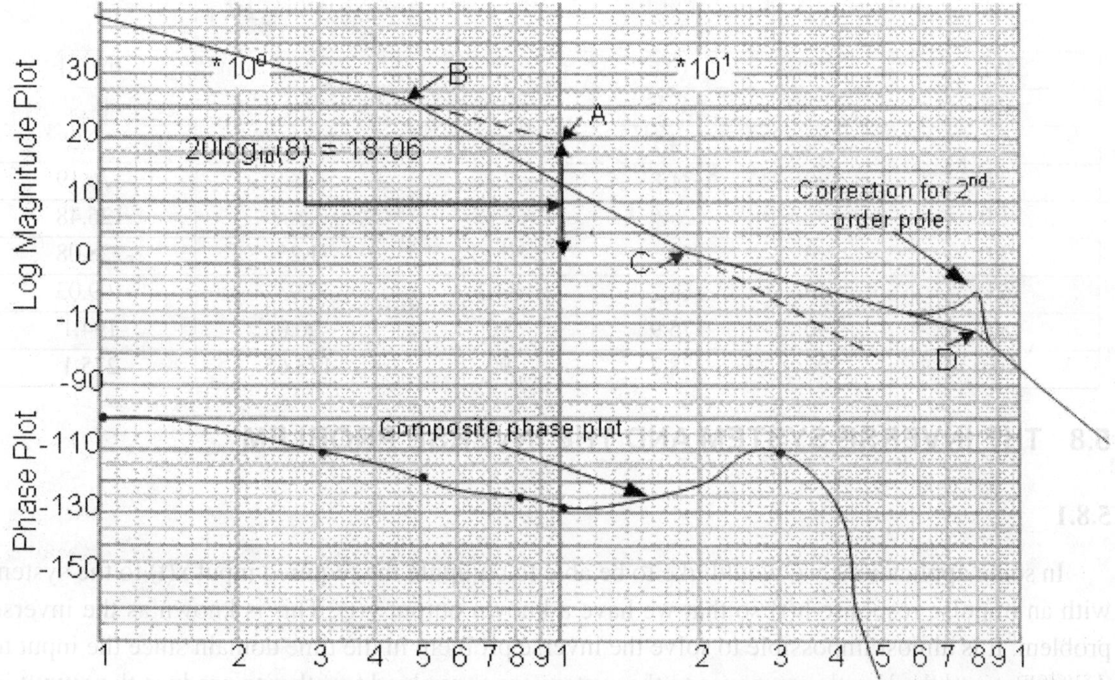

Figure 5.15: Bode plot (log-magnitude and phase) for function given in Equation 5.48

Step 4.

At point D we have a second order under damped pole. Since the pole is a second order pole it will introduce a slope change of 40dB per decade. Hence the slope of the plot from 8 radians/sec will be -60db/decade. Also since the two poles at point D are under damped poles we need to introduce a correction. The damping ratio for these poles is 0.2. Looking at Table 5.5 the correction is about 6.25 dB. This is approximately drawn on the plot. This then completes the magnitude plot for the given function.

Step 5.

To draw the phase plot we will compute the phase shift for the poles and the zeros at various different frequency values and then plot the points on the graph. The phase shift is computed for the poles and the zeros individually and then added together. This is shown in Table 5.6. The bottom half of the plot in Figure 5.15 is the phase plot for the function in Equation(5.51).

Table 5.6: Calculating the phase shift for the function given in Equation (5.51)

Frequency	$\tan^{-1}(j\omega)$	$\tan^{-1}(j\omega/2)$	$\tan^{-1}(j\omega/0.5)$	$\tan^{-1}\left(\dfrac{0.05\frac{\omega}{\omega_{cf}}}{\left(1-\left(\frac{\omega}{\omega_{cf}}\right)^2\right)}\right)$	Total Phase
0.1	-90	0.0	-11.31	0.0	-101.31
0.3	-90	8.5	-30.96	0.0	-112.46
0.5	-90	14.1	-45	0.0	-120.88
0.8	-90	21.8	-57.99	-0.289	-126.19
1.0	-90	26.6	-63.43	-0.363	-126.48
3.0	-90	56.3	-80.53	-1.25	-128.08
5.0	-90	68.2	-84.3	-2.93	-109.03
8.0	-90	75.9	-90	-90.0	-194.1
10.0	-90	78.7	-90	-173.65	-275.1

5.8 THE INVERSE SYSTEM AND THE INVERSE PROBLEM

5.8.1

In some applications we would like to be able to compute the required input x(t) to the system with an impulse response h(t) so that we have a known output y(t). This is known as the inverse problem. It is almost impossible to solve the inverse problem in the time domain since the input to the system and the impulse response to the system are convolved together to produce the output in the time domain. So to solve the inverse problem in the time domain we would need to have something that can calculate inverse convolution. We do not have such a thing yet. May be one of you will become very famous and rich by discovering just such a procedure. In the meantime though we will use the property of the convolution theorem in the frequency domain.

In the frequency domain the input is multiplied with the transfer function of the system to get the output. We all know that the inverse of multiplication is division. Division we know how to do. So when we have the transfer function model

$Y(s) = H(s) \bullet X(s)$ we can solve for X(s) to get $X(s) = H^{-1}(s) \bullet Y(s)$.

In the frequency domain we can view this equation as the transfer function model for a new system that has the same transfer function as $H^{-1}(s)$, the input to this system is Y(s) and the response from this system is X(s). Consider for a moment the new system $H^{-1}(s)$, if the original system H(s) was a proper rational fraction then $H^{-1}(s)$ will contain differentiators, (terms in s) which are in general difficult to implement.

When H(s) is a proper fraction then $H(s) = \dfrac{N(s)}{D(s)}$ and $\deg\{N(s)\} < \deg\{D(s)\}$ then $H^{-1}(s) = \dfrac{D(s)}{N(s)}$ may not be a proper fraction since $\deg\{D(s)\} > \deg\{N(s)\}$. If H(s) and $H^{-1}(s)$ are to be both proper fractions then $\deg\{N(s)\}$ must be equal to the $\deg\{D(s)\}$. When both H(s) and $H^{-1}(s)$ are proper fractions then $H(s) \bullet H^{-1}(s)=1$. In this case if the system and its inverse are cascaded then we have a situation as shown in Figure 5.16.

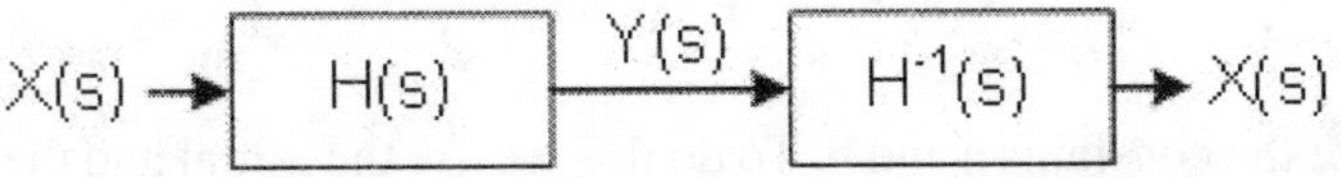

$$X(s) \rightarrow \boxed{H(s)} \xrightarrow{Y(s)} \boxed{H^{-1}(s)} \rightarrow X(s)$$

Figure 5.16: This property of an inverse system is extremely useful for many applications. These applications try to reproduce the original signal. One example of the use of this is in the cell phone that we all use.

As a different application of the inverse system consider the application of an auto pilot for a train car going to a siding yard. We want to park the train car at a known position. If there is a train conductor in the car then the conductor can control the car. If we want to do this on auto pilot then the train has to know what force to apply to first move the car and then to stop the car after it has traveled the required distance. This is where the inverse system comes in play. We know what the result or the outcome is supposed to be, we want to determine the input that will give us this outcome. Consider this example; the train car can be modeled as the following simple input output differential equation

$$M\frac{d^2x(t)}{dt^2} + K_f\frac{dx(t)}{dt} = f(t) \tag{5.52}$$

In this equation x(t) is the position of the train car, f(t) is the force applied, when $f(t) > 0$ then we are driving the train; when $f(t)<0$ then we are applying the brakes and stopping the train car. We wish to move the car from its initial position x(0) = 0 to its final position x(200) = 5280 (one mile in 200 seconds). We also assume that the initial velocity $\dot{x}(0)=0$ and we also want the train stopped after 200 seconds so $\dot{x}(200)=0$. Our train starts from rest and it is at rest at time 200 seconds during which time it has traveled 5280 feet. Writing the system equation and its inverse we get Equation(5.53):

$$X(s) = H(s) \bullet F(s) \qquad \text{and} \qquad H(s) = \frac{1/M}{s\left(s + K_f/M\right)}$$

$$\text{The inverse then is given by } F(s) = H^{-1}(s) \bullet X(s) = \frac{s(s + K_f/M)}{1/M} \bullet X(s) \tag{5.53}$$

Obtaining the straight inverse of this function will give us the driving function x(t). If however we want to make sure that the function x(t) does not contain any impulses then we must make sure that the deg num{F(s)}< deg den{F(s)}. We can do this by properly choosing X(s). Choose X(s) such that deg num{X(s)}< deg den{X(s)}-2. (We choose X(s)-2 because $H^{-1}(s)$ has an excess degree of 2 in the numerator.) If we choose X(s) this way then F(s) will not contain any impulses. To satisfy the degree constraint we can choose x(t) as many different functions, one of these can be $at^3 + bt^2$. Let us see how this function works. Taking the Laplace transform of x(t) we get

$$X(s) = \frac{6a}{s^4} + \frac{2b}{s^3} = \frac{6a + 2bs}{s^4} \tag{5.54}$$

Next we solve for the constants a and b. To do this we use the initial and the final conditions for the position and the velocity that we know. This is shown in Equation(5.55).

$$\begin{aligned}
&\text{Initial conditions: } x(0) = 0 \text{ and } \dot{x}(0) = 0\\
&x(0) = 0 \text{ So } a\cdot(0)^3 + b\cdot(0)^2 = 0\\
&\dot{x}(0) = 0 \text{ So } 3\cdot a\cdot(0)^2 + 2\cdot b\cdot(0) = 0\\
&\text{Final conditions: } x(200) = 5280 \text{ and } \dot{x}(200) = 0\\
&x(200) = 5280 \text{ So } a\cdot(200)^3 + b\cdot(200)^2 = 5280\\
&\dot{x}(0) = 0 \text{ So } 3\cdot a\cdot(200)^2 + 2\cdot b\cdot(200) = 0\\
&\text{Solving these equations we get } a = -0.00132 \text{ and } b = 0.396
\end{aligned} \tag{5.55}$$

With the constants determined we get the driving function F(s) as shown in Equation(5.56). We see that F(s) is a rational function and can now be inverted to get the driving force in the time domain.

$$X(s)=\frac{0.792s-0.00792}{s^4}$$

$$F(s)=\frac{s(s+K_f/M)}{1/M}\bullet\frac{0.792s-0.00792}{s^4}$$

$$=\frac{0.792s^3+\left(0.792\,{}^{K_f}\!/\!_M-0.00792\right)s^2-0.00792\left({}^{K_f}\!/\!_M\right)s}{{}^1\!/\!_M\,s^4} \tag{5.56}$$

The solution that we will get for f(t) by inverting the function in Equation(5.56) is one of the many possible driving force functions. This is not a unique solution. Many other solutions are possible. Often we are interested in some 'Optimum' solution. Once the 'Optimum' criterion is defined then such a solution can be found. Some possible 'Optimum' criteria could be least amount of fuel used; or smallest average velocity; smallest average braking force used; etc. Solutions that are 'Optimized' in this way are a study of automatic control theory. If you are interested in studying this branch of engineering refer to book 1 in the suggested reading material at the end of this chapter.

5.9 CHAPTER SUMMARY

5.9.1 The Laplace Transform:

The Laplace transform is very similar to the Fourier transform; it is not exactly the same. The Laplace transform has the additional negative exponential which the Fourier transform does not have. This makes it possible to find the Laplace transform for many more functions that do not have the Fourier transform. In particular functions that have initial conditions when they are turned on, and for some functions that have a positive exponential. The Laplace transform can be defined as either the two sided or as the one sided transform. Most of the time we will define and use the single sided Laplace transform. The single sided Laplace transform allows us to include initial conditions in system equations and hence represent systems in a realistic manner.

5.9.2 The Properties of the Laplace Transform:

The Laplace transform has many properties that are similar to the Fourier transform. All these properties are listed in detail in Table 5.1 in this chapter. The properties inform us and show us how the Laplace transform behaves under different conditions. We have seen that the Laplace transform is:

Linear:
It obeys the principle of superposition.

A shift in the Time domain:
Corresponds to a rotation in the Laplace domain. This is implemented by multiplying the Laplace domain function by $e^{-s\tau}$. The delay in the time domain function is by τ seconds.

A shift in the Frequency domain:

Corresponds to multiplying the time domain function by an exponential $e^{-s_o t}$. A shift in the frequency domain shifts the entire pole-zero plot either right or left as the case may be by an amount equal to s_o.

Time scaling:

Expanding or contracting the function in the time domain corresponds to collapsing or stretching out the pole-zero plots in the frequency domain.

Initial and Final value theorems:

These theorems tell us how the time domain function behaves during the transient and the steady state time period without having to find the inverse Laplace transform. Using these theorems we can predict what the behavior of the time domain function will be initially when the system starts out and in the steady state.

5.9.3 Inverse Laplace Transform:

The inverse Laplace transform can be obtained by evaluating the inverse integral. This integral is an integral in the complex domain which is not easy to evaluate. It is however easy to use the result of the integral. The result of evaluating the integral is the residues at each pole of the Laplace domain function. The residues for the Laplace function are calculated by using the partial fraction expansion. The function is expanded as a partial fraction and the residues at each pole are determined. Using this partial fraction and the inverse transform pairs given in Table 5.2 the inverse transform is easily determined.

5.9.4 Using Laplace Transform to solve Differential Equations:

Since we can include initial conditions with Laplace transforms we can use Laplace transforms to solve differential equations. We have seen a four step process to solve the differential equations in Section 5.5. The four steps are

- Find the Laplace transform of the differential equation.
- Solve the equation in the Laplace domain. This will be an algebraic equation since the Laplace domain function is an algebraic function.
- Substitute the initial conditions.
- Find the inverse Laplace transform. This is the solution of the differential equation.

5.9.5 Transfer Functions:

Generally we will find that most systems are represented in block diagram form. Block diagrams are generally drawn with the functions in the Laplace domain. In the Laplace domain the input of the block is multiplied by the transfer function of the block to give the output from the block. The different blocks can be connected as cascade, parallel or as feedback connection. In most systems you will see some combination of all the three connections. When you see a feedback connection you will also see a summing junction. To determine the overall transfer function for the system with feedback connections we insert a break in the signal path right after the summing junction. Then from the output side of the break we write equations for the signals as they go through the various blocks till we come to the input side of the break. Now we equate the two signals on the two sides of the break to get the overall transfer function for the system.

5.9.6 Bode Plots:

Once you know the system transfer function you are often interested in determining how the system behaves when subjected to different frequency inputs. This is the job of a frequency response plot. One such plot is the Bode plot. The Bode plot represents the Log-magnitude and the Phase into two separate plots. To draw the Log-magnitude plots we draw the asymptote plots of all the individual poles and the zeros and add them up at all the frequency values to get the overall play of the entire function. To draw the phase plot we make a table of phase shifts for each pole and zero at selected frequency points. Then we add up the individual phase shifts, at each frequency point to get the overall phase shift at selected frequency points. Plotting these phase points vs. frequency gives us the other plot. Generally we add a correction in the magnitude plot when complex conjugate poles and/or zeros are present in the transfer function. The correction is negligible and can be ignored when the damping ratio is greater than 0.65.

5.10 HOMEWORK PROBLEMS

The Laplace Transform

Problem 5.10.1

Obtain the Laplace Transform of the following signals:

a.	$(1 - e^{2t})U(t)$	**b.**	$\delta(t) - \delta(t-10)$
c.	$U(t) - U(t-10)$	**d.**	$(e^{2t} - e^{10t})U(t)$
e.	$(1+e^{-5t}-e^{-2t})U(t)$	**f.**	$\delta(t) - U(t-10)$

Problem 5.10.2

Using the definition of Laplace transform determine the transforms of the following functions:

a.	$e^{-\alpha t}U(t)$	**b.**	$te^{-\alpha t}U(t)$
c.	$e^{-\alpha t}Cos(\beta t)U(t)$	**d.**	$tCos(\beta t)U(t)$
e.	$te^{-\alpha t}Cos(\beta t)U(t)$		

The Laplace Transform Theorems

Problem 5.10.3

You are given that the Laplace Transform of the signal x(t) ⇔ X(s). Using the applicable theorem of Laplace transform determine the transforms of each of the following signals.

a.	$e^{-2t}x(t)$	**b.**	x(at) a>0
c.	x(t)*x(t)	**d.**	x(t-5)U(t-5)
e.	x(t)*x(t-5)	**f.**	$x(t)*[e^{-2t}x(t)]$
g.	tx(t)	**h.**	(t-2)x(t-2)U(t-2)

Problem 5.10.4

Using the Initial value and the Final value theorems determine the initial value and the final value for all the functions in 5.10.6. Compare the initial value and the final value thus obtained by determining the initial value and the final value of the time domain functions that you obtained after you evaluated the inverse Laplace Transforms.

Problem 5.10.5

You are given that the Laplace Transform of the signal $x(t) = 5Sin(3t) = \frac{15}{s^2+9} = X(s)$.

Using the properties and theorems of Laplace transform determine the Laplace Transform of:

a.	5Sin(2 • 3t)U(t)	**b.**	5Sin(3(t-4))U(t-4)	**c.**	5Cos(3t)U(t)
d.	$5e^{-4t}$Sin(3t)U(t)	**e.**	$5e^{-4t}$Sin(3(t-4))U(t-4)	**f.**	$5e^{-4t}$Sin(2 • 3t)U(t)

Inverse Laplace Transform using Partial Fractions

Problem 5.10.6

Use partial fraction expansion to find the inverse Laplace Transform of the following:

a.	$\frac{s+4}{s^2+9s+20}$	b.	$\frac{s^2+4s}{s^2+9s+20}$
c.	$\frac{(s+5)(s+2)}{(s+1)(s+3)((s+1)^2+4)}$	d.	$\frac{(s+4)^2}{(s^2+9s+20)^2}$
e.	$\frac{(s+4)e^{-4s}}{s^2+9s+20}$	f.	$\frac{(s+4)}{s^2(s^2+9s+36.25)}$
g.	$\frac{s(s+4)}{(s^2+9s+20)(s^2+12s+36)}$	h.	$\frac{s^2+4s}{s^3(s^2+9s+20)}$

Solving Differential Equations

Problem 5.10.7

Solve the following differential equations using Laplace Transforms:

a.	$\frac{d^2x(t)}{dt^2}+6\frac{dx(t)}{dt}+5x(t)=e^{-4t}U(t);$ *All initial conditions are zero.*
b.	$\frac{d^3x(t)}{dt^3}+6\frac{d^2x(t)}{dt^2}+11\frac{dx(t)}{dt}+6x(t)=4U(t)-3U(t-2);$ $x(0)=1;\ \left.\frac{dx(t)}{dt}\right\|_{t=0}=2;\ \left.\frac{d^2x(t)}{dt^2}\right\|_{t=0}=3.$
c.	Change the driving function in part 'b' to sin(3t)
d.	$\frac{dx(t)}{dt}+4x(t)+y(t)=U(t);\ \frac{dy(t)}{dt}+3y(t)-x(t)=0;\quad x(0)=2;\ y(0)=3$ Hint: It is not necessary to obtain an equation in terms of x(t) and y(t) alone. Transform the two equations to the Laplace domain, then solve the two equations in the s-domain to get X(s) and Y(s). Now determine the inverse transforms to get the solution for x(t) and y(t) individually. This is an example of interconnected systems.
e.	**Demonstrating Time Invariance:** $\frac{d^2y(t)}{dt^2}+\frac{4dy(t)}{dt}+3y(t)=u(t)$ All initial conditions are zero. After you have determined the response for the given differential equation solve it again but this time change the driving function to u(t-2). Compare the two responses. The second response should have identical shape as the first response but it is delayed in time.
f.	You were given that the initial conditions in part 'e' of this question were all zero. How would you account for non-zero initial conditions? The required initial conditions are both 2 at the starting time of the system. (Hint: Think about what is the starting time for each of the two systems.)
g.	How would the response of the two systems differ in part 'e' of this question if you were given that $y(0^+)=2;$ and $\frac{dy(0^+)}{dt}=0.5$ for both the system examples?

Drawing the Frequency Response Plots (Bode Plots)

Problem 5.10.8

Construct the Bode Plot for the transfer functions given below. Do not forget to add the correction for the complex conjugate poles. Draw the plot from frequency at least one decade below the smallest corner frequency, not counting the pole or the zero at the origin, up to the frequency at least one decade above the highest corner frequency. Do not forget to draw the Phase plots also.

a. $G(s) = \dfrac{200(s+4)}{s(s+1)(s^2+10s+100)}$	**b.** $G(s) = \dfrac{500(s^2+2s+2)}{(s+4)(s^2+81)}$
c. $G(s) = \dfrac{20s(s+4)}{(s+1)(s^2+10s+100)}$	**d.** $G(s) = \dfrac{500(s^2+2s+2)}{(s-4)(s^2+81)}$
e. $G(s) = \dfrac{200(s-4)}{s(s+1)(s^2+10s+100)}$	**f.** $G(s) = \dfrac{100(s^2+5s+4)}{s(s+4)(s^2+81)}$
g. The functions in part 'c' and 'e' are almost the same as each other. Only one zero is shifted from the left half of the s-plane to the right half of the s-plane. Similarly the functions in part 'b' and 'd' are almost the same as each other. Only one pole is shifted from the left half of the s-plane to the right half of the s-plane. Compare the magnitude plots for these pairs of plots. What is the difference between the magnitude plots?	
h. In part 'g' you compared the magnitude of two similar plots. Now compare the phase plots for the same pairs of plots. What is the difference between the phase plots?	

Block Diagrams and System Transfer Functions

Problem 5.10.9

From the block diagrams shown in Figure P5.10.9 determine the overall transfer function for each of the three systems. After you have determined the transfer function move the block $G_1(s)$ from where it is to where signal labeled A is located. Now determine the transfer function of the new block diagram.

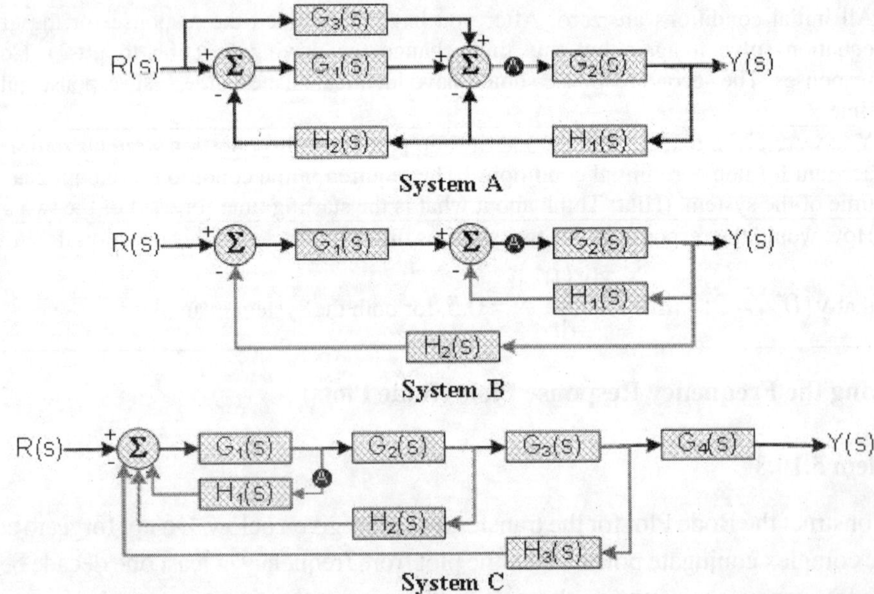

Figure P5.10.9.: Determine the overall transfer function Y(s)/R(s) for the three systems shown

Problem 5.10.10

It is determined that the Block $G_1(s)$ needs to be moved to the point where the signal is labeled "A" but this time the transfer function of the overall system must not be altered. Draw the new block diagram with the block $G_1(s)$ moved to the position "A" without altering the overall transfer function. Hint: You will need to either add another block $G_1(s)$ or the inverse of that block $\{ G_1(s)\}^{-1}$ in other branches.

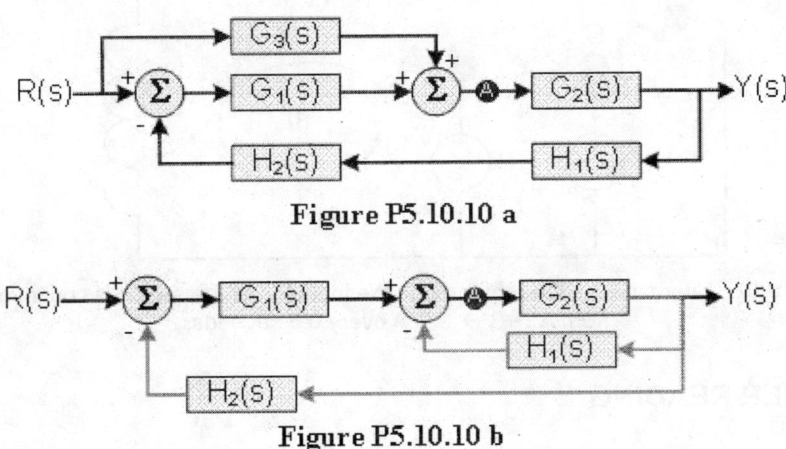

Figure P5.10.10: Determine the overall transfer function Y(s)/R(s) for the two systems shown

Problem 5.10.11

Obtain the voltage across the resistor in Figure P5.10.11 as a function of time for t>0 in each of the three cases shown. For each case assume that $i(0^+) = 0$ and that $v(0^+) = 0$.

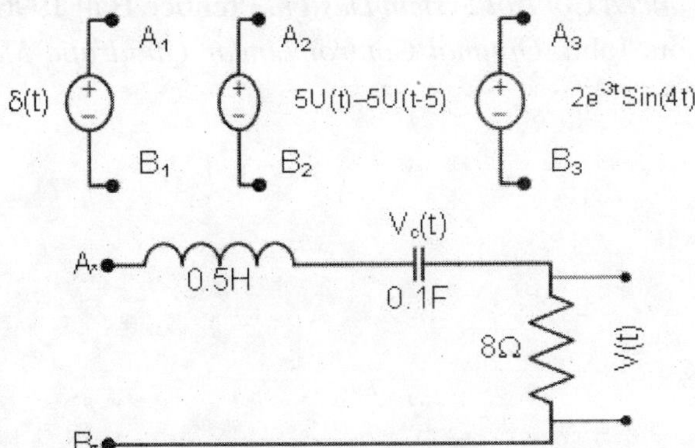

Figure P5.10.11: Connect each of the inputs shown to the circuit one by one and then determine the voltage across the resistor for all time

Problem 5.10.12

Solve for the current through the inductor in the circuit shown in Figure P5.10.12 if the switch is moved according to the following rule: A → B → C → A. Assume that initially the switch is in position A for a very long time and then starts the sequence of moves as shown. After the first move the switch stays in any one position for 0.5 seconds only before going to the next position.

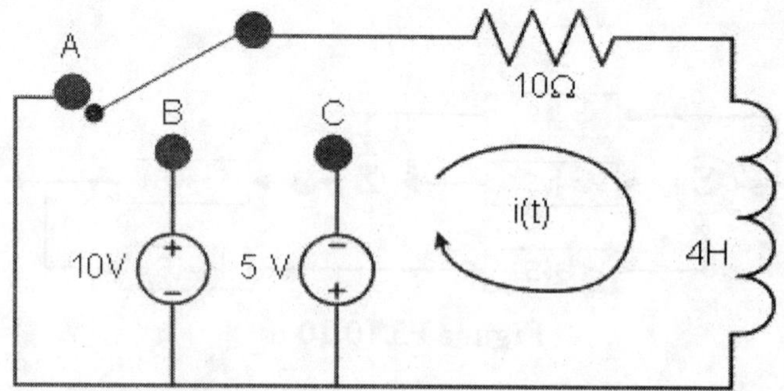

Figure P5.10.12: Determine the Current through the inductor as the switch is continuously moved from A → B → C→ A every 0.5 seconds.

5.11 FURTHER READING

5.11.1

Automatic Control Theory and Applications of Laplace Transforms, Optimization theory is covered in:

1. Borgan W.L., *Modern Control Theory*, Prentice Hall Englewood NJ 1985.
2. Friedland Bernard, *Control System Design – An Introduction to State Space* Methods, McGraw Hill 1986.
3. Friedland Bernard, *Advanced Control System Design*, Prentice Hall 1996.
4. Anderson Brian & Moors John, *Optimal Control Linear Quadratic Methods*, Prentice Hall 1990.

CHAPTER 6

State Space Systems

INTRODUCTION

In the first five chapters of this book we have looked at systems with the transfer function point of view. In this point of view we transform the system into the frequency domain and consider only the input output relations. We solve the system in the frequency domain and then transform the solution back to the time domain. In doing all this we did not get to see what was going on inside the system. The result only gave us the response and nothing else. Often we are interested in knowing what is happening within a system at a particular point. How is a particular capacitor voltage changing or how fast the mass is moving within the system? With the transfer function we could not find that out directly. We can get this information indirectly but with this new representation we will not have to resort to the indirect method.

With the transfer function representation, we had only one input and one output. The transfer function relates this one input to this one output. If there was a second input or a second output we had to define a second or a third system and to find the relation from the second input to the second output, a different system from the second input to the second output has to be defined and then completely solved. A second input to a system could be a wind load on an antenna or some other disturbance. To account for a step change in the wind load to the antenna we will have to define a different system since we have two different input points. With a state space representation there is no limits to the number of inputs and the number of outputs within any one definition. We can easily account for several inputs and several different outputs simultaneously.

The transfer function representation dealt with only the linear system. When there were non-linearity's present in the system we have to either assume that the non-linearity's were small (make the system piece wise linear or some such formulation) or resort to different methods. With the state space representation and the state space solution method that we will use, the solution method remains the same when the system is linear or it is non linear. The state space system can also be extended to time varying systems. With all these advantages over the transfer function method it is no wonder that the state space method is the modern tool that is used by most designers. The special feature of the state space system is the formulation of the matrix equation. The matrix equation is a compact equation which allows large and complicated systems to be studied using the same mathematics tools that you would use for simple systems. In this chapter we explore the state space approach for linear systems.

$$\begin{aligned}
\dot{x}_1 &= a_{11}x_1 + a_{12}x_2 + \cdots + a_{1n}x_n + b_{11}u_1 + b_{12}u_2 + \cdots + b_{1m}u_m \\
\dot{x}_2 &= a_{21}x_1 + a_{22}x_2 + \cdots + a_{2n}x_n + b_{21}u_1 + b_{22}u_2 + \cdots + b_{2m}u_m \\
&\vdots \\
\dot{x}_n &= a_{n1}x_1 + a_{n2}x_2 + \cdots + a_{nn}x_n + b_{n1}u_1 + b_{n2}u_2 + \cdots + b_{nm}u_m
\end{aligned} \tag{6.1}$$

$$\begin{aligned}
y_1 &= c_{11}x_1 + c_{12}x_2 + \cdots + c_{1n}x_n + d_{11}u_1 + d_{12}u_2 + \cdots + d_{1m}u_m \\
y_2 &= c_{21}x_1 + c_{22}x_2 + \cdots + c_{2n}x_n + d_{21}u_1 + d_{22}u_2 + \cdots + d_{2m}u_m \\
&\vdots \\
y_p &= c_{p1}x_1 + c_{p2}x_2 + \cdots + c_{pn}x_n + d_{p1}u_1 + d_{p2}u_2 + \cdots + d_{pm}u_m
\end{aligned} \tag{6.2}$$

6.1 STATE SPACE CONCEPT

The state of a system is the information that you need about the system to be able to predict the response of the system from that time onwards. The way you specify the state of the system is not unique. There are various different combinations of the system parameters that will give us the same information about the system. For example in a circuit with two nodes we can define the voltage at the two nodes as one set of information that will give us the information that we seek about the circuit. For the same circuit we could define the voltage at one node and the sum of the voltages at the two nodes as the second piece of information about the circuit. These two different representations of the circuit are not the same but they both convey the same information to us. The first method conveys the information directly while the second method does the same job in a slightly round about manner. In the same way the state variable representation of a system is not unique. There are many different representations and each one of them will give us the information that we seek about the system in a slightly different manner.

In a linear system with capacitors and inductors the voltage across all the capacitors at $t = t_o$ and the current through the inductors at time $t = t_o$ can be treated as the initial state of the system at time t_o. Knowing how the state variables change tells us how the system is responding. The knowledge of this information and the knowledge of the input will allow us to determine the voltage and the

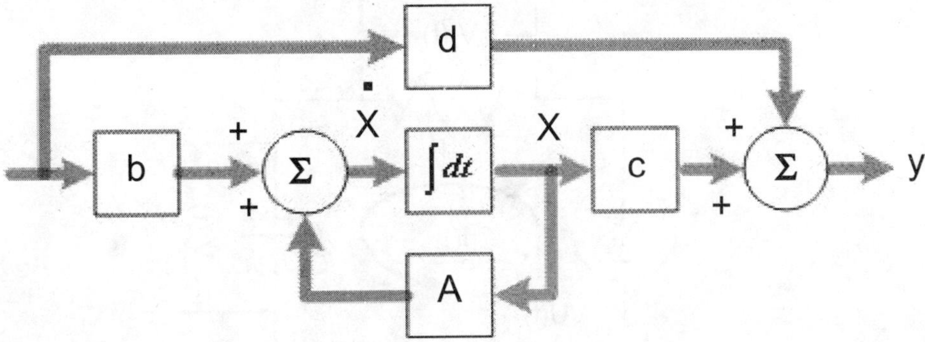

Figure 6.1: The representation of the state variable system showing the relations of the various matrices

currents in the system at any time t where $t > t_o$. Thus we can define the voltages and the currents as the state variables of the system. In general the state of the system is the condition of the energy storage elements. This is only in general so it does not have to be this way. For example we can change one of the state variables in the above example to be the voltage at the capacitor plus some fixed voltage. So now even though the state variable is not the condition of the energy storage element it is indirectly related to the energy storage element. So the state of the system is simply the set of values at time t_o of an appropriately chosen set of variables. These variables are known as the **state variables** of the system.

When we were talking about the transfer function of the system we talked about the order of the system. The order of the system, whether it is represented in the state variable system or in the transfer function, is also related to the number of independent energy storage elements in the system. In an nth order system there will be n independent energy storage elements in the system. So in an nth order system there will also be n state variables. These n state variables will be defined by n first order differential equations. This set of n first order differential equations are known as the state equations of the system. It is often advantageous to think of each state variable as a different dimension in a system. So an nth order system is said to be an n dimension system. A state variable representation defines how the system moves in an n-dimension space. The **state vector** is all the state variables at any instant of time. The state vector at any time t is then the value of each state variable at that time t. The **trajectory** of the system is how the state vector travels in this n dimension space.

Example 6.1

Represent the system shown in Figure 6.2 using the state variable system.

Solution 6.1

The circuit in Figure 6.2 is a simple RC circuit that we have earlier analyzed using a differential equation. To analyze this circuit here we will use the state space method. In the state space method we use state variables. As Equation(6.1) shows we choose a state variable and then write an expres-

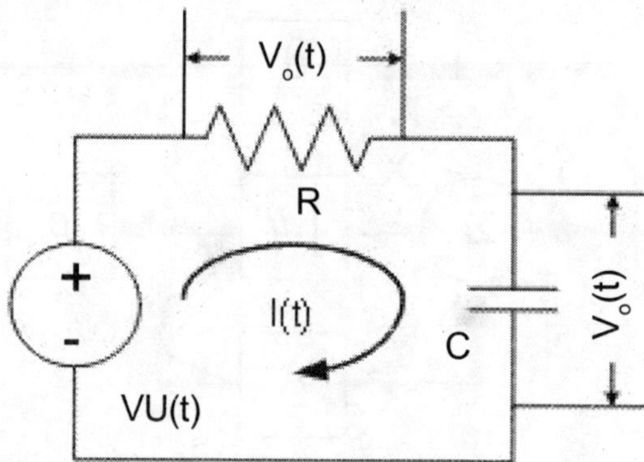

Figure 6.2: Represent the circuit shown as a State variable system

sion that tells what is the rate of change of this variable. Here we will use the voltage across the capacitor, $V_c(t)$ as the state variable. From Equation(6.1) we see that we must determine an equation that relates to the rate of change of the state variable. For this example we know that the voltage across the capacitor changes in proportion to the current flowing through the capacitor or

$$\frac{dV_c(t)}{dt} = \dot{V}_c(t) = \frac{1}{C}I(t).$$

When we substitute for the current in terms of the input voltage and the state variable,

$$I(t) = \frac{1}{R}(V - V_c(t))$$

we get the state variable representation of the system. So for our example the state variable representation is

$$\dot{V}_c(t) = \frac{-1}{RC}V_c(t) + \frac{1}{RC}V.$$

Examine this equation carefully; it is in the same format as Equation(6.1).

On the left hand side we have a first order derivative, on the right hand side we have terms consisting of the state variables and the terms consisting of the input or the driving function. This makes up half of the state variable representation for the system. The other half is the output equation.

The output equation relates the required output quantity in terms of the state variables. Let us decide that we want the voltage across the resistor as the output quantity. So for our example the voltage across the resistor is $V_o(t) = V(t) - V_c(t)$ which is in the format of Equation(6.2). This completes the state variable representation for the circuit of Figure 6.1.

An nth order differential equation can always be written as n first order differential equations. We will see this in more detail in Section 6.4. When we represent the nth order differential equation as n first order differential equations, the n first order differential equations will have all of the inputs and all of the outputs that are present in the nth order State Variable system. The n first order equations can be written as shown in Equation(6.1) and Equation(6.2). Equation (6.1) represents the state equation and Equation (6.2) represents the output equation. These equations can be written in a compact form as shown in Equation (6.3).

$$\dot{x} = Ax + bu$$
$$y = cx + du \tag{6.3}$$

In the representation of Equation (6.3) the **A** matrix is an n-by-n square matrix where n represents the number of state variables in the system. The **b** matrix is an n-by-m matrix. Here m is the number of inputs to the system. The **b** matrix tells us how the m different inputs are driving the state variables. The **c** matrix is a p-by-n matrix. Here p is the number of outputs from the system. The **c** matrix tells us how the n different state variables are combined together to form the p different outputs. The **d** matrix is a p-by-m matrix and corresponds to the direct effect that any particular input has on any particular output. The relations of the various matrices are shown in block diagram form in Figure 6.1. When a system is represented in the state format we will work with the compact form of the system representation shown in Equation (6.3).

Example 6.2

Identify the A; b; c; and d matrices for the circuit in Example 6.1.

Solution 6.2

The state variable equation tells us that the A matrix is the coefficient of the state variable. In this case A = [-1/RC]. The b matrix is the coefficient of the input in the state equation. In this case b = [1/RC]. The c matrix is the coefficient of the state variable in the output equation. In this case c = [-1]. The d matrix is the coefficient of the input in the output equation. In this case d = [1].

Example 6.3

For the system defined by the following equations identify the A, b, c and the d matrices. Also identify the number of inputs and outputs the system has:

a.
$$\dot{x}_1 = -x_1 + x_2 + u_1 \qquad \dot{x}_2 = -x_2$$
$$\dot{x}_3 = -5x_3 - 2u_1 \qquad y = 2x_1 - x_2 + 1.5u_1$$

b.
$$\dot{x}_1 = x_1 + 5x_2 + 2u_1 - 2u_2 \qquad \dot{x}_2 = 3x_1 - 4x_3 + u_1 + 3u_2$$
$$\dot{x}_3 = 2x_1 + 4x_3 + 2u_1 + 2u_2$$
$$y_1 = 4x_1 - 2x_2 + x_3 + 3u_1 + u_2 \qquad y_2 = 2x_1 + x_2 + 5x_3 + u_1 + 2u_2$$

Solution 6.3

The matrices for the system can be directly obtained from the system equations. They are for system:

a.
$$A=\begin{bmatrix}-1 & 1 & 0\\ 0 & -1 & 0\\ 0 & 0 & -5\end{bmatrix} b=\begin{bmatrix}1\\ 0\\ -2\end{bmatrix} c=\begin{bmatrix}2 & -1 & 0\end{bmatrix} d=\begin{bmatrix}1.5\end{bmatrix}$$

This system has one input and it has one output.

b.
$$A=\begin{bmatrix}1 & 5 & 0\\ 3 & 0 & -4\\ 2 & 4 & 0\end{bmatrix} b=\begin{bmatrix}2 & -2\\ 1 & 3\\ 2 & 2\end{bmatrix} c=\begin{bmatrix}4 & -2 & 1\\ 2 & 1 & 5\end{bmatrix} d=\begin{bmatrix}3 & 1\\ 1 & 2\end{bmatrix}$$

This system has two inputs and it has two outputs.

6.1.1 Drawing the Simulation Diagram for a State Variable System:

In the previous chapter we learnt how to draw the block diagrams and how to obtain the system equation from the block diagrams. We did that in the frequency domain. We can do the same in the time domain also. Here we will see how to draw the signal flow diagram (also known as the simulation diagram) for a system in the time domain. To do this we will use the system representation in the State variable format. As we have seen in the state variable format in Equations(6.1) and (6.2). Equation(6.1) is the state equation and that is where we will begin. First notice that the state variable equations are several simultaneous equations. Next each of these equations contains the first derivative of the state variable on the left hand side. What is the derivative of this state variable equal to? That is easy; the derivative of the state variable is equal to the sum of the state variables and the driving function. The driving function is the input and it is known. Since we know that the derivative is equal to a combination of state variables we can determine the derivative as soon as we know the state variables. Once we determine the state variables we can build the derivative of all the state variables. Determining the state variables is also easy; integrate the derivative of the state variables and you will get the state variables themselves.

So the method that we follow is as follows. We first assume that we know exactly what the derivative of each of the state variables is. When we integrate the derivative we will get the corresponding state variable. Once we have the state variable then we can combine the state variables as required to build the derivative of the state variables that we assumed that we knew to begin with. Following these steps will allow us to simulate the system of equations in Equation(6.1). Let us look at a simple example to do this.

Example 6.4

Draw the simulation diagram for system defined by the state equations

$$\begin{bmatrix}\dot{x}_1\\ \dot{x}_2\end{bmatrix}=\begin{bmatrix}2 & -1\\ 0.5 & 3\end{bmatrix}\begin{bmatrix}x_1\\ x_2\end{bmatrix}+\begin{bmatrix}1\\ 2\end{bmatrix}U(t)$$

Solution 6.4

Here we have two state variables so we will begin by assuming that we know exactly what the signal $\dot{x}_1$ is and what the signal $\dot{x}_2$ is. If we know what the two signals are then we can integrate them to get x_1 and x_2. When we complete the integration the state variables x_1 and x_2 will be known. This is shown in step 1 in Figure 6.3.

Now that we know the two state variables and the input signal is always known, we can combine the state variables and the input to build the derivative of the state variables as required by the state variable equation. This is shown in step 2 in Figure 6.3. The two step process builds the state variable equation as required in Equation(6.1).

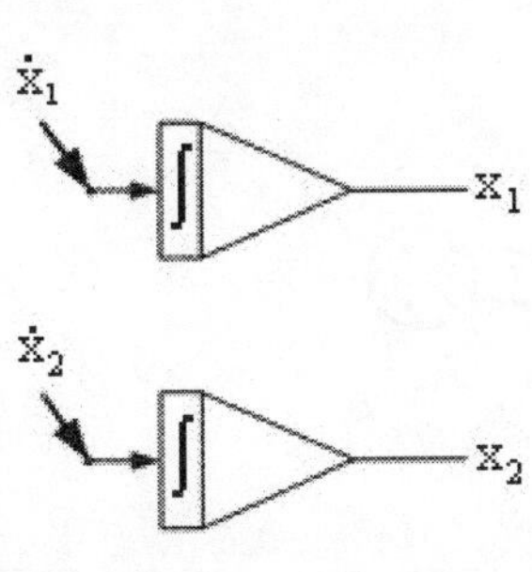

Step 1: Assume you know the derivatives. Integrate to get the state variables.

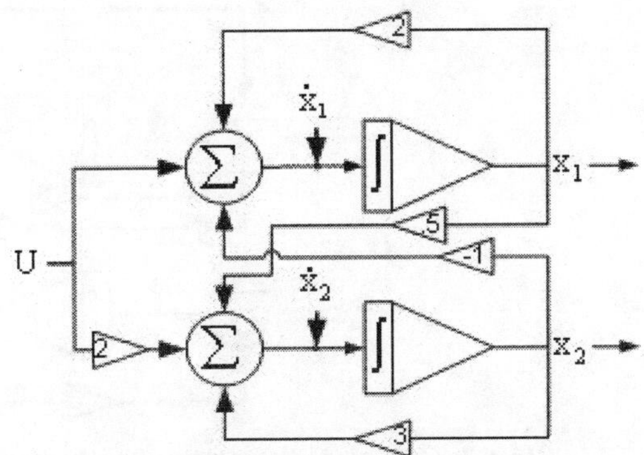

Step 2: Combine the state variables and the input to build the derivatives of the state variables.

Figure 6.3: Building the State Variable Simulation Diagram

Example 6.5

Complete the simulation diagram for system defined by the state equation in Example 6.4 and with the output equation $y = 4x_1 + 3x_2$

Solution 6.5

In Example 6.4 we began and completed the simulation diagram for the state variables. We continue with the same diagram and to that we add the third step; this step will add the simulation for the output equation. In step 2 of Figure 6.3 we had developed the state variables. All that we now need to do is to combine the required state variables to get the output equation. This is done in step 3 of Figure 6.4.

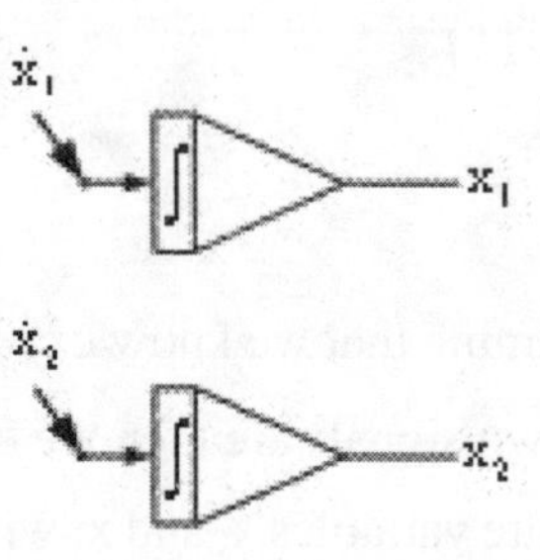

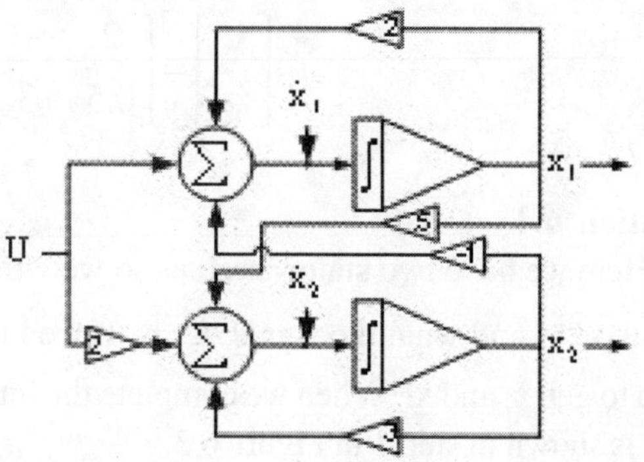

Step 1: Assume you know the derivatives. Integrate to get the state variables.

Step 2: Combine the state variables and the input to build the derivatives of the state variables.

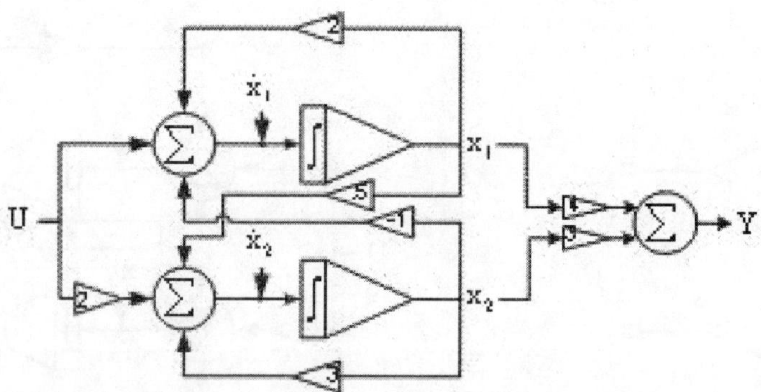

Step 3: Complete the simulation by adding the output equation.

Figure 6.4: Completing the State Variable Simulation Diagram

Example 6.6

Draw the simulation diagram for system 'a' in Example 6.3.

Solution 6.6

The simulation diagram is shown in Figure 6.5. Drawing the state variable diagram is very straight forward if we look at first drawing the simulation diagram for each state variable and then adding to that diagram the simulation diagram for the output.

Example 6.7

Draw the simulation diagram for system 'b' in Example 6.3.

Solution 6.7

The simulation diagram is shown in Figure 6.6. Drawing the state variable diagram is very

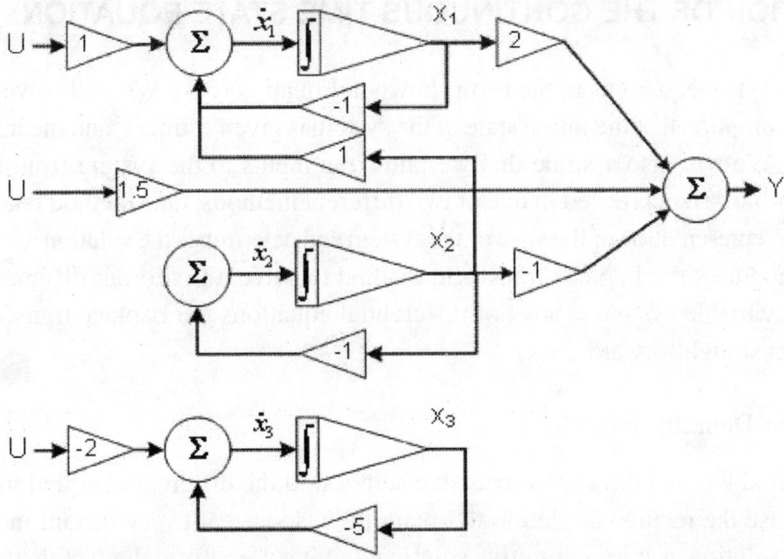

Figure 6.5: Simulation diagram for system defined in System A

straight forward if we look at first drawing the simulation diagram for each state variable and then adding to that diagram the simulation diagram for the output. This system has two inputs and two outputs and this is evident from the simulation diagram also.

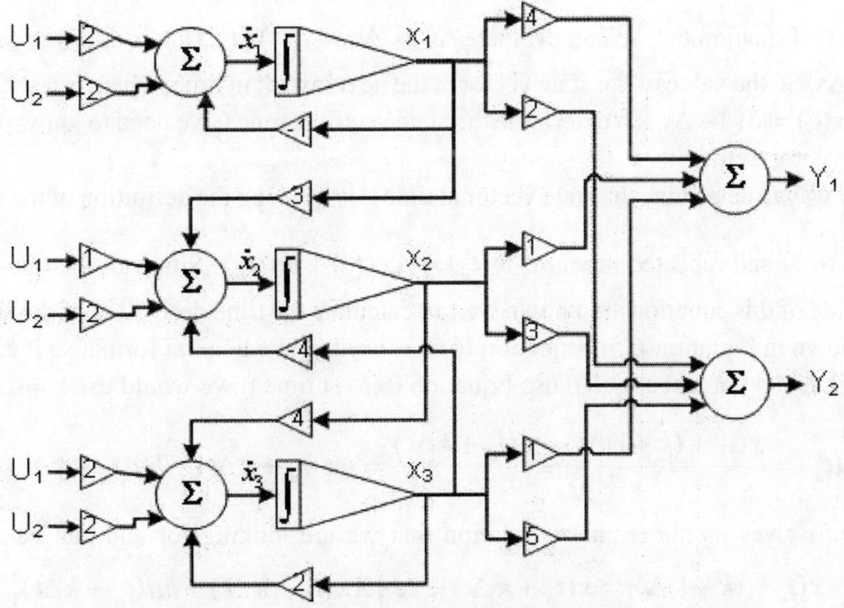

Figure 6.6: Simulation diagram for system defined in System B

6.2 SOLUTION OF THE CONTINUOUS TIME STATE EQUATION

Consider the state equations in the form shown in Equation (6.3). We will solve the state equation with the assumption that the initial state of the system is given at time t_0 and the initial state of the system is $x(t_0)$. We will also assume that we know the inputs to the system from the initial time onwards. The solution can proceed in one of two different methods. One method takes advantage of the time domain representation of the state of the system and determines the solution as time progresses. The other method uses the Laplace transform method to solve n first order differential equations. Since the State variable system is a set of differential equations the Laplace transform method of solution is rather straightforward.

6.2.1 The Time Domain Solution

In this method we first develop a recursive solution to the differential equation. Then as time progresses we use the recursive relation to obtain the response at every instant in time. This is a rather pleasing solution as it is an intuitive solution, but it suffers from the fact that we do not get a closed form solution every time. Completing the solution once will explain the method of solution.

We first define the derivative at say time t_0. This is given by Equation(6.4). This gives us one way of determining the value of the derivative of the state vector at time t_0.

$$\dot{x}(t_o) = \frac{x(t_o + \Delta t) - x(t_o)}{\Delta t} \stackrel{\Delta}{=} \frac{\Delta x}{\Delta t} \tag{6.4}$$

Now using Equation 6.4 we can evaluate **Δx** as $\Delta x = \dot{x}(t_o)\Delta t$. That is at time t_0, x changes by the amount **Δx**. So the value of the state vector at the next instant in time, which is t_1 will be given by $x(t_0 + \Delta t) = x(t_1) = x(t_0) + \Delta x$. To determine the state vector at time t_1 we need to know the derivative of the state vector at time t_0.

Another way to determine the state vector at time t_1 is by using the definition of the system given in Equation (6.3) and repeated here. So $\dot{\boldsymbol{x}}(\boldsymbol{t_o}) = \boldsymbol{Ax}(\boldsymbol{t_o}) + \boldsymbol{bu}(\boldsymbol{t_o})$. Since all the quantities on the right hand side of this equation are known we can calculate the time derivative of the state vector at time t_0 as shown in Equation(6.5). Equation (6.5) is written in a general format so it can be used at any future time and not just at t_0. To use Equation (6.5) at time t_0 we would use $k = 0$.

$$\dot{\boldsymbol{x}}(\boldsymbol{t_o}) = \frac{\boldsymbol{x}(\boldsymbol{t_o} + (\boldsymbol{k}+1)\boldsymbol{\Delta t}) - \boldsymbol{x}(\boldsymbol{t_o} + \boldsymbol{k\Delta t})}{\boldsymbol{\Delta t}} = \boldsymbol{Ax}(\boldsymbol{t_o} + \boldsymbol{k\Delta t}) + \boldsymbol{bu}(\boldsymbol{t_o} + \boldsymbol{k\Delta t}) \tag{6.5}$$

Equation (6.5) gives us the recursive relation that we are looking for and can be re-written as

$$\boldsymbol{x}(\boldsymbol{t_o} + (\boldsymbol{k}+1)\boldsymbol{\Delta t}) = \boldsymbol{x}(\boldsymbol{t_o} + \boldsymbol{k\Delta t}) + \boldsymbol{\Delta t}\left\{\boldsymbol{Ax}(\boldsymbol{t_o} + \boldsymbol{k\Delta t}) + \boldsymbol{bu}(\boldsymbol{t_o} + \boldsymbol{k\Delta t})\right\}$$

This recursive relation is an example of a difference equation. For discrete time systems difference equations play the same role as the differential equations in the continuous time systems. Even though the system that we are right now analyzing is not a discrete time system we are solving the system with very, very small increments in time. With these small increments in time the system simulates a continuous time system and the solution holds. Once we have the state vector at the various instants in time the output vector can be obtained by substituting the state vector in the output equation. This we do in the next section.

Since the state equation is also a differential equation we can solve it like a differential equation. The solution of the state equation can be broken up into the homogenous solution and the particular solution. Remember, to determine the homogenous solution we set the input to zero, to do this in the state system we will set the b matrix to zero. Next taking the lead from the scalar solution (remember that the scalar equation represents a 1-by-1 matrix also) we can write the homogeneous solution as shown in Equation (6.6). In Equation(6.6) x_h represents the homogeneous solution and x_o represents the initial condition which is the value of x(t) at $t=t_o$.

Scalar example:

$$\dot{x} = ax \text{ and } x(t_o) = \boldsymbol{x_o} \tag{6.6}$$

$$\text{The solution is: } x_h(t) = e^{a(t-t_o)}\boldsymbol{x_o}$$

$$\text{Matrix solution is analogous } x_h(t) = e^{A(t-t_o)}\boldsymbol{x_o}$$

In Equation (6.6) we see the term $e^{A(t-t_o)}$. This is a matrix exponential. What does the matrix exponential mean? How do we evaluate this term? We will get an idea about how to evaluate this matrix exponential from the power series expansion of e^{at}. Recollect that

$$e^{at} = 1 + at + a^2t^2/2! + a^3t^3/3! + a^4t^4/4! + \ldots +.$$

Using this same format and recognizing that the coefficient 'a' this time is a square matrix, we get the matrix exponential as shown in Equation(6.7). From Equation (6.7) we see that the expression for e^{At} is a square matrix the same size as the A matrix. So e^{At} is also an n-by-n matrix. This matrix is a very special matrix; one of its peculiarities is the way we get the inverse of this matrix. The inverse of the matrix e^{At} can be easily determined as $(e^{At})^{-1} = e^{-At}$. We will need this information a little later on. For now the Homogeneous solution of the matrix equation is determined as shown in Equation (6.6) using the matrix exponential computed as shown in Equation(6.7).

$$\boldsymbol{e^{At}} = \boldsymbol{I} + \boldsymbol{At} + \frac{\boldsymbol{A^2t^2}}{2!} + \frac{\boldsymbol{A^3t^3}}{3!} + \frac{\boldsymbol{A^4t^4}}{4!} + \cdots + \tag{6.7}$$

Next we will determine the particular solution. Here we will adopt the method of variation of parameters. For this method we must first assume a solution and the solution that we will assume is $x_p(t) = e^{A(t-t_o)}\xi(t)$. Here $\xi(t)$ is the vector that has to be determined. To determine $\xi(t)$ we will first differentiate the assumed particular solution. When we differentiate the particular solution we get Equation(6.8):

$$\dot{x}_p(t) = Ae^{A(t-t_o)}\xi(t) + e^{A(t-t_o)}\dot{\xi}(t) = Ax_p(t) + bu(t)$$
$$\dot{x}_p(t) = Ae^{A(t-t_o)}\xi(t) + e^{A(t-t_o)}\dot{\xi}(t) = Ae^{A(t-t_o)}\xi(t) + bu(t) \qquad (6.8)$$

From Equation (6.8) by examining and rearranging the right hand side we get

$$e^{A(t-t_o)}\dot{\xi}(t) = bu(t) \text{ or } \dot{\xi}(t) = e^{-A(t-t_o)}bu(t) = e^{A(t_o-t)}bu(t).$$

(When you make use of the fact that the two terms on the RHS of Equation(6.8) represent the solution which is ξ(t).) This last equation can be solved by direct integration to get Equation(6.9). Since we know that the homogeneous solution already satisfies the initial conditions, it can be shown that in the particular solution $\xi(t_o)$ has to be 0.

$$\xi(t) - \xi(t_o) = \int_{t_o}^{t} e^{A(t_o-\lambda)}bu(\lambda)d\lambda \qquad (6.9)$$

Then using Equation (6.9) we get the particular solution for the state vector as

$$x_p(t) = e^{A(t-t_o)}\int_{t_o}^{t} e^{A(t_o-\lambda)}Bu(\lambda)d\lambda = \int_{t_o}^{t} e^{A(t-\lambda)}Bu(\lambda)d\lambda$$

Using this particular solution and the homogeneous solution given in Equation (6.6) we get the complete solution as given in Equation (6.10)

$$x(t) = e^{A(t-t_o)}x(t_o) + \int_{t_o}^{t} e^{A(t-\lambda)}Bu(\lambda)d\lambda \qquad (6.10)$$

Very often the matrix exponential $e^{A(t-to)}$ is written as $\phi(t-t_o)$ which is known as the state transition matrix. Using the notation of the state transition matrix we can write Equation (6.10) as shown in Equation(6.11).

$$x(t) = \Phi(t-t_o)x_o + \int_{t_o}^{t} \Phi(t-\lambda)Bu(\lambda)d\lambda \qquad (6.11)$$

Equation (6.11) shows us how the state of the system will change. This is the solution to the system of equations representing the system as shown in Equation(6.1). Next when we substitute the state of the system in the output equation we get the complete solution of the system. This is done for you and the result shown in Equation(6.13). The two equations together represent the state and the response of the system. Both these equations are shown in Equation (6.12) and (6.13).

$$x(t) = \Phi(t-t_o)x_o + \int_{t_o}^{t} \Phi(t-\lambda)Bu(\lambda)d\lambda \qquad (6.12)$$

$$y(t) = c\Phi(t-t_o)x_o + \int_{t_o}^{t} c\Phi(t-\lambda)Bu(\lambda)d\lambda + du(t) \qquad (6.13)$$

Example 6.8

Evaluate the state transition matrix using the series expansion method shown in Equation(6.7) when the A matrix is $\begin{bmatrix} -2 & 0 \\ 0 & -3 \end{bmatrix}$

Solution 6.8

The state transition matrix using the series expansion method is shown here

$$e^{At} = \begin{bmatrix} 1 & 0 \\ 0 & 1 \end{bmatrix} + \frac{1}{1!}\begin{bmatrix} -2 & 0 \\ 0 & -3 \end{bmatrix} t + \frac{1}{2!}\begin{bmatrix} 4 & 0 \\ 0 & 9 \end{bmatrix} t^2 + \frac{1}{3!}\begin{bmatrix} -8 & 0 \\ 0 & -27 \end{bmatrix} t^3 + \frac{1}{4!}\begin{bmatrix} 16 & 0 \\ 0 & 81 \end{bmatrix} t^4$$

$$e^{At} = \begin{bmatrix} 1-2t+2t^2-1.33t^3+0.666t^4 & 0 \\ 0 & 1-3t+4.5t^2-4.5t^3+3.375t^4 \end{bmatrix}$$

$$e^{At} \approx \begin{bmatrix} e^{-2t} & 0 \\ 0 & e^{-3t} \end{bmatrix}$$

This time we were able to write the state transition matrix in a closed form solution. Most of the times it will not be possible to write the state transition matrix in a closed form if we use the series expansion method.

6.2.2 Laplace Transform Solution

The second method for solving the state equation uses the Laplace Transform of the state equation. This method is not as intuitive as the direct time domain method but this method is very attractive as it gives us a closed form solution to the state equation. We first determine the Laplace transform of the state equation; this is shown in Equation (6.14)

$$\boldsymbol{L}[\dot{\boldsymbol{x}}(t) = \boldsymbol{A}\boldsymbol{x}(t) + \boldsymbol{b}U(t)] \Rightarrow s\boldsymbol{X}(s) - \boldsymbol{x}(t_o) = \boldsymbol{A}\boldsymbol{X}(s) + \boldsymbol{b}U(s)$$

$$\text{Rearranging we get } (s\boldsymbol{I} - \boldsymbol{A})\boldsymbol{X}(s) = \boldsymbol{x}(t_o) + \boldsymbol{b}U(s) \tag{6.14}$$

$$\boldsymbol{X}(s) = (s\boldsymbol{I} - \boldsymbol{A})^{-1}\boldsymbol{x}(t_o) + (s\boldsymbol{I} - \boldsymbol{A})^{-1}\boldsymbol{b}U(s)$$

This equation is the solution of the state equation in the Laplace domain. Notice that there are two terms on the right hand side. The first term is due to the initial condition and the second term is due to the input. If the initial condition is zero then the first term will vanish. Using this solution of the state equation we can obtain the solution for the output in the Laplace domain by substituting Equation (6.14) in the output equation. This gives us Equation(6.15). Using Equation (6.15) we can determine the transfer function of a system that is described using the state variable matrices. You will recall that usually the transfer function is described with the system at rest. When a system is at rest, the system has zero initial conditions. When we substitute zero for the initial condition vector in Equation(6.15) we get the transfer function of the system. So the transfer function is given by Equation (6.16)

$$\begin{aligned} Y(s) &= cX(s) + dU(s) \\ Y(s) &= c(sI - A)^{-1} x(t_o) + c(sI - A)^{-1} bU(s) + dU(s) \end{aligned} \tag{6.15}$$

Equation (6.16) is a matrix equation. So if you have several inputs and/or several outputs each term in the Y(s)/U(s) matrix will give you the transfer function of each combination of input and output pair.

$$\frac{Y(s)}{U(s)} = c(sI - A)^{-1} b + d \tag{6.16}$$

This is shown in more detail in Example 6.10 and in Example 6.11 here. It is a direct application of the formula in Equation(6.16).

Example 6.9

Evaluate the state transition matrix by computing (s) = (sI-A)-1 when the A matrix is $\begin{bmatrix} -4 & 0 \\ 0 & -2 \end{bmatrix}$.

Solution 6.9

To compute ϕ(s) we first compute (sI-A). It is $\begin{bmatrix} s+4 & 0 \\ 0 & s+2 \end{bmatrix}$. Now that we have the (sI-A) matrix we next determine the inverse of the (sI-A) matrix. The inverse evaluates to $\begin{bmatrix} \frac{1}{s+4} & 0 \\ 0 & \frac{1}{s+2} \end{bmatrix}$.

This is the state transition matrix in the Laplace transform domain. To get the State Transition matrix in the time domain we find the inverse of this matrix. The state transition matrix in the time domain is $\begin{bmatrix} e^{-4t} & 0 \\ 0 & e^{-2t} \end{bmatrix}$.

Example 6.10

Assume that the system is defined by the following matrices

$A=\begin{bmatrix}-2 & 0\\ 0 & -3\end{bmatrix}$ $b=\begin{bmatrix}0 & 0.5\\ 1 & 0.5\end{bmatrix}$ $c=\begin{bmatrix}3 & -4\end{bmatrix}$ $d=\begin{bmatrix}0 & 1\end{bmatrix}$. Determine all the transfer functions for this system.

Solution 6.10

First we determine the $(sI-A)^{-1}$ matrix:

$$(sI-A)=\begin{bmatrix}s & 0\\ 0 & s\end{bmatrix}-\begin{bmatrix}-2 & 0\\ 0 & -3\end{bmatrix}=\begin{bmatrix}s+2 & 0\\ 0 & s+3\end{bmatrix}$$

Next we will determine the inverse of this matrix $\left[sI-A\right]^{-1}=\begin{bmatrix}\dfrac{1}{s+2} & 0\\ 0 & \dfrac{1}{s+3}\end{bmatrix}$.

Next we use this matrix to determine the transfer functions of the system.

$$\frac{Y(s)}{U(s)}=\begin{bmatrix}3 & -4\end{bmatrix}\begin{bmatrix}\dfrac{1}{s+2} & 0\\ 0 & \dfrac{1}{s+3}\end{bmatrix}\begin{bmatrix}0 & 0.5\\ 1 & 0.5\end{bmatrix}+\begin{bmatrix}0 & 1\end{bmatrix}=\begin{bmatrix}\dfrac{-4}{s+3} & \dfrac{s^2+4.5s+6.5}{(s+2)(s+3)}\end{bmatrix}.$$

The transfer function shows that the system has two inputs and one output. So the transfer function matrix represents two transfer functions. The two represent the transfer functions from each of the two inputs to the one output that we have. As an aside notice the second transfer function. Both the numerator and the denominator have polynomials in s that have an equal highest power. This occurs only when we have a direct connection from the input to the output. (A non zero d matrix).

Example 6.11

Using the state variable representation given for the two input, two output system, which is System b in Example 6.3 determine all the four transfer functions represented by

$$\frac{Y_1(s)}{U_1(s)};\frac{Y_1(s)}{U_2(s)};\frac{Y_2(s)}{U_1(s)}\text{ and }\frac{Y_2(s)}{U_2(s)}$$

Solution 6.11

To determine all the four transfer functions for this system we will resort to Equation 6.16 in the text and to the SCILAB program to do the matrix calculations for us. The matrix calculations are simple but they take a long time to complete by hand. The SCILAB program and the result are given below. Notice that since we have not used the SCILAB function ***'clean'*** the first term in some of the numerators is not zero but a very small term of the order of 10^{-13} and 10^{-14}. If we were to use the clean command in this program the small terms will be replaced by zero.

```
//******************************************
//Transfer Function From State Space Representation//
//First define all the required matrices//
A=[1 5 2;3 0 -4;2 4 0];
b=[2 -2;1 3;2 2];
c=[4 -2 1;2 1 5];
d=[3 1;1 2];
I=eye(A);
//Also define 's' as a variable//
s=poly(0,'s','roots');
Phi=s*I-A;
Phi_inv=inv(Phi);
//Calculate the Transfer Function MAtrix//
TF=c*Phi_inv*b+d;
//******************************************
```

```
!                        2    3                          2   3          !
! - 1.137D-13 + 39s + 5s + 3s        - 276 + 113s - 13s + s             !
!   ----------------------------     ----------------------------       !
!                 2  3                              2  3                !
!          - 3s - s + s                      - 3s - s + s               !
!                                                                       !
!                      2   3                        2    3              !
!  5.684D-14 + 42s + 14s + s         - 252 + 45s + 7s + 2s              !
!  ------------------------------    ---------------------------        !
!                 2  3                            2  3                  !
!          - 3s - s + s                      - 3s - s + s               !
```

The result is a 2x2 matrix that gives us all the four transfer functions that we are interested in. The term in position 1,1 is the transfer function that relates $Y_1(s)$ to $U_1(s)$. Similarly the other three terms are: position 1,2 the transfer function that relates $Y_1(s)$ to $U_2(s)$; position 2,1 the transfer function that relates $Y_2(s)$ to $U_1(s)$; position 2,2 the transfer function that relates $Y_2(s)$ to $U_2(s)$. Using Equation (6.16) and SCILAB obtaining the transfer function from the State Space representation is very simple.

Equation (6.14) is the solution to the state equation in the Laplace domain. When we find the inverse Laplace transform of Equation (6.14) we get the solution of the state equation which is given in Equation (6.17)

$$x(t) = \Phi(t - t_o)x(t_o) + \int_{t_o}^{t} e^{A(t-\lambda)} bu(\lambda)d\lambda \qquad (6.17)$$

When we compare the time domain solution in Equation (6.12) with the inverse Laplace transform of Equation (6.17) we find that $(sI\text{-}A)^{-1}=\phi(s)$ which is the Laplace transform of the state transition matrix or $L^{-1}\left[(sI - A)^{-1}\right] = L^{-1}(\Phi(s)) = \Phi(t - t_o)$. Comparing the second term in Equation (6.13) and the second term in Equation(6.15) we find that $L^{-1}\{(sI\text{-}A)^{-1}bU(s)\}$ is a Laplace inverse of a product of two Laplace domain functions. From the theorems of Laplace transforms you remember that the inverse Laplace transform will be a convolution of the two time domain functions. This is what the second term in Equation (6.13) indicates.

We know that the matrix exponential e^{At} is known as the state transition matrix. Its Laplace transform $\phi(s) = (sI\text{-}A)^{-1}$ is known as the **Resolvent** matrix in mathematical books and publications. In engineering books the matrix $\phi(s) = (sI\text{-}A)^{-1}$ is also known as the **Characteristic Frequency Matrix** or simply the **Characteristic Matrix.** Since the State Transition Matrix is the inverse Laplace transform of the Characteristic Matrix, we get a new method to calculate the state transition matrix. This is done in three simple steps. (Sometimes the steps are not quite so simple and the work involved can be quite tiresome but this method does give us a closed form representation of the state transition matrix.)

- First calculate the (sI-A) matrix.
- Determine the inverse of the (sI-A) matrix.
- Obtain the inverse Laplace Transform of the $\phi(s)$ matrix by determining the inverse of each term in the $\phi(s)$ matrix.

Example 6.12

Given an A matrix $A = \begin{bmatrix} 0 & 1 & 0 \\ 0 & 0 & 1 \\ -9 & -26 & -24 \end{bmatrix}$ determine the state transition matrix using the Laplace transform method.

Solution 6.12

First we determine the $(sI\text{-}A)^{-1}$ matrix: $[sI - A] = \begin{bmatrix} s & -1 & 0 \\ 0 & s & -1 \\ 9 & 26 & s+24 \end{bmatrix}$. We next determine the inverse of this matrix.

This is

$$\frac{1}{s^3+24s^2+26s+9}\begin{bmatrix} s^2+24s+26 & (s+24) & 1 \\ -9 & s^2+24s & s \\ -9s & -(26s+9) & s^2 \end{bmatrix}.$$

Next we determine the inverse Laplace transform of this matrix. It will then give us the state transition matrix. This is given by

$$\begin{bmatrix} -9e^{-2t}+37e^{-3t}-27e^{-4t} & 11e^{-2t}-21e^{-3t}+10e^{-4t} & 0.5e^{-2t}-1e^{-3t}+0.5e^{-4t} \\ -4.5e^{-2t}+9e^{-3t}-4.5e^{-4t} & -22e^{-2t}+63e^{-3t}-40e^{-4t} & -1e^{-2t}+3e^{-3t}-2e^{-4t} \\ -9e^{-2t}-27e^{-3t}-18e^{-4t} & 21.5e^{-2t}-69e^{-3t}+47.5e^{-4t} & 2e^{-2t}-9e^{-3t}+8e^{-4t} \end{bmatrix}$$

From this example we see that the Laplace transform method gives us the state transition matrix in a closed form. It does however require finding the inverse of a matrix and then a lot of inverse Laplace transforms. This is not difficult but it is very time consuming.

6.3 PROPERTIES OF THE STATE TRANSITION MATRIX

The State Transition Matrix is also known as the Fundamental Matrix. This matrix has several interesting and important properties which we should know to make our work with the state variable representation easy. We first note from Equation 6.6 that the State Transition matrix is the solution to the homogeneous state equation. So for the state equation $\dot{x}(t) = Ax(t)$ the solution is $\boldsymbol{x(t) = \Phi(t - t_o)x(t_o)}$. This representation gives us the first insight into the state transition matrix. The state transition matrix tells you how the system will transition from the state of the system at time $t=t_o$ to some time in the future. The state transition matrix moves the state of the system from one time to another time.

An obvious extension of this is that the state transition matrix for no time change or $\phi(t_o-t_o) = I$. This holds true for any time t. This makes perfect sense since we are not asking the state vector to change then the present vector must be multiplied by the identity matrix to give us the present vector back.

The state transition matrix only depends on the time difference. It does not matter how many small or large steps we take to get from one time instant to another time instant. Or in other words

$$\phi(t_3-t_o) = \phi(t_3-t_2)\ \phi(t_2-t_1)\ \phi(t_1-t_o).$$

$$\text{So } x(t_3)=\phi(t_3-t_o)x(t_o)$$

$$\text{and also } x(t_3) = \phi(t_3-t_2)\ \phi(t_2-t_1)\ \phi(t_1-t_o)x(t_o).$$

This is a very important property known as the **semigroup** property. This is a direct consequence of the fact that the state transition matrix is a matrix exponential and that it does not matter how we get to state at time t_3 from a starting time t_0 we always arrive at the same state. We may go through as many intermediate states as we want to but when we arrive at state at time t_3 it is always the same state.

A consequence of the semigroup property is that $\boldsymbol{\phi(t_0\text{-}t_1)\,\phi(t_1\text{-}t_0) = I}$ so the inverse of the state transition matrix is obtained by inverting the order of its arguments or $\boldsymbol{\phi(t_0\text{-}t_1) = [\phi(t_1\text{-}t_0)]^{-1}}$. A consequence of this is that $\boldsymbol{[\phi(t_0)]^{-1} = \phi(-t_0)}$.

Example 6.13

Using the state transition matrix from Example 6.8 find the state of the system x(t) when you are given $\boldsymbol{x}(0) = \begin{bmatrix} -3 \\ 3 \end{bmatrix}$ and $\boldsymbol{b} = \begin{bmatrix} 1 \\ 2 \end{bmatrix}$ and u(t) is a step input at t=0.

Solution 6.13

To determine the state of the system at any time t in the future we use Equation(6.12). The first term in Equation(6.12) is $\phi(t)x_0(t)$. When we evaluate this term we get

$$\begin{bmatrix} 1-2t+2t^2-1.33t^3+0.666t^4 & 0 \\ 0 & 1-3t+4.5t^2-4.5t^3+3.375t^4 \end{bmatrix}\begin{bmatrix} -3 \\ 3 \end{bmatrix}$$

$$= \begin{bmatrix} -3+6t-6t^2+4t^3-2t^4 \\ 3-9t+13.5t^2-13.5t^3+10.1253t^4 \end{bmatrix}.$$

The second term in Equation(6.12) is the integral that evaluates to

$$\int_0^t \Phi(\boldsymbol{\lambda})\boldsymbol{b}u(\boldsymbol{\lambda})\,d\boldsymbol{\lambda}$$

$$= \int_0^t \begin{bmatrix} 1-2\lambda+2\lambda^2-1.333\lambda^3+0.666\lambda^4 & 0 \\ 0 & 1-3\lambda+4.5\lambda^2-4.5\lambda^3+3.375\lambda^4 \end{bmatrix}\begin{bmatrix} 1 \\ 2 \end{bmatrix} 1\,d\lambda$$

$$= \int_0^t \begin{bmatrix} 1-2\lambda+2\lambda^2-1.333\lambda^3+0.666\lambda^4 \\ 2-6\lambda+9\lambda^2-9\lambda^3+6.75\lambda^4 \end{bmatrix} 1\,d\lambda$$

$$= \begin{bmatrix} t-\frac{2}{2}t^2+\frac{2}{3}t^3-\frac{1.333}{4}t^4+\frac{0.666}{5}t^5 \\ 2t-\frac{6}{2}t^2+\frac{9}{3}t^3-\frac{9}{4}t^4+\frac{6.75}{5}t^5 \end{bmatrix}$$

Combining the two terms we get the state of the system as a function of time as

$$\begin{bmatrix} -3+(6+1)t-(6+1)t^2+\left(4+\frac{2}{3}\right)t^3-\left(2+\frac{1.333}{4}\right)t^4+\frac{0.666}{5}t^5 \\ 3-(9-2)t+\left(13.5-\frac{6}{2}\right)t^2-\left(13.5-\frac{9}{3}\right)t^3+\left(10.125-\frac{9}{4}\right)t^4+\frac{6.75}{5}t^5 \end{bmatrix}$$

which can be evaluated for any value of time that we are interested in. This shows that the evaluation of the state in the state variable system is a very simple and a straight forward procedure. It is easily done once the State Transition matrix is evaluated.

Example 6.14

Using the state transition matrix in Example 6.8 find the state of the system x(t) at time t = 1 second when you are given $\boldsymbol{x}(0)=\begin{bmatrix}2\\3\end{bmatrix}$. This we are only going to determine how the system will move when there is no external input to drive it.

a. The time progresses from t=0 to t=1 second in one step.

b. Time progresses from t = 0 to t = 1 second in increments of 0.5 seconds.

c. Time progresses from t = 0 to t = 1 second in increments of 0.2 seconds.

Solution 6.14

The State Transition matrix is given to us in a closed form with time as a variable. We will have to evaluate the state transition matrix for each of the simulation to represent the time jump that we are asking the system to make between the results. The three simulation results are given below.

a. We first evaluate the State Transition Matrix when t = 1 second. This matrix evaluates to $\begin{bmatrix}0.018316 & 0\\ 0 & 0.135335\end{bmatrix}$. Using this state transition matrix the state of the system at time t = 1 will be $\begin{bmatrix}0.036632\\0.406005\end{bmatrix}$. That is the two state variables will have the specified values.

b. We first evaluate the State Transition Matrix when t = 0.5 seconds. This matrix evaluates to $\begin{bmatrix}0.135335 & 0\\ 0 & 0.367879\end{bmatrix}$. The state transition matrix evaluates to a different value since the elapsed time is only 0.5 seconds rather than 1.0 seconds. Using this state transition matrix the state of the system at time t = 0.5 seconds will be $\begin{bmatrix}0.27067\\1.103637\end{bmatrix}$ and at t = 1 second (after we use the same state transition matrix the second time will be $\begin{bmatrix}0.036631\\0.406005\end{bmatrix}$

c. We now evaluate the State Transition Matrix when t = 0.2 seconds. This matrix evaluates to $\begin{bmatrix} 0.449329 & 0 \\ 0 & 0.67032 \end{bmatrix}$. The state transition matrix evaluates to a different value since the elapsed time is only 0.2 seconds rather than 0.5 seconds or 1.0 seconds. Using this state transition matrix the state of the system at time t = 0.2 seconds will be $\begin{bmatrix} 0.898658 \\ 2.01096 \end{bmatrix}$; at t = 0.4 second will be $\begin{bmatrix} 0.403793 \\ 1.327987 \end{bmatrix}$; at t = 0.6 second will be $\begin{bmatrix} 0.181436 \\ 0.890176 \end{bmatrix}$; at t = 0.8 second will be $\begin{bmatrix} 0.081525 \\ 0.596703 \end{bmatrix}$ and at t = 1.0 second will be $\begin{bmatrix} 0.036632 \\ 0.399981 \end{bmatrix}$

We see that all the results are the same at time t = 1 second (within rounding error). This result holds when the system being investigated is a linear time invariant system. This example also demonstrates one of the properties of the state transition matrix. This property was labeled as the semi-group property.

6.4 TRANSFORMING THE TRANSFER FUNCTION TO THE STATE VARIABLE FORMAT

Often we are faced with the question of the equivalence of the state model and the transfer function model. How do we transform one model to the other? Is there one unique way to complete the transform? The answer is obvious; the method to complete the transform is not unique since the state model itself is not unique. Here we will show several different methods to transform from one model to another. Each method provides us with a different representation. The different representations provide us with a different perspective or point of view to get an insight in the state model. Equation (6.18) shows us a general transfer function. We will use this general transfer function to develop a State Model for the system.

$$\frac{Y(s)}{U(s)} = \frac{b_m s^m + b_{m-1}s^{m-1} + b_{m-2}s^{m-2} + \cdots + b_1 s + b_0}{(s+p_1)(s+p_2)\cdots(s+p_{n-1})(s+p_n)} \tag{6.18}$$

6.4.1 Canonical or Diagonal Representation:

For this method we assume that the denominator of the transfer function is available in factored form. This is not a major assumption since today there are many software programs that will factor a polynomial in an instant. This facility is available on many hand held calculators also. So requiring that the transfer function be available in factored form is not a major restriction. Another assumption that we make for the present is that there are no repeated roots in the transfer function. This is a major restriction but there is a work around available and we will look into this also towards the end of this section. At that time we will remove this restriction. So the transfer function is represented as shown in Equation(6.18). The transfer function in Equation (6.18) has n poles and m < n zeros. Also the denominator is available in factored form. We can easily rewrite this transfer function in partial fraction form and write the transfer function as shown in Equation(6.19).

$$\begin{aligned}
\frac{Y(s)}{U(s)} &= \frac{\beta_1}{(s+p_1)} + \frac{\beta_2}{(s+p_2)} + \cdots + \frac{\beta_n}{(s+p_n)} \\
Y(s) &= \beta_1 \frac{U(s)}{(s+p_1)} + \beta_2 \frac{U(s)}{(s+p_2)} + \cdots + \beta_n \frac{U(s)}{(s+p_n)} \\
Y(s) &= \beta_1 X_1(s) + \beta_2 X_2(s) + \cdots + \beta_n X_n(s)
\end{aligned} \tag{6.19}$$

In Equation (6.19) we define each of the partial fractions as $X_i(s) = U(s)/(s+p_i)$. Next we determine the inverse Laplace transform of each of the individual factors as shown in Equation (6.20).

$$\begin{aligned}
X_i(s) &= \frac{U(s)}{(s+p_i)} \qquad \textit{and} \qquad Y(s) = \beta_1 X_1(s) + \beta_2 X_2(s) + \cdots + \beta_n X_n(s) \\
sX_i(s) + p_i X_i(s) &= U(s) \\
\dot{x}_i(t) &= -p_i x_i(t) + u(t) \qquad y(t) = \beta_1 x_1(t) + \beta_2 x_2(t) + \cdots + \beta_n x_n(t)
\end{aligned} \tag{6.20}$$

Combining all the individual equations in Equation (6.20) we get a matrix equation as shown in Equation(6.21)

$$\begin{bmatrix} \dot{x}_1 \\ \dot{x}_2 \\ \vdots \\ \dot{x}_n \end{bmatrix} = \begin{bmatrix} -p_1 & 0 & \cdots & 0 \\ 0 & -p_2 & \cdots & 0 \\ \vdots & \vdots & \ddots & \vdots \\ 0 & 0 & \cdots & -p_n \end{bmatrix} \begin{bmatrix} x_1 \\ x_2 \\ \vdots \\ x_n \end{bmatrix} + \begin{bmatrix} 1 \\ 1 \\ \vdots \\ 1 \end{bmatrix} u(t) \tag{6.21}$$

$$y(t) = \begin{bmatrix} \beta_1 & \beta_2 & \cdots & \beta_n \end{bmatrix} \begin{bmatrix} x_1 \\ x_2 \\ \vdots \\ x_n \end{bmatrix}$$

When we complete the inverse transform for every factor in Equation (6.19) we can write the state equations as shown in Equation(6.21). Notice that the A matrix in this method is completely diagonal. The d matrix in this method will always be zero if the transfer function is a proper transfer function. In a proper transfer function there are more poles than zeros so there is no direct connection from the input to the output. The b matrix in this method is all 1's. This indicates that there is a direct connection from the input to every state variable. This means that each and every state variable is affected by the input directly. We will see later that this is a requirement for **controllability.** The c matrix in this method is made up of all the numerator coefficients of the partial fractions. This means there is a direct contribution from each state variable to the output. A direct contribution from each state variable to the output means that each and every state variable affects the output directly. We will see later that this is a requirement for **observability.** This representation is a very straight forward representation when there are no repeated poles in the transfer function of the system.

$$\frac{Y(s)}{U(s)}=\frac{\beta_1}{(s+p_1)}+\frac{\beta_{21}}{(s+p_2)}+\frac{\beta_{22}}{(s+p_2)^2}+\frac{\beta_3}{(s+p_3)}$$

$$\begin{bmatrix}\dot{x}_1\\ \dot{x}_2\\ \dot{x}_3\\ \dot{x}_n\end{bmatrix}=\begin{bmatrix}-p_1 & 0 & 0 & 0\\ 0 & -p_2 & \mathbf{1} & 0\\ 0 & 0 & -p_2 & 0\\ 0 & 0 & 0 & -p_3\end{bmatrix}\begin{bmatrix}x_1\\ x_2\\ \vdots\\ x_n\end{bmatrix}+\begin{bmatrix}1\\ 0\\ \vdots\\ 1\end{bmatrix}u(t) \tag{6.22}$$

$$y(t)=\begin{bmatrix}\beta_1 & \beta_2 & \cdots & \beta_n\end{bmatrix}\begin{bmatrix}x_1\\ x_2\\ \vdots\\ x_n\end{bmatrix}$$

We now remove the restriction that there are no repeated poles in the transfer function. When there are repeated poles present in the transfer function we will have factors such as $X_i(s)=\dfrac{U(s)}{(s+p_i)}$ *and* $X_{i+1}(s)=\dfrac{U(s)}{(s+p_i)^2}$. Take a close look at the factor defined as X_{i+1}. We can rewrite this factor using the factor $X_i(s)$ as $X_{i+1}(s)=\dfrac{X_i(s)}{(s+p_i)}$. With this definition $\dot{x}_{i+1}(t)=-p_{i+1}x_{i+1}(t)+x_i(t)$. With this modification we can now convert transfer functions with repeated roots as shown in Equation(6.22). The complete procedure to convert a transfer function to state variable format is once again demonstrated in Equation(6.22), so repeated poles are not a difficulty either. Notice that the format for the Equations (6.21) and (6.22) are almost identical. When there are repeated roots we find an additional 1 in the super-diagonal. The process when the root is repeated three times is similar. It is left as an exercise for you to complete at the end of the chapter.

6.4.2 Phase Variable Representation:

To study the Phase Variable Representation consider the system representation in its differential equation form. This will be an nth order differential equation. It is possible to easily convert this nth order differential equation into n first order differential equations. We will use these n first order differential equations to convert the system to a state variable representation. This representation is known as the **Phase Variable Representation.** To complete the conversion we write the transfer function from Equation (6.18) as shown in Equation(6.23). Equation (6.23) shows a third order transfer function but it is simple to generalize once you grasp the specifics of the process.

$$\frac{Y(s)}{U(s)} = \frac{Y(s)}{Z(s)}\frac{Z(s)}{U(s)} = \frac{b_2s^2 + b_1s + b_0}{s^3 + a_2s^2 + a_1s + a_0}$$

$$\frac{Y(s)}{Z(s)} = b_2s^2 + b_1s + b_0 \text{ and } \frac{Z(s)}{U(s)} = \frac{1}{s^3 + a_2s^2 + a_1s + a_0} \tag{6.23}$$

From Equation (6.23) we see that we have two functions. The function Z(s)/U(s) can be easily converted to block diagram form as well as differential equation form as we have seen earlier in Chapter 5. This is done for you in Figure 6.7 and in Equation(6.24).

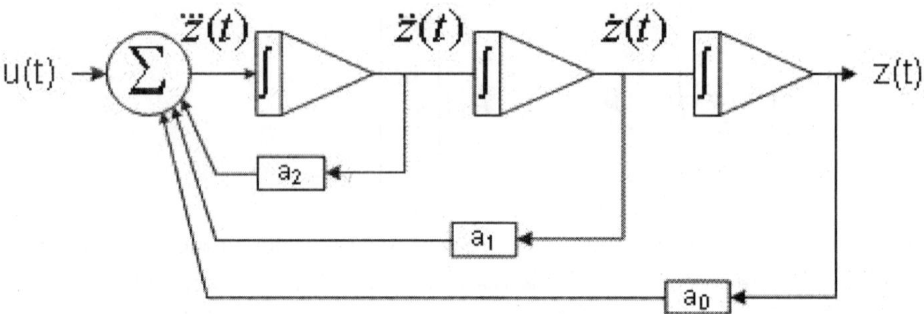

Figure 6.7: Signal flow representation for Equation 6.24

$$\frac{Z(s)}{U(s)} = \frac{1}{s^3 + a_2s^2 + a_1s + a_0} \tag{6.24}$$

$$\left(s^3 + a_2s^2 + a_1s + a_0\right)Z(s) = U(s)$$

Determine the inverse Laplace transform to get

$$\dddot{z}(t) = u(t) - a_2\ddot{z}(t) - a_1\dot{z}(t) - a_0z(t)$$

Next we look at the function Y(s)/Z(s). This function can also be easily converted to block diagram as well as differential equation form. This is done for you in Figure 6.8 and in Equation(6.25).

The z(t) and its derivatives in Figures 6.7 and 6.8 are one and the same so we can combine the two figures together. This is shown in Figure 6.9. Now from Figure 6.7 we can write out the state equations for the system in Phase Variable form. This is done for you in Equation(6.26) and Equation(6.27).

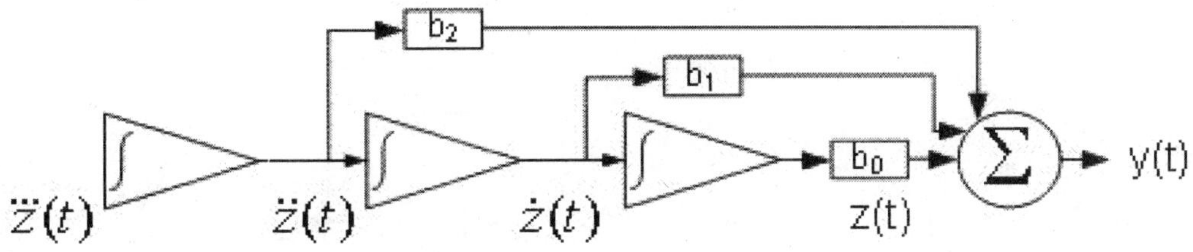

Figure 6.8: Signal flow representation for Equation 6.25

$$\frac{Y(s)}{Z(s)} = b_2 s^2 + b_1 s + b_0 \tag{6.25}$$

$$Y(s) = \left(b_2 s^2 + b_1 s + b_0 \right) Z(s)$$

Take the inverse Laplace transform of this equation to get

$$\mathrm{y(t)} = b_2 \ddot{z}(t) + b_1 \dot{z}(t) + b_0 z(t)$$

$$\begin{aligned} \dot{z}(t) &= \dot{z}_1(t) = z_2(t) \\ \ddot{z}(t) &= \dot{z}_2(t) = z_3(t) \\ \dddot{z}(t) &= \dot{z}_3(t) = -a_2 z_3(t) - a_1 z_2(t) - a_0 z_1(t) + u(t) \\ y(t) &= b_2 z_3(t) + b_1 z_2(t) + b_0 z_1(t) \end{aligned} \tag{6.26}$$

$$\begin{gathered} \begin{bmatrix} \dot{z}_1 \\ \dot{z}_2 \\ \dot{z}_3 \end{bmatrix} = \begin{bmatrix} 0 & 1 & 0 \\ 0 & 0 & 1 \\ -a_0 & -a_1 & -a_2 \end{bmatrix} \begin{bmatrix} z_1 \\ z_2 \\ z_3 \end{bmatrix} + \begin{bmatrix} 0 \\ 0 \\ 1 \end{bmatrix} u(t) \\ y(t) = \begin{bmatrix} b_0 & b_1 & b_2 \end{bmatrix} \begin{bmatrix} z_1 \\ z_2 \\ z_3 \end{bmatrix} \end{gathered} \tag{6.27}$$

From Equation(6.26) and Equation(6.27) and from Figure 6.9 we see that the state variable representation in the Phase variable form has all the numerator coefficients from the transfer function in the '**c**' matrix and they are the feed forward terms. We also see that all the denominator terms from the transfer function appear in the last row of the **'A'** matrix with all the terms in the super diagonal being 1 and the rest of the matrix is all zeros. The **'b'** matrix is also all zeros except for the last entry which is a 1. There is no 'd' matrix as there are no direct connections from the input to the output. With this understanding we can convert a general transfer function expression to state variable format if we develop the matrices individually.

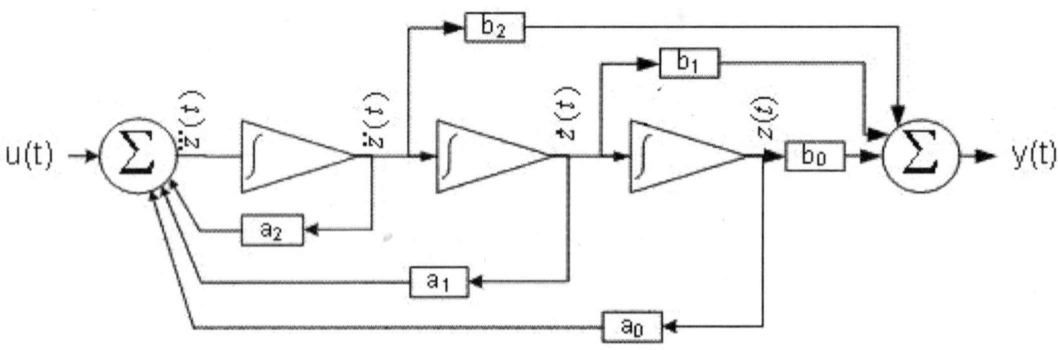

Figure 6.9: Signal flow representation for Equation 6.26 and Equation 6.27

Example 6.15

Starting with the transfer function $\dfrac{Y(s)}{U(s)} = \dfrac{4s^2 + 3s + 5}{s^4 + 15s^3 + 47.1875s^2 + 35.625s + 6.1875}$ determine at least two different state variable representations for this transfer function.

Solution 6.15

We will represent the system defined by the transfer function using the Canonicals and the Phase variable representation for the 'A' matrix.

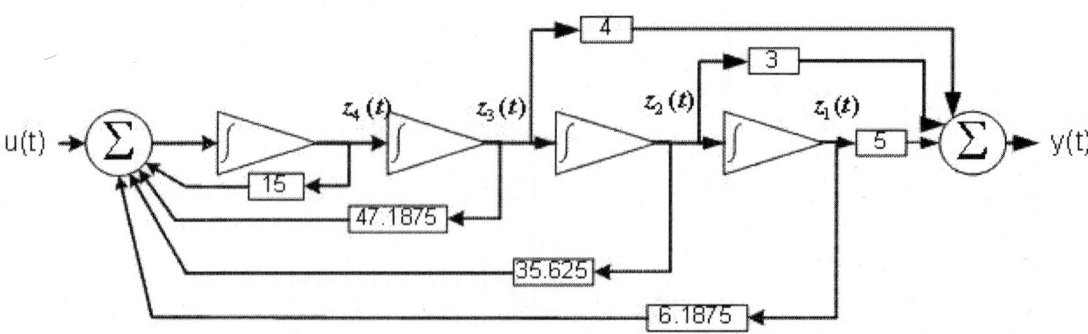

Figure 6.10: Signal flow representation for Example 6.15

a. To get the Canonical representation we will first factor the denominator using SCILAB. When we do this we find that the roots of the denominator are -11; -3; -0.75 and -0.25. Now that we have the roots in the factored form we can write the transfer function in its partial fractions. (The residues can also be determined using the SCILAB function 'residu'. Doing this we get

$$\frac{0.1353}{(s+0.25)}+\frac{0.4848}{(s+3)}-\frac{0.130081}{(s+0.75)}-\frac{0.49}{(s+11)}.$$

Now with this form of the transfer function all the State Matrices can be written directly as

$$A=\begin{bmatrix}-0.25 & 0 & 0 & 0\\ 0 & -3 & 0 & 0\\ 0 & 0 & -0.75 & 0\\ 0 & 0 & 0 & -11\end{bmatrix};b=\begin{bmatrix}1\\1\\1\\1\end{bmatrix};c=\begin{bmatrix}0.1353 & 0.4848 & -0.13 & -0.29\end{bmatrix}$$

b. For a second representation we use the Phase variable canonical form. This representation takes the form

$$\frac{Y(s)}{U(s)}=\frac{Y(s)}{Z(s)}\bullet\frac{Z(s)}{U(s)}$$

$$So\ \frac{Y(s)}{Z(s)}=4s^2+3s+5\ and\ \frac{Z(s)}{U(s)}=\frac{1}{s^4+15s^3+47.1875s^2+35.625s+6.1875}$$

To get the phase variable form we will use the two equations to first draw a simulation diagram. Then from the simulation diagram we can write the Phase variable representation state equations. The signal flow graph is given in Figure 6.10.9.b. The phase variable representation is completed here

$$A=\begin{bmatrix}0 & 1 & 0 & 0\\ 0 & 0 & 1 & 0\\ 0 & 0 & 0 & 1\\ -6.1875 & -35.625 & -47.1875 & -15\end{bmatrix}\ b=\begin{bmatrix}0\\0\\0\\1\end{bmatrix}\ c=\begin{bmatrix}5 & 3 & 4 & 0\end{bmatrix}$$

6.5 OBSERVING THE STATE OF THE SYSTEM–OBSERVERS AND OBSERVABILITY

For a system to be observable all the state variables of the system must be capable of affecting the output of the system. If some individual or a combination of states of the system are not capable of affecting the output of the system then the system is not observable. With this discussion we can write the definition of **Observability:**

An unforced system is said to be observable if and only if, it is possible, to determine any arbitrary initial state of the system at any time T by observing only a finite record of the output of the system, y(t) for t<τ <T.

In this definition there are two very important words. These words tell us that if the system is observable then, the word 'any' tells us that we can determine which state the system began from and the word 'finite' tells us that we can do this in any amount of finite time that we are interested in. If only some but not all the initial states can be predicted then the system is not observable. Observability of a system is determined by computing the Observability matrix. $P_o(T) = \int_0^T \Phi^T(\lambda)c^T c\Phi(\lambda)\, d\lambda$ is a matrix of full rank or the matrix is a non singular matrix.

The matrix $P_0(T)$ is known as the observability Grammian. The proof of this is not very obvious and it is beyond the scope of this book. Those of you who are interested may refer to reference #2 at the end of the chapter for a detailed discussion and proof of the observability Grammian. The observability theorem and its proof is credited to the work done by R.E. Kalman.

The matrix integral that needs to be evaluated is rather difficult and cumbersome to evaluate for a linear time invariant system if all we are interested in doing is determining if the system is observable. It would be nice if there was an easier alternative available to determine this. Fortunately for time invariant systems there is an easier alternative method available. This is done by determining the Observability matrix P_0. This matrix is determined as follows:

$P_o = \left[c^T \mid A^T c^T \mid \left(A^T\right)^2 c^T \mid \cdots \mid \left(A^T\right)^{n-1} c^T\right]$. Once you have determined this matrix we evaluate the rank of the matrix. If the rank of the matrix is n for an n state variable system then the system is observable. (Refer to the SCILAB functions in this chapter to learn how to determine the rank of a matrix.)

The observability matrix for a single input system is an n-by-n square matrix whose columns are made up by multiplying the transpose of the output matrix, c, by successive powers of the transpose of the plant or the system matrix A. So the first column of the controllability is just the 'c^T' matrix. The second column is the result of the matrix product $A^T c^T$. The third column is the matrix product $(A^T)^2 c^T$. This procedure of successively computing the columns continues till we have computed all the n columns for an n state variable system.

The software program that we have been using has a special command that it uses to determine the observability matrix and another command to determine its rank. Both these commands are discussed in more detail in the SCILAB Chapter. Here we just list the two commands for your reference.

```
Po = obsr_mat(A,c)      //This command will place the
                        observability matrix in matrix Po
Prank=rank(Po)          //This command will determine the rank of the observability matrix.
```

6.6 CONTROLLING THE STATE OF THE SYSTEM–CONTROLLERS AND CONTROLLABILITY

For a system to be controllable all the state variables of the system must be capable of being affected by the input. If some individual or a combination of states of the system are not capable of being affected by the input that is applied then the system is not controllable. With this discussion we can write the definition of **Controllability:**

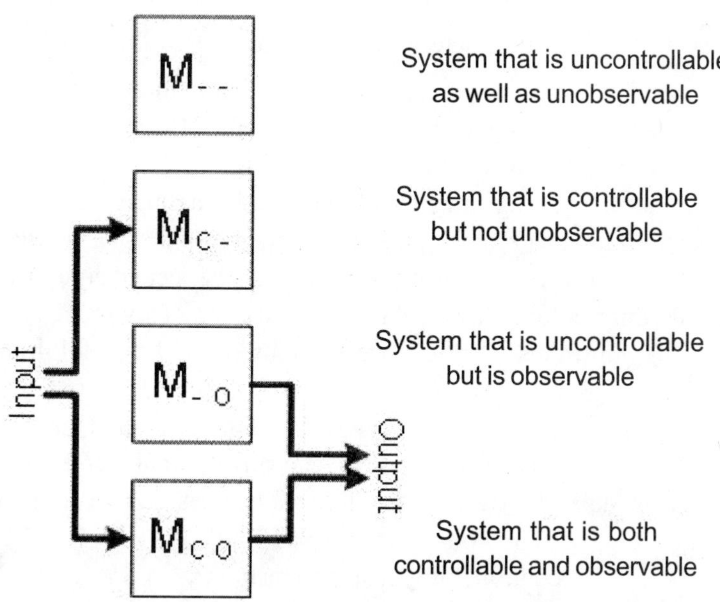

Figure 6.11: Four different classifications of a system

A system is said to be controllable if and only if, it is possible, by means of the input, to transfer the system from any initial state $x(t) = x_i$ *to* ***any*** *other final state* $x_T = x(T)$ *in some* ***finite*** *amount of time* T-$t>0$.

In this definition there are two very important words. These words tell us that if the system is controllable then, the word 'any' tells us that we can take the system to whichever state we may be interested in and the word 'finite' tells us that we can do this in any amount of finite time that we are interested in. So for a time invariant system controllability implies that we can move the system from any beginning state to any final state within some time of our choosing. The controllability theorem states that for a linear time invariant system, the system is controllable if and only if the matrix

$P_c(T) = \int_0^T \Phi(\lambda) b b' \Phi'(\lambda)\, d\lambda$ is a matrix of full rank or the matrix is a non singular matrix.

The matrix $P_c(T)$ is known as the controllability Grammian. The proof of this is not very obvious and it is beyond the scope of this book. Those of you who are interested may refer to reference #2 at the end of the chapter for a detailed discussion and proof of the controllability Grammian. The controllability theorem and its proof is credited to the work done by R. E. Kalman.

The matrix integral that needs to be evaluated is rather difficult and cumbersome to evaluate for a linear time invariant system if all we are interested in doing is determining if the system is controllable. It would be nice if there was an easier alternative available to determine this. Fortunately for time invariant systems there is an easier alternative method available. This time we determine the Controllability matrix P_c. This matrix is determined as follows: $P_c = \lfloor b \mid Ab \mid A^2b \mid \cdots \mid A^{n-1}b \rfloor$. Once you have determined this matrix we evaluate the rank of the matrix. If the rank of the matrix is n for an n state variable system then the system is controllable. (Refer to the appendix on matrix operations to review how to determine the rank of a matrix.)

The controllability matrix for a single input system is an n-by-n square matrix whose columns are made up by multiplying the input matrix, b, by successive powers of the plant or the system matrix A. So the first column of the controllability is just the 'b' matrix. The second column is the result of the matrix product Ab. The third column is the matrix product A^2b. This procedure of successively computing the columns continues till we have computed all the n columns for an n state variable system.

The software program that we have been using has a special command that it uses to determine the controllability matrix and another command to determine its rank. Both these commands are discussed in more detail in the SCILAB Chapter. Here we just list the two commands.

```
Pc = obsr_mat(A,b)        //This command will place the
                          controllability matrix in matrix Pc
Prank=rank(Pc)            //This command will determine the rank of the controllability
                          matrix.
```

With the definitions of controllability and observability we can visualize four types of systems. All the four types of possible systems are shown in Figure 6.11. In Figure 6.11 the system that is labeled M - - is a system that is neither controllable and nor is it observable. The next system that is labeled M_c - is a system that is controllable but it is not observable. The next system that is labeled $M -_o$ is a system that is not controllable but it is observable. The next system that is labeled M_{co} is a system that is both controllable and observable.

6.7 LIAPUNOV STABILITY CRITERIA

Determining whether the system that you designed is stable or not is a very important consideration that every engineer considers. After all it would not be a good idea to design an unstable system. So how do you know if the system that you have designed is stable or not? This question has been investigated by many different investigators and there are many different definitions of stability. It is virtually impossible to determine the stability of a system under every input condition by solving the differential equation that governs the system. So many designers and engineers have spent considerable amount of time to devise a general method that will predict the stability of a system without resorting to solve a set of differential equations. Here we will establish one such method.

Before we try to develop a method to determine stability let us first study how we define stability. One such definition begins with the state equations of the system. The state equations govern how the system responds when an input is applied. We can consider this input as a sudden disturbance that is applied to a system when the system is in stable equilibrium. This disturbance will disrupt the stable equilibrium. When the system is thus disturbed it will move to some state in the vicinity of the previous stable state. But how much will it move? If it moves only a little bit and then rests at this new state position without moving without bound we say that the system has moved to a new stable state. But this movement will also depend on how big the input is. When the input is large the movement from the stable equilibrium state will be large. This concept gives us one very important definition of stability. *When an input, to a relaxed system is bounded, and the output from this system is also bounded then the system is stable*. This is referred to as **BIBO** or **Bounded Input, Bounded Output** stability.

Another definition of stability deals with a system, which when displaced from its stable state returns to its equilibrium state eventually. Such a system is known as an **asymptotically stable** system. An equilibrium state of the system is said to be asymptotically stable, if the system starting from any initial state vector x_0, reaches its stable state as time tends to infinity.

6.7.1 Stability in the Sense of Liapunov

The direct method of Liapunov, which is also known as the second method of Liapunov, allows you to ascertain the stability of the system. The power of the method lies in that it allows us to determine the stability of the system without requiring the solution to the state equations. This method relies upon the idea that at the equilibrium state the total energy of the system is a local minimum.

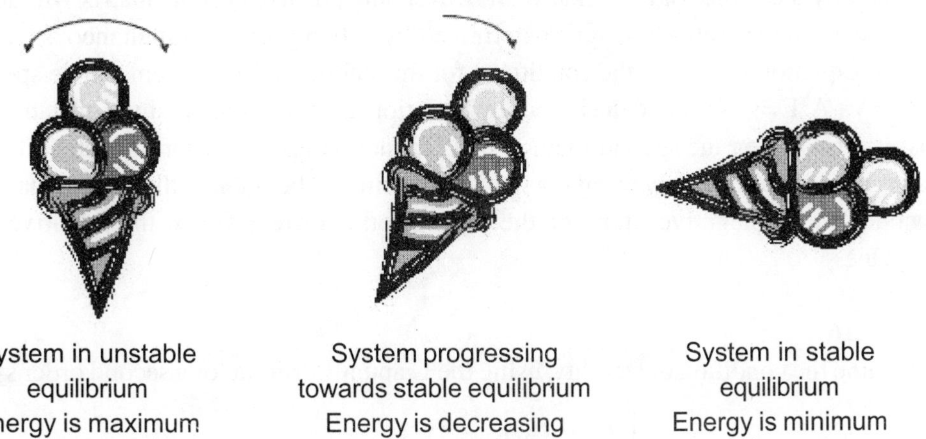

Figure 6.12: System progresses as the energy in the system approaches minimum

Saying this in another way, the system is always reducing the energy that it possesses as it approaches the equilibrium state. The equilibrium exists when the energy of the system is the lowest.

The Liapunov generalization is as follows: Suppose that in the vicinity of the stable state a scalar function **V(x)**, which measures the energy of the system, is created. This function V(x) has continuous first partial derivatives and is a positive function with V(x) = 0 when the system is at its stable state. Further all the first partial derivatives of V(x) in the vicinity of the stable state are negative (decreasing energy) then the system that is represented by the scalar function V(x) is asymptotically stable. This concept is depicted in Figure 6.12.

6.7.2 Generating Liapunov Functions

An explicit method exists for generating the Liapunov functions for a linear system. Consider a system described by the differential equation $\dot{x}(t) = Ax(t)$. For this system select a Liapunov function $V(x) = x^T E x$ where the matrix E has yet to be determined. We first take the time derivative of the energy function so $\dot{V}(x) = x^T E\dot{x} + \dot{x}^T E x$. If we combine this equation with the definition of the system we get

$$\begin{aligned}\dot{V}(x) &= x^T E(Ax) + (Ax)^T Ex \\ &= x^T EAx + x^T A^T Ex \\ &= x^T (EA + A^T E)x = -x^T Fx\end{aligned} \tag{6.28}$$

Since for stability in the sense of Liapunov requires that the function V(x) be a positive definite and its derivative be negative then the matrix E must be positive definite. We will be using this result to investigate the stability of a system. The proof of this theorem is beyond the scope of this book. Since F is an arbitrary symmetric positive definite matrix we can choose F to be the identity matrix. This is generally the choice of the F matrix; however, any positive definite matrix will do. Once the matrix F is chosen the matrix E can be determined by solving several simultaneous equations obtained from Equation(6.28) and the conditions for the stability of the system can be specified. The Equation $EA + A^T E = -F$ is called the Liapunov Equation, as it arises in the study of stability of linear systems. It arises when the second method of Liapunov is used to determine stability. Liapunov equation is just an alternate way of saying that the system will be stable if the system matrix A has its eigen values in the negative plane or the poles of the system are in the negative (left) half of the s-plane.

Example 6.16

Determine the condition of stability, using the Liapunov criteria for a second order system. The system defined by the A matrix $\begin{bmatrix} a_{11} & a_{12} \\ a_{21} & a_{22} \end{bmatrix}$.

Solution 6.16

With the given A matrix we first define an F matrix that is a positive definite matrix. We can choose a 2-by-2 identity matrix for this. Next we use the result of Equation 6.24 to get the equation EA + ATE = -F where F is a positive definite matrix. When we expand this Equation we get $\begin{bmatrix} e_{11} & e_{12} \\ e_{21} & e_{22} \end{bmatrix}\begin{bmatrix} a_{11} & a_{12} \\ a_{21} & a_{22} \end{bmatrix}+\begin{bmatrix} a_{11} & a_{21} \\ a_{12} & a_{22} \end{bmatrix}\begin{bmatrix} e_{11} & e_{12} \\ e_{21} & e_{22} \end{bmatrix}=\begin{bmatrix} -1 & 0 \\ 0 & -1 \end{bmatrix}$. This is a system of equations which when further expanded will give us four equations. Since e12=e21 the equations will reduce to three equations given in Equation(6.29).

$$\begin{aligned} &2e_{11}a_{11} + 2e_{12}a_{21} = -1 \\ &e_{12}a_{22} + (e_{11} + e_{22})a_{21} + e_{12}a_{11} = 0 \\ &2e_{12}a_{12} + 2e_{22}a_{22} = -1 \end{aligned} \tag{6.29}$$

On solving these three equations we get the required conditions for stability of a second order system as a11a22 - a12a21 >0 and a11 + a22 < 0.

6.8 CHAPTER SUMMARY

The State Variable Concept:

The state variable representation is especially useful when the system has several inputs and several outputs. The method of solution or analysis does not change whether you have a big system or a small one; whether you have a single input-single output system or a multiple input-multiple output system. This method can also be extended to time varying systems and the modern software tools make the solution of the state variable representation particularly attractive.

The state of a system is not unique. There are several different ways in which the same system is represented. In general however the state of the system is the behavior of the energy storage elements in the system. So very often you will find the quantity that defines the energy in the energy storage element is chosen as one of the state variables. So when you have a capacitor in the system the voltage across the capacitor will often be chosen as a state variable. Similarly if you have a mass in the system the velocity of the mass will be chosen as one of the state variables. These choices that we have indicated are general not mandatory.

The state of the system is represented by four matrices. The 'A' matrix is the system matrix. It is a square matrix with n rows and n columns. The number of rows and columns represents the number of state variables. The 'b' matrix is the input distribution matrix. This matrix has n rows and m columns. This matrix distributes the 'm' different inputs to the 'n' state variables in the system. The number of columns corresponds to the number of different inputs that are present in the system. The 'c' matrix is the output accumulation matrix. This matrix combines together the state of various state variables to build the response. This matrix has n columns and p rows. The contribution from each of the n state variables is accumulated for each of the p different outputs. The number of rows corresponds to the number of different outputs that may be present in the system. The 'd' matrix is a direct feed through matrix. This matrix tells us if there is any direct connection from an input to an output. This matrix is a p-by-m matrix. This matrix tells us which, if any of the m, inputs are directly connected to any of the p different outputs.

Solving the State of the System:

We solved the state equation in the time domain as well as in the Laplace domain. The time domain solution gave us a recursive relation which tells us how the state of the system will move forward as time progresses. The Laplace domain solution gave us a closed form solution. Both the methods presented us with a matrix exponential in the solution. This matrix exponential is known as the resolvent matrix or the characteristic matrix.

Properties of the State Transition Matrix:

The properties of the characteristic matrix are special. Its inverse is found by negating the time variable in the matrix of $\phi(t)^{-1} = \phi(-t)$. Another special property of this matrix is $\phi(t_3,t_o) = \phi(t_3,t_2)\,\phi(t_2,t_1)\,\phi(t_1,t_o)$. As time moves along the characteristic matrix keeps track of it. This is known as the semi-grouping property. A consequence of this and the inverse property is that $\phi(t_3,t_o)\cdot\phi(t_0,t_3) = I$.

Converting Between Transfer Function and State Variable Format:

The system that is represented in the transfer function form can be converted and represented in the state variable form. So also the system that is represented in the state variable form can be converted and represented in the transfer function form.

Transforming the transfer function to state variable format is mostly done by drawing the signal flow diagram of the differential equation. In the signal flow diagram we have integrators. The output of each of the integrator is defined as a state variable. Depending on how we draw the signal flow graph the state variable representation will come out different. Using the partial factors we saw that the state system had an 'A' matrix that was entirely diagonal. An alternative method to represent the transfer function in the state format used the numerator coefficients of the transfer function in the feed forward path and the denominator coefficients in the feed back path. We called this representation the Phase variable representation.

Observers and Controllers:

In the introduction to this chapter we specified one of the advantages of the state variable system is that we can see and monitor the various states of the system. To do this the system must be observable. A system is observable if we can compute the initial (starting) state of the system, when there is no external input supplied, by watching the output of the system for a finite amount of time. For a linear time invariant system this is determined by computing the rank of the observability matrix. If the observability matrix $P_o = \left[c^T \mid A^T c^T \mid \left(A^T\right)^2 c^T \mid \left(A^T\right)^3 c^T\right]$ is of full rank then the system is observable.

Another advantage of the state variable system is that we can control the various states of the system. To do this the system must be controllable. A system is controllable if we can move the state of the system starting from any initial (starting) state of the system, with some known external input supplied, to any desired final state of the system in a finite amount of time. For a linear time invariant system this is determined by computing the rank of the controllability matrix. The controllability matrix for the system is defined as $P_c = \left[b \mid Ab \mid A^2 b \mid A^3 b\right]$, if this matrix is of full rank then the system is controllable.

Stability of the System:

To determine the stability of the system we examined the second method of Liapunov. The method relies on computing an energy type of a function. Then determining whether the derivative of the function is an increasing or a decreasing function. If this function is a decreasing function then the system is a stable system. To use this method we had to determine the 'E' matrix which was a positive defiant matrix. This 'E' matrix was the one that we used to define the energy type of a function of the system.

6.9 HOMEWORK PROBLEMS

The State Concept

Problem 6.9.1

$$\begin{bmatrix} \dot{x}_1 \\ \dot{x}_2 \end{bmatrix} = \begin{bmatrix} -2 & 0 \\ 0 & -5 \end{bmatrix} \begin{bmatrix} x_1 \\ x_2 \end{bmatrix} + \begin{bmatrix} 0.5 \\ -1 \end{bmatrix} u$$

$$y = \begin{bmatrix} 2 & -1 \end{bmatrix} \begin{bmatrix} x_1 \\ x_2 \end{bmatrix}$$

A state variable system is defined by the following sets of equations.

a. How many state variables are there in this system?

b. How many distinct inputs are there in this system?

c. How many distinct outputs are there in this system?

d. Is there a direct connection from any of the system inputs to any of the system outputs?

Problem 6.9.2

A system is defined by the following sets of equations.

$$\dot{x}_1 = 4x_1 + 4x_2 + 4u_1 - 3u_2$$
$$\dot{x}_2 = 3x_2 - 4x_3 + u_1 - 2u_2$$
$$\dot{x}_3 = 2x_2 + 4x_3 + 2u_1 + 2u_2$$

$$y_1 = 5x_1 - 2x_2 + x_3 + 3u_1$$
$$y_2 = 3x_1 + 4x_2 + 5x_3 + u_2$$

a. Write the state equations in standard form. Identify the A, b, c and d matrices.
b. How many unique inputs, outputs and state variables does this system have?

Problem 6.9.3

A system is defined in the state variable format with the following pertinent matrices.

$$\begin{bmatrix} \dot{x}_1 \\ \dot{x}_2 \\ \dot{x}_3 \end{bmatrix} = \begin{bmatrix} 0 & 1 & 0 \\ 0 & 0 & 1 \\ -2 & -5 & -15 \end{bmatrix} \begin{bmatrix} x_1 \\ x_2 \\ x_3 \end{bmatrix} + \begin{bmatrix} 0 & 1 \\ -1 & 2 \\ 3 & -1 \end{bmatrix} \begin{bmatrix} u_1 \\ u_2 \end{bmatrix}$$

$$y(t) = \begin{bmatrix} 1 & 0 & -2 \\ 0 & -1 & 3 \end{bmatrix} \begin{bmatrix} x_1 \\ x_2 \\ x_3 \end{bmatrix}$$

a. How many unique inputs, outputs and state variables does this system have?
b. Write the individual differential equations and the output equations for this system.

State Transition Matrix

Problem 6.9.4

Evaluate the state transition matrix using the series expansion method when the A matrix is $\begin{bmatrix} -2 & 0 \\ 0 & -3 \end{bmatrix}$

Problem 6.9.5

Evaluate the state transition matrix by computing **ϕ(s) = (sI-A)$^{-1}$** when the A matrix is $\begin{bmatrix} -1 & 0 \\ 0 & -5 \end{bmatrix}$

Problem 6.9.6

In general – using **ϕ(s) = (sI-A)$^{-1}$** – show that a state transition matrix for

$$A = \begin{bmatrix} -\lambda_1 & 0 & 0 \\ 0 & -\lambda_2 & 0 \\ 0 & 0 & -\lambda_3 \end{bmatrix} \text{ is given by } \Phi(s) = \begin{bmatrix} e^{-\lambda_1 t} & 0 & 0 \\ 0 & e^{-\lambda_2 t} & 0 \\ 0 & 0 & e^{-\lambda_3 t} \end{bmatrix}$$

Check your results from Problem 6.9.4 and Problem 6.9.5.

Problem 6.9.7

Determine the state transition matrix using the time domain method for the system in Problem 6.9.1.

Problem 6.9.8

Determine the state transition matrix using the Laplace Transform method for the system in Problem 6.2.

Problem 6.9.9

Determine the state transition matrix using SCILAB program script for the system in Problem 6.9.3.

Problems 6.9.10

Using the state transition matrix that you determined for Problem 4 find the state of the system x(t) at t = 0.7 when you are given $\boldsymbol{x}(0) = \begin{bmatrix} -3 \\ 3 \end{bmatrix}$ and $\boldsymbol{b} = \begin{bmatrix} 1 \\ 2 \end{bmatrix}$ and u(t) is a step input at t = 0.

Problems 6.9.11

Using the state transition matrix that you determined for Problem 6.9.5 find the state of the system x(t) at t = 0.2, 0.4, 0.6, 0.8 and 1.0 when you are given $\boldsymbol{x}(0) = \begin{bmatrix} 4 \\ 3 \end{bmatrix}$ and $\boldsymbol{b} = \begin{bmatrix} 1 \\ 1 \end{bmatrix}$ and u(t) is a step input at t = 0.

Problem 6.9.12

In this chapter we discussed that the purpose of the state transition matrix was to move the state of the system from $t = t_0$ to $t = t_1$. We will use this fact here and determine the state of the system at time t = 1 second using three different state transition matrices.

a. Using the state transition matrix that you obtained for Problem 6.9.9 evaluate the state of the system for the following times t = 0.1 seconds; t = 0.5 seconds and t = 1 seconds. This is done by substituting the various times in the state transition matrix for the variable t.

b. Using the initial state $\boldsymbol{x}(0)=\begin{bmatrix}1\\2\end{bmatrix}$ evaluate the state of the system at time t = 1 second using the state transition matrix evaluated for t = 1 second. This is $\boldsymbol{x}(t=1)=\boldsymbol{\Phi}(t=1)\boldsymbol{x}(0)$.

c. Using the initial state $\boldsymbol{x}(0)=\begin{bmatrix}1\\2\end{bmatrix}$ evaluate the state of the system at time t = 1 second using the state transition matrix evaluated for t = 0.5 seconds. This is done by first multiplying the initial state with the state transition matrix to obtain the state of the system at time t = 0.5 seconds. This state is then used as the starting state and multiplied by the same state transition matrix to get the state of the system at time t = 1 second. This is shown here as

$$\boldsymbol{x}(t=0.5)=\boldsymbol{\Phi}(t=0.5)\boldsymbol{x}(0) \text{ and } \boldsymbol{x}(t=1)=\boldsymbol{\Phi}(t=0.5)\boldsymbol{x}(0.5).$$

d. Repeat the steps in part c of this problem using the state transition matrix for time t=0.1 seconds. For this question you have to determine the state of the system for 10 consecutive times each with an increment of 0.1 seconds.

e. When you finish all the above steps you will find that the state of the system is the same for all the three different evaluation procedures. This shows that the state transition matrix for linear time invariant systems is independent of the starting time and is only dependent on the time difference between the present and the final time. This time difference in our examples were 1 second for part b; 0.5 seconds for part c and 0.1 seconds for part d.

Simulation of a State Variable System

Problem 6.9.13

Draw the simulation diagram for the state variable system described in Problem 6.1, Problem 6.2 and in Problem 6.3.

Problem 6.9.14

Starting with the transfer function $\dfrac{Y(s)}{U(s)}=\dfrac{3s^2+2s+4}{s(s+1)(s+5)^2(s+8)}$ determine the canonical representation for the state variables of the system.

Problem 6.9.15

Starting with the transfer function $\dfrac{Y(s)}{U(s)}=\dfrac{3s^2+2s+4}{s(s+1)(s+5)^2(s+8)}$ determine the phase variable representation for the state variables of the system.

Problem 6.9.16

Starting with the transfer function $\frac{Y(s)}{U(s)} = \frac{4s^2+3s+5}{(s+0.1)(s+0.5)(s+4)(s+10)}$ determine at least two different state variable representations for this transfer function.

Problem 6.9.17

Using the state variable representation given for the two input, two output system in Problem 6.9.1 determine all the four transfer functions represented by $\frac{Y_1(s)}{U_1(s)}; \frac{Y_1(s)}{U_2(s)}; \frac{Y_2(s)}{U_1(s)}$ and $\frac{Y_2(s)}{U_2(s)}$

System Stability

Problem 6.9.18

Use the Laplace transform approach to find **y(t)** for the system defined with the following matrices. Assume zero initial condition and a step input at t = 0 seconds.

$$\boldsymbol{A} = \begin{bmatrix} -1 & 0 & 0 \\ 0 & -3 & 0 \\ 0 & 0 & -5 \end{bmatrix} \quad \boldsymbol{b} = \begin{bmatrix} 0 \\ 1 \\ 2 \end{bmatrix} \quad \boldsymbol{c} = \begin{bmatrix} 1 & 0 & 2 \end{bmatrix} \quad \boldsymbol{d} = \begin{bmatrix} 2 \end{bmatrix}$$

Problem 6.9.19

Determine if all the state variables are controllable by determining the Controllability matrix for the systems represented in Problems 6.9.1; 6.9.2 and 6.9.3.

Problem 6.9.20

Determine if all the state variables are observable by determining the Observability matrix for the systems represented in Problems 6.9.1; 6.9.2 and 6.9.3.

Problem 6.9.21

Determine if the system defined by the A matrix $\begin{bmatrix} 0 & 1 & 0 \\ 0 & \beta & 1 \\ -4 & -2 & -1 \end{bmatrix}$ is a stable system if the value of $\beta = 2$. What is the range of the value of b for the system to be stable? Use Liapaunov criteria to determine the stability criteria.

Problem 6.9.22

If the system in Problem 6.9.18 has a b matrix $\begin{bmatrix} 0 \\ -1 \\ 3 \end{bmatrix}$ is the system controllable?

Problem 6.9.23

If the system in Problem 6.9.18 has a c matrix $\begin{bmatrix} 0 & -1 & 3 \end{bmatrix}$ is the system observable?

Problem 6.9.24

After you have determined the A matrix in the system defined in Problem 6.9.18 determine the eigen values of the matrix. Form an eigen value matrix E by writing all the eigen vectors as columns of the matrix. Determine E^T the transpose of the Eigen vector matrix. Now form a new Matrix as EAE^T. How does this matrix compare with the A matrix of the original system defined in problem 6.9.14?

Problem 6.9.25

Computer Simulation Assignment:

In this computer simulation assignment we will further investigate the validity of the concept covered in Problem 6.9.9 in this chapter. For this assignment we will use the initial state vector of $\boldsymbol{x}(0) = \begin{bmatrix} 1 \\ -2 \\ 3 \end{bmatrix}$

a. Evaluate the state transition matrix for the **A** matrix given in Problem 6.9.12 using the SCILAB functions.

b. Now evaluate the state transition matrix for time 0.01 seconds, -0.05 seconds, 0.2 seconds and 1 second.

c. Compute the state of the system at t = 1 second by using the state transition matrix for t = 1 second.

d. Next compute the state of the system at time t=1 second by using the state transition matrix for t = 0.2 seconds five times in successive order.

e. Next compute the state of the system at time t=1 second by using the state transition matrix for t = 0.01 seconds hundred times in successive order.

f. Next compute the state of the system at time t=1 second by alternately using the state transition matrix for t = 0.2 and t = 0.01 seconds four times in successive order then finish up by using the state transition matrix for t = 0.01, 16 more times.

g. Next compute the state of the system at time t=1 second by sequentially using the state transition matrix for t = 0.2; t = 0.01 and t = -0.05 seconds six times in successive order then finish up by using the state transition matrix for t = 0.01, 4 more times.

h. In each of the cases c, d, e, f and g you should end up with the same state vector. This shows that the state transition matrix not only moves the state of the system forward as time progresses but it can move the state of the even backward in time.

6.10 FURTHER READING

6.10.1

State variable representation of systems is covered in either Mathematics books; Control System Books and Signal and System Books :

1. Ziemer R.E.; Tranter W.H. and Fannin D.R. *Signals and Systems: Continuous and Discrete*, Macmillan Publishing Company, NY 1993.

2. Friedland Bernard, *Control System Design–An Introduction to State Space Methods*, McGraw Hill 1986.

3. Lewis P.H. and Yang Chang. *Basic Control Systems Engineering*, Prentice Hall, NJ. 1997.

CHAPTER 7

The Z - Transform

INTRODUCTION – DISCRETE SIGNALS AND SYSTEMS

In the previous six chapters we have studied systems that were continuous. We analyzed the systems and studied these systems. We now turn our attention to systems that are sampled. A system that is sampled is generally known as a discrete time system. These systems are defined at sampling instants only. These systems are not zero between sampling instants, we just do not know what they are; these systems are just not defined. The discrete time systems take discrete input signals. These input signals are generally obtained by sampling the continuous time input signals. So the discrete time systems are discrete only within the control section. Where they interface with the outside world they are continuous in nature. So why do we bother with the discrete time systems when we can control the systems in the continuous time? The answer is the computer or the microcontroller. Control of systems or the processing of signals is now done by a microprocessor since it can be done by software instead of hardware. Software can be easily changed or altered. To use these and many other advantages systems are nowadays turning more and more to digital or discrete control.

In this chapter we begin by studying how an analog signal is sampled, next we will examine what happens to an analog signal when it is sampled in the time domain as well as in the frequency domain. In Chapter 5 we studied the Laplace Transform and used it for all analysis and design of systems in the analog domain. Remember that the analog system was defined by the differential equation and the Laplace Transform converted the differential equation into an algebraic equation. In an analogous manner we will find that the discrete system is described by a difference equation and the Z-Transform is used for both the analysis and the design of the discrete systems as the Z-transform converts the difference equation into an algebraic equation. In this section we develop the basic properties of the Z-transform and demonstrate how to transform a difference equation to the Z-domain and then how to transform the Z-domain solution back to the time domain.

The Z-Transform for the discrete time systems and the Laplace Transform for Continuous time systems both have similar relationships. We will explore this idea of similarity further when we study the Fourier Transform in a later chapter. In this chapter we define the Z-Transform as a representation which is a sequence of numbers, each number of the sequence having a magnitude and a position. With this representation we will be able to take advantage of the properties of sequences. We will also state and use some results from the Theory of Complex Variables. With this the Z-Transform allows us to use the powerful complex variable theory for discrete time signals and systems just as the Laplace Transform allowed us to use the complex theory for continuous time systems.

In the chapters that follow we will develop the tools necessary to study, analyze and synthesize discrete systems. As we develop these tools we will find that just as the Laplace transform was the principal tool in the analog domain, in the discrete domain the Z-transform is the principal tool.

7.1 SAMPLING A CONTINUOUS TIME SIGNAL

The sampling process begins with a continuous time analog signal x(t). This signal is sampled at regular intervals; this sampling process is similar to taking a snapshot of the signal at regular intervals. This is done by a sampler. The sampled signal from the sampler is first quantized. The quantizing process limits the number of levels that the signal can represent. The quantized signal is finally encoded; the encoding process represents the signal in binary usually. This binary representation of the analog signal is the digital signal that we will be using when we work with discrete time systems. This process is shown in Figure 7.1. Sampling this continuous time signal is analogous to taking a snapshot of the signal at regular and periodic time interval. Say we take the sample every T seconds. Then we get a sequence of numbers which represent the amplitude of the signal x(t) at some time that is a multiple of T. So the first sample will be at t = 0, the second sample will be at t = T the third sample will occur at t = 2T and so on. So the nth sample will occur at t = (n-1)T. This process is shown pictorially in Figure 7.2.

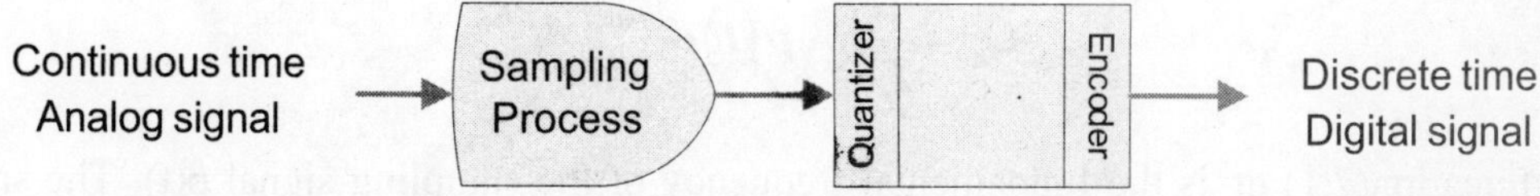

Figure 7.1: The process of converting an analog signal into a digital signal

When we sample a continuous time signal we represent the signal with its amplitude at periodic intervals. This process is shown pictorially in Figure 7.2. Notice in Figure 7.2 the sampled values exactly coincide with the continuous time signal at the sampling instants. So we can view the sampling process as if the signal x(t) is multiplied by the sampling signal. So the signal $x_s(t) = x(t)p(t)$

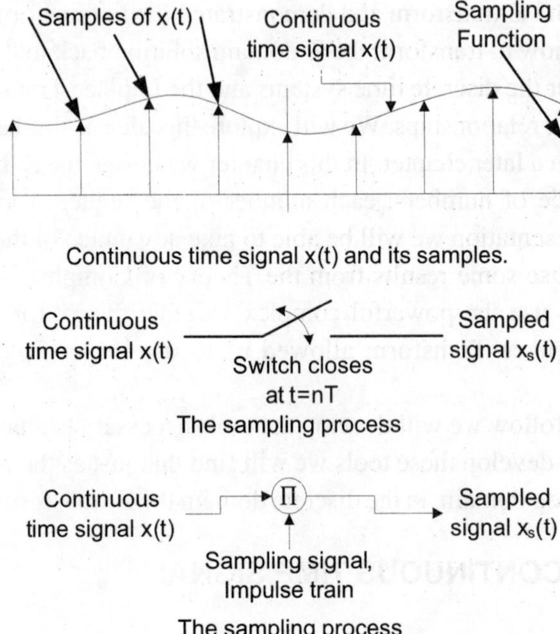

Figure 7.2: The sampling process is equivalent to multiplying the continuous time signal x(t) with an impulse train

where p(t) is the sampling signal. The sampling signal is assumed to be periodical. It is very interesting to see what is the spectrum of the sampled signal $x_s(t)$ and is there any restriction that we must place on the sampling interval so that the spectrum of the original signal x(t) can be recovered from the sampled signal $x_s(t)$. Towards this end we will obtain the Fourier transform of the signal $x_s(t)$.

First let us define the spectrum of the sampling signal p(t). Since p(t) is a periodic signal we can represent it as a Fourier series, doing this we get Equation(7.1).

$$p(t) = \sum_{n=-\infty}^{\infty} C_n e^{jn\omega_o t}$$

$$C_n = \frac{1}{T}\int_{-T/2}^{T/2} p(t) e^{-jn\omega_o t}\, dt \tag{7.1}$$

In Equation(7.1) ω_o is the fundamental frequency of the sampling signal p(t). The sampling interval T and the sampling frequency are related by the relation

$$\omega_o = 2\pi f_o = \frac{2\pi}{T}.$$

Figure 7.2 shows that the sampled signal $x_s(t)$ is obtained by multiplying the analog signal x(t) by the sampling signal p(t) so we can write $x_s(t)$ as shown in Equation(7.2)

$$x_s(t) = \sum_{n=-\infty}^{\infty} C_n x(t) e^{jn\omega_o t} \tag{7.2}$$

We can now determine the spectrum of the sampled signal $x_s(t)$. To do this we will determine the Fourier transform of the sampled signal $x_s(t)$. The Fourier transform of $x_s(t)$ is determined by evaluating the integral in Equation(7.3)

$$X_s(\omega) = \int_{-\infty}^{\infty} \sum_{n=-\infty}^{\infty} \left[C_n x(t) e^{jn\omega_o t} \right] e^{-j\omega t} dt \tag{7.3}$$

Interchange the order of the summation and the integration to get Equation(7.4)

$$X_s(\omega) = \sum_{n=-\infty}^{\infty} C_n \int_{-\infty}^{\infty} x(t)\, e^{-j(\omega - n\omega_o)t} dt \tag{7.4}$$

Notice that the quantity within the integral sign is the Fourier transform of x(t) but with a shift in the frequency domain. This is shown in Equation(7.5)

$$X(\omega - n\omega_o) = \int_{-\infty}^{\infty} x(t)\, e^{-j(\omega - n\omega_o)t} dt \tag{7.5}$$

Using Equation(7.5) in Equation(7.4) we get the Fourier transform of the sampled signal $x_s(t)$ as shown in Equation(7.6)

$$X_s(\omega) = \sum_{n=-\infty}^{\infty} C_n X(\omega - n\omega_o) \tag{7.6}$$

Equation(7.6) shows that the spectrum of the sampled signal is made up of replicas of the spectrum of x(t). These replicas of the spectrum of x(t) are repeated every ω_o frequency. You remember that ω_o is the frequency of the sampling function. We have sampled the signal x(t) at intervals of T seconds. So the relation between the spectrum of x(t) and the spectrum of $x_s(t)$ is as shown in Figure 7.3 and in Equation(7.6). Equation(7.6) shows that each of the translated spectra of X(ω) is multiplied by the Fourier coefficient of the sampling function C_n. We have assumed that the sampling function in Figure 7.2 and in Equation(7.1) is an impulse train. When the sampling function is an impulse train then all the C_n coefficients are unity and all the Fourier coefficients are identical and there is no loss in amplitude from one replica to another. If the sampling function is not an impulse function but a flat top signal then there will be loss of amplitude from one replica to another according to the Fourier coefficients of the C_n of the sampling function.

7.1.1 The Nyquist Criteria for sampled signals:

When we examine Figure 7.3 further we find that each of the replicas exist in their own frequency space. Any two adjacent spectra do not overlap each other in Figure 7.3. This can only occur when the spectrum of x(t) is *band limited.* A signal is a band limited signal when it has a defined high frequency, i.e. the signal has no energy in any frequency that is greater than the defined high frequency. Further because there is no overlap between replicas of X(ω) that make up the spectrum of $X_s(\omega)$ we must also have a specific relation between the highest frequency present in the spectrum of X(ω) and the sampling frequency. This relation can be derived from Figure 7.3. In Figure 7.3 you will notice that the spectrums are centered at a separation of ω_o which is the sampling frequency. Within this sampling frequency we have to have space for the highest frequency ω_h from two replicas of X(ω). This will occur only if Equation(7.7) is satisfied.

$$\omega_o \geq 2\omega_h \tag{7.7}$$

Equation(7.7) is the statement of the famous Nyquist sampling theorem. It says that the sampling frequency must be at least twice as large as the highest frequency present in the signal that is being sampled. Figure 7.3 also shows that if an appropriate low pass filter is available and used then the original signal x(t) can be recovered by passing the sampled signal through a low pass filter.

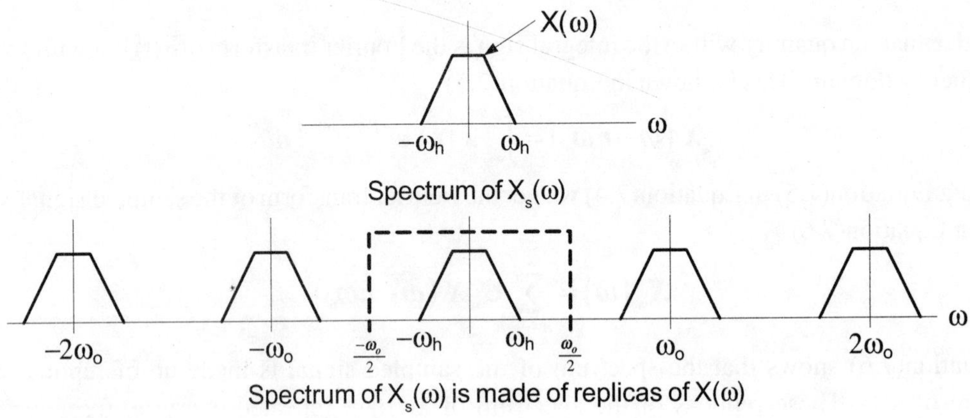

Figure 7.3: Sampling a continuous time signal creates replicas of the sampled signal. The replicas are separated by the sampling frequency

What happens if Equation(7.7) is not satisfied? Look at Figure 7.4. In the top row of Figure 7.4 we see the spectrum of x(t). The next row shows the spectrum when we sample at a rate that is greater than the sampling rate. There is no overlap and each of the replicas is distinct and separate from each other. As we decrease the sampling rate the replicas of the spectrum move closer to each other and when the sampling is done exactly equal to the Nyquist rate the replicas just touch each other. This is shown in the third row in Figure 7.4. Finally when we sample at a rate that is less than the sampling rate the various spectra start to overlap each other. This condition where the spectra overlap is known as *Aliasing.* When aliasing occurs there is loss of information and the original signal can no longer be recovered from the sampled signal. For this reason the signal when it is sampled is sampled at least Nyquist sampling rate.

7.2 RECOVERING THE ORIGINAL SIGNAL FROM THE SAMPLED SIGNAL

Figure 7.3 shows us that to recover the original signal spectra from the sampled signal spectra we can use a Low Pass filter with cutoff frequency equal to ½ω_o. What we see in Figure 7.3 is an ideal reconstruction filter. It is interesting and instructive to see what the reconstructed signal is like.

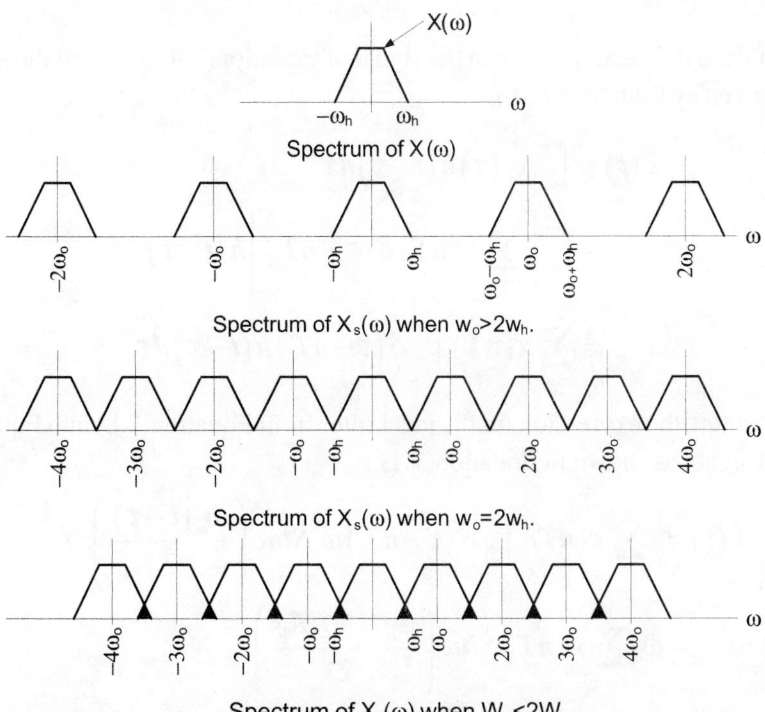

Notice that we have an overlap region

Figure 7.4: When the sampling frequency does not satisfy the Nyquist rate then we have Aliasing and loss of information

To find the reconstructed signal let us determine the time domain function of the ideal filter. If you remember we saw this earlier in Equation(4.37). We will write the function as it applies to the present situation.

$$h(t) = \int_{-\frac{\omega_o}{2}}^{\frac{\omega_o}{2}} e^{j\omega t}\, d\omega = \frac{1}{jt} e^{j\omega t}\Big|_{-\frac{\omega_o}{2}}^{\frac{\omega_o}{2}}$$

$$= \frac{1}{jt}\left[e^{j\frac{\omega_o}{2}t} - e^{j\frac{-\omega_o}{2}t}\right] = \omega_o Sinc\left(\frac{\omega_o t}{2}\right) \tag{7.8}$$

So when we pass the sampled signal through this filter what do we get out of the filter? We will get the answer to that by convolving the filter transfer function with the sampled signal. The sampled signal if you remember is obtained by multiplying the continuous time signal x(t) by the impulse train and is given in Equation(7.9)

$$x_s(t) = \sum_{n=-\infty}^{\infty} x(nT)\delta(t-nT) \tag{7.9}$$

So the output from the ideal filter when the signal of Equation(7.9) is passed through the filter of Equation(7.8) is given by Equation(7.10)

$$\begin{aligned}\hat{x}(t) &= \int_{-\infty}^{\infty} x_s(\tau)h(t-\tau)d\tau \\ &= \int_{-\infty}^{\infty}\left[\sum_{n=-\infty}^{\infty} x(nT)\delta(\tau-nT)\right]h(t-\tau)d\tau \\ &= \sum_{n=-\infty}^{\infty} x(nT)\int_{-\infty}^{\infty}\delta(\tau-nT)h(t-\tau)d\tau\end{aligned} \tag{7.10}$$

When we substitute the expression for the ideal filter from Equation(7.8) into Equation(7.10) we get the recovered signal as shown in Equation(7.11)

$$\begin{aligned}\hat{x}(t) &= \sum_{n=-\infty}^{\infty} x(nT)\int_{-\infty}^{\infty}\delta(\tau-nT)\omega_o Sinc\left(\frac{\omega_o(t-\tau)}{2}\right)d\tau \\ &= \omega_o\sum_{n=-\infty}^{\infty} x(nT)Sinc\left(\frac{\omega_o(t-nT)}{2}\right)\end{aligned} \tag{7.11}$$

Equation(7.11) shows us that the signal $\hat{x}(t)$ is obtained by multiplying the amplitude x(nT) by a sinc function located at t = nT where T is the sampling interval and ω_0 is the multiplier that we need because of the filter amplitude which was chosen to be unity. The Sinc function is a special function. Look at Figure 7.5; it shows two different sinc functions. Examine the sinc function carefully; they pass through zero amplitude periodically. These zero crossings occur exactly at the location of all the other sinc pulses in Equation(7.11). Thus at any one position where t = nT there is contribution from only one pulse, contributions from all the other pulses pass through zero at that location. The contribution from all the other pulses at, t = nT, the location of any pulse is zero. Thus the signal $\hat{x}(t)$ indeed is the same as the signal x(t) at the location of the sinc pulses.

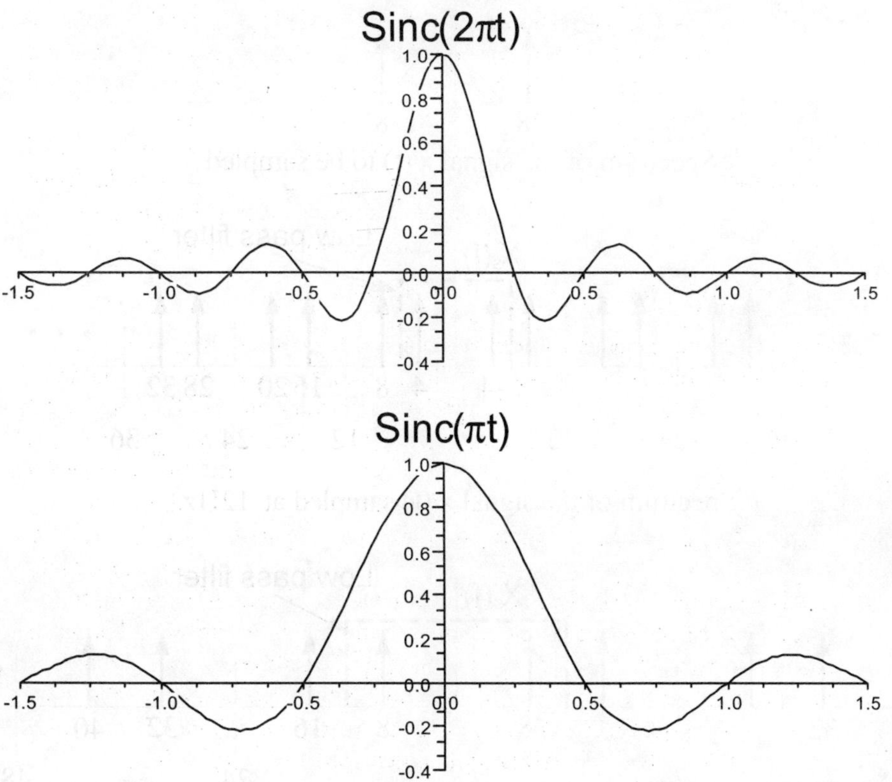

Figure 7.5: Two different sinc functions

Example 7.1

Consider a signal 5Cos(2π8t).

a. Sample this signal at the rate of 12Hz; draw the resulting spectrum; filter the sampled signal with an ideal filter with cutoff 7Hz; identify the resulting signal.

b. Sample this signal at the rate of 24Hz; draw the resulting spectrum; filter the sampled signal with an ideal filter with cutoff 11Hz; identify the resulting signal.

Solution 7.1

Since we have a signal that is a pure tone the highest frequency that is present in the signal x(t) is the frequency of the tone. In this example it is 8Hz. So the spectrum of the signal x(t) is two impulses in the frequency domain at f= ±8 Hz. This is shown in Figure 7.6.

a. We first sample the tone with a sampling rate of 12 Hz. This sampling rate is less than the Nyquist rate (Nyquist rate would be 16 Hz) so the sampled signal creates aliased spectrum.

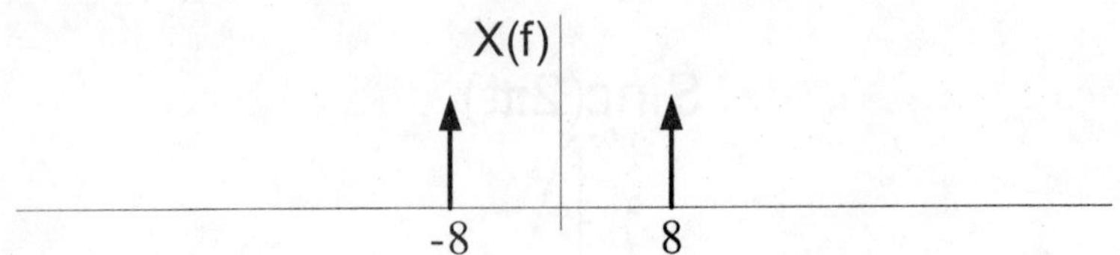

Spectrum of the signal x (t) to be sampled.

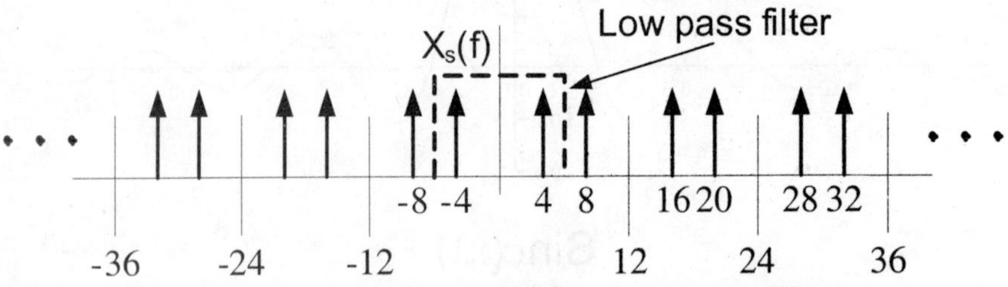

Spectrum of the signal x (t) sampled at 12Hz.

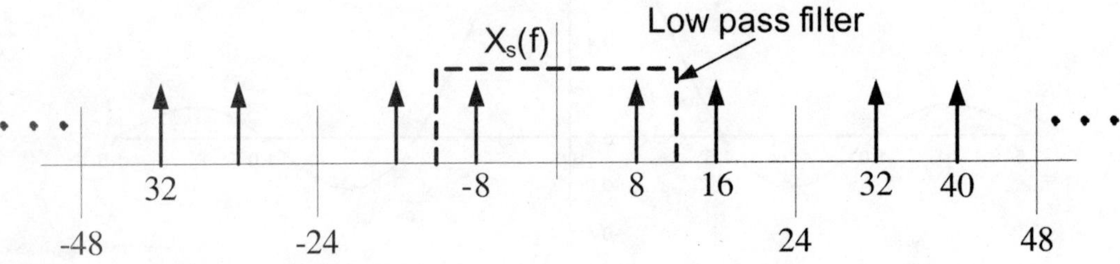

Spectrum of the signal x (t) sampled at 24Hz.

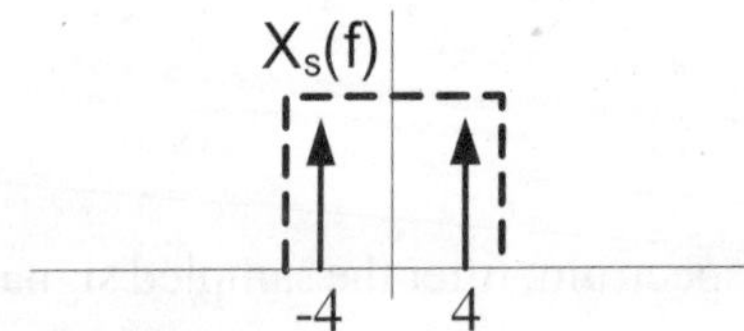

Spectrum of the signal recovered when sampled at 12Hz. Aliasing is evident since sampling is at less than Nyquist rate.

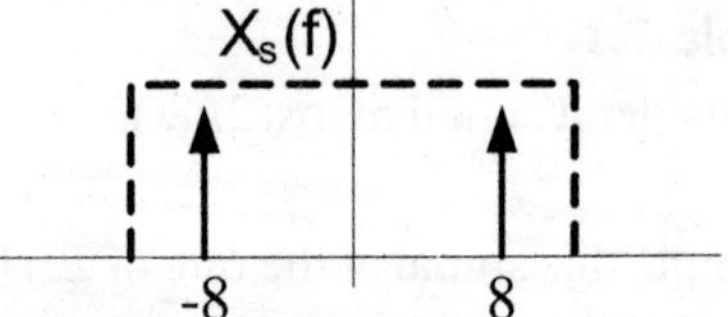

Spectrum of the signal recovered when sampled at 24Hz. Aliasing is absent since sampling is at greater than Nyquist rate.

Figure 7.6: Sampling a band limited signal at less than and greater than Nyquist rate. Aliasing alters the frequency of the recovered signal when the sampling rate is less than the Nyquist rate

When the sampled signal is low pass filtered with a filter with a cutoff frequency of 6 Hz we get a spectrum of signal that has a frequency of 4 Hz and not the original signal which had a spectrum of 8 Hz.

b. We next sample the tone with a sampling rate of 24 Hz. This sampling rate is greater than the Nyquist rate (Nyquist rate would be 16 Hz) so the sampled signal is not aliased. When the sampled signal is low pass filtered with a filter with a cutoff frequency of 12 Hz we get a spectrum of signal that has a frequency of 8 Hz. This is the original signal which had a spectrum of 8 Hz. So when the signal is sampled at a frequency that is greater than the Nyquist rate the original signal is recovered.

Figure 7.6 displays what happens when a band limited signal is sampled.

7.3 THE LINEAR DIFFERENCE EQUATION

Now that we have sampled the analog continuous time signal and have a discrete signal we cannot use differential equations to describe the system since differential equations deal with continuous time signals. The systems in the sampled domain are described by *Difference Equations.* Difference equations allow us to properly represent the input output relations to any given linear time invariant systems. A linear constant coefficient difference equation is the way we express the input and output relations in discrete time systems. A difference shows how the present output is computed using the previous input samples and previous outputs. Since the input is a sampled signal the inputs are provided at discrete instants in time and the outputs are obtained at discrete instants in time. So a typical difference equation will be of the form shown in Equation(7.12)

$$\sum_{k=0}^{N} a_k\, y(n-k) = \sum_{k=0}^{M} b_k\, x(n-k) \tag{7.12}$$

In Equation(7.12) the output is y (n), this output is a combination of the previous N-1 outputs. So y(n-1) is the previous output. Similarly y(n-k) is the kth previous output. Similarly x(n) is the present input and x(n-1) is the previous input, similarly x(n-k) is the kth previous input. Equation(7.12) is a recursive equation and its recursive nature will become evident if we rewrite Equation(7.12) as shown in Equation(7.13)

$$y(n) = \frac{1}{a_0}\left[-\sum_{k=1}^{N} a_k\, y(n-k) + \sum_{k=0}^{M} b_k\, x(n-k)\right] \tag{7.13}$$

In Equation(7.13) we note that y(n) is the present output and it is made up from the previous outputs and present and past inputs. The value N the number of past outputs on which the present output depends is known as the order of the difference equation. The order of the difference equation also tells us the amount of memory in the system being represented. The past values of the output on which the present output depends on can be thought of as initial conditions, since to compute even the very first output we need to know the same number of past outputs. So the past outputs used are treated as initial conditions.

7.3.1 Solving the Linear Difference Equation:

Just as we solved the differential equation earlier using the time domain method (the direct method) and the Laplace transform method (the indirect method) we can solve the Linear Difference Equation also using the time domain method and the transform domain method. Here we will use the direct time domain method. Later in this chapter when we study the Z-transforms we will solve the linear difference equation using the transform method.

The solution of the difference equation is based on the homogeneous solution and the particular solution. The method that we will use here is very similar to the time domain solution method that we used to solve the differential equations.

The Particular Solution:

The particular solution is the solution to the input and it takes the same form as the input. So what ever is the form of the input that is the form of the output as far as the particular solution is concerned. So to solve the particular solution of the form

$$\sum_{k=0}^{N} a_k\, y_p(n-k) = \sum_{k=0}^{M} b_k\, x(n-k) \tag{7.14}$$

We will make a guess at the solution of $y_p(n)$ and our guess will have the same form as the input x(n). So the form of the solution is known. After guessing the solution we will substitute the solution into the difference equation to determine the required constants. The example that follows will make this step clear.

The particular solutions that we assume will depend on the input or the driving functions. In general we always include all the derivatives of the input function as part of the assumed solution. Table 7.1 here summarizes the solutions that we will assume.

Table 7.1: Suggested forms of particular solutions for various input functions.

n^k	$a_0 n^k + a_1 n^{k-1} + \ldots + a_n$
$(\text{Constant})^n$	$a_0(\text{Constant})^n$
$\text{Cos}(\theta n)$ or $\text{Sin}(\theta n)$	$a_1\text{Cos}(\theta n) + a_2\text{Sin}(\theta n)$
$(\text{Constant})^n\{\text{Cos}(\theta n)\}$ or $(\text{Constant})^n\,\text{Sin}(\theta n)\}$	$(\text{Constant})^n\{a_1\text{Cos}(\theta n) + a_2\text{Sin}(\theta n)\}$

The Homogeneous Solution:

The Homogeneous solution begins with the assumption that all the inputs are zero. So we set all the x(n-k)'s to zero in Equation(7.12) and we get Equation(7.15) which has to be solved.

$$\sum_{k=0}^{N} a_k\, y(n-k) = 0 \tag{7.15}$$

To solve Equation(7.15) we make an assumption that the solution is in the form of an exponential sequence. This is similar to the difference equation method that we had used. So forming a characteristic equation to replace the homogeneous equation we get Equation(7.16)

$$\sum_{k=0}^{N} a_k \lambda^{(n-k)} = 0 \tag{7.16}$$

Equation(7.16) is in the form

$$a_0\lambda^n + a_1\lambda^{n-1} + \cdots + a_k\lambda^{n-k} + \cdots + a_N\lambda^{n-N} = 0\,.$$

This is known as the characteristic polynomial of the difference equation. The roots of the characteristic polynomial will enable us to solve the difference equation. We will first assume that the roots are all distinct. When the roots are all distinct then there will be N distinct values of λ that will satisfy Equation(7.16). So the solution to Equation(7.16) for distinct roots is as shown in Equation(7.17)

$$y_h(n) = c_1(\lambda_1)^n + c_2(\lambda_2)^n + \cdots + c_N(\lambda_N)^n \tag{7.17}$$

If all the roots are not distinct then there will be repeated roots present. When we have repeated roots the solution of the characteristic equation has to account for these roots in a slightly different manner. Let us assume that we have root λ_1 repeated ε times. The solution of the characteristic equation will be as shown in Equation(7.18)

$$y_h(n) = c_1(\lambda_1)^n + c_1 n(\lambda_1)^n + \cdots + c_1 n^{\varepsilon-1}(\lambda_1)^n + c_2(\lambda_2)^n + \cdots + c_{N-\varepsilon}(\lambda_{N-\varepsilon})^n \tag{7.18}$$

So the solution to the characteristic equation will be either in the form of Equation(7.17) when all the roots are distinct or Equation(7.18) when there are repeated roots present.

Example 7.2

Determine the complete solution for the difference equation $y(n) - 4y(n-2) = 4n$. Assume that the initial conditions are all zero.

Solution 7.2

The characteristic equation for this difference equation is λ^2-4. The roots of this characteristic equation are $\lambda = \pm 2$. So we can write the homogeneous solution as

$$y_h(n) = ?_1(2)^n + ?_2(-2)^n$$

Next we will choose an assumed particular solution. Since this time the input function is n the solution that we will choose will be

$$y_p(n) = \mathrm{A}n + \mathrm{B}$$

We will now substitute this assumed particular solution in the given difference equation to determine the constants A and B. After we substitute the assumed solution in the given difference equation and equate the coefficients of equal powers on n on both sides we get A = -4/3 and B = -32/9. Now that we have these constants we can determine the coefficients x_1 and x_2 using the given initial conditions. So y(0) = 0 and y(1)=0. Using these conditions we can evaluate the difference equation for y(0) and for y(-1) and equate it to 0. Doing this we get $\chi_1 = 4$ and $\chi_2 = -(4/9)$. So the complete solution for the difference equation is

$$y(n) = 4(2)^n - \frac{4}{9}(-2)^n - \frac{4}{3}n - \frac{32}{9}$$

Example 7.3

Determine the complete solution for the difference equation

$$y(n) + 0.5y(n-1) - y(n-2) = 3n\,U(n).$$

Assume that the initial conditions are y(0) = 0 and y(-1)=0.

Solution 7.3

The characteristic equation for this difference equation is $\lambda^2 + 0.5\lambda - 0.5 = 0$. The roots of the characteristic equation are λ = -1 and λ = 0.5. So the Homogeneous solution for this equation is

$$y_h(n) = ?_1(-1)^n + ?_2(0.5)^n$$

Now that we have the Homogeneous solution we will determine the particular solution. Since the driving function is of the first order the particular solution that we choose will also be of the first order. So choose the particular solution to be An+B. Substitute the particular solution in the given equation and equate coefficients to solve for the constants A and B.

$$An + B + 0.5(A(n-1)+B) - 0.5(A(n-2)+B) = 3n$$

$$(A + 0.5A - 0.5A)n = 3n \qquad \Rightarrow A = 3$$

$$(B + 0.5B - 0.5B) - (0.5A - A) = 0 \qquad \Rightarrow B = -1.5$$

$$y_p(n) = 3n - 1.5$$

So the complete solution will be $y(n) = y_h(n) + y_p(n)$

$$y(n) = \lambda_1(-1)^n + \lambda_2(0.5)^n + 3n - 1.5$$

Next when we use the initial conditions we will be able to solve for the two constants.

$$y(0)=0 \qquad \Rightarrow \lambda_1+\lambda_2-1.5=0$$

$$y(-1)=0 \qquad \Rightarrow \lambda_1(-1)^{-1}+\lambda_2(0.5)^{-1}+3(-1)-1.5=0$$

Solving these two equations we get λ_1=–0.5 and λ_2=2. Now that we know all the constants the complete solution is $-0.5(-1)^n + 2(0.5)^n + 3n - 1.5$. Towards the end of the chapter we will solve this same differential equation using Z-Transforms. Compare the method of solution with that solution method.

7.4 DISCRETE TIME CONVOLUTION SUMMATION

When we analyzed continuous time systems we learnt that when a signal goes through a system and an output from that system is obtained the output from the system is the result of convolution between the input and the impulse response of the system. Discrete time systems also behave in pretty much the same manner. The output from a discrete system is the result of convolution between the input and the impulse response of the system. This time however both the input and the impulse response are discrete. They are not continuous so the convolution cannot be computed by integration; the convolution is computed by a summation. The convolution summation is very similar to the convolution integration. We define the discrete time convolution summation by the expression shown in Equation(7.19)

$$\begin{aligned} y(n) &= x(n)*h(n) \\ &= \sum_{k=-\infty}^{\infty} x(k)h(n-k) \\ &= \sum_{k=-\infty}^{\infty} h(k)x(n-k) \end{aligned} \tag{7.19}$$

The convolution sum is evaluated in pretty much the same manner as the convolution integration. An example will make it clear.

Example 7.4

Determine the convolution of the discrete input signal {u(n)-u(n-4)} with the impulse response $e^{-n}u(n)$.

Solution 7.4

We will demonstrate the convolution both graphically as well as in a tabular manner. Examine Figure 7.7.

We begin by writing the input function as it appears and flipping the impulse response function. The two functions to be convolved are drawn at the top of the figure. The table below the figure

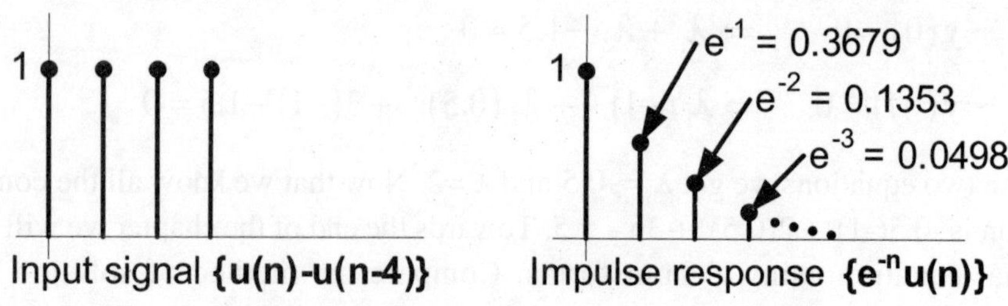

Convolve these two functions together

		1	1	1	1	Result of convolution
n=0	$e^{-4}\ e^{-3}\ e^{-2}\ e^{-1}$	e^{-0}				1
n=1	$\cdots e^{-4}\ e^{-3}\ e^{-2}$	e^{-1}	e^{-0}			1.3679
n=2	$\cdots e^{-4}\ e^{-3}$	e^{-2}	e^{-1}	e^{-0}		1.5032
n=3	$\cdots e^{-4}$	e^{-3}	e^{-2}	e^{-1}	e^{-0}	1.5530
n=4	$\cdots$	e^{-4}	e^{-3}	e^{-2}	e^{-1}	0.5713
n=5		$\cdots$	e^{-4}	e^{-3}	e^{-2}	0.21017
n=6			$\cdots$	e^{-4}	e^{-3}	0.07732
n=7				$\cdots$	e^{-4}	0.028444
n=8					$\cdots$	0.010464

Convolution is carried out by multiplying the numbers in the columns together and then adding the results.

Figure 7.7: Discrete convolution

lists the input function in the top of the columns and the impulse function is flipped and written to the left of the table. For n=0 there is an overlap of only one sample. Whenever we have an overlap of the two functions we multiply the corresponding samples together and add all the results of multiplication. For our example the multiplication proceeds as shown in the table. The table shows the results only for the first 9 steps.

7.5 THE Z-TRANSFORM SUMMATION

In the Equation(7.11) we have seen that when an analog signal is impulse sampled its spectrum is several replicas of the spectrum of the continuous time signal. In Equation(7.9) we showed the relation between the sampled signal and the continuous time signal in the time domain. We wish to find the Laplace transform of the infinite sum on the right hand side of Equation(7.9). This we do in Equation(7.20), in this equation since x(nT) is independent of the variable 't' we can take it out of the integral when we are attempting to find the Laplace. In Equation(7.20) the term $x_s(t)$ represents the sampled version of the signal x(t).

$$L\left[x_s(t)\right] = X_s(s) = L\left[\sum_{n=-\infty}^{\infty} x(nT)\delta(t-nT)\right] \tag{7.20}$$

$$X_s(s) = \int_0^{\infty} \sum_{n=-\infty}^{\infty} x(nT)\delta(t-nT)e^{-st}\,dt = \sum_{n=-\infty}^{\infty} x(nT)\int_0^{\infty}\delta(t-nT)e^{-st}\,dt$$

The last term in Equation(7.20) is the integral of an impulse multiplied by an exponential. This integral evaluates to e^{-snT} due to the property of the impulse function. So the Laplace transform of the sampled signal evaluates to Equation(7.21). Generally the variable Z is substituted for e^{sT} so we get the Z-Transform summation as shown in Equation(7.21). In Equation(7.21) X(z) is the Z-Transform of the sequence x(nT). In this example the sequence x(nT) was obtained by sampling the analog signal x(t). This however is not a necessity to obtain the Z-Transform. Equation(7.21) is the Z-Transform of any sequence of numbers. Further we must remember that the Z-Transform is only obtained for a sequence of discrete numbers or a sequence of sampled values of an analog signal hence we have dropped the subscript 's' that indicated that the sequence was obtained by sampling an analog signal.

$$X_s(s) = \sum_{n=-\infty}^{\infty} x(nT)e^{-snT}$$

$$X(z) = \sum_{n=-\infty}^{\infty} x(nT)z^{-n} = \sum_{n=-\infty}^{\infty} x(nT)z^{-n} \tag{7.21}$$

X(z) the Z-Transform of x(t) is an ordered number sequence. In an ordered number sequence each number has a magnitude and a position. This is so also with a Z-Transform sequence. In Equation(7.21) the right hand side shows this specifically. Each number on the right hand side of Equation(7.21) corresponds to a different value of n. So for any value of n the term x(nT) represents the magnitude of the number and the term z^{-n} represents the position of the number in the sequence. Sometimes this is referred to as sample number as x(nT) corresponds to the nth sample of the analog sequence x(t).

So say for example we have an analog sequence $x(t)=3e^{-2t}Cos(6t)$. If we sample this sequence with the sampling interval being T = 0.01, then the fifth sample x(4T) = x(0.04) = 2.94059 (remember that the first sample is at t=0) and this would be identified in the Z-Transform of x(t) as $2.94059z^{-4}$. The summation in Equation(7.21) that defines the Z-Transform extends from $-\infty$ to $+\infty$. This summation of the Z-Transform then defines the two sided Z Transform and is known as a *two sided* or a *bilateral* Z-Transform. If the summation extended from 0 to $+\infty$ then the defined Z Transform would be known as a one sided or a unilateral Z-Transform.

In Chapter 5 we saw that the Laplace Transform operator 's' is a complex variable. It has a real part and an imaginary part. So we can interpret the 'z' operator in the Z-Transform given in Equation(7.21) as shown in Equation(7.22). In Equation(7.22) we see that the z-operator also tells us the location of the number in the z-plane. The magnitude of z tells us how far from the origin the number is located in the z-plane and the phase tells us the angle of rotation with reference to the positive x-axis. This idea will become more clear when we see how the various regions of the s-plane map into the different regions in the z-plane. Refer to Figure 7.8.

$$z = e^{sT} = e^{(\sigma + j\omega)t} = e^{\sigma t} e^{j\omega t} = |z| \underline{/z} \tag{7.22}$$

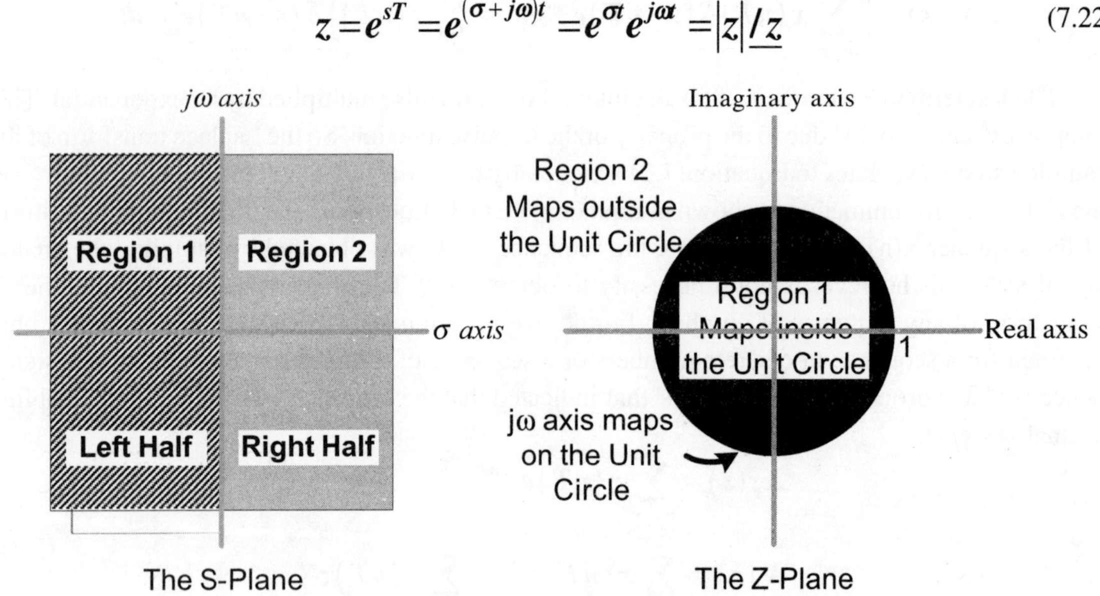

Figure 7.8: The mapping from the s-plane to the z-plane

Region 1:

This region represents the left half of the s-plane in Figure 7.8. In this region the real part of s is negative. With the real part of s negative the magnitude of z which is $e^{\sigma t}$ is always less than 1. In this region ω can be either positive or negative. The phase of z, which is $e^{j\omega t}$ corresponds to rotation in the z-plane will vary between ±180 degrees. The rotation can be either positive or negative depending on the value of ω. So every point in the left half of the s-plane maps into the interior of a circle of radius 1 and centered at the origin, further the entire imaginary axis from the s-plane maps on to the unit circle in the z-plane; the origin from the s-plane maps to the point 1+j0; and the negative real axis from the s-plane maps to the diameter of the unit circle in the z-plane along the real axis. *Thus the entire left half of the s-plane maps to the inside of the unit circle in the z-plane.*

Region 2:

This region corresponds to the right half of the s-plane in Figure 7.8. In this region the real part of s is positive. With the real part of s positive the magnitude of z which is $e^{\sigma t}$ is always greater than 1. In this region ω can be either positive or negative. This means the phase of z, which is $e^{j\omega t}$ corresponds to rotation in the z-plane will vary between ±180 degrees. The rotation can be either positive or negative depending on the value of ω. So every point in the right half of the s-plane maps into the exterior of a circle of radius 1 and centered at the origin. The entire imaginary axis from the s-plane maps on to the unit circle in the z-plane, this is the dividing line between the left half of the s-plane and the right half of the s-plane. The positive real axis is mapped from z=1+j0 to z=-1+j0 but to the exterior of the unit circle.

As we have just seen that $e^{j\omega t}$ represents rotation in the z-plane with the magnitude of z being determined by $e^{\sigma t}$. Since rotation of say $\omega = \omega_1$ or $\omega = \omega_1 + 2\pi$ or $\omega = \omega_1 + 2n\pi$ amounts to the same angle with respect to the positive real axis, the vector with the same σ value but many different angles will fall on top of each other. So a point in the s-plane at $s_1 = -5+j3$ and another point $s_2 = -5+j(3+2\pi)$ will be coincident on each other in the z-plane as they both have the same σ value and their ω values differ by an integral multiple of 2π. With this discussion we can visualize the s-plane divided into infinitely many strips infinite in width and 2π in height. Each one of these strips maps identically one on top of the other strips as the ω values change.

Recall now the discussion that we had about the stability of systems. When the poles of the system lie in the left half of the s-plane then the poles and the system is stable. When the poles of the system lie on the $j\omega$ axis in the s-plane the poles and the system have oscillatory tendency. When the poles of a system lie in the right half of the s-plane the poles and the system are considered unstable. In the previous paragraph we just saw that the left half of the s-plane maps into the inside of the unit circle in the z-plane. So in the z-plane the region inside the unit circle corresponds to the stable region, the unit circle itself corresponds to the oscillatory condition and the region outside the unit circle corresponds to the unstable region.

Example 7.5

Determine the Z-Transform of the sequence defined as follows:

$$x(n) = \begin{cases} 0 & n \leq 0 \\ 2 & n = 1 \\ 1 & n = 2 \\ 3 & n = 3 \\ 1 & n = 4 \\ 0 & n \geq 5 \end{cases}$$

Solution 7.5

From the definition of Z Transform we can write

$$\mathbf{X(z) = 2z^{-1} + 1z^{-2} + 3z^{-3} + 1z^{-4}}$$

This example clearly demonstrates that the Z-transform of a sequence refers to the position of the number in the sequence.

Example 7.6

Determine the Z-Transform of the sequence a^n; $n \geq 0$.

Solution 7.6

We will determine the Z-transform of this sequence using the definition. This shown in Equation(7.23)

$$X(z) = \sum_{0}^{\infty} a^n z^{-n} = \sum_{0}^{\infty} \left(az^{-1}\right)^n \tag{7.23}$$

This series can be written in a closed form only if $az^{-1} < 1$

$$= \frac{1}{1 - az^{-1}} = \frac{z}{z - a}$$

This example illustrates that the Z-transform is also a complex function. Here we see that the Z-transform has a zero at z=0 and a pole at z=a.

7.6 THE REGION OF CONVERGENCE OF THE Z-TRANSFORM SUMMATION

The Z-Transform as defined in Equation(7.21) is in general an infinite power series, depending on the sequence x(nT). If we consider the Equation(7.21) as an operator then we can visualize the Z-Transform as something that converts a sequence x(nT) into a function of z. With this interpretation we can think of z as a complex variable and the Z-Transform with its power series representation. This is what we saw in Example 7.5 and in Equation(7.23). Equation(7.23) does not converge for all values of z, it is valid only when $a < z$. Thus the sequence has a region of convergence. All the values of the variable z for which the sequence of the Z-Transform converges together make up the *Region of Convergence* (ROC). The ROC of the Z-Transform is dependent only on the magnitude of z not the phase of z, so for convergence we need $|X(z)| < \infty$ so we must have the inequality in Equation(7.24) to hold.

$$\sum_{n=-\infty}^{\infty} |x[n]| \bullet \left|z^{-n}\right| < \infty \tag{7.24}$$

The ROC of the Z-Transform in Equation(7.24) is all the values of z such that the inequality holds true. So if for some value of z say $z = z_1$ the inequality in Equation(7.24) holds, then the inequality will hold true for every value of z on a circle with radius $z = z_1$. Thus the ROC in the Z-domain is circular and it grows as a circle or shrinks as a circle. The ROC may extend from some value at $z = z_1$ all the way to $z = \infty$, or it may extend from $z = 0$ to some value $z = z_1$ or it may be a ring starting at $z = z_1$ and ending at $z = z_2$. The three possible shapes are shown in Figure 7.9. So the ROC is always circular with its center at the origin.

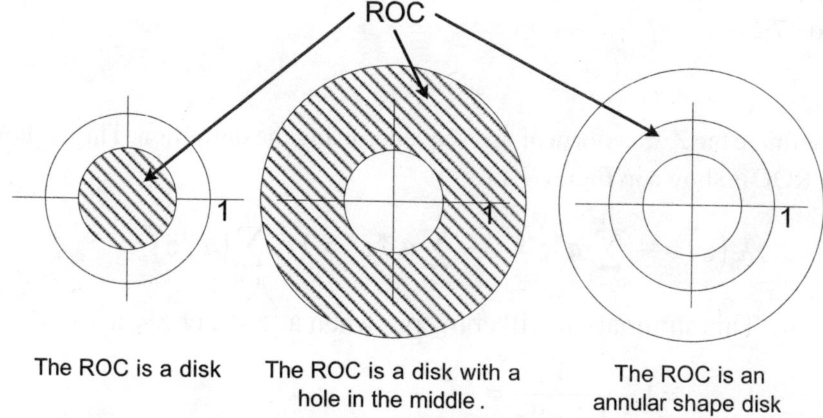

Figure 7.9: Various possible shapes for the Region of Convergence (ROC)

To determine the ROC we make use of the rules for the summation of a sequence and the value of z that just makes the inequality in Equation(7.24) hold true. When we find the value of z that just does not satisfy Equation(7.24) we have identified the boundary of the ROC. In Example 7.5 we determined the ROC for the Z-transform of the sequence a^n; $n \geq 0$. The sequence summation converged only when $az^{-1}<1$. From this we were able to write the ROC as $a < z$ or all the values of z that are greater than the constant a. This is shown in Figure 7.10 and the ROC is the entire Z-plane where $|z| > a$.

Remember that the Z-transform is not complete till you have specified the region of convergence. To emphasize this fact let us determine another Z-transform and the region of convergence in Example 7.6. Then compare the result of this example with the result of Example 7.5.

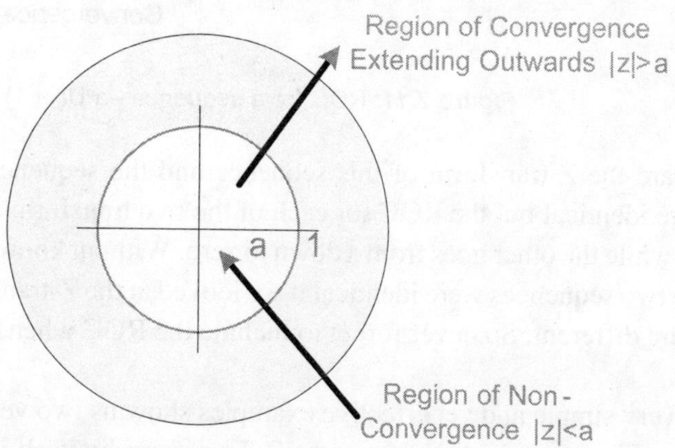

Figure 7.10: ROC for a sequence $a^n u(n)$

Example 7.7

Determine the Z-transform of the sequence $-a^n$; but this time we will make the sequence active when $n \leq -1$. Thus this sequence is a non causal sequence. The Z-Transform of this sequence is given in Equation(7.25)

Solution 7.7

We will determine the Z-transform of this sequence using the definition. This is shown in Equation(7.25). The ROC is shown in Figure 7.11.

$$X(z) = -\sum_{n=-\infty}^{-1} a^n z^{-n} = -\sum_{n=1}^{\infty} a^{-n} z^n = 1 - \sum_{n=0}^{\infty} \left(a^{-1}z\right)^n \tag{7.25}$$

This summation will converge when $a^{-1}z < 1$ or $z < a$

$$= 1 - \frac{1}{1 - a^{-1}z} = \frac{z}{z - a}$$

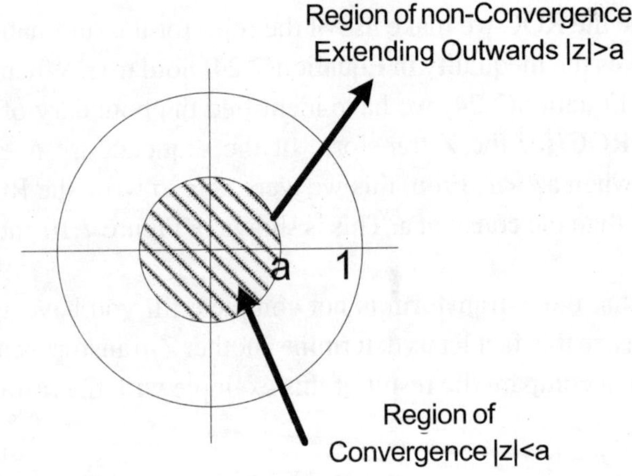

Figure 7.11: ROC for a sequence $-a^nU(-n-1)$

Now compare the Z-transform of this sequence and the sequence in Example 7.5. The two Z-transforms are identical but the ROC for each of the two transforms is different. One goes from a out to infinity while the other goes from a down to zero. Without knowing the ROC we would have thought that the two sequences were identical if we looked at the Z-transform only yet we know that the sequences are different. So never forget to include the ROC when you specify the Z-transform of any function.

These two very simple and yet effective examples show us two very important peculiarities of the Z-Transform. First, that the function of the Z-Transform by itself is not unique; more than one sequence may have the same Z-Transform function. Second, you must always specify the ROC of the Z-Transform else you have left out some very vital information. The Z-Transform expression and the ROC taken together are unique to the sequence.

Example 7.8

Determine the ROC and the Z-Transform for the sequence x[n] = $(½)^n$u[n] + $(-S!)^n$u[n].

Solution 7.8

Look at Equation(7.26). In order to determine the ROC of this function we get two conditions and they both have to be satisfied simultaneously. The two conditions are |z| > ½ and |z| >$^1/_3$. So the ROC for this sequence is |z| > ½ since this condition applies to both the sequences. The ROC is shown in Figure 7.12.

$$X(z)=\sum_{n=0}^{\infty}\left(\tfrac{1}{2}z^{-1}\right)^n+\sum_{n=0}^{\infty}\left(-\tfrac{1}{3}z^{-1}\right)^n=\frac{z}{z-\frac{1}{2}}+\frac{z}{z+\frac{1}{3}} \tag{7.26}$$

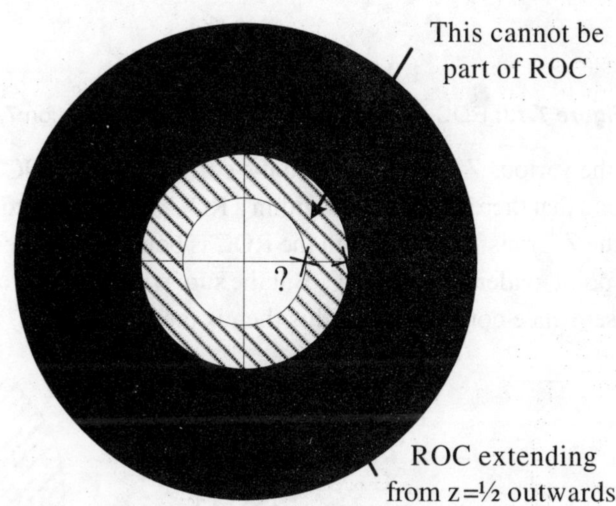

Figure 7.12: ROC in the Z-Plane for function in Equation 7.27

Example 7.9

Determine the ROC and the Z-Transform for the sequence x[n] = $(^3/_8)^n$u[n] – $(½)^n$u[-n-1].

Solution 7.9

Look at Equation(7.27). The ROC of the sequence is an annular ring that extends from z = $^3/_8$ to z = ½. This ROC is shown in Figure 7.13.

$$X(z)=\sum_{0}^{\infty}\left(\tfrac{3}{8}z^{-1}\right)^n-\sum_{-\infty}^{-1}\left(\tfrac{1}{2}z^{-1}\right)^n=\left.\frac{z}{z-\frac{3}{8}}\right|_{ROC\to z>\frac{3}{8}}+\left.\frac{z}{z-\frac{1}{2}}\right|_{ROC\to z<\frac{1}{2}} \tag{7.27}$$

$$X(z) = \left.\frac{z(16z-7)}{8\left(z-\frac{3}{8}\right)\left(z-\frac{1}{2}\right)}\right|_{ROC \rightarrow \frac{3}{8}<z<\frac{1}{2}}$$

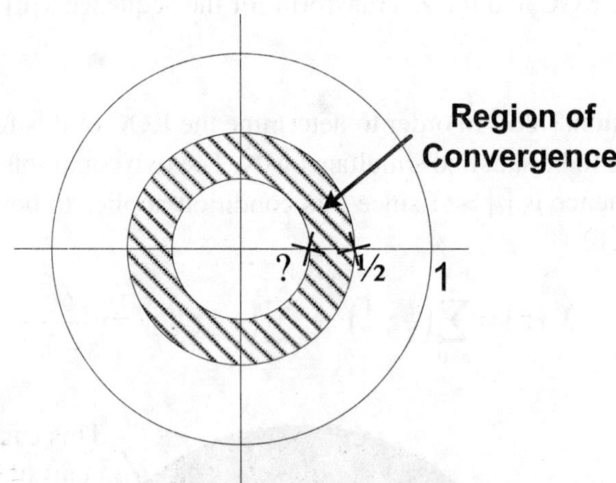

Figure 7.13: ROC in the Z-Plane for function in Equation 7.27

When we look at the various Z-transforms and the corresponding ROC's we find that the ROC is bounded by a pole, and that there are no poles within a ROC. So one way to find the ROC is to look at where the poles of the Z-Transform lay. Then the ROC is bounded by one or more of those poles. It gives you a starting point to identify the ROC. But the sure way is to look at the sequence and find the region where the sequence converges and this then is the ROC.

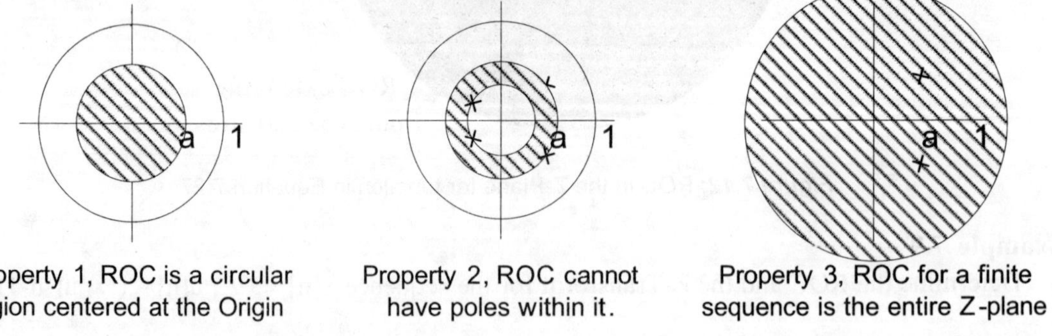

Figure 7.14: ROC in the Z-Plane as discussed in Properties 1, 2 and 3

7.6.1 Properties of the ROC of the Z-Transform

In the previous section we have just seen that the Z-Transform is not complete without specifying the ROC. The ROC of the Z-Transform has some special properties. Knowing these properties of the ROC will enable us to better understand the Z-Transform. Here is a list of the properties of the Z-Transform. The properties are demonstrated in Figures 7.14 and 7.15.

1. The ROC is either a disk, or a ring in the Z-plane centered at the origin.
2. The ROC cannot contain any poles of the Z-Transfer function. It may however contain zeros of the transfer function within it.
3. If x(n) is a finite sequence, say from $n = N_1$, to $n = N_2$ both $N_1 < \infty$ and $N_2 < \infty$ then the ROC is the entire Z-plane except may be at $z = 0$ or at $z = \infty$.
4. *Right Handed Sequence*: A sequence that is zero from $n = -\infty$ to $n = N_1 < \infty$ has its ROC that extends outwards from its outermost pole to infinity possibly including $z = \infty$.
5. *Left Handed Sequence*: A sequence that is zero from $n = N_1 < \infty$ to $n = \infty$ has its ROC that extends inwards from its innermost pole to zero possibly including $z = 0$.
6. *A Two Sided Sequence* A sequence that extends from $n = -\infty$ to $n = +\infty$ will have its ROC as a disk that is bounded on the two sides (inner circle and the outer circle) by poles, at the same time the disk does not contain any poles within it.

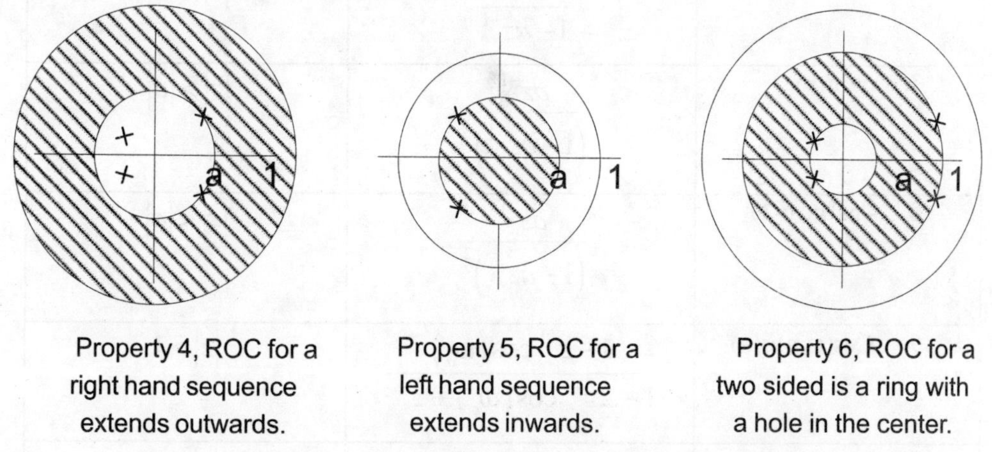

Property 4, ROC for a right hand sequence extends outwards.

Property 5, ROC for a left hand sequence extends inwards.

Property 6, ROC for a two sided is a ring with a hole in the center.

Figure 7.15: ROC in the Z-Plane as discussed in Properties 4, 5 and 6

7.6.2 The Z-Transform of Simple Functions

In the preceding two sections we started with the definition of the Z-Transform and obtained the two sided summation. Then using the property of the function to determine where the function has non zero values and using the properties of the sequence summation we can determine the closed form expression for the Z-Transform. The table below gives us several Z-Transform pairs for some simple functions and their region of convergence.

Sequence	Z-Transform	ROC
1. $\delta(n)$	1	All Z-Plane
2. $u(n)$	$\frac{1}{1-z^{-1}}$	$\lvert z\rvert > 1$
3. $-u(-n-1)$	$\frac{1}{1-z^{-1}}$	$\lvert z\rvert < 1$
4. $\delta(n-m)$	z^{-m}	All Z except 0 if $m > 0$ or ∞ if $m < 0$
5. $a^n u(n)$	$\frac{1}{1-az^{-1}}$	$\lvert z\rvert > \lvert a\rvert$
6. $-a^n u(-n-1)$	$\frac{1}{1-az^{-1}}$	$\lvert z\rvert < \lvert a\rvert$
7. $na^n u(n)$	$\frac{az^{-1}}{\left(1-az^{-1}\right)^2}$	$\lvert z\rvert > \lvert a\rvert$
8. $-na^n u(-n-1)$	$\frac{az^{-1}}{\left(1-az^{-1}\right)^2}$	$\lvert z\rvert < \lvert a\rvert$
9. $\text{Cos}(\omega_o n)u(n)$	$\frac{1-z^{-1}\cos(\omega_o)}{1-2z^{-1}\cos(\omega_o)+z^{-2}}$	$\lvert z\rvert > 1$
10. $\text{Sin}(\omega_o n)u(n)$	$\frac{z^{-1}\sin(\omega_o)}{1-2z^{-1}\cos(\omega_o)+z^{-2}}$	$\lvert z\rvert > 1$
11. $r^n\text{Cos}(\omega_o n)u(n)$	$\frac{1-rz^{-1}\cos(\omega_o)}{1-2rz^{-1}\cos(\omega_o)+r^2z^{-2}}$	$\lvert z\rvert > r$
12. $r^n\text{Sin}(\omega_o n)u(n)$	$\frac{rz^{-1}\sin(\omega_o)}{1-2rz^{-1}\cos(\omega_o)+r^2z^{-2}}$	$\lvert z\rvert > r$

7.7 PROPERTIES OF THE Z-TRANSFORM

Just like the Laplace transform properties helped us to visualize and extend the Laplace transform pairs the Z-Transform properties will also give us further insight to the Z-Transform and allow us to extend the Z-Transform pairs. The Z-Transform properties are similar to the Laplace Transform properties.

$$ax_1(n)+bx_2(n) \overset{z}{\Leftrightarrow} aX_1(z)+bX_2(z) \qquad ROC \Rightarrow R_{x_1} \cap R_{x_2} \tag{7.28}$$

(1) Linearity:

The Z-Transform is a linear transform as shown in Equation(7.28). The Linearity property is easily proved by the definition of the Z-Transform as shown in Equation(7.29). The ROC has now to satisfy both the sequences together. So the ROC for the composite sequence is the intersection of the two ROC's. This assumes that there are no pole zero cancellations when the two Z-Transforms are combined together. If there is a pole zero cancellation then the ROC of the combination could be larger than the two individual ROC's.

$$\begin{aligned} Z\left(ax_1(n)+bx_2(n)\right) &= \sum_{n=-\infty}^{\infty} \left(ax_1(n)+bx_2(n)\right)z^{-n} \\ &= \sum_{n=-\infty}^{\infty} ax_1(n)z^{-n} + \sum_{n=-\infty}^{\infty} bx_2(n)z^{-n} \\ &= aX_1(z)+bX_2(z) \end{aligned} \tag{7.29}$$

(2) Shift in Time:

When the sequence x(n) is shifted in time by say n_0 samples then the Z-Transform of the shifted sequence gets multiplied by z^{-n_0} which places either n_0 poles or zeros depending on the sign of n_0. The sign of n_0 tells us whether the sequence is shifted left or to the right.

$$x(n-n_o) \overset{z}{\Leftrightarrow} z^{-n_o} X(z) \qquad ROC \Rightarrow R_x \ (\pm\, \mathbf{z}=\mathbf{0} \text{ or } \mathbf{z}=\infty) \tag{7.30}$$

The proof of this property directly follows from the definition of the Z-Transform definition. Remember that the quantity n_0 is an integer, if it is a positive integer then the sequence x(n) is shifted right, if it is negative then the sequence x(n) is shifted left. This shifting adds poles to the new Z-Transform either at the origin or at infinity. This change of poles can change the ROC at either the origin or at infinity. The proof is simple and obtained in a straight forward manner by substituting $m = n - n_0$ as given in Equation(7.31).

$$\begin{aligned} Z\left[x(n-n_o)\right] &= \sum_{n=-\infty}^{\infty} x(n-n_o)z^{-n} \qquad \textbf{Let } m = n - n_o \\ &= \sum_{m=-\infty}^{\infty} x(m) z^{-(m+n_o)} \end{aligned} \tag{7.31}$$

$$= z^{-n_o} \sum_{m=-\infty}^{\infty} x(m) z^{-m}$$

$$= z^{-n_o} X(z) \qquad ROC \Rightarrow R_x \ (\pm \mathbf{z=0 \ or \ z=\infty})$$

(3) Multiplication by an Exponential Sequence:

The effect of multiplying the sequence x(n) by a^n is to scale the pole zero locations of the sequence x(n) by the scale factor 'a'. Since the pole zero locations are scaled by the scaling factor a the ROC is also scaled by the scaling factor 'a'.

$$a^n x(n) \overset{z}{\Leftrightarrow} X(z/a) \qquad ROC \Rightarrow |a| R_x \tag{7.32}$$

If 'a' is a positive real number then this property can be viewed as a shrinking or the expanding of the ROC and the entire z-plane. If 'a' is complex with magnitude of a = 1 then this property corresponds to the rotation in the z-plane. Rotation in the z-plane can be interpreted as a frequency shift or a modulation in the z-plane. The proof of this property directly follows from the definition of the Z-Transform definition. In the definition we combine all the terms that are raised to the power of n and re-write the Z-Transform definition. The proof is given in Equation(7.33).

$$Z\left[a^n x(n)\right] = \sum_{n=-\infty}^{\infty} a^n x(n) z^{-n}$$

$$= \sum_{n=-\infty}^{\infty} x(n) \left(a^{-1} z\right)^{-n} \tag{7.33}$$

$$= X\left(a^{-1} z\right) = X\left(\frac{z}{a}\right) \qquad ROC \Rightarrow |a| R_x$$

(4) Differentiation in the Z domain:

The effect of multiplying the sequence x(n) by n is to differentiate the Z-Transform of the sequence. The ROC of this sequence is the same as that of the original sequence with the possible addition or the deletion of the ROC at Z = 0 or at z = ∞.

$$x(n) \overset{z}{\Leftrightarrow} -z \frac{dX(z)}{dz} \qquad ROC \Rightarrow R_x \ (\pm \mathbf{z=0 \ or \ z=\infty}) \tag{7.34}$$

The proof of this property directly follows from the definition of the Z-Transform definition. We begin by differentiating the Z-Transform of x(n). Then we rearrange the various terms to get the result indicated by Equation(7.34). The proof is given in Equation(7.35)

$$X(z) = \sum_{n=-\infty}^{\infty} x(n) z^{-n}$$

$$\frac{dX(z)}{dz} = \sum_{n=-\infty}^{\infty} -nx(n) (z)^{-n-1} \tag{7.35}$$

$$\frac{dX(z)}{dz} = z^{-1}\sum_{n=-\infty}^{\infty} -nx(n)(z)^{-n}$$

$$-z\frac{dX(z)}{dz} = \underbrace{\sum_{n=-\infty}^{\infty} nx(n)(z)^{-n}}_{\text{Definition of Z-Transform of nx(n)}} = Z(nx(n))$$

(5) Time Reversal:

When the sequence is flipped in the time domain or the sequence is run backward then the poles and the zeros of the new sequence are the reciprocals of the poles and the zeros of the original sequence.

$$x(-n) \overset{z}{\Leftrightarrow} X\left(\frac{1}{z}\right) \qquad ROC \Rightarrow \frac{1}{R_x} \tag{7.36}$$

The proof of this property directly follows from the definition of the Z-Transform definition. The ROC $1/R_x$ implies that the ROC is inverted. So if say a point z_a lies in the ROC of R_x then $1/z_a$ lies in the ROC of $1/R_x$. We can state this as follows: if the ROC of x(n) is R_x which is ➔ $r_R < z < r_L$ then the ROC of x(-n) is $1/R_x$ is ➔ $1/r_L < z < 1/r_R$. The proof is given in Equation(7.37).

$$Z[x(-n)] = \sum_{n=-\infty}^{\infty} x(-n)z^{-n} \qquad \text{Let } m = -n$$

$$= \sum_{m=-\infty}^{\infty} x(m)\left(z^{-1}\right)^{-m} \tag{7.37}$$

$$= X\left(z^{-1}\right) = X\left(\frac{1}{z}\right) \qquad ROC \Rightarrow \frac{1}{R_x}$$

(6) Convolution of Sequence:

When a sequence is the input to a discrete time system the output of the system is the convolution of the two sequences (the input and the system sequence). When the two sequences are convolved together their Z-Transforms are multiplied together

$$x_1(n) * x_2(n) \overset{z}{\Leftrightarrow} X_1(z)X_2(z) \qquad ROC \Rightarrow R_1 \cap R_2 \tag{7.38}$$

The proof of this property is a little tricky but it follows from the definition of the Z-Transform of the convolution. The ROC $R_1 \cap R_2$ implies that the ROC is the intersection of the two ROC's. The ROC defined as the intersection is the ROC in general. There may be occasions when the ROC may be larger. This will happen if a pole at the edge of the ROC of one function is canceled by a zero of another function then the ROC may be larger. The proof is given in Equation 7.39.

$$Z[y(n)] = Z[x_1(n) * x_2(n)] = \sum_{n=-\infty}^{\infty} y(n) z^{-n} = \sum_{n=-\infty}^{\infty}\left[\sum_{k=-\infty}^{\infty} x_1(k) x_2(n-k)\right] z^{-n}$$

Inter - change the order of the two summations to get

$$Y(z) = \sum_{k=-\infty}^{\infty} x_1(k)\left[\sum_{n=-\infty}^{\infty} x_2(n-k)\right] z^{-n} \qquad \text{Let } m = n - k \tag{7.39}$$

$$Y(z) = \sum_{k=-\infty}^{\infty} x_1(k) z^{-k} \sum_{m=-\infty}^{\infty} x_2(m) z^{-m} = X_1(z) X_2(z) \qquad ROC \Rightarrow R_1 \cap R_2$$

7.8 THE INVERSE OF THE Z-TRANSFORM

When we analyzed systems with the Laplace transforms the method of solution was to transform the time domain system or function to the Laplace domain, perform the analysis in the Laplace domain and then invert the solution back to the time domain. We will follow this same procedure with the Z-Transform also. Since we need to obtain the inverse transform to get back to the time domain we will study how to get the inverse transform first. There are several formal and informal methods to determine the inverse of the Z-domain function. Here we will examine two different methods, one is the familiar partial fraction expansion and table look up and the other one is very intuitive.

7.8.1 Inverse Z-Transform by Partial Fraction Expansion:

Just as we used partial fraction expansion to find the inverse Laplace transform of an S-domain function that was not in our inverse transform tables we can use partial fraction expansion to find the inverse transform of a Z domain function that is not in our inverse transform tables. The method that we will follow applies to a rational fraction. So the first step is always to begin with a rational fraction. You can always convert a general fraction to a rational fraction by simply dividing the numerator by the denominator. The long division process continues till the numerator polynomial of the remainder is of one degree less than the denominator polynomial.

The long division results in power terms and a rational fraction. The coefficients of the power terms represent the inverse Z transform which will shift the entire Z-Transform sequence. After you have done the necessary long division and you have the denominator that has a higher degree than the numerator then you have a rational fraction and you can begin the method. From here on we will assume that you have the Z-domain function as a rational fraction.

$$X(z) = \frac{b_0 \prod_{k=1}^{M}\left(1 - c_k z^{-1}\right)}{a_0 \prod_{k=1}^{N}\left(1 - p_k z^{-1}\right)} \quad \text{or} \quad X(z) = \frac{b_0 \prod_{k=1}^{M}\left(z - c_k\right)}{a_0 \prod_{k=1}^{N}\left(z - p_k\right)} \tag{7.40}$$

The Z-domain functions are written with either z as the variable or with z^{-1} as the variable. You will come across both these forms but the method to determine the inverse is the same. If you are comfortable using only one form then you can always convert one form to the other by multiplying both the numerator and the denominator by an appropriate (highest) power of z. Then you are always dealing with just one form that you are comfortable with.

To obtain the partial fraction expansion we write the z-domain transfer function in one of the two forms shown in Equation(7.40). Both these forms are used to represent the pole zero function in the z-domain. Starting at either one of these two expressions we can re-write the function as partial fractions. The partial fractions in both the formats at the respective pole locations in the z-domain are shown in Equation(7.41).

$$X(z)=\sum_{k=1}^{N}\frac{A_k}{\left(1-p_k z^{-1}\right)} \quad \text{or} \quad X(z)=\sum_{k=1}^{N}\frac{A_k}{\left(z-p_k\right)} \tag{7.41}$$

Now that we have X(z) written in partial fraction form we can proceed to evaluate the residues. The residues in both the cases are the coefficients A_k's. Once we have each of the residues evaluated the inverse of the Z-domain function can be determined by looking up the Z-transform table. The evaluation of the residues is done in the same manner as we did the evaluation of the residues for the Laplace transform. This is shown in Equation(7.42) for both the forms of writing the Z-domain function.

$$A_k=(1-p_k z^{-1})X(z)\Big|_{z^{-1}=p_k} \quad \text{or} \quad A_k=(z-p_k)X(z)\Big|_{z=p_k} \tag{7.42}$$

Sometimes X(z) may have multiple order poles. If X(z) has multiple order poles then the partial fraction expansion for the two forms will be as shown in Equation(7.43). From Equation(7.43) we see that when we have multiple poles of order S we have to evaluate the C_m residues for each of the S poles. I am sure that you remember from our studies about the Laplace Transform the evaluation of the residues for the multiple poles is slightly different from the evaluation of the simple residues. This different method is shown for you in Equation(7.44) for both the forms in which Z-Transforms are generally written.

$$\begin{aligned} X(z)&=\sum_{k=1}^{K}\frac{A_k}{(1-p_k z^{-1})}+\sum_{m=1}^{S}\frac{C_m}{\left(1-p_k z^{-1}\right)^m} \\ X(z)&=\sum_{k=1}^{K}\frac{A_k}{(z-p_k)}+\sum_{m=1}^{S}\frac{C_m}{\left(z-p_k\right)^m} \end{aligned} \tag{7.43}$$

$$C_{s-k}=\frac{1}{k!(-p_k)^k}\left\{\frac{d^k\left[\left(1-p_k z^{-1}\right)^s X(z)\right]}{d\left(z^{-1}\right)^k}\right\}\Bigg|_{z^{-1}=p_k} \tag{7.44}$$

$$C_{s-k}=\frac{1}{k!}\left\{\frac{d^k\left[\left(z-p_k\right)^s X(z)\right]}{dz^k}\right\}\Bigg|_{z=p_k}$$

Once we have determined the residue at all the poles then the inverse transform is determined by looking up the corresponding pairs in the Inverse Transform Table.

Example 7.10

Determine the inverse Z-transform of the function

$$X(z)=\frac{1}{1-z^{-1}+0.16z^{-2}} \qquad ROC=\begin{cases}|z|>0.8\\|z|<0.2\end{cases}$$

Solution 7.10

This time we are given two different expressions for the ROC for the same Z-domain function. So this is like two separate examples. Consider Case 1 when $|z|>0.8$ and Case 2 when $|z|<0.2$.

Case 1: ROC $|z|>0.8$ We first write X(z) as partial fraction and determine the residues for the partial fractions. This is done in Equation(7.45)

$$X(z)=\frac{1}{1-z^{-1}+0.16z^{-1}}=\frac{A}{1-0.8z^{-1}}+\frac{B}{1-0.2z^{-1}}$$

$$A=\frac{1}{1-0.2z^{-1}}\Bigg|_{z^{-1}=1.25}=1.3333$$

$$B=\frac{1}{1-0.8z^{-1}}\Bigg|_{z^{-1}=5}=-0.3333$$

$$X(z)=\frac{1.333}{1-0.8z^{-1}}-\frac{0.333}{1-0.2z^{-1}} \qquad (7.45)$$

From Equation(7.45) we can directly write the inverse transform since both the sequences are right sequences as $x(n) = [1.333(0.8)^n-0.333(0.2)^n]u(n)$.

Case 2: ROC $|z|<0.2$ We first write X(z) as partial fraction and determine the residues for the partial fractions. This is done in Equation(7.45). Notice that the residues and the partial fraction expansion are not affected by the change in the ROC. From Equation we can directly write the inverse transform as $x(n) = [-1.333(0.8)^n+0.333(0.2)^n]u(-n-1)$ since both the sequences are left sequences (Examine Example 7.7 and Equation (7.25)).

7.8.2 Inverse Z-Transform by Long Division:

We have seen that the Z-Transform of a function can also be written by definition as

$$X(z) = \sum x(n)\, z^{-n}\,.$$

On expanding the right hand side we get Equation(7.46). So if we can manipulate the z-domain expression in the form shown in Equation(7.46) the inverse z-transform can be obtained from inspection. The coefficients of the z^{-n} are the inverse z-transform values at the corresponding sample points. Rewriting X(z) in the form shown in Equation(7.46) is easily done by long division. Before long division is carried out though, we usually write the X(z) expression in terms of z^{-1} rather than in terms of z. Once the expression in X(z) is written as an expression of z^{-1} then the numerator polynomial is divided by the denominator polynomial to get the expression as shown in Equation(7.46).

$$x(z) = x(0) + x(1)z^{-1} + x(2)z^{-2} + x(3)z^{-3} + \cdots \tag{7.46}$$

The long division can be continued for as many terms as we are interested in. This method is the easiest way of finding the inverse z-transform. Even though this method is easy it has one major drawback. This method in general will not give us a result in a closed form expression for the inverse Z-Transform. Many times however the first few terms are sufficient to determine the time domain behavior of the system. Take the case where the time domain system is well behaved and the response approaches an asymptote. In this case the first few terms will take us to the asymptotic value of the system response. This asymptotic value can be checked by the Final Value Theorem for Z-Transforms.

In the SCILAB functions in Section 7.10 in this chapter we introduce a new SCILAB function **LDIV** which will perform the long division for us and gives us the result expressed in Equation(7.46). So the long division does not have to be performed by hand, powerful computer programs are available to do the work for us.

Example 7.11

Repeat Example 7.10 but this time determine the inverse transform for both the cases using long division.

Solution 7.11

Case 1: Since this time the sequences are right hand sequences and the ROC extends outward to infinity both the poles are causal poles. For causal right handed sequences the inverse by long division is directly obtained by dividing the numerator by the denominator as shown here.

Inverse Z-Transform by Long division. Case 1 Example 7.11

$$
\begin{array}{l}
\quad\quad\quad\quad\quad\quad 1+z^{-1}+0.84z^{-2}+0.68z^{-3} \\
1-z^{-1}+0.16z^{-2}\ \big)\ 1 \\
\quad\quad -(1-z^{-1}+0.16z^{-2}) \\
\quad\quad\quad +z^{-1}-0.16z^{-2} \\
\quad\quad\quad -(z^{-1}-\quad z^{-2}+0.16z^{-3}) \\
\quad\quad\quad\quad 0.84z^{-2}-0.16z^{-3} \\
\quad\quad\quad\quad -(0.84z^{-2}-0.84z^{-3}+0.1344z^{-4} \\
\quad\quad\quad\quad\quad 0.68z^{-3}-0.1344z^{-4}
\end{array}
$$

Inverse Z-transform for the Causal sequence
is x(n) = {1, 1, 0.84, 0.68, ... }

Inverse Z-Transform by Long division. Case 2 Example 7.11

$$
\begin{array}{l}
\quad\quad\quad\quad\quad 6.25z^{2}+39.0625z^{3}+205.078125z^{4} \\
0.16z^{-2}-z^{-1}+1\ \big)\ 1 \\
\quad\quad -(1-6.25z^{1}+6.25z^{2}) \\
\quad\quad\quad +6.25z^{1}-6.25z^{2} \\
\quad\quad\quad -(6.25z^{1}-39.0625z^{2}+39.0625z^{3}) \\
\quad\quad\quad\quad 32.8125z^{2}-39.0625z^{3} \\
\quad\quad\quad\quad -(32.8125z^{2}-205.078z^{3}+205.078z^{4} \\
\quad\quad\quad\quad\quad 166.0156z^{-3}-205.078z^{-4}
\end{array}
$$

Inverse Z-transform for the anti Causal sequence
is x(n) = {6.25, 39.0625, 205.078125, ... }

We can also use SCILAB to perform the long division for us. Here we repeat the above two long divisions using the SCILAB function LDIV.

```
//**********************
//Example of Inverse Z-transform by Long division
//**********************
xn=poly([1],'z','c');
xd=poly([1, -1, 0.16],'z','c');
x=ldiv(xn,xd,5)'                // Result of long division. Left sequence.
yn= poly([1],'z','c');
yd=poly([0.16, -1, 1],'z','c');
y=ldiv(yn,yd,5)'                // Result of long division. Right sequence.
```

The result of the SCILAB script is given below.

x =

6.25 39.0625 205.07812 1037.5977 5203.2471

y =

1. 1. 0.84 0.68 0.5456

The SCILAB division can give us the result for either the right hand sequence or for the left hand sequence as you see in the above example. Notice that to change the result from a left sequence to a right sequence all we did was to reverse the order of the coefficients on the divisor.

7.9 THE TRANSFER FUNCTION AND THE POLE LOCATIONS

In the Chapter on Laplace Transforms we have seen that with continuous time systems the transfer function plays a very important role in the analysis and the design of systems. This is also true for discrete time systems. The transfer function of a system relates the input-output relation explicitly in what ever domain you are operating in. In this chapter we are discussing the Z-Transform so the transfer function relates the input to the output in the Z-Domain. This is shown in Figure 7.16.

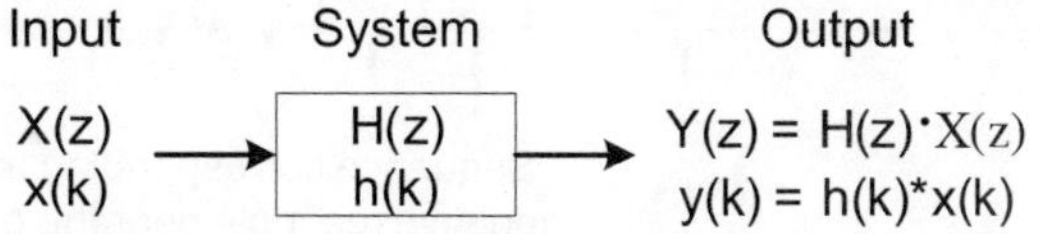

Input	System	Output
X(z) →	H(z)	→ Y(z) = H(z)·X(z)
x(k)	h(k)	y(k) = h(k)*x(k)

Figure 7.16: Figure shows the transfer function relationship in the time and the Z-Domain

In Figure7.16 the system function H(z) is the ratio of the output function Y(z) and the input function X(z) or the **System Function** H(z) = Y(z)/X(z). In the time domain the output sequence y(k) is the convolution of the two time domain sequences h(k) and the input sequence x(k). In the time domain this relation is arrived by the convolution property of Z-transform and Equation(7.38). The sequence h(k) in the time domain is known as the impulse response sequence. Since the output of the system is dependent on the system function is it important to study how the location of the poles and the zeros of the system in the system function affect the system response.

$$Y(z) = H(z) \cdot X(z)$$

$$Y(z) = \frac{A(z)}{(z-p_{h1})(z-p_{h2})\cdots(z-p_{hm})} \frac{B(z)}{(z-p_{x1})(z-p_{x2})\cdots(z-p_{xn})} \qquad (7.47)$$

To study this we will begin with a general function with all distinct poles. The Z-Domain transfer function can be written as shown in Equation(7.47). In Equation(7.47) we see that the output response depends on both the poles of the input as well as the poles of the system function. We can re-write Equation(7.47) so that the response is in its partial fraction form. This is shown in Equation(7.48).

$$Y(z) = H(z) \bullet X(z)$$

$$Y(z) = \frac{a_1 z}{(z - p_{h1})} + \frac{a_2 z}{(z - p_{h2})} + \cdots + \frac{a_m z}{(z - p_{hm})} + \frac{b_1 z}{(z - p_{x1})} + \frac{b_2 z}{(z - p_{x2})} + \cdots + \frac{b_n z}{(z - p_{xm})} \quad (7.48)$$

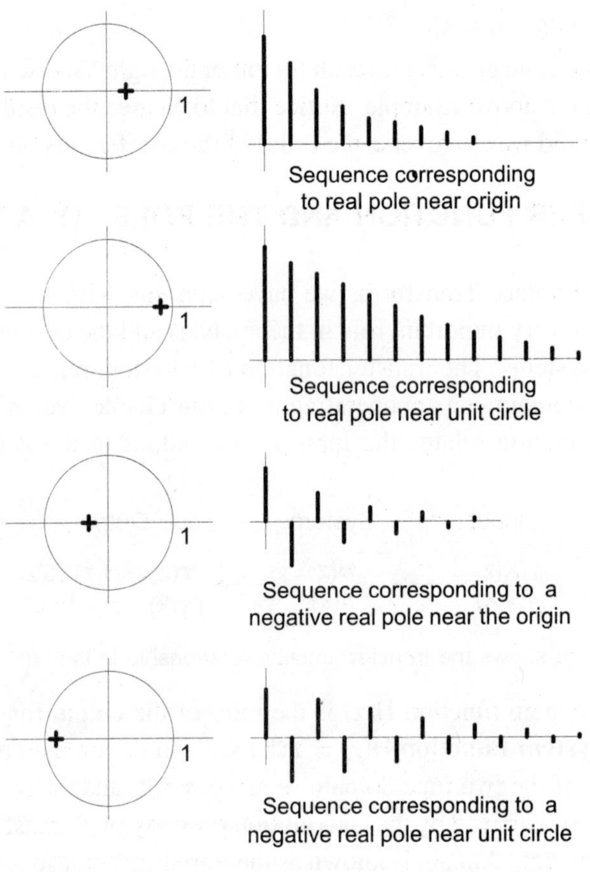

Figure 7.17: Stable sequences for real poles. As the pole approaches the unit circle the sequence persists longer

If we were to find the inverse Z-transform of every term in Equation(7.48) and added the individual sequences then we would get the response in the time domain. This sample inverse transform is shown in Equation(7.49). Equation(7.49) shows that each pole can be used either to produce a specific desired effect on the output or the pole from the system function can be used to counter the undesirable effect from a pole in the input function. This is done by placing a zero in the transfer function exactly where the undesirable pole in the input exists. This is discussed further in the following paragraphs where we discuss how to eliminate an undesirable frequency component in an input.

$$y(k) = a_1\left(p_{h1}\right)^k + a_2\left(p_{h2}\right)^k + \cdots + a_m\left(p_{hm}\right)^k$$
$$+ b_1\left(p_{x1}\right)^k + b_2\left(p_{x2}\right)^k + \cdots + b_n\left(p_{xm}\right)^k \quad (7.49)$$

From Equation(7.48) we can infer that if a pole at p_{hi} is close to the origin ($|p_{hi}| < 1$) then the exponential sequence $(p_{hi})^k$ is a decreasing sequence and the effect due to this pole will be present only for a small time during the transient portion and will gradually die out.

On the other hand if the pole is located very close to and within the unit circle then ($|p_{hi}| \approx 1$ and $|p_{hi}| < 1$), in this case the effect due to this pole will persist for a long time. These poles that are located within the unit circle and very close to it are known as the dominant poles. The dominant poles control the response of the system for most of the time. So as the system poles approach the unit circle the input plays a smaller and smaller role in shaping the response.

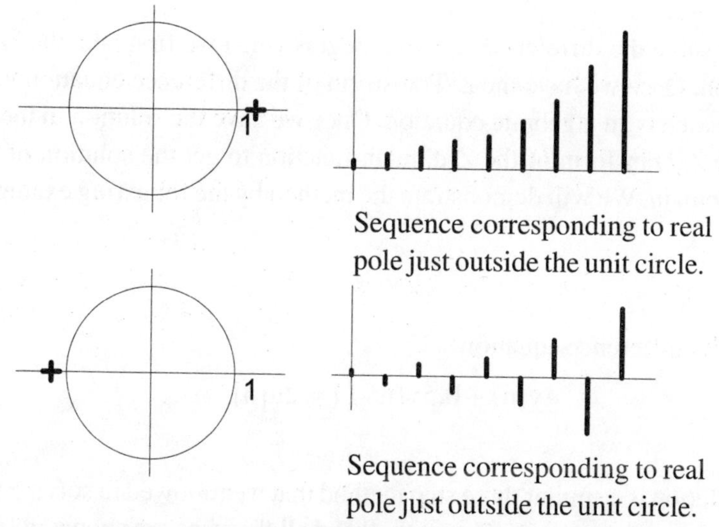

Figure 7.18: Unstable sequences for real poles. As the pole crosses the unit circle the sequence increases without bound

As the poles of the system cross the unit circle then the exponential sequence, $(p_{hi})^k$ for that pole increases without bound and k increases. This pole will make the system unstable. The effect of the various pole locations are shown in Figure 7.17.

Sometimes we wish to suppress or completely eliminate a sinusoidal frequency component from the input. A sinusoidal component in the input of say frequency ω_o will have two complex conjugate poles at $\text{Cos}(\omega_o) \pm j\text{Sin}(\omega_o)$. So if our system has two complex conjugate zeros located at $\text{Cos}(\omega_o) \pm j\text{Sin}(\omega_o)$ then the effect of the sinusoidal frequency will be cancelled by the system zeros. So the effect for the pole locations can be summarized as:

- Poles inside the unit circle - first order or higher - represent stable terms.
- Poles outside the unit circle - first order or higher - represent unstable terms.

- Zeros can appear anywhere in the Z-Plane, inside or outside the unit circle.
- A system is only as stable as its least stable part - the concept of the weakest link.
- When a zero is placed on top of any pole the effect due to that pole is cancelled.

7.10 Z-TRANSFORM SOLUTION TO DIFFERENCE EQUATION

When we were studying Laplace Transforms we saw how the Laplace Transforms could be used to solve differential equations. In the same way that the Laplace transforms can be used to solve differential equations we can use the Z-Transforms to solve difference equations. Earlier in this chapter we saw how the difference equation is solved directly in the time domain. Here we will study the procedure that can be used to solve the difference equation in the Z-transform domain. The procedure to solve the difference equation is similar to the procedure to solve the differential equation and it is given below.

The procedure to solve the difference equation begins when we first take the Z-Transform of the difference equation. Once we have the Z-Transform of the difference equation we solve the Z-Transform equation which is an algebraic equation. Once we have the solution in the Z-domain we determine the inverse Z-Transform of the Z-domain function to get the solution of the difference equation in the time domain. We will demonstrate the method by the following example to solve the difference equation.

Example 7.12

Solve the first order difference equation

$$y[n] + 0.5y[n-1] = 2u[n]$$

Solution 7.12

The method of solution is a similar three step method that we followed in solving the differential equations using the Laplace transforms. The method and all the steps are shown in Equation(7.50).

$$\boldsymbol{y[n]} + 0.5\boldsymbol{y[n-1]} = 2\boldsymbol{u[n]} \qquad \text{Difference Equation}$$

$$Y(z) + 0.5z^{-1}Y(z) = 2\frac{z}{z-1} \qquad \text{Z-Transform of the Equation}$$

$$\frac{Y(z)}{z} = 2\frac{1}{z-1}\frac{1}{z+0.5} = \frac{1.333}{z-1} - \frac{1.333}{z-(-0.5)} \qquad \text{Solution in the Z-Domain}$$

$$Y(z) = \frac{1.333z}{z-1} - \frac{1.333z}{z-(-0.5)}$$

$$\boldsymbol{y(n)} = 1.333\boldsymbol{u(n)} - 1.333(-0.5)^n \qquad \text{Solution in Time Domain} \qquad (7.50)$$

The Time domain solution shows the steady state value to be 1.333 and during the transient portion there is an oscillatory term that decreases as time goes by. In this example we did not have any initial condition. When there is some initial condition present the method is the same but we have to remember to include the initial condition. Let us repeat the same example but this time we will include the initial condition of y[-1] = 2.

Example 7.13

Solve the first order difference equation

$$y[n]+0.5y[n-1]=2u[n]$$

$$y[-1]=2$$

Solution 7.13

The method of solution when we have initial conditions requires us to add the initial condition when we first determine the Z-transform of the difference equations. This method is alas the three step method that we followed in solving the differential equations using the Laplace transforms. The method and all the steps are shown in Equation(7.51)

$$y[n]+0.5y[n-1]=2u[n] \qquad y[-1]=2 \qquad \text{Difference Equation}$$

$$Y(z)+0.5z^{-1}Y(z)+0.5y(-1)=2\frac{z}{z-1} \qquad \text{Z - Transform of the Equation}$$

$$\frac{Y(z)}{z}=2\frac{1}{z-1}\frac{1}{z+0.5}-\frac{0.5*2}{z+0.5} \qquad (7.51)$$

$$Y(z)=\frac{1.33z}{z-1}-\frac{1.33z}{z+0.5}-\frac{z}{z-(-0.5)} \qquad \text{Solution in the Z-Domain}$$

$$y(n)=1.33u(n)-1.33(-0.5)^n u(n)+(-0.5)^n u(n+1) \qquad \text{Solution in Time Domain}$$

Equation(7.51) shows that the procedure for solving a difference equation with or without initial conditions is the same as we outlined in this section. In Example 7.11 we solve the same example that we solved by direct time domain method to show that both the methods give us the same result.

Example 7.14

Determine the complete solution for the difference equation $y(n)-4y(n-2)=4n$. Assume that the initial conditions are all zero. Use the Z-transform method to solve. Compare the solution with the solution of Example 7.2.

Solution 7.14

To solve this using the Z-transform method we will first determine the Z-transform of the difference equation. This is done in Equation(7.52)

$$Y(z)-4z^{-2}Y(z)=\frac{4z^{-1}}{\left(1-z^{-1}\right)^{2}}$$

$$Y(z)=\frac{4z^{-1}}{\left(1-z^{-1}\right)^{2}\left(1-4z^{-2}\right)}=\frac{4z^{3}}{(z-1)^{2}\left(z^{2}-4\right)} \tag{7.52}$$

$$\frac{Y(z)}{z}=\frac{4z^{2}}{(z-1)^{2}\left(z^{2}-4\right)}=\frac{C_1}{(z-1)^{2}}+\frac{C_2}{(z-1)}+\frac{A_3}{(z-2)}+\frac{A_4}{(z+2)}$$

Next we need to determine the four residues. Determining the residues we get

$$C_1=\left.\frac{4z^{2}}{z^{2}-4}\right|_{z=1}=-\frac{4}{3}$$

$$C_2=\left.\frac{d\left(\dfrac{4z^{2}}{z^{2}-4}\right)}{dz}\right|_{z=1}=\left.\frac{8z\left(z^{2}-4\right)-4z^{2}(2z)}{\left(z^{2}-4\right)^{2}}\right|_{z=1}=-\frac{32}{9}$$

$$A_4=\left.\frac{4z^{2}}{(z-1)^{2}(z-2)}\right|_{z=-2}=-\frac{4}{9}$$

$$A_3=\left.\frac{4z^{2}}{(z-1)^{2}(z+2)}\right|_{z=2}=4$$

Now that we have the residues we can write the Z-domain solution of the difference equation. The solution in the Z-domain and in the time domain are given in Equation(7.53)

$$Y(z)=\frac{-4z}{3(z-1)^{2}}+\frac{-32z}{9(z-1)}+\frac{4z}{(z-2)}+\frac{-4z}{9(z+2)}$$

$$y[n]=\left[-\frac{4n}{3}-\frac{32}{9}+4(2)^{n}-\frac{4}{9}(-2)^{n}\right]u[n] \tag{7.53}$$

If you check the solution of Example 7.2 you will see that the two examples have the same solution.

Example 7.15

Determine the complete solution for the difference equation $y(n)+0.5y(n-1)-0.5y(n-2)=3nU(n)$. Assume that the initial conditions are all zero. Use the Z-transform method to solve. Compare the solution with the solution of Example 7.3.

Solution 7.15

To solve this using the Z-transform method we will first determine the Z-transform of the difference equation. This is done in Equation(7.54)

$$Y(z)+0.5z^{-1}Y(z)-0.5z^{-2}Y(z)=\frac{3z^{-1}}{\left(1-z^{-1}\right)^{2}}$$
$$Y(z)=\frac{3z^{-1}}{\left(1-z^{-1}\right)^{2}\left(1+z^{-1}\right)\left(1-0.5z^{-1}\right)} \tag{7.54}$$
$$\frac{Y(z)}{z}=\frac{3z^{2}}{(z-1)^{2}(z+1)(z-0.5)}$$

After we write Equation(7.54) as partial fractions and determine the residues we will be able to determine the inverse transform. This is done in Equation(7.55)

$$\frac{Y(z)}{z}=\frac{C_1}{(z-1)^2}+\frac{C_2}{(z-1)}+\frac{A_3}{(z+1)}+\frac{A_4}{(z-0.5)} \tag{7.55}$$
$$C_1=3;C_2=-1.5;A_3=-0.5;A_4=4$$
$$y[n]=\left[3n-1.5-0.5(-1)^n+2(0.5)^n\right]U(n)$$

From the solution of this example and example 7.14 we see that the Z-transform method is very simple and straightforward and gives us the same answer as the time domain method.

7.10.1 Some Useful SCILAB Functions:

We will examine three more functions of SCILAB which pertain to the work that we have done in this chapter. We will also re-visit another function that is useful for the work that we have done in this chapter. The four functions that we are going to learn are: **LDIV; PDIV; CLEAN** and **RESIDU.** These functions help us in determining the inverse Z transform of a Z-domain function.

• **LDIV:** The LDIV function is used to perform long division between two polynomials and to get the coefficients of the long division. The command is issued as ***x=ldiv(num_poly,deno_poly,#_of_coeff)***. The result of the long division will be in the vector 'x'. The LDIV function is used to perform the long division that we have used in determining the inverse Z-Transform. With the long division performed the result of the long division are the coefficients that represent the time domain sequence which is obtained as shown in Section 7.8.2.

• **PDIV:** The PDIV function is used to reduce a general Z-domain function to a rational function. Once we have the rational function then we can use the partial fraction expansion to determine the inverse Z-transform. The command is issued as ***[Q R] = pdiv(num_poly,deno_poly)***. When the command is executed the result of polynomial division is the quotient polynomial [Q] and the remainder polynomial [R]. These are the Q and the R polynomial in the command. The remainder polynomial divided by the deno_poly will be the rational function that we are looking for.

• **CLEAN:** When working with numbers it is possible that the result of a division will be a very small number very close to zero but not exactly zero. This could be a result of rounding in the computer. To get around this rounding error SCILAB has a very convenient command called CLEAN. The command is issued as ***B=clean(A,esp)***. In this command A is a matrix which has to be cleaned. esp is a small number that is used as the maximum round off error (usually set to 1d-10). Thus the matrix B will be the same as matrix A except for those entries in A that are smaller then ± esp. These entries will be reduced to zero.

• **RESIDU:** The residue command is the same as the one we saw when we were working with Laplace Transforms. This command determines the residue at a particular pole. The command is issued as ***V=residu(p,q1,q2)***. In this command V is the variable where the residue will be found, p is the numerator polynomial q1 is the pole location where we want to determine the residue and q2 is the rest of the denominator polynomial.

7.11 CHAPTER SUMMARY

Discrete time signals are obtained in several different ways. You can either sample a continuous time signal or the signal may be a discrete signal to begin with. It does not matter once you have the signal in the sampled form the analysis is the same. The sampling of a continuous time signal is done by a sampling function which is assumed to be an impulse train. The sampling function and the result of sampling with an impulse train are demonstrated in Figure 7.2.

Once we sample a continuous time signal we can determine the spectrum of the sampled signal. This spectrum of the sampled signal is related to the original continuous time signal. The relations between the frequency spectrum of the continuous time signal and the sampled signals is shown in Figure 7.4 and in Equation(7.6).

The Nyquist criteria for sampled signals gives us the condition necessary for the original signal to be recovered without loss of information. The Nyquist criteria is given in Equation(7.7). If the sampling is done so that the sampling frequency is at least twice the largest frequency present in the continuous time signal then there is no aliasing in the sampled signal. Aliasing results in loss of information. Aliasing of a sampled signal is shown in Figure 7.4.

With continuous time signals and continuous time systems we used the differential equations to describe and analyze the systems. With sampled or discrete time signals we use difference equations. The solution of a discrete time difference equation follows the same general procedure as the solution to the differential equation. We determine the Homogeneous solution and the particular solutions. Both these solutions have undetermined constants that have to be determined. The constants of the particular solution are determined by substituting the solution in the difference equation and equating the coefficients. To determine the constants of the homogeneous solution you use the given initial conditions to solve for the constants.

The Z-Transform summation is for a discrete sequence, this discrete sequence is obtained either by sampling an analog signal or by some discrete process. The summation given in Equation(7.21) and repeated here represents the Z-Transform of a discrete sequence. The Z-Transform definition is $X(z) = \sum x(n)\, z^{-n}$

We derived the Z-Transform from the Laplace Transform of a discrete sequence by replacing e^{st} by z. The Z-transform can be visualized as an ordered number sequence. When viewed in this way the coefficient x(n) represents the magnitude of the number in the sequence and the function z^{-n} represents the position of the number in the sequence. Thus the number $x(4)z^{-4}$ is the fourth number in the sequence and its magnitude is x(4).

Since we have related the Laplace plane to the Z-plane we can also see how the poles and zeros from the Laplace plane map on to the Z-plane. This mapping is rather straightforward. The entire left half of the S-domain maps into the inside of the unit circle in the Z-domain, the imaginary axis maps on to the unit circle and the entire right half of the s-plane maps on to the outside of the unit circle.

The Z-transform of a function must be specified along with its region of convergence. Without the ROC the Z-Transform is not unique to a sequence. The same expression can exist for a different sequence. The Z-Transform along with its ROC is a unique function of a sequence that you have. So you must always remember to include the region of convergence of the Z-Transform. The typical ROC of a function in the Z-domain will have a generally circular shape and the center of the circle is located at the origin. It could be a circular disk, a circular disk with a hole in the center or an annular shaped circular disk. The three possible shapes are shown in Figure 7.9.

The ROC is bounded by poles at its edge. The ROC cannot include any poles within it. The ROC for a limited sequence is the entire Z-plane except perhaps the point $z = 0$ or the area $z = \infty$. The ROC is determined from the sequence the largest/smallest value of z that makes the Z-Transform summation finite.

The properties of the Z-Transform are very similar to the properties of the Laplace Transform. The properties of Z Transform include:

- Linearity $a\,x_1(n) + b\,x_2(n) \overset{z}{\Leftrightarrow} a\,X_1(z) + b\,X_2(z)$

- Shift in Time $x(n-n_o) \overset{z}{\Leftrightarrow} z^{n_o} X(z)$
- Multiplication by an exponential sequence $a^n x(n) \overset{z}{\Leftrightarrow} X\left(z/a\right)$
- Differentiation in the Z-domain $n\,x(n) \overset{z}{\Leftrightarrow} -z\dfrac{dX(z)}{dz}$
- Time Reversal $x(-n) \overset{z}{\Leftrightarrow} X\left(1/z\right)$
- Convolution of two sequences $x_1(n) * x_2(n) \overset{z}{\Leftrightarrow} X_1(z) \cdot X_2(z)$

The inverse Z-Transform is obtained by either partial fraction expansion and table lookup or by long division. For partial fraction expansion we must first convert the Z-domain function into a rational fraction. Once the Z-domain function is a rational fraction then the residues at each of the individual poles can be computed. After the residues are computed the inverse transform can be obtained by table lookup. In order to compute the residues we can use the SCILAB command ***RESIDU.***

To obtain the inverse Z-Transform by long division there is no need to convert the Z-Domain function to a rational fraction. The long division directly gives the time domain sequence that we are looking for with each iteration of the long division. To perform the long division we have a different SCILAB function. This command is ***LDIV.*** The LDIV command will give us as many coefficients as we want.

The two methods of obtaining the inverse transforms have their own advantages. The partial fraction expansion method will give us a closed form expression where as the long division method does not require us to first factor the Z-domain function first.

Just as we had used the Laplace transform to solve differential equations we are able to use the Z-Transform to solve difference equations. The method is the same as the method of solutions of the differential equations. The method of solution of the difference equations is as follows: We first determine the Z-Transform of the difference equation. The Z-transform will change the difference equation into an algebraic equation. So we solve this algebraic equation in the Z-domain. Once we have the solution then we find the inverse transform of the Z-domain solution to get the solution of the difference equation.

7.12 HOMEWORK PROBLEMS

Sampling a signal and Nyquist Criteria.

Problem 7.12.1

Consider a signal x(t) = 3Cos(4πt) - 4Sin(6πt) + 2Cos(8πt). We wish to sample this signal so that the sampling rate is 25% faster than the Nyquist sampling rate.

a. Draw the frequency spectrum of the continuous time signal.

b. Draw the frequency spectrum of the sampled signal.

c. If the sampled signal is passed through an ideal low pass filter with cutoff ½ the sampling frequency what will the frequency spectrum of the recovered signal look like.

Problem 7.12.2

Consider a signal $x(t) = 3\text{Cos}(4\pi t) - 4\text{Sin}(6\pi t) + 2\text{Cos}(8\pi t)$. We wish to sample this signal so that the sampling rate is 25% slower than the Nyquist sampling rate.

a. Draw the frequency spectrum of the continuous time signal.

b. Draw the frequency spectrum of the sampled signal.

c. If the sampled signal is passed through an ideal low pass filter with cutoff ½ the sampling frequency what will the frequency spectrum of the recovered signal look like.

Problem 7.12.3

Consider a signal $x(t) = 3\text{Cos}(24\pi t) - 4\text{Sin}(36\pi t) + 2\text{Cos}(48\pi t)$. We wish to sample this signal so that the sampling rate is 44Hz.

a. Draw the frequency spectrum of the continuous time signal.

b. Draw the frequency spectrum of the sampled signal.

c. If the sampled signal is passed through an ideal low pass filter with cutoff ½ the sampling frequency what will the frequency spectrum of the recovered signal look like.

Difference Equations:

Problem 7.12.4

Explain why you would choose the particular solution for a difference equation as described in Table 7.1. For the following input functions suggest appropriate forms of particular solutions:

a. $(n+n^2)u(n)$

b. $(\text{Cos}(24n\pi) + \text{Sin}(36n\pi))u(n)$

c. $[n(\text{Cos}(24n\pi) + \text{Sin}(36n\pi))]u(n)$

d. $[n\text{Cos}(24n\pi) + \text{Sin}(36n\pi)]u(n)$

e. $[\text{Cos}(24n\pi) + n\text{Sin}(36n\pi)]u(n)$

Problem 7.12.5

Solve the following difference equations with the given initial conditions:

a. $y[n]-2y[n-1]+1.5y[n-2]=3u[n] \quad y[0]=1; y[-1]=0$

b. $y[n-1]-2y[n-2]+1.5y[n-3]=3u[n] \quad y[1]=1; y[2]=0$

c. $y[n]-2y[n-1]+1.5y[n-2]=(3n+2)u[n] \quad y[0]=1; y[-1]=0$

Discrete Convolution Sum:

Problem 7.12.6

This problem shows us a very important concept in transform analysis. Convolution in the time domain is equal to multiplication in the transform domain. We saw this in the Laplace transform domain also.

Consider the signals w(n) = x(n) * y(n). You are given the signal:
x(n) = x(0)=1; x(1)=2; x(2)=-2; x(3)=3; x(4)=2; x(5)=1 and the signal
y(n) = y(0)=2; y(1)=2; y(2)=0; y(3)=-1; y(4)=1.

a. Determine the signal w(n) by performing discrete convolution x(n) with y(n) as shown in Figure7.7

b. Determine the Z-Transform of the two signals x(n) and y(n).

c. Determine the Z-Transform of the signal w(n) by multiplying X(z) and Y(z).

d. Determine the Z-Transform of the signal w(n) directly from the result of part a of this problem.

e. Show that the Z-Transform of W(n) in part d is the same as the Z-Transform of w(n) in part c

Z-Transforms:

Problem 7.12.7

Determine the definition of Z-Transform and identify the ROC for each of the following time domain functions.

a. $x(nT) = A\delta((n-m)T)$.

b. A finite length sequence x(0)=0; x(1)=2; x(2)=0; x(3)=4; x(4)=3; x(5)=2.

c. $x(nT) = a^n U(nT)$ a=0.5

d. $x(nT) = a^n U(nT) - a^{n-4} U((n-4)T)$ a=0.5

Problem 7.12.8

Use the Z-Transform table and the Z-Transform theorems to obtain the Z-Transforms of the following \time domain functions.

a. x(n) = aU(n) -aU(n-5) a > 0

b. x(n) = nU(n)

c. x(n) = n[aU(n) -aU(n-5)] a > 0

d. x(n) = anCos(0.25n)U(n) a > 0

Problem 7.12.9

Find the Z-Transform of the following signals. What is the ROC for each of the functions? How does the pole-zero plot of each of the functions differ from each other?

a. $x(n) = a^{n}U(n)$ $\quad 0 < a < 1$

b. $x(n) = a^{2n}U(n)$ $\quad 0 < a < 1$

c. $x(n) = a^{4n}U(n)$ $\quad 0 < a < 1$

Problem 7.12.10

Consider the signals w(n) = x(n) * y(n). You are given the signal x(n) = 4U(n) - 4U(n-4) and the signal y(n) = 2.5U(n) - 2.5U(n-3).

a. Determine the signal w(n) by performing discrete convolution x(n) with y(n)

b. Determine the Z-Transform of the two signals x(n) and y(n).

c. Determine the Z-Transform of the signal w(n) by multiplying X(z) and Y(z).

d. Determine the Z-Transform of the signal w(n) directly from the result of part a of this problem.

e. Show that the Z-Transform of W(n) in part d is the same as the Z-Transform of w(n) in part c.

Problem 7.12.11

Prove the scaling theorem for Z-Transforms using the following three signals. How is the ROC altered because of the scaling? How does the scaling affect the pole-zero plot of the signal when it is scaled?

a. $X(n) = (0.75)^{n}U(n)$

b. $X(n) = (0.25)^{n}U(n) = \left(\frac{0.75}{3}\right)^{n} U(n).$ $\quad$ Scale factor of 3.

c. $X(n) = (0.9375)^{n}U(n) = (1.25 * 0.75)^{n}\, U(n).$ $\quad$ Scale factor of 1.25.

Z-Transform Theorems:

Problem 7.12.12

You are given a signal x(n) which is a complex signal of the type

$$x(n) = (\alpha^{n} + j\beta^{n})u(n) \qquad \beta < 1 \; and \; \alpha < 1$$

a. Determine the Z-Transform of the signal x(n).

b. Determine the Z-Transform of the signal x*(n)

c. Determine the Z-Transform of the signal x(-n).

d. Determine the Z-Transform of the signal x*(-n)

e. What is the relation between the Z-Transforms that you obtained in steps a and b?

f. What is the relation between the Z-Transforms that you obtained in steps c and d?

Inverse Z-Transforms:

Problem 7.12.13

Find the inverse Z-Transform of the following Z-domain functions by partial fraction expansion. After you have the inverse transform evaluate the first six terms of the series. Assume all the poles correspond to right hand sequences.

a. $\dfrac{1}{2-4z^{-2}+6z^{-3}}$

b. $\dfrac{3z^{-1}+2z^{-2}}{1-0.5z^{-1}+z^{-2}}$

c. $\dfrac{3z^{-1}-33z^{-3}}{1+3z^{-1}-2z^{-2}}$

d. $\dfrac{2+4z^{-1}}{2-3z^{-1}+2z^{-2}}$

Problem 7.12.14

Find the inverse Z-Transform of all the Z-domain functions given in Problem 7.13 by long division. Determine the first six terms of the series. Assume all the poles correspond to right hand sequences. Compare the result with the first six terms obtained in Problem 7.12.13.

Problem 7.12.15

Multiply each of the functions in Problem 7.12.13 by $\mathbf{Z}^{-2}$. Now determine the inverse Z-Transform of these new functions by partial fraction expansion. Determine the first ten terms for each function. What can you say about the inverse Z-Transforms of the functions in Problems 7.12.13 and 7.12.15. Draw the sketch of the corresponding Z-Transforms one below the other. Which property of the Z-Transform does this demonstrate? Assume all the poles correspond to right hand sequences.

Problem 7.12.16

Determine the inverse Z-Transforms of the function given below.
For each of the three ROCs shown, use the partial fraction expansion method.

$$X_1(z)=\frac{4z^{-1}}{1+0.1z^{-1}-0.3z^{-1}}\qquad\begin{cases}ROC_1 & \left|z^{-1}\right|>0.6\\ ROC_2 & \left|z^{-1}\right|<0.5\\ ROC_3 & 0.5<\left|z^{-1}\right|<0.6\end{cases}$$

Problem 7.12.17

Determine the initial values and the final values of all the functions given in Problems 7.12.13 and 7.12.14 using the initial value and the final value theorems. Are the initial values for the corresponding functions in Problems 7.12.13 and 7.12.14 the same? Are the final values for the corresponding functions in Problems 7.12.13 and 7.12.14 the same? Why are the initial values not the same? Why do the final values remain the same even though the initial values change?

Problem 7.12.18

Use the Z-Transform to solve the following difference equations.

a. $y(n) - 0.75y(n-1) - 0.2y(n-2) = 4[U(n-1) - U(n-4)]$

$$y(-1) = 1 \text{ and } y(-2) = -1$$

b. $y(n) - 0.25y(n-1) - 0.2y(n-2) = 2\delta(n-1) + U(n)$

$$y(-1) = 4 \text{ and } y(-2) = 8$$

Problem 7.12.19

You are given a first order differential equation

$$0.2\frac{dy(t)}{dt} + 0.8\,y(t) = x(t) \text{ with } x(t) = 2U(t) \text{ and } y(0) = 2.$$

a. Solve this equation using Laplace Transform.

b. Next approximate the differential Equation with $\frac{dy(t)}{dt} = \frac{y(nT) - y((n-1)T)}{T}$. So now the Differential equation will become a Difference equation. The Difference equation is $\left(\frac{0.2}{T} + 0.8\right)y(nT) - \frac{0.2}{T}y((n-1)T) = x(nT)$. In this equation let $y(-1T) = 2$ and $x(nT) = U(nT)$. Solve this differential equation using Z-Transforms.

c. Show that the two results approach each other as $T \rightarrow 0$.

7.13 FURTHER READING

Z-Transforms and sampled systems are covered in books dealing with Digital Signal Processing. Some of the very good books in this area are:

1. Ziemer R.E.; Tranter W.H. and Fannin D.R. *Signals and Systems: Continuous and Discrete* Macmillian Publishing Company NY 1993.
2. Gordon E. Carlson, *Signals and Linear System Analysis* John Wiley 1998.
3. Alexander Poularikas and Samuel Seely, *Signals and Systems* PWS Kent Publishing, 1991.

CHAPTER 8

The Discrete Transforms

INTRODUCTION

In the first half of this book we have studied the characteristics of the **L**inear **T**ime **I**nvariant (LTI) systems. The fundamental characteristic of these LTI systems is that they do not alter the frequency of the signal. LTI systems only change the phase and the amplitude of the signal as the signal goes through the system. This fact led us to study the Fourier series and the Fourier Transforms of signals. In studying the Fourier series and the Fourier Transform we found that any signal that satisfied the Dirchlet conditions can be represented by a sum of harmonically related sinusoids.

The above paragraph is true for continuous time signals. Can we make a similar statement about discrete time or sampled signals? We sampled the continuous time signal in the previous chapter and determined its Z-Transform but what about its frequency content. Is the sampled system still an LTI system? Is it possible to represent these discrete time signals also by a sum of harmonically related sinusoids? In this chapter we examine the Fourier series and the Fourier transform for discrete time signals. We will examine signals that are time limited (finite length sequences) and sampled signals and see if these signals can indeed be represented by a sum of sinusoidal signals.

The Discrete Fourier Transform (DFT) that we will study in this chapter is a very computationally intensive operation. The computational burden is proportional to the square of the number of samples in the signal. So as the number of samples increases the computational burden can become so large that the computer cannot keep up with the required computations for real time processing. For this reason fast and efficient algorithms have been developed. There are several different algorithms available but we will examine only two that are the most popular. The other algorithms use very similar ideas to do the computations efficiently. These algorithms are together given the name **F**ast **F**ourier **T**ransform (FFT) computation methods.

8.1 THE DISCRETE FOURIER SERIES

When you sample a periodic signal using a periodic impulse sampling function is the resulting sequence also periodic? To answer this question consider the signal $x(t) = A_n Cos(2\pi f_o t)$. This is a periodic signal with period f_o. We will next sample this using impulse sampling with a sampling frequency f_s. After we sample the signal with sampling frequency f_s then we will get a sampled signal which is $x[nT] = A_n Cos(2\pi f_o nT) = A_n Cos\left(2\pi \frac{f_o}{f_s} n\right)$. The question that we want answered is: Is x[nT] a periodic signal? If x[nT] is periodic then we will have x[nT] = x[(n+N)T] where N is the period of the sampled signal. So we must have

$$2\pi(n+N)\frac{f_o}{f_s} = 2\pi n \frac{f_o}{f_s} + 2\pi\lambda$$
$$N\frac{f_o}{f_s} = \lambda \quad or \quad \frac{\lambda}{N} = \frac{f_o}{f_s} \tag{8.1}$$

In Equation(8.1) both λ and N have to be integers. So for a sampled signal to be periodic with period N the ratio of the two frequencies f_o and f_s has to be a rational function. When the ratio of the two frequencies is a rational function then the sampled signal will be a periodic signal. The ratio of the two frequencies is known as the Normalized frequency of the sampled signal. Since the periodicity of the sampled signal depends on the frequency of the sampling signal the same signal can have different periodicity depending on the frequency of the sampling signal.

Example 8.1

A signal x(t) = 5Cos(30πt) is sampled by an impulse sampling train that has a frequency of 100Hz. Is the resulting signal periodic? What is the period if the signal is periodic?

Solution 8.1

This time the frequency of the signal is 15Hz, and the sampling frequency is 100Hz. So the ratio of the two frequencies 15/100 is a rational fraction and hence the sampled signal is a periodic signal.

The period of the periodic signal, in number of samples, is $N = \frac{\lambda f_s}{f_o} = \frac{3 \cdot 100}{15} = 20\ Samples$

Example 8.2

A signal x(t) = 5Cos(30πt) is sampled by an impulse sampling train that has a frequency of 45Hz. Is the resulting signal periodic? What is the period if the signal is periodic?

Solution 8.2

This time the frequency of the signal is 15Hz, and the sampling frequency is 45Hz. So the ratio of the two frequencies 15/45 is a rational fraction and hence the sampled signal is a periodic signal.

The period of the periodic signal, in number of samples, is $N = \frac{\lambda f_s}{f_o} = \frac{1 \bullet 45}{15} = 3\,Samples$

Example 8.3

A signal x(t) = 5Cos(30t) is sampled by an impulse sampling train that has a frequency of 100Hz. Is the resulting signal periodic? What is the period if the signal is periodic?

Solution 8.3

This time the frequency of the signal is $\frac{15}{\pi} Hz$, and the sampling frequency is 100Hz. So the ratio of the two frequencies $\frac{15}{\pi 100} Hz$ is not a rational fraction since π is an irrational number, and hence the sampled signal is not a periodic signal.

Now that we know that the sampled signals can also be periodic signals and we also know that we can determine the Fourier series for periodic signals, what will the Fourier series for this sampled signal be? To get an understanding of the Fourier series of a sampled signal let us look at the frequency spectrum of a simple sampled signal.

Consider a sampled signal given by x[n] = Cos(0.6πn). We will use Euler's theorem to write this signal as

$$\mathbf{x[n]} = \tfrac{1}{2}e^{j2\pi(0.3)n} + \tfrac{1}{2}e^{j2\pi(-0.3)n} \tag{8.2}$$

Equation(8.2) represents two rotating phasors that are rotating at ±0.3 revolutions per sample. This frequency of 0.3 revolutions per sample is the normalized frequency of the phasor. If we know the sampling frequency we could determine the actual frequency of the signal before it was sampled. So the sampled signal has a frequency spectrum just like the analog signal had a frequency spectrum. We saw that in Chapter 7 earlier also. In this Chapter we will extend the idea of the Fourier series to the sampled signal also.

To develop the Fourier series for the discrete time signal we will consider the expansion of the sequence x[n] into a complex exponential sum over the fundamental period of N samples. This sum will exist for all sequences that are absolutely square summable. This condition is similar to the Dirchlet conditions that we required the continuous time signals to satisfy before we were able to expand them into Fourier series. So if a signal satisfies Equation(8.3)

$$\sum_{n=n_1+1}^{n_1+N} |x[n]|^2 < \infty \tag{8.3}$$

Remember that with the continuous time Fourier series we expanded the function into orthogonal basis functions. For the discrete time signal also we will expand the sampled signal by the use of orthogonal basis functions. The basis functions that we will choose are the sampled complex exponential functions

$$\Phi_m[n] = e^{\frac{j2\pi nm}{N}} \tag{8.4}$$

Where the period of the function is N and the fundamental rotates once in N samples. Other harmonically related functions will rotate n times in N samples so for every value of n we will get a different and a unique phasor. There will be a total of N unique phasors that will be used to represent the sampled signal.

As mentioned earlier the basis functions are mutually orthogonal to each other. This is demonstrated in Equation(8.5)

$$\sum_{n=1}^{N} \Phi_m[n]\Phi_p^*[n] = \begin{cases} N & m = p \\ 0 & m \neq p \end{cases} \tag{8.5}$$

There are only N distinct basis functions as shown by Equation(8.6) which shows that the basis functions are periodic with period N.

$$\begin{aligned} \Phi_{m+(\lambda N)}[n] &= e^{\left(\frac{j2\pi n(m+(\lambda N))}{N}\right)} = e^{\left(\frac{j2\pi nm}{N}\right)} e^{\left(\frac{j2\pi n\lambda N}{N}\right)} \\ &= e^{\left(\frac{j2\pi nm}{N}\right)} e^{\left(\frac{j2\pi n}{1}\right)} = e^{\left(\frac{j2\pi nm}{N}\right)} = \Phi_m[n] \end{aligned} \tag{8.6}$$

So the discrete time Fourier series of any sampled signal can be written as shown in Equation(8.7). The basis functions are generally represented with the function W which has a superscript as well as a subscript. The subscript represents the number of samples over which the fundamental basis function is periodic. The superscript represents the harmonic number and the coefficient of the nth sample.

$$\hat{x}[n] = \sum_{m=1}^{N} X_m e^{\frac{j2\pi nm}{N}} = \sum_{m=1}^{N} X_m W_N^{-nm} \tag{8.7}$$

How close does $\hat{x}[n]$ represent x[n]? or how do we determine the coefficients X_m? To determine the coefficients X_m we will begin by setting $\hat{x}[n]$ equal to x[n], multiply it with W_N^{-nm} and sum it over all the N harmonics as shown in Equation(8.8).

$$\begin{aligned} \sum_{n=1}^{N} x[n]W_N^{nk} &= \sum_{n=1}^{N} \hat{x}[n]W_N^{nk} \\ &= \sum_{n=1}^{N}\left[\sum_{m=1}^{N} X_m W_N^{-nm}\right]W_N^{nk} \end{aligned} \tag{8.8}$$

$$= \sum_{m=1}^{N} X_m \left[\sum_{n=1}^{N} W_N^{-nm} W_N^{nk} \right]$$

$$= \sum_{m=1}^{N} X_m \left[\sum_{n=1}^{N} \Phi_m[n] \Phi_k^*[n] \right]$$

$$= NX_k$$

This equation gives us the formula that we need to determine the coefficients of the harmonics that make up the Fourier series of the sampled signal x[n]. Therefore the equation that will give us the Fourier series coefficients for a sampled signal can be computed by using Equation (8.9)

$$X_m = \frac{1}{N} \sum_{m=1}^{N} x[n] W_N^{nm} \tag{8.9}$$

So the pair of Equations(8.7) and (8.9) form the Fourier series pair for discrete time signals.

8.1.1 Properties of the Complex Number W:

- The complex number W and the basis function are one and the same when you examine them carefully. So the properties of the complex number W are the same as the properties of the basis function. In addition to the properties that we have already listed the properties of the complex number W are listed in Table 8.1:

Table 8.1: Properties of the complex number W

1	$W_N^N = e^{\left(\frac{-j2\pi}{N}\right)^N} = e^{-j2\pi} = 1$
2	$W_N^{m+N} = W_N^m W_N^N = W_N^m$ W is periodic with period N
3	$W_N^2 = e^{\left(-j\frac{2\pi}{N}\right)^2} = e^{\left(\frac{-j2\pi}{(N/2)}\right)} = W_{N/2}$
4	$W_N^{N/2} = e^{\left(\frac{-j2\pi N}{2N}\right)} = e^{(-j\pi)} = -1$
5	$\sum_{m=0}^{N-1} W_N^{(n-m)k} = \frac{1-W_N^{(n-m)N}}{1-W_N^{(n-m)}} = \begin{cases} N & n=m \\ 0 & n \neq m \end{cases}$
6	➢ $W^0; W^1; W^2; \cdots; W^{N-1}$ specify equidistant points around the unit circle. This is shown in Figure 8.1.

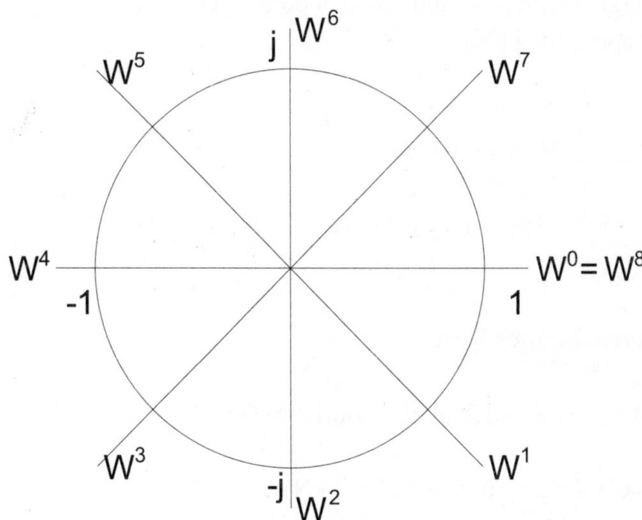

Figure 8.1: Graphical representation of a Complex number $W = e^{-j2\pi n/N}$ for N = 8

Equation(8.7) shows us the definition of the complex number W. The subscript to the Number W tells us the number of samples we have to take in one period. Using Eulers identity we can expand W around the unit circle as shown in Figure 8.1. From Figure 8.1 the properties listed in Table 8.1 become self evident. Remember these very well as we will be using these again in this chapter several times.

Example 8.4

What is the discrete time Fourier Series for 6Cos(6πt) when N is 4, when N is 7 and when N is 15?

Solution 8.4

Since these computations are very tedious and time consuming and do not really add to any understanding we will use a SCILAB script to do the computing work for us. The form of the sampled function is given in Equation (8.10)

$$x(t)\Big|_{t=\frac{n}{N}} = 6Cos\left(3n\frac{2\pi}{T}\frac{T}{4}\right) = 6Cos(1.5\pi n) \qquad (8.10)$$

The SCILAB script computes the Discrete Fourier Series Equation and then the sampled signal itself in the two halves of the script. The script is given below.

```
*****************************************
N=input('How many samples in the Discrete Fourier Series? ');
n=1:N;
```

```
//Build a sampled signal which is sampled at N points per cycle.
x=clean(4*cos(2*%pi*3*(n-1)/N));
X=zeros(1,size(x,'*'));
x_hat=X;
//Determine the Discrete Fourier Series.
for m=1:N
   W=clean(%e^(-%i*2*%pi*(m-1)*(n-1)/N));
   X(m)=clean(1/N*(x*W'));
end
//Print out the Discrete Fourier Series.
X
//Reconstruct the original signal from the Fourier Series
for m=1:N
   W_inv=clean(%e^(%i*2*%pi*(m-1)*(n-1)/N));
   x_hat(m)=clean((X*W_inv'));
end
//Print out the reconstructed signal.
x_hat
******************************************
```

The result when we sample the signal with 4 samples is given below:

How many samples in the Discrete Fourier Series? -->4

X = 0 2. 0 2.

x_hat = 4. 0 - 4. 0

Notice from the computation of the variable x_hat that the original Cosine function is reproduced.

The result when we sample the signal with 7 samples is given below:

How many samples in the Discrete Fourier Series? -->7

X = 0 0 0 2. 2. 0 0

x_hat = 4. - 3.6038755 2.4939592 - 0.8900837 - 0.8900837 2.4939592 - 3.6038755

Notice from the computation of the variable x_hat that the original Cosine function is reproduced.

Next when we sample this signal with 15 equally spaced samples we get

-->How many samples in the Discrete Fourier Series? -->15

X = 0 0 0 2. 0 0 0 0 0 0 0 0 2. 0 0

x_hat = 4. 1.236068 - 3.236068 - 3.236068 1.236068 4. 1.236068 - 3.236068 - 3.236068 1.236068 4. 1.236068 - 3.236068 - 3.236068 1.236068

Notice from the computation of the variable x_hat that the original Cosine function is reproduced.

8.2 DISCRETE TIME FOURIER TRANSFORMS

The **D**iscrete **T**ime **F**ourier **T**ransform (DTFT) of a finite energy discrete signal will give us the frequency content of the discrete signal. In general these signals are infinite in nature, sampled and they are not periodic. They have finite energy. Just as the Fourier Transform gave us the frequency content of the finite time signal the DTFT will give us the frequency content of the finite energy sampled signal. The one sided DTFT is defined as shown in Equation(8.11)

$$\mathbb{F}\{x[n]\} = X(\omega) = X(e^{j\omega}) = \sum_{n=0}^{\infty} x(n)e^{-\omega n} \tag{8.11}$$

The function $F(\omega)$[1] is known as the DTFT of the discrete sequence x[n] and it represents the frequency content that is present in the sequence x[n]. This frequency function $F(\omega)$ is periodic with period 2π which can be seen by replacing ω by $\omega + 2\pi$ in the expression for $F(\omega)$ as shown in Equation(8.12)

$$X(\omega + 2\pi) = \sum_{n=0}^{\infty} x[n]e^{-j(\omega+2\pi)n} = \sum_{n=0}^{\infty} x[n]e^{-j\omega n}\, e^{-j2\pi n} = X(\omega) \tag{8.12}$$

Remember that the Fourier transform of the continuous time signal has infinite range in frequency whereas the DTFT is completely represented by only a finite range of frequencies. This finite range extends from 0 to 2π or from $-\pi$ to π (since the function $F(\omega)$ is periodic in 2π). Any frequency range outside is equivalent to some frequency in this range. This is satisfying since this is what we saw in the previous chapter when we sampled a continuous time signal and looked at its frequency spectrum and found that it was repeated as shown in Figure 7.3 and in Figure 7.4.

The **I**nverse **D**iscrete **T**ime Fourier Transform (IDTFT) can be obtained from the definition of the DTFT as shown below by some mathematical manipulations. We begin with the definition of the DTFT.

$$X(\omega) = \sum_{n=0}^{\infty} x[n]e^{-j\omega n} \tag{8.13}$$

In Equation(8.13) we want to eliminate the term $e^{-j\omega n}$ from the right hand side. To accomplish this we will multiply both sides of the equation by $e^{-j\omega k}$ and then integrate over one period of the DTFT as shown.

$$\int_{-\pi}^{\pi} X(\omega)e^{j\omega k}\, d\omega = \int_{-\pi}^{\pi} \sum_{n=0}^{\infty} x[n]e^{-j\omega n}e^{j\omega k}\, d\omega$$

$$\int_{-\pi}^{\pi} X(\omega)e^{j\omega k}\, d\omega = \int_{-\pi}^{\pi} \sum_{n=0}^{\infty} x[n]e^{j\omega(k-n)}\, d\omega$$

Interchange the order of the integration and the summation to get Equation (8.14)

$$\int_{-\pi}^{\pi} X(\omega)e^{j\omega k}\, d\omega = \sum_{n=0}^{\infty} x[n]\int_{-\pi}^{\pi} e^{j\omega(k-n)} d\omega \tag{8.14}$$

[1] Some authors write this as $X(e^{j\omega})$. We will use $X(\omega)$

The integral on the right hand side of Equation(8.14) can be recognized as the integral of the product of two basis functions which are orthogonal to each other. So the result of the integral will be zero unless the two functions are equal to each other. When they are equal to each other then the result of the integral is 2π. Making use of this fact we get Equation(8.15)

$$\int_{-\pi}^{\pi} X(\omega)e^{j\omega k}\,d\omega = 2\pi x[k]$$

$$or$$

$$x[k] = \frac{1}{2\pi}\int_{-\pi}^{\pi} X(\omega)e^{j\omega k}\,d\omega \tag{8.15}$$

Which is the definition of the IDTFT of a sampled sequence, the pair of equations in Equation(8.13) and in Equation(8.15) form the DTFT pair of synthesis and the analysis equations.

Example 8.5

Determine the DTFT for the sequence $\alpha^n u(n)$ when $\alpha<1$.

Solution 8.5

We use the definition of the DTFT to determine the transform of the given function. $X(\omega) = \sum_{n=0}^{\infty} \alpha^n e^{-j\omega n} = \dfrac{1}{1-\alpha e^{-j\omega}}$

Example 8.6

Determine the Phase spectrum and the Magnitude spectrum of the DTFT determined in Example 8.5.

Solution 8.6

The Magnitude and the Phase spectrum of $X(\omega)$ are easily determined as shown:

$$|X(\omega)| = \left[\frac{1}{1-\alpha e^{-j\omega}}\frac{1}{1-\alpha e^{j\omega}}\right]^{\frac{1}{2}} = \frac{1}{\left(1+\alpha^2-2\alpha Cos(\omega)\right)^{\frac{1}{2}}}$$

$$X(\omega) = \frac{1}{1-\alpha e^{-j\omega}}\frac{1-\alpha e^{+j\omega}}{1-\alpha e^{-j\omega}} = \frac{1-\alpha e^{j\omega}}{1+\alpha^2-2\alpha Cos(\omega)}$$

$$\Phi(\omega) = \tan^{-1}\left(\frac{\alpha Sin(\omega)}{1-\alpha Cos(\omega)}\right)$$

Looking carefully at the magnitude and the phase spectrum we can clearly see that both the functions are periodic with period of 2π.

8.3 PROPERTIES OF THE DISCRETE TIME FOURIER TRANSFORM

Just as with all the other transforms that we have studied, the DTFT also has some of the fundamental properties. As we study these properties we will find that all the properties are very similar to the properties that we came across when we studied the Z-Transform. This is as expected from the previous paragraph.

8.3.1 Linearity:

The DTFT is a linear transform. Equation(8.16) shows the statement of the property. This property is proved directly from the definition of the DTFT as shown in Equation(8.17)

$$F\{ax_1(n)\pm bx_2(n)\}\Leftrightarrow aX_1(\omega)\pm bX_2(\omega) \tag{8.16}$$

$$\begin{aligned}F\{ax_1(n)\pm bx_2(n)\} &\Leftrightarrow \sum_{n=0}^{\infty}\{ax_1(n)\pm bx_2(n)\}e^{-jn\omega}\\ &=\sum_{n=0}^{N-1}ax_1(n)e^{-jn\omega}\pm bx_2(n)e^{-jn\omega}\\ &=aX_1(\omega)\pm bX_2(\omega)\end{aligned} \tag{8.17}$$

8.3.2 Time Shift:

This property shows that a delay or a shift in the time domain corresponds to a rotation in the frequency domain. Equation(8.18) shows the statement of the property. This property is proved directly from the definition of the DTFT as shown in Equation(8.19)

$$\text{F}\{\text{x(n-k)}\}\triangleq e^{-j\omega k}X(\omega) \tag{8.18}$$

$$\text{F}\{\text{x(n-k)}\}=\sum_{n=0}^{\infty}(\text{x(n-k)})e^{-jn\omega} \qquad \text{let n-k = m}$$

$$=\sum_{m=-k}^{\infty}\text{x(m)}\,e^{-j(m+k)\omega}$$

Change the lower limit in the summation to zero as x(m) = 0 for m<0.

$$\begin{aligned}F\{x(n-k)\}&=e^{-jk\omega}\sum_{m=0}^{\infty}\text{x(m)}\,e^{-jm\omega}\\ F\{x(n-k)\}&=e^{-jk\omega}X(\omega)\end{aligned} \tag{8.19}$$

Example 8.7

You are given that x(t) has a DTFT that is X(ω). Using the DTFT properties determine the DTFT of the following:

a. $5^2x(t)$
b. $6^3x(t-5)$

Solution 8.7
For this example we will use the properties that we have just studied
a. Since 5^2 is only a constant we can use property from Equation (8.17) to get the DTFT as $5^2X(\omega)$.
b. This time we will have to use two properties. First since 6^3 is a constant we can use the property from Equation (8.17) and as the function also represents a time delay we will use the property from Equation (8.19) to get the DTFT as $6^3e^{-j5\omega}X(\omega)$

8.3.3 Time Reversal:

This property shows that reversing the time of the sequence in the time domain sequence does not change the magnitude spectrum of the signal in the Fourier domain which is what we should expect as we have not changed the sequence; the phase spectrum however undergoes a sign change (phase reversal). Equation(8.20) shows the statement of the property.

$$F\{x(-n)\} = X(-\omega) \tag{8.20}$$

This property is proved directly from the definition of the DTFT as shown in Equation(8.21)

$$\begin{aligned} F\{x(-n)\} &= \sum_{n=0}^{\infty} x(-n)e^{-j\omega n} \\ &= \sum_{m=-\infty}^{0} x(m)e^{-j(-\omega)m} \\ &= \sum_{m=0}^{\infty} x(m)e^{-j(-\omega)m} = X(-\omega) \end{aligned} \tag{8.21}$$

Example 8.8
Determine the DTFT of the following functions using the properties of the DTFT. $5^{-2}x(-t-7)$

Solution 8.8
First we will rewrite the function as follows: $5^2x\{-(t+7)\}$. For this example we will use the last three properties that we have just studied, first since 5^{-2} is a constant we will use the property given in Equation (8.17), next we will use the property given in Equation (8.19), and then finally we will use the property given in Equation (8.21), to complete the time reverse function as shown below.

$$F\left[5^2x(-t-7)\right] = 5^2e^{j7(-\omega)}X(-\omega) = 5^2e^{-j7\omega}X(-\omega)$$

Notice that the time reversal reverses the sign on ω. Since ω appears at two places in the transform the sign has to be reversed both the times.

8.3.4 Convolution:

To prove this property we begin with the definition of discrete convolution. The statement of the property is given in Equation(8.22)

$$F\{x_1(n) * x_2(n)\} \triangleq X_1(\omega) \bullet X_2(\omega) \tag{8.22}$$

To prove the property we will begin with the definition of convolution, in which we will adjust the summation and re-arrange the terms so that we have two different Discrete Time Fourier transforms. This property is proved in Equation(8.23) and in Equation(8.24)

$$\begin{aligned} F\{x_1(n) * x_2(n)\} &= \sum_{n=0}^{\infty}\{x_1(n) * x_2(n)\}e^{-j\omega n} \\ &= \sum_{n=0}^{\infty}\left\{\sum_{k=0}^{\infty} x_1(k)x_2(n-k)\right\}e^{-j\omega n} \end{aligned} \tag{8.23}$$

In Equation(8.23) we have replaced the Convolution sign by the convolution summation. Now in Equation(8.23) if we let n – k = m and separate the two summations we will get the answer that we are looking for. This is shown in Equation(8.24)

$$\begin{aligned} F\{x_1(n) * x_2(n)\} &= \sum_{n=0}^{\infty}\left\{\sum_{k=0}^{\infty} x_1(k)x_2(m)\right\}e^{-j\omega(m+k)} \\ &= \sum_{n=0}^{\infty} x_2(m)e^{-j\omega m}\sum_{k=0}^{\infty} x_1(k)e^{-j\omega k} \\ &= X_2(\omega)X_1(\omega) \end{aligned} \tag{8.24}$$

8.3.5 Frequency Shift

When the time domain function is multiplied by an exponential sequence the Discrete Time Fourier domain function under goes a shift in the frequency. This property is also sometimes referred to as the Modulation Property. The statement of the property is given in Equation(8.25)

$$F\{e^{j\omega_0 k}x(n)\} = X(\omega - \omega_0) \tag{8.25}$$

The Frequency shift property of the DTFT is proved by directly using the definition of the DTFT and is shown in Equation(8.26)

$$\begin{aligned} F\{e^{j\omega_0 k}x(n)\} &= \sum_{n=0}^{\infty}\left(e^{j\omega_0 k}x(n)\right)e^{-jn\omega} \\ &= \sum_{n=0}^{\infty} x(n)e^{-jn(\omega-\omega_0)} \\ &= X(\omega - \omega_0) \end{aligned} \tag{8.26}$$

Example 8.9

Determine the DTFT of the function $e^{-j5t}x(t-7)$.

Solution 8.9

This time we will use the property given in Equation (8.21) and in Equation (8.26). Since these two properties are duals of each other we get the following:

$$F\left[e^{-j5t}x(t-7)\right]=e^{-j7\omega}X(\omega-5)$$

Did you notice that both the time domain and the frequency domain functions have a very interesting result as both the functions have an exponent and a delay! The delay in the time domain function is in time while in the frequency domain it represents a shift in the frequency.

8.3.6 Multiplication with a Ramp:

The statement of this property is given in Equation(8.27)

$$F\{nx(n)\} \Leftrightarrow -j\frac{dX(\omega)}{d\omega} \tag{8.27}$$

To prove this property we begin with the right hand side of the definition of the Discrete Fourier transform and determine what is the derivative of X(ω). Once we have the derivative we will adjust it so that it matches the function on the left hand side of Equation(8.27). What then remains must be the DTFT of the function f(n) multiplied by a ramp. This is shown in Equation(8.28)

$$\begin{aligned}\frac{dX(\omega)}{d\omega} &= \frac{d\sum_{n=0}^{\infty} x(n)e^{-jn\omega}}{d\omega} = \sum_{n=0}^{\infty} x(n)\frac{de^{-jn\omega}}{d\omega} \\ &= \sum_{n=0}^{\infty} x(n)\left\{-jne^{-jn\omega}\right\} \\ &= -j\sum_{n=0}^{\infty} nx(n)\, e^{-jn\omega}\end{aligned} \tag{8.28}$$

$$F\left[\sum_{n=0}^{\infty} nx(n)\, e^{-jn\omega}\right] = j\frac{dX(\omega)}{d\omega}$$

8.3.7 Modulation:

The statement of this property is given in Equation(8.29)

$$F\left[x(n)Cos(\omega_0 n)\right]=\tfrac{1}{2}\left[X(\omega+\omega_0)+X(\omega-\omega_0)\right] \tag{8.29}$$

To prove this property we begin with the definition of Discrete Time Fourier Transform. Next we will use the Euler's identity to represent the Cos(ω_0n) as two exponentials. Then we will use the Frequency shift property of the DTFT given in Equation(8.26) to prove the modulation property. This property of the DTFT is proved in Equation(8.30)

$$\begin{aligned} F\{Cos(\omega_0 n) f(n)\} &= \sum_{n=0}^{\infty} Cos(\omega_0 n) f(n) e^{-jn\omega} \\ &= \sum_{n=0}^{\infty} \frac{e^{jn\omega_0} + e^{-jn\omega_0}}{2} f(n) e^{-jn\omega} \\ &= \sum_{n=0}^{\infty} \left[\left(\frac{e^{jn\omega_0}}{2} f(n) e^{-jn\omega} \right) + \left(\frac{e^{-jn\omega_0}}{2} f(n) e^{-jn\omega} \right) \right] \\ &= \frac{1}{2} F(\omega - \omega_0) + \frac{1}{2} F(\omega + \omega_0) \end{aligned} \tag{8.30}$$

Example 8.10

Determine the DTFT of the function $ne^{-j5t}x(t-7)$.

Solution 8.10

This time we will use the property given in Equation (8.21) and in Equation (8.26) to account for the delay and the multiplication by the exponent. After we have done this we will use the property in Equation, to account for multiplication by a ramp function as shown here:

$$F\left[ne^{-j5t}x(t-7)\right] = -j\frac{d\left[e^{-j7\omega}X(\omega-5)\right]}{d\omega}$$

In this DTFT if we know the function of X(ω) then we can easily differentiate to get the required result.

8.3.8 Relation between the Z-Transform and the DTFT:

We have now analyzed an infinite sequence using both the Z-transform as well as the DTFT. Is there a relation that exists between the two transforms? The answer can easily be derived when we look at the the transforms and compare them. This is done for you in Equation(8.31)

Z-transform

$$Z\left[x(n)\right] = \sum_{n=0}^{\infty} x(n) z^{-n}$$

Discrete Time Fourier Transform

$$F\left[x(n)\right] = \sum_{n=0}^{\infty} x(n) e^{-j\omega n}$$

Both the transforms are the same when we replace $z=e^{-j\omega}$ (8.31)

So we see that the DTFT is very similar to the Z-transform. Remember that the Z-transform has a magnitude and a rotation (phase). When we make the substitution as indicated by Equation(8.31) we see that the replacement of z by $e^{-j\omega}$ implies that the magnitude of the Z-transform is unity or one. So the DTFT is the same as the Z-transform when the Z-transform is evaluated along the unit circle. It is for this reason that there is so much similarity between the Z-transform and the DTFT theorems

Table 8.2: Properties of the Discrete Time Fourier Transform

1	**Linearity**	$\{af1(n) \pm bf2(n)\}$	$aF_1(\omega) \pm bF_2(\omega)$
2	**Time Shift**	$\{f(n-k)\}$	$e^{-j\omega k} F(\omega)$
3	**Time Reversal**	$\{f(-n)\}$	$F(-\omega)$
4	**Convolution**	$f_1(n) * f_2(n)$	$F_1(\omega) \bullet F_2(\omega)$
5	**Frequency Shift**	$\{e^{j\omega_0 k} f(n)\}$	$F(\omega - \omega_0)$
6	**Multiplication by a Ramp**	$\{nf(n)\}$	$-j\dfrac{dF(\omega)}{d\omega}$
7	**Modulation**	$\{Cos(\omega_0 n)f(n)\}$	$\frac{1}{2}F(\omega - \omega_0) + \frac{1}{2}F(\omega + \omega_0)$

and the properties.

8.4 FOURIER TRANSFORM FOR FINITE LENGTH SEQUENCES

In the previous section we studied the DTFT of finite energy but infinite time signals. When we have finite length (time) signals then many of the entries in the sequence of the Discrete Time signal will be zero, or alternately we can consider the finite time sequence as a truncated sequence of the infinite sequence. Since the sequence is truncated the spectrum of the signal requires special consideration. The finite length sequence that we have now has data points at f(0), f(1), ... f(N-1), look at Figure 8.2. To consider the effect of missing data we proceed as shown in Equation(8.32). We begin by writing the definition of the Discrete Time Fourier Transform. To this definition we will add the restraint posed by having a finite length sequence. This is done by limiting the sum to N-1 terms only since all the remaining terms are zero. Next in this expression we substitute the expression for the

$$\begin{aligned} X_N(\omega) &= \sum_{n=0}^{\infty} x(n)e^{-j\omega n} = \sum_{n=0}^{N-1} x(n)e^{-j\omega n} \\ &= \sum_{n=0}^{\infty}\left[\frac{1}{2\pi}\int_{-\pi}^{\pi} X(\omega')e^{j\omega' n}d\omega'\right]e^{-j\omega n} \\ &= \frac{1}{2\pi}\int_{-\pi}^{\pi} X(\omega')d\omega'\left[\sum_{n=0}^{\infty} e^{j\omega' n}e^{-j\omega n}\right] \\ &= \frac{1}{2\pi}\int_{-\pi}^{\pi} X(\omega')d\omega'\left[\sum_{n=0}^{\infty} e^{-j(\omega-\omega')n}\right] \\ &= \frac{1}{2\pi}\int_{-\pi}^{\pi} X(\omega')\left[W(\omega-\omega')\right]d\omega' \end{aligned} \tag{8.32}$$

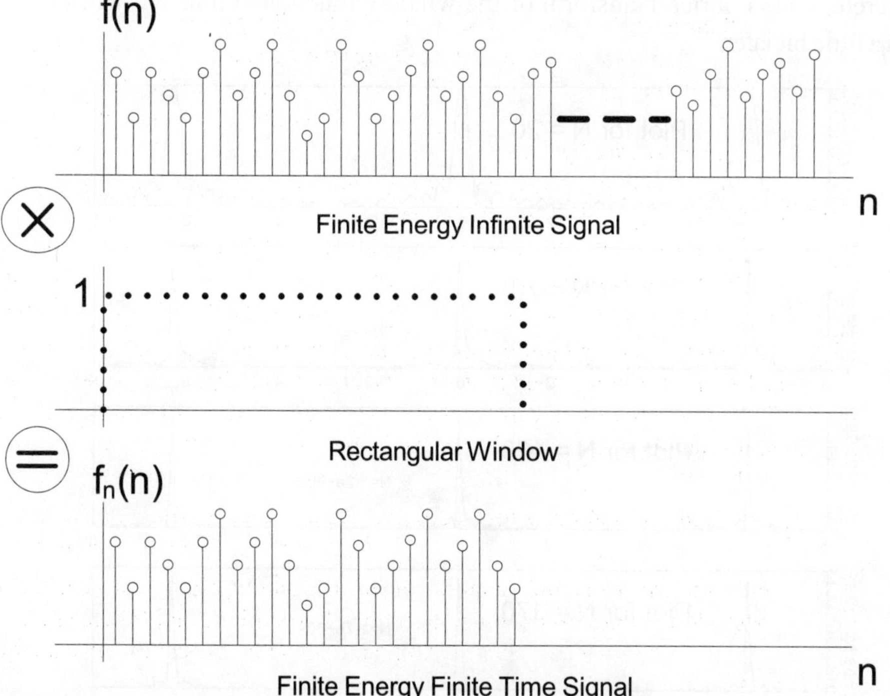

Figure 8.2: Finite energy infinite time signal when multiplied by a rectangular window gives a finite energy finite time signal

inverse transform. This new expression we will rearrange to get Equation(8.32).

Equation(8.32) is a convolution equation. The quantity in the square bracket in the second and the third lines in Equation(8.32) can be thought of as a Fourier transform of some function which we have called as the function W(ω). So the **D**iscrete **F**ourier **T**ransform (DFT) of a finite length sequence is a convolution of the DTFT of the infinite sequence itself with the DTFT of the function W(ω). What is this function W(ω)? Equation(8.33) helps us to find this function. We can think of the function w(n) as the rectangular window function. We saw the same effect when we were studying the FIR filter design. Here since our interest is in the new signal left behind by the windowing process we do not explore the use of different window functions, we only use the rectangular window.

$$W(\omega)=\sum_{n=0}^{N-1} 1e^{-j\omega n}=e^{-j\omega\left(\frac{N-1}{2}\right)}\frac{Sin\left(\frac{\omega N}{2}\right)}{Sin\left(\frac{\omega}{2}\right)} \tag{8.33}$$

The function w(n) must have a unit amplitude from n = 0 to n = (N-1) and it must be zero everywhere else. This function is the rectangular window function w(n) = u(n) - u(n-N). The window function is shown in Figure 8.2. The integral in Equation(8.32) is a very interesting integral. It represents a convolution between the Discrete Time Fourier Transform F(ω) of the sequence f(n) and the Discrete Time Fourier Transform of the window function W(ω). We will talk about this convolution a little bit later.

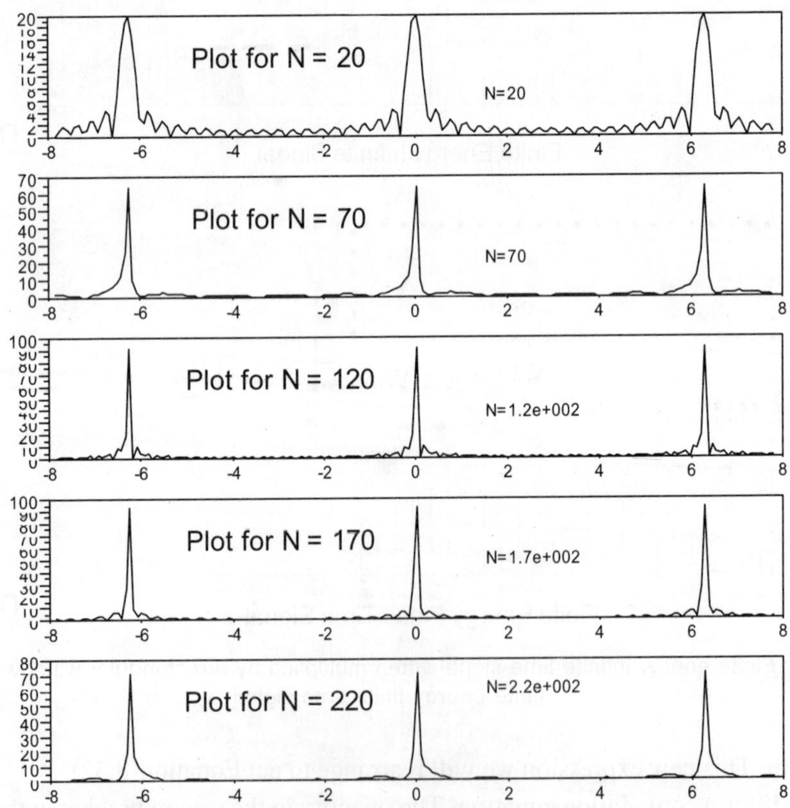

Figure 8.3: Plot of Sin(Nω/2)/Sin(ω/2) for various values of N. Note the amplitude of the plot approaches impulse as N → ∞.

To get the idea of the windowing process consider only the function W(ω). We will examine the window as the window length N becomes larger and larger. In the limit as N → ∞, Equation(8.32) must represent the DTFT of the function f(k) as the sequence f(k) would be infinite with N → ∞. So in this special case (N = ∞) W(ω) must be an impulse. We know that W(ω) must be an impulse function because the impulse functions possess the property that when the impulse function is convolved with any function say f(n), the result of convolution is the original function, f(n), without any alteration. That is to say, when a function is convolved with an impulse the result is the same function. The above explanation makes sense as Equation(8.32) must revert back to Equation(8.13) when the sequence f(n) is an infinite sequence. So what happens to the function W(ω) when N is not ∞? Look at Equation(8.33). When N is not ∞ the amplitude of the function W(ω) has a term Sin(Nω/2)/Sin(ω/2). This term has the property that is similar to that of the impulse function. The graph for Sin(Nω/2)/Sin(ω/2) is given in Figure 8.3. Notice that as N gets to be larger and larger the function approaches an impulse. The function will be an impulse when N → ∞. So the larger the window the closer its spectrum comes to an impulse. Also the larger the window function the two transforms will also approach each other, but we are not so interested in this.

The SCILAB script for the plot in Figure 8.3 is given below:

```
****************************************
SCILAB Script for plot in Figure 8.3
****************************************
for N = 20:50:220
w=-2.5*%pi:(2*%pi)/75:2.5*%pi;
amp=abs(sin(N*w/2)./sin(w/2));
subplot(5,1,(N)/20);plot2d(w,amp);
xstring(1.5,N/4,"N="),xnumb(2,N/4,N)
end
```

Is the rectangular window the only window possible? Not quite. The Fourier Transform spectrum will then depend on the window used. We will study the effect of windowing in a later chapter. In general it has been found that windows other than the rectangular window tend to reduce the ripples in the spectrum of the window. When the ripples are reduced the spectrum of $f_N(n)$ resembles the spectrum of f(n). Typically it has been found that the energy in the main lobe of the window controls the smoothing effect. The wider the main lobe the greater the smoothing effect due to the window.

8.5 DISCRETE FOURIER TRANSFORM

In the previous sections we obtained the discrete sequence by sampling an analog signal. Very often however we obtain the discrete sequence from an experimental setup which is an experimental sequence. The difference between these two methods of obtaining sampled data is that in the former method we know the function that is sampled and hence the function can be used in an integral. In the latter, since the data is obtained from an experiment, we do not know the function behind the sequence so it is impossible to use integrals. Most of the data in practical applications is obtained in this manner. So when the data is obtained experimentally we use **D**iscrete **F**ourier **T**ransform (DFT). Irrespective of how you get the finite length sequence, either by experiment or by sampling a known function, you can always use the DFT for finite length sequences when your sequence is of finite length.

There is a close parallel relation between DFT and the Fourier Transform. In this section we will first define the DFT, and then we will show that the mathematical properties of DFT are similar to the continuous time Fourier transforms. Then finally we will look at a very efficient means of computing the DFT known as the **F**ast **F**ourier **T**ransform (FFT).

So the conditions that we have now are as follows: We have a finite length sequence that is obtained from a sampling process (experimental setup). So we only have the data but we do not know the function behind the numbers. Remember also that the experiment has a definite beginning and an end, so the data that we obtain is a finite length sequence. By definition we will define the DFT as shown in Equation(8.34). We have introduced the complex number W earlier in Table 8.1, in Figure 8.1 and in Equation(8.7).

$$\begin{aligned} X(k) &= \sum_{n=0}^{N-1} x(n) e^{\frac{-jnk}{N}} = \sum_{n=0}^{N-1} x(n) W_N^{nk} \\ x(n) &= \frac{1}{N} \sum_{k=0}^{N-1} X(k) e^{\frac{jnk}{N}} = \frac{1}{N} \sum_{k=0}^{N-1} X(k) W_N^{-nk} \end{aligned} \tag{8.34}$$

Example 8.11 Determine the DFT of the following finite length sequences:

a. $x(n) = \sum_{n=0}^{N-1} ae^{-\alpha n}$

b. $x(n) = \sum_{n=0}^{N-1} a\cos(\alpha n)$

Solution 8.11

To compute the required transforms we will directly use the DFT definition given in Equation (8.34) for both the transforms that we have to compute:

a. Using the first part of Equation (8.34) we get

$$X(k) = \sum_{n=0}^{N-1} ae^{\alpha n} W_N^{nk} = \sum_{n=0}^{N-1} ae^{\alpha n} e^{\frac{-j2\pi nk}{N}} = \sum_{n=0}^{N-1} ae^{\frac{-n(j2\pi k-\alpha)}{N}}$$

The last summation can be rearranged as shown here to get the DFT in a closed form. Once again we are able to do this since we know the function that is sampled to get x[n].

$$X[k] = a\frac{1-e^{-N\left(\frac{j2\pi k-\alpha}{N}\right)}}{1-e^{-\left(\frac{j2\pi k-\alpha}{N}\right)}} = a\frac{1-e^{-(j2\pi k-\alpha)}}{1-e^{-\left(\frac{j2\pi k-\alpha}{N}\right)}}$$

b. In the same way using the first part of Equation (8.34) we get

$$X(k) = \sum_{n=0}^{N-1} a\cos(\alpha n)W_N^{nk} = \sum_{n=0}^{N-1} a\frac{e^{\alpha n}+e^{-\alpha n}}{2}e^{\frac{-j2\pi nk}{N}}$$

$$= \sum_{n=0}^{N-1}\left\{\frac{a}{2}e^{\frac{-n(j2\pi k-\alpha)}{N}} + \frac{a}{2}e^{\frac{-n(j2\pi k+\alpha)}{N}}\right\}$$

The last summation can be rearranged as shown here to get the DFT in a closed form. Once again we are able to do this since we know the function that is sampled to get x[n].

$$X[k] = \frac{a}{2}\frac{1-e^{-(j2\pi k-\alpha)}}{1-e^{-\left(\frac{j2\pi k-\alpha}{N}\right)}} + \frac{a}{2}\frac{1-e^{-(j2\pi k+\alpha)}}{1-e^{-\left(\frac{j2\pi k+\alpha}{N}\right)}}$$

Example 8.12

You are given that the DFT of a signal x[n] is X[k]. A student forms a new signal by the following two methods. What is the relation of the DFT of this new signal so formed with the DFT of the original signal x[n]?

a. Signal $x_1[n]$ formed by catenating n zeros after the signal x[n]. (Zero padding)

b. Signal $x_2[n]$ formed by inserting zeros between successive samples of x[n]

Solution 8.12

To determine the relation of the two DFT's we will determine the DFT of the new signal and manipulate to see if we can relate it to the DFT of the original signal as shown here.

a. We first write the definition of the DFT of the new signal as shown here.

$$X_1[k] = \sum_{m=0}^{M-1} x_1[m]W_M^{mk} = \sum_{m=0}^{\frac{M-1}{2}} x_1[m]W_M^{mk} + \underbrace{\sum_{m=\frac{M}{2}}^{M-1} x_1[m]W_M^{mk}}_{\text{All x[m] here are zero}}$$

$$\underbrace{X_1[2k]}_{\text{Even terms of } X_1[k]} = \sum_{m=0}^{\frac{M-1}{2}} x[n]W_M^{m2k} = \sum_{m=0}^{\frac{M-1}{2}} x[n]W_{M/2}^{mk} = X[k]$$

The above analysis shows that all the even terms of $X_1[k]$ make up the DFT of X[k].

b. This time all the even terms of $x_2[n]$ are zero. We again begin with the definition of $X_2[k]$ as shown here:

$$X_1[k] = \sum_{m=0}^{M-1} x_1[m]W_M^{mk} = \sum_{m=0}^{\frac{M-1}{2}} x_1[2m]W_M^{2mk} + \underbrace{\sum_{m=0}^{\frac{M-1}{2}} x_1[2m+1]W_M^{(2m+1)k}}_{\text{All } x_1[2m+1] \text{ here are zero}}$$

$$\underbrace{X_1[k]}_{\text{First half terms of } X_1[k]} = \sum_{m=0}^{\frac{M-1}{2}} x[m]W_{M/2}^{mk} = X[k]$$

In both these examples what we tried to do is to match the summation on the right hand side to the standard summation. When we got it to be the standard summation we were able to say that this is the DFT of the sequence in the summation. So what is the standard summation for the DFT? The standard summation consists of the following:

a. The summation is over N terms and the summation index begins at zero and goes to (N-1).

b. There are N terms in the sequence x[n]. They may be either real or complex.

c. The super index of W has two indexes, one index (k most of the time) is constant for a particular X[k] while the other index (n most of the time) varies from 0 to (N-1).

d. The sub index of W is N which represents the number of terms in the summation.

In all the homework problems dealing with DFT you should try to adjust the summation so that it results in a standard form summation.

8.6 OPERATIONS ON A FINITE LENGTH SEQUENCE

The DFT is computed for sequences that have N sample points. The sequence sample values for n<0 is zero and for n>(N-1) is also zero. This is true for sequences in both the time and the frequency domain.

8.6.1 Circular Shift:

When we attempt to shift either the time or the frequency domain we end up with the same N sample values but these N sample values are organized in a slightly different manner. Consider a length N = 7 sequence shown in Figure 8.4. The sequence has non zero values only for samples 0

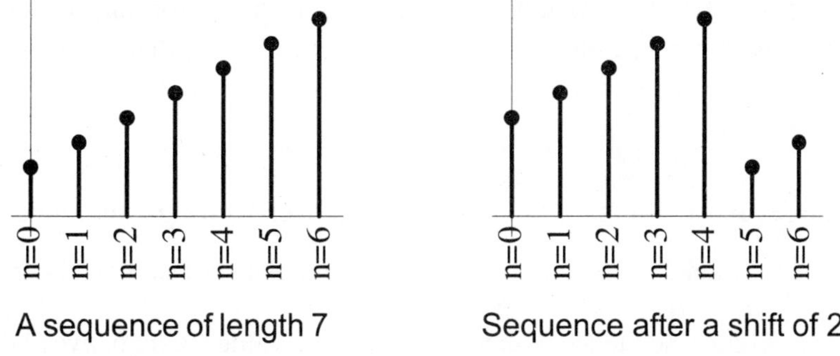

Figure 8.4: Circular shift in a length N sequence

through N-1. All the other sample values are zero. When we shift the sequence by 2 sample points to the left the sequence still has the same N sample points but they are arranged in a slightly different manner. The shifted sequence also has zero values for n<0 and for n>(N-1). So the sequence always stays within sample values zero to (N-1). Such a shift is different from the shift that we have seen in an infinite sequence. Since this shift is different we need to define the shift as a special type or a different type of a shift. This is known as a **Circular Shift**. The circular shifting operation is executed by the modulus operation.

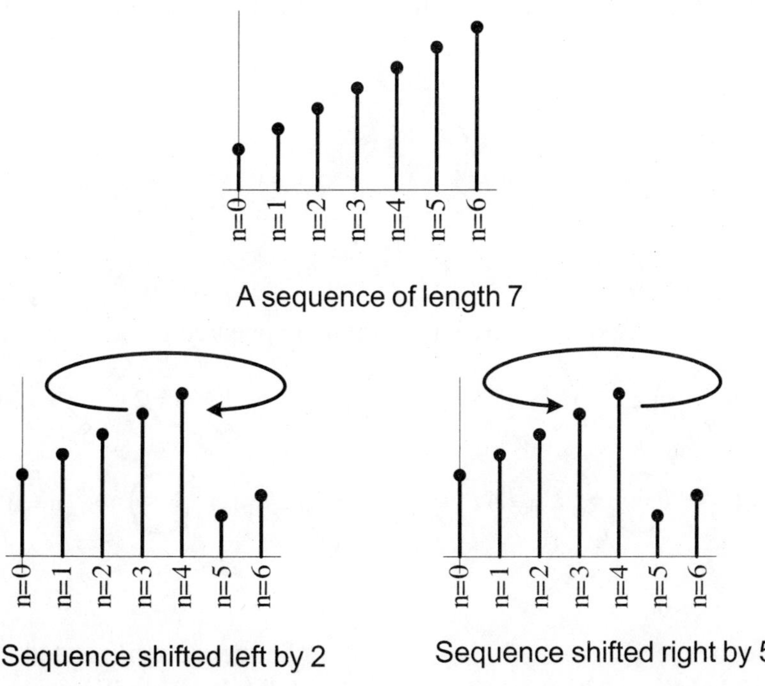

Figure 8.5: Circular shift left by n_0 samples is the same as the circular shift right by $N-n_0$ samples

The modulus operation is the remainder after performing the appropriate division. The modulus operation is written as shown in Equation(8.35). If we let r = $<m>_N$ then r = m + pN; here p is an integer, either positive or negative, so that r always lies between 0 and (N-1).

$$<m>_N = m \text{ modulo } N \tag{8.35}$$

If we shift the sequence in Figure 8.4 by either 2 or 9 or 16 we get the same figure shown in Figure 8.4. So using the modulus operation we define the circular shift as $x_c(n) = x[<n - n_o>_N]$.

So $x_c(n)$ is also a length N sequence with all the N sample values lying between 0 and (N-1). If n_o is positive then we get a right circular shift and if n_o is negative we get a left circular shift. Since the shift is circular a shift of n_o points to the right is the same as a shift of N-n_o to the left as shown in Figure 8.5. A circular shift by an amount greater than N is equivalent to a corresponding shift $<n_o>_N$.

An interesting consequence of the circular shift is the reversal of the sequence. A circularly reversed sequence is $x[<-n>_N] = x[<N-n>_N]$ so we get

$$x[<-n>_N] = \begin{cases} x[<N-n>_N] & 1 \le n \le N-1 \\ x[n] & n = 0 \end{cases} \tag{8.36}$$

All this business becomes perfectly clear if we interpret the sequence as if it is arranged on a 'Lazy Suzan' as shown in Figure 8.6.

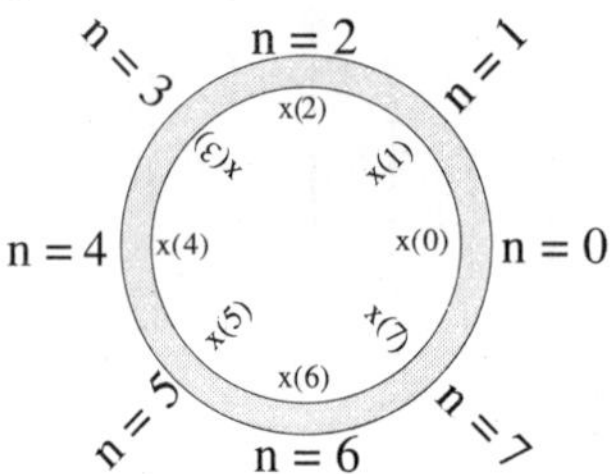

Sequence x[n] as it original appeared .

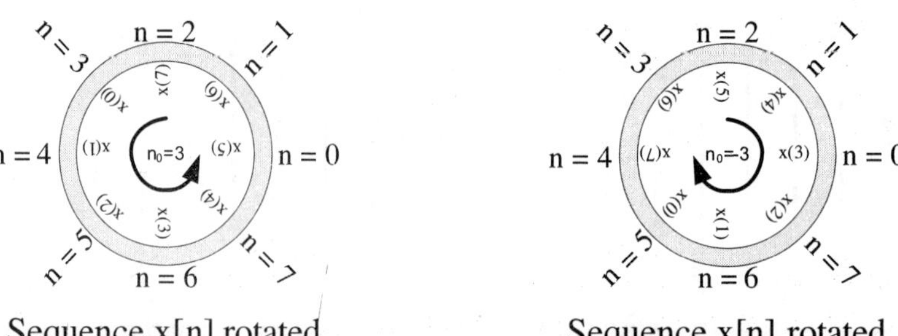

Sequence x[n] rotated right by 3 positions.

Sequence x[n] rotated left by 3 positions.

Figure 8.6: Demonstrating circular shift of a finite sequence

8.6.2 Circular Convolution:

In the previous section we have seen that the shifting operation in finite length sequences is a circular shifting operation. The shift keeps the sequence a length N sequence but it rearranges the ordering of the sequence values. One of the operations that deal with sequences and shifting is the convolution operation. So how is the convolution of finite length sequences computed? With circular shift we get circular convolution which is only slightly different than the linear convolution. The definition of circular convolution is similar to the definition of linear convolution except the sequence that is shifted is shifted circularly. So the definition of circular convolution is as shown in Equation(8.37).

$$y_c[n]=\sum_{m=0}^{N-1} x[m]h[\langle n-m \rangle_N]=x[n] \, \textcircled{N} \, h[n] \tag{8.37}$$

This equation is known as the circular convolution equation and it is written usually as the right hand side of Equation 8.37. The convolution symbol is usually a circle with a number written inside it. The number represents the length of the sequence and hence it tells us how many points to be used in the circular convolution. In circular convolution both the sequences are of the same length. If they are not of the same length and this happens often then the shorter sequence is padded with zeros to make it equal to the longer sequence. Circular convolution is completed as demonstrated in Example 8.13.

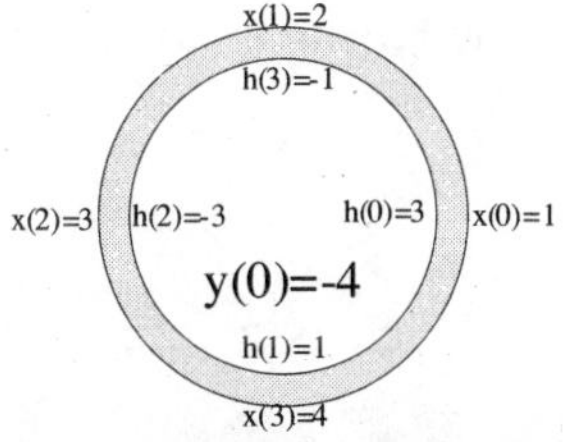

Sequences x[n] and h[-n] ready for the first calculation .

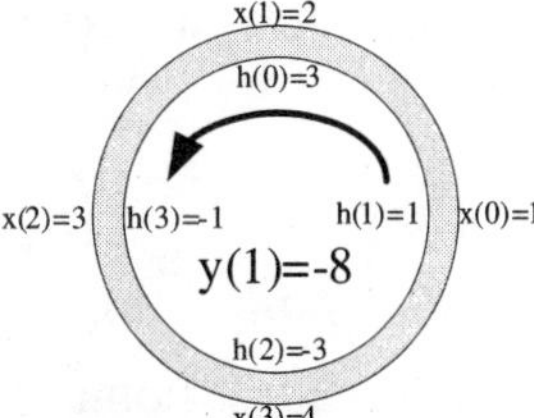

Sequence h[-n] rotated left by 1 position.

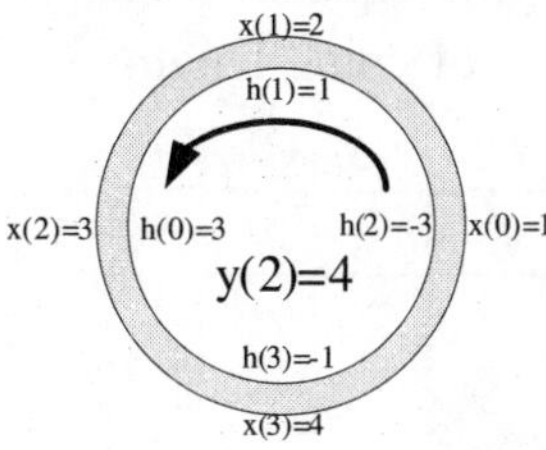

Sequence h[-n] rotated left by 2 positions.

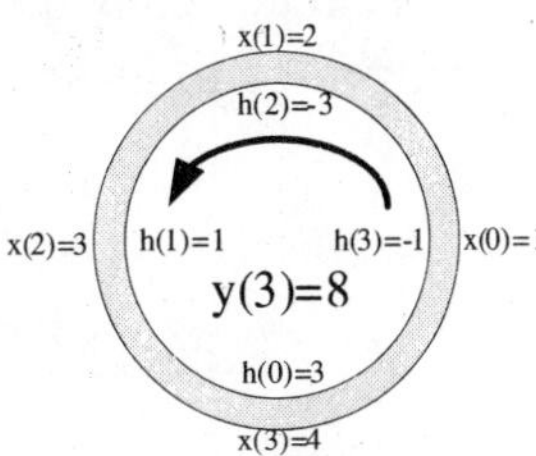

Sequence h[-n] rotated left by 3 positions.

Figure 8.7: Demonstrating the computation of circular convolution using the 'Lazy Susan' diagram for circular shifts

Example 8.13

Convolve the sequence x[n] = [1 2 3 4] with the sequence h[n] = [3 1 -3 -1]

Solution 8.13

Since both the sequences are 4 point sequences the result of convolution will also be a 4 point sequence. The convolution is completed as shown below. We demonstrate each step of the convolution individually:

y[0] =	x[0]h[0] +	x[1]h[3] +	x[2]h[2] +	x[3]h[1]	
y[0] =	(1)(3) +	(2)(-1) +	(3)(-3) +	(4)(1)=	-4
y[1] =	x[0]h[1] +	x[1]h[0] +	x[2]h[3] +	x[3]h[2]	
y[1] =	(1)(1) +	(2)(3) +	(3)(-1) +	(4)(-3) =	-8
y[2] =	x[0]h[2] +	x[1]h[1] +	x[2]h[0] +	x[3]h[3]	
y[2] =	(1)(-3) +	(2)(1) +	(3)(3) +	(4)(-1) =	4
y[3] =	x[0]h[3] +	x[1]h[2] +	x[2]h[1] +	x[3]h[0]	
y[3] =	(1)(-1) +	(2)(-3) +	(3)(1) +	(4)(3) =	8

Notice that we rotate h[n] left by one each step of the convolution to accomplish the circular convolution.

This same circular convolution can be visualized using our 'Lazy Susan' analogy as shown in Figure 8.7. The circular convolution can also be accomplished using a tabular method as shown in Example 8.14.

Example 8.14

Convolve the two finite sequences x[n]=[1 3 5 7] which is a four point sequence with h[n]=[5 4 3 2 1] which is a five point sequence.

Solution 8.14

Since we know that circular convolution is performed with sequences of equal length we will pad the sequence x[n] with zeros to make both the sequences of equal length. So the new sequence

	x(0)	x(1)	x(2)	x(3)	x(4)		
	1	3	5	7	0		
h(0) h(4) h(3) h(2) h(1) →	0	4	3	2	1	y(0) →	41
h(1) h(0) h(4) h(3) h(2) →	1	0	4	3	2	y(1) →	42
h(2) h(1) h(0) h(4) h(3) →	2	1	0	4	3	y(2) →	33
h(3) h(2) h(1) h(0) h(4) →	3	2	1	0	4	y(3) →	14
h(4) h(3) h(2) h(1) h(0) →	4	3	2	1	0	y(4) →	30

Figure 8.8: Performing circular convolution using the tabular method

x[n] = [1 3 5 7 0]. We will perform the convolution using the tabular method as shown in Figure 8.8. Notice that for each step of the convolution we are rotating h[n] by one position so every step will involve all the N entries in both the sequences.

Example 8.15

In Example 8.13 we determined the convolution of two time domain sequences using the convolution process. Determine the convolution of the two time domain sequences by multiplying the DFT of the two time domain sequences.

Solution 8.15

To determine the convolution using the DFT we will first determine the DFT of the two sequences. The DFT of $x_1[n]$ is $X_1[k]$ = [10; -2+2j; -2; -2-2j]

$$X_1[k]=\sum_{n=0}^{3} x_1[n]W_N^{nk}$$

$$X_1[0]=x_1[0]e^0+x_1[1]e^0+x_1[2]e^0+x_1[3]e^0=10$$

$$X_1[1]=x_1[0]e^0+x_1[1]e^{\frac{-j2\pi}{4}}+x_1[2]e^{\frac{-j4\pi}{4}}+x_1[3]e^{\frac{-j6\pi}{4}}$$

$$=1-2j-3+4j=-2+2j$$

$$X_1[2]=x_1[0]e^0+x_1[1]e^{\frac{-j4\pi}{4}}+x_1[2]e^{\frac{-j8\pi}{4}}+x_1[3]e^{\frac{-j12\pi}{4}}$$

$$=1-2+3-4=-2$$

$$X_1[3]=x_1[0]e^0+x_1[1]e^{\frac{-j6\pi}{4}}+x_1[2]e^{\frac{-j12\pi}{4}}+x_1[3]e^{\frac{-j18\pi}{4}}$$

$$=1+2j-3-4j=-2-2j$$

Similarly the DFT of $x_2[n]$ is $X_2[k]$ = [0; 6-2j; 0; 6+2j]

$$X_1[k]=\sum_{n=0}^{3} x_1[n]W_N^{nk}$$

$$X_1[0]=x_1[0]e^0+x_1[1]e^0+x_1[2]e^0+x_1[3]e^0=10$$

$$X_1[1]=x_1[0]e^0+x_1[1]e^{\frac{-j2\pi}{4}}+x_1[2]e^{\frac{-j4\pi}{4}}+x_1[3]e^{\frac{-j6\pi}{4}}$$

$$=1-2j-3+4j=-2+2j$$

$$X_1[2]=x_1[0]e^0+x_1[1]e^{\frac{-j4\pi}{4}}+x_1[2]e^{\frac{-j8\pi}{4}}+x_1[3]e^{\frac{-j12\pi}{4}}$$

$$=1-2+3-4=-2$$

$$X_1[3]=x_1[0]e^0+x_1[1]e^{\frac{-j6\pi}{4}}+x_1[2]e^{\frac{-j12\pi}{4}}+x_1[3]e^{\frac{-j18\pi}{4}}$$

$$=1+2j-3-4j=-2-2j$$

Next we multiply the two DFT to get $X_1[k]X_2[k]$ = [0; -8+16j; 0; -8-16j]

We are now ready to compute the IDFT of the product. This is done as shown below to get the result y[n] = [-4; -8; 4; 8] which is what we had obtained when we used the circular convolution in Example 8.13 earlier.

$$X_1[k] = \sum_{n=0}^{3} x_1[n] W_N^{nk}$$

$$Y[0] = \tfrac{1}{4}\left[0e^0 + (-8+16j)e^0 + 0e^0 + (-8-16j)e^0\right] = -4$$

$$Y[1] = \tfrac{1}{4}\left[0e^0 + (-8+16j)e^{\frac{j2\pi}{4}} + 0e^0 + (-8-16j)e^{\frac{j6\pi}{4}}\right]$$

$$= \tfrac{1}{4}\left[0 + (-8j-16)\,0 + (8j-16)\right] = -8$$

$$Y[2] = \tfrac{1}{4}\left[0e^0 + (-8+16j)e^{\frac{j4\pi}{4}} + 0e^0 + (-8-16j)e^{\frac{j12\pi}{4}}\right]$$

$$= \tfrac{1}{4}\left[0 + (8-16j)\,0 + (8+16j)\right] = 4$$

$$Y[3] = \tfrac{1}{4}\left[0e^0 + (-8+16j)e^{\frac{j6\pi}{4}} + 0e^0 + (-8-16j)e^{\frac{j18\pi}{4}}\right]$$

$$= \tfrac{1}{4}\left[0 + (8j+16)\,0 + (-8j+16)\right] = 8$$

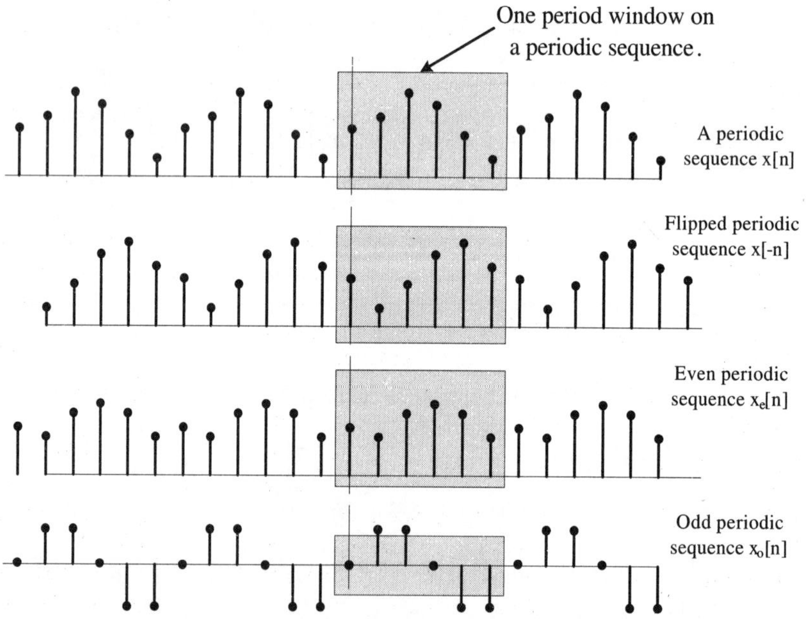

One period window on a periodic sequence.

A periodic sequence x[n]

Flipped periodic sequence x[-n]

Even periodic sequence $x_e[n]$

Odd periodic sequence $x_o[n]$

Figure 8.9: Demonstrating that conjugate symmetric and conjugate anti symmetric sequences of periodic sequences are also periodic with same period. One period of each sequence is highlighted by a window of length one period

8.6.3 Symmetry Properties:

The DFT possesses symmetry properties just like the other Fourier transforms but due to the finite nature of the DFT these properties have to be modified slightly. In general we cannot use the definitions of the conjugate symmetric and the conjugate anti symmetric components that we have used so far. In the definitions we have used earlier we used the sequence x(-n) and x*(-n). This would imply that the sequence extend to the negative range also. This would in effect double the length of the sequence. So using the definitions that we have for a conjugate symmetric and the conjugate anti symmetric sequence the length of the sequence would have to be a length 2N-1 sequence. On the other hand we note that for periodic sequences with period N the conjugate symmetric and the conjugate anti symmetric sequences are periodic sequences with the same period N. This visualization of periodic sequences suggests a possible way to describe the symmetric sequences.

The visualization that we will employ is that we will see the sequence x[n] as one period of a periodic sequence and then we will use this visualization to define the conjugate symmetric and the conjugate anti symmetric sequences of this finite length sequence. Finally we will view the result through a window that is of length N as shown in Figure 8.9. Another way of saying the same thing is to visualize the flipped of the reverser sequence as shifted circularly. This is evident from the second row in Figure 8.9. Notice that the sequence within the window is a circularly shifted sequence. So we can write the definition for a conjugate and a conjugate anti symmetric sequence as shown in Equation(8.38)

$$\begin{aligned} x_{cs}[n] &= \tfrac{1}{2}\{x[n] + x^*[<-n>_N] \qquad 0<n<N-1 \\ x_{ca}[n] &= \tfrac{1}{2}\{x[n] - x^*[<-n>_N] \qquad 0<n<N-1 \end{aligned} \tag{8.38}$$

We will call these as circular conjugate symmetric and circular conjugate anti symmetric sequences. Using the above definitions we can now determine the circular symmetric sequences as shown in Example 8.16.

Example 8.16

Determine the circular conjugate symmetric and circular conjugate anti symmetric parts of a complex finite length sequence

x[n] = [4+3i 5-2i -2-4i -3+3i]

Solution 8.16

In order to determine the circular conjugate symmetric and circular conjugate anti symmetric parts we first determine the conjugate sequence x*[n].

$$x^*[n] = [4-3i,\ \ 5+2i,\ \ -2+4i,\ \ -3-3i]$$

Next we determine the modulo circularly reversed entries for the given sequence. In this sequence since we have 4 entries we will determine modulo 4 values.

$$x^*[<-0>_4] = x^*[0] = \quad 4-3i$$
$$x^*[<-1>_4] = x^*[3] = -\ 3-3i$$
$$x^*[<-2>_4] = x^*[2] = -\ 2+4i$$
$$x^*[<-3>_4] = x^*[1] = \quad 5+2i$$

Using these modulo values we arrive at the reversed sequence which is

$$x^*[<-n>_4] = [4-3i, \ -3-3i, \ -2+4i, \ 5+2i]$$

Finally we arrive at the circular conjugate symmetric and circular conjugate anti symmetric sequences using Equations(8.38) as

$$x_{cs}[n] = \tfrac{1}{2}\left[x[n] + x^*[<-n>_N]\right] = [8, \quad 1-2.5i, \quad 2, \quad 1+2.5i]$$
$$x_{ca}[n] = \tfrac{1}{2}\left[x[n] - x^*[<-n>_N]\right] = [3i, \ 4+0.5i, \ -4i, \ -4+0.5i]$$

We can now very easily verify that $x[n] = ½\{x_{cs}[n] + x_{ca}[n]\}$, also that

$x_{cs}[n] = x^*_{cs}[<-n>_N]$ and that $x_{ca}[n] = -x^*_{ca}[<-n>_N]$

The above discussion also applies to the frequency domain sequence which is the DFT of the finite length sequence x[n] since the transform X[k] is also a finite length sequence so for the frequency domain sequences we will have

$$X_{cs}[k] = \tfrac{1}{2}\left[X[k] + X^*[<-k>_N]\right]$$
$$X_{ca}[k] = \tfrac{1}{2}\left[X[k] - X^*[<-k>_N]\right]$$

8.7 DFT PROPERTIES

Just as with all the other transforms that we have studied, the DFT also has some of the fundamental properties. As we study these properties we will find that all the properties are very similar to the properties that we came across earlier. This is as expected as this transform is very similar to the other transforms. When we are examining these properties and Theorems we will always remember that the sequence x[n] and its DFT X[k] are both finite length sequences and each of length N. In each of these properties we will assume that x[n] ↔ X[k] are a DFT pair and also h[n] ↔ H[k] are a DFT pair.

8.7.1 Linearity:

The Linearity property is listed in Equation(8.39)

$$F\{ax_1[n] + bx_2[n]\} = aX_1[k] + bX_2[k] \tag{8.39}$$

This property is proved directly from the definition of the DFT as shown in Equation(8.40)

$$\begin{aligned} F\{ax_1(n) \pm bx_2(n)\} &= \sum_{n=0}^{N-1}\{ax_1(n) \pm bx_2(n)\}W_N^{nk} \\ &= \sum_{n=0}^{N-1} ax_1(n)W_N^{nk} \pm bx_2(n)W_N^{nk} \\ &= aX_1(k) \pm bX_2(k) \end{aligned} \tag{8.40}$$

8.7.2 Circular Time Shift:

The Circular Time Shift property is listed in Equation(8.41)

$$F\{x\langle n\text{-}p\rangle_N\} \triangleq W_N^{kp}X(k) \tag{8.41}$$

This property shows that a delay or a shift in the time domain corresponds to a rotation in the frequency domain. This property is proved directly from the definition of the DTFT as shown in Equation(8.42)

$$F\{x\langle n\text{-}p\rangle_N\} = \sum_{n=0}^{N-1}(x(n\text{-}p))W_N^{nk} \qquad \text{let } n\text{-}p = m$$

$$F\{x\langle n\text{-}p\rangle_N\} = \sum_{m=-p}^{N-p-1} x(m)W_N^{n(m+p)}$$

We change the limit to zero to N-1 as there are only N values of the sequence and we are using all the N values to carry out the computation. With the limit of N values we can view the sequence as if it is in a circular buffer. So it is the same N values that are used for the computation. We refer to this in more detail when we talk about the circular convolution.

$$\begin{aligned} F\{x(n\text{-}p)\} &= W_N^{np}\sum_{m=0}^{\infty} x(m)W_N^{nm} \\ F\{x(n\text{-}p)\} &= W_N^{np}X(m) \end{aligned} \tag{8.42}$$

8.7.3 Circular Frequency Shift

The Circular Time Shift property is listed in Equation(8.43)

$$F\{W_N^{-np}x[n]\} = X[\langle k-p\rangle_n] \tag{8.43}$$

This property shows that when a time domain sequence is multiplied by an exponential sequence W^{np} then we get a shift in the frequency domain. This property is proved directly from the definition of the DTFT as shown in Equation(8.44)

$$F\left\{W_N^{-np}x[n]\right\}=\sum_{n=0}^{N-1}W_N^{-np}x[n]W_N^{nk}$$

$$=\sum_{n=0}^{N-1}x[n]W_N^{n(k-p)}$$

$$=X\left[<k-p>_N\right] \tag{8.44}$$

8.7.4 Duality:

We have seen this property earlier. We begin with a certain time domain function and we determine its transform, we have a pair. Now if we get a different time domain function which has the same shape as the previous frequency domain function then the transform of this new time domain function will have the same shape as the previous time domain function. That is the transform pair are always duals of each other. Then if we have the N point transform pair $x[n] \leftrightarrow X[k]$ then the DFT of X[n] is a length N sequence and it is shown in Equation(8.45)

$$F\{X[n]\}=Nx\left[<-k>_N\right] \tag{8.45}$$

To prove this property we begin with the definition of the DFT. This is done for you in Equation(8.46). Next substitute the inverse transform expression for X[n]. Re-arrange to get the result that we need. This is done for you in Equation(8.47)

$$F\{X[n]\}=\sum_{n=0}^{N-1}X[n]W_N^{nk} \tag{8.46}$$

$$X[p]=\sum_{p=0}^{N-1}x[p]W_N^{-np}$$

$$F\{X[n]\}=\sum_{n=0}^{N-1}\left[\sum_{p=0}^{N-1}x[p]W_N^{-np}\right]W_N^{nk}$$

$$=\sum_{p=0}^{N-1}x[p]\left[\sum_{n=0}^{N-1}W_N^{-np}W_N^{nk}\right] \tag{8.47}$$

$$=Nx\left[<-k>_N\right]$$

We get the last step in Equation(8.47) since W is a basis function and the summation will be non zero only when p=-k.

8.7.5 Time Reversal:

When a fixed length sequence is reversed then this reversal has to be done so that the sequence stays within the fixed length so this reversal can be viewed as modulo reversal. With this idea the Time Reversal property is listed in Equation (8.48).

$$F\left[x(-n)\right]=X\left[N-K\right] \tag{8.48}$$

The proof of this property is very straight forward and follows directly from the definition of the DFT as shown in Equation(8.49)

$$\begin{aligned}
F\left[x(-n)\right]&=F\left[x\langle -n\rangle_N\right]=F\left[x[N-n]\right]\\
F\left[x(-n)\right]&=\sum_{n=0}^{N-1}x[N-n]W_N^{nk}\\
&=\sum_{m=0}^{N-1}x[m]W_N^{(N-m)k}=W_N^{Nk}\sum_{m=0}^{N-1}x[m]W_N^{-mk}\\
&=X[-k]=X\left[\langle -k\rangle_N\right]=X[N-k]
\end{aligned} \tag{8.49}$$

8.7.6 Real and Imaginary part of the sequence:

In general both the time domain sequence and the frequency domain sequences can be complex quantities. With the complex sequences the real part and the imaginary parts of the sequences can be separated individually as shown in Equation(8.50)

$$\begin{aligned}
F\left[x(n)\right]&=\sum_{n=0}^{N-1}x(n)W_N^{nk}\\
&=\sum_{n=0}^{N-1}\left[x_R(n)+jx_I(n)\right]\left\{Cos\left(\frac{2\pi nk}{N}\right)-jSin\left(\frac{2\pi nk}{N}\right)\right\}\\
X_R[k]&=\sum_{n=0}^{N-1}\left(x_R(n)Cos\left(\frac{2\pi nk}{N}\right)+x_I(n)Sin\left(\frac{2\pi nk}{N}\right)\right)\\
X_I[k]&=\sum_{n=0}^{N-1}\left(x_I(n)Cos\left(\frac{2\pi nk}{N}\right)-x_R(n)Sin\left(\frac{2\pi nk}{N}\right)\right)
\end{aligned} \tag{8.50}$$

Similarly we can determine the transform of the real and the imaginary time sequences as shown in Equation(8.51)

$$\begin{aligned}
F^{-1}\left[X(k)\right]&=\frac{1}{N}\sum_{k=0}^{N-1}X(k)W_N^{-nk}\\
&=\sum_{k=0}^{N-1}\left[X_R(k)+jX_I(k)\right]\left\{Cos\left(\frac{2\pi nk}{N}\right)+jSin\left(\frac{2\pi nk}{N}\right)\right\}\\
x_R[n]&=\sum_{k=0}^{N-1}\left(X_R(k)Cos\left(\frac{2\pi nk}{N}\right)-X_I(k)Sin\left(\frac{2\pi nk}{N}\right)\right)\\
x_I[n]&=\sum_{k=0}^{N-1}\left(X_I(k)Cos\left(\frac{2\pi nk}{N}\right)+X_R(k)Sin\left(\frac{2\pi nk}{N}\right)\right)
\end{aligned} \tag{8.51}$$

Table 8.3: Properties of the Discrete Fourier Transform

	Name of Property	Time Domain	Frequency Domain
1	**Linearity**	$ax_1(n) \pm bx_2(n)$	$aX_1[k] \pm bX_2[k]$
2	**Circular Time Shift**	$x\left[\langle n-p\rangle_N\right]$	$W_N^{kp} X\left[k\right]$
3	**Convolution**	$\sum_{m=0}^{N-1} x_1(m) x_2\left(\langle n-m\rangle_N\right)$	$X_1\left[k\right] \cdot X_2\left[k\right]$
4	**Circular Frequency Shift**	$W_N^{-np} x\left[n\right]$	$X\left[\langle k-p\rangle_n\right]$
5	**Time Reversal**	**x[-n]=x[N-n]**	**X[-k] = X[N-k]**

8.8 LINEAR CONVOLUTION USING DFT

In the previous section we saw that the convolution performed using finite length sequences is a circular convolution which is slightly different than the linear convolution that we have seen. However it is the linear convolution that we must perform when a signal passes through a system. So often we are faced with a question - Can we perform Linear Convolution using finite sequences? The answer to that is a resounding yes. We can indeed perform linear convolution using finite sequences.

The most obvious difference between linear convolution and the circular convolution is that the circular convolution of two length N sequences gives us a result that is also a length N sequence. Whereas when we perform a linear convolution between two length N sequences we get a length 2N-1 sequence. That is the length of the linear convolution is equal to the sum of the two sequences minus 1 (N+M-1). Thus the circular convolution, which only produces a length N result, somehow aliases the result. If we can make sure that aliasing does not take place then the result of the circular convolution and the result of linear convolution will be the same.

8.8.1 Convolution using Finite Length Sequences

In the circular convolution aliasing occurs because all the N points in the sequence are used in performing the convolution for every cycle. In linear convolution as we shift one function under the other the convolution gradually builds up and in the same way as we shift the function out the convolution gradually dies down. We can recreate this same effect in circular convolution if we pad the two functions with N-1 zeros. Now when a zero is under one of the non zero values of the other function the product will not contribute to the convolution and we will avoid the aliasing. This is shown in Figure 8.10.

In Figure 8.10 we see two sequences whose linear convolution is desired. We first make both the sequences as long as the resulting convolution will be by padding zeros. So if one sequence is length M and the other is length N then we make both of them length N+M-1 by padding appropriate

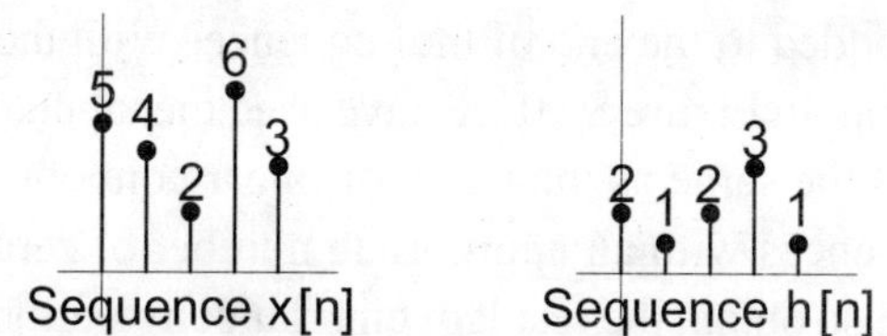

Since both sequences are equal length we pad each sequence with N -1 or 4 zeros.

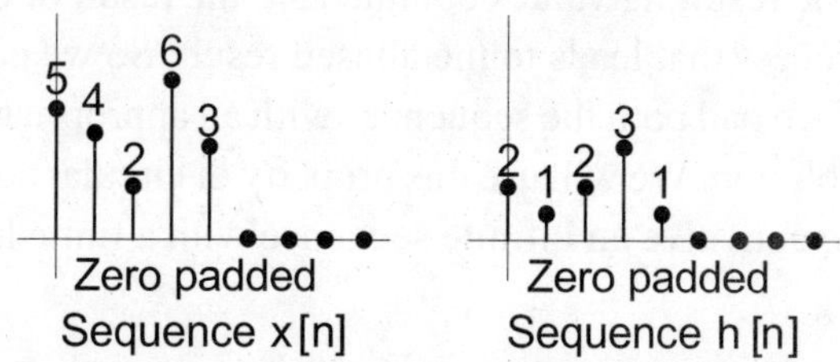

Circular convolution with these two sequences will be the same as linear convolution .

x(0)	x(1)	x(2)	x(3)	x(4)	x(5)	x(6)	x(7)	x(8)	
5	4	2	6	3	0	0	0	0	
2	0	0	0	0	1	3	2	1	y(0) → 10
1	2	0	0	0	0	1	3	2	y(1) → 13
2	1	2	0	0	0	0	1	3	y(2) → 18
3	2	1	2	0	0	0	0	1	y(3) → 37
1	3	2	1	2	0	0	0	0	y(4) → 33
0	1	3	2	1	2	0	0	0	y(5) → 25
0	0	1	3	2	1	2	0	0	y(6) → 26
0	0	0	1	3	2	1	2	0	y(7) → 15
0	0	0	0	1	3	2	1	2	y(8) → 3

Result is the same as linear convolution performed using circular convolution.

Figure 8.10: Performing linear convolution using the circular convolution

number of zeros. The zeros are padded to the end of the sequence. With the sequences lengthened we perform the circular convolution. In Figure 8.10 we have used the tabular method to perform the circular convolution. The result is the same as the result of linear convolution. This happens only because we have padded the sequences with an appropriate number of zeros.

If you look carefully you can also obtain the result of circular convolution from the linear convolution result in Figure 8.10. To do this we wrap the last 4 results around and add the overlapping results. So we wrap y(8) to y(3) and add; wrap y(7) to y(2) and add; wrap y(6) to y(1) and add finally wrap y(5) to y(0) and add. The resulting values obtained are the result of circular convolution. It is this wrapping and adding process that leads to the aliased result. So we can get linear convolution using circular convolution if we pad both the sequences with an appropriate number of zeros before performing the circular convolution. We will use this property of circular convolution in the next two sections where we attempt to convolve an infinite sequence with a finite length sequence.

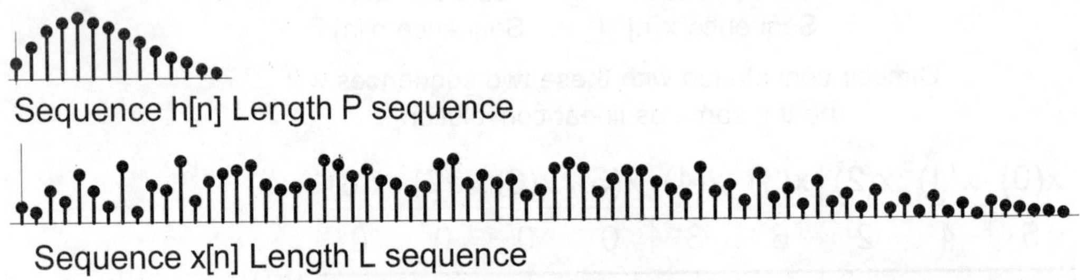

Figure 8.11: The two sequences to be convolved together, h(n) is the short sequence and x(n) is an infinite sequence

Often you have a need to convolve two sequences where one of the sequences is very much larger than the other. Typical relations between the two sequences is shown in Figure 8.11. We can of course make both the sequences equal by padding appropriate number of zeros and then determining the DFT of the two sequences before multiplying them together. After we have multiplied them together we will get a result which we will inverse transform to get the result of convolving the two sequences together. This would require that we determine the DFT and the IDFT of very large sequences. We will see in the next chapter that the computation required to perform the DFT or the IDFT increases by N^2 so as N becomes very large the computation load would become enormous. Besides some times, such as in speech or real time applications we want the result of filtering a signal as the signal is received, we do not have the luxury to store the sequence and then work on the sequence after the entire sequence has been received. In cases such as these we can employ one of the following two methods.

8.8.2 Overlap and Add Method when one sequence is infinite:

Assume that you have two sequences that you have to convolve. One sequence is a shorter sequence which we will call as h[n], and the other sequence is a long sequence, almost infinite in length, which we will call as x[n]. Assume that the sequence h[n] is a length P sequence and the sequence x[n] is a length L sequence. The two sequences are shown in Figure 8.11. We will first divide the sequence x[n] into several shorter sequences of length N. We will choose N to be greater than P. These smaller sequences which are derived from x[n] are shown in Figure 8.12. Before we begin the circular convolution the sequence h[n] and each of the $x_r[n]$, will be extended so that each of the $x_r[n]$ and the sequence h[n] has length N+P-1 by padding zeros to the end of all the sequences.

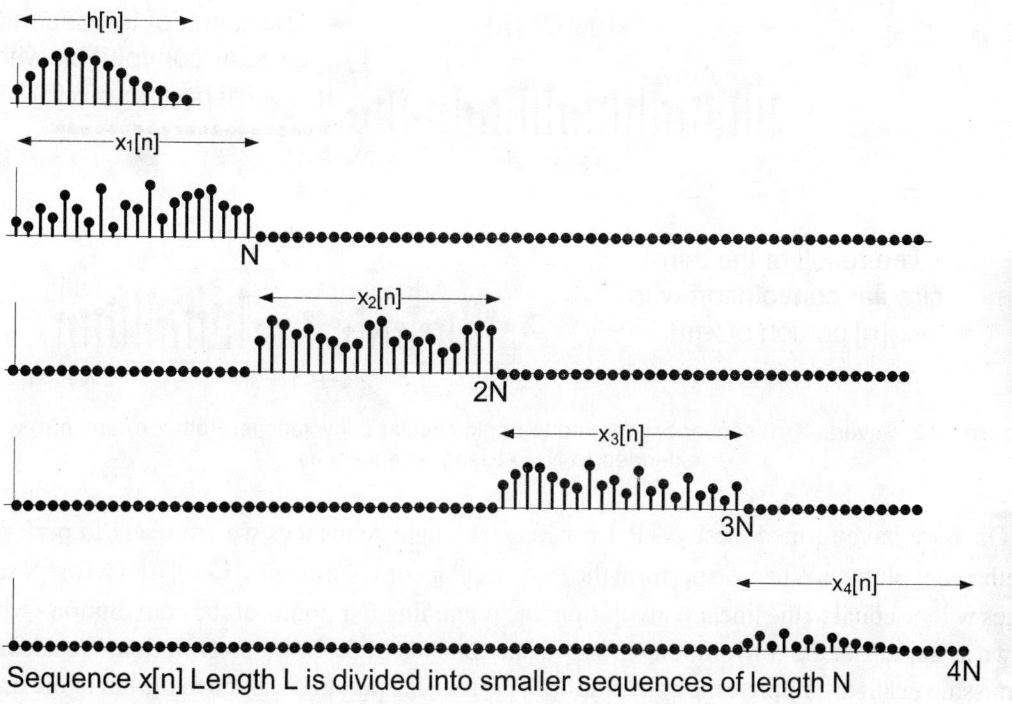

Figure 8.12: Several $X_r(n)$ sequences formed to begin circular convolutions. Both x(n) and h(n) will be extended to N+P-1 length sequences

First the sequence is divided into smaller sequences $x_r[n]$ as shown in Equation(8.52)

$$x[n] = \sum_{r=0}^{\infty} \sum_{m=0}^{N-1} x_r[m - rN] \tag{8.52}$$

where each of the $x_r[n]$ is determined as shown in Equation(8.53)

$$x_r[k] = \begin{cases} x[k + rN] & 0 \le k \le N-1 \\ 0 & \text{Otherwise} \end{cases} \tag{8.53}$$

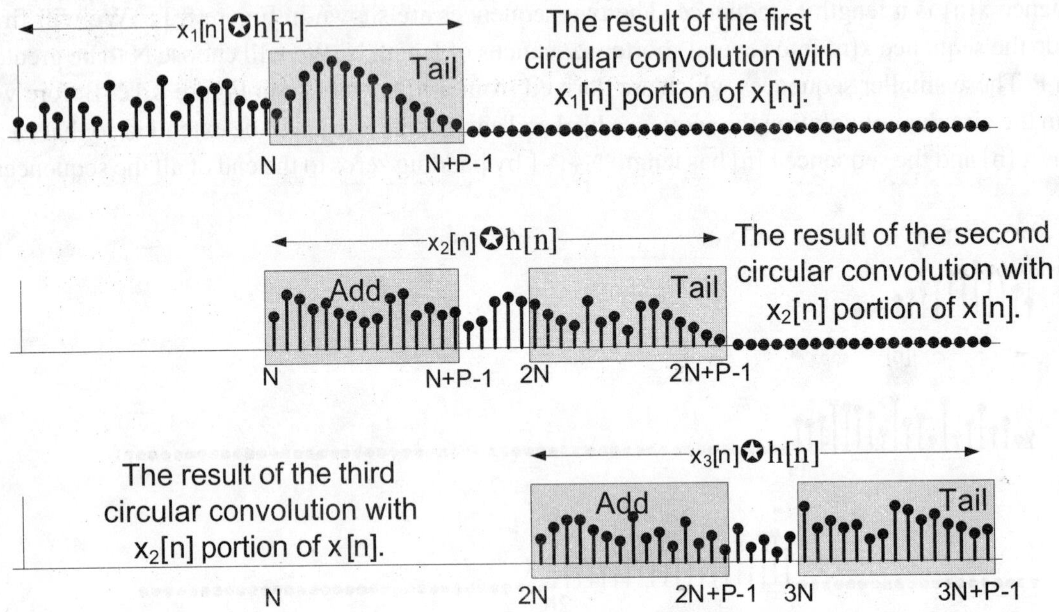

Figure 8.13: Several $X_r(n)$ sequences formed to begin circular convolutions. Both x(n) and h(n) will be extended to N+P-1 length sequences

Once we have formed these N+P-1 (or longer) length sequences we are ready to perform the circular convolution. When we perform the first circular convolution h[n]✪x_1[n] the first N sample values will be equal to the linear convolution, the remaining P-1 points of the convolution - which is known as the 'tail' of the convolution - is only a partial result of the linear convolution. We need to add the missing result to complete the convolution. This missing part to be added to the tail of the result of the first convolution is obtained in the next convolution. This first convolution is shown in Figure 8.13 in the first row. So as Figure 8.13 shows we will divide the result into two parts. Save the first N points and save the (P-1) point tail to be used with the next convolution.

Next we perform the next circular convolution with h[n] and x_2[n], this result is shown in the center row diagram of Figure 8.13. In this convolution the first P-1 points are not equal to linear convolution result. They represent the missing part and are only a partial result which will become complete if we were to add the 'tail' that we have saved from the previous convolution to these P-1 points, since the 'tail' is also of length P-1 points the result of the addition will be possible and it will be the same as the result of linear convolution. The next N-P+1 points will be the correct result of linear convolution so they are stored away. The remaining P-1 points from the present convolution now form the new 'tail' to be used with the next convolution.

Continuing in this manner with successive x_r[n] till we reach the end of the sequence x[n]. The last circular convolution will not leave behind a tail since the function h[n] will shift away and will no longer overlap the function x[n]. So in the last convolution, after we add the tail from the previous convolution, the result that we get is the complete result of convolution.

With this definition of $x_r[n]$ and the understanding of each convolution we get the complete convolution as shown in Equation(8.54)

$$y[n] = h[n] \otimes x[n]$$

$$y[n] = \sum_{r=0}^{\infty} y_r[n - rN] \tag{8.54}$$

where each $y_r[n] = h[n] \circledast x_r[n]$. In each of the convolution sequences $x_r[n]$ have only N non zero points and h[n] have only P non zero points. The result of convolution $y_r[n]$ has N+P-1 non zero points. So when we pick off the N linear convolution points we have the remaining P-1 non zero points - the 'tail' - that need to be added to the P-1 points from the next convolution. This is what we have tried to show in Figure 8.13.

The advantage of the overlap and the add method is that it allows us to determine the DFT of smaller sequences which are easier to complete as the computation time required for an N point DFT is of the order of N^2. With the overlap and add method we are not done after completing the convolution, we have to add a partial result obtained after the next convolution so if time and speed are of essence then we will have to wait longer and this method fails. If speed is not of essence then this is a very efficient method.

8.8.3 Overlap and Save Method

Assume that you have two sequences that you have to convolve. One sequence is a shorter sequence which we wish to convolve with each other. We will call the short sequence as h[n], and the long sequence which is almost infinite in length which we will call as x[n]. The two sequences are shown in Figure 8.11. Here again h[n] is a length P sequence and x[n] is a length L sequence. Again we will divide the sequence x[n] into smaller sequences of length N where N > P. We will choose to divide the sequence x[n] in a special way.

Each successive $x_r[n]$ will be chosen so that it will overlap the first P-1 points in $x_r[n]$ with the last P-1 points from the previous or $x_{r-1}[n]$ sequence. This division of the sequence x[n] is shown in Figure 8.14. We will also pad the first $x_1[n]$ with P zeros in the beginning. These P zeros are padded before we begin the convolution. So we can define $x_r[n]$ as shown in Equation(8.55)

$$x_r[n] = x[n + r(N - P + 1) - P + 1] \qquad 0 \le n \le N - 1 \tag{8.55}$$

We will also pad h[n] with N-P zeros so both the sequences will be length N sequences. Now that we have both sequences of length N we are ready to complete the circular convolution.

When the circular convolution is completed the result contains some points that are useless and the remaining points that are the result of the linear convolution. In the result of circular convolution the first P points are useless so we will discard them. The remaining N-P points are the result of linear convolution and these points are saved. We will now perform the next convolution between h[n] with $x_2[n]$. Remember when we formed $x_2[n]$ we overlapped $x_2[n]$ with $x_1[n]$ for P points. These P points are at the end of $x_1[n]$ and at the beginning of $x_2[n]$. This overlap is shown in Figure 8.14.

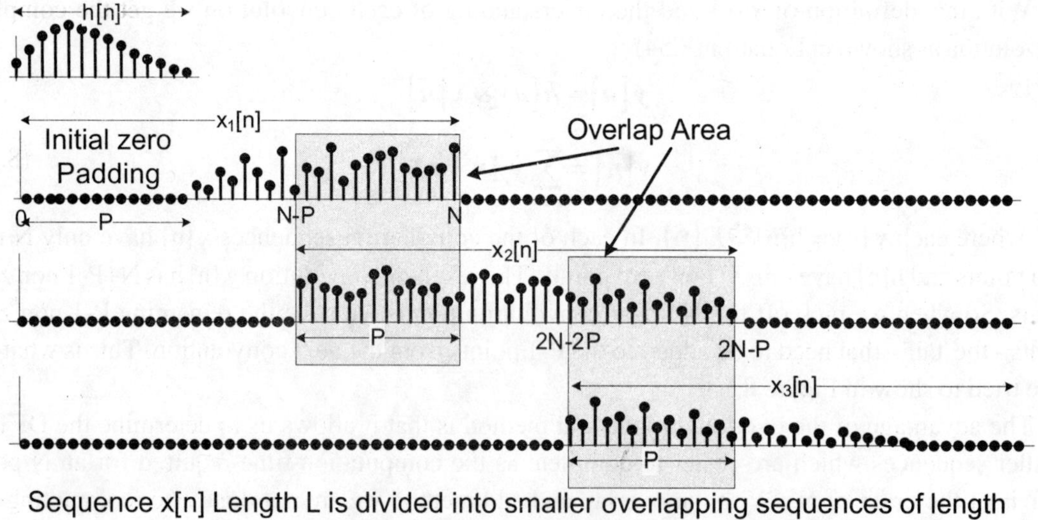

Figure 8.14: Several $X_r(n)$ sequences formed to begin circular convolutions. Only the h(n) sequence will be extended to length N sequence

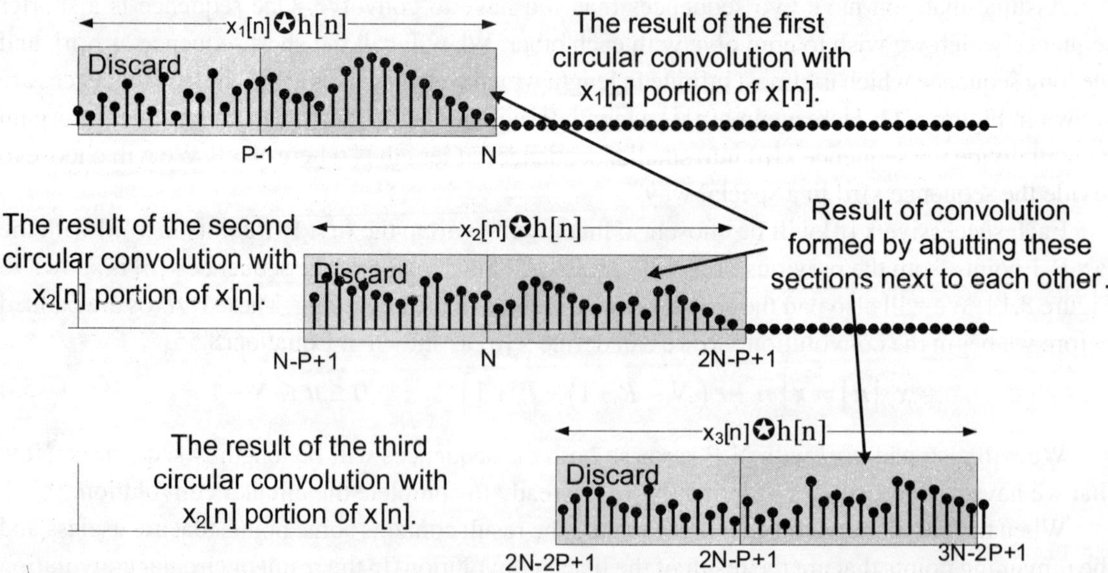

Figure 8.15: Circular convolution result for Overlap and Save method. Notice that the first P-1 points of each convolution are discarded. The remaining N–P+1 points are saved as they form the result that we are looking for.

As the convolution proceeds we build up the result as shown in Figure 8.15. As the result for each intermediate convolution is obtained we first discard the first P points of the convolution and save the remaining N-P points. So with each convolution we get additional N-P points appended to the result. The result is built up by abutting the points from each successive convolution. The circular convolution of each section $x_r[n]$ with h[n] is written as $y_r[n]$. Here each $y_r[n] = h[n] \circledast x_r[n]$ and each of the $y_r[n]$ are combined together as $y[n]=\sum_{r=0}^{\infty} y_r\left[n-r(N-P+1)+P-1\right]$

The advantage of the overlap and save method is that it allows us to determine the DFT of smaller sequences which are easier to complete as the computation time required for an N point DFT is of the order of N^2. With the overlap and save method we are done after completing the partial convolution for a few terms, so if time and speed are of essence then we usually use this method. This method however wastes some computations as we have to compute the DFT of the overlap portion of the sequence twice.

8.9 COMPUTING THE DFT USING THE FFT

The DFT is a very useful and a widely used algorithm. Because of its very wide use there has been tremendous interest in how the DFT is computed. Let us first investigate what is required to compute the DFT and then we will investigate how we can do it more efficiently.

Brute Force Computation of the DFT:

When we are computing the DFT we are in general dealing with complex numbers, both the x[n] and the W are complex numbers. When we want to complete a complex multiplication

$$\mathbf{(a+bi)(x+yi) = (ax+by)+i(bx+ay)}$$

we need to complete 4 real multiplications and 2 real additions. So to complete the DFT computation which contains all complex arithmetic we will need to complete the computation shown in Equation(8.56)

$$\begin{aligned} X[k] &= \sum_{n=0}^{N-1} x[n] W_N^{nk} \\ &= \left[x[0]e^0 + x[1]e^{\frac{-j2\pi(1)k}{N}} + x[2]e^{\frac{-j2\pi(2)k}{N}} + \cdots + x[N-1]e^{\frac{-j2\pi(N-1)k}{N}} \right] \end{aligned} \tag{8.56}$$

Equation(8.56) shows us that to compute any one value of X[k] we need to perform N complex multiplications and N-1 complex additions. Since there are N different X[k] values we will need to complete N^2 complex multiplications and N(N-1) complex additions. As N becomes larger and larger these computations take a significant amount of time. Even for a modest size of N=1024 we will need to perform 2^{20} complex multiplications and almost just as many complex additions. This will tax even the most modern of all computers. So if we can come up with a clever algorithm that will reduce the computation effort then it will be most welcome.

There are several such algorithms, they are all collectively known by a graphic name of **F**ast **F**ourier **T**ransform (FFT). The FFT is not a new or a different transform. The FFT is just a clever way of computing the DFT so that we do not have to perform so many different complex multiplications and complex additions.

8.9.1 Decimation in Time:

We begin describing this algorithm with the assumption that the sequence x[n], which is a length N sequence is a sequence of even length (N is even). If it is not then we can always pad the sequence with one extra sample point which is zero to make its length even. To compute the DFT of an even length sequence we will write the DFT computation as shown in Equation(8.57)

$$
\begin{aligned}
X[k] &= \sum_{n=0}^{N-1} x[n] W_N^{nk} \\
X[k] &= \underbrace{\sum_{n=0}^{\frac{N}{2}-1} x(2n) W_N^{2nk}}_{\text{All the even entries of } x(n)} + \underbrace{\sum_{n=0}^{\frac{N}{2}-1} x(2n+1) W_N^{(2n+1)k}}_{\text{All the odd entries of } x(n)}
\end{aligned} \tag{8.57}
$$

The computation shown in Equation(8.57) computes the DFT for the sequence x(n) but notice how we have arranged the computation. The first summation represents all the even position values of x(n) while the second summation represents all the odd position values of x(n). With a little thought and algebra we can modify the two summations in Equation(8.57) as shown in Equation(8.58)

$$
\begin{aligned}
W_N^{2nk} &= e^{\frac{j2\pi(2n)k}{N}} = e^{\frac{j2\pi(n)k}{N/2}} = W_{\frac{N}{2}}^{nk} \\
W_N^{(2n+1)k} &= e^{\frac{j2\pi(2n+1)k}{N}} = e^{\frac{j2\pi k}{N}} e^{\frac{j2\pi(n)k}{N/2}} = W_N^k W_{\frac{N}{2}}^{nk}
\end{aligned} \tag{8.58}
$$

When we substitute Equation(8.58) into Equation(8.57) we get Equation(8.59)

$$
X[k] = \underbrace{\sum_{n=0}^{\frac{N}{2}-1} x(2n) W_{N/2}^{nk}}_{\frac{N}{2}\text{ point DFT}} + \underbrace{W_N^k \sum_{n=0}^{\frac{N}{2}-1} x(2n+1) W_{N/n}^{nk}}_{\frac{N}{2}\text{ point DFT}} \tag{8.59}
$$

In Equation(8.59) the two summations are each N/2 point DFT calculations. So we have effectively reduced one N point DFT to 2; N/2 point DFT's. With this change the computation effort required now is of the order of $2(N/2)^2$. So by rearranging the terms in a special way we have reduced the amount of computations required. Can we do this type of division again? Yes we can as long as the new (and smaller) sequences also contain even number of entries in them. We can keep on dividing x(n) into its even and odd entries. In the limit if we begin with N being a power of 2 ($N=2^{\upsilon}$) then the computation effort required reduces to $N\log_2(N)$ complex multiplications and a similar number of complex additions. This leads to an enormous reduction of effort when N is large.

What we have just done using equations is demonstrated pictorially in Figure 8.16. In Figure 8.16 the left hand side represents two N/2 point DFT's which are combined together as shown to form the DFT of the entire N point sequence. Then as we explained earlier these two N/2 point DFTs can also be computed by dividing the N/2 points into even and odd points to get N/4 point sequences. This is shown in Figure 8.17. As explained earlier this idea can be extended till each sequence is only a 1 point sequence and then the sequences are combined together as shown in Figure 8.18 for a complete 16 point sequence. Notice that in Figure 8.16 the input sequence is not in normal form but it is in a shuffled form. This way the output sequence that we get comes out in straight or normal form.

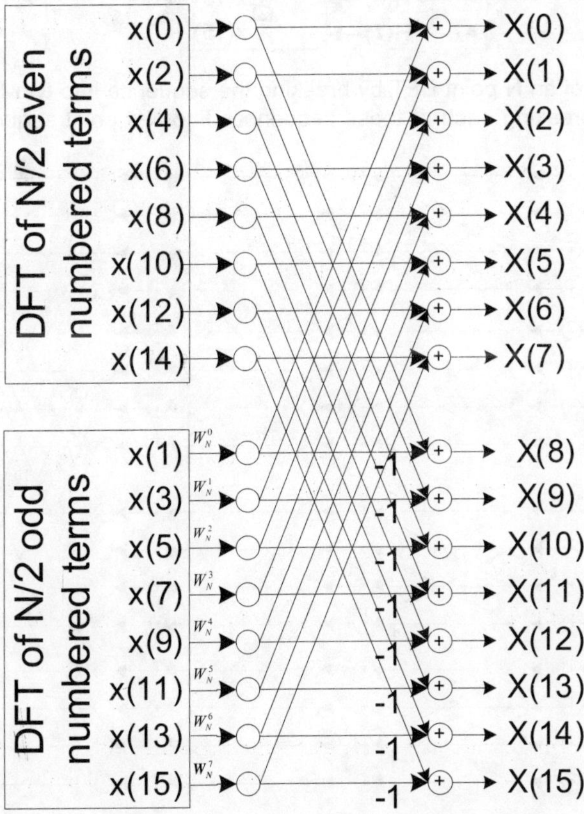

Figure 8.16: Computation of an N point DFT by breaking the sequence into two N/2 point sequences

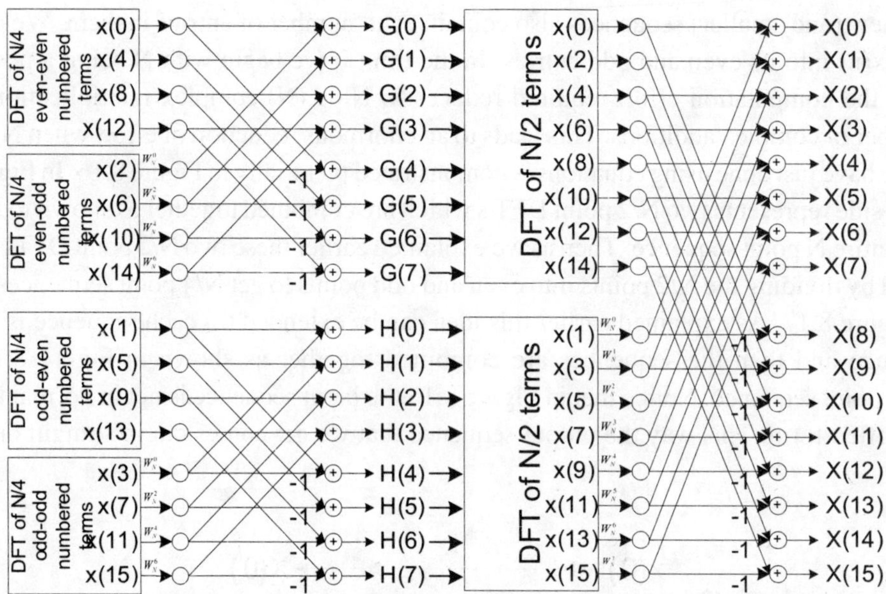

Figure 8.17: Computation of an N point DFT by breaking the sequence into two N/2 point sequences, and again breaking each of those sequences into N/4 point sequences

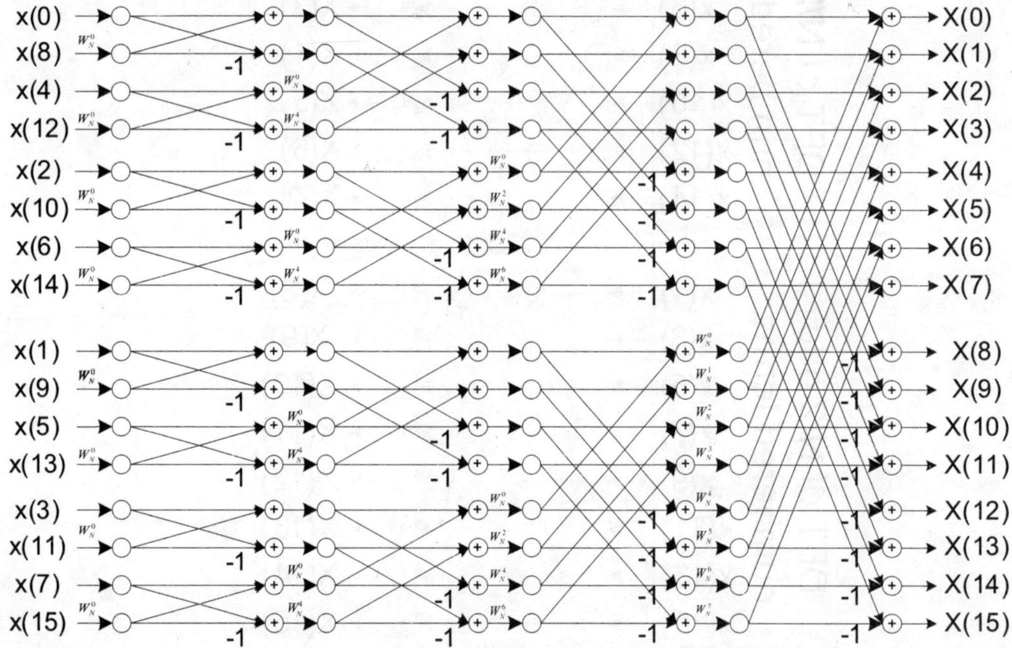

Figure 8.18: Computation of an 16 point DFT by successively breaking the sequence into two N/2 point sequences. Decimal in Time.

8.9.2 Decimation in Frequency:

We begin describing this algorithm with the assumption that the sequence x[n], which is a length N sequence is a sequence of even length (N is even). If it is not then we can always pad the sequence with one extra sample point which is zero to make its length even. To compute the DFT of an even length sequence we will write the DFT computation as shown in Equation(8.60)

$$X[k]=\sum_{n=0}^{N-1} x[n]W_N^{nk}$$

$$X[k]=\underbrace{\sum_{n=0}^{\frac{N}{2}-1} x(n)W_N^{nk}}_{\text{First half entries of } x(n)} + \underbrace{\sum_{m=0}^{\frac{N}{2}-1} x\left(m+\tfrac{N}{2}\right)W_N^{\left(m+\frac{N}{2}\right)k}}_{\text{Second half entries of } x(n)} \tag{8.60}$$

The computation shown in Equation(8.60) computes the DFT for the sequence x[n] but this time we have arranged the computation so that the first summation uses only the first half of the terms while the second summation uses only the last half of the terms. Next consider first the computation of all the even terms for X[k]. With a little thought and algebra we can modify the summations in Equation(8.60) as shown in Equation(8.61) and in Equation(8.62). These two equations give us the even portion and the odd portion of the DFT individually. Just as we did for the decimation in time algorithm we can carry this algorithm also further by taking each N/2 point DFT and further dividing it into N/4 and so on. A diagram similar to Figure 8.18 is given in Figure 8.19 for the decimation in Frequency algorithm. Notice that in this algorithm the input numbers are entered in order but the final result appears in a shuffled form.

$$X[2k]=\underbrace{\sum_{n=0}^{\frac{N}{2}-1} x(n)W_N^{n2k}}_{\text{First half entries of } x(n)} + \underbrace{\sum_{m=0}^{\frac{N}{2}-1} x\left(m+\tfrac{N}{2}\right)W_N^{\left(m+\frac{N}{2}\right)2k}}_{\text{Second half entries of } x(n)}$$

$$X[2k]=\underbrace{\sum_{n=0}^{\frac{N}{2}-1} x(n)W_{N/2}^{nk}}_{\text{DFT of } \frac{N}{2} \text{ terms}} + \underbrace{W^k\sum_{m=0}^{\frac{N}{2}-1} x\left(m+\tfrac{N}{2}\right)W_{N/2}^{mk}}_{\text{DFT of } \frac{N}{2} \text{ terms}}$$

$$X[2k]=\sum_{n=0}^{\frac{N}{2}-1}\left[x(n)+x\left(n+\tfrac{N}{2}\right)\right]W_{N/2}^{nk} \tag{8.61}$$

$$X[2k+1]=\underbrace{\sum_{n=0}^{\frac{N}{2}-1} x(n)W_N^{n(2k+1)}}_{\text{First half entries of } x(n)} + \underbrace{\sum_{m=0}^{\frac{N}{2}-1} x\left(m+\tfrac{N}{2}\right)W_N^{\left(m+\frac{N}{2}\right)(2k+1)}}_{\text{Second half entries of } x(n)}$$

$$X[2k+1]=\underbrace{\sum_{n=0}^{\frac{N}{2}-1} x(n)W_N^n W_{N/2}^{nk}}_{DFT\ of\ \frac{N}{2}\ terms}+\underbrace{W^k\sum_{m=0}^{\frac{N}{2}-1} x(m+\tfrac{N}{2})W_N^m W_N^{N/2} W_{N/2}^{mk}}_{DFT\ of\ \frac{N}{2}\ terms}$$

$$X[2k+1]=\sum_{n=0}^{\frac{N}{2}-1}\left[x(n)-x(n+\tfrac{N}{2})\right]W_N^n W_{N/2}^{nk} \tag{8.62}$$

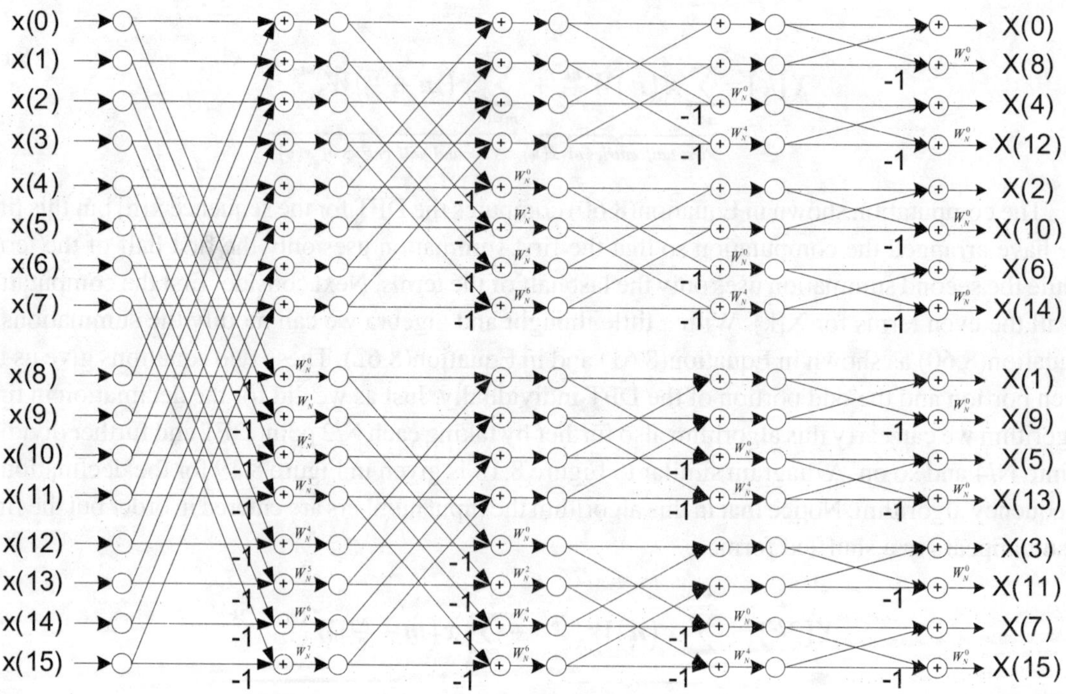

Figure 8.19: Computation of an 16 point DFT by successively breaking the sequence into two N/2 point sequences. Decimal of Frequency.

In Equation(8.62) we see the odd entries of the result. The two terms are subtracted from each other since $W_N^{N/2}=-1$ so all the second half terms are subtracted.

8.10 CHAPTER SUMMARY

8.10.1 Discrete Fourier Series:

We began this chapter with the study of the Discrete Fourier Series. At that time we saw that a periodic signal that is sampled periodically may or may not itself be periodic. The conditions for the sampled signal to be periodic are that the ratio of the signal frequency and the sampling rate of the sampling signal be a rational number.

8.10.2 The Complex Number W:

To continue our studies we introduced a special notation to represent the sampling instants around the unit circle. This was done by means of the complex number W. Table 8.1 lists some of the commonly used properties of the complex number W. We will find that using the notation of W will greatly ease our analysis of the sampled signals.

8.10.3 Discrete Time Fourier Transforms:

Now that we have sampled a periodic signal we have an infinite length signal (since all periodic signals are of infinite length). The DTFT allows us to study the properties of the sampled signal in the frequency domain just as the Fourier Transform allowed us to study the properties of the continuous time signal in the frequency domain. As we studied the DTFT we saw that there were many similarities between the Fourier Transform and the DTFT which is to be expected as by sampling the signal we have only modified the frequency content not drastically altered the frequency information contained in the signal. The properties of the DTFT are listed in Table 8.2.

8.10.4 Fourier Transform for Finite Length Sequence:

The DTFT was obtained for infinite length and finite energy signals. If we limit the infinite length signal to say one period of the signal then we get a finite energy finite length signal. This is just one of the ways to get a finite energy finite length signal. Once we have the finite length signal we will treat it as if it represents one period of an infinite length signal. Since the other periods contain the same information that is present in this one period we can determine the properties of the entire signal by examining the properties of just the one period of the signal.

8.10.5 Discrete Fourier Transform:

Determining the Fourier transform of the finite length signal leads us to the DFT. The DFT assumes that the finite length sequence is a periodic sequence and computes the DFT of the sequence. In this case both the time domain sequence and the frequency domain sequences are of equal length, they are both assumed to be periodic sequences and they are both discrete sequences. The computation of the DFT is very computationally intensive, it is of the order of N^2 but there are many similar computations that can be combined together so that the computational burden is substantially reduced. This gives us two very efficient methods; Decimation in Time and Decimation in Frequency; that reduce the number of computations to be of the order of $N\log_2(N)$ which is a substantial savings since both the time domain and the frequency domain sequences are complex sequences.

8.11 HOMEWORK PROBLEMS

The Discrete Fourier Series:

8.11.1 Determine if the following signals after being sampled as shown are periodic. If the signals are periodic determine the period of each signal in number of samples.

a. x(t) = 5Cos(50t) Signal sampled at 50; 500; 100π samples/sec.
b. x(t) = 5Cos(50πt) Signal sampled at 50; 500; 100π samples/sec.
c. x(t) = 5Cos(50t)Sin(22t) Signal sampled at 50; 500; 100π samples/sec.
d. x(t) = 5Cos(50πt) Sin(22t) Signal sampled at 50; 500; 100π samples/sec.
e. x(t) = 5Cos(50t)Sin(22t) Signal sampled at 50; 500; 100π samples/sec.
f. x(t) = 5Cos(50πt) Sin(22πt) Signal sampled at 50; 500; 100π samples/sec.

8.11.2 You are given that a particular sampled signal is a periodic signal. Write an expression for at least two signals that when sampled as shown will have a period as required. One of the two signals is a product signal of the type Cos(mt)Sin(nt).

a. Period of the signal 33 samples per second. Sampled at 100 samples per second.
b. Period of the signal 50 samples per second. Sampled at 60 samples per second.
c. Period of the signal 30 samples per second. Sampled at 80 samples per second.
d. Period of the signal 33 samples per second. Sampled at 15π samples per second.
e. Period of the signal 50 samples per second. Sampled at 80π samples per second.
f. Period of the signal 40 samples per second. Sampled at 50π samples per second.

8.11.3 What is the Discrete Time Fourier Series for all the signals given in Homework Problem 8.11.1 when the sampled signal is a periodic signal?

8.11.4 Using a SCILAB script determine the values of the Discrete Time Fourier Series by evaluating the summation of the Discrete Time Fourier Series.

Properties of the complex number W:

8.11.5 Prove the following properties of the complex number W

a. Prove $\frac{1}{N}\sum_{m=0}^{N-1}\sum_{n=0}^{N-1} W_N^{m-n} = 1$

b. Prove $\left[W_N^{-N}\right] = 1$

Properties of the Discrete Time Fourier Transform:

8.11.6 You are given that the DTFT of x(t) is X(ω) and the DTFT of h(t) is H(ω). Now using the properties of the DTFT determine the DTFT of all the following functions.

a. $ax[n] + b^2h[n]$. a>0 and b>0
b. atx[n] a>0
c. a[n-5]x[n-5] a>0
d. $a[n-5]x[n-5] + b^2h[n]$. a>0 and b>0
e. $a[n-5]x[n] + b^2h[n]$. a>0 and b>0
f. $a[-n-5]x[-n-5] * b^2h[n]$. a>0 and b>0
g. $a[-n-5]x[-n-5] * b^2h[-n]$. a>0 and b>0
h. $a[-n-5]x[-n] * b^2h[-n]$. a>0 and b>0

8.11.7 Using a SCILAB script determine the DTFT of all the periodic functions in Problem 8.11.1

Fourier Transform for Finite Length Sequences

Discrete Fourier Transform:

8.11.8 The following signals are sampled for one second. That gives you a finite length sequence. Determine the DFT of the resulting sequence. (Remember these sampled signals do not have to be periodic to start with.)

a. 5Cos(4t) Sampled at the rate of 10 samples per second.
b. 5Cos(4πt) Sampled at the rate of 10 samples per second.
c. 5Cos(4t) Sampled at the rate of 3π samples per second.
d. 5Cos(4πt) Sampled at the rate of 3π samples per second.
e. 5Cos(4t)Sin(5t) Sampled at the rate of 10 samples per second.
f. 5Cos(4πt)Sin(5πt) Sampled at the rate of 3π samples per second.

8.11.9 You are given that the DFT of the signal x[n] is X[k]. Now form the following new signals and relate the DFT of the new signal to the DFT of the original signal:

a. Signal $x_1[n]$ is formed by catenating signal x[n] to itself. $x_1[n] = [x[n],x[n]]$

b. Signal $x_2[n]$ is formed by inserting two zeros between successive samples of signal x[n], thus forming a signal that is three times as large as signal x[n].

Overlap and Add Method/Overlap and Save Method

8.11.10 Write a SCILAB program to compute the convolution of a short sequence h[n] of length 50 with a long sequence x[n] of length 525.

a. Use the Overlap and Add method. How many different sections do you have to split the computations so that you will complete the convolution?

b. Use the Overlap and Save method. How many different sections do you have to split the computations so that you will complete the convolution?

c. Which method is the more economical method in terms of the number of computations required?

d. What do you have to do to the two sequences if this convolution was to be performed using direct circular convolution?

e. What is the gain in the computation efficiency of the methods in a and b over the method in d?

CHAPTER 9

Digital Filter Design

INTRODUCTION

The difference equations that we studied and investigated in the chapter on Z-transforms are a description of a discrete system just as the differential equation is the description of a continuous time system. What the difference equation tells us is the response to the system when we have an input presented to the system. The difference equation tells us what the nth output from the system will be. This same characterization can also be used to describe the digital filters which are used in systems to perform special tasks. The digital filters that we will explore in this chapter are characterized by their impulse responses. Since it is the impulse response that really describes the system, we convolve the input that we have on hand with the impulse response to get the output from the system.

Impulse responses for digital filters are characterized as either **F**inite **I**mpulse **R**esponse (FIR) or they are characterized as **I**nfinite **I**mpulse **R**esponse (IIR). In this chapter we will study both the FIR and the IIR filters. The two types of filters have a lot of similarity and a lot of things that are common but they are also very much different. Because of their differences we will study them independently one at a time. As we are studying please make an effort to see what the similarities between the two filters are.

One very glaring difference between the two types of filter design techniques is the phase response of the two filters. For most applications the phase response is not too critical but when the phase has to be maintained then only the linear phase or the zero phase filters have to be used. Both types of filters, the FIR and the IIR filters can be designed to have zero or linear phase, we however almost always use the FIR filters to design zero or linear phase filters because they can be designed to replicate this property so very easily and at the same time when we design the FIR filters to replicate this property we get an added bonus of symmetrical coefficients in the implementation of the filter.

9.1 LINEAR PHASE RESPONSE

9.1.1 Group Delay and Phase Delay:

Exact linear phase is one of the main attractions for the design and the use of FIR filters. In the earlier chapters we have seen that when a signal passes through a filter it suffers an amplitude change as well as a phase change. This phase change that the signal undergoes is identified as either a phase delay or as group delay.

The phase delay of the filter is the amount of time delay that each frequency component of the signal suffers in going through the filter. Mathematically, the phase delay is the negative of the phase angle divided by the frequency so the phase delay is defined as shown in Equation(9.1)

$$\tau_p = -\frac{\theta(\omega)}{\omega} \tag{9.1}$$

The group delay of the filter is the amount of time delay that the composite signal suffers at each frequency in going through the filter. Mathematically, the group delay is the negative of the derivative of the phase angle with respect to the frequency so the group delay is defined as shown in Equation(9.2)

$$\tau_g = -\frac{d(\theta(\omega))}{d\omega} \tag{9.2}$$

A filter is said to have a linear phase response if the phase characteristics of the filter satisfy one of the two conditions given in Equation(9.3)

$$\theta(\omega) = -\alpha\omega \qquad or \qquad \theta(\omega) = \beta - \alpha\omega \tag{9.3}$$

In both these relations α and β are constants. It can readily be shown that when a filter satisfies the first of the two conditions then the filter will have constant group delay since

$$\tau_p = -\frac{\theta(\omega)}{\omega} = -\frac{-\alpha\omega}{\omega} = \alpha$$

as well as constant phase delay since

$$\tau_g = -\frac{d(\theta(\omega))}{d\omega} = -\frac{d(-\alpha\omega)}{d\omega} = \alpha,$$

while if the filter satisfies the second of the two conditions then it will have only constant group delay. Please verify this on your own.

9.1.2 Symmetry Conditions in Linear Phase Filters:

Linear phase filters come in several different varieties. To see what criteria a filter has to meet for it to be a linear phase filter let us examine the phase response of the filter and equate it to a linear phase condition as shown in Equation(9.3). The DTFT of an FIR filter can be written as shown in Equation(9.4)

$$H(\omega)=\left|H(\omega)\right|e^{j\theta(\omega)}=\sum_{n=0}^{N-1}h[n]e^{-j\omega n} \qquad (9.4)$$

Where the magnitude and the phase responses can be individually written as shown in Equation(9.5)

$$\left|H(\omega)\right|=M(\omega) \quad \textit{and} \quad -\theta(\omega)=\tan^{-1}\left[\frac{\mathrm{Im}(H(\omega))}{\mathrm{Re}(H(\omega))}\right] \qquad (9.5)$$

So for a filter to be a linear phase filter the phase of the filter will have to be proportional to the frequency as shown in Equation(9.6)

$$\theta(\omega)=\alpha\omega=\tan^{-1}\left[\frac{\mathrm{Im}(H(\omega))}{\mathrm{Re}(H(\omega))}\right]$$

$$=\tan^{-1}\left[\frac{\sum_{n=0}^{N-1}h[n]\,Sin(\omega n)}{\sum_{n=0}^{N-1}h[n]\,Cos(\omega n)}\right] \qquad (9.6)$$

After doing some algebra and trigonometry on Equation(9.6) we get the condition that we need to identify linear phase filters. This is shown in Equation(9.7)

$$\tan(\alpha\omega)=\frac{Sin(\tau\omega)}{Cos(\tau\omega)}=\left[\frac{\sum_{n=0}^{N-1}h[n]\,Sin(\omega n)}{\sum_{n=0}^{N-1}h[n]\,Cos(\omega n)}\right]$$

$$\sum_{n=0}^{N-1}h[n]\,Cos(\omega n)Sin(\alpha\omega)=\sum_{n=0}^{N-1}h[n]\,Sin(\omega n)Cos(\alpha\omega)$$

$$\sum_{n=0}^{N-1}h[n]\left[Cos(\omega n)Sin(\alpha\omega)-Sin(\omega n)Cos(\alpha\omega)\right]=0$$

$$\sum_{n=0}^{N-1}h[n]\left[Sin((n-\alpha)\omega)\right]=0 \qquad (9.7)$$

The solution to the last equation in Equation(9.7) will give us two different conditions, satisfying any one of these conditions will give us a filter that has linear phase. One of the solutions to the last equation in Equation(9.7) is $\alpha\omega=\frac{(N-1)\omega}{2}$ and the conditions on the filter coefficients are given in Equation(9.8)

$$h[n]=h[N-n-1]\begin{cases} n=0,1,2,\cdots,\dfrac{N-1}{2} & N\ Odd \\ n=0,1,2,\cdots,\left(\dfrac{N}{2}-1\right) & N\ Even \end{cases} \tag{9.8}$$

That is the filter has to be positive symmetric for the filter to have linear phase. The other solution to the last equation in Equation(9.7) will give us a filter which is negative symmetric and the solution is $\alpha\omega=\frac{\pi}{2}-\frac{(N-1)\omega}{2}$ and in this case the conditions on the filter coefficients are given in Equation(9.9)

$$h[n]=-h[N-n-1]\begin{cases} n=0,1,2,\cdots,\dfrac{N-1}{2} & N\ Odd \\ n=0,1,2,\cdots,\left(\dfrac{N}{2}-1\right) & N\ Even \end{cases} \tag{9.9}$$

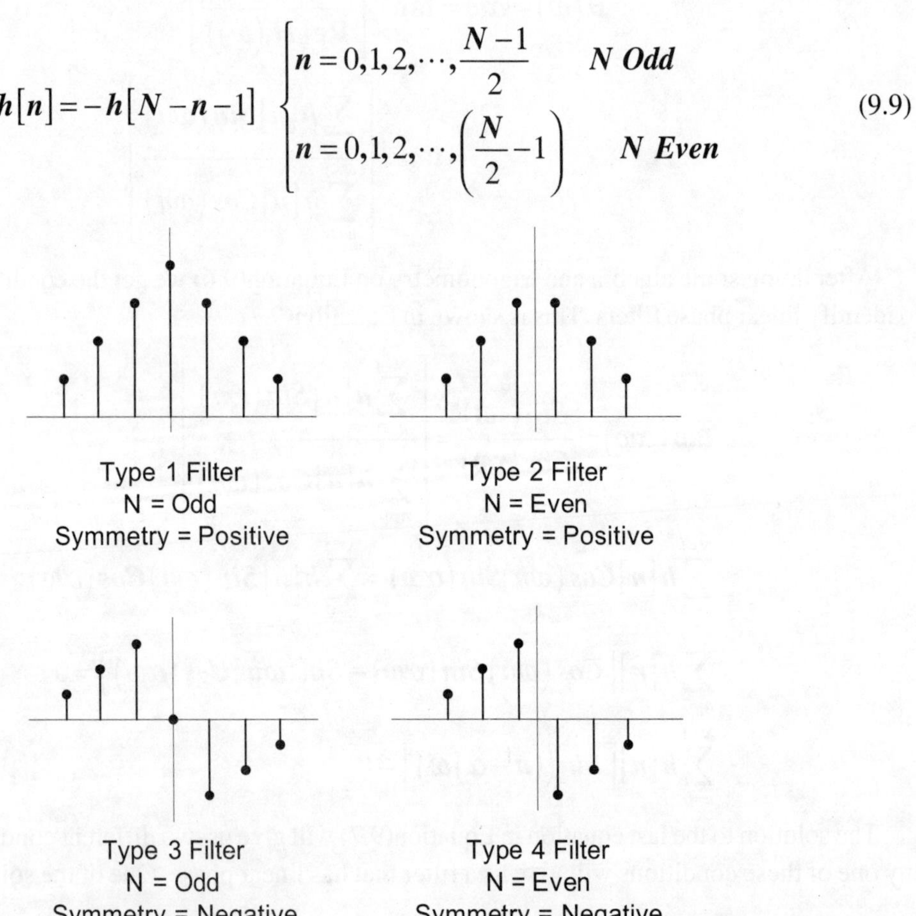

Figure 9.1: Four different types of filters showing the various different types of symmetry in the filter coefficients

With two different conditions for linear phase filters and the length of the filter being either odd or even there are exactly four different types of linear phase filters. The four types of filters come from the permutations of N - odd or even and from symmetry - positive or negative. The various different types of symmetries in the filter coefficients are shown in Figure 9.1.

Each of the four types of filters have their particular type of responses. For example the Type 2 filter (positive symmetric even length) is always zero at frequency f = 0.5 (half the sampling frequency) so this type of a filter is unsuitable for a high pass filter.

The Type 3 filter (negative symmetric odd length) and the Type 4 filter (negative symmetric even length) both introduce a 90^0 phase shift and have a response that is zero at f = 0 so these types of filters are unsuitable for low pass filters. Further the Type 3 filter (negative symmetric odd length) is also zero at f = 0.5 so this type of filter is unsuitable for a high pass filter. The Type 3 and the Type 4 filters are both used to design the differentiators and the Hilbert transformers.

The Type 1 filter (positive symmetric odd length) is the most versatile of all the types of filters as it can be used to meet most different requirements.

9.2 FINITE IMPULSE RESPONSE FILTERS

The FIR filters are non recursive filters. This means that the next output that you will get from the filter is based only on the present input and the past inputs. It does not take into account what the past outputs were, the present output is independent of the past outputs. Since these filters are independent of any and all the past outputs there is no feedback involved, there is no positive feedback or negative feedback. Since there is no feedback these filters are always stable. If you remember from your earlier studies that positive feedback is required for systems to become unstable. For the FIR filters since there is no feedback the filters are always stable.

The design of the FIR filters is approached from two different points of view. In both these points of view we begin with the frequency domain function which we will invert to get the time domain function. We call the two different ways in which you can design the FIR filters the Windowing method and the Frequency Sampling method. The windowing method relies on the Discrete Time Fourier Transform (DTFT) while the frequency sampling method relies on the Discrete Fourier Transform (DFT).

As we study the methods of the design of the FIR filters and examine their responses we will find that the length of the filter is a parameter that is not exactly defined. Further we will find that the width of the transition band, the band between the pass band and the stop band, is directly affected by the length of the filter. Longer the filter the narrower the transition band will be. So it is important to have an idea about the length (size, order) of the filter. In general there is no direct relation between the transition band and the length of the filter so many trial and error attempts are made with varying lengths of the filter to see which length of the filter best meets the transition width specifications. Even though we will determine the length of the filter by trial and error it is very helpful to get an approximate idea of what the length of the filter should be. For this many empirical formulas have been developed and these formulas are used to estimate the length of the filter as a first attempt. Remember that these are empirical formulas so they will only give you a ball park figure, and not an exact value.

Herman's Empirical Formula:

$$N = \frac{D(\delta_p \delta_s)}{\Delta F} - f(\delta_p \delta_s)\Delta F + 1 \tag{9.10}$$

In the formula in Equation(9.10) the term F is the required width of the transition band in terms of normalized frequency. The term $D(\delta_p \delta_s)$ is a polynomial defined in Equation(9.11) and the coefficients in the polynomial all have values as shown in Equation(9.12)

$$D(\delta_p \delta_s) = \log_{10}(\delta_s)\left[a_1\left(\log_{10}(\delta_p)\right)^2 + a_2\left(\log_{10}(\delta_p)\right) + a_3\right] + \left[a_4\left(\log_{10}(\delta_p)\right)^2 + a_5\left(\log_{10}(\delta_p)\right) + a_6\right] \tag{9.11}$$

$$a_1 = 5.309\text{x}10^{-3} \quad a_2 = 7.114\text{x}10^{-2} \quad a_3 = -4.761\text{x}10^{-1}$$
$$a_4 = -2.661\text{x}10^{-3} \quad a_5 = -5.941\text{x}10^{-2} \quad a_6 = -4.761\text{x}10^{-2} \tag{9.12}$$

And the term $f(\delta_p \delta_s)$ is dependent on the ripple in the pass band and the stop band as shown in Equation(9.13)

$$f(\delta_p \delta_s) = 11.01217 + 0.51244\left[\log_{10}(\delta_p) - \log_{10}(\delta_s)\right] \tag{9.13}$$

Since this is an empirical formula it gives us an approximate result. As you might imagine there are many different empirical formulas. Another empirical that is very similar to the formula used for the Kaiser window (we will talk about the Kaiser window later in this chapter) is as shown in Equation(9.14)

$$N = \frac{-10\log_{10}(\delta_p \bullet \delta_s) - 15}{14\frac{(f_s - f_p)}{F}} + 1 \tag{9.14}$$

9.2.1 The Windowing approach to FIR filter design:

Earlier we have seen that when we sample an analog signal or an analog function the frequency spectrum of the sampled signal is periodic replicas of the frequency spectrum of the analog function. Since the frequency spectrum of an FIR filter is periodic and we know that this periodic function can be expressed as a linear combination of complex exponentials so we get Equation(9.15)

$$H_d(\omega) = \sum_{n=-\infty}^{\infty} h_d[n] e^{-jn\omega}$$
$$h_d[n] = \frac{1}{2\pi}\int_{-\pi}^{\pi} H_d(\omega) e^{jn\omega} d\omega \tag{9.15}$$

So the basic design procedure of this type of filter begins with a desired frequency response (one period) of the filter. To get the Filter coefficients $h_d[n]$ we begin with a desired frequency response labeled as $H_d(\omega)$ in Equation(9.15). Next we determine the IDTFT of this desired filter response. Once the IDTFT is obtained we will get the desired filter coefficients $h_d[n]$. This is the filter in the time domain that we are looking for. In order to implement this filter we have two problems that we need to overcome:

1. $h_d[n]$ is an infinite sequence. We have to limit this sequence to a finite length sequence. So the first problem that we have to overcome is to devise a scheme that will permit us to truncate the infinite sequence to a finite sequence.
2. $h_d[n]$ is a non-causal sequence. Notice that h_d has coefficients for both positive as well as negative values of n. Since we need our filter to be a causal filter we have to convert the filter we obtain after truncation into a filter sequence that is a causal sequence. For this we will have to find a scheme to delay the filter.

In order to overcome both the problems stated above we will truncate the sequence; which is obtained in Equation(9.15) by a process known as 'Windowing'. Windowing is a process that limits the sequence to ±N sample points instead of to ± ∞ sample points. When we limit the sequence by windowing then the resulting sequence will be finite. Now that the sequence is finite we will shift the sequence - that is delay the sequence by N sample points. The delaying process will shift the entire sequence so that the delayed filter is a causal finite sequence, no more negative values of n in this filter. This is shown below by the use of Z transforms. We have used Z transforms only because it is easier to visualize the position of the sequence since the coefficient of z tells you the position of the sequence. So Equation(9.16) is the goal that we want to work towards. Let us see how we will get to it.

$$H(z) = \sum_{n=-\infty}^{\infty} h_d[n]z^{-n} = \sum_{n=-\frac{N-1}{2}}^{\frac{N-1}{2}} h_d[n]z^{-n}$$

Delay the filter by N/2 sample points to get

$$= z^{-\left(\frac{N-1}{2}\right)} \sum_{n=-\frac{N-1}{2}}^{\frac{N-1}{2}} h_d[n]z^{-n} = z^{-\left(\frac{N-1}{2}\right)} \left[h_d(0) + \sum_{n=1}^{\frac{N-1}{2}} h_d[n]\left[z^{n} + z^{-n}\right] \right] \tag{9.16}$$

The two actions that we performed, truncation and delay affect the filter in different ways. First the multiplication by the delay function does not alter the magnitude function in any way so the shape of the magnitude response of the filter stays same in the frequency domain; it's the phase response of the filter that is altered by the delay operation. The truncation of the filter abruptly is like saying that we are going to view this filter through a rectangular window that stretches from –N/2 to +N/2. This truncation by a rectangular window is produced by multiplying the infinite sequence with another sequence that has unit values in the window and zero values outside the window. The multiplication of two functions in the time domain results in convolution in the frequency domain. Convolution of the two functions in the frequency domain introduces oscillations near a discontinuity. These oscillations that are introduced are known as Gibbs Phenomena. The Gibbs Phenomena can be reduced by choosing a proper window function; for example a window function that has sides that are tapering towards cutoff rather than sides that abruptly cutoff the amplitude to zero will reduce the oscillations or the Gibbs phenomena. We introduce and discuss the choice of different window functions, their use and their implementation a little bit later. First let us look at an example of how the filter is designed.

Example 9.1

(a) Use the DTFT method to design a low pass filter so that the desired frequency response is:

$$H_d(\omega)=\begin{cases}1 & for\ |\omega|\le\omega_p \\ 0 & \omega_p\le|\omega|\le\Omega/2\end{cases}$$

(b) Convert this filter to a causal filter by using a rectangular window if the filter has to be at most 11 sample points.

Solution 9.1

(a) We first determine the infinite desired filter coefficients in the time domain. So

$$h_d[n]=\frac{1}{2\pi}\int_{-\pi}^{\pi}H(\omega)e^{j\omega n}d\omega$$

$$=\frac{1}{2\pi}\int_{-\omega_p}^{\omega_p}e^{j\omega n}d\omega=\frac{1}{n\pi}Sin(n\omega_p)$$

$$h_d[n]=\frac{\omega_p}{\pi}Sinc(n\omega_p)$$

This is the infinite sequence of the filter coefficients. We will limit these coefficients and then delay them to build the finite filter.

(b) Now we have to limit the filter to 11 points so we will multiply this filter using a rectangular window with N = ± 5 so $H_d(z)=\sum_{n=-5}^{5}h_d[n]z^{-n}$

Now that we have truncated the filter we need to delay this filter by 5 sample points. When we delay the windowed filter we will get the resulting filter function as:

$$H_d(z)=z^{-5}\left[\sum_{n=-5}^{5}h_d[n]z^{-n}\right]$$

$$H_d(z)=h_d(0)z^{-5}+h_d(-1)z^{-4}+h_d(-2)z^{-3}+h_d(-3)z^{-2}$$
$$+h_d(-4)z^{-1}+h_d(-5)+h_d(1)z^{-6}+h_d(2)z^{-7}$$
$$+h_d(3)z^{-8}+h_d(4)z^{-9}+h_d(5)z^{-10}$$

Example 9.1 shows a causal filter with a cutoff frequency w_p which has been truncated to 11 sample points. In part b of the example we have delayed the filter by 5 sample points so the filter is also causal. Now is a good time to analyze and see what we have just accomplished by windowing and to see the result of our actions.

The Effect of Windowing:

To study the effect of windowing let us begin with the infinite sequence for the filter given in Equation(9.15). We want this sequence limited from -N to +N so the resulting desired sequence will be

$$h[n] = \begin{cases} h_d[n] & -N \le n \le N \\ 0 & Otherwise \end{cases}$$

In general we can achieve this by multiplying the desired impulse response with a finite duration window w[n] so $h[n] = w[n]h_d[n]$. Here the window w[n] is given by Equation(9.17)

$$w[n] = \begin{cases} 1 & -N \le n \le N \\ 0 & Otherwise \end{cases} \tag{9.17}$$

As we mentioned earlier this product in the time domain results in convolution in the frequency domain or the filter transfer function now with the windowing will be as shown in Equation(9.18).

That is H(ω) is a periodic convolution of the Fourier transform of the desired frequency response $H_d(\omega)$ with the Fourier transform of the window. This is shown in Figure 9.2. The top figure shows the two functions in Equation(9.18) which are to be convolved together. The bottom figure shows the

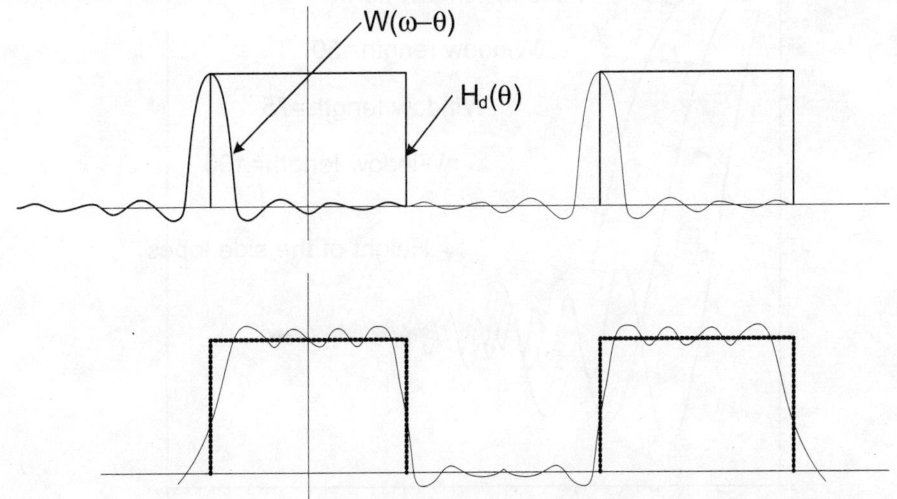

Figure 9.2: The convolution process implied by the truncation operation on the desired filter response. Truncation leads to convolution

$$H(\omega)=\frac{1}{2\pi}\int_{-\pi}^{\pi} H_d(\theta)W(\omega-\theta)d\theta \tag{9.18}$$

approximate result of convolution with the shape of the desired filter also drawn by a dashed line. Notice that the shape of the resulting filter is approximately the same as the desired filter but the obtained filter has some ripples that are present. These ripples are introduced because the window functions do not have an ideal impulse as its Fourier transform. The closer we come to the impulse as the Fourier transform of the window the smaller the ripples will be. This is the goal of the windows that we will be using. So by controlling the shape of the window we try to achieve a Fourier transform of the window that is an impulse.

Different Windows:

The rectangular window function that we have used has a main lobe and side lobes. After we window the infinite desired filter we will have a finite windowed filter. From Figure 9.2 we see that this windowed filter has ripples. We see the ripples in the resulting filter after windowing the desired filter response because the window function has a main lobe that has width to it. We see the ripples also because 100% of the energy is not contained in the main lobe of the window function. So the choice of windows is governed by our desire that our window length should be as small as possible which reduces the computation effort required to implement the filter, while having the main lobe of the windows' Fourier transform as narrow as possible. These two requirements are conflicting requirements. We can quickly see that these requirements are conflicting both mathematically and

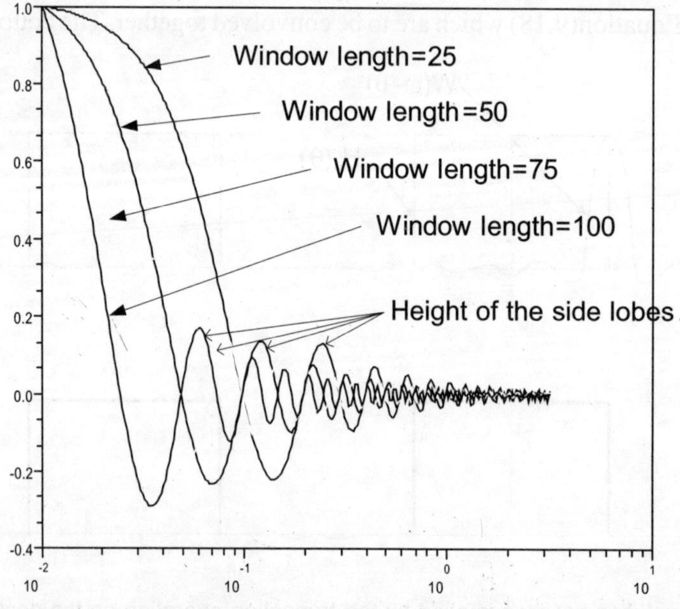

Figure 9.3: Plot of the Fourier transform of the rectangular window of different lengths

$$
\begin{aligned}
W(\omega) &= \sum_{n=0}^{N} e^{-j\omega n} \\
&= \frac{1-e^{-j\omega N}}{1-e^{-j\omega}} \\
&= e^{-j\frac{\omega(N-1)}{2}} \frac{Sin(\omega N/2)}{Sin(\omega/2)}
\end{aligned} \tag{9.19}
$$

intuitively as shown in Equation(9.19).

Equation(9.19) is the Fourier transform of the rectangular window. A plot of the positive frequency half of this window is shown in Figure 9.3 for windows of various lengths, the negative frequency half is a mirror image of this plot. From the plot we see two things that are directly obvious. First as the length of the window gets longer the main lobe gets narrower. So the length of the window directly controls how wide the main lobe of the window will be. Now notice the height of the first side lobe. They are the same no matter the length of the window. The length of the window does not affect in any way the height of the side lobes; it only controls the width of the main lobe. So for a very narrow main lobe width the window length must be very long. In the limit if the window length is infinite then the width of the main lobe will disappear and the response will become an impulse.

Intuitively also we can see the same result. Before we windowed the desired response to limit it to a finite length the desired filter response had infinite length. This infinite length desired response was exactly equal to the response that we wanted. There were no externally introduced ripples. This was because the window through which we were seeing the desired response was infinite in length. So an infinite length window gave us a response that was the same as the desired response.

What we have just seen is that the length of the window does not alter the ripples in the window in any way. The length of the window only controls the width of the main lobe. So what does control the height of the side lobes? The height of the side lobes is controlled by the shape of the window. The shape of the rectangular window has a sharp cutoff at the edge of the window. What if we taper the window gradually to the edge of the window? That is the idea that is used to design different types of windows.

The frequency response of the rectangular window has a main lobe that contains most of the energy and it comes close to an impulse but it is not an impulse. If we can find an alternate window that has a frequency response that resembles an impulse response more than a rectangular window then such a window will not introduce so many ripples, or if the window contains more of the windows energy in the main lobe then the ripples will be reduced. There are several different windows that come closer to having more of the window's energy in the main lobe than the rectangular window. These windows are Triangular, Hamming, Hanning, Blackman and the Kaiser windows. The more popular windows that are used are defined as follows:

Bartlett (Triangular)	$w[n]=\begin{cases}2n/M & 0\le n\le M/2\\ 2-2n/M & M/2\le n\le M\\ 0 & \text{Otherwise}\end{cases}$
Hamming	$w[n]=\begin{cases}0.5-0.5Cos(2\pi n/M) & 0\le n\le M\\ 0 & \text{Otherwise}\end{cases}$
Hanning	$w[n]=\begin{cases}0.54-0.46Cos(2\pi n/M) & 0\le n\le M\\ 0 & \text{Otherwise}\end{cases}$
Blackman	$w[n]=\begin{cases}0.42-0.5Cos(2\pi n/M)+0.08Cos(4\pi n/M) & 0\le n\le M\\ 0 & \text{Otherwise}\end{cases}$

A plot of the four windows is given below in Figure 9.4.

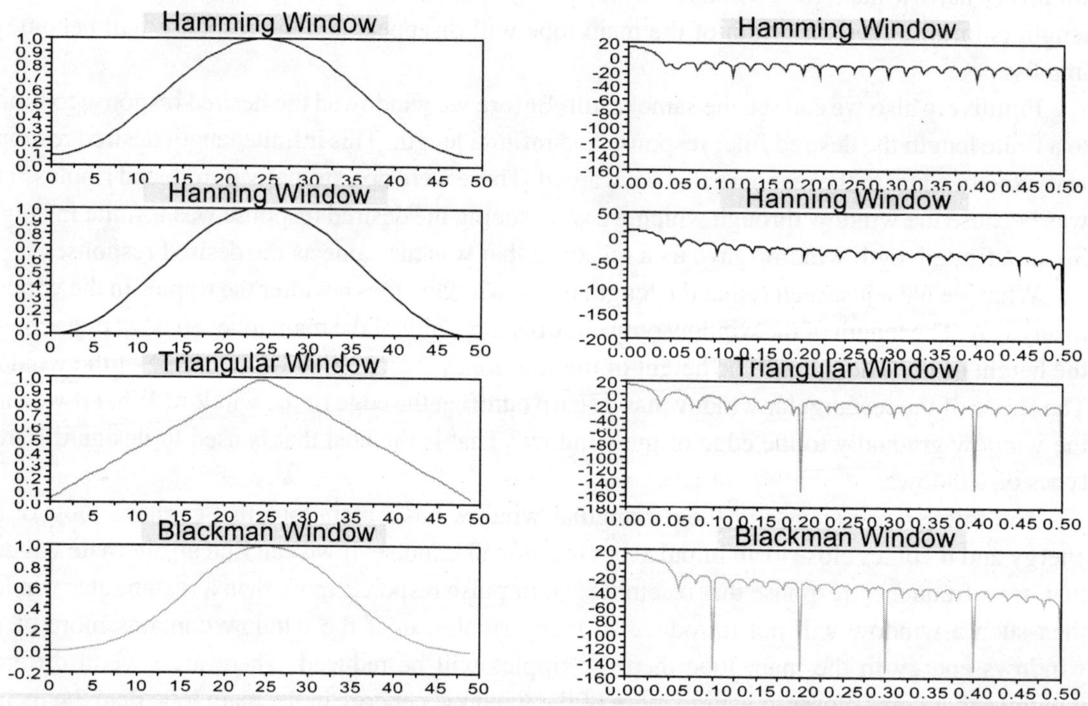

Figure 9.4: The four different windows in the time domain and also in the Frequency domain. Notice the increase in the width of the main lobe and the increase in attenuation of the various windows. The height of the first side lobe. As the attenuation in the stop band increases the width of the main lobe also increases.

How we use any of these windows to design an FIR filter is demonstrated in Example 9.2, Example 9.3 and discussed here. To design an FIR filter we begin with a desired frequency response, next we find the IDTFT to get the filter in the time domain that is infinite in length and non causal. This filter is an infinite filter so we restrict the filter to a finite length by windowing it. To window the filter we multiply it with one of the window functions above. Then to complete the filter we delay the windowed filter by N/2 points. So the process to use one of the four windows above is exactly the same as it was for the use of the rectangular window.

Example 9.2

(a) Design a filter that has a cutoff frequency of 300 Hz and has a sampling frequency of 1000 Hz:

$$H_d(\omega) = \begin{cases} 1 & for\,|f| \le 300 \\ 0 & 300 \le |f| \le 500 \end{cases}$$

(b) Plot the frequency response of the resulting filter with the Rectangular window as well as the Hamming window.

Solution 9.2

(a) We first determine the infinite desired filter coefficients in the time domain. So

$$h_d[n] = \frac{1}{2\pi}\int_{-\pi}^{\pi} H(\omega)e^{j\omega n}d\omega$$

$$= \frac{1}{F_s}\int_{-f_p}^{f_p} e^{j2\pi fn}df = \frac{1}{n\pi F_s}Sin(2\pi f_p n)$$

$$h_d[n] = \frac{3}{5}Sinc(2\pi f_p n)$$

The above filter is an infinite filter so we limit it with the use of a rectangular window of size 128. The SCILAB script for the filter is given below and the plot of the filter is given in Figure 9.5. Figure 9.5 shows plots with both the Rectangular window and the Hamming window.

```
*****SCILAB Script for the FIR filter in Figure FIR.3*****
n=0:1:127;N=size(n,'*');
h=clean(3/5*sinc(3*(n-N/2)*%pi/5));
[hmag fr]=frmag(h,256);
subplot(211);plot2d(1000*fr,20*log10(hmag),style=color('green'))
xtitle('Plot of FIR with Rectangular window')
hm=window('hm',N);
wh=h.*hm;
```

```
[whmag fr]=frmag(wh,256);
subplot(212);plot2d(1000*fr,20*log10(whmag),style=color('green'))
xtitle('Plot of FIR with Hamming window')
```

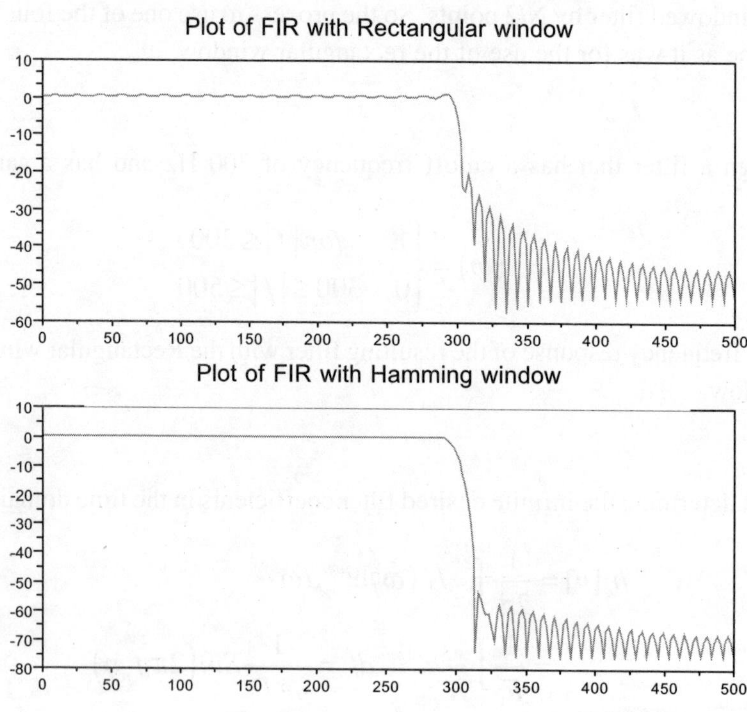

Figure 9.5: Plot of an FIR filter with a 300 Hz cutoff

The plot on the top in Figure 9.5 is for the Rectangular window. Notice that with the Rectangular window there are some ripples that are still present. The ripples are not present when we used the Hamming window which is the bottom graph in Figure 9.5. This is because the Hamming window gradually tapers towards the edges rather than an abrupt cutoff found in the rectangular window. Another interesting fact to notice between the two plots is the height of the first side lobe. For the rectangular window the height of the side lobe is only about 18 dB down while the height of the first side lobe for the Hamming window is almost 38 dB down. The final fact that you should notice is the width of the transition band. The transition band from the pass band to the stop band is narrower in the Rectangular window than it is in the plot with the Hamming window. We will talk about these three properties of the various windows at the end of this section. One more example will be extremely useful here.

Example 9.3

(a) Design a filter that has a stepped response with a first cutoff at 200 Hz that will attenuate the signal down by 80% and the second cutoff at 300 Hz that is to take the desired filter response down to zero. The required stepped response for the filter is shown in Figure 9.6:

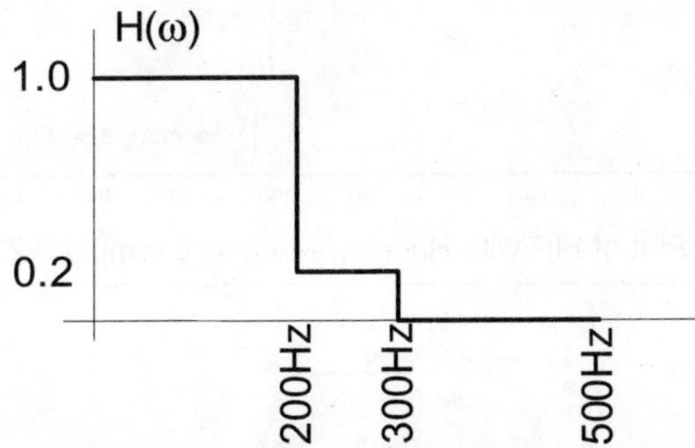

Figure 9.6: Determine an FIR filter to represent this stepped frequency response

$$H_d(\omega) = \begin{cases} 1.0 & 0 \le |f| \le 200 \\ 0.2 & 200 \le |f| \le 300 \\ 0 & 200 \le |f| \le 500 \end{cases}$$

(b) Plot the frequency response of the resulting filter with the Rectangular window as well as the Hanning window.

Solution 9.3

(a) We first determine the infinite desired filter coefficients in the time domain. (In determining the desired response we have treated this filter as two filters, one having a pass band gain of 0.8 in the frequency range -200 to +200 and another that has pass band gain of 0.2. Putting both the filters together will give us the filter as shown in Figure 9.6.) This time since the desired frequency response is stepped to two levels we will account for that by breaking up the integral in several ranges as shown here:

$$h_d[n] = \frac{1}{F}\left[\int_{-\omega_1}^{\omega_1} 0.8e^{j\omega n}\, d\omega + \int_{-\omega_2}^{\omega_2} 0.2e^{j\omega n}\, d\omega\right]$$

$$= \frac{1}{2\pi}\left[2*0.8*\omega_1 Sinc(n\omega_1) + 2*0.2*\omega_2 Sinc(n\omega_2)\right]$$

Next we can use a SCILAB script to draw the frequency response plot for this filter. The script is given below and the plot is drawn in Figure 9.7. Please notice the same three effects that we listed in Example 9.2 are also present here.

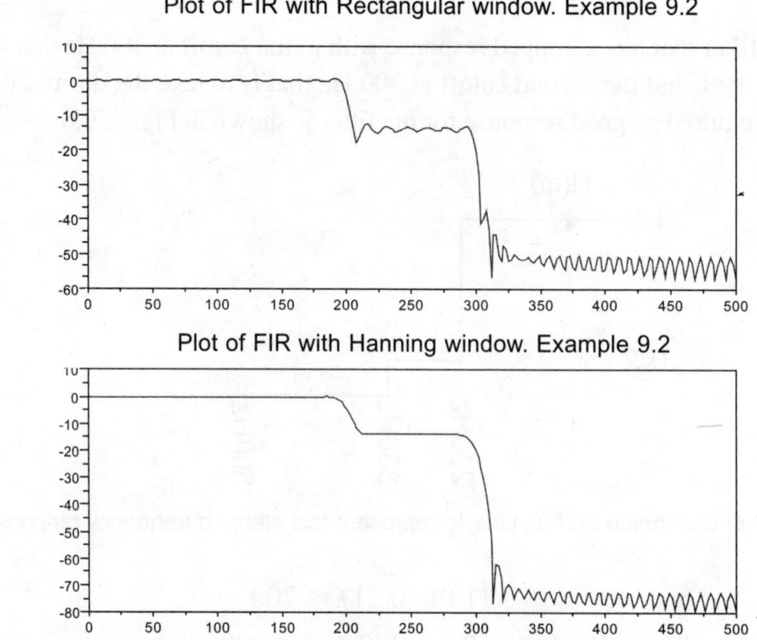

Figure 9.7: Plot of an FIR filter with a stepped response at ω1 = 200 and then at ω2 = 300

```
******SCILAB Script for the FIR filter in Figure FIR.5******
n=0:1:127;
N=size(n,'*');
hs=clean(.32*sinc(2*%pi*(n-N/2)/5)+.12*sinc(3*%pi*(n-N/2)/5));
hn=window('hn',N);
[hsmag fr]=frmag(hs,256);
subplot(211);
plot2d(1000*fr,20*log10(hsmag))
whs=hs.*hn;
whsmag=frmag(whs,256);
subplot(212);plot2d(1000*fr,20*log10(whsmag))
```

So what we get from windowing is that the length of the window controls the width of the main lobe. When we make the window long, the width of the main lobe will be narrow. See the effect on the width of the main lobe on the Rectangular window as the length of the window is increased in Figure 9.8.

Making the length of the window longer also increases the computational effort required to implement the filter. The length of the window does not have any effect on the attenuation provided by the window in the stop band. The attenuation provided by the window in the stop band is entirely controlled by the shape of the window. So the Hamming window provides the same attenuation every time it is used and so also the Hanning window. The length of the window does not alter the attenuation provided by the window.

So for the window design procedure we first determine how much attenuation we require in the stop band by the filter and determine a window shape that will provide the required attenuation. Once the required attenuation is obtained by the window shape we determine the length of the window

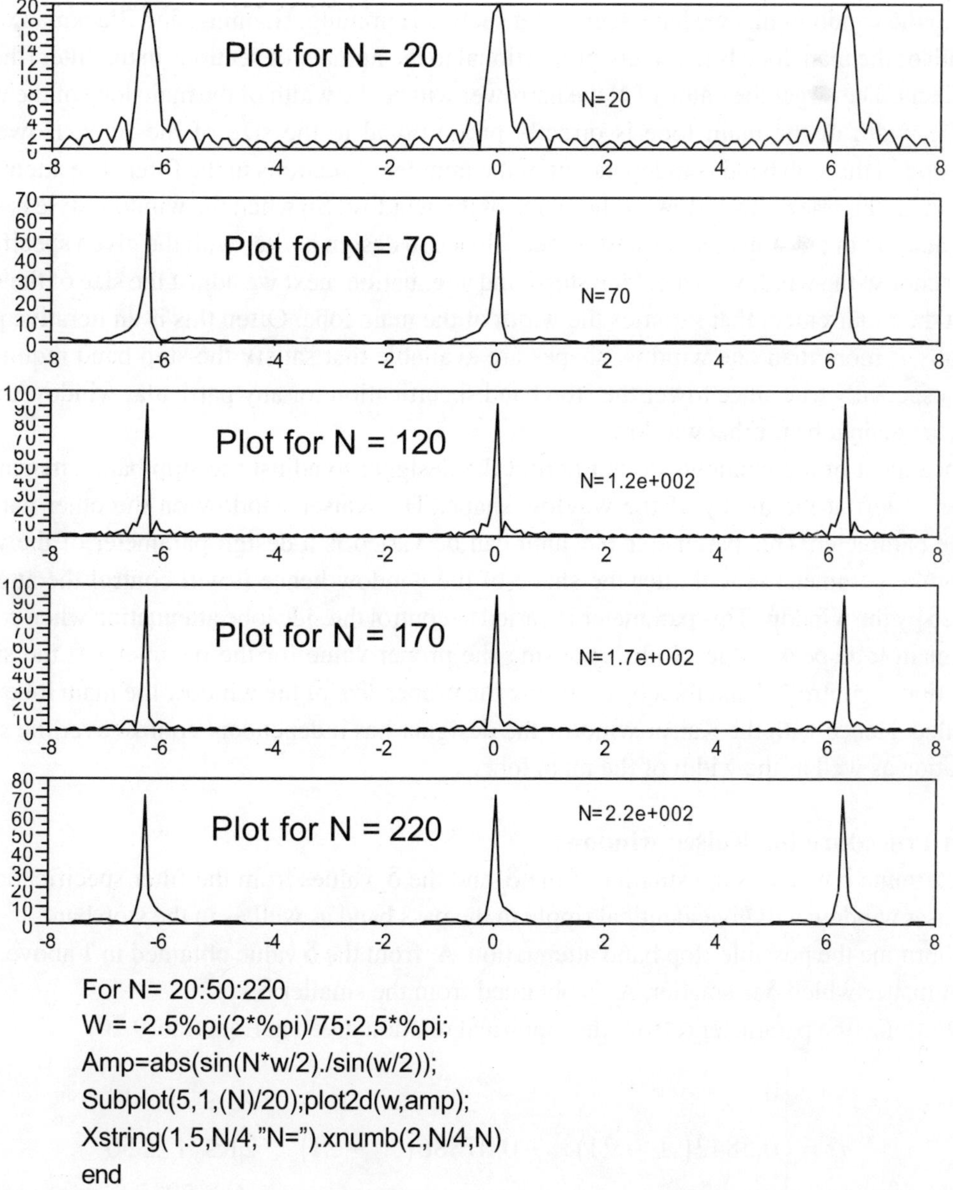


```
For N= 20:50:220
W = -2.5%pi(2*%pi)/75:2.5*%pi;
Amp=abs(sin(N*w/2)./sin(w/2));
Subplot(5,1,(N)/20);plot2d(w,amp);
Xstring(1.5,N/4,"N=").xnumb(2,N/4,N)
end
```

Figure 9.8: Several plots of the Rectangular window as the length of the window increases. Note the amplitude of the plot approaches impulse as N → ∞

required, by using the empirical formulas shown in Equation(9.10) or in Equation(9.14), and following that up by trial and error, by examining the width of the transition band. Since the Triangular, the Hamming, the Hanning and the Blackman window have only one parameter that we can alter they are able to meet only one requirement.

The Kaiser Window:

In all the windows that we have seen so far such as Hamming, Hanning, and Blackman windows the width of the main lobe is inversely proportional to the number of sections in the filter (the length of the filter). The larger the value of N the narrower will be the width of the main lobe of the window. Thus the width of the main lobe is directly proportional to the size of the filter. However the attenuation in the stop band is independent of the number of sections in the filter. The attenuation is a function of the selected window or the shape of the window. So when the window style is selected the attenuation in the stop band is determined. Hence to design a filter with the given specifications we first choose the window to meet the stop band attenuation, next we adjust the size of the window to meet the requirement that satisfies the width of the main lobe. Often this is an iterative process; especially if more than one window shapes are available that satisfy the stop band requirements. This is especially true since lower the stop band specification for any particular window the wider will be the main lobe for that window.

Since most of the windows do not permit the designer to adjust the stop band attenuation the designer is left at the mercy of the window shape. The Kaiser window on the other hand has a variable parameter. This parameter α which can be varied is a design parameter of the window. Varying the parameter α will alter the shape of the window hence it will control the attenuation provided by the window. This parameter is varied to control the side lobe attenuation when compared to the main lobe peak value. So by choosing the proper value for the parameter α the side lobe attenuation is controlled and then by choosing the proper size of the window the main lobe width is controlled. Hence with the Kaiser window the designer has independent control over the side lobe attenuation as well as the width of the main lobe.

Design Procedure for Kaiser window:

1. Determine $\boldsymbol{\delta}$ which is the smaller of the $\boldsymbol{\delta_s}$ and the $\boldsymbol{\delta_p}$ values from the filter specifications. The Kaiser window will give identical ripple in the pass band as well as in the stop band.
2. Determine the possible stop band attenuation $\mathbf{A_s}$ from the $\boldsymbol{\delta}$ value obtained in 1 above. (It does not matter which $\boldsymbol{\delta}$ is smaller. $\mathbf{A_s}$ is obtained from the smaller $\boldsymbol{\delta}$.)
3. Determine the parameter α from the empirical relation given in Equation(9.20)

$$\alpha = \begin{cases} 0 & A_s \le 21 \\ 0.5842(A_s - 21)^{0.4} + 0.07886(A_s - 21) & 21 \le A_s \le 50 \\ 0.1102(A_s - 8.7) & A_s \ge 50 \end{cases} \tag{9.20}$$

4. We next determine the parameter **D** from the empirical design equations given in Equation(9.21). This parameter D will enable us to determine the length of the required filter.

$$D = \begin{cases} 0.9222 & A_s \leq 21 \\ \dfrac{A_s - 7.95}{14.36} & A_s > 21 \end{cases} \tag{9.21}$$

5. Now that we have determined the parameter D we can calculate the required Filter order as shown in Equation(9.22)

$$N = \frac{D * \text{Sampling Freq}}{\left(\Delta f = \left|f_s - f_p\right|\right)} + 1 \tag{9.22}$$

6. With the order of the filter known and the shape parameter **α** also computed we are finally ready to determine the window coefficients that will define the filter as shown in Equation(9.23). In the equation to compute the window coefficients the function $I_o(x)$ $I_o(x)$ is the zero order modified Bessel function of the first kind.

$$W_{kn}(n) = \frac{I_o\left\{\alpha\left[1 - \left(\dfrac{2n}{N-1}\right)^2\right]^{1/2}\right\}}{I_o(\alpha)} \qquad -(N-1)/2 \leq n \leq (N-1)/2 \tag{9.23}$$

7. With all the window coefficients known we can finally determine the filter coefficients as $h[n] = W_{kn}(n)h_d[n]$; $n \leq (N-1)/2$

8. Finally we make the filter causal by shifting the coefficients by (N-1)/2 sample points to the right.

Example 9. 4

Design a filter to meet the following specifications. Use the Kaiser window.
Pass Band Magnitude: $|H(\omega)| < 1 \pm 0.02$ dB
Pass Band edge frequency: $\omega_p < 0.5\pi$
Stop Band Magnitude: $|H(\omega)| < 0.015$ dB
Stop Band edge frequency: $\omega_p < 0.6\pi$

Solution 9.4

First we need to determine the filter coefficients. Since this is a simple Low Pass Filter the filter coefficients are directly obtained as we did in Example 9.1. After we have obtained the filter coefficients we will design the Kaiser window to meet the required specifications.

We need to first determine the parameter A as required in step 2 above. For this we need to get $\delta = \min(\delta_p, \delta_s)$. This time it is the specification for the stop band so $\delta = 0.015$dB. This translates to $A = -20\log_{10}(0.015) = 36.478$.

Now that we have determined the parameter A we can determine the parameter α using the empirical relation given in step 3 above. With $A = 36.478$ we get $\alpha = 2.968$.

The next parameter that we need to determine is D which is given in Step 4 above. For our example with $A>21$ the parameter $D = 1.96$.

With the parameter D determined we can determine the size of the filter. For this we have step 5. From step 5 above we get the filter order as 39.73.

Finally we are now ready to determine the filter coefficients. Using Equation(9.23) all the filter coefficients can be computed.

The function $I_0(x)$ is the zero order modified Bessel function of the first kind. This function is not a common function so computing it with a simple calculator is not very easy. Many engineers have determined approximations that can be used to compute the Bessel function. This approximation is given by a series expansion given in Equation(9.24). In Equation(9.24) the summation is carried out till L terms are used. L is typically chosen by the engineer to be some suitable number. Choosing $L > 10$ provides plenty of accuracy, L is never chosen to be greater than 25.

$$I_o(x) = 1 + \sum_{k=1}^{L} \left[\frac{\left(\frac{x}{2}\right)^k}{k!} \right]^2 \qquad L \leq 25 \tag{9.24}$$

9.2.2 Frequency Sampling

Since the digital filter that we are trying to design is a finite length filter, why not start with a finite number of frequency samples and take advantage of the powerful DFT computation techniques

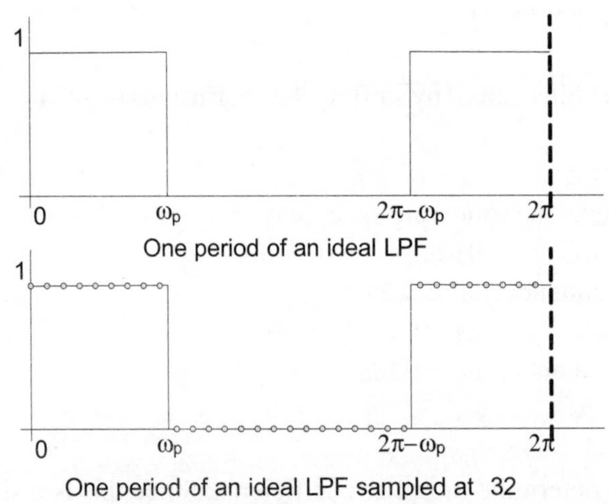

Figure 9.9: Samples of one period of the desired frequency response to be used to design an FIR filter

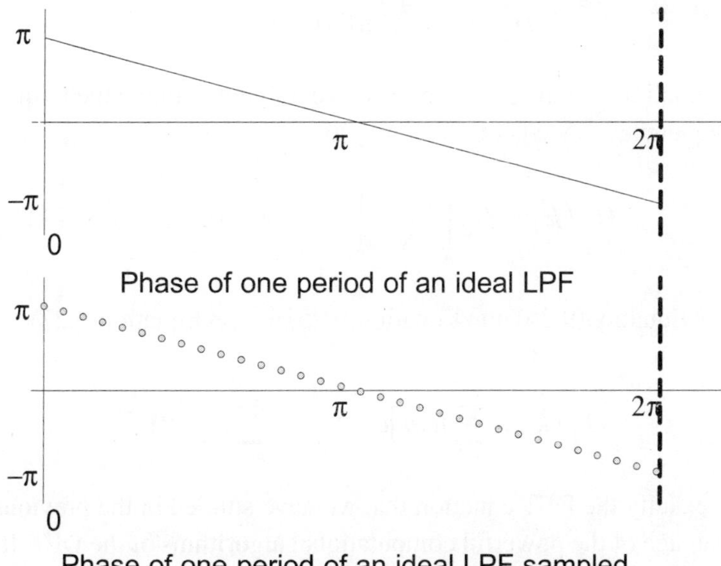

Figure 9.10: Linear phase of one period of an FIR filter. Add this phase to the magnitude of the filter to complete the design of the FIR filter using the Frequency sampling method

available to perform the required computations. That is the idea behind the Frequency sampling approach of FIR filter design. So we begin the frequency sampling design method with the entire period of the desired filter frequency response drawn as shown in the top of Figure 9.9. We will now sample the frequency response at N equally spaced points in frequency. This will give us the magnitude of the frequency response of the filter that we need. To the magnitude response we have to add the required phase of the frequency response. Remember that this is a linear phase filter so we will add linear phase to the magnitude response of the filter. The phase response over one period of the frequency response will be as shown in Figure 9.10.

In the frequency sampling method of FIR filter design we begin by specifying the desired frequency response like the one shown in Figure 9.9 just like we did in the window method. Since the desired frequency response is periodic with period 2π we sample the desired frequency response at equally spaced frequency values over one period. When we sample the desired frequency response we are determining N sample values that are $2\pi/N$ radians apart. Remember that N can be either even or odd.

Just as in the window method, our goal here is also to obtain h[n] the FIR filter coefficients from the equally spaced frequency specifications. While we are trying to determine the filter coefficients we will remember to exploit the basic property of symmetry so that the filter designed by the frequency sampling method also exhibits the property of linear phase. To see how we design the filter using the frequency sampling method we begin with the desired frequency response as shown in Equation(9.25)

$$H_d(\omega) = \sum_{n=0}^{N-1} h[n] e^{-j\omega n} \tag{9.25}$$

Notice that the summation is finite over N points. We will next sample the frequency response at N equally spaced frequencies so we get Equation(9.26)

$$H_d(k) = H_d\left(\frac{2\pi k}{N}\right) \qquad k = 0,1,2,\cdots(N-1) \tag{9.26}$$

When we substitute Equation(9.26) into Equation(9.25) we get Equation(9.27)

$$H_d(k) = \sum_{n=0}^{N-1} h[n] e^{\frac{-j2\pi nk}{N}} = \sum_{n=0}^{N-1} h[n] W_N^{nk} \tag{9.27}$$

Equation(9.27) is exactly the DFT equation that we have studied in the previous chapters. So this method takes advantage of the powerful computational algorithms of the DFT. It is a simple matter to invert the frequency samples and get the filter coefficients in terms of the sampled frequency values. To see this multiply Equation(9.27) by W_N^{-nk} and sum the result over all the N values to get Equation(9.28)

$$\sum_{k=0}^{N-1} H_d(k) W_N^{-nk} = \sum_{k=0}^{N-1}\left[\sum_{n=0}^{N-1} h[n] W_N^{nk}\right] W_N^{-nk} \tag{9.28}$$

As we have seen earlier the right hand side of Equation(9.28) reduces to Nh[n] so the equation that defines the filter coefficients is given by Equation (9.29)

$$h[n] = \frac{1}{N} \sum_{k=0}^{N-1} H_d(k) W_N^{-nk} \tag{9.29}$$

In Equation(9.29) $H_d(k)$ are the samples of the desired frequency response of the filter. I am sure that you remember that the IDFT in general gives us a complex sequence h[n]. However since we plan to implement this FIR filter with only real components all the filter coefficients of the sequence h[n] must be real coefficients. From the symmetry properties in Section 8.6.3 we know that for h[n] to be real we must have H(k) = H*(N-k). This symmetry condition along with the symmetry condition on h[n] (we need this because we want the FIR filter to have linear phase) we can reduce the number of frequency specifications to about half (N/2 when N is even; (N-1)/2 when N is odd). So the equations required to determine the filter coefficients are considerably reduced. In particular when you are given a desired response as

$$H(\omega) = |H(\omega)| e^{j\omega n}$$

This is the desired frequency response that we want. It has been separated into the magnitude and the phase response. Next we will sample this response at N equally spaced points in one period of the response to get Equation(9.30)

$$H(k) = \left| H\left(\frac{2\pi k}{N}\right) \right| e^{-j\frac{2\pi kn}{N}} \tag{9.30}$$

Now that we have the frequency samples H(k) we can determine the IDFT to determine the FIR filter coefficients h[n]. The following design examples will clarify the design method to design the linear phase FIR filters based on the frequency sampling method.

Example 9.5

Determine the coefficients of a linear phase filter of length 59 which has a symmetric unit sample response and a frequency response that satisfies:

$$\left| H_d\left(\frac{2\pi k}{59}\right) \right| = \begin{cases} 1 & k = 0,1,2,3,\cdots,23 \\ 0.2 & k = 24 \\ 0 & k = 25,26,27,28,29 \end{cases}$$

Solution 9.5

Since we know that h[n] has to be linear phase and symmetric we know that h[n] = h[59-n] and the condition on the frequency samples will be

$$H_d\left(\frac{2\pi k}{59}\right) = H_d^*\left(\frac{2\pi(59-k)}{59}\right).$$

For this example we are given the magnitude response and we have to add the phase response to the magnitude response before we determine the IDFT of the given frequency response. Since the phase has to be linear with frequency the response for k = 0 to 29 can be written as

$$\left| H_d\left(\frac{2\pi k}{59}\right) \right| e^{-j\frac{2\pi kn}{59}}.$$

After we have added the phase for the samples from k = 0 to k = 29 we can determine the frequency response coefficients for k = 30 to k = 59 by making use of the symmetry condition H*(59-k) = H(k). This will give us all the terms of the frequency response for one period. Now we are ready to determine the IDFT to get the filter coefficients in the time domain.

Using the frequency sampling method to design the FIR filter we find that the frequency response at the frequency sample points chosen is exact while the frequency response in between the sample points is an interpolated value. One sample of the design of a low pass filter is shown in Figure 9.11 with the SCILAB script for the program included. The script shown is valid only for odd number of samples but a script for even number of samples is similar to the included program. Notice how the SCILAB script closely follows Example 9.5 above.

```
N=59;Nc=24;
//Build the magnitude response.
H=ones(1,N+1);
H(Nc+1:(N+1-Nc))=0;
H(Nc+1)=0.2;H(N+1-Nc)=H(Nc+1);
//Build the Phase response
ph1=clean(exp(-%i*2*%pi*(N-1)/(2*N)*(0:((N-1)/2))));
ph2=clean(exp(%i*2*%pi*((N-1)/2)*((N+1)/2:(N))/N));
ph =[ph1 conj(ph2)];
//Frequency Response
FRQ=0*ones(1,N+1);
FRQ=H.*ph;
//Plot the Frequency Response
h=clean(dft(FRQ(1:N),1));
[Hmag fr] = frmag(real(h),256);
plot2d(fr,20*log10(Hmag),style=color('red'))
```

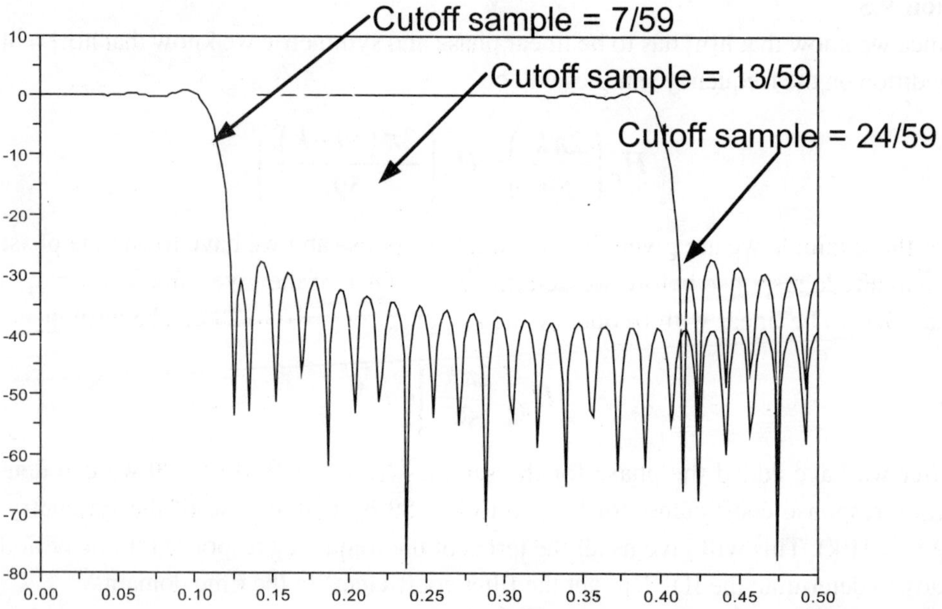

Figure 9.11: Several filters designed using the Frequency sampling method. The various plots are drawn by changing the sample point when the cutoff occurs. The SCILAB script for the program is included in the text chapter

9.3 INFINITE IMPULSE RESPONSE FILTERS

We saw that the FIR filter design begins with the required response in the frequency domain and proceeds entirely in the discrete domain. We do not transform the filter to the analog domain. On the other hand the design of the IIR filters is based largely on the design of analog filters. So for these filters we will begin with the specifications in the discrete domain which we will transform to the analog domain, design the filter in the analog domain and then transform the designed filter back to the discrete domain. These back and forth transformations give us different characteristics in the filters based on the method of the transformations.

Earlier in Chapter 4 we learnt about the characteristics of analog filters, what they are and what they represent. In Section 4.4.1 we saw how to design the analog filters that exhibit the Butterworth characteristics and in Section 4.4.2 we saw how to design the analog filters that exhibit the Chebychev characteristics. We can use either of these methods to design the analog filters that we are going to transform. In Section 4.4.3 we studied filter transformations. The filter transformations are still valid for this purpose also. So once we have the specifications of the required filter in the analog domain then the filter can be designed in any way that we know. It is this freedom that makes this method of designing IIR filters very attractive. The attractive points are:

1. The analog design methods give us a closed form solution of the required filter.
2. The design methods of analog filter are very well known and understood.
3. Many applications require digital simulations of analog filters so this gives us a method to simulate analog filters in the digital domain.

In the following discussion since we have two different types of filters we will use the subscript 'A' to indicate that we are dealing with the analog filter such as $H_A(s)$ or $h_a(t)$, and we will use the subscript 'D' to indicate that we are dealing with the filter in the discrete domain such as $H_D(z)$ or $h_d[n]$. Also the analog domain filter will refer to the continuous time argument while the discrete time filter will refer to the discrete time argument.

To transform the filter from the analog domain to the discrete domain we can proceed using any one of the methods that will transform the s-plane to the z-plane. Obviously we want a stable filter to transform to a stable filter so the transformation should be such that it will transform the entire left half of the s-plane to the interior of the unit circle in the z-plane. There are several such transformations available and in this section we will explore the two that are the most popular.

Even though we design the filter first in the analog domain and then transform it back to the discrete domain it is not absolutely given that this is the only way to design IIR filters. The domain (analog or digital) where the problem of designing the filter is solved will determine where the filter can be used. Thus contrary to popular belief a great deal of IIR filter design does not intrinsically depend on continuous time filter design but instead makes use of a wide body of knowledge that is available in literature on the design of such filters.

9.3.1 Impulse Invariance Method of Filter Design:

The most intuitive transformation of the filter would be to match the impulse response of the filter in the analog and the digital domain. We define and characterize the filters by their impulse responses so what could be better than getting the impulse response that you want in the analog domain and then transforming it to the discrete domain so the impulse response has the same or similar characteristics. That is the idea behind the impulse invariance method.

In this transform method we sample the analog filter at equally spaced points on the impulse response of the analog filter. So in effect we are sampling an analog function so that

$$h_a(t)_{t=nT} = h_a[nT] = h_d[n].$$

In this equation T is the sampling period. We can see right away that since we are sampling there is a distinct possibility that the digital filter could be aliased if the analog filter is not sufficiently band limited. Aliasing will be avoided only if the analog filter is sufficiently band limited. A low pass analog filter could be sufficiently band limited but a high pass filter which permits high frequencies to pass through will not be band limited and will suffer from severe distortion. Even with low pass filters extreme care has to be exercised so that the discrete filters are not aliased.

To investigate impulse invariance design technique we begin with a typical low pass filter in the analog domain. Consider the system function of the low pass filter written in partial fraction form as shown in Equation(9.31)

$$H_A(s) = \sum_{k=1}^{N} \frac{\alpha_k}{s - s_k} \tag{9.31}$$

We first determine the impulse response of this filter by determining the inverse Laplace transform of the filter. The impulse response of the filter is shown in Equation(9.32)

$$h_a(t) = \sum_{k=1}^{N} \alpha_k e^{s_k t} U(t) \tag{9.32}$$

Now that we have the impulse response of the filter that we need we will sample this filter with a sampling period T so that the effect of aliasing is minimum. The sampled filter is shown in Equation(9.33)

$$h_d[n] = h_a[nT] = \sum_{k=1}^{N} \sum_{n=0}^{\infty} \alpha_k e^{s_k nT} \tag{9.33}$$

We can quickly write the right hand side of Equation(9.33) in its Z-transform form as shown in Equation(9.34)

$$H(z) = \sum_{k=1}^{N} \frac{\alpha_k}{1 - e^{s_k T} z^{-1}} \tag{9.34}$$

This is the filter in the discrete domain designed through the impulse invariance method. To form a direct connection between the filters in the analog domain and the discrete domain compare Equation(9.31) with Equation(9.34). One gives us the filter in the analog domain and the other gives us the filter in the discrete domain. Both the filters are written in their partial fraction form. In this form the numerators of both the filters are exactly the same. So the residues from the analog domain transform as they are to the discrete domain with no change at all. The poles from the analog domain are mapped to the corresponding poles in the discrete domain by mapping the pole from ($s-s_k$) to a corresponding pole at $1-e^{s_k T}z^{-1}$ so this method directly maps the poles from one domain to the poles in the other domain. Since the stable poles from the analog domain are mapped to the stable region (magnitude of the poles is $e^{s_k T}$ and since s_k is less than 0 the pole is a stable pole as the magnitude is less than 1) in the discrete domain a stable filter in the analog domain will map to a stable filter in the discrete domain.

Even though the Impulse invariance method maps stable poles to the stable region the mapping only maps the poles. The zeros of the analog filter, if there are any are not mapped like the poles. They are mapped where they come out. The discrete filter could and does have zeros, could have more or less zeros than the analog filter but they are not mapped in any particular way. So the impulse invariance method does not map the S-plane to the Z-plane; it rather maps only the poles from the S-plane to the Z-plane.

Even though the name of the method and the procedure to perform the transform suggest that this method should be used when the shape of the impulse response is to be maintained, this is not the motivating factor behind the impulse invariance method. We use the impulse invariance method when the filter is first band limited and the shape of the frequency response is to be maintained. The shape of the frequency response is to be kept intact. Although the impulse invariance method introduces aliasing the relation between the frequency of the analog response and the digital response is linear. Since the relation of the frequency response is linear the shape of the response is unaltered and it is maintained when the transform is complete.

So the impulse invariance method is used when we want to design a low pass filter and the shape of the frequency response is a key design consideration.

Example 9.6

Determine the impulse invariant digital filter that corresponds to the second order Butterworth filter.

Solution 9.6

The transfer function of a second order Butterworth filter is

$$H(s)=\frac{1}{s^2+1.414s+1}=\frac{1}{(s+0.707+j0.707)(s+0.707-j0.707)}$$

First we must determine the transfer function in its partial fraction form. The partial fraction form requires that we compute the residues at the two poles. The partial fraction form is

$$H(s) = \frac{0.707j}{s + 0.707 + 0.707j} + \frac{-0.707j}{s + 0.707 - 0.707j}$$

Next in this equation for each pole which is represented by $s+s_i$ we replace it by $1-e^{-sT}z^{-1}$ which will give us the required impulse invariant digital filter that corresponds to the second order Butterworth filter.

$$H[z] = \frac{0.707j}{1 - e^{-(0.707+0.707j)T} z^{-1}} + \frac{-0.707j}{1 - e^{-(0.707-0.707j)T} z^{-1}}$$

9.3.2 Bilinear Transformation

This method of transforming an analog filter to a digital filter is algebraic in nature. In this method we approximate the continuous time integral with the trapezoidal rule. This method of approximating the integral with the trapezoidal rule is pretty standard when an integral is to be approximated. The trapezoidal rule is shown in Figure 9.12. In Figure 9.12 the area under the curve between the time t_1 and t_0 is given by the trapezoidal Equation(9.35)

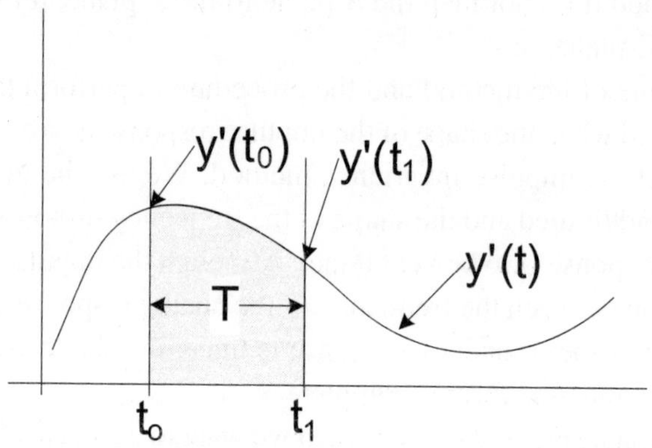

Figure 9.12: Demonstrating the trapezoidal rule of integration

$$\textit{Trapezoidal Rule} = \frac{T}{2}\left[y'(t_1) + y'(t_0)\right] \tag{9.35}$$

We will use this in the derivation of the bi-linear transformation. To begin consider the differential Equation(9.36)

$$\alpha_1 \frac{dy_a(t)}{dt} + \alpha_0 y_a(t) = \beta_0 x(t) \tag{9.36}$$

We can write the filter transfer function pertaining to this differential equation, which will be the system function for this differential equation and it is shown in Equation(9.37)

$$H_a(s) = \frac{\beta_o}{\alpha_1 s + \alpha_0} \tag{9.37}$$

The integral of the differential of a function between the limits t_0 and t_1 is given as shown in Equation(9.38)

$$\begin{aligned} y_a(t) &= \int_{t_0}^{t_1} 1 dy_a(\tau) + y_a(t_0) \\ t_1 = nT; &\quad t_0 = (n-1)T \\ y_a(nT) &= \int_{(n-1)T}^{nT} 1 dy_a(\tau) + y_a((n-1)T) \end{aligned} \tag{9.38}$$

We can now approximate the last integral Equation(9.38) by the trapezoidal rule given in Equation(9.35) to get Equation(9.39)

$$y_a(nT) = \frac{T}{2}\left[\frac{dy_a(nT)}{dt} + \frac{dy_a((n-1)T)}{dt}\right] + y_a((n-1)T) \tag{9.39}$$

Also the discrete version of Equation(9.36) will be used to represent the system in the discrete domain. The difference equation will be as shown in Equation(9.40)

$$\frac{dy(nT)}{dt} = -\frac{\alpha_0}{\alpha_1} y[nT] + \frac{\beta_0}{\alpha_1} x[nT] \tag{9.40}$$

When we substitute Equation(9.40) in Equation(9.39) we get the bilinear transform equation after a little bit of algebra. This is shown in Equation(9.41)

$$y_a[nT] = y_a[(n-1)T] + \frac{T}{2}\begin{bmatrix} -\frac{\alpha_0}{\alpha_1} y[nT] + \frac{\beta_0}{\alpha_1} x[nT] \\ -\frac{\alpha_0}{\alpha_1} y[(n-1)T] + \frac{\beta_0}{\alpha_1} x[(n-1)T] \end{bmatrix} \tag{9.41}$$

When we determine the Z-transform of Equation(9.41) then we get Equation(9.42)

$$H[z] = \frac{y[nT]}{x[nT]} = \frac{y[z]}{x[z]} = \frac{\beta_0}{\alpha_1 \frac{2}{T}\frac{1-z^{-1}}{1+z^{-1}} + \alpha_0} \tag{9.42}$$

Equation(9.42) represents the filter in the discrete domain which we obtained when we took the analog filter given in Equation(9.37) and approximated the integral with the trapezoidal rule. So both these equations represent the same filter, one in the analog domain and the other in the discrete domain. Now compare the two equations, we can get Equation(9.42) from Equation(9.37) by making a simple algebraic substitution shown in Equation(9.43)

$$s = \frac{2}{T}\frac{1-z^{-1}}{1+z^{-1}} \tag{9.43}$$

We can easily and quickly invert Equation(9.43) to get the transform from the Z domain to the s-domain. This equation is given in Equation(9.44)

$$z = \frac{1+\frac{T}{2}s}{1-\frac{T}{2}s} \tag{9.44}$$

When we consider the mapping of the s-plane to the z-plane the algebraic mapping maps the left half of the s-plane to the interior of the unit circle in the z-plane. So a stable filter in the analog domain will map to a stable filter in the discrete domain. This mapping is however not linear mapping. The frequency from the analog domain is not linearly mapped to the discrete domain. This is shown in Equation(9.45) which shows us how the imaginary axis in the s-plane is mapped from the s-plane to the z-plane. Since we are mapping the imaginary axis σ in the s-plane is zero so in the z-plane the mapping occurs around the unit circle as shown in Equation(9.45)

$$s = \sigma + j\omega_a = \frac{2}{T}\left[\frac{1-e^{-j\omega_d}}{1+e^{-j\omega_d}}\right] = \frac{2}{T}\frac{e^{\frac{j\omega_d}{2}}}{e^{\frac{j\omega_d}{2}}}\left[\frac{e^{\frac{j\omega_d}{2}} - e^{\frac{-j\omega_d}{2}}}{e^{\frac{j\omega_d}{2}} + e^{-j\omega_d}}\right] = j\frac{2}{T}\tan\left(\frac{\omega_d}{2}\right)$$

$$\omega_a = \frac{2}{T}\tan\left(\frac{\omega_d}{2}\right) \qquad \omega_d = 2\tan^{-1}\left(\frac{\omega_a T}{2}\right) \tag{9.45}$$

We see from Equation(9.45) that the relation between the analog frequency and the discrete frequency is a tangent relation and since the tangent function is a non linear function the mapping of the frequency is non linear. This non linear effect is known as warping and it is shown in Figure 9.13

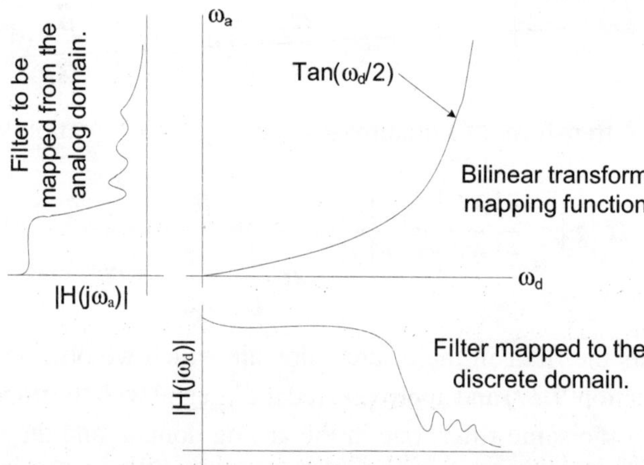

Figure 9.13: Illustration of the frequency distortion that takes place during bilinear transformation

where an analog frequency response $|H(\omega_a)|$ is transformed by bilinear transformation to give us the frequency response of the discrete filter $|H(\omega_d)|$. The warping effect takes the low frequency region and stretches it out on the right hand side of the unit circle while the high frequency region is all scrunched up towards the left hand side of the unit circle.

The warping effect can be and generally is compensated for by pre-warping the frequency requirements. This is shown in the next section.

Example 9.7

Determine the digital filter that corresponds to the second order Butterworth filter by using bilinear transform.

Solution 9.7

The transfer function of a second order Butterworth filter is

$$H(s) = \frac{1}{s^2 + 1.414s + 1}$$

For bilinear transform we substitute directly for the s terms in the analog expression by the substitution given in Equation(9.43). This will give us the discrete filter that we are looking for as shown here

$$H(z) = \frac{1}{\left[\frac{2}{T}\frac{1-z^{-1}}{1+z^{-1}}\right]^2 + 1.414\left[\frac{2}{T}\frac{1-z^{-1}}{1+z^{-1}}\right] + 1}$$

In the above discussion we have the term T which represents the sampling time. What should this be and how is this chosen? It is an interesting fact that if you start with the specifications in the discrete domain, transform them to the analog domain where you design the filter and then transform the filter back to the discrete domain then the sampling time does not participate in the design process. One example will make this clear.

Example 9.8

Determine the digital filter, with a 3dB cutoff frequency of 0.3π rad/sec, by transforming an equivalent first order analog filter by using bilinear transform.

Solution 9.8

In this example we are told what the 3dB cutoff frequency in the discrete domain is. So we will first transform this discrete domain frequency to the analog domain frequency using the frequency transform relation given in Equation(9.45). The equivalent analog domain 3dB cutoff frequency is

$$\omega_a = \frac{2}{T}\tan\left(\frac{\omega_d}{2}\right) = \frac{2}{T}\tan\left(\frac{0.3\pi}{2}\right) = \frac{2}{T}(0.51) = \frac{1.02}{T}$$

Notice that since we do not know the value of the sampling time T we have left it as it is. Now we will design an analog low pass filter that has a cutoff frequency that is 1.02/T radians/sec. The requirement said that we need a first order filter. This filter is given below.

$$H_a(s) = \frac{\frac{1.02}{T}}{s + \frac{1.02}{T}}$$

We are now ready to convert this filter to its discrete equivalent using bilinear transform. To do this we substitute for s from Equation(9.43) so we get the discrete filter as

$$H_d(z) = \frac{\frac{1.02}{T}}{\frac{2}{T}\frac{1-z^{-1}}{1+z^{-1}} + \frac{1.02}{T}} = \frac{1.02\left(1+z^{-1}\right)}{3.02 - 0.98z^{-1}}$$

Look at the final discrete time filter. It does not have the sampling time as the parameter. In completing the design we are performing the transform and its inverse. When we go around this way the effect of the sampling time is negated since it is divided once and it is multiplied the other time. So when you have to design discrete filters using bilinear transform and you are given the specifications in the discrete domain you can treat the sampling time as 1 and ignore it completely.

9.3.3 Prewarping

Of the two methods that we have learnt so far to transform an analog filter to its discrete equivalent the Impulse Invariant method is applicable only for the low pass filters but it preserves the frequency relations as it is a linear transformation. The bi-linear transformation is an algebraic transform but it warps the frequency so the frequency in the analog domain and the frequency in the discrete domain are related by the tangent function.

In Bi-linear design to finally have a discrete filter meeting a specified magnitude response we must first prewarp the critical frequencies from the discrete filter to the analog filter, then design the analog filter with these prewarped frequencies and then when we perform the bilinear transform to get the discrete filter the transformation will unwrap the prewarped frequency so we will end up with the magnitude response that was required in the discrete domain to begin with.

The prewarping is done for as many critical frequencies as there are specified in the discrete domain. So if you need a particular attenuation at a particular frequency in the discrete domain you would prewarp that frequency from the discrete domain to the analog domain to determine the analog frequency that has to have the specified attenuation. Once this information is known in the analog domain the filter with that attenuation is designed and then transformed to the discrete domain. The filter in the discrete domain will have the attenuation required at the frequency specified.

Prewarping is just transforming the frequency from the discrete domain to the analog domain by the prewarping equation given in Equation(9.45). To illustrate the procedure of designing an IIR low pass filter by bilinear transformation we present the following example.

Example 9.9

Design a Butterworth low pass filter with a pass band edge frequency ω_p of 0.3π radians/sec, pass band ripple is less than 0.5dB, stop band edge frequency ω_s of 0.6π radians/sec, with minimum stop band ripple more than 15dB. Use bilinear transformation with pre-warping.

Solution 9.9

We will begin by transforming the discrete domain specifications to the analog domain by prewarping the frequencies. So the pass band and the stop band edge frequencies in the analog domain will be

$$\omega_{ap} = \frac{2}{T}\tan\left(\frac{0.3\pi}{2}\right) = \tan\left(\frac{0.3\pi}{2}\right) = 0.51$$

$$\omega_{as} = \frac{2}{T}\tan\left(\frac{0.75\pi}{2}\right) = \tan\left(\frac{0.75\pi}{2}\right) = 2.4142$$

Since we are transforming the discrete frequency to analog frequency and then back again to the discrete frequency the sampling time T will be immaterial so we have chosen it to be 2. We could have chosen it to be any value. From the pass band and the stop band frequencies and the attenuations specified we need to determine the order of the filter. Using Equations(4.44), (4.45) and (4.46) from Chapter 4, we will determine the order of the required filter. With the specifications that we have we determine that $\delta = 4.7337$, $A^2 = 31.6227$, $\varepsilon^2 = 0.12201$ and $\delta_1 = 0.01365$. With these specifications we get N=1.777 = 2. So we need a second order Butterworth filter which is

$$H_a(s) = \frac{1.0}{(s)^2 + 1.414(s) + 1.0}$$

This second order filter has a cutoff frequency of 1 radian/sec. So we need to transform this filter from a prototype filter to the required filter. For this we need to first determine the 3dB cutoff frequency. The 3dB cutoff frequency can be determined from Equation 4.45. Using the two equations will give us two slightly different answers. But they are close to each other. The equation that you use depends if meeting the pass band specification is critical or meeting the stop band specification is the critical specification. For this example we get 1.0263. So we need to transform the filter to the 3dB cutoff frequency of 1.0263 radian/sec. The second order Butterworth filter with this 3dB cutoff frequency is

$$H_a(s) = \frac{1.0}{\left(\frac{s}{1.0263}\right)^2 + 1.414\left(\frac{s}{1.0263}\right) + 1.0} = \frac{1.0533}{s^2 + 1.4512s + 1.0533}$$

Now that we have the designed filter in the analog domain we are ready to transform it to the discrete domain by bilinear transform. Remember from the earlier step that we have chosen T to be 2 so we must continue using the same value of T. Thus we get the filter that we are looking for as

$$H_d(z) = \frac{1.0533}{\left(\frac{1-z^{-1}}{1+z^{-1}}\right)^2 + 1.3512\left(\frac{1-z^{-1}}{1+z^{-1}}\right) + 1.0533}$$

The steps are many but they are simple and straightforward.

9.4 FREQUENCY TRANSFORMATION FOR DIGITAL FILTERS

Earlier in Chapter 4 we have seen how to transform a prototype analog low pass filter designed using normalized frequency to a desired type of filter. (Low pass, High pass, Band pass or Band stop filter.) This was done by frequency scaling and transformation. It allowed us to complete the design of a convenient filter at a convenient frequency range.

After we have designed the analog filter and we have transformed the analog filter to the discrete type it is most probably a low pass filter. This is because we most probably designed the filter as a low pass filter in the analog domain or we transformed the filter using the impulse invariance method. Remember, due to aliasing in the impulse invariance method, this method is applicable only to the low pass filters. So we need a method to scale as well as transform the discrete time filters.

To make sure that we have no confusion between the variables we will use the subscript L to indicate the low pass filter that we have. So $H_L(*)$ will indicate the transfer function of the low pass filter that we begin with. Also z_L will indicate the z-domain variable of the low pass filter that we begin with. So $H_L(z_L)$ is the original low pass discrete time filter that we begin with. Similarly we will use the subscript D to indicate the filter that we desire. It does not matter what type of a filter we desire. We will use the subscript D. So z_D is the z-domain variable of the desired filter and $H_D(z_D)$ is the transfer function of the desired filter. So the L subscript indicates the starting filter which is a low pass filter and the D subscript indicates the target filter which can be any type of filter including another low pass filter.

The most general form of the discrete filter algebraic transform is given by Equation(9.46)

$$F(z) = \pm \prod_{k=1}^{K} \left(\frac{z - \lambda_k}{1 - \lambda_k^* z} \right) \tag{9.46}$$

In Equation(9.46) the parameter λ_k can be a complex value and if it is a complex quantity then it occurs along with its complex conjugate. So it is either real or occurs as a complex conjugate pair. Further to make sure that a stable filter will always map to a stable filter the magnitude of λ_k is always less than 1 so $|\lambda_k| < 1$.

Low Pass to Low Pass Transformation:

To transform a proto type low pass filter $H_L(z_L)$ with a 3dB cut off frequency ω_L to another low pass filter $H_D(z_D)$ with a 3dB cut off frequency ω_D we will use the transformation in Equation(9.46).

The transformation is given in Equation(9.47)

$$z_L^{-1} = \frac{z_D^{-1} - \lambda}{1 - \lambda z_D^{-1}} \tag{9.47}$$

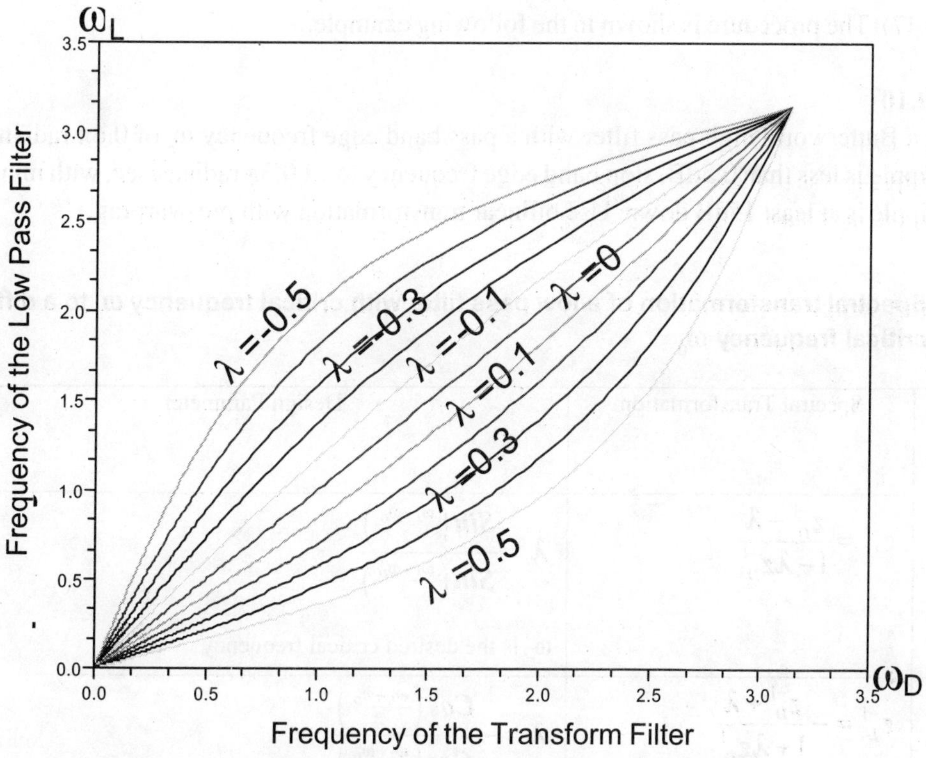

Figure 9.14: Plot of Equation 9.48 for various values of λ. Only the plot for λ = 0 is a linear plot

In this transformation since we have only one value of λ it is a real value. To get a better idea about what the transformation does it is instructive to examine this transformation around the unit circle where $z = e^{j\omega}$. Substitute for z and simplify Equation(9.47) to get Equation(9.48)

$$\tan\left(\frac{\omega_L}{2}\right) = \frac{1+\lambda}{1-\lambda}\tan\left(\frac{\omega_D}{2}\right) \tag{9.48}$$

This frequency transformation equation is again a non linear equation. A plot of Equation(9.48) for various values of λ is shown in Figure 9.14. The plot is linear only for λ = 0. Equation(9.48) is also the equation that will tell us what value of λ is to be used to perform the required transformation. In Equation(9.48) since we know the two frequencies ω_L and ω_D we can compute the required value of λ. Solving for λ we get Equation(9.49)

$$\lambda = \frac{Sin\left(\frac{\omega_L - \omega_D}{2}\right)}{Sin\left(\frac{\omega_L + \omega_D}{2}\right)} \tag{9.49}$$

Once we obtain the value of l then the required substitution equation can be determined by using Equation(9.47). The procedure is shown in the following example.

Example 9.10

Design a Butterworth high pass filter with a pass band edge frequency ω_p of 0.6π radians/sec, pass band ripple is less than 0.5dB, stop band edge frequency ω_s of 0.3π radians/sec, with minimum stop band ripple is at least 15dB down. Use bilinear transformation with pre-warping.

Table 9.1: Spectral transformation of a low pass filter with critical frequency ω_L to a different filter with critical frequency ω_D

Required Filter Type	Spectral Transformation	Design Parameter
Low Pass	$z_L^{-1} = \frac{z_D^{-1} - \lambda}{1 - \lambda z_D^{-1}}$	$\lambda = \frac{Sin\left(\frac{\omega_L - \omega_D}{2}\right)}{Sin\left(\frac{\omega_L + \omega_D}{2}\right)}$ ω_D is the desired critical frequency
High Pass	$z_L^{-1} = -\frac{z_D^{-1} + \lambda}{1 + \lambda z_D^{-1}}$	$\lambda = -\frac{Cos\left(\frac{\omega_L + \omega_D}{2}\right)}{Cos\left(\frac{\omega_L - \omega_D}{2}\right)}$ ω_D is the desired critical frequency
Band Pass	$z_L^{-1} = -\frac{z_D^{-2} - \frac{2\lambda\sigma}{\sigma+1} z_D^{-1} + \frac{\sigma-1}{\sigma+1}}{\frac{\sigma-1}{\sigma+1} z_D^{-2} - \frac{2\lambda\sigma}{\sigma+1} z_D^{-1} + 1}$	$\lambda = \frac{Cos\left(\frac{\omega_{D2} + \omega_{D1}}{2}\right)}{Cos\left(\frac{\omega_{D2} - \omega_{D1}}{2}\right)}$ $\sigma = Cot\left(\frac{\omega_{D2} - \omega_{D2}}{2}\right)\tan\left(\frac{\omega_L}{2}\right)$ ω_{D2} and ω_{D1} are the desired upper and lower critical frequencies.
Band Stop	$z_L^{-1} = -\frac{z_D^{-2} - \frac{2\lambda}{1+\sigma} z_D^{-1} + \frac{1-\sigma}{1+\sigma}}{\frac{1-\sigma}{1+\sigma} z_D^{-2} - \frac{2\lambda}{1+\sigma} z_D^{-1} + 1}$	$\lambda = \frac{Cos\left(\frac{\omega_{D2} + \omega_{D1}}{2}\right)}{Cos\left(\frac{\omega_{D2} - \omega_{D1}}{2}\right)}$ $\sigma = \tan\left(\frac{\omega_{D2} - \omega_{D2}}{2}\right)\tan\left(\frac{\omega_L}{2}\right)$ ω_{D2} and ω_{D1} are the desired upper and lower critical frequencies.

Solution 9.10

Here we have to design a high pass filter and we are given the required specifications. We can transform the high pass requirements to the analog domain. Once we have the high pass requirements in the analog domain we can transform the filter to be a low pass filter in the analog domain and design the filter. Once we have the low pass filter in the analog domain then we can transform it back to be a high pass filter in the analog domain and then transform it back to be a discrete time filter by the bilinear transform.

As an alternative we can transform the filter from the high pass to a low pass filter in the discrete domain, then transform the low pass filter to the analog domain, design the filter and then transform it back to the discrete domain. This discrete filter can then be scaled to become a discrete high pass filter. For this example we will follow this procedure.

The above procedure showed us how to transform a Low pass filter to another Low pass filter at a different frequency. Other transforms are similarly completed by substituting a z_D domain expression for every z_L in the low pass filter. However just as here each transform requires that we first determine the parameter λ that will complete the transform from the cutoff frequency that we have to the cutoff frequency that we need. These transforms along with the expression to determine the parameter λ are given in Table 9.1.

In Table 9.1 we see that the transform is always from a low pass filter to a different type of filter that is desired. In performing the required transform we need to determine either one or two parameters depending on the type of filter that is desired. We need to determine only one parameter; λ if the target filters have only one cutoff frequency; we need to determine two parameters λ and δ if the target filters have two cutoff frequencies. Another point to consider carefully is as follows. If the filter that you have is not a low pass filter but is a different type of filter then you will first have to determine the equivalent low pass filter and then from the obtained low pass filter we transform to the desired filter. This is not a big hardship or does not require actual two transforms; you would just determine the equivalent substitutions required for each transform and then complete the transform in one step. An example of this is given below.

Example 9.11

You are given a high pass filter with a transfer function as shown in Equation (9.50) which has a cutoff frequency of 0.4.

$$H[z] = \frac{0.4 + z}{1 + 0.4z} \tag{9.50}$$

Convert this digital filter to another High pass filter with cutoff frequency of 0.6.

Solution 9.11

Since we are given a High pass filter and we want another High pass filter we first need to transform to a low pass filter which we will then transform back to a high pass filter as follows.

a. Determine λ. This is given by the ratio of the sine of the cutoff frequencies so we need to pick the cutoff frequency of the low pass filter. Say we choose the cutoff frequency of the low pass filter to be 0.2 then we can calculate λ using Equation(9.51)

$$\lambda = \frac{Sin\left(\frac{\omega_H - \omega_D}{2}\right)}{Sin\left(\frac{\omega_H + \omega_D}{2}\right)} = \frac{Sin(0.1)}{Sin(0.3)} = 0.3378 \tag{9.51}$$

b. Determine substitution for z_H. Using this value of λ we can determine the required transform substitution to get the low pass filter as shown in Equation (9.52). So we substitute z term in the high pass filter with the equivalent term in Equation(9.52). This gives us the required low pass filter.

$$z_H^{-1} = \frac{1 + \lambda z_L}{\lambda + z_L} = \frac{1 + 0.3378 z_L}{0.3378 + z_L} \tag{9.52}$$

c. Determine λ for second transform. Next to get the required High pass filter we will once again calculate a new value of l as shown in Equation (9.53) and use this to transform the low pass filter to the required high pass filter.

$$\lambda = \frac{Sin\left(\frac{\omega_L - \omega_D}{2}\right)}{Sin\left(\frac{\omega_L + \omega_D}{2}\right)} = \frac{Sin(-0.2)}{Sin(0.4)} = -0.51 \tag{9.53}$$

d. Determine substitution for z_L. Finally we have the required value of λ so we can complete the transform by first determining the required substitution as shown in Equation (9.54)

$$z_L^{-1} = \frac{z_D^{-1} - \lambda}{1 - \lambda z_D^{-1}} \tag{9.54}$$

As you can see that this is a process that requires a lot of patience and a great deal of algebra. This process is almost never followed as designing a new digital filter will be considerably less work than doing the work indicated here. We however do need the transform from the low pass filter to the various different types of filters since we may need to transform a low pass filter to a different type of filter. We usually design the analog filters as low pass filters so if we are going to use an IIR filter which is first designed in the analog domain then this will be a low pass filter. We then convert the low pass filter to the discrete domain and hence we will have a low pass filter in the discrete domain. This low pass filter can then be transformed to the type of filter required by using the substitutions given in Table 9.1.

9.5 FIR VERSUS IIR FILTERS

There are many reasons for using either the FIR filters or the IIR filters. A brief study of these issues will give us the background that we need in deciding what type of filter we should use when we are given a choice and can choose either an IIR filter or an FIR filter.

First we talk about the FIR filters:

FIR filters with exact linear phase are easy to design. This simplifies the approximation problem in many cases especially when frequency non linearity is harmful. Such examples are in speech processing, data transmission, phase modulated systems. A second advantage of FIR filters is that efficient realizations exist as both recursive as well as non recursive structures. FIR filter structures that are realized non recursively are always stable.

The disadvantages of FIR filters are that the filter requires a large number of taps to adequately approximate the sharp cutoff filters. Remember the transition band is proportional to the size of the filter and for a narrow transition band we need a large number of taps in the filter. The FIR filters that are designed are always non causal, so to make them causal the filter has to be delayed. The amount of delay is not always equal to an integer number of samples. This non integer number of sample delays can lead to problems in some signal processing applications. The delay in the filter also makes it very difficult to implement these filters in real time.

Next we talk about the IIR filters:

In contrast to FIR filters the IIR filters have their own advantages and disadvantages. First the IIR filters are obtained in a nice closed form formula. So these filters are compact and can be implemented with many fewer delay elements. Fewer delay elements implies fewer computations and fewer storage requirements. There is a vast literature of design methods of analog filters which are used to design the IIR filters. In this literature all the peculiarities and nuances of the filters are known and can be utilized. So there is no ambiguity in the design of the analog filters.

On the other hand the disadvantages of IIR filters are that they do not display linear phase response. It is possible to design an IIR filter and then compensate for the phase of the filter by an all pass compensating network but the design of the combined two filters lead us back to a filter that is of comparable size compared to an FIR filter that has linear phase and the magnitude characteristics to match so there is no advantage. To get linear phase from an IIR filter we would need the filter to satisfy the condition that $H(z) = H(z^{-1})$. Such a transfer function will have poles that are mirror images on both sides of the unit circle. So for every pole that was inside the unit circle we would also have a pole outside the unit circle. This would lead to an unstable filter. Since the IIR filters use feed back it is possible that the filter that you design could be an unstable filter if you are not careful during the design phase.

9.6 CHAPTER SUMMARY

9.6.1 Linear Phase Response

The filter response has two components to it, magnitude and the phase. Very often we are interested in the phase response being linear while meeting the required magnitude response. Linear phase response is obtained when the phase response of the filter is $\theta(\omega) = -\alpha\omega$ or $\theta(\omega) = \pi - \alpha\omega$. With the first condition we get both the group delay and the phase delay that are constant while with the latter condition we get only the group delay that is constant. We will use both these conditions in designing linear phase filters.

9.6.2 Finite Impulse Response Filter

In designing the FIR filters we use one of the two available methods—the Window method or the Frequency Sampling method. (Other methods are also available but these two are the most popular and easy to use.)

9.6.2.1 Window Design Method:

The FIR design method begins with the frequency response that we desire to have. Next we determine the IDTFT of the desired filter response. This gives us an infinite sequence, so to limit the sequence and make it finite we will window the sequence. This will make the sequence finite. This finite sequence is a non causal sequence so to make the filter implementable we will delay the sequence by N/2 sample points to get a causal finite length filter.

The effect of windowing is to convolve the frequency response of the window with the frequency response of the desired filter to get the resulting filter. So if the frequency response of the window is an impulse then we will get the resulting filter that is exactly the same as the desired filter. Unfortunately the window frequency response only come close to the impulse function so the resulting filters are slightly smeared based on the style and the size of the window. The shape of the window determines the attenuation provided by the window while the size of the window determines the width of the transition band. It is for this reason that the size of the window is determined mostly by trial and error.

The standard windows such as the Hamming, the Hanning and the Blackman windows have only the size parameter that is adjustable; the shape of the window is predetermined. On the other hand the Kaiser window has two adjustable parameters. The two parameters are the shape parameter α and the size of the window N. Thus the Kaiser window can be fine tuned to meet both the required attenuation as well as the width of the transition band.

9.6.2.2 Frequency Sampling Method:

In the frequency sampling method also we begin with a desired frequency response of the filter. Next we sample one period of the magnitude response at N equally spaced (in frequency) points. This gives us the magnitude of the required filter. To the magnitude we will add the required linear phase of the filter. Once we have added the linear phase to the magnitude we will have N sample points in the frequency domain. When we determine the IDFT of these N sample points we will get the N point filter coefficients in the time domain. This is the filter that we are looking for.

9.6.3 Infinite Impulse Response Filters

The infinite impulse response or the IIR filters are designed by transforming an analog filter to its digital equivalent. In the chapter we have studied two different methods to transform the filters. They are the Impulse invariance and the Bilinear transform.

For the Impulse Invariance method we begin by writing the filter in the partial fraction form where each pole is identified individually. Then we transform each individual pole from the analog domain to the discrete domain to get the discrete filter. This method transforms the shape of the frequency response linearly from the analog domain to the discrete domain. This method however does not transform the zeros of the analog filter to the discrete domain. Also, this method, because of the sampling involved can be used only when the required filter is sufficiently band limited. Thus this method is not appropriate to transform high pass or band stop filters.

Bilinear transform is the other method that we have discussed. With Bilinear transform we substitute for every occurrence of the analog variable with an equivalent expression in the discrete domain. This substitution is an algebraic substitution and leads to a non linear transform of the frequency profile. The nonlinearity of the frequency mapping has a tangent relation so to get the frequency response that you want or need in the discrete domain you need to first pre-warp the critical frequencies from the discrete domain to the analog domain. After pre-warping when we perform the bilinear transform we will get the frequency response that we wanted. In performing this round trip from the discrete domain to the analog domain and back again we get an added bonus in that the sampling time becomes immaterial and hence we can choose any convenient value that we need.

9.6.4 Frequency Transformation for Digital Filters

Just as we were able to transform the filter from the prototype low pass analog filter to any other type of analog filter at any frequency, we can also transform a prototype low pass discrete filter to a required type of filter centered at the required frequency. This transformation requires that we determine a special set of parameters and once we have determined these parameters then it is just a matter of direct substitution to transform one type of filter to another type of a filter.

9.6.5 FIR versus IIR Filters

The FIR filters as we have seen are designed to duplicate the linear phase requirement which gives us constant group delay and may also give us constant phase delay. The FIR filters are all zero filters so they are always stable. To get the same magnitude response from an FIR filter that is obtainable from an IIR filter we will need a much larger FIR filter than the IIR filter. The IIR filters have both the poles and zeros, because of the presence of the poles in the filter IIR filters have feedback and when there is feedback there is a possibility that the filter may be an unstable filter. All IIR filters are not unstable but they have a potential to be unstable.

9.7 HOMEWORK PROBLEMS

FIR Filter Design

Problem 9.7.1

Design an FIR linear phase filter to approximate the following ideal frequency response.

a. Determine the coefficients for a 25 tap filter based on the window method using a rectangular window.

b. Plot the magnitude and the phase response of the frequency response of the filter.

c. Repeat parts a, and b of Problem 9.7.1 using the Hamming window.

d. Repeat parts a, and b of Problem 9.7.1 using the Bartlett window.

$$H_d(\omega) = \begin{cases} 1 & |\omega| \le \frac{\pi}{6} \\ 0 & \frac{\pi}{6} \le |\omega| \le \pi \end{cases}$$

Problem 9.7.2

Determine an FIR linear phase filter to approximate the following ideal band pass frequency response.

a. Determine the coefficients for a 25 tap filter based on the window method using a rectangular window.

b. Plot the magnitude and the phase response of the frequency response of the filter.

c. Repeat parts a, and b of Problem 9.7.1 using the Hamming window.

d. Repeat parts a, and b of Problem 9.7.1 using the Bartlett window.

$$H_d(\omega) = \begin{cases} 0 & |\omega| \le \frac{\pi}{6} \\ 1 & \frac{\pi}{6} \le |\omega| \le \frac{\pi}{3} \\ 0 & \frac{\pi}{3} \le |\omega| \le \pi \end{cases}$$

Problem 9.7.3

The Figure P.9.3 shows the frequency response of an ideal differentiator. Using a 51 tap filter determine the coefficients of an ideal linear phase differentiator.

a. Determine the coefficients for a 51 tap filter based on the window method using a rectangular window.

b. Plot the magnitude and the phase response of the frequency response of the filter.

c. Repeat parts a, and b of Problem 9.7.3 using the Hanning window.

d. Try to design the filter using 52 taps. Comment on what you observe.

e. The filter in Figure P.9.3 is a full band differentiator. Design the differentiator if you need the differentiator to differentiate frequencies only up to $\pi/3$ instead of till $\pm\pi$

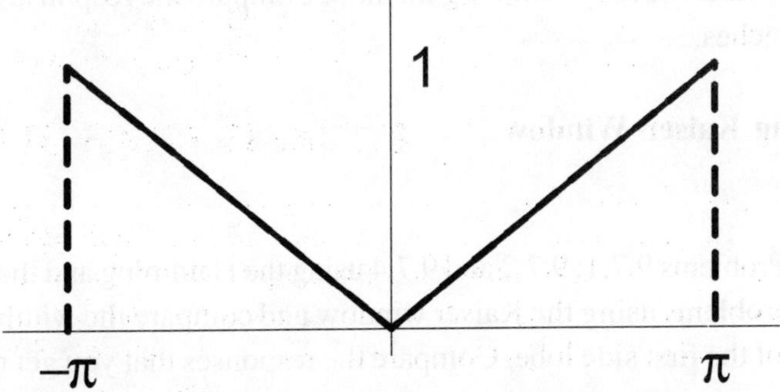

Figure P. 9.3: Magnitude response of an ideal Differentiator

Problem 9.7.4

The Figure P.9.4 shows the frequency response of an ideal band pass filter. Using a 61 tap filter determine the coefficients of an ideal linear phase band pass filter.

a. Determine the coefficients for a 61 tap filter based on the window method using a rectangular window.

b. Plot the magnitude and the phase response of the frequency response of the filter.

c. Repeat parts a, and b of Problem 9.7.4 using the Hanning window.

d. Try to design the filter using 52 taps. Comment on what you observe.

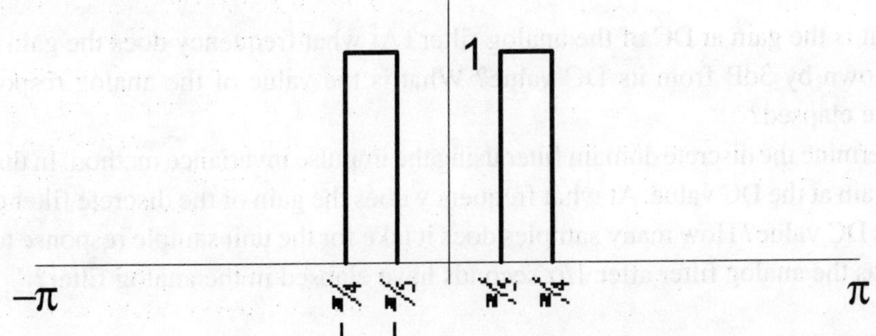

Figure P. 9.4: Magnitude response of an ideal Band Pass Filter

Filter Design Using Frequency Sampling

Problem 9.7.5

You attempted Problems 9.7.1; 9.7.2; 9.7.3 and 9.7.4 using the window method. Repeat these four problems using the frequency sampling method. Compare the responses that you get using the two different approaches.

Filter Design Using Kaiser Window

Problem 9.7.6

You attempted Problems 9.7.1; 9.7.2 and 9.7.4 using the Hamming and the rectangular windows. Repeat these three problems using the Kaiser window and compare the width of the transition band and the attenuation of the first side lobe. Compare the responses that you get using the two different approaches.

IIR Filter Design

Problem 9.7.7

We wish to compare the performance of a Low pass filter that is transformed from an analog filter to a discrete filter. For this purpose we will employ a first order Butterworth low pass filter given by the transfer function

$$H(s) = \frac{\alpha}{s+\alpha} \Leftrightarrow h_a(t) = e^{-\alpha t}$$

a. What is the gain at DC of the analog filter? At what frequency does the gain of the analog filter drop down by 3dB from its DC value? What is the value of the analog response after $1/\alpha$ seconds have elapsed?

b. Determine the discrete domain filter using the impulse invariance method. In this digital filter what is the gain at the DC value. At what frequency does the gain of the discrete filter drop down by 3dB from its DC value? How many samples does it take for the unit sample response to decay to the same value as the analog filter after $1/\alpha$ seconds have elapsed in the analog filter?

Problem 9.7.8

Repeat Problem 9.7.5 but this time determine the discrete filter using bilinear transformation. Assume that the bilinear transformation is done with the assumption that T = 2.

Problem 9.7.9

An analog signal x(t) is a sum of two signals $x_1(t)$ and $x_2(t)$. The spectrum of the two signals is shown in Figure Problem 9.9. The signal x(t) is band limited to 40KHz. This signal x(t) is sampled at the rate of 1 sample every 10mSec to get the signal x[n]. It is desired to suppress the signal $x_2(t)$ by passing the sequence x[n] through a digital low pass filter which has the following specifications: $d_p = 0.02$; $w_p = 15.0$ KHz; $d_s = 0.01$; $w_s = 25.0$ KHz;

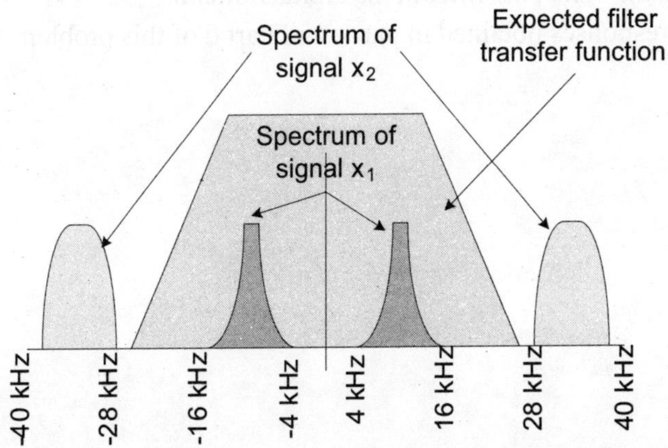

Figure P. 9.9: Spectrum of signal x[n] and the spectrum of desired filter.

a. Design an FIR windowed filter to meet the given specifications. Which window would be acceptable? What is the required length of the filter?

b. Design an FIR frequency sampled filter that has the same size as the windowed filter in part a above.

c. Design an IIR filter to meet the specifications given. Do this as follows:

1. Determine the minimum order of a Butterworth filter to meet the given specifications. Convert the analog Butterworth filter using the bilinear transform method. Before designing the required analog filter remember to pre-warp the two critical frequencies.

2. Determine the minimum order of a Chebyshev filter to meet the given specifications. Convert the analog Chebyshev filter using the impulse invariance transform method.

Problem 9.7.10

Repeat problem 9.7.9 with the following changes. Instead of a low pass filter use a band pass filter with stop band bands at 20 KHz and 50 KHz and the pass band from 28 KHz to 40 KHz. This will allow you to separate the signal $x_2[n]$ from the composite signal x[n]. We can do this in several different ways. Try all the following methods:

a. Design all the required filters as specified in the problem.

b. Take all the designed filters in part a and b in problem 9.7.9 and transform them to the frequency range of interest using the transform equations given in Table 9.1 in the text.

c. Take the analog filters designed in part c in problem 9.7.9 and transform the analog filter to the band pass filter before transforming the filter to the digital domain.

d. Take the filters designed and transformed to the digital domain in part c in problem 9.7.9; transform the digital filter to the band pass filter in the digital domain.

e. Compare the filter responses obtained in part c and part d of this problem.

CHAPTER 10

Discrete State Space Systems

INTRODUCTION

Earlier in Chapter 6 we saw how the continuous time systems can be represented by a state variable representation. The state variable representation allowed us to view the system from a different perspective and gave us an insight about how the various internal states of the system behaved.

In this chapter we will see that the discrete time systems can also be represented by a state variable representation and that this representation is very similar to the representation of the continuous time systems with all the similar benefits that we obtained when we represented the continuous time system in the state variable format.

In discrete time systems as in continuous time systems, we will describe the system using a set of difference equations instead of differential equations. The difference equations describe the unique relations between the state of the system, the input applied to the system and the output obtained from the system. Since we are dealing with causal, linear, time invariant systems the output described by the difference equation at the present sample time is related to the present and past inputs and past outputs.

The state description and analysis of any system is facilitated by representing the system in a compact form as a matrix. The matrix representation allows us to analyze complex systems, multiple inputs multiple outputs system using relatively simple matrix operations. The discrete time system, just like the continuous time system was, is represented by simultaneous first order equations. This time the equations are difference equations instead of differential equations.

10.1 STATE EQUATIONS AND SIGNAL FLOW GRAPHS FROM DIFFERENCE EQUATIONS

The discrete time systems are represented in state variable representation form as shown in Equation(10.1)

$$\begin{aligned} x(k+1) &= Ax(k) + Bu(k) \\ y(k) &= Cx(k) + Du(k) \end{aligned} \tag{10.1}$$

In Equation(10.1) the four matrices A, B, C and D are constant matrices for time invariant systems. We will be focusing only on these systems in this chapter. The expanded form for the system state equations are presented in Equation(10.2) and (10.3)

$$\begin{bmatrix} x_1(k+1) \\ x_2(k+1) \\ \vdots \\ x_n(k+1) \end{bmatrix} = \begin{bmatrix} A_{11} & A_{12} & \cdots & A_{1n} \\ A_{21} & A_{22} & \cdots & A_{2n} \\ \vdots & \vdots & \ddots & \vdots \\ A_{n1} & A_{n2} & \cdots & A_{nn} \end{bmatrix} \begin{bmatrix} x_1(k) \\ x_2(k) \\ \vdots \\ x_n(k) \end{bmatrix} + \begin{bmatrix} B_{11} & B_{12} & \cdots & B_{1p} \\ B_{21} & B_{22} & \cdots & B_{2p} \\ \vdots & \vdots & \ddots & \vdots \\ B_{n1} & B_{n2} & \cdots & B_{np} \end{bmatrix} \begin{bmatrix} u_1(k) \\ u_2(k) \\ \vdots \\ u_n(k) \end{bmatrix} \tag{10.2}$$

$$\begin{bmatrix} y_1(k) \\ y_2(k) \\ \vdots \\ y_q(k) \end{bmatrix} = \begin{bmatrix} C_{11} & C_{12} & \cdots & C_{1n} \\ C_{21} & C_{22} & \cdots & C_{2n} \\ \vdots & \vdots & \ddots & \vdots \\ C_{q1} & C_{q2} & \cdots & C_{qn} \end{bmatrix} \begin{bmatrix} x_1(k) \\ x_2(k) \\ \vdots \\ x_n(k) \end{bmatrix} + \begin{bmatrix} D_{11} & D_{12} & \cdots & D_{1p} \\ D_{21} & D_{22} & \cdots & D_{2p} \\ \vdots & \vdots & \ddots & \vdots \\ D_{q1} & D_{q2} & \cdots & D_{qp} \end{bmatrix} \begin{bmatrix} u_1(k) \\ u_2(k) \\ \vdots \\ u_p(k) \end{bmatrix} \tag{10.3}$$

The equations show that the A matrix is a square matrix with n rows and columns where there are n state variables in the system. The B matrix is a n×p matrix. It has n rows and p columns where p represents the number of inputs to the system. The C matrix is a q×n matrix. It has q rows and n columns where q represents the number of outputs to the system. The D matrix is a q×p matrix. It has q rows and p columns where p represents the number of inputs to the system and q represents the number of outputs from the system.

Discrete time systems are represented by higher order difference equations which can be converted to a set of simultaneous first order differential equations. These first order equations are then arranged as shown in Equations(10.2) and (10.3) to convert the system to the state representations. The next example will make the method clear.

Example 10.1

Convert the system represented by the following difference equation in a state variable format.

$$y(k)+\alpha_1 y(k-1)+\alpha_2 y(k-2)+\alpha_3 y(k-3)$$
$$=\beta_0 u(k)+\beta_1 u(k-1)+\beta_2 u(k-2)$$

Solution 10.1

To convert the difference equation to a State Variable representation we begin with a reduced difference equation. The reduced equation in our example is given in Equation(10.4)

$$\gamma(k)+\alpha_1\gamma(k-1)+\alpha_2\gamma(k-2)+\alpha_3\gamma(k-3)=u(k) \tag{10.4}$$

Next we will multiply Equation(10.4) by β_0 to get Equation(10.5)

$$\beta_0\{\gamma(k)+\alpha_1\gamma(k-1)+\alpha_2\gamma(k-2)+\alpha_3\gamma(k-3)\}=\beta_0\{u(k)\} \tag{10.5}$$

To continue we will next delay Equation(10.4) by one sample and multiply it by β_1 to get Equation(10.6)

$$\beta_1\{\gamma(k-1)+\alpha_1\gamma(k-2)+\alpha_2\gamma(k-3)+\alpha_3\gamma(k-4)\}=\beta_1\{u(k-1)\} \tag{10.6}$$

And finally we will delay Equation(10.4) by two samples and multiply it by β_2 to get Equation(10.7)

$$\beta_2\{\gamma(k-2)+\alpha_1\gamma(k-3)+\alpha_2\gamma(k-4)+\alpha_3\gamma(k-5)\}=\beta_2\{u(k-2)\} \tag{10.7}$$

If we add the three Equations(10.5), (10.6) and (10.7) together and rearrange them we get the equation that is shown in Equation(10.8)

$$\begin{aligned}
&\{\beta_0\gamma(k)+\beta_1\gamma(k-1)+\beta_2\gamma(k-2)\}\\
&\quad+\alpha_1\{\beta_0\gamma(k-1)+\beta_1\gamma(k-2)+\beta_2\gamma(k-3)\}\\
&\quad+\alpha_2\{\beta_0\gamma(k-2)+\beta_1\gamma(k-3)+\beta_2\gamma(k-4)\}\\
&\quad+\alpha_3\{\beta_0\gamma(k-3)+\beta_1\gamma(k-4)+\beta_2\gamma(k-5)\}\\
&\qquad=\beta_0\{u(k)\}+\beta_1\{u(k-1)\}+\beta_2\{u(k-2)\}
\end{aligned} \tag{10.8}$$

In Equation(10.8) if we make the following four assignments

$$\begin{aligned}
&\{\beta_0\gamma(k)+\beta_1\gamma(k-1)+\beta_2\gamma(k-2)\}=y(k)\\
&\{\beta_0\gamma(k-1)+\beta_1\gamma(k-2)+\beta_2\gamma(k-3)\}=y(k-1)\\
&\{\beta_0\gamma(k-2)+\beta_1\gamma(k-3)+\beta_2\gamma(k-4)\}=y(k-2)\\
&\{\beta_0\gamma(k-3)+\beta_1\gamma(k-4)+\beta_2\gamma(k-5)\}=y(k-3)
\end{aligned} \tag{10.9}$$

After making the assignments we substitute each of the assignments in Equation(10.8) then Equation(10.8) is just a restatement of equation that defined the original difference equation. Next we will define the state variables as shown in Equation(10.10). Notice that $\gamma(k-3)$ is the term that has the most delay in the reduced equation that we defined in Equation(10.4) so we begin with that term.

$$\begin{aligned}
&\gamma(k-3)=x_1(k)\\
&\gamma(k-2)=x_2(k)=x_1(k+1)\\
&\gamma(k-1)=x_3(k)=x_2(k+1)\\
&\gamma(k)=x_3(k+1)=u(k)-\alpha_1\gamma(k-1)-\alpha_2\gamma(k-2)-\alpha_3\gamma(k-3)\\
&\gamma(k)=x_3(k+1)=u(k)-\alpha_1x_3(k)-\alpha_2x_2(k)-\alpha_3x_1(k)
\end{aligned} \tag{10.10}$$

Then we can define the system state equations as shown in Equation(10.11)

$$\begin{bmatrix} x_1(k+1)\\ x_2(k+1)\\ x_3(k+1)\end{bmatrix}=\begin{bmatrix}0 & 1 & 0\\ 0 & 0 & 1\\ -\alpha_3 & -\alpha_2 & -\alpha_1\end{bmatrix}\begin{bmatrix} x_1(k)\\ x_2(k)\\ x_3(k)\end{bmatrix}+\begin{bmatrix}0\\0\\1\end{bmatrix}u(k) \tag{10.11}$$

And using the first equation in Equation(10.9) and substituting for the $\gamma(\cdot)$ from Equation(10.10) we get the required output equation which is shown in Equation(10.12)

$$\{\beta_0\gamma(k)+\beta_1\gamma(k-1)+\beta_2\gamma(k-2)\}=y(k)$$

$$\left\{\begin{aligned}&\beta_0u(k)-\beta_0\alpha_1x_3(k)-\beta_0\alpha_2x_2(k)\\ &\qquad-\beta_0\alpha_3x_1(k)+\beta_1x_3(k)+\beta_2\gamma x_2(k)\end{aligned}\right\}=y(k)$$

$$y(k)=\left[(-\beta_0\alpha_3)\ \ (\beta_2-\beta_0\alpha_2)\ \ (\beta_1-\beta_0\alpha_1)\right]\begin{bmatrix} x_1(k)\\ x_2(k)\\ x_3(k)\end{bmatrix}+[\beta_0]u(k) \tag{10.12}$$

So the two sets of Equations(10.11) and (10.12) form the state variable representation for the difference equation given in the statement of the problem. It is interesting to see the signal flow graph that would represent the state variable format of the system shown in Equations(10.11) and (10.12). Example 10.2 shows this.

Example 10.2

Represent the state variable system defined by Equations(10.11) and (10.12) using a signal flow graph.

Solution 10.2

We begin the representation of the state system by a signal flow graph by starting with the individual state equations given in Equation(10.11). First note that the state variables $x_1(k)$ and $x_2(k)$ are related by a delay only. Similarly state variables $x_2(k)$ and $x_3(k)$ are related by a delay only. Once we have these then we can build the signal flow graph for state variable $x_3(k+1)$ as shown in Figure 10.1.

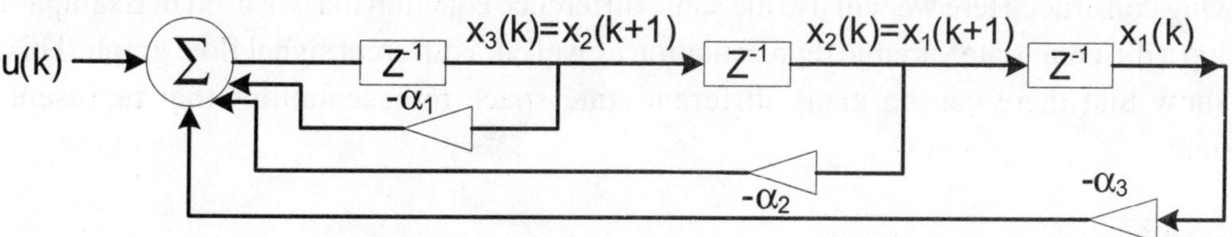

Figure 10.1: Signal flow graph to represent the state Equation for the system given in Example 10.1

Next to this plot we want to add the signal flow graph for the output equation. The signal flow graph for the output equation only is given in Figure 10.2. Since there is no feedback involved in the signal flow graph for the output equation the drawing is very straightforward. The signal flow graph for the output equation is shown in Figure 10.2.

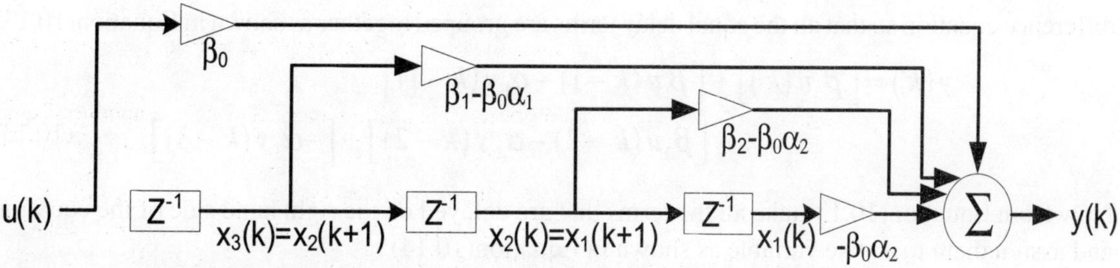

Figure 10.2: Signal flow graph to represent the output Equation for the system given in Example 10.1

Now examine both the individual signal flow graphs carefully. Both of them use the same state variables and there are three delay elements in both the graphs. So it is a simple matter to combine the two individual signal flow graphs into one to get the signal flow graph for the entire state space system. This is shown in Figure 10.3.

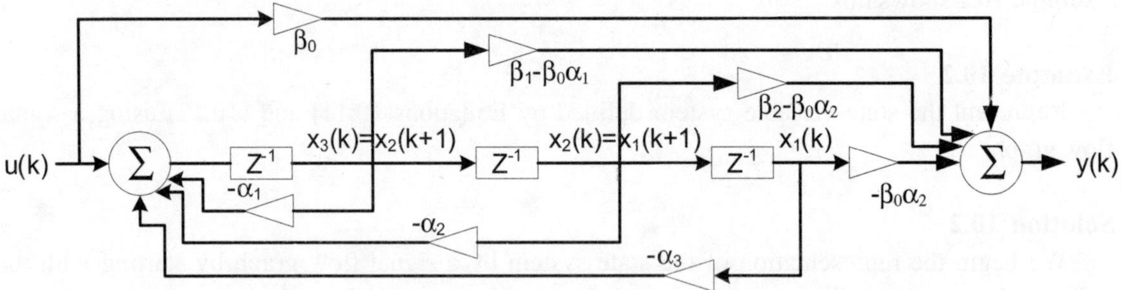

Figure 10.3: Signal flow graph to represent the State System discussed in Example 10.1

As an alternate way of converting a difference equation to a state space representation consider the following construct. Here we will use the same difference equation that we used in Example 10.1 and develop a different state variable representation as well as a different signal flow graph. This just goes to show that there can be many different state space representations that represent the same system.

Example 10.3

Convert the system represented by the following difference equation in a state variable format.

$$y(k)+\alpha_1 y(k-1)+\alpha_2 y(k-2)+\alpha_3 y(k-3)$$
$$=\beta_0 u(k)+\beta_1 u(k-1)+\beta_2 u(k-2)$$

Solution 10.3

To convert the difference equation to a State Variable representation we will begin by writing the difference equation so that all the equal delay terms are grouped together as shown in Equation(10.13)

$$y(k)=\left[\beta_0 u(k)\right]+\left[\beta_1 u(k-1)-\alpha_1 y(k-1)\right]$$
$$+\left[\beta_2 u(k-2)-\alpha_2 y(k-2)\right]+\left[-\alpha_3 y(k-3)\right] \tag{10.13}$$

Now from Equation(10.13) take all the terms that are delayed on the right hand side of the equation and assign them to a state variable as shown in Equation(10.14)

$$x_3(k)=\left[\beta_1 u(k-1)-\alpha_1 y(k-1)\right]$$
$$+\left[\beta_2 u(k-2)-\alpha_2 y(k-2)\right]+\left[-\alpha_3 y(k-3)\right] \tag{10.14}$$

With state variable $x_3(k)$ defined we can determine what the output y(k) will be in terms of this state variable. Substitute Equation(10.14) into Equation(10.13) and we get the required expression for the output as shown in Equation(10.15)

$$y(k)=\beta_0 u(k)+x_3(k) \tag{10.15}$$

Now that we have defined the state variable $x_3(k)$ we can determine what $x_3(k+1)$ will be. This is shown in Equation(10.16)

$$\begin{aligned} x_3(k+1)=&\left[\beta_1 u(k)-\alpha_1 y(k)\right] \\ &+\left[\beta_2 u(k-1)-\alpha_2 y(k-1)\right]+\left[-\alpha_3 y(k-2)\right] \end{aligned} \tag{10.16}$$

Now from Equation(10.16) take all the terms that are delayed on the right hand side of the equation and assign them to the next state variable as shown in Equation(10.17)

$$x_2(k)=\left[\beta_2 u(k-1)-\alpha_2 y(k-1)\right]+\left[-\alpha_3 y(k-2)\right] \tag{10.17}$$

Now that we have defined the state variable $x_2(k)$ we can determine what $x_2(k+1)$ will be. This is shown in Equation(10.18)

$$x_2(k+1)=\left[\beta_2 u(k)-\alpha_2 y(k)\right]+\left[-\alpha_3 y(k-1)\right] \tag{10.18}$$

We continue this process of defining a state variable and then obtaining its next sample till all the delayed terms in the equation are used up. For our example we need to do this only one more time. So from Equation(10.18) take all the terms that are delayed on the right hand side of the equation and assign them to the next state variable as shown in Equation(10.19)

$$x_1(k)=\left[-\alpha_3 y(k-1)\right] \tag{10.19}$$

Now that we have defined the state variable $x_1(k)$ we can determine what $x_1(k+1)$ will be. This is shown in Equation(10.20)

$$x_1(k+1)=\left[-\alpha_3 y(k)\right] \tag{10.20}$$

Now that we have the definitions of all the required state variables we need to put them in the proper format. The format that we need the state variables in is rather standard. Every expression has to be in terms of the other state variables. So we will go about converting the right hand side of Equations(10.16), (10.18) and (10.20) in terms of the other state variables. We begin with Equation(10.16). The last two terms in Equation(10.16) are exactly the same as the right hand side of Equation(10.17), we will also substitute from Equation(10.15) for y(k). So making the substitution we get Equation(10.21)

$$\begin{aligned} x_3(k+1)&=\beta_1 u(k)-\alpha_1 y(k)+x_2(k) \\ &=\beta_1 u(k)-\alpha_1\left[\beta_0 u(k)+x_3(k)\right]+x_2(k) \\ &=x_2(k)-\alpha_1 x_3(k)+(\beta_1-\alpha_1\beta_0)u(k) \end{aligned} \tag{10.21}$$

Similarly when we begin with Equation(10.18) and make the substitution of Equation(10.20) and (10.15) we get Equation(10.22)

$$\begin{aligned} x_2(k+1) &= \left[\beta_2 u(k) - \alpha_2 y(k)\right] + \left[x_1(k)\right] \\ &= \beta_2 u(k) - \alpha_2\left[\beta_0 u(k) + x_3(k)\right] + x_1 \\ &= x_1(k) - \alpha_2 x_3(k) + (\beta_2 - \alpha_2\beta_0)u(k) \end{aligned} \tag{10.22}$$

Finally when we begin with Equation(10.20) and make similar substitutions we get Equation (10.23)

$$\begin{aligned} x_1(k+1) &= -\alpha_3 y(k) \\ &= -\alpha_3\left[\beta_0 u(k) + x_3(k)\right] \\ &= -\alpha_3 x_3(k) - \alpha_3\beta_0 u(k) \end{aligned} \tag{10.23}$$

Equations(10.21), (10.22) and (10.23) form the three state equations for the difference equations which can be written in matrix notation as shown in Equation(10.24)

$$\begin{bmatrix} x_1(k+1) \\ x_2(k+1) \\ x_3(k+1) \end{bmatrix} = \begin{bmatrix} 0 & 0 & -\alpha_3 \\ 1 & 0 & -\alpha_2 \\ 0 & 1 & -\alpha_1 \end{bmatrix} \begin{bmatrix} x_1(k) \\ x_2(k) \\ x_3(k) \end{bmatrix} + \begin{bmatrix} (-\alpha_3\beta_0) \\ (\beta_2 - \alpha_2\beta_0) \\ (\beta_1 - \alpha_1\beta_0) \end{bmatrix} u(k) \tag{10.24}$$

And the output equation can also be written a matrix notation as shown in Equation(10.25)

$$\left[y(k)\right] = \begin{bmatrix} 0 & 0 & 1 \end{bmatrix} \begin{bmatrix} x_1(k) \\ x_2(k) \\ x_3(k) \end{bmatrix} + [\beta_0]u(k) \tag{10.25}$$

Equations(10.24) and (10.25) represent the difference equation in the state variable format.

Example 10.4

Represent the state variable system defined by Equations(10.24) and (10.25) using a signal flow graph.

Solution 10.4

We begin the representation of the state system by a signal flow graph by starting with three delay elements since we have three states in the system. The output sides of the delay elements represent the state variable and the input side represents the advanced state variable. Next we will individually build the advanced state variable individually from the three Equations(10.21), (10.22) and (10.23). This is shown in Figure 10.4.

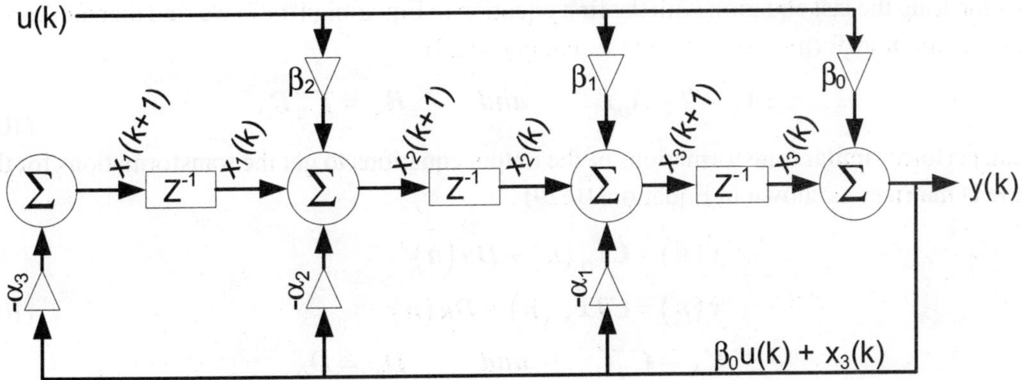

Figure 10.4: Signal flow graph to represent the State System discussed in Example 10.3

10.2 TRANSFORMING STATE REPRESENTATION

Now that we have seen that the same system can have several different state representations the obvious question that you would ask is as follows: Is it possible to transform one state representation to another? The answer to this question is obviously yes! Frequently it so happens that the state variables used in one representation are not as convenient as the state variable representation in another representation. We can always get the state variables in a different representation by reformulating the state equations, but it would be nice if we can take the state representation that we have and transform it to a different format. So to transform the state variable representation we have to determine the new set of matrices A_N; B_N; C_N; and D_N matrices from the set of old matrices A_O; B_O; C_O; and D_O. The transforming that we are proposing will transform the old state vector from x_O to the new state vector x_N. The transformation that we are proposing is a linear transform such as the one shown in Equation(10.26)

$$\boldsymbol{x_O} = \boldsymbol{T}\boldsymbol{x_N} \tag{10.26}$$

In Equation(10.26) x_N is the new state vector. The transformation matrix T is a non singular square matrix that has the same size as the number of state variables. In completing the transform we will assume that T is a constant matrix. (This assumption is not necessary but makes things a lot easier. If T is not a constant matrix then we will also have terms that are the first derivatives of T and they will have to be included.)

We begin with the original or the old state variable representation. In that equation we will replace the old state vector with a new state vector from Equation(10.26) as shown in Equation(10.27)

$$\begin{aligned}
\boldsymbol{x_O}(\boldsymbol{n}+1) &= \boldsymbol{A}\boldsymbol{x_O}(\boldsymbol{k}) + \boldsymbol{B}\boldsymbol{u}(\boldsymbol{k}) \\
\boldsymbol{T}\boldsymbol{x_N}(\boldsymbol{n}+1) &= \boldsymbol{A}\boldsymbol{T}\boldsymbol{x_N}(\boldsymbol{k}) + \boldsymbol{B}\boldsymbol{u}(\boldsymbol{k}) \\
\boldsymbol{x_N}(\boldsymbol{n}+1) &= \boldsymbol{T}^{-1}\boldsymbol{A}\boldsymbol{T}\boldsymbol{x_N}(\boldsymbol{k}) + \boldsymbol{T}^{-1}\boldsymbol{B}\boldsymbol{u}(\boldsymbol{k})
\end{aligned} \tag{10.27}$$

Comparing the last equation with the first equation in Equation(10.27) we find that the A and the B matrices are transformed as shown in Equation(10.28)

$$A_N = T^{-1}A_O T \qquad and \qquad B_N = T^{-1}B_O \tag{10.28}$$

We can perform similar transformations of the output equations to get the transformations for the C and the D matrices as shown in Equation(10.29)

$$\begin{aligned} y(n) &= Cx_O(n) + Du(n) \\ y(n) &= CTx_N(n) + Du(n) \\ C_N &= C_O T \qquad and \qquad D_N = D_O \end{aligned} \tag{10.29}$$

The transformed system or the new representations of the state variables are said to be similar to the original (old) representation of the state variables. Similar matrices have the same characteristic polynomials.

Example 10.5

Given the state representation of discrete system as

$$A = \begin{bmatrix} 8 & 6 \\ 2 & 4 \end{bmatrix} \; B = \begin{bmatrix} 0 \\ 1 \end{bmatrix} \; C = \begin{bmatrix} 1 & -1 \end{bmatrix} \; D = \begin{bmatrix} 1 \end{bmatrix}$$

Convert it to an alternate representation using the transformation matrix $T = \begin{bmatrix} -1 & -1 \\ -2 & 1 \end{bmatrix}$

Solution 10.5

To complete the conversion we need to first determine the inverse matrix for the T matrix given to us. Using SCILAB we get the inverse matrix as $T^{-1} = \frac{1}{3}\begin{bmatrix} -1 & -1 \\ -2 & 1 \end{bmatrix}$. With this inverse matrix we can determine the new set of matrices using Equation(10.28) and Equation(10.29)

$$A_N = T^{-1}A_O T = \frac{1}{3}\begin{bmatrix} -1 & -1 \\ -2 & 1 \end{bmatrix}\begin{bmatrix} 8 & 6 \\ 2 & 4 \end{bmatrix}\begin{bmatrix} -1 & -1 \\ -2 & 1 \end{bmatrix} = \begin{bmatrix} 10 & 0 \\ 10 & 2 \end{bmatrix}$$

$$B_N = T^{-1}B_O = \frac{1}{3}\begin{bmatrix} -1 & -1 \\ -2 & 1 \end{bmatrix}\begin{bmatrix} 0 \\ 1 \end{bmatrix} = \begin{bmatrix} -\frac{1}{3} \\ \frac{1}{3} \end{bmatrix}$$

$$C_N = C_O T = \begin{bmatrix} 1 & -1 \end{bmatrix}\begin{bmatrix} -1 & -1 \\ -2 & 1 \end{bmatrix} = \begin{bmatrix} 1 & -2 \end{bmatrix}$$

$$D_N = D_O$$

Thus the four new matrices will transform the system to a different representation of the same system.

Consider the following algebraic equation **Ax = λx**. In this equation **A** is an nxn matrix, **x** is an unknown column vector, λ is a scalar which is very often a complex variable such as s or z. We can rewrite the above equation as **(A - λI)x = 0**. This last equation has a non trivial solution if and only if $\mathbf{det}(A-\lambda I)=|A-\lambda I|=0$.

This equation is known as the characteristic equation of the matrix **A** and the roots of this equation is known as the **eigen** values of matrix **A**. Corresponding to each eigen value of matrix **A** there exists a non zero column vector **X** that satisfies the characteristic equation. The value of X that satisfies the characteristic equation, for any specific eigen value λ_i, is known as the eigen vector of the matrix **A**. The eigen vectors can be determined as shown in Example 10.6.

Example 10.6

Determine the eigen vectors of the square matrix $A=\begin{bmatrix}8 & 6\\ 2 & 4\end{bmatrix}$

Solution 10.6

First we determine the characteristic equation for the given **A** matrix. From the characteristic equation we will determine the eigen values of the matrix **A**. The characteristic equation and its roots are:

$$\mathbf{det}(A-\lambda I)=\lambda^2-12\lambda+20=0=(\lambda-2)(\lambda-10)$$

Now that we know the characteristic equation and the roots of characteristic equation which will be the eigen values of the matrix A. The eigen values of the characteristic equation are 10 and 2. For these two eigen values we can determine the eigen vectors as shown below in Equations(10.30) and (10.31)

$$(A-10I)x=0 \Rightarrow \begin{bmatrix}(8-10) & 6\\ 2 & (4-10)\end{bmatrix}\begin{bmatrix}x_{11}\\ x_{21}\end{bmatrix}=0 \qquad (10.30)$$

$$(A-2I)x=0 \Rightarrow \begin{bmatrix}(8-2) & 6\\ 2 & (4-2)\end{bmatrix}\begin{bmatrix}x_{12}\\ x_{22}\end{bmatrix}=0 \qquad (10.31)$$

The solution to Equation(10.30) is $x_{11}=3x_{12}$ and the solution to Equation(10.31) is $x_{21}=-x_{22}$. We can arbitrarily choose x_{11} = 1 and x_{21} = 1 then we get the two eigen vectors. When we put the two vectors together as a matrix then we get a new matrix $\begin{bmatrix}3 & 1\\ 1 & -1\end{bmatrix}$. This matrix that is formed using the eigen vectors is a very special matrix. To see what is so special about the matrix let us call this matrix as a **T** matrix and determine its inverse first and then determine **T⁻¹AT**.

$$T^{-1} = \frac{1}{4}\begin{bmatrix} 3 & -1 \\ 1 & 1 \end{bmatrix}$$

$$T^{-1}AT = \frac{1}{4}\begin{bmatrix} 1 & 1 \\ 1 & -3 \end{bmatrix}\begin{bmatrix} 8 & 6 \\ 2 & 4 \end{bmatrix}\begin{bmatrix} 3 & 1 \\ 1 & -1 \end{bmatrix} = \begin{bmatrix} 10 & 0 \\ 0 & 2 \end{bmatrix}$$

Look carefully at the result of the matrix multiplication $T^{-1}AT$. The result is a diagonal matrix which has the eigen values of the matrix A along the main diagonal. If we take the eigen vector matrix and its inverse as the state equation transformation matrices in Equation(10.28) and in Equation(10.29) then we will get the state representation of the system that represents the A matrix in its diagonal form. This form of the A matrix allows us to view what is happening to each state variable individually.

Example 10.7

Given the state representation of discrete system as

$$A = \begin{bmatrix} 5 & 4 & 3 \\ 2 & 1 & 0 \\ 1 & 2 & 4 \end{bmatrix} \quad B = \begin{bmatrix} 1 \\ 2 \\ -1 \end{bmatrix} \quad C = \begin{bmatrix} 0.5 & 2 & -1 \end{bmatrix} \quad D = \begin{bmatrix} 1 \end{bmatrix}$$

Convert it to an alternate representation that is a diagonal representation using the eigen vector matrix for matrix A

Solution 10.7

First we determine the characteristic equation for the given **A** matrix. From the characteristic equation we will determine the eigen values of the matrix A. The characteristic equation and its roots are:

$$\det(A - \lambda I) = \lambda^3 + 10\lambda^2 - 18\lambda - 3 = 0 = (\lambda + 0.15_{33941})(\lambda - 2.58_{36302})(\lambda - 7.56_{97639})$$

The eigen values of the characteristic equation are 3, 4 and 5. For these three eigen values we can determine the eigen vectors as shown below in Equations(10.32), Equation(10.33) and Equation(10.34)

$$(A + 0.15_{33941} I)x = 0 \Rightarrow \begin{bmatrix} (5 + 0.15_{33941}) & 4 & 3 \\ 2 & (1 + 0.15_{33941}) & 0 \\ 1 & 2 & (4 + 0.15_{33941}) \end{bmatrix}\begin{bmatrix} x_{11} \\ x_{12} \\ x_{13} \end{bmatrix} = 0 \quad (10.32)$$

$$\left(A-2.58_{36302}I\right)x=0\Rightarrow\begin{bmatrix}(5-2.58_{36302}) & 4 & 3\\ 2 & (1-2.58_{36302}) & 0\\ 1 & 2 & (4-2.58_{36302})\end{bmatrix}\begin{bmatrix}x_{21}\\ x_{22}\\ x_{23}\end{bmatrix}=0 \quad (10.33)$$

$$\left(A-7.56_{97639}I\right)x=0\Rightarrow\begin{bmatrix}(5-7.56_{97639}) & 4 & 3\\ 2 & (1-7.56_{97639}) & 0\\ 1 & 2 & (4-7.56_{97639})\end{bmatrix}\begin{bmatrix}x_{31}\\ x_{32}\\ x_{33}\end{bmatrix}=0 \quad (10.34)$$

The solution to Equation(10.32) is

$$-0.57_{6695}x_{11}=x_{12}=-0.34_{269}x_{13},$$

the solution to Equation(10.33) is

$$0.79_{1815}x_{21}=x_{22}=-1.97_{1106}x_{23}$$

and the solution to Equation(10.34) is

$$3.28_{4882}x_{31}=x_{32}=1.48_{0457}x_{33}.$$

To get to the solutions listed we have arbitrarily chosen $x_{12} = x_{22} = x_{32} = 1$ and then solved for the other variables. This gives us an eigen vector matrix and its inverse that are

$$T=\begin{bmatrix}-0.57_{6695} & 0.79_{1815} & 3.28_{4882}\\ 1 & 1 & 1\\ -0.34_{269} & -1.97_{1106} & 1.48_{0457}\end{bmatrix} \quad T^{-1}=\begin{bmatrix}0.39_{29711} & 0.87_{06458} & 0.28_{38434}\\ 0.20_{75709} & -0.03_{09594} & -0.43_{96525}\\ 0.18_{54002} & 0.16_{03136} & 0.15_{58091}\end{bmatrix}$$

Using these vectors the new system that we get is as follows

$$A_N=T^{-1}A_OT=\begin{bmatrix}-0.15_{33941} & 0 & 0\\ 0 & 2.58_{36302} & 0\\ 0 & 0 & 7.56_{97639}\end{bmatrix}$$

$$B_N=T^{-1}B_O=\begin{bmatrix}0.39_{29711} & 0.87_{06458} & 0.28_{38434}\\ 0.20_{75709} & -0.03_{09594} & -0.43_{96525}\\ 0.18_{54002} & 0.16_{03136} & 0.15_{58091}\end{bmatrix}\begin{bmatrix}1\\ 2\\ -1\end{bmatrix}=\begin{bmatrix}1.06_{44771}\\ 0.58_{53042}\\ 0.35_{02183}\end{bmatrix}$$

$$C_N=C_OT=\begin{bmatrix}0.5 & 2 & 1\end{bmatrix}\begin{bmatrix}-0.57_{6695} & 0.79_{1815} & 3.28_{4882}\\ 1 & 1 & 1\\ -0.34_{269} & -1.97_{1106} & 1.48_{0457}\end{bmatrix}=\begin{bmatrix}2.05_{43425} & 4.36_{70135} & 2.16_{1984}\end{bmatrix}$$

And since $D_N = D_O$ the D matrix is the same and does not change. Examine the A matrix, it is a diagonal matrix and along the main diagonal we see the eigen values of the A matrix. The four matrices together give us an alternate representation of the original system. Remember we have not changed the system. The system is the same, we have only changed the representation that we are going to use for the system.

10.3 SOLUTIONS TO DISCRETE TIME STATE EQUATIONS

The solution to the discrete state equation is obtained in a manner that is very similar to the continuous time state equation solution. We begin, as we did for the continuous time systems, with the homogeneous state equation as shown in Equation(10.35)

$$x(n+1) = Ax(n) \tag{10.35}$$

To solve this homogeneous discrete state equation we will begin with an initial state vector $x(n_o)$ at time n_o. Starting with this known state vector we determine what the state vector will be at each successive sample times. This calculation is shown in Equation(10.36)

$$\begin{aligned} x(n_o+1) &= Ax(n_o) \\ x(n_o+2) &= Ax(n_o+1) = A^2x(n_o) \\ \vdots \quad & \quad \vdots \quad\quad\quad \vdots \\ x(n_o+k) &= Ax(n_o+k-1) = A^k x(n_o) \end{aligned} \tag{10.36}$$

To get a general solution for the homogeneous equation we will substitute $n=n_o+k$ in Equation(10.36) to get Equation(10.37)

$$x(n) = A^{n-n_o} x(n_o) \tag{10.37}$$

When $n_o=0$ we get Equation(10.38)

$$x(n) = A^n x(0) \tag{10.38}$$

Often we replace $\Phi(n,n_o) = A^{n-n_o}$ or $\Phi(n) = A^n$. Here the matrix Φ (n) is known as the state transition matrix and it is a square matrix with the same size as the matrix A. The solution of the general state equation will also proceed in the same manner. We will begin with an initial vector as shown in Equation(10.39)

$$x(n_o+1) = Ax(n_o) + Bu(n_o) \tag{10.39}$$

Starting with this we compute the state vector at the next sampling instant as shown in Equation(10.40)

$$\begin{aligned} x(n_o+2) &= Ax(n_o+1)+Bu(n_o+1) \\ &= A\{Ax(n_o)+Bu(n_o)\}+Bu(n_o+1) \\ &= A^2x(n_o)+ABu(n_o)+Bu(n_o+1) \end{aligned} \tag{10.40}$$

If we continue this process for k sampling instants we get Equation(10.41)

$$\begin{aligned} x(n_o+k) &= Ax(n_o+k-1)+Bu(n_o+k-1) \\ &= A^k x(n_o)+\sum_{m=n_o}^{n_o+k-1} A^{n_o+k-m-1}Bu(m) \end{aligned} \tag{10.41}$$

To get a general solution for the general equation we will substitute $n=n_o+k$ in Equation(10.41) to get Equation(10.42)

$$x(n)=A^{n-n_o}x(n_0)+\sum_{m=n_o}^{n-1} A^{n-m-1}Bu(m)$$

$$x(n)=\Phi(n-n_o)x(n_o)+\sum_{m=n_o}^{n-1}\Phi(n-m-1)Bu(m) \tag{10.42}$$

This last equation gives us a state vector at any time after the initial time. It shows that the state vector is a sum of two terms. The first term corresponds to the contribution due to the initial state vector and the second term represents the contribution by the input. This gives us the trajectory that the state vector takes. Now that we know the state vector at any time we can determine the complete response from the system when we substitute the state vector in the output equation. This is shown in Equation(10.43)

$$y(n)=Cx(n)+Du(n) \tag{10.43}$$

$$y(n)=C\Phi(n-n_o)x(n_o)+\sum_{m=n_o}^{n-1}C\Phi(n-m-1)Bu(n)+Du(n)$$

Since in linear systems we are often interested in the impulse response of the system we can replace the driving function u(n) by an impulse δ(n) then the response due to the impulse will be found when the initial state vector is set to zero. Then in Equation(10.43) when we do this we get the second and the third terms and replace them by the impulse response of the system h(n) as shown in Equation(10.44)

$$h(n)=\sum_{m=n_o}^{n-1}C\Phi(n-m-1)B\delta(n)+D\delta(n) \tag{10.44}$$

Example 10.8

Determine the solution to the system shown in Figure 10.5 for the sampling instants n = 0, 1, 2 and 3 assuming that the system shown is at rest at n = 0 and u(n) = unit step input at n = 0.

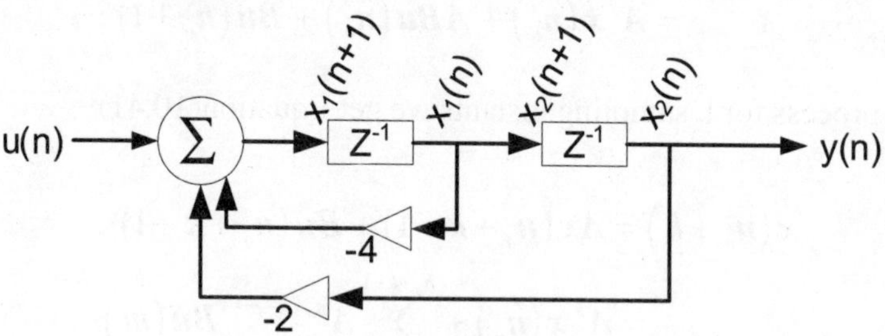

Figure 10.5

Solution 10.8

First we determine the state equations for the system from the given figure. The state equations can be written as shown in Equation(10.45)

$$\begin{bmatrix} x_1(n+1) \\ x_2(n+1) \end{bmatrix} = \begin{bmatrix} -4 & -2 \\ 1 & 0 \end{bmatrix} \begin{bmatrix} x_1(n) \\ x_2(n) \end{bmatrix} + \begin{bmatrix} 1 \\ 0 \end{bmatrix} u(n) \tag{10.45}$$

$$y(n) = \begin{bmatrix} 0 & 1 \end{bmatrix} \begin{bmatrix} x_1(n) \\ x_2(n) \end{bmatrix}$$

The state vector for n=1 and the solution for n=0 will be

$$\begin{bmatrix} x_1(0+1) \\ x_2(0+1) \end{bmatrix} = \begin{bmatrix} -4 & -2 \\ 1 & 0 \end{bmatrix} \begin{bmatrix} 0 \\ 0 \end{bmatrix} + \begin{bmatrix} 1 \\ 0 \end{bmatrix} 1 = \begin{bmatrix} 1 \\ 0 \end{bmatrix}$$

$$y(0) = \begin{bmatrix} 0 & 1 \end{bmatrix} \begin{bmatrix} 0 \\ 0 \end{bmatrix} = 0$$

Next using the known state vector at n=1 we get the state vector at n=2 and the solution for n=1 as

$$\begin{bmatrix} x_1(1+1) \\ x_2(1+1) \end{bmatrix} = \begin{bmatrix} -4 & -2 \\ 1 & 0 \end{bmatrix} \begin{bmatrix} 1 \\ 0 \end{bmatrix} + \begin{bmatrix} 1 \\ 0 \end{bmatrix} 1 = \begin{bmatrix} -3 \\ 1 \end{bmatrix}$$

$$y(1) = \begin{bmatrix} 0 & 1 \end{bmatrix} \begin{bmatrix} 1 \\ 0 \end{bmatrix} = 0$$

Next using the known state vector at n=2 we get the state vector at n=3 and the solution for n=2 as

$$\begin{bmatrix} x_1(2+1) \\ x_2(2+1) \end{bmatrix} = \begin{bmatrix} -4 & -2 \\ 1 & 0 \end{bmatrix}\begin{bmatrix} -3 \\ 1 \end{bmatrix} + \begin{bmatrix} 1 \\ 0 \end{bmatrix}1 = \begin{bmatrix} 11 \\ -3 \end{bmatrix}$$

$$y(2) = \begin{bmatrix} 0 & 1 \end{bmatrix}\begin{bmatrix} -3 \\ 1 \end{bmatrix} = 1$$

Next using the known state vector at n=3 we get the state vector at n=4 and the solution for n=3 as

$$\begin{bmatrix} x_1(3+1) \\ x_2(3+1) \end{bmatrix} = \begin{bmatrix} -4 & -2 \\ 1 & 0 \end{bmatrix}\begin{bmatrix} 11 \\ -3 \end{bmatrix} + \begin{bmatrix} 1 \\ 0 \end{bmatrix}1 = \begin{bmatrix} -37 \\ 11 \end{bmatrix}$$

$$y(3) = \begin{bmatrix} 0 & 1 \end{bmatrix}\begin{bmatrix} 11 \\ -1 \end{bmatrix} = -3$$

This example clearly shows how the solution will proceed.

10.4 Z-TRANSFORM SOLUTION TO THE STATE EQUATIONS

A student might often wonder; is it possible to get a closed form solution for the state equation or do we have to rely on the step by step solution as depicted in Example 10.8? The answer to this is obvious; a closed form solution is definitely available. If you think back with the continuous time systems we used the Laplace transform to obtain the closed form solution for the continuous time state variable system. For the discrete system we will use the Z-transform to determine the solution in the closed form system. The Z domain solution proceeds as follows, we begin with the state equation as shown in Equation(10.46)

$$\boldsymbol{x}(\boldsymbol{n}+1) = \boldsymbol{A}\boldsymbol{x}(\boldsymbol{n}) + \boldsymbol{B}\boldsymbol{u}(\boldsymbol{n})$$

$$\boldsymbol{y}(\boldsymbol{n}) = \boldsymbol{C}\boldsymbol{x}(\boldsymbol{n}) + \boldsymbol{D}\boldsymbol{u}(\boldsymbol{n}) \tag{10.46}$$

If we determine the Z-transform of Equation(10.46) then we get Equation(10.47)

$$z\boldsymbol{X}(z) = \boldsymbol{A}\boldsymbol{X}(z) + \boldsymbol{B}\boldsymbol{U}(z) + z\boldsymbol{x}(0)$$

$$\boldsymbol{Y}(z) = \boldsymbol{C}\boldsymbol{X}(z) + \boldsymbol{D}\boldsymbol{U}(z) \tag{10.47}$$

The relations shown in Equation(10.47) are valid because the transform of a vector or a matrix is the transform of each entry of the vector or the matrix. Since in our example we are dealing with the Z-transform the Z-transform of the A matrix will be the Z-transform of each individual element of the A matrix. So the Z-Transform of the x(n+1) can be written as shown in Equation(10.48)

$$Z\begin{bmatrix} x_1(n+1) \\ x_2(n+1) \end{bmatrix} = \begin{bmatrix} zX_1(z) - zx_1(0) \\ zX_2(z) - zx_2(0) \end{bmatrix} = \begin{bmatrix} zX_1(z) \\ zX_2(z) \end{bmatrix} - \begin{bmatrix} zx_1(0) \\ zx_2(0) \end{bmatrix} \tag{10.48}$$
$$= zX(z) - zx(0)$$

After we do the required algebra we can write the two equations in Equation(10.47) as shown in Equation(10.49)

$$\begin{aligned} X(z) &= [zI - A]^{-1} BU(z) + [zI - A]^{-1} zx(0) \\ Y(z) &= \left(C[zI - A]^{-1} B + D\right)U(z) + C[zI - A]^{-1} zx(0) \end{aligned} \tag{10.49}$$

In Equation(10.49) the output equation gives us information about the impulse response or the transfer function. We get this information when we set the input to a unit impulse and set the initial conditions to zero. When we do this we get the impulse response as shown in Equation(10.50)

$$H(z) = \left(Cz^{-1}\Phi(z)B + D\right)\; H(z) = \left(C[zI - A]^{-1} B + D\right) \tag{10.50}$$

As we have seen earlier the state space representation is generally written with the resolvent matrix. The resolvent matrix $\Phi(n) = A^n$ the transform of this matrix is therefore given in Equation(10.51)

$$\Phi(z) = Z\{\Phi(n)\} = Z\{A^n\} = z[zI - A]^{-1} = \left[I - z^{-1}A\right]^{-1} \tag{10.51}$$

With the definition in Equation(10.51) we get the transfer function or the impulse response as $H(z) = \left(Cz^{-1}\Phi(z)B + D\right)$.

With these definitions we can determine the time sequence vector y(n) corresponding to the Z domain solution Y(z). To get this solution we need to determine the inverse transform of the solution Y(z). The inverse transform of Y(z) is obtained just as we obtained the inverse transform of any Z-domain function. The following example will make this method clear.

Example 10.9

Determine the solution to the system shown in Figure 10.6 using the z-domain method and assuming that the system shown is at rest at n=0 and u(n) = unit step input at n=0.

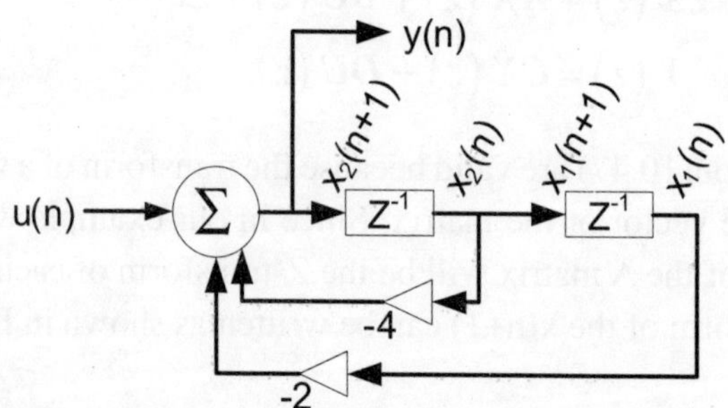

Figure 10.6

Solution 10.9

First we determine the state equations for the system from the given figure. The state Equations can be written as

$$\begin{bmatrix} x_1(n+1) \\ x_2(n+1) \end{bmatrix} = \begin{bmatrix} 0 & 1 \\ -2 & -4 \end{bmatrix} \begin{bmatrix} x_1(n) \\ x_2(n) \end{bmatrix} + \begin{bmatrix} 0 \\ 1 \end{bmatrix} u(n)$$

$$y(n) = \begin{bmatrix} -2 & -4 \end{bmatrix} \begin{bmatrix} x_1(n) \\ x_2(n) \end{bmatrix} + [1] u(n)$$

Next we need to determine the resolvent matrix. So we will next determine the matrix $[zI-A]^{-1}$

$$[zI - A]^{-1} = \begin{bmatrix} z & -1 \\ 2 & z+4 \end{bmatrix}^{-1} = \frac{1}{z^2+4z+2} \begin{bmatrix} z+4 & 1 \\ -2 & z \end{bmatrix}$$

We also need the Z transform of the input function. Since this time the input function is a unit step function its Z transform is $U(z) = \dfrac{z}{z-1}$. Since the initial conditions are given as zero we can write the Z domain solution for the system as shown in Equation(10.52)

$$\begin{aligned} Y(z) &= \left(C\Phi(z)z^{-1}B + D\right)U(z) \\ &= \left(\begin{bmatrix} -2 & -4 \end{bmatrix} \frac{\begin{bmatrix} z+4 & 1 \\ -2 & z \end{bmatrix}}{z^2+4z+2} \begin{bmatrix} 0 \\ 1 \end{bmatrix} + 1 \right) \frac{z}{z-1} \\ &= \frac{z^3}{(z-1)(z^2+4z+2)} \end{aligned} \tag{10.52}$$

Now if we determine the inverse Z transform of the last equation in Equation(10.52) we will get the response y(n) as time goes by.

10.5 OBSERVING THE STATE OF THE SYSTEM

Observability is a property that describes the structural features of a dynamic system. Here we discuss and present some of the known results for linear time invariant systems. A system is said to be observable if for any state vector x(0) there is a finite value of N such that the state vector x(0) can be computed from the observation of the n-1 previous outputs. This would be possible only if every state variable of the system has a direct influence on the output of the system.

Consider a system described by Equation(10.53)

$$\begin{aligned} x(n+1) &= Ax(n) \\ y(n) &= Cx(n) \end{aligned} \tag{10.53}$$

In Equation(10.53) we have not included the driving function or the input since the input is known for all time. So it can be accounted for as shown in the next section. If the input is not known (such as a disturbance, and we are not dealing with that in this book) then we have an entirely different problem. Let us determine the successive outputs from the system defined in Equation(10.53).

$$\begin{aligned} y(0) &= Cx(0) \\ y(1) &= Cx(1) = CAx(0) \\ y(2) &= Cx(2) = CA^2x(0) \\ &\vdots \qquad \vdots \\ y(n-1) &= Cx(n-1) = CA^{n-1}x(0) \end{aligned}$$

Writing this equation in matrix form we get the result that we want as shown in Equation(10.54). The system will be observable if the matrix on the right hand side is a non-singular matrix. Since this matrix is a non singular matrix it can be inverted.

$$\begin{bmatrix} y(0) \\ y(1) \\ \vdots \\ y(n-1) \end{bmatrix} = \begin{bmatrix} C \\ CA \\ \vdots \\ CA^{n-1} \end{bmatrix} x(0) \tag{10.54}$$

The matrix transpose of the matrix on the right hand side is known as the observability matrix which is shown in Equation(10.55)

$$O = \left[C^T \vdots \;\; A^T C^T \vdots \;\; \cdots \;\; \left(A^T\right)^{n-1} C^T \vdots \right] \tag{10.55}$$

When the system is observable then the matrix O is a matrix that has an inverse. When we determine the inverse of the observability matrix we will be able to determine the initial state vector as shown in Equation(10.56)

$$x(0) = O^{-1} \begin{bmatrix} y(0) \\ y(1) \\ \vdots \\ y(n-1) \end{bmatrix} \tag{10.56}$$

Example 10.10

Determine if the system shown in Figure 10.6 is an observable system. If it is observable then determine the observability matrix.

Solution 10.10

The system described in Figure 10.6 has the following matrices

$$C=\begin{bmatrix}-2 & -4\end{bmatrix} \quad A=\begin{bmatrix}0 & 1\\ -2 & -4\end{bmatrix}$$

With these matrices we can determine the Observability matrix as $O=\begin{bmatrix}-2 & -4\\ -4 & 16\end{bmatrix}$. Since this matrix is not a singular matrix and it has full rank which is a rank of 2 the system described in Figure 10.6 is an observable system.

Example 10.11

Now that we know that the system in Figure 10.6 is observable what should the initial state vector be when the previous two outputs have been observed?

Solution 10.11

Since we know the previous two outputs we will use Equation 10.56 to determine the state vector that was present at the time when we started to record the outputs. The state vector will be determined as follows

$$\begin{bmatrix}y(0)\\ y(1)\end{bmatrix}=\begin{bmatrix}C\\ CA\end{bmatrix}x(0)$$

$$x(0)=\begin{bmatrix}C\\ CA\end{bmatrix}^{-1}\begin{bmatrix}y(0)\\ y(1)\end{bmatrix}$$

Where and how do we use the observers? Students often ask what is the use of observers? The main reason for observers occurs in feedback control systems. In the state variable representation of feedback control system we need to have access to the state variables so that we may use them for

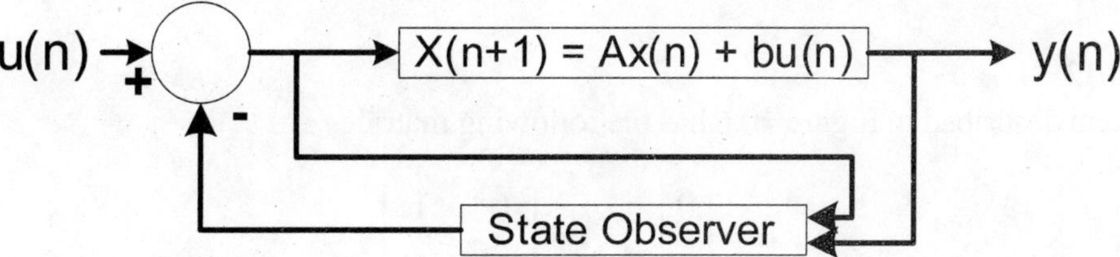

Figure 10.7: How the Observer is used in the system

the required feedback. Examine Figures 10.5, 10.6 or any of the other figures, you see that the state variables need to be made available for feedback. Often in many systems you either do not have access available to the individual state variables or there is no one point in the system that can be identified as a point where the state variable can be measured. If the state variable is not available then how can we cause it to be fed back to complete the system? The answer is the State Observer. It is the state observer that we have built in the above section. A typical system that uses an observer will look like the system shown in Figure 10.7.

10.6 CONTROLLING THE STATE OF THE SYSTEM

The easiest way to understand controllability of a system is to consider a time-invariant discrete system. For this consider the system $\boldsymbol{x}(\boldsymbol{n}+1)=\boldsymbol{Ax}(\boldsymbol{n})+\boldsymbol{Bu}(\boldsymbol{n})$ with zero initial condition. The solution to this system was determined in Equation(10.42) and is given here also in Equation(10.57)

$$\boldsymbol{x}(\boldsymbol{n})=\sum_{m=0}^{n-1}\boldsymbol{A}^{n-m-1}\boldsymbol{Bu}(\boldsymbol{m})$$

$$\boldsymbol{x}(\boldsymbol{n})=\boldsymbol{Bu}(\boldsymbol{n}-1)+\boldsymbol{ABu}(\boldsymbol{n}-2)+\cdots+\boldsymbol{A}^{n-1}\boldsymbol{Bu}(0) \tag{10.57}$$

The controllability problem then is to make the vector x(n) equal to any pre-assigned vector by choosing appropriate control inputs u(0), u(1), …, u(n-1). When the control is scalar then x(n) is simply a linear combination of vectors $\{\boldsymbol{B},\boldsymbol{AB},\cdots,\boldsymbol{A}^{n-1}\boldsymbol{B}\}$. In order for x(n) to equal any vector that we want it to be (that is control it in such a way that it reaches the state that we want it to be) the vectors above must span the entire space and hence must satisfy the condition $\boldsymbol{rank}\{\boldsymbol{B},\boldsymbol{AB},\cdots,\boldsymbol{A}^{n-1}\boldsymbol{B}\}=\boldsymbol{n}$. If this condition is met then the system will be controllable and it will be possible to move the system to any state vector that you want only by controlling what input you provide to the system.

Example 10.12

Determine if the system shown in Figure 10.6 is a controllable system. If it is controllable then determine the controllability matrix.

Solution 10.12

The system described in Figure 10.6 has the following matrices

$$\boldsymbol{B}=\begin{bmatrix}0\\1\end{bmatrix}\quad \boldsymbol{A}=\begin{bmatrix}0 & 1\\-2 & -4\end{bmatrix}$$

With these matrices we can determine the Controllability matrix as $C = \begin{bmatrix} 0 & 1 \\ 1 & -4 \end{bmatrix}$. Since this matrix is not a singular matrix and it has full rank which is a rank of 2 the system described in Figure 10.6 is a controllable system.

Example 10.13

Now that we know that the system in Figure 10.6 is controllable what should the input sequence be so that the system reaches a known state vector?

Solution 10.13

From Equation(10.57) we can determine the required state vector as shown in Equation(10.58)

$$\begin{aligned} \boldsymbol{x}(2) &= \boldsymbol{Bu}(1) + \boldsymbol{ABu}(0) \\ \boldsymbol{x}(2) &= \begin{bmatrix} 0 \\ 1 \end{bmatrix} \boldsymbol{u}(1) + \begin{bmatrix} 0 & 1 \\ -2 & -4 \end{bmatrix} \begin{bmatrix} 0 \\ 1 \end{bmatrix} \boldsymbol{u}(0) \\ \boldsymbol{x}(2) &= \begin{bmatrix} 0 \\ \boldsymbol{u}(1) \end{bmatrix} + \begin{bmatrix} \boldsymbol{u}(0) \\ -4\boldsymbol{u}(0) \end{bmatrix} = \begin{bmatrix} \boldsymbol{u}(0) \\ \boldsymbol{u}(1) - 4\boldsymbol{u}(0) \end{bmatrix} \end{aligned} \tag{10.58}$$

It is now a simple matter to choose u(0) and u(1) so that the state vector reaches the condition required within two sample time instants.

10.7 CHAPTER SUMMARY

Just as we were able to convert the differential equation to a state variable format for a continuous time system we can convert a difference equation to a state variable format for a discrete time system. The conversion methods for both the continuous time and the discrete time systems are very similar to each other. In this chapter we discussed two different methods to convert the difference equation to the state variable format. Both the methods give us a representation that is known as the phase variable representation. In one representation the input is shown directly connected to only one state variable while the output is a sum of all the state variables while in the other representation the input is directly connected to all the state variables but the output is taken only from one state variable. This just shows that the state variable representation is not unique and several different representations are possible for the same system.

Representing the state variable system in several different formats was emphasized in the next section where we saw how we can transform a state variable representation to a different state variable representation by a simple similarity transform. The similarity transformation is accomplished by using a non singular n-by-n matrix to complete the transform. One particular similarity transform that is often done is the similarity transform that converts any state variable representation to a diagonal representation. In the diagonal representation all the state variables are de-coupled and can be examined individually. To transform the state variable representation to the diagonal format we use the Eigen Vector matrix to perform the transformation.

The solution of the discrete time state equation can be accomplished step by step by using the obtained state vector in the output equation and then computing the next state vector by using the present state vector in the system equation. The discrete time solution is ideally suited for the software program that we have been using. The solution of the discrete state representation is also possible with the Z-transform. The Z-transform solution is very similar to the Laplace transform solution and it is obtained in the same manner.

Observing the state of the system and designing observers are very important with the state variable representation since with all state variable representations it is necessary to feedback the state of the system. To feedback the state of the system it is necessary to have access to the state variables. In many systems the state variables are either not accessible or are not physical quantities that can be monitored. In cases like these it becomes difficult or impossible to monitor the state of the system. It is in these cases that a state observer is used.

Controlling the state of the system and designing the controllers are very important with the state variable system also since this permits us to determine the input required to get the state of the system to the desired end point as it follows the prescribed trajectory. The trajectory of the system is the various states of the system as it moves from one state to another state.

10.8 HOMEWORK PROBLEMS

State Variable Representation

Problem 10.8.1

Determine the state variable representation for the following difference equations so that the input is connected to only one state variable. This is similar to the representation that we developed for Figure 10.3:

a. $y(n-3) + 2y(n-2) + 4y(n-1) - 6y(n) = 4u(n)$
b. $y(n-3) + 4y(n-1) - 6y(n) = 4u(n-2) + 2u(n-1) + u(n)$
c. $y(n-5) + 2y(n-3) + 4y(n-1) = 4u(n-2) + 2u(n-1)$
d. $y(n-3) - 8y(n-2) + 4y(n-1) - 6y(n) = 4u(n-3) + u(n)$
e. $y(n-3) + 2y(n-2) + 4y(n-1) - 6y(n) = 4u(n-2)$

Problem 10.8.2

Represent the difference equations given in Problem 10.8.1 using the phase variable state variable representation so that the output is connected to only one state variable. This is similar to the representation that we developed for Figure 10.4.

Transforming the State of the System

Problem 10.8.3

For all the state variable representations that are third order in Problem 10.8.1 and Problem 10.8.2 use the similarity transform matrix $T = \begin{bmatrix} 0 & 1 & 0 \\ 0 & 0 & 1 \\ 1 & 2 & 3 \end{bmatrix}$ to transform the system to an alternate state variable representation. Remember to transform the output equation also.

Problem 10.8.4

Convert system 'a' from Problem 10.8.1 to a diagonal representation using the eigen vector matrix. Since system 'a' from Problem 10.8.1 also has two other similar representations in Problem 10.8.2 and in Problem 10.8.3 convert these representations of system 'a' to a diagonal representation using their own eigen vector matrices. Do you get the same (or similar) systems in all the three cases? This is an informal way of showing that the state variable representation is not unique.

Signal Flow Graphs

Problem 10.8.5

Draw the signal flow graph for all the systems represented in Problem 10.8.1, and in Problem 10.8.2.

Solutions of the System

Problem 10.8.6

In Problem 10.8.1 through Problem 10.8.4 we obtained four different representations for system a. For each of the representations determine the first 10 output values. This way you are able to verify that all the four representations of the system a are indeed identical.

Problem 10.8.7

In Problem 10.8.1 through Problem 10.8.4 we obtained four different representations for system a. For each of the representations determine the Z transform solution. This way you are able to verify that all the four representations of the system a are indeed identical.

Observers and Controllers

Problem 10.8.8

Which of the systems described in Problem 10.8.1 are observable? For all the observable systems determine the observer that will allow you to observe the state of the system.

Problem 10.8.9

Which of the systems in Problem 10.8.1 are controllable. For the controllable systems determine the required input sequence so that the state of the system moves to a location where each of the state variable is unity.

APPENDIX I

SCILAB

APPENDIX 1.1 – Introduction

SCILAB is a powerful computing environment provided as software that can be easily downloaded freely via the internet. SCILAB is currently widely used in education and as well as industry throughout the world. In this chapter we attempt to give you as much information as required for you to get started to write your own SCILAB script. When you download the SCILAB program you will also get a help file with the program. The help file gives you help about all the commands along with the meanings, the use and some examples of the command.

The objective of this chapter is to get you started so that you can follow all the developments that we have completed for you in the text and also for you to try things that have been left for you to try on your own. The best way to learn this subject is to try things out. So when you see an equation or a formula program it in SCILAB, draw a graph representing the variation of one parameter to learn the effect of that parameter on the formula. The numerous practical examples given in the book and those suggested in the exercise sets will get you started and serve as a basis for developing other applications on your own.

The way we have used the software in the book is to go beyond a simple software package. We have tried to incorporate the software package as a tool to be used to understand and to further the explanation given in the text. As they say a picture is worth a thousand words, so it is with graphs. One graph is worth a lot of written text or explanation.

Appendix 1.a Organization of this Chapter:

The first objective of this chapter is to give the student and the professional a description of most of the commands in SCILAB. This small chapter cannot do justice to all the commands neither it can list all the commands. So this chapter will serve as an introduction to the various commands that can be used in SCILAB. As the commands are introduced we will try to demonstrate the use of the particular commands by explanation and example.

However learning to use this software package is like learning to play the game of Bridge. Bridge is a card game that most students learn the rules of in the dormitory while going to college. But they learn to really play good bridge only after they have played the game for many years after learning the rules, so also with this software package. I learnt the rules of this package many years ago but I am still learning the various different nuances that are present in the package only now.

Appendix 1.b What is SCILAB?

SCILAB is a powerful interactive programming environment that makes the task of numerical computing and data manipulation easy to accomplish. SCILAB does this by being an interpreted high level language that has a very large collection of built in functions, integrated graphics, data manipulation capability and an ability to incorporate programming languages such as FORTRAN or C.

SCILAB is a powerful programming language with syntax that is easy to use and understand. The programming language has all the elements of a modern high level language. The elements of this programming language include assignment operations, loop control, conditional execution as well as functions. Further since the basic element in SCILAB is an array instead of a single variable (although single variables are also present and possible) each command works on an array. As a result you need far fewer commands than you would need in either C or in FORTRAN. Since the arrays are all represented as matrices it is now easier to perform matrix operations with single commands.

SCILAB is an interpreted command language so when SCILAB is presented with a command it is executed. The user can see the result of the command immediately and if an error is made the command can be modified right then and there. The modified command is executed immediately and the result examined. This way the interpreted language is much more powerful than the alternative which requires an entire program to be written and compiled before execution begins. This way you can examine and verify the data after each command rather than having to plan out a series of commands and manipulations on the data and only seeing the result at the end. The interpreted language is also more suited for experimentation which we plan to do throughout this book. With the interpreted language you can experiment with various different values for individual parameters and see the results immediately.

Appendix 1.c Installation

As mentioned earlier, SCILAB is available free and can be downloaded at http//www.scilab.org. The process for installation of SCILAB will depend on the operating system that you are using. The information for installing for the system that you are using is also available at the web site where you will download the program. I would recommend that you install the compiled version and not the binary version.

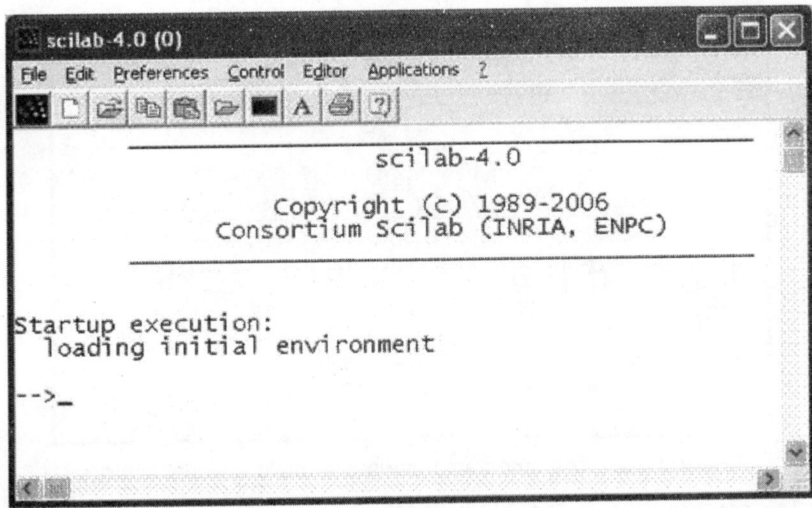

Figure A.1: SCILAB's command window that opens up when you start the program

Appendix 1.d The First Steps

(i) When you run SCILAB it will open a command window like the one shown in Figure A.1. This is the window for the Windows operating system. It might differ if you are using a different operating system. This is an inter-active window where the user can enter commands at the SCILAB command prompt. The command prompt is (-->). The command is completely entered with a carriage return. On receiving the carriage return SCILAB will execute the command and present you with an answer. After the answer is presented the command prompt will be seen and you can now enter the next command.

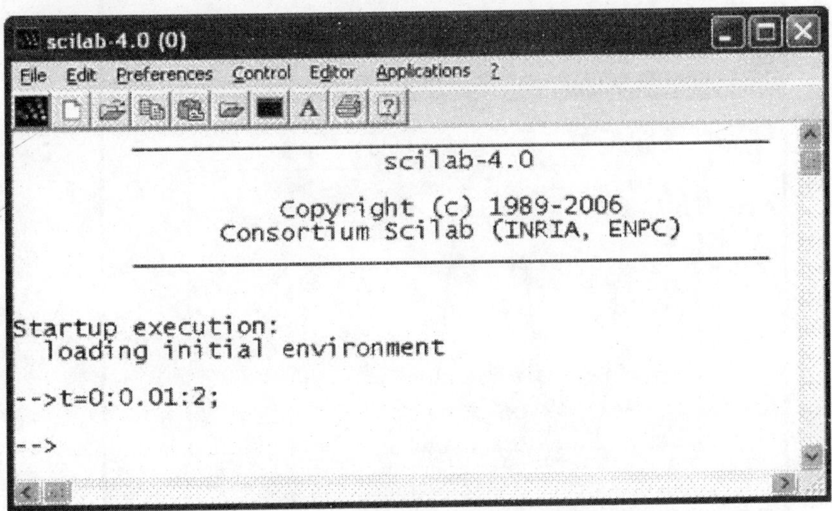

Figure A.2: The time vector is built

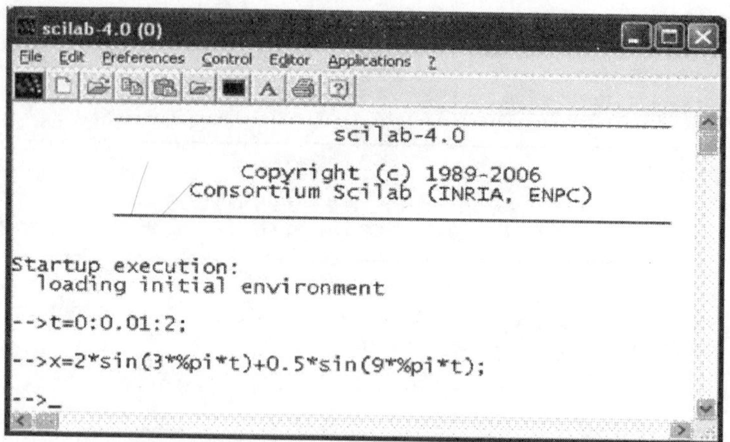

Figure A.3: The time vector is used to build a signal vector

(ii) A typical SCILAB session will consist of issuing commands, examining the result, and then going back to edit the command or to continue with the next step of the simulation. SCILAB can also

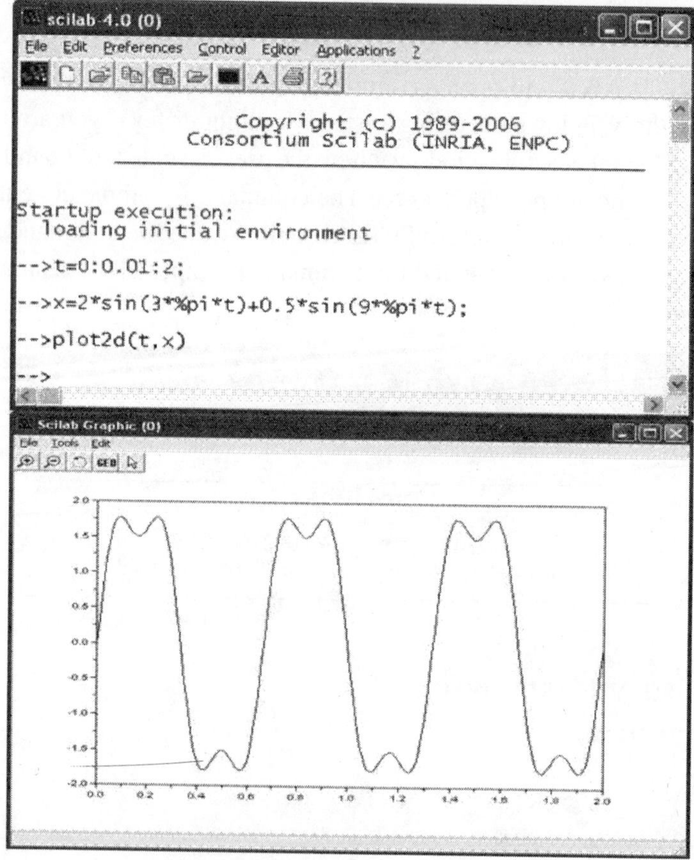

Figure A.4: The Plot of a time vector

be run from stored programs. These stored programs are presented to the SCILAB program and the program will execute them one command at a time. The result of the individual commands will be used in the following commands. For example suppose you want to build a time vector 2Sin(3πt) + 0.5Sin(9πt) and then draw a plot the steps would be as follows. First we define a time vector as shown in Figure A.2. The time vector is assigned to the variable t in Figure A.2. The variable t is a vector with the first entry as zero and the last entry as 2. Next we will use this time vector that we have built to build a time function as required and shown in Figure A.3. Figure A.3 shows that the command to build the data vector places the result in variable x. Variable x is also a vector and it is built by completing the calculation indicated for each value of the t vector. So now we have two vectors (t and x) that are the same size so we can use these two vectors to draw the plot of the data. This plot is drawn with the vector x along the x-axis against the time vector t along the y-axis. This is shown in Figure A.4. This exercise was intended to show you that SCILAB is indeed a very simple and an easy software package that you can learn easily and quickly.

APPENDIX 1.2 – The Language of SCILAB

SCILAB as a program works on objects but these objects are never declared explicitly. They have dynamic type and their sizes can change dynamically according to the operations and the functions that are used to assign a value to these objects. The following session will illustrate this.

- **Assigning a value to a variable:**

Assign a value of 35 to variable xx in SCILAB. To accomplish this command is a simple assignment statement:

```
-->xx=35
 xx =
   35.
-->
```

Notice that SCILAB has now assigned a value of 35 to the variable xx. We did not define what the variable was; it was dynamically assigned to be a constant. Now change the assignment to the same variable and make it a 2 × 2 matrix by the following SCILAB command:

```
-->xx=[1 3;4 6]
 xx =
   1.   3.
   4.   6.
-->
```

The dynamic assignment has now changed variable xx to now be the 2 × 2 matrix and it is no longer 35 as we had first defined.

So to define a constant just assign the value to the variable.

To define a matrix assign the values within a square bracket, enter the matrix row by row, separate the entries in a row by a space or a comma, separate the rows by a semi-colon.

- **Complex values**

SCILAB permits us to first define and then to use complex numbers also. Complex numbers are specified by the key operator 'i'. So to define a variable to be a complex number a command such as ***a = 3 + 4*%i*** will define 'a' as the complex number with 3 as the real part and 4 as the imaginary part. Once you have the complex numbers defined you can do arithmetic with these complex numbers and the arithmetic will be performed according to the rules of complex numbers. So for example you want to define a vector of 10 complex values that increases the real part by 2 every successive value and decreases the imaginary part by 1.5 each successive value then the SCILAB script will be as follows:

```
v = [1 2 3 4 5 6 7 8 9 10] // defines a vector from 1 to 10.
a = 2-1.5*%i // defines the complex multiplier.
vector = a*v // computes the vector that we want.
```

The result that we get from SCILAB is:

```
v =
  1.  2.  3.  4.  5.  6.  7.  8.  9.  10.
a =
  2. - 1.5i
vector =
     column 1 to 6
  2. - 1.5i  4. - 3.i  6. - 4.5i  8. - 6.i  10. - 7.5i  12. - 9.i
     column  7 to 10
  14. - 10.5i  16. - 12.i  18. - 13.5i  20. - 15.i
```

- **Building a regular vector**

In Figure A.2 we built a time vector that had equal spaced entries from a starting value to an ending value. Vectors such as that vector are used very often in SCILAB. SCILAB permits us to build these vectors in several different ways.

t = start : increment : end

A command as the one shown here will build a vector from a specified starting value (first entry) to a specified ending value (last entry) with an additive increment (middle entry). The example shows how the command will be executed.

Example: Define the variable t as a vector with first entry as 0.0 and the last entry as 1.0 with the in between values spaced regularly and increasing by 0.1.

Answer: t = 0:0.1:1 → 0, 0.1, 0.2, 0.3, 0.4, 0.5, 0.6, 0.7, 0.8, 0.9, 1.0

t = linspace(start, end, number of entries)

This command is similar to the earlier command. Here also we have a start value and an end value specified. This time instead of specifying an additive increment we specify the number of entries we want to have in the array.

Example: Define the variable t as a vector with first entry as 0.0 and the last entry as 1.0 with eleven in between values that are spaced regularly.

Answer: t = linspace(0,1,11) → 0, 0.1, 0.2, 0.3, 0.4, 0.5, 0.6, 0.7, 0.8, 0.9, 1.0

As you can see both the commands are identical. In this second command we have used the command word "linspace" which creates linearly spaced values. There is a second command that is similar to this command and it creates a vector that has values that have the same ratio in two adjacent entries. This command is known as "logspace" and it is demonstrated as shown below.

t = logspace(start, end, number of entries)

This command creates logarithmically spaced entries. This time however the start entry is taken as $10^{start\ value}$ and similarly the end value is taken as $10^{end\ value}$ and the number of entries have a product relationship as shown below in the example.

Example: Define the variable t as a vector with first entry as 10^0 and the last entry as 10^2 with six in between values spaced logarithmically.

Answer: t = logspace(0,2,6) → 1, 2.511886, 6.3095734, 15.848932, 39.810717, 100.

The example shows that we have created a logarithmically spaced array. The ratio between any two entries is 2.511886. The first entry is 10^0 which is 10 to the power of the start value and the last entry is 10^2 which is 10 to the power of the end value.

- **Arithmetic**

Different arithmetic operations are performed with the same operator precedence that we are familiar with so we perform multiplies and divides first and then the plus and the minus. In an expression the precedence is evaluated from left to right in operations that have equal precedence. You can always change the order of execution by proper use of parenthesis, as the examples below show us.

Example: x=4*5-6/3 = 18

Example: x=4*(5-6)/3 = -1.333333

- **Matrix Operations**

Matrix operations are performed in the same way as you would expect. If the matrices are conformal then matrix operations will be performed.

- **Special Matrix Operations**

In addition to the normal matrix operations there are some special matrix operations. These operations are not performed according to the rules of matrix operations. For example if you have an array (a row matrix) that has 10 elements and another array (a row matrix) that also has 10 elements and you wanted to form another array (a row matrix) that is formed by element by element product

of the two arrays then the matrix operations will not perform this operation. This is done by using the period to modify the operation. This is shown in the example below. This operation takes a little getting used to so try out several different examples.
Example: Define two row vectors and perform an element by element product of the two vectors.

Answer: t=1:1:5; → t = 1, 2, 3, 4, 5
x=0.1:0.1:0.5 → x= 0.1, 0.2, 0.3, 0.4, 0.5
t.*x → ans = 0.1, 0.4, 0.9, 1.6, 2.5

- **User Defined Functions**

Just like you can define used defined functions in other programming languages you can also define functions in SCILAB also. Once the function is defined you can use the function by invoking the function in your commands. All SCILAB commands that we will see as we go forward in this chapter are defined as functions. To define a function you begin with a key word **functions**, write out the function name, define the function and end the function with a key word **endfunction.** The following defines a function to calculate the sin of specified angle.

Example: Define a function that will calculate the Sine of the value supplied.
Answer: Function y = foo(x,g); y = g(x); endfunction

In the definition above foo is the name of the function, this function takes two parameters x and g. The value computed for the function is g(x).

To use the function you call the function by using its name and providing it with the required number of parameters. In our example if we call the function with the following command xx=foo(1.5,sin) then the result that we get back is 0.997495 which is the value sin(1.5) which is what we asked the function to compute.
So to define a function you begin with the key word **function**.
Next you specify the name of the function along with the parameters that the function needs.
Next you define what the function has to calculate. This does not have to be just one command, it can be several different commands.This can also be a call to a different function that has been defined earlier elsewhere.

When all the required commands have been specified you end the function definition by the key word **endfunction.**

- **Branching**

Conditional execution is also possible in SCILAB just as in other programming languages by the use of the **If** statement. The simplest form of the branching instruction is a simple command as:

if <condition> then <statement> end

This command is similar to the conditional execution in many of the high level programming languages. If the specified condition is true then execute the specified statement else skip the statement. Just as in other high level programming languages this simple **if** statement can be modified with the use of the else statement, this is shown below.

if <condition> then <true statement> else <false statement> end

In this example when the condition is true then the true statement is executed, if the condition is false then the false statement is executed.

Example: Execute the function foo defined above if the value of the variable a is less than 30, else decrease the variable a by 5.
Answer: Assume that the variable a is assigned as shown in this statement and the function foo is also assigned as shown then the second statement will execute as desired.

```
a=40; function y=foo(x,g); y=g(x);endfunction;
if(a<30) then y=foo(a,sin); else a=a-5;end
```

- **Looping**

Iterative executions are also possible within SCILAB just as they are possible with other high level programming languages. With SCILAB loops or iterative execution can be executed by either the **for** command or the **while** command. The two commands are similar to each other and they are used as follows:

for variable = expression, statements, end

In the above command the **for** statement first assigns the value of the expression to the variable, then it will execute all the statements till the end statement. This completes one iteration of the **for** statement. At the end of the execution the program will go back to the **for** statement, if the expression is a vector then the variable will take on the value of the next element of the vector and the group of statements will be executed again. This process will continue till all the elements of the vector are used up. The example below shows how this statement is executed.

Example: Write a **for** loop that will execute several statements as the loop variable is assigned the values 1, 5, 6, 8 successively.
Answer: The following command will execute the statements between the **for** and the **end** statement as the loop control variable x takes on the specified values.
for x=[1 5 6 8], statements to be executed, end

while expression, true statements, else false statements, end

In the above command the **while** statement will evaluate the expression. If the expression evaluates to a **true** condition then the true statements will be executed. At the end of the execution of the true statements the condition will be checked again. As long as the condition evaluates to a true condition the true statements will continue to execute. The first time the expression evaluates to a false condition the group of false statements will be executed. The false statements get executed only once. So as soon as the evaluated condition is false the **while** statement evaluates the false statements and then terminates. The example below shows how this statement is executed.

Example: Write a **while** loop that will execute several statements as the loop as long as the loop control variable is > 1. The variable is successively divided by 2 at the completion of the true statements.
Answer: The following command will execute the statements between the **while** and the **else** as long as the variable a>1. During the execution the variable a is divided by 2. Then the condition is tested again. As soon as the variable a is either equal to or less than 2 the else conditions are executed and the **while** statement is terminated.

while (a>1) <true statements, a=a/2>, else <false statements>, end

APPENDIX 1.3 – Drawing Graphs

SCILAB can draw graphs either in 2-D or in 3-D. Since we have used only 2-D plots we will be discussing only 2-D plots over here. 3-D plots are also possible and you can learn about these from the help file that you will download with the program. The command for a simple 2-D plot is as shown below:

plot2d(x-variable, y-variable)

The command above says that you can draw a plot once you have defined the values for the x-axis in the x-variable and the values for the y-axis in the y-variable. The plot you get with the specified command is a simple plot that does not look very good. We can make the plot a little pretty by adding title for the plot and for the axis as well as changing the color of the plot. We can also draw several plots on the same graph. All these things are discussed below.

Placing a title for the plot as well as for the two axes:

xtitle('Title to be assigned for the plot','Title for the X-axis','Title for the Y-axis')

The following example will demonstrate the use of the two commands.

Example: Draw the graph of a Sin wave and place a title on the graph, the X-axis and the Y-axis.
Answer: The following sequences of commands will first draw the plot and then place the required titles on the graphs.

```
t=0:0.01:1;ct=cos(4*%pi*t),plot2d(t,ct);
xtitle('My First Plot','X-axis Time','Y-axis Cosine')
```

As you can see that drawing a graph is a very simple matter and adding titles is not difficult either. To make the graphs a little prettier you can add color to the graphs. You will not be able to see the change in color of the graph in the text book but when you try it out on your computer screen you will see that the graph is drawn with a different color. To draw a graph with a different color you add a style command to the plot command. This is done as follows. The command draws the same graph

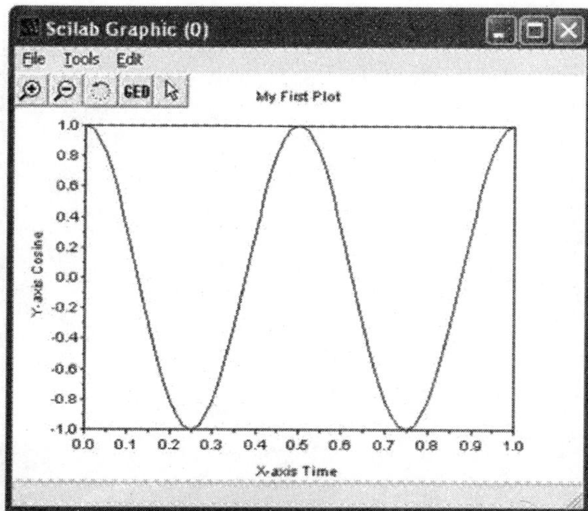

Figure A.5: Cosine plot with Titles for the plot and the axes

as the one drawn in Figure A.5 but this time the cosine curve is drawn in green color. You can choose any different color that you want. So if you wanted a red graph replace the word green by the word red and so on. All the colors that SCILAB understands can be chosen this way.

```
t=0:0.01:1;ct=cos(4*%pi*t);plot2d1(t,ct,style=color('green'))
```

If you have two or more curves that you want drawn on the same graph then SCILAB will plot them automatically for you on the same plot while adjusting the axis at the same time. This is demonstrated in Figure A.6. In Figure A.6 we add the graph of 2Cos($8\pi t$) to the graph of Figure A.5. The new graph is drawn in Green color. The second graph is drawn with the same time vector but a new computation for the Cosine value using the command:

```
ct2=2*cos(8*%pi*t);plot2d(t,ct2,style=color('green'))
```

Until now we have drawn just one graph on one page. It is possible to have several subgraphs on one page. To draw a subgraph we first tell SCILAB how many graph windows we want drawn on one page and in which window do we want to draw the next plot in. The graph is divided into rows and columns of windows by a command such as:

subplot(# of Rows, # of columns, Window number for the next graph)
So a command such as **subgraph(3,2,5)** will divide the graph paper in three rows of two columns each and plot the next plot in window number 5. The windows are numbered with the top left window being window number 1 and then counting successively across the row and then down to the next row. The example below shows the graphs drawn on subplots.

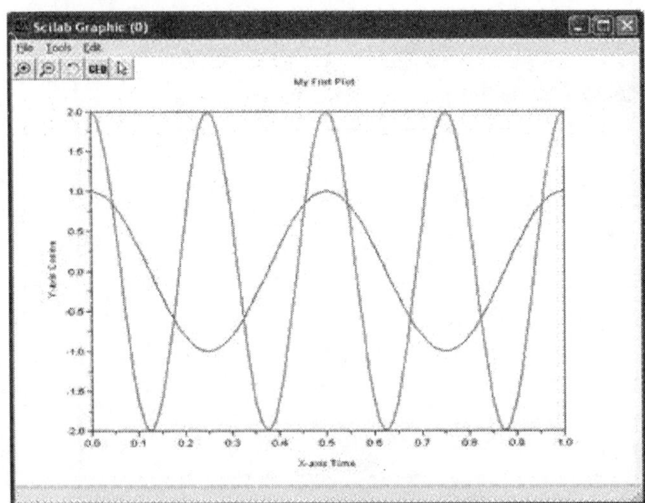

Figure A.6: A second plot added to the first plot. Notice the change in color of the second graph and the scaling of the axis

Example: Draw the first six harmonics of Cos(2πt) on a single graph paper using six subplots.
Answer: The following sequences of commands will draw the six plots and then place them as subplots as required on a single graph paper. The plots are shown in Figure A.7.

```
t=0:0.01:1;
for i=1:6
ct=cos(2*i*%pi*t);
subplot(2,3,i);
plot2d(t,ct);
end
```

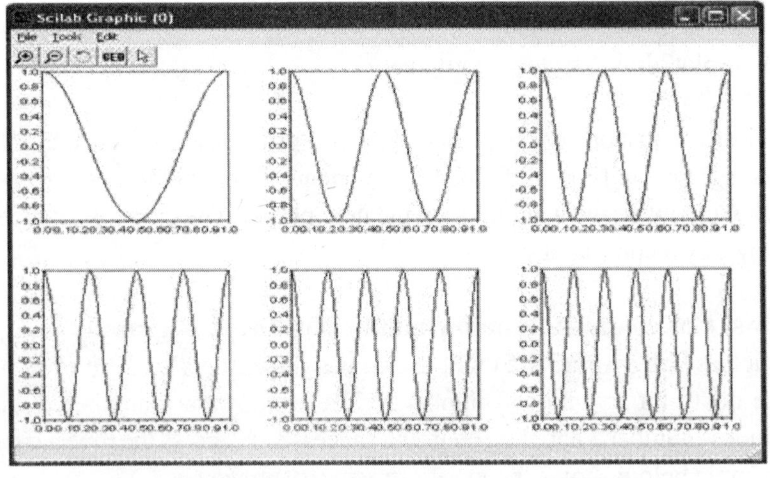

Figure A.7: Plot of six graphs using the subplot command

APPENDIX 1.4 – Other Useful SCILAB Functions

In the book we have used other SCILAB functions which are described here:

• Poly

This function defines a polynomial in a variable that you can specify. The polynomial can be specified either by listing the coefficients of each term or by specifying the roots of the polynomial. Here are two examples. Assume that v is a vector that has 10 entries from 1 to 10 spaced by 1. The first command defines the polynomial in the variable p using the first 5 entries in the vector v as the coefficients of the polynomial. The second command defines the polynomial in the variable p using the first 5 entries in the vector v as the roots of the polynomial.

```
>P1=poly(v(1:5),'p','coeff') //Define polynomial in variable p using coefficients.
 P1 =
   1 + 2p + 3p^2 + 4p^3 + 5p^4
>P2=poly(v(1:5),'p','roots') //Define polynomial in variable p using roots of polynomial.
 P2 =
 - 120 + 274p - 225p^2 + 85p^3 - 15p^4 + p^5
```

We can do normal arithmetic with the polynomials also. For example we can divide one polynomial by the other to get

```
>P3=P1/P2
P3 =
         1 + 2p + 3p^2 + 4p^3 + 5p^4
     ------------------------------------
-120 + 274p - 225p^2 + 85p^3 - 15p^4 + p^5
```

Or when we add the two polynomials we get

```
>P4 = P1+P2
 P4 =
-119 + 272p - 222p^2 + 89p^3 - 10p^4 + p^5
```

• Defining a system

You define a system by telling SCILAB the numerator polynomial and the denominator polynomial of an open loop system within the **syslin** command. So if in the above examples we wish to use P1 as the numerator polynomial and P2 as the denominator polynomial to define a system then the system will be as follows:

```
->sys=syslin('c',P1,P)
 sys =
```

$$\frac{1 + 2p + 3p^2 + 4p^3 + 5p^4}{-120 + 274p - 225p^2 + 85p^3 - 15p^4 + p^5}$$

In the above example the variable **sys** is now defined as a linear system as we can now analyze the system.

• **Frequency Response Plots**

In the book we have drawn the Bode plot. Along with the Bode plot we can also draw the Nyquist plot as well as the Nichols plot. The Bode plot is two separate plots, one is the magnitude plot while the other is the phase plot. To draw any of the frequency response plots you have to first define a system as shown above. Once you have the system defined the plot can be drawn. As an example assume that we have defined a system as done above then the Bode plot of the system **sys** will be drawn as:

bode(sys)

Similarly the other plots can be drawn. By changing the command to nyquist we get the **Nyquist** plot and by changing the command to **chart** we get the Nichols plot for the system defined by the variable **sys.**

• **Signal Processing Commands:**

While studying the Fourier transforms we have used the FFT command to quickly determine the Fourier transform of a vector. This command can be used to either compute the Fourier transform or the inverse Fourier transform of a vector. The command is used as follows:

V=fft(v,-1) // in this command V is the Fast Fourier Transform of the vector v.

APPENDIX 1.5 – Table of Common Derivatives

$\dfrac{d\left[x^{n}\right]}{dx} = nx^{n-1}$	$\dfrac{d\left[Ln(x)\right]}{dx} = \dfrac{1}{x}$
$\dfrac{d\left(e^{ax}\right)}{dx} = ae^{ax}$	$\dfrac{d\left[Sin(ax)\right]}{dx} = aCos(ax)$
$\dfrac{d\left[Cos(ax)\right]}{dx} = -aSin(ax)$	$\dfrac{d\left[Tan(ax)\right]}{dx} = aSec^{2}(ax)$
$\dfrac{d\left[Cos^{-1}(ax)\right]}{dx} = \dfrac{-a}{\sqrt{1-(ax)^{2}}}$	$\dfrac{d\left[Sin^{-1}(ax)\right]}{dx} = \dfrac{a}{\sqrt{1-(ax)^{2}}}$
$\dfrac{d\left[f(x)g(x)\right]}{dx} = f(x)\dfrac{d\left[g(x)\right]}{dx} + g(x)\dfrac{d\left[f(x)\right]}{dx}$	
$\dfrac{d\left[\dfrac{f(x)}{g(x)}\right]}{dx} = \dfrac{g(x)\dfrac{d\left[f(x)\right]}{dx} - f(x)\dfrac{d\left[g(x)\right]}{dx}}{g^{2}(x)}$	

APPENDIX 1.6 – Table of Common Integrals

$\int a dx = ax$	$\int u dv = uv - \int v du$
$\int f(ax) dx = \frac{1}{a} \int f(x) dx$	$\int x^n dx = \frac{x^{n+1}}{n+1} \quad n ^{1} -1$
$\int \frac{1}{x} dx = \begin{matrix} \ln(x) \text{ if } x > 0 \\ \ln(-x) \text{ if } x < 0 \end{matrix} = \ln(\lvert x \rvert)$	$\int e^x dx = e^x$
$\int \text{Sin}(x) dx = -\text{Cos}(x)$	$\int \text{Cos}(x) dx = \text{Sin}(x)$
$\int \text{Tan}(x) dx = \ln(\text{Sec}(x)) = -\ln(\text{Cos}(x))$	$\int \text{Cot}(x) dx = \ln(\text{Sin}(x))$
$\int \text{Cos}^2(x) dx = \frac{x}{2} + \frac{\text{Sin}(2x)}{4}$ $= \frac{1}{2}(x + \text{Sin}(x)\text{Cos}(x))$	$\int \text{Sin}^2(x) dx = \frac{x}{2} - \frac{\text{Sin}(2x)}{4}$ $= \frac{1}{2}(x - \text{Sin}(x)\text{Cos}(x))$
$\int \frac{dx}{x^2 + a^2} = \frac{1}{a} \text{Tan}^{-1}\left(\frac{x}{a}\right)$	$\int \frac{dx}{x^2 - a^2} = \frac{1}{2a} \ln\left(\frac{x - a}{x + a}\right)$
$\int \frac{dx}{a^2 - x^2} = \frac{1}{2a} \ln\left(\frac{a + x}{a - x}\right)$	$\int \frac{dx}{\sqrt{x^2 + a^2}} = \ln\left(x + \sqrt{x^2 + a^2}\right)$
$\int \frac{dx}{\sqrt{x^2 - a^2}} = \ln\left(x + \sqrt{x^2 - a^2}\right)$	$\int x^n e^{ax} dx = \frac{1}{b} x^n e^{bx} - \frac{n}{b} \int x^{n-1} e^{ax} dx$
$\int x^n \text{Sin}(bx) dx$ $= -\frac{x^n}{b} \text{Cos}(bx) + \frac{n}{b} \int x^{n-1} \text{Cos}(bx) dx$	$\int x^n \text{Cos}(bx) dx$ $= \frac{x^n}{b} \text{Sin}(bx) - \frac{n}{b} \int x^{n-1} \text{Sin}(bx) dx$

APPENDIX 1.7 – Table of Common Laplace Transforms and Theorems

Time Domain Function	Laplace Transform
$\delta(t)$	1
1	$\frac{1}{s}$
$e^{-\alpha t}$	$\frac{1}{s+\alpha}$
$Sin(\alpha t)u(t)$	$\frac{\alpha}{s^2+\alpha^2}$
$Cos(\alpha t)u(t)$	$\frac{s}{s^2+\alpha^2}$
Frequency shift $e^{-\alpha t}x(t)$	$X(s+\alpha)$
$e^{-\beta t}Sin(\alpha t)u(t)$	$\frac{\alpha}{(s+\beta)^2+\alpha^2}$
$e^{-\beta t}Cos(\alpha t)u(t)$	$\frac{(s+\beta)}{(s+\beta)^2+\alpha^2}$
Differentiation $\frac{dx(t)}{dt}$	$sX(s)-x(0^-)$
Delay $x(t-t_0)u(t-t_0)$	$e^{-st_0}X(s)$
Convolution $x_1(t)*x_2(t)$	$X_1(s)X_2(s)$
Initial Value $x(0^+)$	$\underset{s\to\infty}{Limit}\ sX(s)$
Final Value $\underset{t\to\infty}{Limit}\ x(t)$	$\underset{s\to 0}{Limit}\ sX(s)$
Integration $\int_{-\infty}^{t} x(\lambda)d\lambda$	$\frac{X(s)}{s}+\frac{x^{(-1)}(0^-)}{s}$
Time Scale $x(at)u(t)$	$\frac{1}{\lvert a\rvert}X\left(\frac{s}{a}\right)$

APPENDIX 1.8 – Table of Z-Transforms and Theorems

Discrete Time Function	Z-Transform	Region of Convergence
$\delta(n)$	1	
$u(n)$	$\dfrac{1}{1-z^{-1}}$	$z>1$
$e^{-\alpha n}=\left(e^{-\alpha}\right)^n=K^n$	$\dfrac{1}{1-e^{-\alpha}z^{-1}}=\dfrac{1}{1-Kz^{-1}}$	$z>K$
n	$\dfrac{z^{-1}}{\left(1-z^{-1}\right)^2}$	$z>1$
$Sin(bn)$	$\dfrac{Sin(b)z^{-1}}{1-2Cos(b)z^{-1}+z^{-2}}$	$\left(1-2Cos(b)z^{-1}+z^{-2}\right)>0$
$Cos(bn)$	$\dfrac{1-Cos(b)z^{-1}}{1-2Cos(b)z^{-1}+z^{-2}}$	$\left(1-2Cos(b)z^{-1}+z^{-2}\right)>0$
$e^{-\alpha n}Sin(bn)$	$\dfrac{e^{-\alpha}Sin(b)z^{-1}}{1-2e^{-\alpha}Cos(b)z^{-1}+e^{-2\alpha}z^{-2}}$	$\left(1-2e^{-\alpha}Cos(b)z^{-1}+e^{-2\alpha}z^{-2}\right)>0$
$e^{-\alpha n}Cos(bn)$	$\dfrac{1-e^{-\alpha}Cos(b)z^{-1}}{1-2e^{-\alpha}Cos(b)z^{-1}+e^{-2\alpha}z^{-2}}$	$\left(1-2e^{-\alpha}Cos(b)z^{-1}+e^{-2\alpha}z^{-2}\right)>0$

APPENDIX 1.9 – Fourier Transform Pairs and Theorems

Definition $x(t)=\frac{1}{2\pi}\int_{-\infty}^{\infty}X(\omega)e^{j\omega t}d\omega$	$X(\omega)=\int_{-\infty}^{\infty}x(t)e^{-j\omega t}dt$
$\delta(t)$	1
1	$2\pi\delta(\omega)$
$u(t)$	$\frac{1}{j\omega}+\pi\delta(\omega)$
$e^{-\alpha t}u(t) \quad \text{Re}(\alpha)>0$	$\frac{1}{\alpha+j\omega}$
$te^{-\alpha t}u(t) \quad \text{Re}(\alpha)>0$	$\frac{1}{(\alpha+j\omega)^2}$
$e^{-\alpha\|t\|}u(t) \quad \text{Re}(\alpha)>0$	$\frac{2\alpha}{\alpha^2+\omega^2}$
Scale Change $x[at]$	$\frac{1}{\|a\|}X\left[\frac{\omega}{a}\right]$
Time Reversal $x(-t)$	$X(-\omega)$
Conjugation $x^*(t)$	$X^*(-\omega)$
Time Shift $x(t-t_0)$	$e^{-j\omega t_0}X(\omega)$
Frequency Shift $e^{j\omega_0 t}x(t)$	$X(\omega-\omega_0)$
Convolution $x_1(t)*x_2(t)$	$X_1(\omega)X_2(\omega)$
Time Differentiation $\frac{dx(t)}{dt}$	$j\omega X(\omega)$

APPENDIX 1.10 – Discrete Fourier Transform Pairs and Theorems

Definition	$x(n) = \frac{1}{N}\sum_{k=0}^{N-1} X(k) W_N^{-nk}$	$X(k) = \sum_{n=0}^{N-1} x(n) W_N^{nk}$
Symmetry	$\frac{1}{N} X(n)$	$x(-k)$
Time Shift	$x(n-i)$	$W_N^{ni} X(k)$
Frequency Shift	$W_N^{-ni} x(n)$	$X(k-i)$
Even Functions	$x_e(n)$	$\sum_{n=0}^{N-1} x_e(n) Cos(nk) = X_e(k)$
Odd Functions	$x_o(n)$	$-j\sum_{n=0}^{N-1} x_o(n) Sin(nk) = X_o(k)$
Time Reversal	$x(-n)$	$X(-k)$
Conjugate Functions	$x^*(n)$	$X^*(-k)$

References

1. **M. Abramowitz and I.A. Stegun,** editors. *Handbook of Mathematical Functions.* Dover Publications, New York NY, 1972.
2. **J.W. Adams and A.N. Wilson Jr.** A new approach to FIR digital filters with fewer multipliers and reduced sensitivity. *IEEE Transactions on Circuits and Systems.* Pages 277 - 283, May 1983.
3. **J.W. Adams.** FIR digital filters with least squares stop bands subject to peak gain constraints. *IEEE Transactions on Circuits and Systems.* Pages 376 - 388, April 1991.
4. **R.C. Agarwal and J.W. Cooley.** New Algorithm for Digital Convolution. *IEEE Transactions on Acoustics Speech and Signal Processing.* Pages 392 - 410, October 1997
5. **C.S. Burns, A.W. Soewito and R.A. Gopinath.** Least squared error FIR filter design with transition bands. *IEEE Transactions on Signal Processing.* Pages 1327 - 1340 1992.
6. **J.C. Candy and G.C. Temes.***Over sampling methods for A/D and D/A conversion.* Pages 1 - 25 IEEE press New York N Y 1992.
7. **D.S.K. Chan and L.A. Rabiner.** Analysis of quantization errors in the direct form for finite impulse response digital filters. *IEEE Transactions on Audio and Electroacoustics.* Pages 339 - 342, April 1981
8. **J.Chun and N.K. Bose.** Fast evaluation of an integral occurring in Digital Filtering applications. *IEEE Transactions on Signal Processing.* Pages 1982 - 1986 August 1995.
9. **J.M. Cioffi and Y.S. Byun.** *Adaptive Filtering. Handbook for Digital Signal Processing* Chapter 15 Pages 1085 - 1142. Wiley Interscience New York N Y 1993.
10. **J.W. Cooley and J.W. Tukey.** *An algorithm for machine calculation of complex Fourier series.* Math Computation 297 - 301 1965.

11. **R.E. Crochiere and A.V. Oppenheim.** *Analysis of Linear Digital Networks*. Proceedings IEEE Pages 581 - 595 1975.

12. **A.Fettweis.** A simple design method of maximally flat delay digital filters. *IEEE Transactions on Audio and Electroacoustics*. 112 - 114 June 1972.

13. **P.Garde.** All pass crossover systems. *Journal of the Audio Engineering Society*. 575 - 584 September 1980.

14. **B.Gold and K.L.Jordan.** *A note on Digital Filter Synthesis*. Proceedings IEEE Pages 1717 - 1718 October 1968.

15. **D.J. Goodman and M.J. Carey.** Nine Digital Filters for decimation and interpolation. *IEEE Transactions on Acoustics Speech and Signal Processing*. Pages 121 - 126 April 1977.

16. **S.S. Haykin and R. Carnegi.** *New Method of Synthesizing linear digital filters based on convolution integral*. IEE Proceedings Pages 1063 - 1072 June 1970.

17. **J.P.J. Heemskerk and K.A.S. Immink.** Compact Disk: System Aspects and Modulation. *Philips Technical Review* Pages 157 - 165 1982.

18. **L.B. Jackson.** *Digital Filters and Signal Processing*. Kluwer, Boston Ma. 3rd Edition 1996.

19. **N.S. Jayant.** *Digital Coding of Speech waveforms*. Proceedings IEEE Pages 611 - 632 May 1974.

20. **J.D. Johnston.** A filter family designed for use in quadrature mirror filter banks. Proceedings *IEEE International Conference on Acoustics Speech and Signal Processing* Pages 291 - 294 April 1980.

21. **J.F. Kaiser.** Non-recursive digital filter design using the I0-Sinh window function. Proceedings 1974 *IEEE International Symposium on Circuits and Systems*. Pages 20 - 23 San Francisco CA April 1974.

22. **I. Koren.** *Computer Arithmetic Algorithms*. Prentice Hall Englewoods Cliffs NJ 1993.

23. **T.I. Laakso, V. Valimiki, M. Karjalainen and U.K. Laine.** Splitting the Unit delay. *IEEE Signal Processing Magazine*. Pages 30 - 60 January 1996.

24. **N. Levinson.** *The Wiener RMS criterion in digital filter prediction Joint Math Physics*. Pages 261 - 278 1947.

25. **I.S. Lin and S.K. Mitra.** Overlapped Block Digital Filtering. *IEEE Transactions on Circuits and Systems II*: Analog and Digital Signal Processing. Pages 586 - 596 August 1996.

26. **A. Mahanta, R.C. Agarwal and S.C. Dutta Roy.** FIR filter structures having low sensitivity and roundoff noise. *IEEE Transactions on Acoustics Speech and Signal Processing*. Pages 913 - 920 December 1982.

27. **K. Meerkötter.** Realization of limit cycles free second order digital filters. Proceedings 1976 *IEEE International Symposium on Circuits and Systems*. Pages 295 - 298 1976.

28. **W.L. Mills, C.T. Mullis and R.A. Roberts.** Digital filter realizations without overflow oscillations. *IEEE Transactions on Acoustics Speech and Signal Processing*. Pages 334 - 338 August 1978.

29. **S.K. Mitra and A. Makur.** Warped discrete Fourier Transform. Proceedings *IEEE workshop on Digital Signal Processing.* Bryce UT. August 1998.
30. **S.K. Mitra and H. Babic.** Partial Fraction Expansion of rational Z-transforms. *Electronics Letters* Pages 1726-1730 September 1998.
31. **Y. Neuvo and S.K. Mitra.** Complementary IIR digital filters. Proceedings *IEEE International Symposium on Circuits and Systems.* Pages 234 - 237 Montreal Canada May 1984.
32. **P. Papamichalis.** *Digital Signal Processing Applications with the TMS 320 Family, Theory, Algorithms and Implementations.* Volume 3. Prentice Hall Englewoods Cliffs NJ 1990.
33. **J. G. Proakis and D.G. Manolakis.** *Digital Signal Processing: Principles Algorithms and Applications.* Prentice Hall Englewoods Cliffs NJ 2nd Edition 1992.
34. **L.R. Rabiner & B. Gold.** *Theory and Application of Digital Signal Processing.* Prentice Hall, Englewood Cliffs NJ. 1975.
35. **V. Ramachandran.** Determination of discrete transfer function from its real (or imaginary) parts on the unit circle. *IEEE Transactions on Acoustics Speech and Signal Processing,* Pages 440 - 442 March 1989.
36. **P.A. Regalia; S.K. Mitra & J. Fadavi.** Implementations of real digital filters using complex arithmetic. *IEEE Transactions on Circuits and Systems.* Pages 345 - 354 April 1987.
37. **P.A. Regalia; S.K. Mitra & P.P. Viadyanathan.** *The Digital all pass network: A versatile signal processing building block.* IEEE Proceedings Pages 19 - 37 January 1988.
38. **I.W. Selsnick, M. Lang and C.S. Burns.** A modified algorithm for constrained least square design of multiband FIR filters without specified transaction bands. *IEEE Transcations on Signal Processing,* Pages 497 - 501 February 1998.
39. **S.M. Spangenberg, I. Scott, S. McLaughlin, G.J.R. Povey, D.G.M. Cruickchank & P.M. Grant.** An FFT based approach for fast acquisition in spread spectrum communication systems. *Wireless Personal Communications.* Pages 27 - 55 May 2000.
40. **S. Thurnhofer.** Two dimensional Teager filters. In S. K. Mitra and G Sicuranza, Editors *Nonlinear Image processing,* Chapter 6. Academic Press New York, NY. 2000.
41. **A. Williams & F.J. Taylor.** *Electronic Filter Designers Handbook,* McGraw Hill New York NY. 3rd Edition 1995.
42. **D. Yellin & E. Weinstein.** Multi-channel signal separation: Methods and Analysis. *IEEE Transactions on Acoustics Speech and Signal Processing.* Pages 106 - 118 January 1996.
43. **T-H. Yu, S.H. Mitra, and H. Babic.** *Design of linear phase FIR Notch filters.* Sadhana Pages 133 - 155. November 1990.